KJE 6819 HAT

REGULATING SERVICES IN THE EUROPEAN UNION

Regulating Services in the European Union

VASSILIS HATZOPOULOS

OXFORD
UNIVERSITY PRESS

OXFORD
UNIVERSITY PRESS

Great Clarendon Street, Oxford, OX2 6DP,
United Kingdom

Oxford University Press is a department of the University of Oxford.
It furthers the University's objective of excellence in research, scholarship,
and education by publishing worldwide. Oxford is a registered trade mark of
Oxford University Press in the UK and in certain other countries

© V. Hatzopoulos 2012

The moral rights of the author have been asserted

First Edition published in 2012

Impression: 1

British Library Cataloguing in Publication Data

Data available

Library of Congress Cataloging in Publication Data

Library of Congress Control Number 2012934412

ISBN 978–0–19–957266–3

Printed and bound by
CPI Group (UK) Ltd, Croydon, CR0 4YY

In memory of my father

Preface: Object of the Book and Methodology

A. The importance of services and the relevance of studying their regulation

'The Single Market has been, and remains, the cornerstone of Europe's integration and sustainable growth. But this major European project requires renewed political determination so that it can fulfil all its potential.'[1] If the above statement, by the President of the EU Commission, holds true, then it is worth asking 'what is there in the single market?'. The shortest answer to this question would be 'services'. Over 70 per cent of member states' GDP comes from the provision of services.[2] About the same percentage accounts for the actual level of employment in services,[3] while the numbers climb to over 95 per cent when it comes to the creation of new employment. What is more, the development of the service sector corresponds to a steady trend: 'while in the manufacturing industry production rose at an annual rate of 0.3 per cent over the period 2000–2008, in services, the annual turnover growth rate varied from 1.7 per cent in "hotels and restaurants" to 6.7 per cent in "water transport"'.[4]

Any initiative to re-launch the single market, therefore, bears essentially on services. Such a re-launch seems all the more necessary in view of the fact that cross-border provision of services accounts for only 5 per cent of the EU's GDP, compared with 17 per cent for manufactured goods traded within the single market.[5] On a different measure, services account for only 24 per cent of total EU trade.[6]

---

[1] Mission letter from the President of the European Commission to Professor M. Monti, Pres (2009) D/2250, entrusting Professor M. Monti with the preparation of a Report on the future of the Single Market. The result of this was the Report, 'A New Strategy for the Single Market' (9 May 2010), available at <http://ec.europa.eu/bepa/pdf/monti_report_final_10_05_2010_en.pdf> (last accessed on 17 November 2011).

[2] See eg Monteagudo, J., and Diexr, A., 'Economic Performance and Competition in Services in the Euro Area: Policy Lessons in Times of Crisis' European Economy Occasional Papers No. 53/2009, EU Commission/DG Economic and Financial Affairs, available at <http://ec.europa.eu/economy_finance/publications/publication15841_en.pdf>, at 22 (last accessed on 17 November 2011); as it shall be explained in ch 1, statistical data about services is highly contestable; therefore, on a different (slightly predated) count, services account only for 54 per cent of EU GDP and 67 per cent of employment. See also Communication COM (2004) 83 final, 'Report on Competition in Professional Services', at 6.

[3] Ibid.

[4] Ibid, at 10.

[5] Communication COM (2010) 608 final, 'Towards a Single Market Act: For a Highly Competitive Social Market Economy—50 Proposals for Improving Our Work, Business and Exchanges with One Another', at 3–4.

[6] House of Lords, Inquiry into Re-launching the Single Market—Written Evidence (22 October 2010), at 2, available at <http://www.parliament.uk/documents/lords-committees/eu-sub-com-b/singlemarketinquiry/singlemarketwe221010.pdf> (last accessed on 20 November 2011).

Therefore, to anyone wondering why the provision and trade of services matter for the EU, over 50 years after the foundations of the single market were laid by the Rome Treaty, the short answer would be 'it's the economy, Stupid'.[7] However, as M. Monti observes, there is more than the economy: the integration project itself is at stake, since the single market represents its foundation.[8]

Nonetheless, both the economic and the integration objectives can be questioned today, since there is both an 'integration fatigue' and, especially since the 2008 crisis, a 'market fatigue', too.[9] In addition, the financial crisis prompted the realization that the internal market, in general, and the market for services, in particular, may not be pursued on purely market terms. The issue of efficiently regulating the internal market once again became paramount. The more so, since the economic sector most severely hit by the crisis has been services.[10] Turning this observation on its head, it has been observed that 'improving the economic performance of services is not only important for long-term growth, but this is also essential in a period of economic crisis'.[11] This is so, for at least four reasons: a. since services account for an important share of household expenditure, lower prices of services help preserve the purchasing power of consumers and to cushion the impact of the crisis on the most vulnerable segment of the population; b. services contribute to a large extent to the adjustment capacity of the European economy because they have large interactions with manufacturing, as suppliers (utilities) or users (tourism) of intermediate inputs, and because they are a vector of technology diffusion (ICT services); c. as many services are labour intensive, well-functioning services can more easily absorb workers affected by restructuring; d. most reforms needed to improve the functioning of services' markets do not involve an upfront budgetary cost.[12] Moreover, it is now sufficiently documented, on economic grounds, that the quality and content of regulation have a direct bearing on economic growth.[13]

Interest in the way the internal market is being regulated is not new; instead, it has been pervasive since the publication of the 1962 General Programmes.[14] The 1985 White Paper on 'Completing the Internal Market'[15] initiated a sustained

---

[7] James Carville, Bill Clinton's political strategist in the 1992 election, placed a sign over his desk in the Little Rock headquarters: 'It's the economy, Stupid!'. For a campaigner fixed on a need for a central theme, the sign encapsulated a pointed response to the question 'What is the campaign about?'.

[8] Monti Report, 2010, n 1.

[9] Ibid.

[10] Monteagudo, J., and Diexr, A., 2009, n 2, at 6.

[11] Ibid, at 7.

[12] Ibid.

[13] See eg Blankart, C., Baake, P., and Jansen, C., 'Growth and regulation' in Galli, G., and Pelkmans, J. (eds), *Regulatory Reform and Competitiveness in Europe, 1: Horizontal Issues* (Cheltenham/Northampton: Edward Elgar Publishing, 2000) 40–80; and much earlier, Hindley, B., and Smith, A., 'Comparative Advantage and Trade in Services' (1984) 7 *The World Economy* 369–89; the latter authors, however, insist more on the role of regulation for the promotion of R&D and of innovation.

[14] General Programmes for the suppression of restrictions to the freedom of establishment and free provision of services [1962] OJ 2/36 and 2/32, respectively.

[15] White Paper COM (1985) 310 final, 'Completing the Internal Market'.

reflection on the best way to regulate the internal market. This led to the successful achievement (overall) of the '1992' objective of a fully operational internal market. Thereafter, an important body of sector-specific hybrid and experimental regulation followed, aimed at adapting traditionally monopolistic network-based activities to the internal market requirements. The horizontal 1997 'Single Market Action Plan'[16] and the 1999 'Financial Services Action Plan'[17] were intended to give a fresh push to market integration. Then, a few months after the 2000 Lisbon summit had recognized the importance of services for the achievement of the set goals (a competitive market with high employment and sustainable environment-friendly development), the Commission put forward 'An Internal Market Strategy for Services',[18] and two Communications on business-related and professional services,[19] which were to set the scene for the first ever horizontal 'Services Directive'.[20] This has been the single most disputed text of secondary legislation ever to be adopted by the EU legislature and has been drastically amended during the negotiation process—the Parliament has proposed over 300 amendments to the text submitted to it by the Commission. In the form finally adopted, the Services Directive imposes a set of procedural rules (securing self-discipline and cooperation between national administrations), but very few, if any, substantive rules.[21] This may explain the fact that, as the deadline for the Directive's implementation was expiring, the Commission tried to revitalize the internal market and commissioned the Monti Report.[22] On the basis of this Report, the Commission published, on October 2010, its Communication 'Towards a Single Market Act', whereby it puts forward some 50 actions for the short and medium term, which could re-launch the European economy.[23]

---

[16] Commission Communication of 4 June 1997 Action plan for the single market CSE (97)1 final, available at <http://ec.europa.eu/internal_market/strategy/docs/plan_en.pdf> (last accessed on 17 November 2011).

[17] Commission Communication of 11 May 1999, 'Implementing the Framework for Financial Markets: Action Plan COM(1999) 232 final'.

[18] Communication COM (2000) 888 final, 'An Internal Market Strategy for Services'.

[19] Communication COM (2003) 747 final, 'The Competitiveness of Business-Related Services and their Contribution to the Performance of European Enterprises', and Communication COM (2004) 83 final, 'Report on Competition in Professional Services', respectively.

[20] European Parliament and Council Directive 2006/123/EC on services in the internal market [2006] OJ L376/36.

[21] See in more detail, the discussion in ch 6.

[22] Monti Report, 2010, n 1.

[23] Communication COM (2010) 608 final, n 5. Following the suggestions made in the Monti Report, the Commission shifts back from the term 'internal market' to 'single market'; in this respect, Professor M. Monti thinks that 'From a conceptual and communication point of view, "single" seems more appropriate than "internal". Firstly, citizens of any EU country are likely to understand the term "internal market" as referring to their own domestic market, rather than the EU-wide market. Secondly, when used with non-European interlocutors, the expression European "internal market" may convey a flavour of closure, of "fortress Europe", that in general is far from reality and that it is not in the EU's interest to nurture. Thirdly, "single" is a more committing description. In fact, the market for any particular good or service within the EU is "internal" by definition, but requires actions by policy makers and market participants, if it is to be really "single", rather than fragmented' (Monti Report, 2010, n 1, at fn 1).

Among these proposals, an important proportion is vertical in nature and directly concerned with specific service activities (transport, e-commerce, business-related services, banking, etc), others touch in a horizontal way upon the way services are provided (posted workers, public procurement), while others affect the inputs used for service production (copyrights, standards, authentication, and network security). Moreover, the vast majority of the second half of the proposals, under the general title 'Restoring confidence by putting Europeans at the heart of the single market', concerns services almost exclusively. Out of the 50 proposals put forward by the Commission in its 2010 Communication, very few do not have a bearing, direct or indirect, on the provision of services.

In addition, the importance of services as the driving force of the internal market is being acknowledged by the Commission itself in its 'Europe 2020' Communication:

'The single market was conceived before the arrival of Internet, before information and communication technologies became the one of the main drivers of growth and before services became such a dominant part of the European economy. The emergence of new services (eg content and media, health, smart energy metering) shows huge potential, but Europe will only exploit this potential if it overcomes the fragmentation that currently blocks the flow of on-line content and access for consumers and companies.'[24]

It is, therefore, no exaggeration to state that the recent upsurge for the internal market constitutes, in fact, an effort to complement and push further the substance-less Services Directive.

Indeed, since the Classic Community Method (CCM) has reached its limits in the field of services (through the issuance of the Services Directive) without delivering the desired outcomes, and given that the economic conjecture in Europe demands some coordinated action in order to foster production and competitiveness in the area of the EU's comparative advantage, namely the provision of services, the quest of alternative or complementary means of regulating services becomes paramount. The ambition of the present book is to contribute to this debate.

This objective becomes all the more intriguing, since a brief examination of the legislation enacted so far in the field of services shows that the EU has been extremely timid in the area, especially if compared with the field of goods. With the notable exception of the Services Directive, the EU has legislated on a sector-specific, often uncoordinated, sometimes even experimental manner, and has lacked a solid intellectual background of guiding principles, as well as of legislative techniques.[25]

The legislative inertia has been compensated for, to a large extent, by the judiciary, who gradually developed a very important body of core principles. Indeed, there is no way one can study the rules applicable to the provision of

---

[24] Communication COM (2010) 2020, 'Europe 2020: A Strategy for Smart, Sustainable and Inclusive Growth', at 20.
[25] See the overview of existing legislation provided in ch 6.

services in the EU without paying due attention to the judgments of the Court of Justice of the EU (CJEU). Contrary to what happens in most other areas of the law, where the legislature sets some basic principles to be subsequently interpreted/ applied by the courts, in the field of services, it has been the Court that set the principles: the Posted Workers Directive, the Services Directive and the recent Patients' Rights Directive[26] all provide examples where the legislature has intervened *ex post* in order to consolidate, codify, rationalize, and, often, restrict the scope of principles and rules introduced by the Court.[27] Indeed, on some occasions, the Court has gone so far as to provoke hostile reactions, from both scholars and the general public.[28] It is submitted that the Court's well-intended activism in favour of the free movement of services has reached its limits and that any further step towards the more integrated and competitive market economy that the EU badly needs must now be made in a constitutionally more orderly way; concerns about legitimacy, coherence, and efficiency plead in favour of less casuistic and more coordinated forms of regulation. The relative failure of the CCM, witnessed by the complex and timid text of the Services Directive, calls for the study of alternative regulatory means and methods.

The timing of this book is also relevant. By virtue of the screening exercise orchestrated by the Services Directive, the member states have communicated to the Commission some thousands of measures which (may) obstruct trade in services. Going through all these measures will put the Commission, for the first time ever, in a position to grasp the regulatory needs and difficulties in this area of the law. Therefore, in the years to come the Commission is likely to put forward more and more focused regulatory proposals for the free provision of services; the Services Directive itself provides for fresh initiatives. In order for such initiatives to make sense, however, a thorough understanding of the legal position pertaining to services and of the various regulatory options available is crucial.

B. Structure of the book—methodology

In order to provide such an understanding, it is necessary first to establish the basic principles governing the provision of services within the EU, as they have been

---

[26] Proposal for a Directive COM (2008) 414 final, on the application of patients' rights in cross-border healthcare.

[27] European Parliament and Council Directive 96/71/EC concerning the posting of workers in the framework of the provision of services [1997] OJ L18/1; European Parliament and Council Directive 2006/123/EC on services in the internal market [2006] OJ L376/36; Proposal for a Directive COM (2008) 414 final, n 26. For these, see the discussion in ch 6.

[28] See eg Scharpf, F., 'The Only Solution Is to Refuse to Comply with ECJ Rulings' (2009) 4:1 *Social Europe J* 16, also available at <http://www.social-europe.eu/2009/04/interview-the-only-solu-tion-is-to-refuse-to-comply-with-ecj-ruling> (last accessed on 17 November 2011) calling for civil disobedience to the Court's case law, after the *Viking* and *Laval* judgments, for which see in ch 5 (Case C-438/05 *International Transport Workers' Federation and Finnish Seamen's Union v Viking Line ABP and OÜ Viking Line Eesti* [2007] ECR I-10779 and Case C-341/05 *Laval un Partneri Ltd v Svenska Byggnadsarbetareförbundet, Svenska Byggnadsarbetareförbundets avdelning 1, Byggettan and Svenska Elektrikerförbundet* [2007] ECR I-11767).

developed by the Court, then to look at the way in which these have been put to work by the legislature, and thereafter, to examine the extent to which alternative ways of regulation could be used to achieve comparable objectives.

More specifically, the structure of the present book develops as follows: Chapter 1 is intended to offer a basic literature review on the two overarching themes of the book, namely *services* and *regulation*. Chapter 2 delves into the legal definition of services under EU law, by examining the core question 'what is in a market?' and how the boundaries between market and non-market activities are drawn within the EU; by the same token, the concept of services of general (economic) interest is explored. Chapters 3 and 4 look into the concept of restrictions to the free provision of services and to justifications for such restrictions. Chapter 5 briefly examines the various areas 'regulated' through case law, while Chapter 6 looks on the manifestations of legislative initiative in the area of services. Chapter 7 explores how private regulation has been used for regulating services and examines the limitations thereof. Chapter 8 turns to non-regulatory means of regulating services, such as the Open Method of Coordination (OMC), the powers given to various EU agencies, to national regulatory authorities, and to networks thereof. Chapter 9 concludes with some speculative thoughts on the way 'new governance' could be effectively used in order to promote trade in services. Chapter 10 summarizes the previous chapters and gives an insight into future directions.

The approach followed is both positivist and normative. The author's intention has been that these two aspects are present in every single chapter of the book: a description of the legal situation and of the relevant literature is, ideally, followed by normative thoughts on how things could be made to work. Moreover, the structure of the book is intended to convey a dynamic paradigm, since the first chapters are more positivist and oriented to past experience, while the later ones are more normative and provide an outlook on the future.

In the effort to build these two approaches, the analysis has 'trespassed' into sciences of which the author has much less mastery than of law: this applies to the use of basic statistics and to the extensive references to political and administrative science work. Both experiments have been extremely rewarding experiences to the author, and, hopefully, will not prove catastrophic for the relevant sciences nor for the readers.

The book's venture into statistics has been prompted by the observation made above that, in the field of services more than in relation to any other EU fundamental freedom, the Court has played a major role in setting the applicable principles. The original idea has been that, if further regulation in the field of services is to be proposed, the wealth of the Court's case law should be studied, not only in terms of the principles established, but also in terms of the areas of economic activity touched and of the kinds of restrictions identified. In other words, in order to single out the areas in which future regulation may be necessary and the kinds of restrictions it is to face, one needs to look into the experience so far. The Services Directive was intended to be a step in this direction; instead, the lack of a comprehensive quantitative study of the Court's case law, the important exceptions and exclusions foreseen already in the draft Directive as put forward by Commissioner Bolkestein (the Bolkestein draft) and, of course, the highly unsatisfactory text which ensued from the CCM decision-making process, underlined all more graphically the need for a fresh study of the relevant case law. With the above in mind, a quantitative study of the full body of cases concerning services was undertaken, covering the relevant case law since the beginning of the EEC in 1958;[29] the quantitative study covers the period to June 2009.[30] The study is intended to be as complete as possible; it does not purport, however, to be fully exhaustive, as many cases having some impact on trade in services primarily concern other areas of EU law (the other freedoms, citizenship, competition law, transport, flanking policies, etc) and are difficult to pick up in a comprehensive manner. Instead of proceeding in some requalification leading to yet another classification of existing case law, the collection of cases taken in the study is based on the classifications of the EUR-Lex database combined with those of the Court (interestingly the two do not fully correspond): all cases which appear under the category 'services' in the two EU databases have been included. The corpus has been further enriched, on the judgment of the author, with a few cases recorded under different headings which are, nonetheless, highly relevant to the area of services.

In the first count, the study covered only those cases in which the Treaty provisions on services are applied, alone or together with some rule of secondary legislation. Cases which exclusively concern the application of some Regulation, Directive, or Decision in the area of services have been left out. Both preliminary rulings (Article 267 TFEU) and proceedings against member states (Article 258 TFEU) have been included. A total of 283 cases have been recorded.[31] These have been used in various classifications. It is worth noting that out of those cases, almost half (125) have been delivered by the Full Court or, after the entry into force of the Nice Treaty, the Grand Chamber of the Court of Justice, typically with the intervention of numerous member states.

While the quantitative study does not go beyond the end of June 2009, the law and corresponding bibliography in this book is up to date as of the end of December 2010.

Vassilis Hatzopoulos

Athens/Komotini February 2010

---

[29] Interestingly enough, though, the first services case only reached the Court in 1974 (Case 155/73 *Giuseppe Sacchi* [1974] ECR 409).

[30] This study would not have been possible without the precious help of Diane Grisel, a College of Europe alumna and PhD candidate at the University of Geneva. The relevant database has been developed jointly and has been fleshed out essentially by her relentless efforts. We are jointly responsible for any errors or misrepresentations made therein.

[31] See Appendix, Case Law Processed in the Spreadsheet.

Acknowledgements

After having wandered around in various stimulating areas of EU law, ranging from institutional, political, procedural, internal market and competition matters, to issues related to the areas of freedom, security, justice, and LGBT rights, with this book I chose to revisit the origins of my academic career: services.

Therefore, I cannot but acknowledge the defining impact on my academic personality exerted by my early professors, Denys Simon, Robert Kovar, and David O'Keeffe: if they have nothing to do with the making of this book, they contributed greatly to forming its author. Without knowing it, Elias Mossialos contributed too, by instigating my interest in healthcare, thus refreshing my (then faded) interest in services. Paul Demaret and Inge Govaere gave me the opportunity to teach at the College of Europe, Bruges, and even created a seminar broadly bearing the title of the present book; indirectly but surely they contributed both in terms of intellectual stimuli and discussions, and in terms of access to valuable bibliographic sources. Tamara Hervey and Aris Georgopoulos gave me the opportunity to test some of my ideas before the wonderful crowd of the University of Nottingham, while the *CML Rev* people (Alison McDonnel in particular) systematically encouraged me to 'get some exposure' on this area of the law.

Erika Szyszcack's long experience and motherly manners have guided me both in relation to the general direction followed and with regard to specific issues touched by the book. Catherine Barnard, Lawrence Gormley, and Tony Prosser have very usefully reviewed parts of this book akin to their respective interests, and I am highly indebted to all of them.

The two people whose help has been absolutely decisive for the completion of the present book are Diane Grisel, a College of Europe alumnus and PhD candidate at the University of Geneva, who has helped me with the early classifications and all the statistics of this book, and Christos Malamataris, a Cantab LLM alumnus, who has edited, corrected, and critically reviewed the draft. His work has been brought to perfection by the infallible OUP editor.

Most importantly, I would like to thank my grown-up family—actually I started thinking about this book at the same time as I started thinking about new arrivals, and I managed to have two (arrivals, not books!)—for their patience and love.

Contents Summary

Contents

Table of Cases

Table of Cases

Table of Legislation

DECISIONS

List of Abbreviations

ACER	Agency for the Cooperation of Energy Regulators
AFSJ	area of freedom, security, and justice
AG	Advocate General
AIFM	alternative investment fund manager
Art	article
AVMS	audiovisual media services
B2B	business to business
B2C	business to customer
BEPG	Broad Economic Policy Guidelines
BER	block exemption Regulations
BEREC	Body of European Regulators for Electronic Communications
CCCTB	common consolidated corporate tax base
CCM	Classic Community Method
CDE	*Cahiers de Droit Européen*
CEBR	Centre for Economics and Business Research
CEBS	Committee of European Banking Supervisors
CEER	Council of European Energy Regulators
CEIOPS	Committee of European Insurance and Occupational Pensions Supervisors
CEN	Comite Européenne de Normalisation
CENELEC	Comite Européenne de Normalisation Electrotechnique
CERP	European Committee for Postal Recognition
CESR	Committee of European Securities Regulators
CFI	Court of First Instance
ch	chapter
CJEU	Court of Justice of the European Union
CML Rev	*Common Market Law Review*
CoC	Code of Conduct
CoCom	Communications Committee
COEES	Confederation of European Security Services
CoOP	country of origin principle
CoR	Committee of Regions
COTIF	Convention pour le Transport International Ferroviaire

CPA	Classification of Products by Activity
CPC	Central Product Classification
CPV	Common Procurement Vocabulary
CRA	credit rating agency
CSDP	Common Security and Defence Policy
CSR	corporate social responsibility
CUP	Cambridge University Press
CYEL	*Cambridge Yearbook of European Legal Studies*
DG	Directorate General
EACEA	Education, Audiovisual and Culture Executive Agency
EACI	Executive Agency for Competitiveness and Innovation
EAHC	Executive Agency for Health and Consumers
EASA	European Aviation Safety Agency
EBA	European Banking Authority
EBL Rev	*European Business Law Review*
ECHR	European Convention of Human Rights
ECJ	European Court of Justice
ECOSOC	Economic and Social Committee
ECPR	European Committee of Postal Regulators
ECR	European Court Reports
ECSC	European Coal and Steel Community
ECtHR	European Court of Human Rights
ECTS	European Credit and Transfer Accumulation System
ed	editor
EEC	European Economic Community
EES	European employment strategy
EIOPA	European Insurance and Occupational Pensions Authority
EL Rev	*European Law Review*
ELJ	*European Law Journal*
EMSA	European Maritime Safety Agency
EMU	Economic and Monetary Union
ENISA	European Network and Information Security Agency
EP	European Parliament
ERA	European Railway Agency
ERC	European Research Council
ERG	European Regulators Group
ERGEG	European Regulatory Group for Energy and Gas
ERGPS	European Regulators Group for Postal Services

ERSA	European Rail Safety Agency
ERTMS	European Rail Traffic Management System
ESA	European Supervisory Authorities
ESFS	European System of Financial Supervision
ESMA	European Securities and Markets Authority
ESRB	European Systemic Risk Board
ETSI	European Telecommunications Standards Institute
ETSO	European Transmission System Operators
EU	European Union
EUMC	European Monitoring Centre on Racism and Xenophobia
Eur	European
FDI	foreign direct investment
FEG	Federation Européenne des Guides
fn	footnote
FOC	flag of convenience
FRA	EU Agency for Fundamental Rights
GATS	General Agreement on Trade in Services
GATT	General Agreement on Tariffs and Trade
GDP	gross domestic product
GSM	Global System for Mobile Communications
GTE	Gas Transmission Europe
ICT	information communications technology
IGC	Intergovernmental Conference
IM	internal market
IMC	internal market clauses
IMF	International Monetary Fund
IMI	internal market information
Int	international
IPPP	institutionalized private public partnership
IRA	independent regulatory authority
IRG	Independent Regulators Group
ISIC	International Standard Classification
IT	information technology
ITF	International Transport Workers Federation
J	journal
JEPP	*Journal of European Public Policy*
L	Law
LGBT	lesbian, gay, bisexual, and transgender

LIEI	*Legal Issues of Economic Integration*
MFN	most favoured nation (principle)
MR	mutual recognition
MSITS	Manual of Statistics of International Trade in Services
n	note
NACE	Nomenclature Statistique des Activités Economiques dans la Communauté Européenne
NAP	national action plan
NAICS	North American Industry Classification
NCA	National Competition Authority
NESGI	non-economic service of general interest
NGO	non-governmental organization
No.	number
NRA	national regulatory authorities
OECD	Organization of Economic Cooperation and Development
OJ	Official Journal
OLAF	Office de la Lutte Antifraude
OMC	Open Method of Coordination
ONP	open network provision
ORPI	overriding reasons in the public interest
OUP	Oxford University Press
para	paragraph
PPP	private public partnership
R&D	research & development
RAXEN	Racism and Xenophobia Network
REA	Research Executive Agency
Rec	recital
Rev	Review
RIA	Regulatory Impact Assessment
RTDE	*Revue Trimestrielle de Droit Européen*
SD	Services Directive
SEC	Secretariat-General
SGEI	service of general economic interest
SGI	service of general interest
SHEC	safety, health, environment, and consumer
SIC	standard industrial classification
SME	small and medium-sized enterprise
SRB	sustainable responsible business

SSGI	social service of general interest
TCN	third-country national
TEN-T EA	Trans-European Transport Network Executive Agency
TEU	Treaty for the European Union
TFEU	Treaty on the Functioning of the European Union
TVWF	television without frontiers
UK	United Kingdom
UN	United Nations
UNCTAD	United Nations Conference on Trade and Development
US	United States
v.	versus
WEP	West European Politics
WTO	World Trade Organization
YEL	*Yearbook of European Law*

1

Regulation and Services:
Basic Conceptual Background

The title of this book bears on three main topics: services, regulation, and the European Union (EU). This first chapter is intended to show how these three components fit with one another, and to explain why it is important for anyone with an interest in the EU to consider the issue of services regulation. This issue, of course, is equally crucial at the EU and the international level, since services account for the most important part of national GDPs in developed countries and the international trade in services is on the increase. For EU member states, however, the EU constitutes by far the most important level for service regulation, since, during the last two decades, the rules developed in tandem by the EU legislature and judiciary set the scene not only for trading services across borders, but also for the very provision of services within each individual member state. National regulatory choices, despite the theoretical shield of formal competence share (expressly consecrated by the Lisbon Treaty) and subsidiarity, are far from being intact. EU regulation encroaches upon them both directly, in areas of shared competence, and indirectly, in areas where member states retain their regulatory powers, but 'must nevertheless comply with Community law when exercising those powers'.[1]

At the international level, the most important source of obligations in the area of services is the General Agreement on Trade in Services (GATS), signed in 1994 as part of the Treaty establishing the World Trade Organization (WTO). The GATS has a normative content which is complex (both in the way the Agreement is structured and in the way the various provisions relate to one another), unclear (the precise content of the main obligations stemming from the Agreement is open to various interpretations—as confirmed by the few GATS opinions delivered by the WTO Dispute Settlement bodies), and uneven (each signatory member is only bound to the extent of its own commitments). Hence, unsurprisingly, one of the chief objectives of the ongoing Doha round of negotiations is the revision of the GATS. Notwithstanding the revision process, the GATS does create a framework of legal obligations on EU member states, albeit one that is felt much more loosely than the impact of EU regulation. Indeed, one of the issues for EU regulation is

---

[1] According to the expression regularly used by the CJEU in areas such as taxation, healthcare and education.

that it needs itself to be GATS-compatible, in order to ensure that member states do not violate their commitments; not to mention the EU's own obligations as a signatory to the GATS.[2] In addition to the complex, unclear, and uneven character of the GATS, there are at least two reasons why the TFEU has a more important impact on service regulation. First and foremost, for the time being, the GATS remains essentially an instrument of negative integration: it is about deregulation and better regulation at the national level, but regulation produced at the GATS level is scarce.[3] Secondly, the GATS rules are restricted to market opening, but do not impose, as yet, any competition discipline at the global level.[4] As it shall be seen in the following chapters, however, the regulation of services in the EU takes place as much through the internal market rules as through the EU competition rules.

For these reasons, the EU level of service regulation has been chosen as the most meaningful one to examine the way in which services are, or may be, regulated.

A. Services

It is a commonplace to read or hear that we live in a 'service society', that over 70 per cent of the wealth produced by developed nations is through service provision, and that almost all new employment opportunities currently emerge in the field of services. Few people, however, are sure about what services actually represent. Indeed, the only people certain of the definition of 'services' are those who have never seriously thought about them. Once one starts reading about services, one is flabbergasted by the ambiguity that reigns in relation to them, examined under any discipline: economics, social sciences, law. The ambition of the present section is not to add to the fast-growing bibliography, both vertical and interdisciplinary, on services, but rather to cherry-pick elements from pre-existing analyses, which will make the advances in the following chapters more intelligible. First, a quick glance will be had at the economic definition of services and the linked social realities, then services as a legal category under the EU legal system will be briefly presented.

---

[2] Princen, S., 'EC Compliance with WTO Law: The Interplay of Law and Politics' (2004) 15 *Eur J of Int L* 555–74.

[3] The mandates given to that effect by the GATS, notably in the area of internal regulation (Art VI), safeguard measures (Art X), and subsidies (Art XV) have so far failed to deliver any binding text, while the Agreement on Public Procurement (Art XIII) is only a plurilateral one, essentially based on the EU experience.

[4] Warner, M., 'Competition policy and GATS' in Sauvé, P., and Stern, R. (eds), *GATS 2000: New Directions in Services Trade Liberalization* (Washington DC: Harvard/Brookings Institution Press, 2000) 364–98; for the potential of the GATS on internal regulation, however, see Wouters, J., and Coppens, D., 'GATS and domestic regulation: Balancing the right to regulate and trade liberalization' in Alexander, K., and Andenas, M. (eds), *The World Trade Organization and Trade in Services* (The Hague: Brill, 2008) 207–36; and more extensively, Delimatsis, P., *International Trade in Services and Domestic Regulations, Necessity, Transparency and Regulatory Diversity* (Oxford: OUP, 2008).

1. Services in real-economic terms

a. Brief history of (scientific interest in) services

It is a commonplace to state that services only became important in the 1970s and that, before that, they constituted a category broadly ignored by economists and social scientists alike. This is true only if one looks back to the last couple of centuries. The image becomes much more diversified by looking further back. A few snapshots from history may testify to this. Food collectors and hunters possessed very little in terms of goods, but were quite proficient in getting organized to ensure that the services mutually provided (food collection, hunting, securing the village, cooking, childcare, etc) guaranteed the survival of their families and societies. Classical Athens and Rome were both societies where services dominated: defence and public security, leisure, sport, education, justice, sanitation, etc. The production of goods, at this time, depended to a large extent on the provision of services (defence, public security, justice) and was essentially left to servants.[5] More importantly, the quality of the polity and the means of its citizens to identify with it were directly linked to the quality of the services provided. More than a necessary prerequisite for the production of material goods,[6] services were seen as the main import of the state. In the Middle Ages, average people possessed very little and the earth belonged to the aristocracy; the feudal system was based on the sovereign offering security and other services (such as justice, sanitation, religious services, etc) against chores offered by the vassals. It was with the industrial revolution and the advent of manufacturing that property became paramount and that wealth came to be counted on the basis of the quantity of goods produced, owned, and traded. From the eighteenth century on, the only services considered to have some added value were commerce, transport, and financial services.[7] This lack of interest in services prevailed, although in industrialized states services accounted for an important part of wealth production even by the nineteenth century: in 1851, more than 45 per cent of the UK's national income was derived from service activities (trade, transport, the professions, and so on).[8]

Services came to be recognized as a distinct economic category only in the mid-twentieth century under the opaque terminology of 'tertiary sector'. Defined by

---

[5] Rubalcaba, L., *The New Service Economy: Challenges and Policy Implications for Europe* (Cheltenham/Northampton: Edward Elgar Publishing, 2007), at 16–17.

[6] For recent expressions of this idea see Huysmans, J., 'A Foucaultian View on Spill-over: Freedom and Security in the EU' (2004) 7 *J of Int Relations and Development* 298–314; Bigo, D., Carrera, S., and Guild, E., 'The Challenge Project: Final Policy Recommendations on the Changing Landscape of European Liberty and Security' (2009) CEPS Paper available at <http://www.ceps.eu/book/challenge-project-final-policy-recommendations-changing-landscape-european-liberty-and-security> (last accessed on 5 November 2011).

[7] Ibid.

[8] Bryson, J., and Daniels, P., 'Worlds of services: from local service economies to offshoring or global sourcing' in Bryson, J., and Daniels, P. (eds), *The Handbook of Services Industries* (Cheltenham/Northampton: Edward Elgar Publishing, 2007) 1–16, at 1; they cite the work of Dean, P., and Cole, W., *British Economic Growth 1688–1959* (Cambridge: CUP, 1962).

A.G.B. Fisher and C. Clark in the early 1940s, taken on by J. Fourastié in 1949, and reformulated by W.W. Rostow in 1953, the tertiary sector covered all which could not be described as agriculture or manufacture.[9] It took another 20 years before W.J. Baumol's seminal paper on unbalanced growth was published (1967) and yet another decade or two before the economic characteristics and regulatory needs of services started being systematically explored. This delay was largely underpinned by the lack of coherent numerical data, itself caused, among other things, by the absence of commonly accepted service classifications, as well as measurement units.

b. Definition—classifications

Services cover so many and so very different economic activities that even today it is debated whether services are a useful category at all.[10] More importantly—and this is a characteristic bearing important legal consequences, especially in the EU framework—'services' may refer to a group of activities, such as trading, playing, driving; and at the same time, to the products/results of these activities, such as sales, concerts, journeys.[11]

Since the 'tertiary' sector came to be identified by opposition to the other two, agriculture and manufacturing, most definitions of services tend to be negative, their focus being on the immaterial/intangible nature of services. Several authors have tried to turn the negative characteristics of services into positive definitions. Although general catch-all definitions are undeniably useful,[12] it is preferable for the present purposes to look into the specific characteristics of services. In this direction, L. Rubalcaba has identified four negative features which he has 'reversed' in order to explore the positive features of services.[13] He contrasts a) the immaterial and non-tangible nature of services to their usefulness or benefit to the service recipient; b) the fact that services are non-transportable to the fact that they are produced and consumed simultaneously; c) the fact that services are non-cumulative, non-storable, and non-quantifiable to the fact that they procure some change to a good or to a person and that they are the result of a dialogue relationship and of interaction between the provider and the recipient; and finally,

---

[9] For a discussion of the above classification, see Rubalcaba, L., 2007, n 5, at 24; Petit, P., 'The political economy of services in tertiary economies' in Bryson, J., and Daniels, P. (eds), *The Handbook of Services Industries* (Cheltenham/Northampton: Edward Elgar Publishing, 2007) 77–97, at 79.

[10] Illeris, S., 'The nature of services' in Bryson, J., and Daniels, P. (eds), *The Handbook of Services Industries* (Cheltenham/Northampton: Edward Elgar Publishing, 2007) 19–33.

[11] The double nature of services as an activity and as an end-product is an attribute having important consequences on the regulatory means deployed for regulating services. Hence, it constitutes a recurrent theme of this work.

[12] One of the most widely recognized definitions of services has been given by Hill, P., 'On Goods and Services' (1977) 23 *Rev of Income and Wealth* 315–38, at 318. According to him, 'a service may be defined as a change in the condition of a person, or of a good belonging to some economic unit, which is brought about as the result of the activity of some other economic unit, with the prior agreement of the former person or economic unit'.

[13] Rubalcaba, L., 2007, n 5, at 20–3; he is more analytical and identifies seven criteria, but here similar ones have been grouped together and only four have been maintained.

d) the non-predictable character of services to the creation of a transitive relation-ship between the provider and the recipient.[14] S. Illeris reasons along the same lines, but further draws some basic consequences: a) the importance of proximity, b) the need for trust between provider and recipient, c) the limited opportunities for economies of scale, and d) the high demand elasticity of most (but not all) services.[15]

The descriptions above of the residual category of services make it clear that its actual content may be extremely varied and heterogeneous. This heterogeneity is a source of difficulties both at the analytical and at the statistical level.[16]

i. Analytical classifications

From an analytical point view, it is hardly an exaggeration to state that there are as many classification proposals as there are academics writing on services. Depending on the viewpoint adopted, various—often overlapping—classifications have been proposed:[17]

  i. on the basis of the recipient: intermediary/final services; business services/ individual services;

  ii. on the basis of their integration into the economic cycle: production services/distribution services/personal services/social services;

  iii. on the basis of their object: services on goods/services on information/ services on persons/pure public services;

  iv. on the basis of the intensity of innovation/sophistication needed for their provision: highly sophisticated services/non-sophisticated services;

  v. on the basis of the standardization involved: serial services/highly individua-lized services;

  vi. on the basis of their temporal dimension: instant services/temporary-permanent services/storable services;

  vii. on the basis of their geographical dimension: services offered *in situ*/con-sumable at a distance.

Further classifications are proposed by social scientists from non-economic disci-plines. Moreover, classifications are advanced concerning the entities providing services (rather than the services themselves). For instance, on the basis of customers

---

[14] Rubalcaba, L., 2007, n 5, at 22.

[15] Illeris, S., 2007, n 10, at 25–7.

[16] It is worth reproducing the following note, attached to the UN CPC classification v.1 (21 Febru-ary 2002): '28. Among the variety of criteria generally used for distinguishing between goods and services (tangible versus intangible, storable versus non-storable or transportable versus non-transportable), none provides a valid, practical, and unambiguous distinction between goods and services in all cases. While the product content of most CPC subclasses can be identified as being goods or services, in some cases this cannot be resolved easily. Examples of borderline cases are photographs, computer tapes or meals or drinks in restaurants.'

[17] See for the discussion of the various classifications, Rubalcaba, L., 2007, n 5, at 23–7; Illeris, S., 2007, n 10, at 29–33; and Howells, J., 'The nature of innovation in services' in OECD, *Innovation and Productivity in Services: Industry, Services and Trade* (Paris: OECD, 2001) 57–82.

served per day, one can distinguish between professional services, service shops, and mass services. There may also be classifications on the basis of the personnel involved: professional, technical, and related workers; administrative and managerial workers; clerical, and related workers; sale workers and service workers.[18]

For EU purposes, one important category is that of business-related services. Indeed, in 2003 the Commission adopted a broadened definition of 'business-related services' which encompasses: a) business services, themselves divided into knowledge-intensive *professional* services (IT consulting, research and development, R&D, etc) and operational *industrial* services (cleaning, security, etc); b) distribution services; c) network services; and d) financial services.[19] These represent over 55 per cent of employment in the EU and, according to the Commission, could grow much more if several conditions were fulfilled: greater market integration in order to foster competitiveness, better inputs (qualified employment, information and communication technologies, R&D, etc), greater transparency of services markets, better knowledge of the sector, and even use of services across regions.[20] Indeed, as the statistical data compiled for the present book shows, the vast majority of cases brought before the CJEU relate to business-related services.[21]

ii. Statistical classifications

From a statistical point of view, the above polyphony inevitably leads to divergent or incompatible classifications which, in turn, make it difficult to adduce comparable statistical data. The United Nations (UN) have, accordingly, developed the International Standard Classification (ISIC) of all industrial activities, grouping together enterprises that produce the same type of goods or services or use similar processes (ie the same raw materials, process of production, skills, or technology). The first ISIC classification was issued in 1948, and was subsequently revised in 1958, in 1968 (version 2), and then again in 1989 (version 3). ISIC version 4 was officially released on 11 August 2008. In parallel, the UN have also released the Central Product Classification (CPC) which covers goods and services (2000). CPC subsequent version 2 was completed on 31 December 2008. ISIC and CPC are connected, the difference being that the former classifies activities (ie industries), while the latter classifies products (goods and services).

The EU has developed its Statistical Classification of Economic Activities in the European Community (*Nomenclature statistique des activités économiques dans la Communauté Européenne* (NACE)), which was revised in 2002 (version 1.1) and

---

[18] For these two classifications see Illeris, S., 2007, n 10, at 31.

[19] Communication COM (2003) 747 final, 'The Competitiveness of Business-related Services and their Contribution to the Performance of European Enterprises'; and Communication COM (2004) 83 final, 'Report on Competition in Professional Services'.

[20] For a recent account of the importance of business services and the means for their development see Giovanneti, G., Guerrieri, P., and Quintieri, B. (eds), *Business Services: The New Frontiers of Competitiveness* (Cosenza: Rubbettino Editore, 2010).

[21] Further on this, see in ch 5.

then again in 2010 (version 2).[22] NACE version 2 is already applied by the EU institutions and its use has been extended to National Accounts and Balance of Payments statistics as of September 2011. NACE is completely consistent with ISIC version 2, but more detailed. Linked to the NACE at the EU level, one can also find the Classification of Products by Activity (CPA), which corresponds to the UN's CPC.[23] Alongside these classifications other more purpose-specific classifications of services have been established, in particular in the framework of the services procurement Directives (now Directives 2004/17 and 2004/18[24]) or the Common Procurement Vocabulary, last amended in 2008.[25]

The UN's ISIC and EU's NACE broadly distinguish the same 21 categories, as follows (NACE version 2):

A. Agriculture, forestry, and fishing
B. Mining and quarrying
C. Manufacturing
D. Electricity, gas, steam, and air-conditioning supply
E. Water supply, sewerage, waste management, and remediation activities
F. Construction
G. Wholesale and retail trade, repair of motor vehicles and motorcycles
H. Transportation and storage
I. Accommodation and food service activities
J. Information and communication
K. Financial and insurance services
L. Real estate activities
M. Professional, scientific, and technical activities
N. Administrative and support service activities
O. Public administration and defence, compulsory social security
P. Education
Q. Human health and social work activities
R. Arts, entertainment, and recreation
S. Other service activities

---

[22] Different classifications have also been developed in the US, such as the Standard Industrial Classification (SIC) and the North American Industry Classification System (NAICS).

[23] Council Regulation 3696/93/EC on the statistical classification of products by activity (CPA) in the European Economic Community [1993] OJ L342/1.

[24] European Parliament and Council Directive 2004/17/EC coordinating the procurement procedures of entities operating in the water, energy, transport and postal services sectors [2004] OJ L134/1 and European Parliament and Council Directive 2004/18/EC on the coordination of procedures for the award of public works contracts, public supply contracts and public service contracts [2004] OJ L134/114.

[25] European Parliament and Council Regulation 2195/2002/EC on the Common Procurement Vocabulary (CPV) [2002] OJ L340/1, modified by Commission Regulation 213/2008/EC amending Regulation (EC) No 2195/2002 of the European Parliament and of the Council on the Common Procurement Vocabulary (CPV) and Directives 2004/17/EC and 2004/18/EC of the European Parliament and of the Council on public procurement procedures, as regards the revision of the CPV [2008] OJ L74/1.

T. Activities of households as employers, undifferentiated goods, and services-producing activities for own use

U. Activities of extraterritorial organizations and bodies.

Compared to the earlier version, the 2010 NACE classification brought remarkable changes: it merged into single categories several non-service activities (eg agriculture and forestry merged with fishing), split services previously dealt with together in separate groups (for instance, water supply is distinguished from electricity and gas) and recognized new service categories (such as professional, scientific, and technical activities, and also administrative and support service activities); overall, it is clearly more service-oriented.

Another important classification in the area of services stems from the GATS. The GATS covers all services, but for those 'supplied in the exercise of governmental activity' (Article I(3)b). Signatory states are bound to respect the basic most-favoured-nation principle (MFN) together with general transparency and reasonableness obligations for all services. Most importantly, however, GATS signatory states have undertaken commitments, submitted schedules, in respect of specific sector activities, distinguishing between each one of the four supply modes.[26] In order to schedule commitments, signatory states have drawn upon a classification scheme based on the UN system and incorporated in a working document of the WTO secretariat at the time of negotiations, known under its code name as 'W/120'.[27] The GATS classification includes 12 categories of services, as follows: a) tourism, b) financial services, c) communications, d) business services, e) transport, f) construction, g) environmental services, h) leisure, i) distribution, j) health, k) education, l) other services.

iii. Classifications on the basis of information asymmetries

In addition to the analytical and statistical classifications above, there is yet another categorization of services, based on the degree of information asymmetries incorporated therein. If the analytical and statistical classifications are important for economic purposes, the distinction based on information asymmetries is crucial for evaluating the kind and degree of regulation needed for different types of services.[28] A tripartite distinction may be drawn between a) *search services*, the quality of which can be evaluated in advance, provided some re-*search* is done by the service recipient (eg tourist/hotel/restaurant services), b) *experience services*, the quality of which may only be evaluated after consumption (eg hairdresser's/architect's services), and c) *credence services*, the quality of which may not be evaluated

---

[26] These are explained in detail in subsection A(1)e.

[27] The full reference of this document being *MTN.GNS/W/120;* the role of document W/120 in interpreting the actual content of national schedules has been lengthily discussed by the WTO Dispute Settlement Body and by the Appeal Body in case WTO/A (07/04/2005), *US Gambling*, WT/DS285/AB/R available at <http://www.worldtradelaw.net/search/searchreports.htm> (last accessed on 5 November 2011).

[28] For a brief presentation of the distinction, see Rubalcaba, L., 2007, n 5, at 21.

even after consumption (eg medical/surgical treatments, legal services) and in which trust is a paramount feature.

This distinction, common in the area of goods, becomes all the more important in the area of services: while most goods correspond to the two first categories, services rarely fall within the first, mostly come under the second, and very often fall under the third. Service providers, by the use of common standards, labels, trademarks, franchises, codes of conduct, and the like, try to bring services from the latter towards the former categories. Regulators, on their part, tend to secure a minimal level of trust by imposing strict entry and/or exercise requirements. Therefore, credence services call for more intensive regulation than search, or even experience services.

c. Economic characteristics

i. Productivity in services

The two most influential economic thinkers of all time, A. Smith and K. Marx, despite their fundamentally divergent viewpoints, agree on (at least) one thing: that services bear no (intrinsic) economic value. According to A. Smith:

'The sovereign, for example, with all the officers both of justice and war who serve under him, the whole army and navy, are unproductive labourers... Their service, how honourable, how useful, or how necessary so ever, produces nothing for which an equal quantity of service can afterwards be procured... In the same class must be ranked, some of the grave and most important, and some of the most frivolous professions: churchmen, lawyers, physicians, men of letters of all kinds; players, buffoons, musicians, opera-singers, opera-dancers etc... Like the declamation of the actor, the harangue of the orator, or the tune of the musician, the work of all of them perishes in the very instant of its production.'[29]

For K. Marx, equally, wealth was defined as human labour accumulated in products that can be owned.[30]

Today, however, wealth is understood as a high degree of satisfaction of human needs.[31] Clearly, services play an important role in this. Moreover, the distinction of productive (ie engaged in agriculture and manufacture) from unproductive labour (ie engaged in service activities) no longer corresponds to economic reality. Instead, the production, consumption, and trade of services constitute the main source of wealth and employment. Furthermore, services are increasingly incorporated into goods' production in general (via market research, product design, development and testing, advertising) and especially into manufacturing (smart-phones and computers have little value without their embedded software and content).[32] This has prompted several authors to talk of 'a complex process of

---

[29] Smith, A., *The Wealth of Nations* (Harmondsworth: Penguin Books, 1977) 430–1.

[30] Illeris, S., 'The nature of services' in Bryson, J., and Daniels, P. (eds), *The Handbook of Services Industries* (Cheltenham/Northampton: Edward Elgar Publishing, 2007) 19–33, at 28.

[31] Ibid.

[32] See Bryson, J., and Daniels, P. 'Worlds of services: from local service economies to offshoring or global sourcing' in Bryson, J., and Daniels, P. (eds), *The Handbook of Services Industries* (Cheltenham/Northampton: Edward Elgar Publishing, 2007) 1–16, at 5.

hybridisation, whereby the categories of manufacturing and services are becoming increasingly blurred',[33] or, more ambitiously, of a 'servindustrial society', where 'the differentiation of a product is reached by means of material-immaterial combinations within the good-service continuum'.[34]

In view of these developments, economic theory, beginning in the middle of last century, gradually recognized the economic importance of services.[35] The development of common classifications and the availability of statistical data in recent decades[36] gave a considerable boost to this effort.

Nonetheless, even today there is a substantial literature dedicated to the question of productivity in services.[37] The most prominent view opposing productivity in services comes from W.J. Baumol, who identified a productivity 'disease'.[38] Since in services work is used as an end rather than as a means (as in the production of goods), productivity in the field may be only marginally increased through the use of machines, standardization, technological innovations, and the like.[39] In an economy where wages are established on the basis of growth productivity, costs in less dynamic sectors are relatively higher over time. Increased costs will reduce demand and, therefore, employment will gradually diminish and disappear unless activities are subsidised. Therefore, according to W.J. Baumol, sectors such as theatre, handicraft, *haute cuisine* and, on a different account, public services, will either be subsidized or disappear. *Haute cuisine* is still there and thriving, however, and W.J. Baumol's model has been contested by other scholars, both concerning its assumptions and its outcomes.[40]

Moreover, despite the dire predictions of Baumol, the productivity of services has been quite high, and the use of ICTs and other technologies, combined with the effort to standardize services have increased the productivity of services even further.[41] Empirical research shows that service sectors such as transport, communication, financial services, distributive services, and ICT-related services register productivity growths comparable to manufacturing industries. Other, more traditional sectors, such as social and personal services, business-related services, hotel and restaurant services, register low or even negative productivity.[42] What is more,

---

[33] See Bryson, J., and Daniels, P. 'Worlds of services: from local service economies to offshoring or global sourcing' in Bryson, J., and Daniels, P. (eds), *The Handbook of Services Industries* (Cheltenham/Northampton: Edward Elgar Publishing, 2007) 1–16, at 7.

[34] Rubalcaba, L., 2007, n 5, at 27, 29.

[35] See very briefly at the beginning of the present chapter; in some more detail, see Rubalcaba, L., 2007, n 5, at 16–23 and Illeris, S., 2007, n 30, at 19–25.

[36] See the discussion under subheading A(1)b(ii).

[37] See eg Rubalcaba, L., 2007, n 5, at 80–95, who dedicates an entire chapter of his book; see also Petit, P., 'The political economy of services in tertiary economies' in Bryson, J., and Daniels, P. (eds), *The Handbook of Services Industries* (Cheltenham/Northampton: Edward Elgar Publishing, 2007) 77–97.

[38] Baumol, W.J., 'Macroeconomics of Unbalanced Growth: the Anatomy of Urban Crisis' (1967) 57 *American Economic Rev* 415–26.

[39] Productivity is understood as the increase in the value added per unit of employment used; see Rubalcaba, L., 2007, n 5, at 89.

[40] For this criticism, see briefly Petit, P., 2007, n 37, at 80.

[41] Ibid, at 83.

[42] Rubalcaba, L., 2007, n 5, at 93.

it should be noted that the productivity of services can vary at different points in time (it tends to be high at the setup of fresh service activities but slows down thereafter) and in different countries. Therefore, no hard and fast conclusions may be reached concerning services' productivity.

ii. Economic data on services

The divergent classifications of services, as discussed above, also reflect the way services are presented in statistics and, inevitably, how they are accounted for, at both the domestic and the international level. In this respect, at least three types of difficulty should be mentioned.

First, since different countries and different trading blocks follow different classifications, the data provided is not fully homogeneous and comparable: activities which may be dealt as goods in one system may be counted as services under another. This problem is further exacerbated by the fact that government service activities are sometimes not accounted for, depending on the overarching ideological beliefs and the political arrangements prevailing in the different countries.

Secondly, since services are provided and traded in many distinct ways, a fuller picture of the role they play in domestic production and international trade would require that employment and immigration statistics are also taken into account. The latter further add to uncertainty, especially as the classifications followed therein are typically based on specific time-thresholds which do not necessarily correspond to the actual duration of a given service provision. Indeed, the duration of a service provision may well extend over one calendar year, in which case the service provider will typically cease to appear in the immigration statistics and will be accounted for as domestic workforce.

Thirdly, one of the four modes of trade in services,[43] foreign direct investment (FDI), is not accounted for in the services statistics, but rather in the capital movement accounts.[44]

In order to tackle these issues, the Manual on Statistics of International Trade in Services (MSITS) was jointly developed in 2002 by the UN, the EU, the IMF, the OECD, the UNCTAD, and the WTO.[45] Being a 'manual', the document only provides a framework for national account-keeping, and constitutes no more than a suggestion to the competent authorities of the states.

For all the reasons mentioned above, today, the national statistics on services correspond only roughly to each other, while the EU, the OECD, and the UNCTAD continue to publish statistical data following slightly diverging approaches. This, in turn, means that even the most sophisticated economic studies on services are based on numerous assumptions and on 'more-or-less

---

[43] For which see in more detail, under subheading A(1)e(iii).

[44] For all these problems, see, in more detail, Maurer, A., Marcus, Y., Magdeleine, J., and d'Andrea, B., 'Measuring trade in services' in Mattoo, A., Stern, R., and Zanini, G. (eds), *A Handbook of International Trade in Services* (Oxford: OUP, 2008) 133–68.

[45] Available at <http://www.oecd.org/dataoecd/32/45/2404428.pdf> (last accessed on 5 November 2011).

accurate proxies'; this is why they are typically introduced with very strong disclaimers.[46]

d. Factors affecting service provision

Understanding the way service provision develops and identifying the factors that affect it calls for two approaches: one *dynamic*, looking down on service production from a historical and evolutionary perspective, and one *static*, analysing a 'snapshot' of service production today.

i. A dynamic perspective[47]

The presentation below seeks to demonstrate how service provision evolved and grew in significance over time. It follows a chronological order, in the sense that one factor led to the other; all five factors, however, currently contribute to the rise of the economic importance of services.

Urbanization has been an important factor in the development of service economies. It increases the density of demand for services, a condition particularly important for the development of non-transportable and non-storable services (such as education, services of hairdressers, aestheticians, etc). By the same token, urbanization reduces the average cost for the production of services and allows for economies of scale for service providers. It also reduces the total cost of service consumption from the recipient's point of view: since the cost incorporates the time of both providers and recipients (since co-production is required), when these are located in close vicinity, such cost is minimized.

Motorization has played its role, in two ways. First, the transportation of goods from the periphery to the centre and the greater ease of commuting, have made possible the development of urban centres—reinforcing the effects of urbanization. Secondly, motorized service recipients are more mobile and can move towards the services they desire. In this way, the creation of service hubs, such as shopping malls, multiplex movie theatres, sports clubs, and the like has been made possible.

The *modernization* of societies is a third major factor which has affected the development of the service economy; in at least four ways. For one thing, in modern, complex societies, demand for sophisticated services has developed: IT services, specialized health (and healing) services, spas, tourism, and fine arts, to state but a few. Secondly, many activities which were traditionally carried out within the household are now being externalized: laundry, ironing, hairdressing,

---

[46] See eg Monteagudo, J., and Diexr, A., 'Economic Performance and Competition in Services in the Euro Area: Policy Lessons in Times of Crisis' European Economy Occasional Papers 2009/53, EU Commission/DG Economic and Financial Affairs, available at <http://ec.europa.eu/economy_finance/publications/publication15841_en.pdf>, at 18 (last accessed on 5 November 2011): 'these findings should be considered with caution: first because of the high degree of heterogeneity that characterises the service sectors; second, because the analysis is carried out at a relatively aggregated level on the basis of a battery of relatively simple publicly available data; third, because there are significant data limitations in services both in terms of availability and quality'.

[47] For a detailed presentation of this dynamic analysis, see Janson, J.O., *The Economics of Services: Development and Policy* (Cheltenham/Northampton: Edward Elgar Publishing, 2006).

mani/pedicures. This trend is further encouraged, thirdly, by feminine emancipation and the participation of women in economic life. These activities, which were carried out in-house without being counted, are now paid for and counted in the balance books. A fourth, extremely important trend of modern societies, which accounts for an important rise in the amount of services is the outsourcing of governmental services.

ICTs play an important role both by allowing for the provision of new services and by offering the means for greater bulk and better quality of more traditional services. By transforming telecommunications and communications, ICTs impact on both the demand and the supply (and availability) of services. Moreover, through the unprecedented capacities of information and data management, ICTs transform several non-storable and non-tradable services into services which may be traded at a distance.

A final factor stressing the importance of services as an economic activity is *globalization.*[48]

ii. A static perspective

The development of the service economy means that there is increased demand for, and supply of, services. The factors described in the previous section affect both demand and supply. Supply, however, is also affected by other, more technical, factors, notably by regulation. Regulation may allow or prohibit certain service activities, impose conditions on their exercise, and affect their cost. This is why regulatory reform has been a major priority in the field of services, more so than in other fields.

iii. External factors—policies

In addition to services regulations, a series of other regulations and policies affect the development of services. It is not the place here to discuss these in detail; instead, a mere enumeration is sufficient to demonstrate their variety and the complexities they bring to the service economy. A first policy area, having direct impact on service provision, is innovation and R&D policy.[49] Employment regulation is yet another factor, flexibility offering a better fit to the plastic nature of service provision. Educational and vocational training policies are also important. The same is true for standardization and quality assurance policies. Regional policy may have a role to play in the way service activities are developed. At a further remove, one may cite policies favouring entrepreneurship, as well as policies

---

[48] See the discussion in subsection A(1)c.

[49] See Rubalcaba, L., 2007, n 5, at 96–125. See also Howells, J. 'Services and innovation: conceptual and theoretical perspectives' in Bryson, J., and Daniels, P. (eds), *The Handbook of Services Industries* (Cheltenham/Northampton: Edward Elgar Publishing, 2007) 34–44; and, in the same edited volume, Miles, I., 'Knowledge-intensive services and innovation', at 277–94, and also 'Part IV: Services, Technology and Innovation', at 277–376. Moreover, see Howells, J., 'The nature of innovation in services', at 277–94, and also 'Part IV: Services, Technology and Innovation', at 277–376. Moreover, see OECD, *Innovation and Productivity in Services: Industry, Services and Trade* (Paris: OECD, 2001) 57–82.

promoting the collection of data and the compilation of reliable statistics. Last but not least, consumer protection and taxation have a direct bearing on the development of service provision.

e. Trade in services—globalization

i. Globalization and services

It has been stated[50] that globalization is one of the factors favouring the development of the service economy. Indeed, several authors have explained that the relationship between services and globalization is a two-way one:[51] services bring forward globalization which, in turn, favours the production of services.

Services support globalization in at least five ways. First, by establishing transport and communication networks, services establish links between geographically distant places and constitute the basic infrastructure that makes globalization possible: they eliminate distance. Secondly, service companies wishing to develop abroad often have recourse to multi-national firms providing business services (such as financial services, consultants, accountants, recruiting, etc). Thirdly, the creation of new specialized services for niche-markets, and of services clusters, strengthens specialization at the international level, which in turn brings more trade transactions across borders. Fourthly, the creation of specialized service clusters creates market asymmetries and attracts multi-national firms towards those specialization hubs. Last but not least, services bring dynamism into local economies which, in turn, translates into international trade.

Globalization supports the development of services in as many ways. First, it allows for competition at a larger scale, thus enhancing service provision. Secondly, it brings down protectionist measures, cultural and linguistic obstacles, and distances, thus increasing the amount of services which may be traded over borders. This is of particular interest to small and medium enterprises (SMEs) which might not overcome such hurdles on their own; the vast majority of service-providing companies are SMEs. Thirdly, globalization creates a goldmine of opportunities for consultants, accountants, lawyers, and the like, who specialize in transnational operations. Fourthly, the development of big multi-national (global) service firms (eg in the field of hotel services) creates high expectations for service quality, raising, thus, further the level.

Notwithstanding the mutual influences mentioned above, there are several limits to the interaction between services and globalization. For one thing, most service-providing undertakings are not big enough to become players at the global level: the need for specialization and individualization of services, relatively low productivity and fewer opportunities for economies of scale, mean that service companies rarely

---

[50] See the discussion under subheading A(1)d(i).

[51] Rubalcaba, L., 2007, n 5, at 126–63; see also Rubalcaba-Bermejo, L., and Cuadrado-Roura, J., 'Services in the age of globalisation: explanatory interrelations and dimensions' in Cuadrado-Roura, J., Rubalcaba-Bermejo, L., and Bryson, J.R. (eds), *Trading Services in the Global Economy* (Cheltenham/Northampton: Edward Elgar Publishing, 2002) 27–57.

grow large. Secondly, since service provision requires co-production, a big proportion of trade in services takes place through FDI and does not translate into direct
trade flows. Despite the fact that services account for over 70 per cent of the GDP
of most trading countries, trade in services only accounts for 25 per cent of total
trade and FDI in services only accounts for 50 per cent of total FDI.[52] Trade and
FDI, however, are not the only ways in which services go global.

ii. Globalization of services—modes of service trade
According to L. Rubalcaba-Bermejo and J. Cuadrado-Roura,[53] there are four key
dimensions to service globalization: a) flows (of services themselves, capital and
manpower), b) networks (agreements and technology transfers), c) frameworks
(standardization, diversification of global services, etc), and d) brands and trademarks.

Looking closer into the first—and most prominent—component of service
globalization, namely 'flows', the following sub-categories may be identified:
FDI, international trade, and movement of production factors. FDI may take the
form of either mergers and acquisitions or 'greenfield' investment. International
trade may consist of cross-border transactions (supplies, purchases), consumption
abroad (eg tourism), and intra-firm transactions. Finally, movement of production
factors may involve human resources and/or capital.

It is essentially 'flows' which are regulated at the international level. Indeed, the
GATS foresees four modes of service delivery across borders: i. transnational
provision, where services alone cross the borders, ii. consumption abroad, iii.
establishment of the provider abroad, and iv. movement of natural persons.[54]

Before elaborating on the legal rules applicable to globalization in services,
however, it is worth asking the essential question of what determines comparative
advantage in the field of services?

f. From freedom to comparative advantage in services: the role of regulation

i. In an ideal world: freedom as a key component of the services economy
The importance of freedom as a platform from which the production of services
may flourish has been highlighted by L. Rubalcaba in the following terms:

'co-production, interaction, personalization, co-responsibility and participation. All these
highlight the role of two or more parties in building the economy. To ensure the correct
provision of service, at least one offerer and one petitioner must agree to their transaction
plans with an active and free attitude. Freedom is essential to reach an optimal service

---

[52] OECD, 2001, n 49.

[53] Rubalcaba-Bermejo, L., and Cuadrado-Roura, J., 2002, n 51, at 42–4. This view has been
followed further by Daniels, P., 'A global service economy?' in Bryson, J., and Daniels, P. (eds), *The
Handbook of Services Industries* (Cheltenham/Northampton: Edward Elgar Publishing, 2007) 103–25,
at 104–5.

[54] More in detail for the GATS four modes of service provision, see the discussion under
subheading A(2)a.

provision . . . The quality of the service depends on the freedom allowed for the practise [sic] of a co-responsible economic action.'[55]

It will be explained[56] that there are several good reasons for restricting freedom through regulation. While doing so, however, regulators should keep in mind that they are restricting one of the fundamental and inherent characteristics of services.

ii. In real world: good regulation as a decisive component of comparative advantage in service production

Services are based on the personal work of the service provider (the material support, if any, is of secondary importance) to such an extent that several authors have talked of 'personality as a commodity': 'service workers rent their "smiles", emotions, expertise, appearance and emotional intelligence, as well as their muscular capacity for wages, salaries or consultancy fees'.[57] Next to personality, the quality of information at the disposal of the service provider determines to a large extent the quality of the services provided. Indeed, it may be said that the provision of services consists of the application/adaptation of pre-existing information to the specific needs of any given service recipient: the lawyer, the surgeon, the hairdresser, and so many other service providers apply the general knowledge of their respective art, to the case, body, or head of their clients.

If knowledge and other elements of personality are the main service ingredients, then exogenous factors such as geography, climate, and natural resources generally have a very limited role to play, with the exception of specific categories of services, such as tourism and healthcare. Moreover, since the provision of services does not typically require heavy investment and infrastructure, the migration of service activities is considerably less costly than that of good-producing activities.[58]

Service migration, however, may be restricted by the fact that many services are 'co-produced' and require the simultaneous (typically physical) presence of both the provider and the recipient. This limitation may, nonetheless, be overcome by better (electronic) communications and greater travel opportunities. Distance as a problem to service provision is further exacerbated by the key role that *trust* occupies in service provision: service recipients are more likely to trust a provider locally established, known to other family/society members, rather than some 'invisible' provider. This explains why many service undertakings wishing to export services choose to do so through FDI, by acquiring stakes or the control of undertakings locally established, and by hiring local personnel.

Further, service migration may be restricted by regulatory (including tax) measures, making access to the activity or to financial resources expensive or impossible.

---

[55] Rubalcaba, L., 2007, n 5, at 39.

[56] See the developments under heading B of the present chapter.

[57] Bryson, J., and Daniels, P., 'Worlds of services: from local service economies to offshoring or global sourcing' in Bryson, J., and Daniels, P. (eds), *The Handbook of Services Industries* (Cheltenham/Northampton: Edward Elgar Publishing, 2007) 1–16, at 8 and 10; see also Warf, B., 'Embodied information, actor networks, and global value-added services' in Bryson, J., and Daniels, P. (eds), *The Handbook of Services Industries* (Cheltenham/Northampton: Edward Elgar Publishing, 2007) 379–94.

[58] For the various kinds of service migration, see nn 61 *et seq*, and the corresponding text.

In view of the above, the elements which determine comparative advantage in service provision seem to be the following:[59] i. the existence of well-educated and skilled personnel, ii. functional and cheap telecommunication networks, allowing the service provider to have easy access to the necessary information and enhanced contact with service recipients, iii. good transport, through air, water, or land, bringing providers and recipients closer to one another, iv. ease of access to credit, insurance, etc, in order to set up shop, and v. a business-friendly regulatory (including tax) environment. The above elements, in turn, develop positive externalities, such as the accumulation of specific knowledge and experience, and set the conditions for the creation of specialized service hubs (eg the City of London or Silicon Valley).

2. In legal terms

Given that there is no single generally accepted definition of what services are in economic terms, it comes as no surprise that there is nothing akin to a coherent legal definition either. Indeed, any legal definition of services would run the risk of being too comprehensive, as it would embrace investment and labour movement; and at the same time, too restrictive, as it would be difficult to give it the dynamic and extendible scope necessary to cover a field in plain expansion.[60] Therefore, both the GATS and the TFEU have recourse to empirical, or descriptive, means of defining services.

The GATS applies to all services, but for those 'supplied in the exercise of governmental activity' (Article I(3)b). The exception of 'governmental activity' seems to be restricted to mere official authority and purely governmental functions (in economic terms, purely public goods) and does not extend to social, welfare, educational services, and the like (in economic terms, merit goods).[61] For the rest, the GATS contains no other definitional element concerning the concept of services. The lack of any such definition is mitigated, however, by the fact that signatory states have scheduled their commitments on a service by service basis, based on the classification of document W/120.[62] Therefore, GATS signatories need worry only marginally about a generally accepted concept of services, since their contractual obligations are set out separately for each type of service, and indeed for each mode of trans-border provision.

---

[59] Hindley, B., and Smith, A., 'Comparative Advantage and Trade in Services' (1984) 7 *The World Economy* 369–89, at 386–7.

[60] Laüchli, S., 'The Concept of a Service under the GATS and under the EC Treaty' Paper presented for the Master Degree of the College of Europe, Bruges (2000), under the supervision of Eeckhout, P., available at the Library of the College of Europe, Bruges.

[61] Adlung, R., 'Public Services and the GATS' (2006) 9 *J of Int Economic L* 455–85; Krajewski, M., 'Protecting a shared value of the union in a globalized world: services of general interest and external trade' in van de Gronden, J. (ed), *EU and WTO Law on Services: Limits to the Realization of General Interest Policies within the Services Markets?* (Alphen aan den Rijn: Kluwer Law International, 2009) 187–213.

[62] For which see the analysis in subheading A(1)b(ii).

a. Services supply modes under the GATS and the TFEU

While the GATS does not offer any definition of the concept of services, it is, nonetheless, quite precise in respect of their modes of delivery. Article I(2) describes four modes of supply which are brought under its realm:

> *Mode 1,* 'cross-border trade', covers situations where the service alone crosses the borders, while the provider and the recipient interact at a distance. This mode covers ICT services, telemedicine, consultations from a distance, and its subject matter is constantly expanding.

> *Mode 2,* 'consumption abroad', covers situations where the service recipient moves towards the service provided in another state; this mode typically covers tourism, healthcare, and education.

> *Mode 3,* 'commercial presence', corresponds to situations where foreign service providers get commercially established in the territory of another state. Such establishment may take the form of setting up a new entity in the host state (greenfield FDI), or of acquiring participation in already existing entities through mergers and acquisitions.

> *Mode 4,* 'presence of natural persons', covers the services supplied provisionally by foreign natural persons, either employed or self-employed, on the territory of the host state.

These four modes offer much clearer guidance on the type of transactions which are covered by the GATS, than the very vague and imprecise wording of Article 56 TFEU.[63] Indeed, the latter does not clearly distinguish between the various forms of service provision. It has been up to the Court, through its case law, to flesh up the relevant Treaty provisions and to define their scope of application. The difference of the two regimes can be easily explained. An analytical categorization of the various delivery modes has not been necessary for the EU, since member states are bound by a unitary set of rules and principles for all supply modes. In the GATS framework, on the other hand, the distinction between the four supply modes has been instrumental, since the signatory states have had to offer specific commitments for each individual mode.

The CJEU has progressively widened the scope of the Treaty in order to cover all modes of service delivery. The legal categories recognized by the Court only partly correspond to the four GATS modes. Indeed, mode 1 is common to both legal orders. Data collected for the purposes of the present book shows that, out of 283 CJEU cases on services, 100 correspond to mode 1 GATS. They include TV and advertising

---

[63] On this issue see the extremely enlightening article by Krajewski, M., 'Of modes and sectors: external relations, internal debates, and the special case of (trade in) services' in Dashwood, A., and Maresceau, M. (eds), *Law and Practice of EU External Relations: Developments in the EU External Relations Law* (Cambridge: CUP, 2008) 172–215; see also Eeckhout, P., 'Constitutional concepts for free trade in services' in de Búrca, G., and Scott, J., *The EU and the WTO, Legal and Constitutional Issues* (Oxford/Portland: Hart Publishing, 2001) 211–35.

services,[64] insurance,[65] financial services,[66] the management of copyright, patents, and other intellectual property rights,[67] auditor services,[68] lotteries,[69] interim placement services,[70] leasing,[71] postal services,[72] sea transport,[73] medical examinations,[74] and telecom services,[75] to state the most important categories.

Mode 2 covers situations where the service recipient moves to another state to receive services. This delivery mode has been relatively rare in the past, but is becoming increasingly common. Two reasons explain this late 'awakening' of mode 2 of service delivery at EU level. Several of the services concerned with this mode of delivery, especially education and healthcare, have been traditionally organized as part of a public service and, as such, have remained outside the realm of the EU Treaty; this has radically changed in the last 10 years and is currently undergoing a profound modification.[76] In parallel, the CJEU's definition of 'remuneration' has

---

[64] See eg Case 52/79 *Procureur du Roi v Debauve* [1980] ECR 833; Case 62/79 *SA Coditel v Ciné Vog Films* [1980] ECR 881; Case 352/85 *Bond van Adverteerders and others v Netherlands* [1988] ECR 2085; Case C-260/89 *ERT v DEP and Sotirios Kouvelas* [1991] ECR I-2925; Case C-288/89 *Stichting Collectieve Antennevoorziening Gouda v Commissariaat voor de Media* [1991] ECR I-4007; Case C-148/91 *Vereniging Veronica Omroep Organisatie v Commissariat voor de Media* [1993] ECR I-487; Case C-23/93 *TV10 SA v Commissariat voor de Media* [1984] ECR I-4795; Case C-11/95 *Commission v Belgium (cable TV)* [1996] ECR I-4115; Case C-34–36/95 *Konsumentombudsmannen v de Agostini and TV-Shop* [1997] ECR I-3843; Case C-6/98 *Arbeitsgemeinschaft Deutscher Rundfunkanstalten v PRO Sieben Media AG* [1999] ECR I-7599; Case C-405/98 *Konsumentombudsmannnen (KO) v Gourmet International Products AB (GIP)* [2001] ECR I-1795.

[65] See eg Case 205/84 *Commission v Germany (insurance)* [1986] ECR 3755; Case 206/84 *Commission v Ireland (co-insurance)* [1986] ECR 3817; Case 220/83 *Commission v France (co-insurance)* [1986] ECR 3663; Case 252/83 *Commission v Denmark (co-insurance)* [1986] ECR 3713; Case 168/85 *Commission v Italy (insurance)* [1986] ECR 2945; Case C-204/90 *Bachmann v Belgium* [1992] ECR I-249; Case C-118/96 *Safir v Skattemyndigheten i Dalarnas Län* [1998] ECR I-1897; Case C-136/00 *Rolf Dieter Danner* [2002] ECR I-8147.

[66] See eg Case C-384/93 *Alpine Investments v Minister van Financiën* [1995] ECR I-1141; Case C-484/93 *Svensson and Gustavsson v Ministre du Logement et d'Urbanisme* [1995] ECR I-3955; Case C-222/95 *Société Civile Immobilière Parodi v Banque H. Albert de Bary et Cie* [1997] ECR I-3895.

[67] See eg Case 395/87 *Ministère Public v Jean-Luis Tournier* [1989] ECR 2521; Case C-76/90 *Säger v Dennemeyer & Co Ltd* [1991] ECR I-4221; Case C-17/92 *Federación de Distribuidores Cinematográficos v Estado Español et Uniòn de Productores de Cine y Television* [1993] ECR I-2239.

[68] See eg Case C-106/91 *Claus Ramrath v Ministre de la Justice and l'Institut des réviseurs d'entreprises* [1992] ECR I-3351.

[69] See eg Case C-275/92 *Her Majesty's Customs and Excise v Schindler* [1994] ECR I-1039; Case C-124/97 *Markku Juhani Läärä, Cotswold Microsystems Ltd and Oy Transatlantic Software Ltd v Kihlakunnasyyttäjä (Jyväskylä) and Suomen valtio* [1999] ECR I-6067; Case C-243/01 *Criminal proceedings against Piergiorgio Gambelli and others* [2003] ECR I-13031.

[70] See eg Case C-55/96 *Job Centre coop. arl.* [1997] ECR I-7119.

[71] See eg Case C-294/97 *Eurowings Luftverkehrs AG v Finanzamt Dortmund-Unna* [1999] ECR I-7447; Case C-36/02 *Omega Spielhallen-und Automatenaufstellungs-GmbH v Oberburgermeisterin der Bundesstadt Bonn* [2004] ECR I-9609.

[72] See eg Joined cases C-147 & 148/97 *Deutsche Post AG v Gesellschaft für Zahlungssysteme mbH GZS and Citicorp Kartenservice GmbH* [2000] ECR I-825.

[73] See eg Joined cases C-430 & 431/99 *Inspecteur van de Belastingdienst Douane, district Rotterdam v Sea-Land Service Inc and Nedlloyd Lijnen BV* [2002] ECR I-5235.

[74] See eg Case C-496/01 *Commission v France (medical laboratories)* [2004] ECR I-2351; Case C-39/04 *Laboratoires Fournier SA v Direction des verifications nationals et internationals* [2005] ECR I-2057.

[75] See eg Joined cases C-544 & 545/03 *Mobistar SA v Commune de Fleron and Belgacom Mobile SA v Commune de Schaerbeek* [2006] ECR I-7723.

[76] For more on this trend, see the discussion in ch 5.

been widened, thus bringing an ever-increasing category of activities under the EU definition of 'services' and the corresponding legal rules (Articles 56 *et seq* TFEU).[77] Secondly, service recipients have become increasingly aware of the possibilities for receiving services abroad and of their rights in this respect; such rights do not only stem from the rules on services, but also from those on citizenship.[78] Out of the 283 cases brought before the Court, only 32 corresponded to this mode of delivery. Among these, in 27 cases service recipients moved alone in the host member state in order to receive services there, while in the remaining five, they moved to another member state together with the service provider. Of the latter, four concern tourist guides and their right to accompany tourists of their own nationality in other member states.[79] The fifth case concerned Greek port levies which used to be higher for vessels connecting Greece to other member states (typically cruise boats carrying non-Greek passengers) compared to levies on 'cabotage' services within Greece (typically flying the Greek flag and transporting Greek passengers).[80] It is, however, the remaining 27 which are much more intriguing since, some tourist cases aside,[81] they illustrate the trend of seeking healthcare and education in other member states.[82]

Mode 3 GATS, on the other hand, escapes, in principle, the EU definition of services (Article 56 TFEU), since it amounts to the distinct legal category of 'establishment' (Article 49 TFEU) and partly to capital movements (Article 63 TFEU). This, however, has not prevented the Court from scrutinizing national rules governing the establishment of service providers under the rules on services. This has occurred in cases where the national rules governing establishment were also applicable to occasional service provision and/or whenever the duration of the provision could not be ascertained from the facts of the case. Indeed, from a total of

---

[77] See the discussion under subheading A(2)b.

[78] On the impact of citizenship on the provision of social services see, among many, Faist, T., 'Social Citizenship in the European Union: Nested Membership' (2001) 39 *JCMS* 37–58 and, on a more critical note, Katrougalos, G., 'The (Dim) Perspectives of the European Social Citizenship' Jean Monnet Working Paper No. 5/07, also available at <http://centers.law.nyu.edu/jeanmonnet/papers/07/070501.html> (last accessed on 5 November 2011); Newdick, C., 'Citizenship, Free Movement and Healthcare: Cementing Individual Rights by Corroding Social Solidarity' (2006) 43 *CML Rev* 1645–68; Wernicke, S., 'Au nom de qui? The ECJ between Member States, Civil Society and Citizens' (2007) 13 *ELJ* 380–407. More generally, on the recent upsurge of citizenship in EU law, see the following contributions from the special issue of *ELJ*: Besson, S., and Utzinger, A., 'Introduction: Future Challenges of European Citizenship: Facing a Wide-Open Pandora's Box' (2007) 13 *ELJ* 573–90; Jacobs, F., 'Citizenship of the EU: A Legal Analysis' (2007) 13 *ELJ* 591–610; Epiney, A., 'The Scope of Article 12: Some Remarks on the Influence of European Citizenship'(2007) 13 *ELJ* 611–22; Kostakopoulou, D., 'EU Citizenship: Writing the Future' (2007) 13 *ELJ* 623–46.

[79] Case C-154/89 *Commission v France (tour guides)* [1991] ECR I-659; Case C-180/89 *Commission v Italy (tourist guides)* [1991] ECR I-709; Case C-198/89 *Commission v Greece (tourist guides)* [1991] ECR I-727; Case C-375/92 *Commission v Spain (tourist guides)* [1994] ECR I-923.

[80] Case C-269/05 *Commission v Greece (harbour dues)* [2007] ECR I-4.

[81] Case 186/87 *Cowan v Le Trésor Public* [1989] ECR 195; Case C-274/96 *Criminal Proceedings against Horst Otto Bickel and Ulrich Franz* [1998] ECR I-7637; Case C-348/96 *Criminal Proceedings against Donatella Calfa* [1999] ECR I-11; Case C-224/97 *Erich Ciola v Land Vorarlberg* [1999] ECR I-2517; Case C-388/01 *Commission v Italy (museums)* [2003] ECR I-721; Case C-215/03 *Salah Oulane v Minister voor Vreemdelingenzaken en Integratie* [2005] ECR I-1215.

[82] For the corresponding case law, see the relevant headings in ch 5.

Table 1.1. Correspondence of cases decided by the CJEU to GATS modes

GATS mode	No. of cases
Mode 1: Cross-border trade	100
Mode 2: Consumption abroad—recipient moving alone	27
Consumption abroad—provider and recipient moving together	5
Mode 3: Establishment abroad (of service provider)	52
Mode 4: Physical presence—provider	59
Physical presence—provider's personnel	37
Indeterminate	3
Total	283

283 cases handled by the Court during the relevant period, 52 concern restrictions on the establishment of service providers.

Mode 4 GATS covers the situation primarily envisaged by the EU Treaty's founding fathers: service providers moving temporarily to another member state to offer their services. This category, in turn, breaks down to: a) the movement of the service providers (natural persons) themselves, which is the situation primarily envisaged by the Article 56 TFEU (59 cases), b) the movement of the personnel of the service providing undertaking, known under the EU jargon as 'posted workers' (37 cases). See Table 1.1 for a breakdown of 283 cases decided by the CJEU, which correspond to the four GATS modes.

If supply modes have not been much of a problem under the EU law, since they are all subject to the same rules, the actual definition of services has raised considerable difficulties. The latter have been nurtured by the cryptic definitional elements offered in the Treaty itself. Three difficulties flowing from the Treaty terms are presented below (b, c, d).

b. Services as activities or as outcomes?

Article 56 TFEU seems indeterminate as to whether it envisions services as activities or as the outcomes of such activities: it states that 'restrictions on the freedom to provide services within the Union shall be prohibited . . .' (services as outcomes comparable to goods) ' . . . in respect of nationals of member states who are established in a Member State other than that of the person for whom the services are intended' (services as human activities dependent on the situation of the service provider/recipient). This ambivalence is, in turn, reflected in the kinds of rules which service provision is subject to: on some occasions, the approach adopted follows from the rules on free trade of goods, while in others it is the movement of physical persons which prevails. Finally, in some cases, services are dealt with as a category on their own. The distinction above loses its relevance as the broad legal principles applicable to all freedoms grow closer one to the other.[83] Some differences *in law* still prevail, however. Moreover, the kinds of restrictions to each one of the above freedoms (goods/persons) are different *in fact* and it is not always easy to deal with them through a single set of rules.[84] This explains why in chapters 3 and 4, where the criteria for the violation of the rules on services and for justifications will be discussed, developments concerning the full body of the fundamental freedoms are examined first, and only at a subsequent stage does the analysis turn to special rules or principles applicable to the field of services.

c. Normally provided for remuneration?

Article 57 TFEU makes clear that not all services come under the Treaty rules; only those which are 'normally provided for remuneration' do so. This, in turn, raises two questions. For one thing, it is unclear what the use of the word 'normally' stands for. One way of reading 'normally' is as meaning 'usually'; this would suggest that services which are usually provided for remuneration remain under the scope of the Treaty, even when, exceptionally, they are provided for free. Or, inversely, that services which are normally provided for free evade the Treaty rules even where, exceptionally, the recipient is made to pay for them; such a reading, however, is countered by the Court's case law in the field of healthcare, where the starting point for the Court's reasoning is precisely the fact that mobile patients have had to pay for their treatments and thus the free movement rules should be available to them.[85] Another, more subtle, option would be to read 'normally' as embodying a judgment of value: is it 'normal' to pay for healthcare? This interpretation of the term 'normally' gives it real weight, but introduces an essentially political variable in the legal rule. In actual fact, the Court has completely ignored this term and, instead, has focused on offering a comprehensive definition of remuneration.

Thus, secondly, the question of what constitutes remuneration is raised, and how it should relate to the service offered. According to the Court, 'the essential characteristic of remuneration lies in the fact that it constitutes consideration for the service in question and is normally agreed upon between the provider and the recipient of the service'.[86] This definition, however, has been considerably widened. In *Deliège*, the Court accepted that *non-professional* athletes could receive remuneration for their 'services' in an indirect way, through TV broadcasting rights, sponsorship, participation in publicity campaigns, etc. In healthcare cases, the

---

[83] On the convergence of freedoms, see, among many, Hatzopoulos, V., 'Trente ans après les arrêts fondamentaux de 1974, les quatre libertés: quatre?' in Demaret, P., Govaere, I., and Hanf, D. (eds), *30 Years of European Legal Studies at the College of Europe—30 ans d'études juridiques européennes au Collège d'Europe: Liber Professorum 1973/74–2003/04* (Brussels: Peter Lang, 2005) 185–201; and more recently, Tryfonidou, A., 'Further Steps on the Road to Convergence Among the Market Freedoms' (2010) 35 *EL Rev* 36–56.

[84] Oliver, P., and Roth, W.-H., 'The Internal Market and the Four Freedoms' (2004) 41 *CML Rev* 407–41; and more recently Oliver, P., 'Of Trailers and Jet-Skis: Is the Case Law on Article 34 TFEU Hurtling in a New Direction' (2010) 33 *Fordham Int'l LJ* 1423–71.

[85] For this case law see the relevant subheading in ch 5.

[86] Case 263/86 *Belgium v Humbel* [1988] ECR 5365, para 17.

Court accepted that 'the payments made by the sickness insurance funds [for treatment delivered to insured patients], *albeit set at a flat rate*, are indeed the consideration for the hospital services and unquestionably represent remuneration for the hospital which receives them'.[87] Thus, remuneration was found to exist not only in triangular situations,[88] where a third party pays for the recipient's service, but, more importantly, also in situations where the correlation between services received and money paid is only indirect, if not economically non-existent. Further, in *Danner* and *Skandia*,[89] the Court accepted that remuneration can be paid well in advance for a service which is to be delivered over 30 years later, namely the payment of an old-age pension. The above judgments present a concept of remuneration which is extremely wide and flexible.[90] Indeed, the only service activities which evade the relevant Treaty rules are these which lack *any* economic character.[91]

d. A residual legal category?

Article 57 TFEU further states that it applies to service activities 'in so far as they are not governed by the provisions relating [to the other free movement rules]'. Drafted at a time when economic theory largely ignored services or, at best, defined them by opposition to goods, as a residual category, Article 57 TFEU should hardly come as a surprise. Economic reality, however, has evolved since 1957 and, in tandem, so has the legal interpretation of services under the TFEU. The Court's position has evolved greatly in this respect, in relation to all the other Treaty freedoms.

i. Free movement of capital

At a time when the liberalization of capital movements had been denied direct effect[92] and was still one more item in the European Council's overloaded agenda, the Court held that the freedom to receive services in other member states bore with it the right to carry the necessary funds for paying for such services.[93] In this way, the Treaty rules on services created inroads on the rules on capital movement. Such inroads have been constantly present in the Court's case law ever since.[94]

---

[87] Case C-157/99 *B.S.M. Geraets-Smits v Stichting Ziekenfonds VGZ and H.T.M. Peerbooms v Stichting CZ Groep Zorgverzekeringen* [2001] ECR I-5473, para 58 (emphasis added).

[88] Which has already been accepted since Case C-352/85 *Bond van Adverteerders and others v Netherlands* [1988] ECR 2085, para 16.

[89] Case C-136/00 *Rolf Dieter Danner* [2002] ECR I-8147; Case C-422/01 *Försäkringsaktiebolaget Skandia (publ) and Ola Ramstedt v Riksskatteverket* [2003] ECR I-6817.

[90] For more extensive developments on this case law, see Hatzopoulos, V., and Do, U., 'Overview of the Case Law of the ECJ in the Field of Free Movement of Services 2000–2005' (2006) 43 *CML Rev* 923–91.

[91] For more details on the economic character of service activities, see the discussion in ch 2.

[92] Case 203/80 *Criminal proceedings against Guerrino Casati* [1981] ECR 2595.

[93] Joined cases 286/82 & 26/83 *Luisi and Carbone v Ministero del Tesoro* [1984] ECR 377.

[94] See eg Case C-484/93 *Svensson and Gustavsson v Ministre du Logement et d'Urbanisme* [1995] ECR I-3955 and its annotation by Hatzopoulos, V. (1996) 33 *CML Rev* 659–89; Case C-250/95 *Futura Participations SA & Singer v Administration des Contributions (Luxembourg)* [1997] ECR I-2471

ii. Free movement of goods

The borderline between services and goods has been designed progressively, around three core ideas. In its early case law, the Court used a very simple—indeed simplistic—criterion, by distinguishing on the basis of the material/immaterial nature of the activities concerned.[95] Subsequently, the Court adopted a more useful approach, whereby it would identify the core aspect of any given activity (as bearing on goods or services) and then apply the relevant rules to the entire activity, on the basis of the maxim that the accessory follows the principal.[96] This approach has evolved further and now the Court does not limit its enquiry to the material/immaterial nature or to the core aspect of any activity, but also looks at the economic rationale behind it. Hence, for instance, leasing contracts are dealt with under the rules on services irrespective of the actual value of the goods at stake,[97] and so is the installation of slot machines, despite the fact that the machines used may be imported from another member state.[98]

iii. Freedom of establishment

Even more ingenious has been the way in which the Court gradually expanded the scope of the rules on services over situations which would, under an orthodox reading of the Treaty, qualify as 'establishment'. In a development parallel to the one described above (for the distinction between goods and services), the Court first adopted simplistic criteria, such as the existence of infrastructure[99] or the duration (but also the regularity, periodicity, or continuity) of the activity:[100] as soon as any of these conditions were met, the situation shifted from 'services' to 'establishment'. In its most recent case law, however, the Court seems to be abandoning the temporal criterion in favour of a more economic one. Indeed, the Court seems ready to treat economic activities which qualify as services under Article 56 TFEU, irrespective of their duration. Hence, in *Schnitzer*[101] the Court held that a Portuguese construction company, which had been on a construction site in Germany for over three years could, nevertheless, invoke the rules on services, in order to evade the full application of the relevant German legislation. The Court acknowledged that the nature of the activity is readily ascertainable and can safely lead to

and its annotation by Hatzopoulos, V. (1998) 35 *CML Rev* 493–518; and in a bolder manner Case C-452/04 *Fidium Finanz AG v Bundesanstalt für Finanzdienstleistungsaufsicht* [2006] ECR I-9521.

[95] Case 155/73 *Giuseppe Sacchi* [1974] ECR 409; such approach corresponds to the vague 'negative' definition of services discussed in subsection A(1)b.

[96] This approach was launched for the first time in Case C-275/92 *Her Majesty's Customs and Excise v Schindler* [1994] ECR I-1039.

[97] See eg Case C-36/02 *Omega Spielhallen-und Automatenaufstellungs-GmbH v Oberburgermeisterin der Bundesstadt Bonn* [2004] ECR I-9609; Case C-330/07 *Jobra Vermögensverwaltungs-Gesellschaft mbH v Finanzamt Amstetten Melk Scheibbs* [2008] ECR I-9099.

[98] Case C-6/01 *Associação Nacional de Operadores de Máquinas Recreativas (Anomar) and others v Estado português* [2003] ECR I-8621.

[99] Case 205/84 *Commission v Germany (insurance)* [1986] ECR 3755.

[100] Case C-55/94 *Reinhard Gebhard v Consiglio dell'Ordine degli Avvocati e Procuratori di Milano* [1995] ECR I-4165, para 27.

[101] Case C-215/01 *Bruno Schnitzer* [2003] ECR I-14847.

Table 1.2. Free movement of services and other freedoms in the CJEU case law

Other freedom examined	*No. of cases*
Free movement of goods	27
Free movement of workers	42
Freedom of establishment	119
Free movement of capital	25
None	70
Total	283

legal qualifications, while its duration, periodicity, etc. are not.[102] Some months later, the Court ruled on the compatibility with Article 56 TFEU of a Portuguese law which concerned undertakings offering private security services. The fact that this piece of legislation applied only to undertakings operating on Portuguese territory for periods exceeding a calendar year was held not to be relevant.[103] These developments, however, do not devoid the legal category of 'establishment' of any content. They merely mean that there is a presumption that any service activity will be subject to the rules on services, unless it clearly requires long-term establishment in the host member state, such as the operation of a pharmacy.[104]

The above 'qualitative' developments are confirmed by 'quantitative' data. Out of a total of 283 cases decided on the basis of the Treaty rules on services, those which are exclusively concerned with the provision of services are the small minority. Indeed, in 213 cases, some other fundamental freedoms were also at stake. From these 213, 27 cases relate to the free movement of goods, 42 to the free movement of workers, 25 to the free movement of capital, while the remaining 119 put at stake the freedom of establishment (see Table 1.2).

This general observation confirms the economic analysis, according to which services are 'intermediary' economic products, intrinsically linked to the production and distribution of goods and to the movement of production factors, ie workers and capital. The same observation denies the idea, unskilfully expressed in Article 57 TFEU, that services are a legally residual category: if this were indeed the case, all these 213 occurrences would have been dealt with solely under the other Treaty provisions—and no reference would be made to Article 56 TFEU.

The analysis will now turn to examine more closely all these cases where compatibility of national measures was not only examined against the free movement of services, but also some other freedom.

So far as the free movement of goods is concerned, in four cases the Court does not acknowledge the 'goods' dimension of the case at all. Of the remaining 23,

---

[102] Ibid, para 39.
[103] Case C-171/02 *Commission v Portugal (private security firms)* [2004] I-5645.
[104] Case C-393/08 *Emanuela Sbarigia v Azienda USL RM/A e.a.* [2010] OJ C 234/6.

Table 1.3. CJEU's reasoning in relation to other freedoms: Goods

CJEU's reasoning in relation to other freedoms: Goods	No. of cases
Goods dimension not acknowledged	4
Restriction to goods only incidental—not dealt with	6
Both freedoms examined—same reasoning	5
Both freedoms examined—different reasoning	7
Situation only examined under the goods rules	5
Total	**27**

in six the Court finds the restriction to the free movement of goods to be only incidental to a restriction on the provision of services and a necessary consequence thereof, and does not specifically deal with it.[105] In five cases, on the other hand, the services dimension is subsumed to goods.[106] In the remaining 12 cases, the Court dealt with both freedoms; interestingly enough, in only five of them was the reasoning identical for both freedoms,[107] while in the remaining seven, there are differences at the level of the violation—never at the level of justification.[108] More specifically, two cases account for the existence of a specific Treaty provision (Article 35 TFEU) prohibiting only discriminatory measures which hinder goods' exports,[109] two for the *Keck* case law,[110] while the remaining three are explained by more substantial (and less legalistic) differences. See Table 1.3.

Compared to the free movement of goods, convergence of the rules on services is statistically more pronounced with the other personal freedoms.

---

[105] See eg Case C-275/92 *Her Majesty's Customs and Excise v Schindler* [1994] ECR I-1039; Case C-36/02 *Omega Spielhallen-und Automatenaufstellungs-GmbH v Oberburgermeisterin der Bundesstadt Bonn* [2004] ECR I-9609; in yet another one, the Court acknowledges that both freedoms are at stake, but only deals with services, since the referring court has failed to provide the necessary information concerning goods; see Case C-124/97 *Markku Juhani Läärä, Cotswold Microsystems Ltd and Oy Transatlantic Software Ltd v Kihlakunnasyyttäjä (Jyväskylä) and Suomen valtio* [1999] ECR I-6067.

[106] See eg Case 155/73 *Giuseppe Sacchi* [1974] ECR 409; Case C-96/94 *Centro Servizi Spediporto Srl v Spedizioni Marittima del Golfo Srl* [1995] ECR I-2883; Case C-20/03 *Criminal proceedings against Marcel Burmanjer, René Alexander Van der Linden and Anthony De Jong* [2005] ECR I-4133.

[107] See eg Case C-124/97 *Markku Juhani Läärä, Cotswold Microsystems Ltd and Oy Transatlantic Software Ltd v Kihlakunnasyyttäjä (Jyväskylä) and Suomen valtio* [1999] ECR I-6067; Joined cases C-34–36/95 *Konsumentombudsmannen v de Agostini and TV-Shop* [1997] ECR I-3843; Case C-390/99 *Canal Satélite Digital SL v Administracìon General del Estado* [2002] ECR I-607.

[108] Case 251/83 *Eberhard Haug-Adrion v Frankfurter Versicherungs-AG* [1984] ECR 4277; Case C-260/89 *ERT v DEP and Sotirios Kouvelas* [1991] ECR 2925; Case C-272/91 *Commission v Italy (Lottomatica)* [1994] ECR I-1409; Case C-379/92 *Criminal proceedings against Matteo Peralta* [1994] ECR I-3453; Case C-6/98 *Deutscher Rundfunkanstalten v PRO Sieben Media* [1999] ECR I-7599; Case C-405/98 *Konsumentombudsmannnen (KO) v Gourmet International Products AB (GIP)* [2001] ECR I-1795; Case C-355/00 *Freskot AE v Elliniko Dimosio* [2003] ECR I-5263.

[109] Case 251/83 *Eberhard Haug-Adrion v Frankfurter Versicherungs-AG* [1984] ECR 4277; Case C-379/92 *Criminal proceedings against Matteo Peralta* [1994] ECR I-3453.

[110] Case C-6/98 *Deutscher Rundfunkanstalten v PRO Sieben Media* [1999] ECR I-7599; Case C-405/98 *Konsumentombudsmannnen (KO) v Gourmet International Products AB (GIP)* [2001] ECR I-1795.

Table 1.4. CJEU's reasoning in relation to other freedoms: Workers

CJEU's reasoning in relation to other freedoms: Workers	*No. of cases*
Workers privileged	8
Services privileged	3
Both freedoms examined—same reasoning	25
Both freedoms examined—different reasoning	6
Total	42

Table 1.5. CJEU's reasoning in relation to other freedoms: Establishment

CJEU's reasoning in relation to other freedoms: Establishment	*No. of cases*
Services subsumed/ignored	21
Establishment subsumed/ignored	13
Abuse of rights	14
Both freedoms examined—same reasoning	60
Both freedoms examined—different reasoning	11
Total	119

In respect of the free movement of workers (see Table 1.4), out of 42 cases where both sets of rules could be applied, the Court chose: i. to privilege the workers aspect over the services aspect in eight,[111] ii. to ignore or to subsume the worker's perspective to that of services in three,[112] and iii. to deal with both freedoms in 31. Among the latter, in 25 the Court followed the same line of reasoning for both freedoms. The remaining six are cases typically involving some authorization, registration, or permit requirement, which may be imposed on workers wishing to establish themselves in another member state, but not to the occasional service provider.[113]

As regards the freedom of establishment, out of 119 cases which could be dealt with under both Treaty freedoms, the Court decided not to apply the rules on services in 21 (see Table 1.5). These correspond to situations where the

[111] See eg Case 196/87 *Steymann v Staatssecretaris van Justitie* [1988] ECR 6159; Case C-164/94 *Georgios Aranitis v Land Berlin* [1996] ECR I-135; Case C-313/01 *Christine Morgenbesser v Consiglio dell'Ordine degli avvocati di Genova* [2003] ECR I-13467.

[112] See eg Case C-3/95 *Reisebüro Broede v Gerd Sandker* [1996] ECR I-6511; Case C-422/01 *Försäkringsaktiebolaget Skandia (publ) and Ola Ramstedt v Riksskatteverket* [2003] ECR I-6817.

[113] See eg Case 147/86 *Commission v Greece (private schools)* [1988] ECR 1637; Case 263/86 *Belgium v Humbel* [1988] ECR 5365; Case C-55/98 *Skatteministeriet v Bent Vestergaard* [1999] ECR I-7641; Case C-279/89 *Commission v UK (fisheries)* [1992] ECR I-5785; Case C-379/92 *Criminal proceedings against Matteo Peralta* [1994] ECR I-3453; Case C-355/98 *Commission v Belgium (private security)* [2000] ECR I-1221; Case C-283/99 *Commission v Italy (private security)* [2001] ECR I-4363.

permanence of the establishment justifies more stringent and/or different requirements than the temporary service provision. They mainly cover four categories:
i. cases concerning the requirement of a registration, membership of a professional
association, etc,[114] ii. cases relevant to the mutual recognition of professional
qualifications,[115] iii. cases about differential tax treatment based on the place of
residence/establishment,[116] and iv. cases dealing with language requirements.[117]
On the opposite side, in 13 cases, the Court has found the freedom of establishment to be secondary or subsumed to the free provision of services and has only
dealt with them under the latter. In 14 cases, moreover, the establishment rules
have been given preference on the basis of the 'abuse of rights' doctrine. Finally, in
71 cases the Court has examined the restrictions under both freedoms. Of those,
the same reasoning was followed in 60.[118] The 11 cases in which the Court has
applied differently the rules on establishment from the rules on services account for
situations where the permanence of the establishment of the service provider
justified the requirement of a registration/authorization[119] or the application of
the more stringent national requirements;[120] or to tax cases, where residence is the
determining factor.[121]

The above quantitative data clearly supports the idea that all personal freedoms
are dealt with under the same legal principles; the relatively rare occasions in which
different principles apply are justified by objective factual differences and correspond to the largely uncontested idea that a short-term/temporary trans-border
economic activity may not be subject to all the requirements of a full and

---

[114] Case 246/80 *C. Broekmeulen v Huisarts Registratie Commissie* [1981] ECR 2311; Case C-55/94
Reinhard Gebhard v Consiglio dell'Ordine degli Avvocati e Procuratori di Milano [1995] ECR I-4165;
Case C-355/98 *Commission v Belgium (private security)* [2000] ECR I-1221; Case C-79/01 *Payroll
Data Services (Italy) Srl, ADP Europe SA and ADP GSI SA* [2002] ECR I-8923.

[115] Case C-104/91 *Colegio Oficial de Agentes de la Propriedad Immobiliaria v José Luis Aguirre Borrell
and others* [1992] ECR I-3003; Case C-319/92 *Salomone Haim v Kassenzahnärztliche Vereinigung
Nordrhein* [1994] ECR I-425; Case C-340/89 *Vlassopoulou v Ministerium für Justiz, Bundes-und
Europaangelengheiten Baden-Württemberg* [1991] ECR I-2357; Case C-232/99 *Commission v Spain
(doctor's recognition)* [2002] ECR I-4235; Case C-31/00 *Conseil national de l'ordre des architectes v
Nicolas Dreessen* [2002] ECR I-663.

[116] Case C-291/04 *Criminal proceedings against Henri Léon Schmitz* [2006] ECR I-59.

[117] Case C-424/97 *Salomone Haim v Kassenzahnärztliche Vereinigung Nordrhein* [2000] ECR
I-5123.

[118] It is true that in some of them, the same activity was envisioned from opposite viewpoints: as a
restriction to the right of establishment of the foreign service provider, and as a restriction to the right
to receive services of the customers/clients/patients of the host state: see eg Case C-334/02 *Commission
v France (income tax)* [2004] ECR I-2229.

[119] Case 292/86 *Gullung v Conseil de l'ordre des avocats du barreau de Colmar* [1988] ECR 111; Case
C-379/92 *Criminal proceedings against Matteo Peralta* [1994] ECR I-3453; Case 263/99 *Commission v
Italy (transport consultants)* [2001] ECR I-4195.

[120] Case C-70/95 *Sodemare SA and others v Regione Lombardia* [1997] ECR I-3395; Case C-355/98
Commission v Belgium (private security) [2000] ECR I-1221; Case C-145/99 *Commission v Italy
(lawyers)* [2002] ECR I-2235; Case C-215/01 *Bruno Schnitzer* [2003] ECR I-14847; Case C-496/
01 *Commission v France (medical laboratories)* [2004] ECR I-2351; Case C-171/02 *Commission v
Portugal (private securities)* [2004] ECR I-5645; Case C-514/03 *Commission v Spain (private security)*
[2006] ECR I-963.

[121] Case C-522/04 *Commission v Belgium (occupational pension schemes)* [2007] ECR I-5701.

permanent establishment.[122] This, in turn, confirms the conclusion that the Treaty distinction between workers, establishment, and services does not bear any intrinsic normative value—other than offering specific legal bases for secondary legislation. It also demonstrates that the GATS division into the four modes of service provision is more valuable, as it corresponds better to genuine regulatory needs.

Convergence is also observed between the rules on services and those on the free movement of capital. Out of 25 cases putting both freedoms at stake, in five the Court privileged the rules on capital movement over those on services, while in another 13, it moved in the opposite direction. In the seven remaining cases, the Court reasoned in identical terms of both freedoms, and applied them in the same way.

Any doubt which could subsist after all the above statistical data as to the 'residual' character of the rules on services has been expressly dismissed by the Court's formal pronouncement in *Fidium Finanz*, in which the Court held that the definition of Article 57 TFEU 'does not establish any order of priority between the freedom to provide services and the other fundamental freedoms'.[123]

B. Regulation

1. Regulation: basic concepts

As explained above,[124] regulation plays a pervasive role in the provision of services: not only from a purely 'regulatory' perspective, by determining who may provide services, to whom, under which conditions, and so on, but also from an 'economic' perspective, since it is a crucial determinant of comparative advantage in the provision of services.

a. Defining regulation

Understanding what regulation is and how it affects production processes is no easy task, despite (or because of?) the fact that in recent years regulation has gained its status as an autonomous field of study.[125] Indeed, depending on the viewpoint adopted, several definitions of regulation may be proposed.[126] As G. Majone has

---

[122] The idea may not be as uncontested as it may seem: when transposing the Services Directive (European Parliament and Council Directive 2006/123 (EC) on services in the internal market [2006] OJ L376/36), the UK screened all its legislation to comply with the 'stricter' rules on occasional service provision, thus submitting even permanently established service providers to the more lenient rules applicable to temporary service provision.

[123] Case C-452/04 *Fidium Finanz AG v Bundesanstalt für Finanzdienstleistungsaufsicht* [2006] ECR I-9521, para 32.

[124] See the discussion under subheading A(1)f(i).

[125] For an excellent and handy presentation of the various issues raised by the study of regulation, see Morgan, B., and Yeung, K. *An Introduction to Law and Regulation: Text and Materials* (Cambridge: CUP, 2007).

[126] Ogus, A., 'Comparing Regulatory Systems: Institutions, Processes and Legal Forms in Industrialised Countries' Centre on Regulation and Competition Working Paper No. 35/2002, also

explained, the term is used in different ways in the US and the EU.[127] T. Prosser further demonstrates that within the EU itself regulation is seen in two very distinct ways.[128] Despite these, and at a high level of abstraction and simplification, it may be said that regulation is based on the co-existence (to differing degrees) of three capacities on the part of the regulator: standard-setting, information-gathering or monitoring, and behaviour-modification.[129]

Regulation may be approached in a 'state-' and 'rule-centric' manner, whereby
i. the state is the primary locus for articulating the collective goals of a community, ii. the state is characterized by a strictly hierarchical nature, and iii. command is the primary mode of shaping behaviour.[130] Such an approach, however, can be questioned on numerous accounts, both empirical and analytical.[131]

A wider approach has been proposed, which examines the relationships between the state and the range of other actors, institutions, and techniques. Dubbed 'decentred regulation', this analysis seems to offer a more complete view of the role of regulation.[132]

This distinction has more than purely analytical value, as it corresponds to two paradigms of regulation in Europe, namely, the Continental and the Anglo-Saxon.[133]

Under both visions, law always has a role to play, either as the main means of regulation (state-centric regulation) or in a more limited way (decentred regulation). In the latter paradigm, law may be seen as performing a double task: a) facilitative, in the sense that it is an instrument for shaping social behaviour, either by proscribing conduct and threatening sanctions for its violation, or by creating and policing the boundaries of a space for free and secure interaction between participants; and b) expressive, either by legitimizing coercion or by reflecting shared or agreed standards of morality.[134]

---

available at <http://www.regulationbodyofknowledge.org/documents/060.pdf> (last accessed 5 November 2011).

[127] Majone, G., *Deregulation or Re-regulation* (London: Pinter, 1990), at 7–8.

[128] See n 139, and the corresponding text.

[129] Hood, C., Rothstein, H., and Baldwin, R., *The Government of Risk* (Oxford: OUP, 2001), at 23; for a more complete definition of regulation, see Black, J., 'Critical Reflections on Regulation' LSE Centre for the Analysis of Risk and Regulation Discussion Paper 04/2002, available at <http://www.lse.ac.uk/collections/CARR/pdf/DPs/Disspaper4.pdf> (last accessed on 5 November 2011), at 20: 'regulation is the sustained and focused attempt to alter the behaviour of others according to defined standards or purposes with the intention of producing a broadly identified outcome or outcomes, which may involve mechanisms of standard-setting, information-gathering and behaviour-modification'.

[130] For these three components of the state-centric approach, see Morgan, B., and Yeung, K., 2007, n 125, at 4.

[131] Ibid, at 43–52.

[132] Black, J., 'Decentring Regulation: The Role of Regulation and Self Regulation in a "Post Regulatory" World' (2001) 54 *Current Legal Problems* 103–46.

[133] Prosser, T., *Law and the Regulators* (Oxford: OUP, 1997) 1–5.

[134] Morgan, B. and Yeung, K., 2007, n 125, at 5–6.

b. Explaining regulation

There are various theories explaining why regulation emerges and/or which goals it should be pursuing: public interest theories, private interest theories, and institutionalist theories.[135] The first series of theories is the most widely acclaimed and the most useful one, at least for the purposes of the present study: it serves not only an explanatory function, but also provides a prescriptive, analytical framework of what regulation is and what it should be about. This is why it is presented in some detail below. The other two sets of theories are more explanatory than prescriptive.

Private interest theories are grounded on the hypothesis that regulation is the result of actions of individuals or groups motivated to maximize their self-interest; under this setup, public interest may or may not be served. Indeed, the very existence of a validly expressed 'public interest' is questioned and the likelihood of 'regulatory failure' and 'regulatory capture' is stressed. From a political point of view, the absence of any strong umpire allows the regulatory arena to be shaped by a political process in which inequality of resources inevitably gives some groups advantage over others. From an economic point of view, regulation is conceptualized as a good subject to forces of 'supply' and 'demand' in the political arena. Therefore, regulatory behaviour is analogous to market behaviour, but market outcomes are seen as preferable to regulatory ones, since regulatory outcomes are 'all-or-nothing', less flexible, and collective (hence, they need to be made simultaneously). It comes as no surprise that private interest theories of regulation favour economic freedom and extensive deregulation.[136]

Institutionalist theories 'consider institutional dynamics to have, in a sense, a "life of their own" in regulatory regimes, such that they will often shape the outcomes of regulation in surprising ways, given the preferences and interests of regulatory participants'. What is more, they 'blur the differences between public and private actors, and between public and private interests'.[137]

Public interest theories of regulation, on the other hand, are based on the assumption that regulation is necessary for, and justified by, pursuance of the general interest. A fundamental hiatus, however, is drawn between those who consider that such public interest may only bear on welfare economics and be essentially 'market correcting', and those who envision public interest in a broader manner, as incorporating substantive political approaches; indeed, in this latter

---

[135] For a more detailed discussion of these issues, see ibid, at 16–78. The analysis which follows draws extensively on this work.

[136] Further on private choice theories, see Croley, S., 'Theories of Regulation: Incorporating the Administrative Process' (1998) 98 *Columbia L Rev* 56–65; Brown, P., 'The Failure of Market Failures' (1992) 21 *J of Socio-Economics* 1–24; Charles, W., 'A Theory of Nonmarket Failures' (1979) 55 *The Public Interest* 114–33.

[137] Both quotations taken from Morgan, B., and Yeung, K., 2007, n 125, at 53; further on institutionalist theories, see Ayers, I., and Braithwaite, J., *Responsive Regulation: Transcending the Deregulatory Debate* (Oxford: OUP, 1992); Hancher, L., and Moran, M., 'Organizing regulatory space' in Hancher, L., and Moran, M. (eds), *Capitalism, Culture and Regulation* (Oxford: Clarendon Press, 1989) 271–95.

view, regulation should be aimed at more than 'market making' and encompass broader policy/polity objectives.[138]

In the European context, one of the most vocal promoters of this latter position is T. Prosser.[139] In his latest, highly articulate work, T. Prosser presents two visions of regulation:[140] 'regulation as intrusion on private autonomy', pursuing merely allocative efficiencies along the lines of competition law; and 'regulation as an enterprise', pursuing broader social objectives and public service in particular.

Under the former approach (the intrusion paradigm), regulation is seen as a means to which recourse should be had only exceptionally and temporarily. Regulation should be aimed at either 'regulating monopoly, mimicking the effect of market forces through implementing controls on prices and on quality of service' or 'creating the conditions for competition to exist and policing it to ensure that it continues to exist'.[141] Under this approach, 'the rationale for regulation [is] an economic one rather than one of social engineering'.[142] Social engineering through the provision of public services according to the values of solidarity is the objective of the latter vision of regulation (enterprise paradigm). The former approach gives absolute prevalence to private autonomy. By contrast, the latter 'rather than starting from individual rights...starts from the duties of the community to secure such inclusiveness, resting both on a moral sense of equal citizenship and a more prudential goal of minimizing social fragmentation'.[143]

The characteristics of the two visions of regulation, according to T. Prosser, are summarized in Table 1.6.[144]

Each approach is based on distinctive values; the intrusion approach is founded on economic concepts of efficiency and on consumer choice, while the enterprise approach draws upon social and economic rights and social solidarity. A central argument is that each of these paradigms bears value and importance on its own, and that it is a mistake to see public service as simply a correction for market failure. Rather, which approach is chosen will depend more on which values need to be promoted in each different context.[145]

There is, however, a clear advantage of the restrictive vision of regulation (the intrusion paradigm) over the more expansive one (the enterprise paradigm):

---

[138] See eg Sunstein, C., *After the Rights Revolution: Reconceiving the Regulatory State* (Cambridge MA: Harvard University Press, 1990).

[139] This idea is pervasive in T. Prosser's work for some time now. See Prosser, T., *Law and the Regulators* (Oxford: OUP, 1997) 5–14; it also transcends the structure of Prosser, T., *The Limits of Competition Law: Markets and Public Services* (Oxford: OUP, 2005) and it is made even more explicit in Prosser, T., *The Regulatory Enterprise: Government, Regulation and Legitimacy* (Oxford: OUP, 2010), a book entirely dedicated to pieces of regulation and regulatory bodies which primarily pursue the 'second' vision of regulation. For this vision, see more in the following paras.

[140] Prosser, T., 2010, n 139, at 1–20. Chapter 1 of this book bears the title 'Introduction: Two Visions of Regulation and Four Regulatory Models'; for the four models, see in more detail in the following paragraphs.

[141] Prosser, T., 1997, n 139, at 5.

[142] Ibid, at 7.

[143] Prosser, T., 2005, n 139, at 35.

[144] Ibid, at 5–6.

[145] Prosser, T., 2005, n 139, at vii (foreword); ibid, at 38.

Table 1.6. The two visions of regulation (after T. Prosser)

	Regulation as intrusion	*Regulation as enterprise*
Objective	Maximization of economic efficiency	Economic and social/distributive goals
Institutional arrangements	Independence of regulators is key	Collaborative enterprise between regulatory agencies and other government bodies
Regulatory tools	Preference for clear rules	Discretion more important than rules; accountability for discretion through procedural means
Other means of coordination	Contractual relationships, self- and co-regulation	Self-regulation only on the basis of delegation
Relationship between regulators/ regulatees	Analogous to a contract aiming at stability and calculability	Complex network of interaction between a large number of stakeholders
Deliberation and expression of outside interests	Regulator receives evidence through consultation, etc (but limited in order to avoid regulatory capture)	Direct representation of stakeholder interests (eg board membership) and public decision making
Regulatory accountability	Private law mechanisms (contract, tort law)	Public law mechanisms: parliamentary scrutiny and judicial review

the former may enjoy greater legitimacy, since it is easier to grasp its objectives, to monitor its implementation, and to evaluate its efficiency. Regulation as an enterprise, on the other hand, because it pursues objectives which embody political choices, and are not quantifiable, is more difficult to legitimize. Legitimacy, however, may be secured, according to T. Prosser, by additional procedural means ensuring participation, deliberation, and transparency.[146]

c. Regulation's objectives

The broad vision presented above of regulation and its proceduralization explains the widening of regulation's objectives. According to a classical account, regulation may pursue one or more of the following objectives:[147] a. control of monopoly power and monopoly profits (but not rents), b. addressing externalities, c. compensation for inadequate information and information asymmetries, d. preventing excessive (and thus destructive) competition, e. ensuring that production of important goods as well as the use of scarce or else valuable resources is rationalized,

---

[146] Again, all of T. Prosser's books illustrate this point, which is summarily presented in Prosser, T., 2010, n 139, at 6–11.
[147] Breyer, S., *Regulation and Its Reform* (Cambridge MA: Harvard University Press, 1982).

f. limitation of moral hazard, g. protection of consumers, workers, or other groups (also referred to as paternalism). These objectives are typically accounted for under four more general headings: a. natural monopolies or oligopolies—market failures, b. information asymmetries, c. externalities, and d. social and equity considerations.[148]

A large—and more ideological—vision of regulation, however, such as the one advocated by T. Prosser, inevitably calls for a more ideological analysis of regulatory models. Indeed, while the four grounds enumerated above look more like 'excuses' justifying regulation (regulation as an undesirable necessity), T. Prosser reasons more in terms of objectives pursued by regulation (regulation as a deliberate choice). For this reason, he identifies four such objectives. The fact that regulation seeks to maximize efficiency and consumer choice is duly acknowledged. In addition, however, regulation may serve both fundamental human rights (individualistic, rights-based approach) and social solidarity (social solidarity, endowment-based approach). Fourthly, an important degree of regulation is self-sustaining as it is aimed at legitimizing regulation through regulatory participation and deliberation.

All the classifications mentioned above are useful—and indeed, many more useful categories could be proposed. It is worth noting, however, that while the two classifications proposed above come from the US or international experience, T. Prosser's view is grounded in the reality of the EU. Indeed, it is not disputed that regulation in the EU is not exclusively—and some times not even primarily—about market efficiency. As will be shown in the course of this book, although EU regulation starts from an essentially economic standpoint (and corresponding competences), the EU has progressively and increasingly been sensitive both to the rights-based and socially imbued objectives of regulation and to the need for proceduralization and rationalization of regulatory processes. The ever-increasing attachment of the EU to the concept of services of general interest, both by means of sector-specific hard rules and by means of horizontal soft law instruments, accounts for the first tendency.[149] The quality and legitimacy of regulation has also become a major theme in the EU, especially since the adoption of the 2001 White Paper on Governance, the 2002 Communication on Better Regulation, and the 2003 Inter-institutional Agreement on Better Law-making.[150]

---

[148] See eg Ogus, A., 'The regulation of services and the public–private divide' in Caffagi, F., and Muir-Watt, H. (eds), *The Regulatory Function of European Private Law* (Cheltenham/Northampton: Edward Elgar Publishing, 2009) 3–15; Basedow, J., 'Economic regulation in market economies' in Basedow, J., Harald, B., Hopt, K., Kanda, H., and Kono, T. (eds), *Economic Regulation and Competition* (The Hague/London/NY: Kluwer Law International, 2002) 1–24; Gamberale, C., and Mattoo, A., 'National regulations and liberalisation of trade in services' in English, P., Hoekman, B., and Mattoo, A. (eds), *Development, Trade and the WTO: A Handbook* (Washington/Paris: The World Bank/Economica, 2004) 230–51.

[149] See, in more detail, the discussion in ch 2.

[150] White Paper COM (2001) 428 final, 'European Governance', Communication COM (2002) 275 final, 'European Governance: Better Lawmaking', at 2, and Interinstitutional Agreement on Better Lawmaking [2003] OJ C321/1, respectively. See also the discussion in ch 9.

2. Regulation: the EU peculiarities

a. Multi-level regulation—regulatory competition

i. Multi-level regulation

It is a truism to state today that the EU has established a multi-level system of governance. It is not surprising either that the ensuing regulation is multi-layered. This is especially so, if a broad concept of regulation is used—as is the case in the present study. The various layers of regulation and the difficulties in approaching it are the result of two sets of factors, relating to the way the EU operates and the regulatory means it uses.

The way the EU operates can be said to generate regulatory complication, under at least four perspectives. *First*, the 'vertical' competence share between the EU and its member states creates considerable difficulties. Not only is the dividing line often blurred (although Articles 3 to 6 TFEU partly cure this), but, more importantly, the distinction between exclusive, shared, concurrent, coordinated, and support powers is drawn on the basis of political, not real-life criteria. The upshot of this is that, more often than not, a single piece of regulation will transcend two or more kinds of competences. Therefore, it will be difficult to trace both its author and the procedure followed for its adoption. The same difficulty arises, *secondly*, from the 'horizontal' competence-share between the various EU institutions: the role played by each institution is different in every different formal procedure, while informal decision-making processes, notably comitology, account for an increasing number of regulations; the image is further complicated by the involvement of EU agencies, national regulatory authorities, and networks thereof. *Thirdly*, the emerging role of regional and sub-regional authorities, as active participants in EU regulation, adds to the complexity. *Fourthly*, the increasing influence of stakeholders, either through direct delegation of regulatory powers to them, or through more indirect means of participation and consultation further blurs the origin and nature of regulation.

As for the regulatory means in the EU system, it should be noted that alternatives to regulation, typically aimed at some kind of coordination (the Open Method of Coordination being the emblematic expression) bring to the fore fresh means of regulation, such as standards, benchmarks, indicators, and the like.

ii. Regulatory competition

What is more, the multitude of regulators at the national, supranational, and infra-national level, combined with the ill-defined boundaries of competence-share among them, become the source of regulatory competition.

'The term "regulatory competition" refers to a process whereby legal rules are selected (and de-selected) through competition between decentralised, rule-making entities (which could be nation states or other units such as regions or localities). Three justifications are normally given for regulatory competition: firstly, it allows the content of rules to be matched more effectively to the preferences or *wants* of the consumers of law (citizens and others affected); secondly, it promotes diversity and experimentation in the search for effective legal solutions; and thirdly, by providing mechanisms for preferences to be expressed and alternative solutions compared, it promotes the flow of information on effective law making.'[151]

Nonetheless, regulatory competition in the EU brings trouble both at the political and at the legal levels.[152] At the former, acute problems can be created, as deregulatory spirals and a race to the bottom can be caused. Moving to the legal level, regulatory competition is conceptually fundamentally opposed to harmonization; the latter, however, has been and still is one of the core regulatory objectives of the EU.

b. Regulation through internal market—competition law

The multitude of regulatory sources and the (direct or indirect) role played by private actors has one further, purely legal, implication. Since the EU Treaties are fundamentally treaties signed between states, they typically impose obligations on states. For the sake of completeness, however, (and unlike the GATS) the TFEU foresees basic competition rules addressed to private undertakings. Therefore, next to the horizontal internal market (free movement) and to the other sector-specific Treaty rules (transport, education, health, etc), which both describe and circumscribe state-imposed regulation, the EU competition rules also have an important part to play. This is all the more true in relation to services' regulation, since in this area most regulations are process- rather than product-related and are, very often, the fruit of self- or else private regulation.[153]

The interplay between free movement and competition rules as means of service regulation is confirmed by statistics. From Table 1.7 it can be seen that from a total of 283 cases decided by CJEU on the basis of the Treaty rules on services, in at least 57 competition rules were also held to apply. Depending on the factual setting of the cases in question, 13 cases concern the prohibition of concerted practices (Article 101 TFEU), 21 cases relate to prohibited abuses of a dominant position (Article 102 TFEU) and four dealt with the grant of state aids (Article 107 TFEU).

---

[151] Barnard, C., and Deakin, S., 'Market access and regulatory competition' in Barnard, C., and Scott, J. (eds), *The Law of the Single European Market: Unpacking the Premises* (Oxford: Hart Publishing, 2002) 197–224, at 199, Jean Monnet Working Paper No. 9/2001, also available at <http://www.jeanmonnetprogram.org/papers/01/012701.html> (last accessed on 5 November 2011); much earlier, see Scharpf, F., 'Introduction: The Problem-solving Capacity of Multi-level Governance' (1997) 4 *JEPP* 520–38; Ogus, A., 'Competition between National Legal Systems: A Contribution of Economic Analysis to Comparative Law' (1999) 48 *Int & Comparative L Q* 405–18; see also Davies, G., 'The Legal Framework of Regulatory Competition', SSRN online paper (2006), available at <http://papers.ssrn.com/sol3/papers.cfm?abstract_id=903138> (last accessed on 5 November 2011).

[152] Issues related to the regulation of services are briefly discussed in ch 6.

[153] For the distinction between product- and process-oriented rules and the regulatory implications thereof, see ch 6. For private regulation and the means of its control, see the developments in ch 8.

Table 1.7. Application of the competition rules in the case law on services

Competition rule applicable	No. of cases
Article 101 TFEU	13
Article 102 TFEU	21
Article 106 TFEU	19
Article 107 TFEU	4
Total	57

Last but not least, Article 106 TFEU on public undertakings and the provision of services of general economic interest has been involved in 19 cases.

This finding raises, in turn, the question of the way the various Treaty rules are coordinated (if at all) and how they are reflected in the regulation (of EU or member state origin) applicable to the field of services. This issue is extensively discussed in the following chapter.

2

Economic v. Non-economic Services

The economic rules, or put more ambitiously, the economic constitution of the Treaty,[1] only apply to economic activities. This general principle remains valid, even if some authors strive to demonstrate that certain Treaty rules also apply in the absence of an economic activity,[2] and despite the fact that non-economic (horizontal) Treaty provisions (eg principle of non-discrimination, rules on citizenship) are also applicable in the absence of any economic activity.[3]

The distinction between economic and non-economic activities thus takes on a constitutional significance in the EU context, as it serves to delineate the scope of application of the core EU rules. In other words, the distinction is a means of dividing competences between the EU and the member states.

The initial EEC Treaty, having an exclusively economic character, did not contain any key to the above distinction, which was deemed to be external to its scope of application. The situation, however, gradually changed under the impact of two developments. First, successive modifications have brought within the Treaty's realm policies which do not qualify as economic as such, although they might have influence on the economy; for example those concerning culture, education, and healthcare. Secondly, the gradual deregulation (at the national level) and re-regulation (at the EU level) of network and other industries offering services traditionally considered as non-economic, revealed the urgent need to delimit the scope of application of EU rules.

The latter development has also prompted the ongoing debate on the nature and content of services of general interest in the EU, as well as the even more complex question of the competence-share for defining them. It is in the framework

---

[1] Amongst the most prominent supporters of the idea that the EU Treaties may be seen as an economic constitution, see Joerges, C., 'A renaissance of the European Economic Constitution?' in Neergard, U., Nielsen, R., and Roseberry, L. (eds), *Integrating Welfare Functions into EU Law* (Copenhaguen: DJØF Publishing, 2009) 29–52; see also, on a more pessimistic tone, Joerges, C., 'What Is Left of the European Economic Constitution?: A Melancholic Eulogy' (2005) 30 *EL Rev* 461–89, also available at <http://www.direitogv.com.br/AppData/Event/Paper2020Joerges.pdf> (last accessed on 5 November 2011); Baquero-Cruz, J., *Between Competition and Free Movement: The Economic Constitutional Law of the European Community* (Oxford/Portland: Hart Publishing, 2002).

[2] Odudu, O., 'Economic activity as a limit to Community law' in Barnard, C., and Odudu, O. (eds), *The Outer Limits of EU Law* (Oxford/Portland: Hart Publishing, 2009) 225–43.

[3] See also the Commission Staff Working Document SEC (2006) 516, 'Annex to the Communication on Social Services of General Interest in the EU (COM (2006) 177 final)', s. 1.1.1; more recently see Report COM (2010) 630/4, 'EU Citizenship Report 2010: Dismantling the Obstacles to EU Citizens' Rights'.

of this controversy that the most important attempts to draw the line between economic and non-economic activities has taken place, leading to a series of constitutional adjustments (Article 14 TEU, Protocol No. 26, Article 36 of the Charter of Fundamental Rights). This debate, however, as was to be expected, has been essentially political in nature and has stopped short of delivering clear-cut definitions.

Beyond the political debate, an attempt to distinguish economic from non-economic activities from a legal point of view is being pursued by the CJEU and by the Commission in its competition decision making; this has not delivered spectacular results either.

The distinction between economic and non-economic activities is fraught with legal and technical intricacies—the latter generated by dynamic technological advances and regulatory experimentation. More importantly, however, the distinction is pregnant with political and ideological significance and misunderstandings and terminological confusions. It took almost a century and a lengthy cold war to reach a globally accepted definition of what *is* a market. The further question, of what is *in* a market, is still the topic of extremely heated debates, both at the national and at the supranational level.[4] Different solutions have prevailed at different times in different continents and, even, countries. Today, however, under the pressure of globalization and worldwide competition and due to the impact of WTO and the GATS, the trends tend to converge.

Economic theory offers helpful classifications, but is much less clear about the actual content of each one of the proposed categories. A basic distinction is drawn between private and public goods (although the term 'goods' typically refers to services, in the economic sense of the term). Public goods are distinguished from ordinary (private) goods, because they have two special features: a) they are *non-rivalrous* in consumption, in the sense that, once produced, an infinite number of consumers can enjoy them without increased production cost or diminished enjoyment by other consumers; moreover, b) they are *non-excludable*, in the sense that the producer cannot prevent non-purchasers from enjoying the benefits of the services produced. Therefore, there is not sufficient interest by private providers to supply such services, as they fear they would not be able to reap the full benefit of their investment/effort.[5] Hence, the state steps in and offers such services, usually financed through general taxation. Typical examples of public services could be police, national security, traffic light operation, emergency services, refuse collection and management, and the like. A further category has been devised, standing between public and private goods (= services) and is termed 'merit

---

[4] In the context of the EU, see already Mortelmans, K., 'The Common Market, the Internal Market and the Single Market: What's In a Market?' (1998) 35 *CML Rev* 101–36.

[5] See eg Stiglitz, J., *Economics of the Public Sector* (London: W.W. Norton, 2000) 128–9; and more recently, Kaul, I., Grunberg, I., and Stern, M.A., 'Defining global public goods' in Kaul, I., Grunberg, I., and Stern, M.A. (eds), *Global Public Goods: International Cooperation in the 21st Century* (Oxford: OUP, 1999) 2–19.

goods'.[6] These are services which are so meritorious that the state holds that, if they were left to market forces alone, the level of their consumption would be too low, because their price would be too high; hence it intervenes in order to obtain a higher level of consumption. This is achieved through heavily subsidizing or offering for free such services, through resources from tax or compulsory contributions. Typical examples of such services are health and education.[7]

The above economic classifications, however, have barely made it into any legal instrument.

The GATS is silent about the existence of various categories of services. It is supposed to apply to all services, but for the ones 'supplied in the exercise of governmental authority'.[8] This exception is globally understood to be a very limited one,[9] confined to the exercise of *imperium*, and, thus, agnostic to the economic classifications of services discussed above. The absence of any specific rule or exception about 'public' or 'merit' services in GATS may be explained either by the fact that such services were not considered important enough by the negotiators, or that GATS' impact on the liberalization of such services has been judged as unimportant. In view of the fact that under GATS signatory states are essentially bound to the extent of their express commitments, the latter explanation seems more plausible. Nonetheless, the assumption that in the absence of specific commitments the GATS leaves intact the signatory states to freely regulate services can be doubted. Indeed, some basic obligations under GATS, notably those stemming from Articles II, III and (partly) VI (the most-favoured-nation principle, transparency, and domestic regulation, respectively) are applicable in all circumstances, irrespective of any specific commitment. Be that as it may, it remains the case that the GATS does not contain any specific rules distinguishing different categories of services on the basis of their economic, social, or other merits.

In the EU legal system the Treaty has, ever since 1957, contained what has now become Article 106(2) TFEU, demonstrating from the beginning some sensibility towards services meriting special attention: the Treaty rules could be set aside, if this were necessary for the accomplishment of objectives of general interest. The precise content of Article 106(2) has given rise to great controversy, both at the

---

[6] Musgrave, R.A., 'A Multiple Theory of Budget Determination' (1957) 17 *FinanzArchiv* 331–43, also available at <http://www.mohr.de/fileadmin/user_upload/Zeitschriften/musgrave_budget_determination.pdf> (last accessed on 5 November 2011).

[7] For a recent and interesting discussion of this classification under the realm of the state aid rules, see Fiedziuk, N., 'Towards a More Refined Economic Approach to Services of General Economic Interest' (2010) 16 *Eur P L* 271–88.

[8] Article I(3)b GATS.

[9] Krajewski, M., 'Protecting a shared value of the union in a globalized world: services of general interest and external trade' in van de Gronden, J. (ed), *EU and WTO Law on Services: Limits to the Realization of General Interest Policies within the Services Markets?* (Alphen aan den Rijn: Kluwer Law International, 2009) 187–213; Adlung, R., 'Public Services and the GATS' (2006) 9 *J of Int Economic L* 455–85; Ruiz-Fabri, H., and Crontiras, J.P., 'L'OMC et les services' Rapport IDDRI 2/2003, also available at <http://www.iddri.org/Publications/Collections/Idees-pour-le-debat/id_0310_ruiz&fabri.pdf> (last accessed on 5 November 2011).

judicial and at the doctrinal level;[10] some authors even claim that it serves no purpose whatsoever.[11] What is certain, however, is that for many years this provision had been idle, only to be 're-invented' in the early 1990s. Nowadays, following the entry into force of the Lisbon Treaty, with its arsenal of provisions concerning services of general interest (in the TEU, in the Protocols and in the Charter), the scope of Article 106(2) appears even less clear.[12] In any case, it remains beyond doubt that in the EU, some services do require special attention.

It is also clear that the question 'what is in a market' is essentially raised when it comes to services. Goods are generally in the market, provided they have some market value,[13] even a negative one.[14] Indeed, any tangible good incorporates some value or needs to be disposed of, at some cost. Only goods which are per se illegal (use restrictions being a separate question),[15] and which are generally accepted as such[16] are outside the market. Therefore, non-market goods are confined to narcotic drugs, child pornography, and a few other goods.[17] Alongside those, there is a special regime concerning the export of dual-use goods.[18] Moreover, even if they are not moved for an economic purpose (ie traded), goods retain an intrinsic economic value and are, in principle, within the market.[19] Therefore, the category of non-market goods is so restricted that most textbooks spend no more than a line or, at best, a paragraph on this question.

It is in the field of services that the question of 'what is in a market' gains all its importance and requires exhaustive examination. Any tentative answer needs to

---

[10] Some of these controversies are raised in the developments of the present chapter, where the corresponding bibliography is to be found.

[11] Davies, G., 'What does Article 86 actually do?' in Krajewski, M., Neergard, U., and van de Gronden, J. (eds), *The Changing Legal Framework for Services of General Interest* (The Hague: TMC Asser Press, 2009) 51–67.

[12] See the analysis under subheading B(6)c.

[13] Case 7/68 *Commission v Italy (works of art)* [1968] ECR 618, English special edition 423.

[14] Case C-2/90 *Commission v Belgium (Walloon waste)* [1992] ECR I-4431.

[15] See the discussion in ch 3.

[16] This means that it is not enough that a good is considered as illegal in a single member state. See eg Case 34/79 *Regina v Maurice Donald Henn and John Frederick Ernest Darby* [1979] ECR 3795; Case 121/85 *Conegate Limited v HM Customs & Excise* [1986] ECR 1007.

[17] For narcotics, see Case 50/80 *Joszef Horvath v Hauptzollamt Hamburg-Jonas* [1981] ECR 385; Case 221/81 *Wilfried Wolf v Hauptzollamt Düsseldorf* [1982] ECR 3681; Case 294/82 *Senta Einberger v Hauptzollamt Freiburg* [1984] ECR 1177; for an overview of the relevant case law, see Case C-137/09 *Marc Michel Josemans v Burgemeester van Maastricht* [2010] not published in the ECR, available only in Spanish and French, see [2009] OJ C141/57, paras 87–91 (AG).

[18] Council Regulation 1334/2000/EC setting up a Community regime for the control of exports of dual-use items and technology [2000] OJ L159/1; on this topic, see in a very comprehensive way, Koutrakos, P., *Trade, Foreign Policy and Defence in EU Constitutional Law: The Legal Regulation of Sanctions, Exports of Dual-use Goods and Armaments* (Oxford: Hart Publishing, 2001); more recently, Dashwood, A., 'Dual-use goods: (mis)understanding Werner and Leifer' in Arnull, A., Eeckhout, A., and Tridimas, T. (eds), *Continuity and Change in EU Law: Essays in Honour of Sir Francis Jacobs* (Oxford: OUP, 2008) 354–60; and more briefly, see Michel, Q., 'The European Union Dual-use Export Control Regime' (2008) 40 *ESADRA Bulletin* 41–5, also available at <http://esarda2.jrc.it/db_proceeding/mfile/B_2008_040_10.pdf> (last accessed on 5 November 2011).

[19] Odudu, O., 'Economic activity as a limit to Community law' in Barnard, C., and Odudu, O. (eds), *The Outer Limits of EU Law* (Oxford/Portland: Hart Publishing, 2009) 225–43, at 239, where further references to various AGs and authors.

look in two directions. First, the political debate about the contours of the concept of services of general interest, non-economic by nature, and their opposition to services of general *economic* interest (Section A) will be examined. Then the focus will shift to the various techniques followed by the Court in order to accommodate the application of the Treaty rules to certain activities which may not, as a matter of fact, be provided within the market (Section B).

A. The political distinction between economic and non-economic services

1. What is there in a name?

Distinguishing between economic and non-economic activities is a very delicate task which the EU lacks both the technical means and the political legitimacy to undertake. Therefore, in order to overcome this ideological, and thus inconclusive, dilemma (a), the EU institutions have developed various concepts, often overlapping but allowing for some rationalization, based on a triple legal distinction (b).

a. From sterile dilemmas . . .

The TFEU Treaty, in Article 106(2), makes express reference to 'services of general *economic* interest' (SGEIs) and allows for exceptions to the Treaty rules where this is necessary for the provision of such services. This rule has been included in the Treaty since its very inception, in 1957. The concept of 'services of general interest' (SGIs), on the other hand, only made its entry in the EU regulatory arena with the 1996 Commission Communication on 'Services of General Interest in Europe'.[20] As the Commission has subsequently clarified, SGEIs are a sub-category of the more general category of SGIs. SGIs also include *non-economic* services, which are not caught by the Treaty (but may be caught by the general principles thereof).[21]

Economic and legal developments, however, have left the above dichotomy begging for further elaboration, in particular in relation to healthcare and social services. Although in its early Communications, the Commission clearly excluded such services from the scope of SGEIs (and hence, from the application of Treaty rules), the Court's case law in these last 15 years has made clear that, even when provided and/or funded by public entities, healthcare and social services are indeed

---

[20] Communication COM (1996) 443 final, 'Services of General Interest in Europe' [1996] OJ C281/3.

[21] See Communication COM (2007) 725, 'Services of General Interest, Including Social Services of General Interest: A New European Commitment', at 2.1. This view is confirmed in the Commission's most recent document in this area, the Guide on the application to SGEI, and in particular SSGI, of the European rules on state aid, public procurement, and the internal market, pre-published on the website for the 3rd Forum on SSGI organized by the Belgian Presidency. The document is only available in French, <http://www.socialsecurity.fgov.be/eu/docs/agenda/26–27_10_10_guide_commission.pdf> (last accessed on 5 November 2011).

subject to the Treaty rules.[22] Presumably, this is the reason why the Commission next to SGIs and SGEIs has recognized a third category, that of Social Services of General Interest (SSGI).[23] SGIs have been constitutionalized as a legal category (albeit with unclear content) in Protocol No. 26 of the Lisbon Treaty.

Further, it has to be recalled that before having recourse to the concept of SGI, the EU legislature had come to grips with a more technical concept, that of 'universal service'. This earlier concept had been put forth in the course of the gradual liberalization of network industries, in order to oblige the market forces to provide the socially desirable level of service. The concept is most developed in the field of electronic communications.[24]

As if the terminology were not confusing enough, the Court in its seminal judgment in *Altmark*[25] also revived the term 'public service obligations', which had fallen into oblivion, then repealed, together with its bearing Regulation 1191/69.[26] This confusion in terminology has been subsequently alleviated by the Court itself which held that the concept of SGEI in Article 106(2) TFEU and that of 'public service obligations' in *Altmark* are the same.[27] These two terms will henceforth be used interchangeably. Unsurprisingly, these developments and the confusing diversity of concepts employed have nurtured voluminous legal and political science commentary.[28]

---

[22] See, in relation to healthcare, the analysis and references in ch 5.

[23] See White Paper COM (2004) 374 final, 'Services of General Interest', and COM (2007) 725, n 21. See also the documentation of the conference organized by the Observatory for the Development of Social Services in Europe (28–29/06/2004, Brussels), *Social Services of General Interest in the EU: Assessing their specificities, potential and needs*, also available at <http://www.socialplatform.org/module/FileLib/ConferenceReportdocumentationDEENFR.pdf> (last accessed on 5 November 2011); see also SSIG, *Social Services of General Interest in the Internal Market of the 21st Century, The Reform Treaty, The New State of Affairs* (December 2007), also available at <http://www.ssig-fr.org> (last accessed on 5 November 2011); since then an evaluation of SSGIs takes place at a biannual basis, see, for the latest such evaluation, Commission Staff Working Paper SEC (2010) 1284 final.

[24] See de Streel, A., and Queck, R., 'Services d'intérêt général et communications électroniques' in Louis, J.V., and Rodriguez, S. (eds), *Les services d'intérêt économique général et l'UE* (Bruxelles: Bruylant, 2006) 338–84; for a recent CJEU interpretation of the concept, in the field of electronic communications, see Case C-222/08 *Commission v Belgium (electronic communications)* [2010] nyr, para 40.

[25] Case C-280/00 *Altmark Trans GmbH and Regierungspräsidium Magdeburg v Nahverkehrsgesellschaft Altmark GmbH, and Oberbundesanwalt beim Bundesverwaltungsgericht* [2003] ECR I-7747; further on this judgment, see in subsection B(5)d.

[26] Council Regulation 1191/69/EEC on action by Member States concerning the obligations inherent in the concept of a public service in transport by rail, road and inland waterway [1969] OJ English Special Edition I, p. 276, as amended by Council Regulation 1893/91/EEC amending Regulation (EEC) No 1191/69 on action by Member States concerning the obligations inherent in the concept of a public service in transport by rail, road and inland waterway [1991] OJ L169/1; now repealed by the European Parliament and Council Regulation 1370/2007/EC on public passenger transport services by rail and by road [2007] OJ L315/1.

[27] Case T-289/03 *British United Provident Association Ltd (BUPA), BUPA Insurance Ltd and BUPA Ireland Ltd v Commission of the European Communities* [2008] ECR II-81, para 162.

[28] For the most important recent official initiatives in the field, see the relevant Commission webpage, at <http://ec.europa.eu/services_general_interest/index_en.htm> (last accessed on 5 November 2011). A normative analysis of the topic is offered in the excellent contributions contained in the edited volumes by Krajewski, M., Neergard, U., and van de Gronden, J. (eds), *The Changing Legal Framework for Services of General Interest* (The Hague: TMC Asser Press, 2009); van de Gronden, J.

This varied terminology is symptomatic of the lack of clear concepts in the definition of economic and non-economic services. It can also be explained by the existence of divergent ideological agendas. In the early 1990s, in the wild 'deregulation' years, a neat opposition had been marked between, on the one hand, aggressive neo-liberalists (typically of Anglo-Saxon origin), pushing for a complete collapse of the existing boundaries between economic and non-economic activities, and, on the other hand, conservative statists (typically of Continental origin) preaching the virtues of the (then) existing paradigm. The latter's attachment to the *service public* and related terminology has led the former to invent their own terminology to avoid the words '*service public*'. Therefore, different terms often reflect identical ideas, simply marking the divergent ideological approaches of their users, rather than objective differences between the realities described.[29] This, of course, does not make it any easier to comprehend the various terms used.

b. ... to workable three-prong distinctions

The dust from the above battle of ideologies has now settled and both sides have the assurance of not being fully evicted from the scene. Traditional *service public* is being reviewed all over Europe, including in its motherland, France.[30] At the same time, however, the very value of *service public* is now enshrined in the EU Treaties and protected by its institutions, notably by the Court. Further, the recent financial crisis, and the role the states needed to play, has shown beyond any doubt that markets alone may not deliver.

A further difficulty is connected to the fact that the very same term may be used to express different content. In particular, in the successive Commission documents, a steady reinforcement of the economic side of the balance, at the expense of the non-economic, is readily observed.[31] Indeed, for the purposes of EU law, the distinction between economic and non-economic activities appears to

---

(ed), *EU and WTO Law on Services: Limits to the Realization of General Interest Policies within the Services Markets?* (Alphen aan den Rijn: Kluwer Law International, 2009); Neergaard, U., Nielsen, R., and Roseberry, L. (eds), *Integrating Welfare Functions into EU Law: From Rome to Lisbon* (Copenhagen: DJØF Publishing, 2009); Potvin-Solis, L. (ed), *La libéralisation des services d'intérêt économique général en réseau en Europe* (Bruxelles: Bruylant, 2010); Louis, J.V., and Rodriguez, S. (eds), *Les services d'intérêt économique général et l'UE* (Bruxelles: Bruylant, 2006); Bauby, P., Coing, H., and de Toledo, A. (eds), *Les services publics en Europe: pour une régulation démocratique* (Paris: Publisud, 2007); see also Cox, H., Fournier J., and Girardot, M. (eds), *Les services d'intérêt économique général en Europe: régulation, financement, evaluation, bonnes pratiques* (Paris: CEEP/CIRIEC, 2000); and more recently, Eckert, G., 'La distinction entre les services d'intérêt général économique et les services d'intérêt général non-économiques' in Potvin-Solis, L. (ed), *La libéralisation des services d'intérêt économique général en réseau en Europe* (Bruxelles: Bruylant, 2010) 3–21.

[29] This need to move beyond already established national paradigms (and terms) also explains the Commission's choice not to use the term '*service public*' in any operational way; see COM (2007) 725, n 21.

[30] See, among many, Dreyfus, M., 'France' in Krajewski, M., Neergard, U., and van de Gronden, J. (eds), *The Changing Legal Framework for Services of General Interest* (The Hague: TMC Asser Press, 2009) 269–90.

[31] For a clear description of this tendency, see the discussion in subsection A(2)iii.

be an oversimplification. Rather, the qualification of the various activities operates at three levels.

First, SGI is a catch-all term which stands for all services which may, under certain conditions, trigger special attention from member states, and thus demand special arrangements under EU law. SGIs are divided into SGEIs on the one hand, and 'non-economic services of general interest' (NESGIs), on the other.[32] The latter are not caught by the core Treaty rules, but it would seem that the very distinction between the two categories is subject to EU scrutiny for its proportionality.[33] As the Commission itself acknowledges,[34] there are some certainties at the extremities of each of the two categories, but haze persists in the middle. Purely public services connected to the exercise of official authority clearly qualify as NESGIs. At the other extreme, network-based services, such as telecommunications and electricity definitely fall into the category of SGEIs. Between the two, the Commission has identified an intermediate category of 'social service of general interest' (SSGI); it is not mentioned whether SSGIs qualify as economic or non-economic, but they form a category of their own, lying somewhere in the middle. As such, they have become the object of autonomous study by the Commission.[35]

Secondly, SGEIs are the ones for which member states may claim special treatment under Article 106(2), the *Altmark* case law, and the accompanying texts of secondary or soft law.[36] Not all SGEIs, however, necessarily relate to the social and other welfare of member states.

Thirdly, SGEIs may contain two groups of services: a core of services strictly connected to the social and welfare choices of a state and an outer circle of services which, without directly serving any specific welfare function, are nonetheless necessary in order to raise the funds necessary for financing the core SGEIs.[37] Hence, for instance, the need to provide postal services to the entire national territory (*core SGEI*) justifies the reservation of some economically profitable services in favour of the SGEI provider (*fundraising SGEI*).[38] See Figure 2.1.

---

[32] The name and the legal category of NESGIs have been formally introduced in the EU legal order by the Lisbon Treaty and its Protocol No. 26.

[33] Further on the issue of competence, see under subheading A(3).

[34] Communication COM (2007) 725, see n 21.

[35] For the last evaluation, see Commission Staff Working Paper SEC (2010) 1284 final.

[36] For which see under B(6).

[37] For the various ways of funding SGEIs see, among many, Szyszczak, E., 'Financing Services of General Economic Interest' (2004) 67 *Modern L Rev* 982–92; and more recently Lichère, F., 'Le financement des charges de services d'intérêt économique général' in Potvin-Solis, L. (ed) *La libéralisation des services d'intérêt économique général en réseau en Europe* (Bruxelles: Bruylant, 2010) 60–74.

[38] Some authors have been tempted to use the term 'universal service' in order to designate the 'core SGEIs' (eg Sauter, W., 'Services of General Economic Interest and Universal Service in EU law' (2008) 33 *EL Rev* 176–93). Such association will be resisted here, because 'universal service' is a concept developed by the Commission and, more generally the EU legislature, in the framework of the liberalization of network-based industries; however, it is not widely used outside these industries and has anyway been largely ignored by the Court. Although 'universal service' represents the Commission's attempt to dub the '*service public* word' and basically bears the same characteristics (of universality, accessibility, quality, reasonable price, etc) with core SGEIs, by its very name, it inevitably puts the stress on universality.

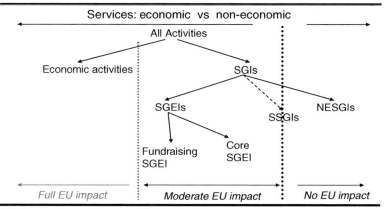

SGI: Service of general interest, SGEI: Service of general economic interest, SSGI:
Social services of general interest, NESGI: Non-economic service of general interest

Figure 2.1. Services: Economic v. non-economic

From the categorizations above, it is clear that there is an important discrepancy between, on the one hand, a restrictive definition of non-economic activities and, on the other hand, an important body of activities which are deemed to be economic but are connected (directly or indirectly) to social or welfare objectives. Therefore, a clear-cut dichotomy according to which economic activities automatically entail the application of EU rules and, conversely, non-economic activities evade EU law altogether can only be sustained subject to further qualification. Indeed, in Figure 2.1, three areas, rather than two, can be identified. At one extreme is the area of mainstream economic services, fully subject to the internal market and competition rules. At the other extreme are NESGIs, on which EU law should have no direct impact. The fact that EU law should leave unscathed member states' powers to provide NESGIs has been constitutionalized in the form of Article 2 of Protocol No. 26 of the Lisbon Treaty. The most controversial category, however, lies in the middle; it concerns services which can in principle be marketed, but are nevertheless subject to some special or else derogatory regime under EU law, be it under Article 106(2) TFEU, under the *Altmark* case law, or under some overriding reason of public interest (ORPI).[39] The fact that such services should benefit from a special regime finds its general expression (since the Treaty of Amsterdam) in Article 14 TFEU and a more specific (and long-standing) expression in Article 106(2) TFEU.

Operating along these lines, the divide between economic and non-economic activities under EU law loses its dramatic and ideological dimension and becomes

---

[39] For the various possibilities, see the analysis under heading B.

more of a gradated and technocratic issue. By the same token, economic categories are complemented by more flexible, legal ones. In other words, the tension between the two extremes (economic and non-economic services) is in some way 'absorbed', by the third 'middle' category of services, which are economic but nonetheless subject to a 'managed' version of the Treaty rules. While the political debate strives to define the outer limits of the two extreme categories, the everyday application of the Treaty (by the Commission and Court) focuses more on defining the scope of SGEIs and the rules applicable to them.

2. Content of SGIs/SGEIs

If SGEIs serve to soften the dividing lines between economic and non-economic activities, the limits and content of SGEIs themselves remain hotly debated and highly contested issues. In this respect, the Treaty is (understandably) silent (with the exception of Article 345 TFEU, declaring the EU's agnosticism concerning the property regime of assets). The General Court, as recently as early 2008, has acknowledged that:[40]

'[i]t must be made clear that in Community law . . . there is no clear and precise regulatory definition of the concept of an SGEI mission and no established legal concept definitively fixing the conditions that must be satisfied before a Member State can properly invoke the existence and protection of an SGEI mission'.

In order to establish the borders between the three categories identified above, attention has to be paid to the sources of SGI rules within the EU legal order (a), the approaches pursued by the institutions and the stakeholders in this respect (b), and the main qualities/characteristics that SGI should fulfil in order to qualify for special treatment under EU law (c).

a. Sources of SGI rules

i. The Treaty
Since the entry into force of the Treaty of Lisbon in December 2009, three kinds of provisions have been added into primary law, in addition to Article 106 TFEU.[41]

Article 14 TFEU
Article 14 TFEU exclusively concerns SGEIs. It consists of two paragraphs. In the first, it is recognized that SGEIs form part of the shared values of the Union and that they should operate in 'conditions, particularly economic and financial

---

[40] Case T-289/03 *BUPA* [2008] ECR II-81, para 165.

[41] For an early assessment of the new rules, see Sauter, W., 2008, n 38; Neergaard, U., 'Services of general (economic) interest: what aims and values count?' in Neergaard, U., Nielsen, R., and Roseberry, L. (eds), *Integrating Welfare Functions into EU Law* (Copenhagen: DJØF Publishing, 2009) 191–224; Wernicke, S., 'Taking stock: the EU institutions and services of general economic interest' in Krajewski, M., Neergard, U., and van de Gronden, J. (eds), *The Changing Legal Framework for Services of General Interest* (The Hague: TMC Asser Press, 2009) 69–79.

conditions, which enable them to fulfil their mission'; these conditions, however, should be 'without prejudice' to the Treaty rules on public undertakings (106 TFEU) and state aids (93 and 107 TFEU). Further, it is stated that establishing such conditions is the responsibility of both 'the Union and the Member States, each within their respective powers'. It is also made clear that the above holds true only 'within the scope of application of the Treaties'—thus implying that there are aspects which evade the Treaty altogether. In the second paragraph, the EU legislature is given a legal basis to regulate SGEI provision, 'without prejudice to the competence of Member States'.

Although the two paragraphs seem, at first glance, somehow antagonistic, in reality they are quite coherent in that they convey a strong message as to the shape of things to come. If member states' views still prevail today in the way that SGEIs are defined and organized, such autonomy is subject to a double constraint: member states are not only obliged to act in accordance with the general Treaty rules, but they are also 'encouraged' to take into account the way SGEIs are organized by their peers. If self-disciplined (*decentred*) coordination fails, however, Article 14(2) TFEU acts like a regulatory default, allowing for *centralized* coordination.

Article 36 of the EU Charter of Fundamental Rights
Article 36 of the Charter of Fundamental Rights basically reproduces the content of Article 14(1) TFEU. The former's added value, more symbolic than practical, is restricted to recognizing that respect for SGEIs is not merely an operational principle of the EU, but a fundamental right. The two provisions together may argue in favour of a 'horizontal' or 'streamlined' application of the relevant rules, covering all provisions of the Treaty. It is worth noting, however, that within the Charter social security, social assistance, and healthcare are protected in Articles 34 and 35, respectively. The existence of separate charter provisions for social and healthcare services, gives a clear indication that the Charter's drafters did not consider those to be economic and, hence, to qualify as SGEIs under Article 36.

Protocol No. 26 'On Services of General Interest'
Protocol No. 26 'On Services of General Interest' also brings some added value, since it is the first text of primary law recognizing SGIs as a legal category. The precise scope of the Protocol, however, is difficult to ascertain since the combined reading of its two Articles is somewhat puzzling. Article 1 refers to SGIs and underlines the basic conditions that both member states and the Union should strive to secure (the role of the local level, diversity, quality, safety, etc); Article 2 refers to NESGIs and creates for them a safe haven from EU law. It is unclear whether the two paragraphs should be read in contrast, as being mutually exclusive (the first only covering SGEIs and the second only NESGIs), or whether the second paragraph covers a sub-category (NESGIs) of the general category (SGIs). Some authors argue in favour of the first option.[42] Others find that the Protocol

---

[42] Wernicke, S., 2009, n 41, at 71.

'illustrates an inability on the part of the Member States to conceptualise within the EU legal framework what is they want from SGEI'.[43] The view supported here, already implied when dealing with terminology issues,[44] is that Article 1 refers to *all* SGIs, economic and non-economic alike, while the second specifically addresses the latter category (NESGIs). This reading is corroborated by the drafting of the provisions at stake: Article 1 is of a general, declaratory nature, while Article 2 sets out a clear competence reservation. At any rate, it is implausible that member states would exercise the competence reserved to them under Article 2 of the Protocol and organize NESGIs in a way which does not respect the principles set out in Article 1; therefore, the principles enunciated in Article 1 also apply for Article 2 services and the latter are a sub-category of the former. In any event, if Protocol No. 26 is to add anything to the EU legal order, this will not be by way of clarifying the various concepts at stake, but rather by describing the characteristics of SGIs.

ii. Secondary law
In secondary law, there are two main categories of texts dealing with SGIs, in fact exclusively with SGEIs (as there would be no legal basis in the Treaty to regulate NESGIs): sector-specific and horizontal; the former predate the latter.

Sector-specific texts
Sector-specific texts dealing with SGIs may be further subdivided into two categories.

The first, and for many years the only, text of EU secondary legislation to deal with 'public service' was Regulation 1191/69, in the area of transport.[45] Transport has been a common policy since the founding Treaties in 1957. This explains why the issue of securing public service was first raised in this context. This Regulation, recently repealed and replaced by Regulation 1370/2007, may be viewed as a category of its own. Not only does it predate, by more than two decades, any other EU attempt to regulate SGIs, but it is also the only text of EU legislation to use the term 'public service'. Both the definitions used and the rules introduced are less sophisticated overall (or more naïve?) than subsequent legislation: public service obligations are defined as 'obligations which the transport undertaking in question, if it were considering its own commercial interests, would not assume or would not assume to the same extent or under the same conditions', and their basic characteristics are 'the obligation to operate, the obligation to carry, and tariff obligations'.[46] From a more substantive point of view, the Regulation concerns a market globally more 'contestable' than fixed network markets (such as telecommunications, gas, or electricity) and describes the conditions under which states may award public service contracts to transport undertakings, while adequately compensating them

---

[43] Sauter, W., 2008, n 41, at 173; the same criticism is also adopted in Neergaard, U., 2009, n 41, at 205.
[44] See the discussion under subheading A(1)a.
[45] Regulation 1191/69 [1969] OJ English Special Edition I, p. 276, as amended by Regulation 1893/91[1991] OJ L169/1; now repealed by Regulation 1370/2007 [2007] OJ L315/1.
[46] Regulation 1370/2007, n 26, Arts 2(1) and 2(2), respectively.

for public service obligations. These requirements have been detailed further in Regulation 2007/1370, rendered necessary after the Court's judgment in *Altmark*.[47]

The second category of texts of secondary legislation dealing with SGI (even though it is called 'universal service' in this framework) consists of all the sector-specific Directives on the re-regulation of the network industries: electronic communications, energy, postal services. Despite referring to 'universal service' in an all-encompassing way, two different regulatory techniques are used for securing it.

The first one, used in the energy sector, follows the same pattern as Regulation 1191/69 (on transport), based on the principle of subsidiarity. In their successive forms, Directives regulating respectively electricity and gas supply,[48] both contain an Article 3 named 'Public Service Obligations and Customer Protection'. This provision entrusts member states with the duty to secure 'in the general economic interest, public service obligations which may relate to security, including security of supply, regularity, quality and price of supplies, and environmental protection, including energy efficiency, energy from renewable sources and climate protection'. Social objectives, such as the protection of vulnerable customers, are also mentioned as part of universal service. Following the principle of subsidiarity and in order to allow for differentiation at the regional level, it is up to the states to define in more detail the precise content of public service obligations. More importantly, it is up to them to undertake long-term planning and to 'implement appropriate measures [which] may include, in particular, the provision of adequate economic incentives, using, where appropriate, all existing national and Community tools'.[49]

This model of securing universal service, based on subsidiarity, may be contrasted with the more centralized model, followed for example in the postal sector. The postal sector Directive 97/67 defines universal service obligations as 'involving the permanent provision of a postal service of specified quality at all points in their territory at affordable prices for all users'.[50] Then, the content of universal service is further set out, in relation to the size and weight of postal items and to the

---

[47] Case C-280/00 *Altmark* [2003] ECR I-7747; for which see under B(3).

[48] See, for electricity, European Parliament and Council Directive 96/92/EC concerning common rules for the internal market in electricity [1997] OJ L27/20; European Parliament and Council Directive 2003/54/EC concerning common rules for the internal market in electricity and repealing Directive 96/92/EC [2003] OJ L176/37; European Parliament and Council Directive 2009/72/EC concerning common rules for the internal market in electricity and repealing Directive 2003/54/EC [2009] OJ L211/55; for gas, European Parliament and Council Directive 98/30/EC concerning common rules for the internal market in natural gas [1998] OJ L204/1; European Parliament and Council Directive 2003/55/EC concerning common rules for the internal market in natural gas and repealing Directive 98/30/EC [2003] OJ L176/57; European Parliament and Council Directive 2009/73/EC concerning common rules for the internal market in natural gas and repealing Directive 2003/55/EC [2009] OJ L211/94.

[49] See eg Directive 2009/72, n 48, Art 3(7).

[50] European Parliament and Council Directive 97/67/EC on common rules for the development of the internal market of Community postal services and the improvement of quality of service [1998] OJ L15/14, Art 3(1). The Directive has been later modified by European Parliament and Council Directive 2002/39/EC amending Directive 97/67/EC with regard to the further opening to competition of Community postal services [2002] OJ L176/21.

periodicity of clearance and delivery thereof.[51] What is more, the Directive foresees that universal service may be financed through the award of exclusive rights and harmonizes the kinds of services which may be the subject of such rights.[52]

The field of electronic communications is the one in which the regulation of universal service is the most complete. An early Commission Communication on this issue[53] has given way to successive Directives. The most recent one, Directive 2002/22, as amended by Directive 2009/136,[54] is dedicated to securing universal service and constitutes the most advanced text of EU law concerning SGI. Not only does it define the main characteristics of universal service in its domain, but it also describes thoroughly the content of each one of them: availability of universal service, full geographical coverage, enquiry services and directories, measures for disabled end users, affordability, quality, etc. Moreover, the Directive contains detailed rules for calculating the cost of universal service. Last but not least, it foresees two ways for meeting such cost, either by spreading it over all market participants, or by setting up some compensation mechanism overseen by the national regulatory authorities (NRAs).

This brief overview of the regulatory means adopted in order to secure universal service in the network-based industries shows that solutions vary considerably, at least in three respects. First and foremost, there is the competence issue, of whether it is for the member states or the Union to define the precise conditions of universal service. Next goes the question of how universal service is financed: in transport, state funding may be used, subject to transparency obligations; in energy, EU funding could also be made available; in the field of postal services, it is through the maintenance of limited exclusivity that universal service is to be funded; in electronic communications, it is through mutual compensation or through the creation of a fund. Thirdly, it should be noted that not only the actual definition but also the main characteristics of universal service may be altered from one sector to another.

Despite such variations, however, sector-specific legislation on universal service bears a common consequence: pre-emption. To the extent that the way to secure universal service is foreseen by EU legislation, member states' freedom to impose restrictions on the relevant activities is limited. Or, to use the terminology here introduced,[55] 'universal service' corresponds to 'core SGEI'; if the way to fund such

---

[51] Directive 97/67, n 50, Art 3(3)–(7).

[52] Ibid, Art 7; it is the reduction of weight of reserved postal items which has led to the amendment of this Directive, by Directive 2002/39 (n 50).

[53] Communication COM (1993) 159 final, 'on the consultation on the review of the situation in the Telecommunications services sector'.

[54] European Parliament and Council Directive 2002/22/EC on universal service and users' rights relating to electronic communications networks and services (Universal Service Directive) [2002] OJ L108/51 and European Parliament and Council Directive 2009/136/EC amending Directive 2002/22/EC on universal service and users' rights relating to electronic communications networks and services, Directive 2002/58/EC concerning the processing of personal data and the protection of privacy in the electronic communications sector and Regulation (EC) No 2006/2004 on cooperation between national authorities responsible for the enforcement of consumer protection laws [2009] OJ L337/11, respectively.

[55] See the discussion under subheading A(1)b.

a core SGEI is foreseen by some sector-specific EU text, member states may no longer institute any exclusive or special rights in the area.

The Services Directive

The Services Directive[56] applies to SGEIs in a horizontal but restricted manner. NESGIs are completely excluded from the Directive's scope, according to Article 2 (2)(a) (an unnecessary provision added during political negotiations on the Directive, since the EU would in any case lack competence to regulate NESGIs). At the same time, the added value of the Directive in relation to SGEIs remains unclear. Some of them, such as telecommunications, transport, and healthcare are excluded altogether from the Directive's scope (Article 2(2)).[57] But even the SGEIs which do come within the Directive's scope are still excluded from the free provision of services principle, which is provided for in Article 16; this is spelt out in Article 17(1). Therefore, the only way in which the Directive may affect the provision of SGEIs is through enhanced administrative cooperation and procedural simplification.[58] The Directive's limited impact on SGEIs largely corresponds to the Court's pre-existing case law, but follows the opposite underlying logic. Whilst the Court generally respects the member states' choices on financing SGEIs, subjecting them to a (loose) proportionality control, Article 17(1) of the Directive excludes such services in a blanket way from the principle of 'free provision of services'; thus not allowing for proportionality control to be carried out. It remains to be seen how the Directive will be interpreted in the light of the Treaty provisions.[59]

iii. Soft law

Ever since the 1996 Communication on SGEIs, the Commission has put considerable effort in defining the concept of SGIs and on drawing the line between economic and non-economic activities.[60] This first Communication was updated in 2001 in order to account for the entry into force of the Amsterdam Treaty (in 1999) and of (what has now become) Article 14 TFEU. This Communication has been furthered by the Commission Report to the Laeken European Council, in particular in respect of its implications for the application of Treaty rules.[61] In 2002, the Commission issued a Communication on the horizontal evaluation of SGEIs; this Communication was of a more methodological nature and concerned

---

[56] European Parliament and Council Directive 2006/123/EC on services in the internal market [2006] OJ L376/36 (Services Directive).

[57] Note that also the Services Directive considers healthcare not to be a NESGI, and therefore, specifically excludes it from its scope.

[58] On these aspects of the SD see ch 6.

[59] On the first such occasion, in a case involving construction services and thus completely unrelated to SGEIs, the Court seemed to be paying lip-service to the Services Directive (n 56) and preferred to reason directly by reference to Treaty provisions, see Case C-458/08 *Commission v Portugal (construction services)* [2010] nyr.

[60] Communication COM (1996) 443 final, 'Services of General Interest in Europe' [1996] OJ C281/3.

[61] Communication from the Commission, 'Services of General Interest in Europe' [2001] OJ C17/4; COM (2001) 597 final, 'Report to the Laeken European Council—Services of General Interest'.

only network-based services, which clearly qualify as SGEIs. Therefore, it offered little by way of definitions.[62] The same year, a Report on the application of the state aid rules on SGEIs was issued, but pending the proceedings in *Altmark*, the Commission itself acknowledged that it could not offer definitive views.[63] In 2003, it launched a big consultation on the basis of a Green Paper.[64] A White Paper followed in May 2004.[65] More than a year later, the Commission, taking stock of the Court's judgment in *Altmark*, issued the Monti/Kroes package 'for state aid in the form of public service compensation'. This consists of three documents, one Directive modifying the Transparency Directive,[66] one Decision granting block exemptions for specific kinds of aids and undertakings,[67] and one 'Framework', stating the Commission's approach for all cases not covered by the block exemption.[68] Thereafter, in 2006, in order to appease the anxiety connected to the adoption of the Services Directive (and to set out in the form of soft law provisions that were severed from it), the Commission published a Communication dedicated to 'Social Services of General Interest'.[69] Next came the 2007 Communication 'Services of General Interest, Including Social Services of General Interest', supported by three staff documents, one on the progress made since the 2004 White Paper, one containing frequently asked questions (FAQs) on state aid, and a final one containing FAQs on public procurement in the area of SGEIs.[70] These have been updated after the entry into force of the Lisbon Treaty to become a more comprehensive Guide.[71] Further, some elements on the distinction between SGEIs

[62] Communication COM (2002) 331 final, 'A Methodological Note for the Horizontal Evaluation of Services of General Economic Interest'; this has been further elaborated by the Commission Staff Working Document SEC (2004) 866, 'Horizontal Evaluation of the Performance of Network Industries Providing Services of General Economic Interest'.

[63] COM (2002) 636 final, 'Report from the Commission on the State of Play in the Work on the Guidelines for State Aid and Services of General Economic Interest (SGEIs)'.

[64] Green Paper COM (2003) 270 final, 'on Services of General Interest'. See also the Report on the ensuing consultation (SEC (2004) 326).

[65] White Paper COM (2004) 374 final, 'Services of general interest'.

[66] Commission Directive 2005/81/EC amending Directive 80/723/EEC on the transparency of financial relations between Member States and public undertakings as well as on financial transparency within certain undertakings [2005] OJ L312/47. Previously, see Commission Directive 80/723/EEC of the Commission on the transparency of financial relations between Member States and public undertakings [1980] OJ L195/35.

[67] Commission Decision 2005/842/EC on the application of Article 86(2) of the EC Treaty to State aid in the form of public service compensation granted to certain undertakings entrusted with the operation of services of general economic interest [2005] OJ L312/67.

[68] Community framework for State aid in the form of public service compensation [2005] OJ C297/4.

[69] COM (2006) 177 final.

[70] Communication COM (2007) 725, 'Services of General Interest, Including Social Services of General Interest: A New European Commitment'.

[71] Guide on the application to SGEI, and in particular SSGI, of the European rules on state aid, public procurement, and the internal market, pre-published on the website for the 3rd Forum on SSGI organized by the Belgian Presidency. The document is only available in French, <http://www.socialsecurity.fgov.be/eu/docs/agenda/26-27_10_10_guide_commission.pdf> (last accessed on 5 November 2011).

and NESGIs can be found in the Handbook on the implementation of the Services Directive.[72]

These and other more technical documents by the Commission, as well as the opinions issued by the European Parliament, the Economic and Social Committee (ECOSOC), and the Committee of the Regions (CoR), make for a lengthy (and often passionate) debate about the boundaries of the market and the role of the state;[73] to which lawyers and political scientists have added a thick layer of literature.[74]

The evolution of the Commission's thinking on the distinction between economic and non-economic activities cannot be traced here in detail. It has been presented in a brilliant manner by D. Damjanovic and B. de Witte.[75] These authors explain how, progressively, under the impact of Commission's initiatives, the Court's case law, and the legislature's work, the boundaries of application of EU law have been greatly displaced. They distinguish five categories of services, in decreasing order of state involvement: a. exercise of public authority (eg army, police, justice), b. core social services (eg social assistance, social security), c. core welfare services (eg healthcare, education), d. services provided by public utilities (electricity, gas, water), and e. fully competitive services (all the rest). They contend that under the initial Treaty of Rome constellation, only category (e) was fully subject to the Treaty rules, with (d) benefiting from Article 106(2) TFEU; the rest constituted national prerogatives. In the current context, however, services of type (e) are subject to the general Treaty rules, while (d) are fully regulated by secondary legislation; group (c) becomes increasingly subject to the internal market and the competition rules, within the boundaries of Article 106(2) TFEU, while (b) comes to be increasingly affected by Treaty rules, at least the ones concerning free movement of people and citizenship; only (a) remains sheltered from the application of EU law.

This picture is confirmed by the indicative definitions given by the Commission in its 2007 Communication. On the non-economic end, the Commission cites core public services (in the economic sense) 'such as police, justice and statutory social security schemes', while on the economic end, it refers to (the non-contested category of) network-based services, such as electricity and gas distribution, postal

---

[72] Handbook on the implementation of the Services Directive, available at <http://ec.europa.eu/internal_market/services/docs/services-dir/guides/handbook_en.pdf> (last accessed on 5 November 2011).

[73] The Commission has dedicated a webpage on this topic where all relevant documents are posted; see <http://ec.europa.eu/services_general_interest/index_en.htm> (last accessed on 5 November 2011); the fact, however, that this page was last updated in February 2008 may be of some significance.

[74] See the works cited in n 28.

[75] Damjanovic, D., and de Witte, B., 'Welfare values and welfare integration under the Lisbon Treaty' in Neergaard, U., Roseberry, L., and Nielsen, R. (eds), *Integrating Welfare Functions into EU law: From Rome to Lisbon* (Copenhagen: DJØF Publishing, 2009) 53–94; it is true that the authors do not reason exclusively on the basis of the Commission's activity, but i. a big part of their analysis does concern this institution, and ii. in its Communications, the Commission is supposed to be describing the state of the law as it results from the practice of all the institutions—therefore, the chapter is fully relevant in order to understand and assess the content of the Commission-originated soft law.

services, and the like.[76] The Commission, further, states that the distinction between the two 'cannot be given a priori and requires a case by case analysis', since 'the reality of these services is often specific and differs widely from one Member State to another, and indeed from one local authority to another'.[77] The Commission does contend, however, that 'in practice, apart from activities in relation to the exercise of public authority, to which internal market rules do not apply by virtue of Article 45 of the EC Treaty, it follows that the vast majority of services can be considered as "economic activities" within the meaning of EC Treaty rules on the internal market'.[78]

More interestingly, in the Services Directive Handbook, the Commission states that

'whether a service which a Member State considers to be of general interest is of an economic or a non-economic nature has to be determined in the light of the case law of the ECJ . . . In any case, it will not be possible for Member States to consider all services in a specific field, for example all education services, as non-economic services of general interest.'[79]

Two conclusions follow from this. *First*, that the distinction between economic and non-economic activity is ultimately an EU issue, controlled by the CJEU—albeit only for manifest error.[80] *Secondly*, and most importantly, it may be observed that contrary to states, which put into place (educational, healthcare, etc) *systems*, EU reasoning is made on the basis of specific *services* cherry-picked among other similar (but more marketable) services, from within the *systems* set by the states. It is submitted that this opposition between the member states reasoning in terms of *systems* and the EU reasoning in terms of *services* is quintessential for understanding the tensions accruing between the two legal orders in relation to the provision of SGEIs.

iv. Case law

More than through soft law, the concept and the regime applicable to SGIs have been developed by the Court's case law. The Court, however, approaches the distinction in a very technical manner, in order to provide specific answers to the questions put to it, and tends to sidestep the deeper, ideological questions. The importance and the high degree of technicality of the Court's case law call for a separate examination of the matter.[81] For reasons of completeness, however, the

---

[76] COM (2007) 725, n 70, at 4.

[77] Ibid, at 5.

[78] Ibid; it is not clear whether the same finding applies in respect to the application of competition rules.

[79] Handbook, n 72, at 11.

[80] See the analysis in subsection A(3)a; see also the Guide, n 71, question No. 2.7, where the Commission cites as example of manifest error the case of port cargo services (Case C-179/90 *Merci convenzionali porto di Genova* [1991] ECR I-5886).

[81] See the developments under heading B; for a brief overview see Dap, S., 'La prise en compte jurisprudentielle de la position particulière des opérateurs de SIEG sur le marché européen' in Potvin-Solis, L. (ed) *La libéralisation des services d'intérêt économique général en réseau en Europe* (Bruxelles: Bruylant, 2010) 75–99.

Court's case law has also been mentioned at this point, as it is probably the single most important source of definitions and rules on SGIs.

b. Approaches to the definitions of SGIs

The role of SGIs in the EU has been extensively discussed both at the political and the doctrinal level, especially since the introduction, by the Treaty of Amsterdam, of (what is now) Article 14 TFEU and the first Commission Communication on the matter.[82] A very important debate about the content and categories of SGIs took place on the occasion of the Commission's White and Green Papers of 2003 and 2004, respectively.[83] Four contextual elements need be emphasized in order to grasp the positions expressed. *First*, consultation took place at a time when sector-specific legislation (in the areas of telecommunications, energy, railway transport, etc) was being revised in order to reinforce universal service obligations. *Secondly*, it was launched only a couple of years after the Court openly acknowledged the possibility of applying the Treaty rules on healthcare and social security and the stakeholders were still in shock. *Thirdly*, this consultation ran parallel, to some extent, with the Convention's work on the draft Constitution which was expected to constitutionalize SGIs. *Fourthly*, the first draft of the Services Directive was in gestation.

The European Parliament, in its Resolution on the 2003 Green Paper,[84] put forward a quite expansive vision of NESGIs, including education, public health-care, social housing, social security, as well as services related to pluralism of information and cultural diversity. Next to this broad category, considered as non-economic, the Parliament suggested that remaining activities be qualified as economic or non-economic on the basis of a set of criteria: the (commercial or non-commercial) objective of the service, the level of public funding and of private investment, profit-making or (at least) cost-covering objective, the existence of objective reasons why it would be preferable to organize the service locally rather than through an award procedure at the EU level, the obligation to secure social rights, and the role for social cohesion. An even longer list of criteria has been put forward by representatives of the non-market organizations;[85] the latter, however, stopped short from excluding from the Treaty scope entire activity sectors.

The criteria put forward both by the European Parliament and the non-market organizations share two characteristics. *First*, they are essentially functional in the sense that they adduce the *nature* of the activity from the *conditions* in which it is exercised. *Secondly*, they are backward- instead of forward-looking, since they tend

---

[82] Communication COM (1996) 443 final, 'Services of General Interest in Europe' [1996] OJ C281/3.

[83] Green Paper COM (2003) 270 final, 'on Services of General Interest', and White Paper COM (2004) 374 final, 'Services of General Interest'.

[84] Adopted on 14 January 2003, 2003/2152(INI), rapporteur P. Herzog; see point 22.

[85] For these see Dony, M., 'Les notions de "service d'intérêt general" et "service d'intérêt écono-mique general"' in Louis, J.V., and Rodriguez, S. (eds), *Les services d'intérêt économique général et l'UE* (Bruxelles: Bruylant, 2006) 4–38, at 33.

to define the *future* regime of services on the basis of *past* experience. In both ways, such criteria serve more as a means to conserve the status quo, rather than as genuine tools for the regulation of services in the future.

In a more pragmatic manner, the Committee of Regions (CoR) has proposed to establish a list, on the basis of the Court's case law, containing all activities which are typically of a non-economic nature.[86] Such a list would not be easy to establish, as the Court tends to reason on a case by case basis and not on the basis of grand principles. Moreover, the degree of legal certainty offered by such a list would be limited. *First*, there are as many ways to organize the provision of 'sensitive' activities as there are member states; and the Court's case law suggests that 'the devil is in the detail'.[87] *Secondly*, such a list would offer legal certainty only for activities which have given rise to some judicial pronouncement, and no others.

All three approaches discussed above (European Parliament, non-market organizations, CoR) reveal the anxiety of their respective authors to take the ball away from the Court and to contain the Commission's activism (even if it is expressed by means of soft law).

The same concern animates, to a large extent, the proposal for a framework Directive on SGEIs, as such an instrument would repatriate responsibility from the Commission back to the member states (in the Council). This may also explain the Commission's unwillingness to lend its support to the initiative, despite the fact that a proposal to that effect, submitted by the Socialist Group of the European Parliament with the support of the Green and the Communist MEPs,[88] has been favourably received by many commentators.[89] It has to be noted, however, that if some political groups have increased the pressure for the adoption of a framework Directive, the European Parliament as a body has lessened its pressure in this respect:[90] from an early call on the Commission 'to define the scope and nature of services of general interest, together with the principles underlying them, and to specify more closely both the level of services necessary for accomplishing EU

---

[86] Committee of Regions Opinion on the 'Green Paper on Services of General Interest' [2004] OJ C73/8.

[87] See the developments under heading B.

[88] The draft proposal is available at <http://www.socialistsanddemocrats.eu/gpes/media3/documents/1927_PL_text_project_directive_en_revised_060530.pdf> (last accessed on 5 November 2011).

[89] See eg Rodrigues, S., 'Towards a general EC framework instrument related to SGEI? Political considerations and legal constraints' in Krajewski, M., Neergard, U., and van de Gronden, J. (eds), *The Changing Legal Framework for Services of General Interest* (The Hague: TMC Asser Press, 2009) 255–66; see also earlier, Rodriguez, S., 'Les services d'intérêt économique général et l'UE: Acquis et perspectives' in Louis, J.V., and Rodriguez, S., (eds), *Les services d'intérêt économique général et l'UE* (Bruxelles: Bruylant, 2006) 421–39; de Vries, S., 'Harmonisation of Services of General Economic Interest: Where there is a Will There is a Way!' in van de Gronden, J. (ed), *EU and WTO Law on Services: Limits to the Realization of General Interest Policies within the Services Markets?* (Alphen aan den Rijn: Kluwer Law International, 2009) 139–58; van de Gronden, J., 'The Services Directive and Services of General (Economic) Interest' in Krajewski, M., Neergard, U., and van de Gronden, J. (eds), *The Changing Legal Framework for Services of General Interest* (The Hague: TMC Asser Press, 2009) 233–54.

[90] See in more detail on the role of the Parliament, Rodrigues, S., 2009, n 89, at 257–8.

objectives and the regulatory framework needed to ensure success',[91] it then moved to a more moderate request to the Commission 'to define the common principles on which services of general interest are based on an appropriate tier of subsidiarity';[92] subsequently, it has even restricted the (material) ambition of its call 'to create more legal certainty in the area of social and healthcare SGI and to formulate a proposal for a sector-specific directive [. . .] in those fields in which it is appropriate to do so'.[93]

Despite their shortcomings, the positions of the stakeholders described above have not been wholly unsuccessful. For one thing, the restrictive view thus orchestrated has resulted in considerably limiting the scope of the Services Directive and in multiplying the exceptions thereto and exclusions thereof. Further, it has removed any Commission temptation to legislate in this field, on the basis of Article 106(3). The positions, however, may also be seen to have backfired. In view of the clearly expressed unwillingness of the institutional actors to pursue the rationalization of the various concepts and legal categories, the Intergovernmental Conference (IGC) which transformed the failed Constitutional Treaty into the Lisbon Treaty, added paragraph 2 in Article 14 TFEU, thus providing an express legal basis for EU legislative action in the area.

3. EU impact on SGIs

The gradual involvement of the EU in defining the concept of SGIs and in describing the respective scopes of NESGIs and SGEIs, together with the sector-specific rules on network industries were bound, sooner or later, to affect the provision of SGIs by the member states. While the actual provision of SGIs unquestionably remains an issue for the member states, the EU impact manifests itself at two levels: at the competence level (a) and at the content level (b).

a. The competence issue—who has the responsibility to determine the scope of SGIs?

In the introduction to the present chapter, it was explained that the distinction between economic and non-economic activities, a politically and ideologically charged topic, takes on a special constitutional function within the EU context: it serves as a competence moderator. Unavoidably then, the regulation of SGIs is fraught with complex competence issues in need of clarification.

Indeed, member states' (initially unfettered) competence in the field of SGIs is now cross-checked under EU law provisions, in at least four successive steps.

i. The first issue raised is that of drawing the line between services which qualify as purely economic and SGIs, to which member states are allowed to give special

---

[91] Resolution PE 222.618 final [1998] OJ C14, para 5.
[92] Resolution PE 296.3 final [2002] OJ C140 E, para 36.
[93] Document P6_TA(2006)380, para 17, on the report of B. Rapkay (Socialist Group, DE).

status; a further question is the way that SGIs break down to SGEIs and NESGIs. From the analysis above, it stems that these issues are very delicate and the EU lacks both the competence and the legitimacy to second-guess choices made by member states in this respect. However, in practice, the EU does two things. *First*, through the various consultations, documents of soft law, and case-specific judgments delivered by the Court, the EU creates a frame of reference offering some general guidance as to the boundaries of the markets and the role of the state. This broad guidance is further fleshed out in the exchange of techniques and practices that takes place in the framework of the social Open Method of Coordination (OMC).[94] *Secondly*, the EU institutions, and prominently the Court, may *in extremis* control the choices made by member states, to ensure that the *effet utile* of the Treaty rules is not systematically circumvented. Thus, in *BUPA*, the General Court held that:[95]

'[a]s regards competence to determine the nature and scope of an SGEI mission within the meaning of the Treaty, and also the degree of control that the Community institutions must exercise in that context, . . . Member States have a wide discretion to define what they regard as SGEIs and that the definition of such services by a Member State can be questioned . . . only in the event of manifest error'.

ii. Turning to SGEIs, it has already been explained[96] that they may be of two types: either strictly corresponding to the needs in general interest (the 'core SGEIs') or indirectly related to the general interest but serving to finance the former category ('fundraising SGEIs'). Traditionally, member states used to reserve entire activity sectors and cross-subsidize indistinctively. Nowadays, under the impact of EU law, the paradigm has shifted: only those services which are (economically) strictly *necessary* and which are (materially) sufficiently *connected* to 'core SGEIs' may be reserved and remain subject to special or exclusive rights, together with 'core SGEIs'. Both these criteria (necessity and proximity) are controlled by EU law. Both, however, are subject to minimal control by the CJEU; this was very well illustrated in *Glöckner*. The decision of the German authorities to reserve (and award without a tendering procedure) non-urgent patient transport together with emergency ambulance services was held to be necessary in order to avoid cream-skimming; moreover, the two activities were found to be closely connected, without further ado, in view of their characteristics and the way they have been traditionally offered.[97]

---

[94] For the OMC see ch 8; see also, among many, Hatzopoulos, V., 'Why the Open Method of Coordination Is Bad for You: A Letter to the EU' (2007) 13 *ELJ* 259–92, with extremely extensive bibliographical references.

[95] Case T-289/03 *BUPA* [2008] ECR II-81, para 166; see also ibid, para 168, where it is stated that 'the control which the Community institutions are authorised to exercise over the use of the discretion of the Member State in determining SGEIs is limited to ascertaining whether there is a manifest error of assessment'.

[96] In the analysis under subheading A(1)b.

[97] Case C-475/99 *Firma Ambulanz Glöckner v Landkreis Südwestpfalz* [2001] ECR I-8089, paras 61 and 60, respectively. It is worth mentioning that from the Court's description of the facts in *Glöckner*, it results that in Germany non-urgent ambulance services had been traditionally offered separately, before the Court's judgment! The fact that the Court nonetheless allows the 'junction' of non-urgent to urgent services shows that the 'necessity and proximity' test followed is quite relaxed.

iii. Once the scope of SGEI has been defined according to the two steps above, the third issue raised is the extent to which its provision justifies derogations from the Treaty rules, under Article 106 TFEU or otherwise. At this level, national competence is constrained by the EU rules in an increasingly intrusive way. The EU has gradually developed a series of characteristics that an SGEI should fulfil in order to qualify for derogations under the Treaty rules. These characteristics stem originally from the national legal orders, mainly the *service public* tradition, but have eventually been transcribed into EU law. A regulatory trade-off is organized under the auspices of, or at least with the consent of, the EU: as long as member states manage to provide a SGEI within prescriptions (of quality, continuity etc) acceptable to the EU,[98] the latter is ready to tolerate derogations to its own rules.

This regulatory trade-off is expressly and specifically organized in network industries: the Directives foresee, in greater or lesser detail, the 'universal service' obligations which should be complied with by member states; at the same time, they introduce derogations from the mainstream Treaty rules. The same regulatory trade-off is also present in all other SGEIs, but operates within the framework of the proportionality test, under the control of the Court. In *Corbeau, Almelo, Deutsche Post, Glöckner*, and other cases,[99] the Court agreed to set aside the relevant competition rules to the extent that this was necessary for the provision of a service fulfilling several conditions which the Court specifically enumerated: universal coverage, full territorial coverage, good quality, and reasonable tariffs.[100] In *Glöckner*, it further stressed that SGEI should be provided in economic terms which do not 'jeopardise the quality and reliability of that service'.[101] If, however, these characteristics are not fulfilled by the incumbent, the proportionality test will shift and then, there will be no justification for departing from the Treaty rules.

An alternative version of such a regulatory trade-off was proposed in *Altmark*: the first *Altmark* condition requires the state authorities themselves to define the characteristics that SGEI provision should fulfil and to make them known to the public and to the Commission. In this context, the price to pay for avoiding the EU rules on state aids is that the EU be informed of the content of SGEI and that it monitors, within the context of the proportionality principle, the fulfilment of such conditions. Therefore, through the regulatory trade-off described above, the EU constrains the member states as to the minimum quality characteristics that SGEIs should fulfil; this is the only means to justify exceptions to the application of the Treaty rules.

---

[98] For the characteristics which should be met by SGEIs in order to justify derogations from the Treaty rules, see the discussion in subsection A(3)b.

[99] Case C-320/91 *Criminal proceedings against Paul Corbeau* [1993] ECR I-2533, Case C-393/92 *Municipality of Almelo and others v NV Energiebedrijf Ijsselmij* [1994] ECR I-1477, Joined cases C-147 & 148/97 *Deutsche Post AG v Gesellschaft für Zahlungssysteme mbH GZS and Citicorp Kartenservice GmbH* [2000] ECR I-825, and C-455/99 *Glöckner*, n 97.

[100] See Case C-320/91 *Corbeau*, n 99, para 15.

[101] Case C-455/99 *Glöckner*, n 97, para 61 *in fine*.

iv. Finally, there is the issue of financing. EU law impinges on the way SGEIs are financed by mandating transparency (*ex post*) and rationalization (*ex ante*).[102] Transparency can be achieved in two ways. First, different service activities should be subject to separate accounting, so that their precise cost—and any cross-subsidization thereto—may be identified. Depending on the specifics of each case and the set of EU rules applicable, this requirement stems from the Transparency Directive,[103] from the sector-specific liberalization Directives, from the logic of *Corbeau* and subsequent case law, from *Altmark* case law and the related legislative package, or from the need to set and publish tendering documents. Depending on the source of the transparency obligation, the above elements are further subject to adequate publicity and, under circumstances, have to be communicated to the Commission.[104] Transparency wards off preferential or otherwise irrational funding from public authorities. Furthermore, rationalization stems from the *Altmark* package (the second *Altmark* condition: *ex ante* calculation of the cost of SGEIs), as well as from the very logic of public procurement: under both sets of rules, public authorities are required to estimate in advance the cost of the projected services, neither system allows for last-minute top ups. This may lead to rationalization both at the level of public authorities and at the level of the entities entrusted with the actual provision of the SGEI: the former are put under pressure to develop powerful cost-calculating tools (something which has been missing for many years from core sectors of SGEI, such as healthcare provision), while the latter are given incentives to control costs (an objective also served by the fourth *Altmark* condition—no compensation for inefficiencies).[105]

As long as these requirements are complied with, member states enjoy wide discretion to determine the actual amount of funding that they allocate to the entities providing SGEIs. This was implied in *Glöckner*, where the Court accepted that the level of reliability and quality of the service provided is to be determined by each individual member state. In a more explicit manner, the General Court in *BUPA* held that:[106]

'[g]iven the discretion enjoyed by a Member State in defining an SGEI mission and the conditions of its implementation, including the assessment of the additional costs incurred in discharging the mission, which depends on complex economic facts, the scope of the control which the Commission is entitled to exercise in that regard is limited to one of manifest error... Furthermore, it follows that the Court's review of the Commission's assessment in that regard must also observe the same limit'.

It follows that, sector specific rules aside, member states remain the masters of the services they provide to their citizens and that their competence to define, fund, and

---

[102] The requirements are being presented in the chronological order they emerged.
[103] Directive 2006/111/EC [2006] OJ L 318/17, Arts 1(2) and 4.
[104] Such an obligation follows directly from Art 5 of Directive 80/723, as well as from the *Altmark* case law and legislative package (Case C-280/00 *Altmark* [2003] ECR I-7747).
[105] The *Altmark* case law and its implications are extensively discussed under subheading B(3).
[106] Case T-289/03 *BUPA* [2008] ECR II-81, para 220.

provide SGEIs is to a large extent unconstrained by EU law. EU rules are, in principle, applicable but are, in fact, applied in a manner that largely accommodates national choices. Only in extreme situations of manifest error may such choices be controlled by the Commission or the Court. There is thus little that EU law does to affect the definition and the provision of SGEIs at the political level.

At the administrative/managerial level, however, the EU is having an ever-increasing impact on the way SGEIs are organized and funded. This occurs in two ways. *First*, the characteristics of the services provided are being defined at the EU level. In the framework of the regulatory trade-offs described above, the EU, as an offset for waiving the application of its own rules, assumes a monitoring role over the characteristics of the services provided by member states. Moreover, *secondly*, through the technical requirements it imposes for the provision of SGEIs, the EU enforces transparency, rationalization, and accountability of national authorities in respect of the services they keep away from the market.[107]

b. The content issue—what conditions should SGIs fulfil in order to receive special treatment?

i. Description

As explained above, the provision of SGEIs sidesteps the application of EU rules to the extent that such SGEIs comply with some basic requirements which distinguish them from normal, marketable services. A thriving Continental literature on *service public* has offered the EU a solid intellectual background on which to build its own SGEI requirements.[108] The oft-celebrated *lois de Rolland*, according to which public services should always satisfy the principles of continuity, equality of treatment, and adaptability[109] have served as the first reference point for the EU institutions in building the EU concept of SGEI. The process has been piecemeal and was accomplished through the concurrent contribution of various institutions.

After a long gestation period, initiated by the sector-specific Communications and Directives on universal service, nurtured by the occasional judgment of the Court, and crystallized by the various horizontal Commission Communications, it has become possible to identify the main characteristics of SGEI.[110] Protocol No. 26 of the Lisbon Treaty (Article 1, last indent) has transformed these characteristics

---

[107] An explicit manifestation of this trend is offered by the recent judgment of the Court in Case C-271/08 *Commission v Germany (old-age insurance)* [2010] nyr.

[108] For a recent overview of the relevant literature and a critical assessment of the impact EU law has had on *service public* in France see Dreyfus, M., 'France' in Krajewski, M., Neergard, U., and van de Gronden, J. (eds), *The Changing Legal Framework for Services of General Interest* (The Hague: TMC Asser Press, 2009) 269–90.

[109] Rolland, L., *Précis de Droit Administratif* (Paris: Dalloz, 1938) 18; actually Rolland was codifying pre-existing doctrine and practice and his 'laws' have been quintessential for any *service public* for almost a century; only in recent years, under the impact of neo-liberalist economic theories and of EU law, have these 'laws' been questioned.

[110] See eg Dony, M., 'Les notions de "service d'intérêt général" et "service d'intérêt économique général"' in Louis, J.V., and Rodriguez, S. (eds), *Les services d'intérêt économique général et l'UE* (Bruxelles: Bruylant, 2006) 4–38, at 37.

into constitutional norms (albeit of uncertain legal value). This Treaty provision foresees that 'the shared values of the Union in respect of SGEIs [. . .] include in particular [. . .] a high level of quality, safety and affordability, equal treatment and the promotion of universal service and of user rights'. These requirements were further spelled out by the Commission in its 2007 Communication. They reflect, to a large extent, the old *lois de Rolland*, reshuffled, made more precise, and put into the EU context. The 'EU *lois de Rolland*', as explained in the 2007 Communication, are the following:

a. '*High level of quality, safety and affordability*' encompasses 'access to services, including cross-border services; the value for money and financial affordability of services, including special schemes for people on low incomes and with special needs, which is particularly important in the case of social services; physical safety, reliability and continuity; high quality and choice; transparency and access to information from providers and regulators'.[111]

b. '*Equal treatment and universal service*' require 'ensuring equal treatment between women and men and combating all forms of discrimination in accessing services of general economic interest. Where an EU sector-specific rule is based on the concept of universal service, it should establish the right of everyone to access certain services considered as essential and impose obligations on service providers to offer defined services according to specified conditions, including complete territorial coverage and at an affordable price'.[112]

c. Finally, *upholding 'user rights'* calls for 'the existence of independent regulators with appropriate staff and clearly defined powers and duties. These include powers of sanction, in particular the ability to monitor the transposition and enforcement of universal service provisions. These also require provisions for the representation and active participation of consumers and users in the definition and evaluation of services, the availability of appropriate redress and compensation mechanisms, and the existence of a review clause allowing requirements to be adapted over time to reflect new social, technological and economic developments'.[113]

ii. Comment

Several comments may be made in respect of the above characteristics that SGEIs should fulfil.

First, it may be observed that some issues, such as 'affordable price' and 'adaptability' are recurrent and, in different forms, appear in more than one heading above: a clear sign that the appropriation by the EU of the concept of *service public* has not been without intellectual casualties.

Further, *secondly*, the most innovative item in this EU definition of SGEI characteristics comes under the third heading, 'user rights'. Original as this may

---

[111] Communication COM (2007) 724 final, 'A Single Market for 21st Century Europe', at 10.
[112] Ibid, at 10.
[113] Ibid, at 10–11.

seem under the Continental experience, it is much less so under the Anglo-Saxon system of 'common carrier'. The latter system is based more on the citizen-consumer model rather than the citizen-taxpayer. Consumers' interests are not secured through special (administrative) procedures before special (administrative) jurisdictions, but on the basis of 'common law' and general consumer rights. Consumers in the Anglo-Saxon system have the opportunity to express their disapproval as to the poor quality of the service received in the framework of regular monitoring processes rather than in the occasional election ballot. Monitoring is secured by specialized agencies occasionally having regulatory competences.[114] It may be expected, therefore, that next to the sector-specific NRAs foreseen by the individual Directives on electronic communications, energy, etc, horizontal SGEI monitoring bodies will surface within the national legal orders. Or, since the pressure for abolishing sector-specific legislation and the corresponding regulators is already high, in the medium term a horizontal SGEI regulator/monitoring authority could emerge.[115]

Thirdly, the precise content of all the above requirements expressed in Protocol No. 26 of the Lisbon Treaty and in the 2007 Communication on SGEIs still needs to be clarified. What does 'high level of quality' amount to? Or even more controversially, what is a 'high level of affordability'—if affordability can ever have 'levels' . . . ? Even less controversial, or else general, requirements, such as 'universal coverage', are not as straightforward as they may prima facie seem. This is illustrated in the General Court's recent case law.

In *BUPA*, the General Court held the requirement of universal coverage to be satisfied in a situation where only 50 per cent of the population was actually covered.[116] Not only did the Court choose to ignore such quantitative data, but it also made some unprecedented qualitative qualifications. The General Court held that:[117]

'the fact that the SGEI obligations in question have only a limited territorial or material application or that the services concerned are enjoyed by only a relatively limited group of users does not necessarily call in question the universal nature of an SGEI mission within the meaning of Community law'.

The General Court further explained that:[118]

'the compulsory nature of the service in question is an essential condition of the existence of an SGEI mission within the meaning of Community law. That compulsory nature must be

---

[114] For the Anglo-Saxon model and its comparison with the Continental model of *service public*, see Amato, G., 'Citizenship and public services: some general reflections' in Freedland, M. and Sciarra, S. (eds), *Public Services and Citizenship in European Law: Public and Labour Law Perspectives* (Oxford: Clarendon Press, 1998) 145–56; Harlow, C., 'Public service, market ideology and citizenship' in Freedland, M. and Sciarra, S. (eds), *Public Services and Citizenship in European Law: Public and Labour Law Perspectives* (Oxford: Clarendon Press, 1998) 48–56.

[115] For the sector-specific regulation and the corresponding regulators, as well as for the arguments for and against the abolition of such regulation, see the analysis in ch 6.

[116] Case T-289/03 *BUPA* [2008] ECR II-81.

[117] Ibid, para 187.

[118] Ibid, para 188.

understood as meaning that the operators entrusted with the SGEI mission by an act of a public authority are, in principle, required to offer the service in question on the market in compliance with the SGEI obligations which govern the supply of that service'.

The General Court even went as far as to hold that:[119]

'the possibility that an insurer may voluntarily withdraw from the Irish [Private Medical Insurance] PMI market does not affect the continuity of the supply of the PMI service concerned and, accordingly, the universality and accessibility of that service'.

Further, in relation to affordability (examined under the perspective of universality), the Court held that 'the fact that the prices of PMI services are neither regulated nor subject to a ceiling does not affect their universal nature either'.[120]

These findings hardly correspond to either the Commission's views about universality, or the etymology of the word used. However, the fact that quality and accessibility are paramount in the definition of SGEI and that universality follows may also be ascertained by the order in which these different values are enumerated in Article 1 of Protocol No. 26.[121]

Further, while dealing with the universality issue in *BUPA*, the General Court itself expressly disavowed the Commission's soft law instruments by stating that:

'the applicants' restrictive understanding of the universal nature of an SGEI, based on certain Commission reports or documents, the content of which, moreover, is not legally binding, is not compatible with the scope of the discretion which Member States have when defining an SGEI mission'.[122]

Such instances of inter-institutional conflict may only complicate the understanding of already complex concepts, such as SGEI; especially in an area where, as explained above, soft law is extensively used. It has to be noted that the judgment in *BUPA* not only runs counter to the Commission's vision of SGEIs, but also, and more importantly, nearly overturns the CJEU judgment in *Altmark*. *BUPA* is, overall, a contestable judgment which has been appealed against, but the appeal was withdrawn after the Irish Government amended the contested risk equalization scheme. Therefore, the significance attributable to the ruling in *BUPA* is questionable, but its mere pronouncement shows that even after the 'constitutionalization' of the SGEI characteristics in Protocol No. 26, many uncertainties remain.

B. The legal distinction

When it comes to the actual application of the Treaty rules on the various services, the Court needs to reach concrete solutions. On a politically charged topic,

---

[119] Ibid, para 196.

[120] Ibid, para 202.

[121] This explains that the use of the term 'universal service' in order to describe the core SGEIs, as suggested by Sauter, W., 'Services of General Economic Interest and Universal Service in EU Law' (2008) 33 *EL Rev* 176–93 is being resisted here.

[122] Case T-289/03 *BUPA*, n 116, para 187.

however, even the CJEU's judgments can occasionally be highly political, either by the substantive rule they introduce,[123] or by the grand statements they contain.[124] Political judgments serve as legal benchmarks, permitting the Court to resolve the bulk of more technical questions put to it on a regular basis. In most cases, however, the Court tries to reach moderate solutions, while avoiding grand statements of principle. Indeed, a thorough analysis of the Court's case law shows that it has regularly sidestepped qualifying an activity as being economic (or non-economic), by making use of alternative criteria.

The fact that such criteria, however, are often used inconsistently, sporadically, and with different weight in every single case has led several commentators to the conclusion that the qualification of any given activity as economic differs depending on whether the Court approaches it from the internal market or from the competition perspective.[125] Although some (few) valid arguments may indeed be put forward for such a differentiated approach, it has always been the author's view that an apple is an apple, irrespective of whether it is observed wearing green, red or blue lenses. This holds all the more true if at stake is not an apple, but a competence moderator, having constitutional implications for the functioning of the EU.[126]

In order to test this hypothesis, the analysis followed scrutinizes, step by step, the reasoning of the Court both under the internal market and under the competition rules. This exercise shows that only rarely does the Court openly discuss the very nature of the activity, while in most cases it reaches solutions by looking to other, less political, factors. Indeed, the cases brought before the Court are decided on the basis of answers to six basic questions: a. the nature (public/private) of the body at the origin of the measure, b. the nature (economic/non-economic) of the activity, c. the object of the measure (economic regulation/material regulation of an activity, such as sport, etc), d. the existence of mitigating factors to the violation of

---

[123] For the leeway left to member states in order to finance services they deem of general interest, see eg Case C-320/91 *Criminal proceedings against Paul Corbeau* [1993] ECR I-2533, and Case C-475/99 *Firma Ambulanz Glöckner v Landkreis Südwestpfalz* [2001] ECR I-8089.

[124] See eg Case C-438/05 *International Transport Workers' Federation and Finnish Seamen's Union v Viking Line ABP and OÜ Viking Line Eesti* [2007] ECR I-10779, para 79, and Case C-341/05 *Laval un Partneri Ltd v Svenska Byggnadsarbetareförbundet, Svenska Byggnadsarbetareförbundets avdelning 1, Byggettan and Svenska Elektrikerförbundet* [2007] ECR I-11767, para 105, for the statement that the EU does not only have an economic, but also a social objective.

[125] See eg Odudu, O., 'Economic Activity as a Limit to Community Law' in Barnard, C. and Odudu, O. (eds), *The Outer Limits of EU Law* (Oxford/Portland: Hart Publishing, 2009) 225–43; see also Schweitzer, H., 'Competition Law and Public Policy: Reconsidering an Uneasy Relationship: The Example of Article 81' EUI Law Working Paper No. 30/2007, also available at <http://cadmus.eui.eu/dspace/bitstream/1814/7623/3/LAW-2007-30.pdf> (last accessed on 6 November 2011), at 3; see also Case C-205/03P *Federación Española de Empresas de Tecnología Sanitaria (FENIN) v Commission of the European Communities* [2006] ECR I-6295 (AG).

[126] In the same sense, see Idot, L., 'Concurrence et libre circulation: Regards sur les derniers développements' (2005) *Revue des Affaires Européennes* 391–409, at 370; and more recently, Neergaard, U., 'Services of general (economic) interest: what aims and values count?' in Neergaard, U., Nielsen, R., and Roseberry, L. (eds), *Integrating Welfare Functions into EU Law* (Copenhagen: DJØF Publishing, 2009) 191–224.

the EU rules (rule of reason, *de minimis*, etc), e. the applicability of exceptions (expressly provided by the Treaty or judge-made), and f. the applicability of Article 106(2).[127]

Not all of the questions are dealt with in every single case, nor are they always formulated in the above sequence or in comparable terms. Led by judicial economy, the Court gives priority to the question(s) offering the most credible solution, in view of the specifics of each case, with the least judicial effort. There are very few cases, if any, where all the questions are raised by the Court. Taken together, however, the various cases may be systematized, offering a blueprint of the Court's approach, capable of universal application. In order for the argument to be more accurate the general internal market law (free movement rules) is distinguished from the more specific public procurement rules, while the competition rules concerning private conduct (Articles 101 and 102) are distinguished (whenever necessary) from the ones on state aid (Article 107). Moreover, Article 106(2), instituting an express exception in consideration of the nature of the activities concerned, is distinguished from other grounds of exception.

1. Nature of the body subject to the rules

a. Free movement

For the free movement rules to apply, the principle is simple: only public entities, central or decentralized, are subject to them. This, however, has been extended in two directions. *First*, entities created, run or otherwise controlled by the state are assimilated to it, irrespective of their legal nature. Therefore, a development body established by the state,[128] an informal trade council,[129] as well as a private society entrusted with special rights[130] have all been held to be subject to the internal market rules. The concept of state has further been stretched in the case law concerning the direct effect of Directives, to include private undertakings under the direct or indirect control of the state.[131] *Secondly*, entities, even private in nature, which exercise de jure or de facto some regulatory activity must also respect the internal market rules: sports associations or federations,[132] professional

---

[127] Article 106(2) is a Treaty exception and could well be integrated in category (e), but is being kept distinct, since it is the only Treaty provision specifically aimed at 'setting aside' services which require some protection from market forces.

[128] Case 102/86 *Apple and Pear* [1988] ECR 1443.

[129] Case 249/81 *Commission v Ireland (buy Irish)* [1982] ECR 4005.

[130] Joined Cases 266 & 267/97 *R v Royal Pharmaceutical Society of Great Britain, ex p Association of Pharmaceutical Importers and others* [1989] ECR 1295.

[131] Case C-188/89 *A. Foster v British Gas* [1990] ECR I-3313; Case C-271/91 *M. H. Marshall v Southampton and South West Hampshire Health Authority* [1993] ECR I-4367.

[132] Case 36/74 *Walrave and Koch* [1974] ECR 1405; Case 13/76 *Gaetano Donà v Mario Mantero* [1976] ECR 1333; Case C-415/93 *Union royale belge des sociétés de football association ASBL v Jean-Marc Bosman, Royal club liégeois SA v Jean-Marc Bosman and others, and Union des associations européennes de football (UEFA) v Jean-Marc Bosman* [1995] ECR I-4921; Joined cases C-51/96 & C-191/97 *Deliège* [2000] ECR I-2549; Case T-313/02 *Meca-Medina* [2004] ECR II-3291.

associations,[133] insurance funds,[134] trade unions,[135] and even automobile associations.[136]

b. Public procurement

Public procurement rules and principles only apply to contracting authorities or, in the broader terms used in Directive 2004/17,[137] to contracting entities. The same is true about the 'procurement principles' devised by the Court's case law and based on transparency (also referred to as 'the transparency case law').[138] Contracting authorities/entities must be sufficiently connected to the state; given that the aim of the procurement rules is to ensure that *public* money reaches the market in a transparent and objective way, their scope is confined to entities managing public money. As soon as an entity gains enough independence, either managerial or financial, so as not to be either managing 'public' money or influenced in its decisions by the state, then the rules cease to apply.[139] Accordingly, contracting entities are the state and its sub-divisions, as well as 'bodies governed by public law': these are bodies which i. have legal personality, ii. are established for the specific purpose of meeting needs in the general interest, not having an industrial or commercial character, and iii. are financed for the most part, are subject to management supervision or have an administrative, managerial, or supervisory board, whose majority is appointed by the state or its sub-divisions.

Condition (ii) above already feeds into the second main question asked by the Court, of the *nature of the activity* pursued, and will be examined in more detail below.[140]

Condition (iii), which is the one directly concerned with the *nature of the entity*, is in fact very similar to the test followed for the application of the internal market rules: irrespective of the legal nature of the entity concerned, the rules apply to the extent that the entity's conduct can be attributed to the state. Through a highly

---

[133] Case 292/86 *Gullung v Conseil de l' ordre des avocats du barreau de Colmar* [1988] ECR 111; Case C-309/99 *Wouters* [2002] ECR I-1577; Case C-506/04 *Graham J. Wilson v Ordre des avocats du barreau de Luxembourg* [2006] ECR I-8613; Joined cases C-94 & 202/04 *Federico Cipolla v Rosaria Fazari, née Portolese and Stefano Macrino and Claudio Capopart v Roberto Meloni* [2006] ECR I-11421.

[134] See, among several cases, Case C-158/96 *Köhll* [1998] ECR I-1931, Case C-157/99 *Smits-Peerbooms* [2001] ECR I-5473, and all the recent case law concerning the free movement of patients.

[135] Case C-438/05 *Viking* [2007] ECR I-10779; Case C-341/05 *Laval* [2007] ECR I-11767.

[136] Case C-49/07 *Motosykletistiki Omospondia Ellados NPID (MOTOE) v Elliniko Dimosio* [2008] ECR I-4863.

[137] European Parliament and Council Directive 2004/17/EC coordinating the procurement procedures of entities operating in the water, energy, transport and postal services sectors [2004] OJ L134/1 (the Utilities Directive).

[138] For this case law, see ch 6. See also Hatzopoulos, V., and Stergiou, H., 'Public procurement for healthcare services: from theory to practice' in van de Gronden, J., Krajewski, M., Neergaard, U., and Szyszczak, E. (eds), *Health Care and EU Law* (The Hague: TMC Asser Press, 2011).

[139] Under the Utilities Directive, n 137, the same logic is also applied at the level of *activities* (as opposed to entities): as long as any given activity 'is directly exposed to competition on markets to which access is not restricted', it automatically ceases falling into the scope of the Directive (Art 30(1)).

[140] See the discussion in subsection B(2).

technical body of case law, the Court has considerably extended the reach of the procurement rules, by stretching the concept of contracting authorities/entities.[141]

Differences between the free movement and the procurement rules lie at three levels.

First, it should be remembered that the procurement rules are more technical and more demanding to comply with; it is in this framework that the condition of state control and state financing has been judicially developed. Judgments such as *Mannesmann Anlagenbau, University of Cambridge,* and *Bayerischer Rundfunk* are much more explicit about the required link (between the entity and the state) than any free movement judgment.[142] Next to this pseudo-difference, there is a *second* one which is more substantial. The fact that a body exercises regulatory activity does not suffice to bring it under the procurement rules (as would be the case in free movement rules). In this respect, public procurement rules differ from free movement rules and come closer to state aid rules: it is the public origin of financial resources which matters, not the regulatory powers tentatively enjoyed by the entity concerned. *Thirdly*, and most importantly, it has already been identified above that the definition of contracting authorities/entities is not only based on criteria concerning the entities themselves, but also on criteria concerning the activity pursued by the entity. In this respect too, the public procurement rules look like the ones on competition and state aid, to which the analysis now turns.

c. Competition rules: private conduct and state aids

The application of competition rules, both those concerning private conduct and those on state aid rests on the qualification of the entities concerned (acting or beneficiaries) as 'undertakings'. Such a qualification is agnostic as to the legal nature of the entity concerned. In its seminal judgment in *Höfner*, the Court held that:

'in the context of competition law...the concept of an undertaking encompasses every entity engaged in an economic activity regardless of the legal status of the entity and the way in which it is financed'.[143]

In subsequent cases the Court further explained that the entity concerned need not be a profit-making undertaking, but may as well be a non-profit-making body.[144]

---

[141] See Sauter, W., and Schepel, H., *State and Market in EU Law: The Public and Private Spheres of the Internal Market before the EU Courts* (Cambridge: CUP, 2009) 51–5.

[142] Case C-44/96 *Mannesmann Anlagenbau* [1998] ECR I-73; Case C-380/98 *University of Cambridge* [2000] ECR I-8035; Case C-337/06 *Bayerischer Rundfunk* [2007] ECR I-11173.

[143] Case C-41/90 *Höfner and Elser* [1991] ECR I-1979, para 21. A somehow more helpful definition was offered in the early ECSC Case 19/61 *Mannesman AG v High Authority of the ECSC* [1962] ECR 357, para 371 and Joined Cases 17/61 & 20/61 *Klöckner-Werke AG and Hoesch AG v High Authority of the ECSC* [1962] ECR 325, para 341: 'an undertaking is constituted by a single organisation of personal, tangible and intangible elements, attached to an autonomous legal entity and pursuing a given long term economic aim'.

[144] See eg Case C-244/94 *Fédération Française des Sociétés d'Assurance, Société Paternelle-Vie, Union des Assurances de Paris-Vie and Caisse d'Assurance et de Prévoyance Mutuelle des Agriculteurs (FFSA) v Ministère de l'Agriculture et de la Pêche* [1995] ECR I-4013, para 21.

Therefore, contrary to the internal market rules, where the *nature of the entity* is the only (free movement) or the main (public procurement) criterion on which their application rests, for competition rules, such a nature is completely irrelevant. What counts for the application of competition rules is the *nature of the activity*.[145]

d. General assessment of the nature of the entity criterion

From the above, it becomes clear that the nature of the entity is of absolute importance for free movement rules, as it is the exclusive criterion for their applicability; it is of relative importance for the public procurement rules, as state control/financing constitutes one important criterion (out of three) for their applicability; and it is of no importance at all for the competition rules. This, further, means that, as far as this criterion goes, the different sets of rules are not mutually exclusive and the same entity may be subject to more than one set.

2. Nature of the activity

a. Free movement

As stated above, critical for the application of free movement rules is the public nature of the entity involved. The nature of the activity only comes into play in the form of an exception, or rather two exceptions.

Article 45(4) TFEU provides an exception to the free movement of workers in public service. At the same time, Article 51 TFEU expressly foresees that the right of establishment and (in combination with Article 62 TFEU) the free provision of services do not apply to activities which are connected, in the host state, with the exercise of official authority. These exceptions have been interpreted in a restrictive manner.

The concept of public service under Article 45(4) TFEU has been held to be a concept of EU law, confined to activities (not entire posts)[146] which involve substantial participation in the state's effort to exercise its functions and/or to safeguard the general interest, thus requiring a special relationship of allegiance to the state.[147] Similarly, the concept of public authority under Article 51 TFEU has been restricted to activities genuinely

---

[145] The same point is made in the Communication COM (2007) 725, 'Services of General Interest, Including Social Services of General Interest: A New European Commitment', at 5, where it is stated that 'in the area of competition law, according to the Court of Justice, it is not the sector or the status of an entity carrying out a service (eg whether the body is a public undertaking, private undertaking, association of undertakings, or part of the administration of the State), nor the way in which it is funded, which determines whether its activities are deemed economic or non-economic; it is the nature of the activity itself'.

[146] Case C-451/03 *Servizi Ausiliari Dottori Commercialisti Srl v Giuseppe Calafiori* [2006] ECR I-2941, para 47; Case C-173/94 *Commission v Belgium (employment in the public service)* [1997] ECR I-3265, and Case 290/94 *Commission v Greece (employment in the public service)* [1996] ECR I-3285.

[147] See also Sauter, W., and Schapel, H., 2009, n 141, at 61; see also, among many, Case 225/85 *Commission v Italy (employment in the NRC)* [1987] ECR 2625; Case C-4/91 *Annegret Bleis v Ministère de l'Education Nationale* [1991] ECR I-5627; Case C-473/93 *Commission v Luxembourg (employment in the public service)* [1997] ECR I-3207.

involving the exercise of authority and involving some power of decision—not mere preparatory or other collateral functions.[148] It has been observed, however, that the exercise of authority need not necessarily take the form of coercion, but may also concern civil aspects of public authority, such as the registration of births, marriages, and deaths.[149]

Next to these Treaty provisions whereby the application of the free movement rules may be sidestepped on grounds of public authority, a second ground seems to have been advanced by the Court—solidarity. The fulfilment, by the state, of its solidarity obligations towards its citizens was held to exclude the economic character of activities which could be provided in market conditions.[150] In *Sodemare*, a case decided under the freedom of establishment rules, the Court held that, since the rule that only non-profit-making bodies could engage in an activity connected to the general welfare (old people's homes) was dictated by solidarity, it could not be scrutinized under Treaty rules.[151] Similarly, in *Freskot*, a case decided under Article 56 TFEU, the Court found that the compulsory insurance scheme for farmers pursued an objective of social policy, 'given that the rate of the contribution is fixed independently of the risk facing each farm and that, in general, the national legislature sets a uniform rate both for the contributions paid and the benefits granted'; thus, it could not possibly violate the free provision of services rule.[152] Further in this judgment, and essentially for the same reasons, the Court also found the competition rules on state aid to be inapplicable.[153] More recently, in *Piatkowski*, the Court refused to scrutinize, under the rules on free movement of workers and establishment, a Dutch measure on the calculation of social security contributions, given that such a measure was part of 'a system of social security based on principles of solidarity'.[154]

It is true that the concept of solidarity has been developed and used essentially in the framework of (circumventing) competition rules[155]—and much less in the

---

[148] See eg Case C-404/05 *Commission v Germany (organic agricultural products)* [2007] ECR I-10239; Case C-393/05 *Commission v Austria (organic agricultural products)* [2007] ECR I-10195.

[149] See Sauter, W., and Schapel, H., 2009, n 141, at 65, with reference to Case C-405/01 *Collegio de Oficiales de la marina mercante Espanola* [2003] ECR I-10391. This position, however, may need readjustment in view of the judgments delivered by the Court while this book was under print, in Case C-52/08 *Commission v Portugal (notaries)* [2011] ECR nyr and Case C-53/08 *Commission v Austria (notaries)* [2011] ECR nyr.

[150] See, in this respect, Neergaard, U., 'In search of the role of "solidarity" in primary law and the case law of the ECJ' in Neergaard, U., Nielsen, R., and Roseberry, L. (eds), *The Role of Courts in Developing a European Social Model: Theoretical and Methodological Perspectives* (Copenhagen: DJØF Publishing, 2010) 97–138.

[151] Case C-70/95 *Sodemare* [1997] ECR I-3395, which has been further refined in subsequent judgments of the Court and its scope was restricted, but it has not been overturned.

[152] Case C-355/00 *Freskot* [2003] ECR I-5263, paras 67 and 57–59. In fact, in the latter paragraphs, the Court concludes that the benefits provided by ELGA (the fund) did not constitute services at all, while in paras 67 *et seq* the Court holds that even if some activities could be singled out as constituting services, any restrictions thereto could be justified 'on the ground of overriding public interest relating to a social policy objective' (para 69).

[153] Ibid, paras 76–88.

[154] Case C-493/04 *L.H. Piatkowski v Inspecteur van de Belastingdienst grote ondernemingen Eindhoven* [2006] ECR I-2369, para 38.

[155] For which, see the discussion under subheading B(2)c.

framework of the internal market.[156] In the free movement case law, solidarity-related arguments, such as the maintenance of the financial balance of the health-care[157] and social security systems,[158] tend to come up at a later stage of the Court's reasoning, as overriding reasons in the public interest (ORPIs).[159] This, however, does not preclude the solidarity element, whenever it is overarching, to be taken into account by the Court already at the stage of the qualification of the activity, in order to exclude altogether the application of the free movement rules.[160]

b. Public procurement

As stated above, the nature of the activity pursued constitutes, technically, one of the three tests for identifying a 'contracting authority/entity' (the other two being the existence of legal personality and state control). Therefore, technically, it is integrated in the first question, that of the nature of the entity. In this framework, however, the issue of the activity pursued is always treated separately. Indeed, according to Article 1(9) of Directive 2004/18,[161] the first condition for identifying a body governed by public law is that it be 'established for the specific purpose of meeting needs in the general interest, *not having an industrial or commercial character*'. According to the Court, such needs:

'are generally needs which are satisfied otherwise than by the availability of goods and services in the market place and which, for reasons associated with the general interest, the State chooses to provide itself or over which wishes to retain a decisive influence'.[162]

Three remarks need be made in respect of the nature of the activities which make an entity qualify as a contracting entity.[163]

First, the fact that some competition by private undertakings may or does actually exist, does not automatically rule out the possibility that such activities

---

[156] See Neergaard, U., 2009, n 150, at 123.

[157] See eg C-157/99 *Smits-Peerbooms* [2001] ECR I-5473 and all the recent case law concerning the free movement of patients.

[158] See eg Case C-76/05 *Herbert Schwarz and Marga Gootjes-Schwarz v Finanzamt Bergisch Gladbach* [2007] ECR I-6849.

[159] For which, see the discussion in ch 4.

[160] Hervey, T., ' "Social Solidarity": a buttress against internal market law?' in Shaw, J. (ed), *Social Law and Policy in an Evolving EU* (Oxford: Hart Publishing, 2000) 31–47, also available at <http://aei. pitt.edu/2294/1/002338_1.PDF> (last accessed on 6 November 2011); she observes that the same ambivalence of solidarity is also true in relation to the competition rules, since, eg in *Albany*, the Court found that the activity in question did not possess sufficient solidarity features to be brought altogether outside the scope of the Treaty, but could, nonetheless, justify an exception under Art 106(2) TFEU (Case C-67/96 *Albany International BV v Stichting Bedrijfspensioenfonds Textielindustrie* [1999] ECR I-5751).

[161] European Parliament and Council Directive 2004/18/EC on the coordination of procedures for the award of public works contracts, public supply contracts and public service contracts [2004] OJ L134/114 (the Public Procurement Directive).

[162] See eg Case C-360/96 *BFI Holding BV* [1998] ECR I-6821, paras 50–51, and Case C-18/01 *Korhonen* [2003] ECR I-5321, para 47.

[163] Further on this issue, see Bovis, C., *EC Public Procurement: Case Law and Regulation* (Oxford: OUP, 2006) ch 7; Arrowsmith, S., *The Law of Public and Utilities Procurement* (London: Sweet & Maxwell, 2005) ch 5.

are offered by the public entity in the general interest.[164] It is only when the entity in question 'operates in normal market conditions, aims to make a profit, and bears the losses associated with the exercise of its activity' that the Court is satisfied that it is not going to take economically unsound decisions; only then will the Court leave the entity unconstrained by public procurement rules.[165] It should be noted that the very same conditions of profit seeking and, more decisively, of cost bearing are also used by the Court—in reverse—in order to ascertain the existence of undertakings.[166]

Secondly, if the entity's activities are partly 'in the general interest' and partly within the market, the entity is subject to the procurement rules even for contracts which relate to its purely competitive activities. This 'infection' or 'contamination' theory[167] was introduced by the Court in *Mannesmann* and confirmed ever since.[168]

Thirdly, contrary to the definition of SGEIs, or to the concept of solidarity, for which the Court tries to put forward its own set of criteria and to control *in extremis* the choices made by the member states,[169] member states seem to have a free hand in deciding the activities which they keep for themselves, thus subjecting them to the procurement rules. This vision stems from the excerpt quoted above ('. . . the State chooses to . . .'). Moreover, it is in conformity with the innate rationale of the public procurement rules: their objective is not to constrain the member states' choices concerning the services they offer to their population, but rather to make sure that, when providing for their citizens, member states respect the principles of objectiveness, transparency, and equal treatment. It is in the teleology of the procurement rules to have a wide scope of application and the Court has no reason to try to restrict national choices.

In other words, *regulation* by the state is always presumed to have some impact on economic activity and is, thus, subject to the free movement rules—unless some direct connection to the exercise of public authority can be shown. *Economic dealings* of the state, on the other hand, are either within the market, in which case the competition rules do, in principle, apply to them; or they operate in the pursuance of general interest, in which case the public procurement rules apply to them. Neither qualification excludes altogether the application of EU law and,

---

[164] C-18/01 *Korhonen*, n 162, paras 43–44, where the Court gives two reasons for such a finding: first, that even if there is competition, a body financed or controlled by the state may nonetheless be guided by non-economic considerations; secondly, that it is hard to imagine any activities that could not in any circumstances be carried out by private undertakings.

[165] Ibid, para 51.

[166] See eg C-309/99 *Wouters* [2002] ECR I-1577, paras 48–49.

[167] For the use of the term 'infection', see Sauter, W., and Schepel, H., *State and Market in EU Law: The Public and Private Spheres of the Internal Market before the EU Courts* (Cambridge: CUP, 2009), at 54; however, the term 'contamination' seems to be describing more accurately the legal situation.

[168] Case C-44/96 *Mannesmann Anlagenbau* [1998] ECR I-73, para 26, subsequently confirmed, inter alia, in Case C-373/00 *Truley* [2003] ECR I-1931, para 56, and Case C-18/01 *Korhonen*, n 162, para 58.

[169] For the control by the Court of the concept of SGEI put forward by the member states, see the analysis at subheading A(3)a(iv).

therefore, there is no teleological argument in favour of one or the other interpretation. On the contrary, the Court has consistently interpreted the concept of a contracting authority extremely widely.[170]

These observations make clear that the notion of serving needs of general interest, for the purposes of public procurement, is much wider than the concept of the exercise of public authority, for the purposes of the free movement rules. In economic terms, it could be said that the former correspond to 'merit goods' while the latter is confined to a restrictive vision of 'public goods'. This makes sense, since the purpose of the two sets of rules is different: under the free movement rules 'public authority' serves as a ground for excluding the application of the fundamental freedoms, while under the procurement rules, 'needs of general interest' serve as a ground for establishing EU competence over national procurement practices.

What makes much less sense, however, is that many entities which qualify as undertakings under the competition rules are simultaneously constrained by the public procurement rules.[171]

c. Competition rules: private conduct and state aid

It has been briefly explained above (subheading B(1)C) that for the application of competition rules, the nature of the entity involved is completely irrelevant. What does count, on the other hand, is the activity pursued. Such activity must satisfy two requirements to qualify as economic. First, it should consist 'in offering goods and services in a given market'. Buying into a market does not, on its own, qualify as an economic activity, if the purchase is not connected to a commercial activity.[172] Secondly, the entity offering goods and services should bear the financial risks of the activity[173]—an activity which need not be pursued for profit,[174] but which is 'capable of being carried on, at least in principle, by a private undertaking with a view to profit'.[175] This last condition is interpreted in an extremely wide manner, the criterion used being that the activity in question 'has not always been and is not necessarily' exercised outside the market.[176] It has been observed in this respect that 'it is not actual competition or even potential competition that is relevant, but hypothetical competition'.[177]

---

[170] Sauter, W., and Schapel, H., 2009, n 141, at 53.

[171] Further on this issue, see under subheading d(ii).

[172] See eg a highly authoritative, although thoroughly disputed, judgment in Case C-205/03P *FENIN* [2006] ECR I-6295, para 25; for this judgment see, among many, Krajewski, M., and Farley, M., 'Non-economic Activities in Upstream and Downstream Markets and the Scope of Competition Law after *FENIN*' (2007) 32 *EL Rev* 111–24.

[173] See eg Case C-309/99 *Wouters* [2002] ECR I-1577, paras 48–49.

[174] Case C-244/94 *FFSA* [1995] ECR I-4013, para 21.

[175] Case C-364/92 *SAT Fluggesellschaft mbH v Eurocontrol* [1994] ECR I-43, para 9.

[176] Case C-41/90 *Höfner* [1991] ECR I-1979, para 22.

[177] Sauter, W., and Schapel, H., 2009, n 141, at 82.

These two conditions make for a very extensive concept of 'undertaking', made even broader by the Court's expansive view of the concept of 'associations of undertakings' contained in the Treaty.[178]

There are, however, two boundaries to the scope *ratione materiae* of competition rules, stemming from the nature of the activity pursued. First, there are cases where the activity carried out by the entity concerned bears the mark of public authority.[179] There is a second category of cases where the activity is a manifestation of the principle of solidarity.[180] Both the exercise of public authority and the carrying out of solidarity functions transform an otherwise economic activity to a non-economic one.

In order to ascertain whether an activity is sufficiently connected to the exercise of public authority, the Court examines a. its nature, b. its aim, and c. the rules to which it is subject.[181] This last criterion (c), as is also the case for public procurement, allows the states some leeway in determining the scope of application of the competition rules. However, unlike public procurement, national regulatory choices are 'cross-checked' by reference to the nature and the aim of the activity. The test, therefore, is not merely a subjective one, depending on the free will of member states, but rather objective, since it is primarily connected to the very characteristics of the activity.

The case law is more abundant concerning solidarity, but it is not always easy to know in advance how direct a relationship to solidarity an activity must have, so as not to qualify as economic.[182] From a relatively long series of judgments concerning essentially pension and healthcare funds,[183] it follows that elements

---

[178] See eg Case C-309/99, n 173, paras 48–49.

[179] See eg Case C-364/92 *Eurocontrol*, n 175; Case C-343/95 *Diego Calì & Figli Srl v Servizi ecologici porto di Genova SpA (SEPG)* [1996] ECR I-1547; Case T-155/04 *SELEX Sistemi Integrati SpA v Commission of the European Communities* [2006] ECR II-4797.

[180] See, for the first application of this trend, Joined cases C-159 & 160/91 *Christian Poucet v Assurances Générales de France and Caisse Mutuelle Régionale du Languedoc-Roussillon* [1993] ECR I-637; see also Case C-218/00 *Cisal di Battistello Venanzio & C. Sas v Istituto nazionale per l'assicurazione contro gli infortuni sul lavoro (INAIL)* [2002] ECR I-691; and Joined cases C-264, 306, 354 & 355/01 *AOK Bundesverband and others v Ichthyol-Gesellschaft Cordes, Hermani & Co and others* [2004] ECR I-2493; on this (and other) case law, see very authoritatively, Hervey, T., 2000, n 161; see also Dougan, M., 'Expanding the frontiers of EU citizenship by dismantling the territorial boundaries of the national welfare states?' in Barnard, C., and Odudu, O. (eds), *The Outer Limtis of EU Law* (Oxford/Portland: Hart Publishing, 2009) 119–65; generally on the issue of solidarity, see also Houtepen, R., and Ter Meulen, R., 'New Types of Solidarity in the European Welfare State' (2000) 8 *Health Care Analysis* 329–40; White, J., 'Rethinking Transnational Solidarity in the EU' (2003) 20 *Perspectives* 40–57; and on a more philosophical tone, see recently the edited volume by Karagiannis, N., *European Solidarity* (Liverpool: LUP, 2007).

[181] See Case C-343/95 *Calì*, n 179, paras 22–23, and the AG opinion in this same case, paras 41–42.

[182] See, in this respect, Neergaard, U., 'In search of the role of "solidarity" in primary law and the case law of the ECJ' in Neergaard, U., Nielsen, R., and Roseberry, L. (eds), *The Role of Courts in Developing a European Social Model: Theoretical and Methodological Perspectives* (Copenhagen: DJØF Publishing, 2010) 97–138; Ross, M., 'The value of solidarity in European public services law' in Krajewski, M., Neergaard, U., and van de Gronden, J. (eds), *The Changing Legal Framework for Services of General Interest* (The Hague: TMC Asser Press, 2009) 81–99.

[183] See C-244/94 *FFSA* [1995] ECR I-4013; Case C-70/905 *Sodemare* [1997] ECR I-3395; Case C-67/96 *Albany* [1999] ECR I-5751; Joined cases C-115–157/97 *Brentjens Handelsonderneming BV v*

which would point to a non-economic activity, include:[184] (a) a social objective pursued, (b) the compulsory nature of participation/contribution, (c) the contributions paid being related to the income of the insured person, not to the nature of the risk covered, (d) the benefits accruing to insured persons not being directly linked to contributions paid by them, (e) the benefits and contributions being determined under the control or the supervision of the state, (f) strong overall state control, (g) the funds collected being redistributed, and not capitalized and/ or invested, (i) cross-subsidization between different schemes, and (j) the non-existence of competitive schemes offered by private operators.[185] None of these elements seems to be decisive on its own and, indeed, many of them may be criticized. In particular, requirements (a), (b), (f), and (i) above have all been accused for failing to account for the diversity of social systems in the EU and for countering modernization and rationalization efforts.[186]

Furthermore, the Court has developed a theory of 'severability' in the field of competition law whereby:

'since the Treaty provisions on competition are applicable to the activities of an entity which can be severed from those which it engages as a public authority, the various activities of an entity must be considered individually and the treatment of some of them as powers of a public authority does not mean that it must be concluded that the other activities are not economic'.[187]

The existence and precise scope of a theory of severability is, however, unclear. Though commonly used in cases involving public authority activities, the theory has been resisted (admittedly only on procedural grounds) by the Grand Chamber of the Court in *FENIN* in relation to solidarity activities.[188]

Stichting Bedrijfspensioenfonds voor de Handel in Bouwmaterialen [1999] ECR I-6025; and Case C-219/ 97 *Maatschappij Drijvende Bokken BV v Stichting Pensioenfonds voor de Vervoer-en Havenbedrijven* [1999] ECR I-6121, respectively. On these three cases, Idot, L., 'Droit Social et droit de la concurrence: confrontation ou cohabitation: A propos de quelques développements récents'(1999) 9:11 *Europe* 4–8; Case C-218/00 *Cisal*, n 180; Case T-319/99, *Federación Española de Empresas de, Tecnología Sanitaria (FENIN) v Commission* [2003] ECR II-357, upheld by the Court in Case C-205/03P *FENIN* [2006] ECR I-6295; Case C-355/00 *Freskot* [2003] ECR I-5263; Joined cases C-264/01, C-306, 354 & 355/01 *AOK*, n 180.

[184] Note that these are broadly the same, but taken from the reverse side, to the ones used to identify contracting entities (see under subheading B(2)b).

[185] For a more detailed analysis of those criteria, see Hatzopoulos, V., 'Health law and policy: the impact of the EU' in de Búrca, G. (ed), *EU Law and the Welfare State: In Search of Solidarity* (Oxford: OUP, 2005) 123–60. For a critical view of the Court's meddling with social funds, see also Kessler, F., 'Droit de la concurrence et régimes de protection sociale: un bilan provisoire' in Kovar, R., and Simon, D. (eds), *Service public et Communauté Européenne: entre l'intérêt général et le marché, Vol. I* (Paris: La documentation française, 1998) 421–46, at 430, where further reference to other commentators.

[186] Hervey, T., 2000, n 160.

[187] Case T-155/04 *SELEX Sistemi Integrati*, n 179, para 54; and before that, see Case C-82/01 P *Aéroports de Paris v Commission of the European Communities* [2002] ECR I-9297, paras 75 *et seq.*

[188] One of the arguments put forward by the plaintiffs, and ignored by the Court, was that the Sistema Nacional de Salud (SNS) (the Spanish health system) was not only providing services to the population for free, but was in parallel engaging into the commercial provision of healthcare, in particular to the attention of foreign nationals; see C-205/03P *FENIN*, n 183, para 9.

d. General assessment of the activity criterion

i. Convergence—coherence

It is clear from the above that in all four fields of law examined, the qualification of an activity as being economic or non-economic follows the same basic pattern: activities are presumed to be economic, unless they are shown to be connected either to public authority, or to solidarity: the identification of an activity embodying authority or solidarity will exclude the application of free movement and competition rules, but at the same time, will trigger the application of public procurement rules. For the purposes of public procurement, 'activities in the general interest' cover a wider category than simple public authority and solidarity measures, since the decision of the member state to retain decisive influence over specific activities is enough to subject such activities to the procurement rules.

The concept of public authority which serves to exclude the application of the rules on free movement (under Article 51 TFEU), and on competition (under the above-mentioned case law of the Court) seems to have common grounding. Similarly, the concept of solidarity seems to be unique and its effects on the application of the various sets of rules comparable. Moreover, both concepts are EU concepts and subject to the control of the CJEU.

In addition, the requirement that *undertakings* bring goods/services *into* the market fits perfectly with the opposite requirement that *contracting entities* operate *outside* the market. An entity which buys (without selling) into the market and then offers (for free) to the population is not an undertaking;[189] it is, nonetheless, subject to the public procurement rules. Similarly, the condition that an undertaking should bear the risks of its own operations combines well with the idea that entities which shift their risks to the state are subject to the procurement rules.[190]

Therefore, a systemic coherence seems to be emerging from the application of the concepts discussed: the free movement and competition rules apply whenever there is a market, in order to ensure competition *in* the market. The procurement rules apply whenever the exercise of authority, solidarity, or other state function exclude competition from the market; they are designed to secure competition *for* the market. By the same token, it seems prima facie that any given entity is either an undertaking or a contracting authority, but never both.

ii. Dissonance—confusion

This idyllic vision, however, collapses once the analysis gets into the details. Several overlaps may be identified. *First,* from a normative viewpoint, it is problematic that two separate questions (ie the nature of the entity and the nature of the activity) are dealt with indistinctly (and often confusingly), for the purposes of public procurement and competition. *Secondly,* while the solidarity argument has been extensively tested as a means of excluding the application of competition rules, it has only rarely

---

[189] Ibid.
[190] See the discussion in subsection B(2)b.

been used in the same way under free movement rules.[191] *Thirdly*, 'needs of general interest' in the sense of public procurement have been interpreted in too wide a manner, in at least three respects: a. the Court, in the procurement context, rarely examines the proportionality of the decision of member states to reserve a certain type of activity; b. the existence of some competition from other (private) undertakings does not automatically exclude the application of procurement rules; c. the theory of 'contamination' means that an entity may be subject to the procurement rules for activities for which it is subject to full competition. *Fourthly*, on the competition side, 'undertaking' has also been interpreted to be too wide a concept, especially in view of a. the fact that even hypothetical competition is enough, and b. the uncertainties of the theory of 'severability' (the same entity may qualify as an undertaking for some of its activities and as a public authority for others).

Such differences, moreover, account for the fact that several entities may, at the same time, be subject to competition *and* public procurement rules. This is especially true for entities engaged in the provision of services broadly associated to the general interest, such as healthcare.[192] This seems to be an undesirable outcome, as the two sets of rules should be mutually exclusive. From a systemic viewpoint, it has been shown that they are deemed to cover different situations and to achieve different outcomes (competition *in* the market *v.* competition *for* the market). The two qualifications are supposed to be opposites: 'the exercise of an economic activity' is the criterion for identifying an undertaking, while, on the other hand, a contracting entity is one which 'does not pursue an activity of economic or commercial nature'. One of the fundamental principles of market economy is that economic operators should be free to contract with whomever they wish:[193] any given entity may not be subject simultaneously to free competition and to the restrictive and time-consuming rules on public procurement.

3. The object of a measure

The third question examined by the Court has to do with the object of any given measure. There is great controversy in the legal literature whether measures restricting trade should be tested only as to their object or also as to their effect. Under WTO law, the most authoritative expression of the idea that only the object

---

[191] As noted above, in the free movement case law, solidarity is essentially expressed through the 'financial equilibrium' ORPI; see also the discussion under subheading B(5).

[192] See on this issue, Hatzopoulos, V., 'Public procurement and state aid in national healthcare systems' in Mossialos, E., Permanand, G., Baeten, R., and Hervey, T. (eds), *Health Systems Governance in Europe: The Role of EU Law and Policy* (Cambridge: CUP, 2010) 381–420; Hatzopoulos, V., 'Financing National Health Care in a Transnational Environment: The Impact of the EC Internal Market' (2009) 26 *Wisconsin Int L J* 761–804; more generally, on the topic, see Bovis, C., 'The conceptual links between state aid and public procurement in the financing of services of general interest' in Krajewski, M., Neergard, U., and van de Gronden, J. (eds), *The Changing Legal Framework for Services of General Interest* (The Hague: Asser Press, 2009) 149–70; Bovis, C., 'Financing Services of General Interest in the EU: How Do Public Procurement and State Aids Interact to Demarcate between Market Forces and Protection?' (2005) 11 *ELJ* 79–109.

[193] This 'freedom to deal' is known in competition law as the 'Colgate doctrine' from the US Supreme's Court judgment in *United States v Colgate & Co*, 250 US 300 (1919).

should be taken into account comes from D. Regan.[194] The argument goes that purely protectionist measures should be struck down, while measures having as their primary aim to protect something valued by any given state/constituency should be left unscathed. Fellow states in an international agreement or international institutions are not in a position to second-guess political choices and legitimate preferences of democratic constituencies. Moreover, if they act rationally, states will not systematically try to introduce 'beggar-thy-neighbour' regulation. This vision, however, over-restrictive as it is to the scope of international trade rules, does not seem to have prevailed in the WTO practice, which instead seems to be following something akin to an 'object and effects' doctrine.[195]

In the EU it has become clear, ever since the founding free movement judgments,[196] that an effect-based approach should be taken into account. This has led to judicial excesses, denounced by several authors,[197] and even by the Court itself, notably in *Keck*.[198] Legal doctrine has come up with various theories in order to re-centre the EU's focus on measures which are truly restrictive of trade: discrimination, the *de minimis* rule, remoteness, and double burdens, to state but a few.[199] One of the most recent and remarkable such attempts to 'restrict restrictions' comes from C. Barnard, who proposes a qualified 'market access' test, whereby all measures restricting market access would be caught, unless genuinely non-discriminatory.[200] This, in practice, is not very different from using intent as

---

[194] Regan, D., 'Judicial Review of Member-State Regulation of Trade within a Federal or Quasi-federal System: Protectionism and Balancing, Da Capo' (2001) 99 *Michigan L Rev* 1853–902; see also Regan, D., 'What Are Trade Agreements For?: Two Conflicting Stories Told by Economists, with a Lesson for Lawyers' (2006) 9 *J Int Economic L* 951–88; and more recently, in the EU context, Regan, D., 'An outsider's view of *Dassonville* and *Cassis de Dijon*: on interpretation and policy' in Poiares Maduro, M., and Azoulai, L. (eds), *The Past and the Future of EU Law: The Classics of EU Law Revisited on the 50th Anniversary of the Rome Treaty* (Oxford: Hart Publishing, 2010) 465–73.

[195] For a discussion of the relevant case law see, among many, Leroux, E., 'Eleven Years of GATS Case Law: What Have We Learned?' (2007) 10 *J of Int Economic L* 749–93; Ortino, F., 'Treaty Interpretation and the WTO Appellate Body Report in US-Gambling: A Critique' (2006) 9 *J of Int Economic L* 117–48; and Leitner, K., and Lester, S., 'WTO Dispute Settlement from 1995 to 2005: A Statistical Analysis' (2006) 9 *J of Int Economic L* 219–31.

[196] Such as Case 8/74 *Procureur du Roi v Dassonville* [1974] ECR 837; Case 33/74 *Johannes Hervicus Maria van Binsbergen v Bestuur van de Bedrijfsvereniging voor de Metaalnijverheid* [1974] ECR 1299; Case 2/74 *Jean Reyners v Belgian State* [1974] ECR 631; Case 120/78 *Rewe-Zentral AG v Bundesmonopolverwaltung für Branntwein (Cassis de Dijon)* [1979] ECR 649.

[197] For most 'classic' criticism, see Case C-145/88 *Torfaen Borough Council v B & Q plc* [1989] ECR I-3851 (AG); White, E.L., 'In Search of the Limits to Article 30 of the EEC Treaty (1989) 26 *CML Rev* 235–80; Mortelmans, K., 'Article 30 of the EEC Treaty and Legislation Relating to Market Circumstances: Time to Consider a New Definition?' (1991) 28 *CML Rev* 115–36.

[198] Joined cases C-267 & 268/91 *Criminal proceedings against Bernard Keck and Daniel Mithouard* [1993] ECR I-6097.

[199] For a recent restatement of the relevant literature and some further thoughts, see Spaventa, E., 'The outer limits of the Treaty free movement provisions: some reflections on the significance of *Keck*, remoteness, and *Deliège*' in Barnard, C., and Odudu, O. (eds), *The Outer Limits of EU Law* (Oxford/Portland: Hart Publishing, 2009) 245–69; for a more detailed discussion of the various tendencies, see ch 3.

[200] Barnard, C., 'Restricting Restrictions: Lessons for the EU from the US?' (2009) 68 *Cambridge LJ* 575–606.

the main guide for qualifying obstacles to trade, although it is conceptually different.

The Court, however, has so far not given in to such a restrictive definition of restrictions. It has, nonetheless, indicated that the object of the measures brought to it is to be taken into account in two ways: either to set a (rebuttable) presumption of being innocuous, where their object is to regulate selling arrangements,[201] or to exclude measures from its scrutiny all together, when they are alien to the regulation of economic activity. It is this latter category which is of interest here.

a. Free movement

The most explicit expression of the idea that some regulations are, by nature, alien to the exercise of economic activity, is the Court's judgment in *Deliège*, concerning sporting rules. In this judgment, the Court held that:

'the Treaty provisions concerning freedom of movement for persons do not prevent the adoption of rules or practices [imposing restrictions] for reasons which are not of an economic nature, which relate to the particular nature and context of such [activity]'.[202]

Or, put differently, 'those rules do not constitute restrictions on freedom of movement because they concern questions of purely sporting interest and, as such, have nothing to do with economic activity'.[203] Therefore, the subject matter of the measures takes them outside the scope of the free movement rules, to the extent that limitations thereto are 'inherent' in the nature of the measures.[204]

It is unclear whether this line of reasoning is only applicable in the field of sport. Some authors tend to bring this case law together with that on 'remoteness', 'selling arrangements', and other cases in which the Court has refused the existence of any restrictive effect on trade.[205] The judgments in *Deliège* and *Meca-Medina*, however, may be seen as the expression of the broader idea that the object of some regulations is so clearly non-economic that it cannot possibly be held to be market-distorting. This latter reading may be confirmed by reference to the other fields of the present heading.

b. Public procurement

For the procurement rules to apply, there needs to be a contract. This is expressed by criterion (i) of a 'contracting authority', ie the requirement that the awarding entity has legal personality (the other two being state control and the pursuance of some activity in the general interest).[206] If a public entity entrusts another public entity with the execution of a given mission, there is no contract between two

---

[201] Joined cases C-267 & 268/91 *Keck*, n 198.
[202] Joined cases C-51/96 and C-191/97 *Deliège* [2000] ECR I-2549, para 43.
[203] Case C-519/04P *David Meca-Medina and Igor Majcen v Commission of the European Communities* [2006] ECR I-6991, para 31.
[204] Joined cases C-51/96 & C-191/97 *Deliège*, n 202, para 64.
[205] See Spaventa, E., 2009, n 199, at 266–7.
[206] See more under subheading B(1)b.

different legal persons and the situation is closer to the concept of delegation. Furthermore, public money does not enter the market, but remains within the confines of the state and the situation has thus no relevance for EU law.

The way member states organize, merge or else restructure their services, in order to fulfil their obligations towards their citizens, is '*cuisine interne*' and need not be constrained by the formal procurement rules. According to the Court's judgment in *Teckal*[207] and subsequent case law, such 'in-house' arrangements are not caught by the procurement rules and principles. This is true as long as a. awarding entities exercise over the appointed entity control which is similar to that exercised over their own departments, and b. the appointed entity's essential activities are carried out for the authorities which own it. The 'in-house' doctrine, introduced with great circumspection in the early Court judgments,[208] has been consolidated and its scope has been extended by the recent judgments in *ASEMFO v Tragsa* and, more importantly, *Coditel*.[209] The technicalities of the 'in-house' doctrine need not detain us here.[210] What is important, however, is that this doctrine supports the idea that the organizational/operational arrangements adopted by member states in order to discharge their obligations towards their citizens are, by their nature, alien to the procurement rules. This principle and its legal implications are extremely important in an era of advanced state divestiture and intense experimentation with flexible tools for the provision of services to the public (creation of undertaking-like public companies, Public Private Partnerships, Public Public Partnerships, etc). What is more, just like the sporting rules above, such arrangements are not captured by the free movement rules, although they do affect the market, because their primary aim is different and they are indispensable for the attainment of such an aim.

c. Competition—private conduct

In the 'trilogy' cases concerning supplementary pension funds,[211] the Court invented yet another use for solidarity, apart from the (dis)qualification of

---

[207] Case C-107/98 *Teckal Srl v Comune di Viano and Azienda Gas-Acqua Consorziale (AGAC) di Reggio Emilia* [1999] ECR I-8121.

[208] See eg Case C-26/03 *Stadt Halle and RPL Recyclingpark Lochau GmbH v Arbeitsgemeinschaft Thermische Restabfall-und Energieverwertungsanlage TREA Leuna* [2005] ECR I-1; Case C-458/03 *Parking Brixen GmbH v Gemeinde Brixen and Stadtwerke Brixen AG* [2005] ECR I-8612; Case C-410/04 *Associazione Nazionale Autotrasporto Viaggiatori (ANAV) v Comune di Bari and AMTAB Servizio SpA* [2006] ECR I-3303.

[209] Case C-295/05 *Asociación Nacional de Empresas Forestales (Asemfo) v Transformación Agraria SA (Tragsa) and Administración del Estado* [2007] ECR I-2999; Case C-324/07 *Coditel Brabant SA v Commune d'Uccle and Région de Bruxelles-Capitale* [2008] ECR I-8457.

[210] For a recent account of all the relevant case law, see Frenz, W., and Schleissing, P., 'The never ending story of "in-house" procurement' in Krajewski, M., Neergard, U., and van de Gronden, J. (eds), *The Changing Legal Framework for Services of General Interest* (The Hague: TMC Asser Press, 2009) 171–87; Kaarresalo, T., 'Procuring In-house: The Impact of the EC Procurement Regime' (2008) 17 *Public Procurement L Rev* 242–54; see also the various contributions in Comba, M., and Treumer, S. (eds), *The In House Providing in European Law* (Copenhagen: DJØF Publishing, 2010).

[211] Case C-67/96 *Albany* [1999] ECR I-5751, Cases C-155–157/97 *Brentjens* [1999] ECR I-6025, and Case C-219/97 *Drijvende* [1999] ECR I-6121, respectively. On these three cases, see Idot, L.,

economic activity.[212] The question put to the Court was whether sector-specific collective agreements making affiliation compulsory to a single fund per sector infringed competition rules. The Court found that the pension schemes in question were not sufficiently impregnated with solidarity and held that the funds qualified as undertakings.[213] It also submitted, however, that the agreements concluded between employers and employees, making affiliation to the above 'undertakings' compulsory, lay outside the scope of Article 101 TFEU.[214] In order to reach this conclusion, the Court referred to the *nature* and the *purpose* of the agreements. Regarding the former, the Court held that such agreements were the fruit of social dialogue, a form of negotiation enshrined in the EU Treaty (Article 152 TFEU). As for the latter, ie the purpose of the agreement, the Court found that it contributed directly to improving one of the employees' working conditions, namely, their remuneration.[215] The Court explained that:

'It is beyond question that certain restrictions of competition are inherent in collective agreements between organisations representing employers and workers. However, the social policy objectives pursued by such agreements would be seriously undermined if management and labour were subject to Article 85(1) [now Article 101(1) TFEU].'[216]

In these judgments, again, the idea is clearly expressed that agreements, the *nature and purpose* of which are primarily non-economic, are not caught by the Treaty economic rules (here, rules on competition), even if they do have restrictive effects; at least to the extent that such restrictive effects are 'inherent' to the measures.

Subsequent judgments have outlined the limits of such an approach. In *Pavlov*, the Court made clear that the conclusion of collective agreements between professionals exercising a liberal profession was not foreseen in the Treaty, and therefore, could not benefit from the above exclusion from the competition rules.[217] More importantly, in *Viking*, the Court restrictively applied the 'inherent' condition, as it held that it is not 'inherent' to 'the very exercise of trade union rights and the right to take collective action that [the Treaty] fundamental freedoms will be prejudiced'.[218] These cases, nonetheless, do not call into question the principle that some agreements, because of their 'inherent' content, are excluded from the scope of the competition rules.

'Droit Social et droit de la concurrence: confrontation ou cohabitation: A propos de quelques développements récents'(1999) 9:11 *Europe* 4–8.

[212] For which, see the analysis under subheading B(2)c.

[213] For the criteria used to determine whether there is sufficient solidarity, see in subsection B(2)c.

[214] Case C-67/96 *Albany* [1999] ECR I-5751, para 64; Case C-115–117/97 *Brentjens* [1999] ECR I-6025, para 61; and Case C-219/97 *Drijvende* [1999] ECR I-6121, para 51.

[215] See eg Case C-219/97 *Drijvende* [1999] ECR I-6121, paras 49–50.

[216] Ibid, para 46.

[217] Joined cases C-180–184/98 *Pavel Pavlov and others v Stichting Pensioenfonds Medische Specialisten* [2000] ECR I-6451, para 69.

[218] Case C-438/05 *Viking* [2007] ECR I-10779, para 52.

d. General assessment of the object of the measure

From the analysis above, it becomes clear that alongside the nature of the entity and of the activity pursued, the 'nature and object' of the measure/agreement involved are also taken into account. In other words, the Court recognizes that in some circumstances, even if the effects of a measure/agreement do restrict the application of EU rules, the object of the measure/agreement serves to obliterate the restrictive effects. In this sense, it may be said that the Court does follow an idiosyncratic reverse 'object and effects doctrine', whereby a *positively valued object* serves to legitimize *negatively valued effects*; subject to a strict test of proportionality, expressed through the condition that restrictions should be 'inherent' in the measure.

4. Mitigating factors—threshold of interference

Measures/agreements which are in breach of Treaty rules are, occasionally, left unscathed. This is because the level of annoyance they provoke is not intolerable. This may be the case either because the level of interference is too low (*de minimis*) or too uncertain (remoteness); or because the interference is necessary for the achievement of some other objective internal (ancillary restrictions) or external (rule of reason) to the measure/agreement examined.

It is not the place here to elaborate on these theories, as each of these would require separate monographs. Very briefly, however, it may be shown how they all serve the same function, as part of the wider discussion on the economic/non-economic activity conundrum.

a. Free movement

The Court, while defining the concept of restriction in an extensive way, has nonetheless, provided 'escape routes' through which national measures forego its scrutiny. In this way, the Court consciously mitigates the intensity of its own control over national measures, thus allowing member states some leeway to pursue their regulatory choices without being subject to a strict test of necessity and proportionality. These various escape routes are discussed in some detail in the following chapter dedicated to the concept of 'restriction'.

b. Public procurement

The same objective is openly followed in the field of public procurement, in several ways. *First*, the Public Procurement Directives apply to operations whose economic value is higher than a given threshold. Thresholds differ depending on the object of procurement (goods and services on the one hand, construction on the other), on whether the purchasing authority belongs to the central or decentralized administration, and on the activity concerned by the operation, utilities being subject to different thresholds; they are regularly revised. Thresholds clearly stand for a *de minimis* principle. *Secondly*, utilities procurement is subject to different (more flexible) rules than the ones applicable to the other sectors. *Thirdly*, even within traditional sectors, different services are listed in different Annexes, and are, thus, subject to different rules. Therefore, for example, rail and water transport, as well as education, healthcare, and social services (all enumerated in Annex IIB of the Directive 2004/18) are only subject to the 'light' procurement regime, namely the use of objective standards in the tendering documents and post-award publicity. *Fourthly*, the Directives only cover classic procurement procedures, to the exclusion of concession contracts and Public Private Partnerships. All these arrangements leave member states with considerable leeway to organize the provision of services they deem 'sensible', outside the strict constrains of the procurement regime—but still subject to the procurement principles.[219]

c. Competition rules—private conduct

Several factors within the definitions of Article 101 and, to a lesser extent, Article 102 TFEU operate as 'mitigating factors'.

In Article 101(1) alone, well before the question of an exemption by virtue of Article 101(3) is ever raised, there are several doctrines which limit the scope of application of the Treaty. Article 101(1) prohibits agreements, etc 'which have as their object or effect the prevention, restriction or distortion of competition within the common market'. The EU Courts and the Commission have been interpreting the above condition flexibly, by clearing collusive conduct which, on balance, is more in favour than to the detriment of competition. This practice is comparable to the American 'rule of reason' doctrine and indeed, has been qualified as such within the EU framework.[220] An issue which is highly disputed in EU legal doctrine is whether the balancing exercise imbued by the rule of reason also encompasses non-economic considerations; such debate has been nurtured by some isolated judgments of the Court, such as *Wouters* and *Meca-Medina*.[221]

Furthermore, next to the 'rule of reason' (or as part of it),[222] the Courts and the Commission have also developed the doctrine of 'ancillary restraints': restrictions

---

[219] For which, see the discussion in ch 5.

[220] The issue of the precise content and scope of the rule of reason doctrine cannot be tackled here. See, however, Joliet, R., *The Rule of Reason in Antitrust Law: American, German and Common Market Laws in Comparative* (The Hague: Martinus Nijhoff, 1967); Fasquelle, D., *Droit américain et droit communautaire des ententes: Etude de la règle de raison* (Paris: Joly, 1993); and more briefly, Steindorff, E., 'Article 85 and the Rule of Reason' (1984) 21 *CML Rev* 639–46; Korah, V., 'The Rise and Fall of Provisional Validity: The Need for a Rule of Reason in EEC Antitrust' (1981) 3 *Northwestern J Int L and Business* 320–57; see *contra* Whish, R., and Surfin, B., 'Article 85 and the Rule of Reason' (1987) 7 *YEL* 1–38; Black, O., 'Per Se Rules and Rules of Reason: What Are They?' (1997) 3 *Eur Competition L Rev* 289–94.

[221] For reasons of coherence, these cases will be examined in more detail under subheading B(5)c, despite the fact that they are technically part of an expanded 'rule of reason' doctrine.

[222] For a thorough presentation of the various doctrinal positions, see Werden, G., 'The Ancillary Restraints Doctrine' Paper presented in the ABA 54th Antitrust Law Spring Meeting (2006), also available at <http://www.abanet.org/antitrust/at-committees/at-s1/pdf/spring-materials/2006/werden06.pdf> (last accessed on 6 November 2011).

which are strictly necessary to the achievement of the main purpose of the agreement and proportionate thereto, are admitted. Especially used in the area of mergers, this doctrine has also been enshrined into successive Commission Notices.[223]

Furthermore, in order to be caught by Article 101(1), collusion needs to 'affect trade between member states'. If, however, the effect is not appreciable, then the prohibition of Article 101(1) will not apply. The *de minimis* doctrine was introduced into EU competition law by the CJEU as early as 1969 and has been fleshed out by successive Commission Notices.[224]

Moreover, the concept of concerted practice has, to some extent, been limited by the theory of oligopolistic interdependence. According to this theory, in oligopolistic markets, parallel pricing is only rational and may not, on its own, account for a concerted practice.[225] Despite the fact that this theory has been criticized both in economic terms,[226] as well as in competition law terms,[227] and that it has been very restrictively perceived by the Court,[228] the fact that it is up to the Commission to prove an alleged concerted practice does give some practical significance to this theory.

Similarly, in the framework of Article 102 TFEU, which prohibits the abuse of dominance, both the concept of dominance and that of abuse are flexible, subject to various—often pro-monopolistic—interpretations.[229] Dominance is questioned by the doctrine of contestability.[230] Abuse, for its part, may be refuted by the existence of some objective justification and/or on efficiency grounds,[231] despite the existence of some 'special responsibility' on the charge of dominant undertakings.[232]

---

[223] For the one currently in force, see Commission Notice on restrictions directly related and necessary to concentrations [2005] OJ C56/24.

[224] Case 5/69 *Franz Völk v S.P.R.L. Ets J. Vervaecke* [1969] ECR 295. See also the Commission Notice on agreements of minor importance which do not appreciably restrict competition under Article 81(1) of the Treaty establishing the European Community (*de minimis*) [2001] OJ C 368/13.

[225] Hall, R., and Hitch, C., 'Price Theory and Business Behaviour' (1939) 2 *Oxford Economic Papers* 12–45; Stigler, G., 'The Kinked Oligopoly Demand Curve' (1947) 55 *J of Political Economy* 431–9; Osborne, D. 'A Duopoly Price Game' (1974) 41 *Economica* 157–75; Bhaskar, V., 'The Kinked Demand Curve: A Game-Theoretic Approach' (1988) 6 *Int J of Ind Organization* 373–84.

[226] See eg Stigler, G., 1947, n 225.

[227] See eg Whish, R., *Competition Law*, 8th edn (Oxford: OUP, 2008) 547.

[228] See eg Case 48/69 *Imperial Chemical Industries (ICI) Ltd v Commission of the European Communities* [1972] ECR 619; Case 172/80 *Gerhard Züchner v Bayerische Vereinsbank AG* [1981] ECR 2021.

[229] See, in general, Joliet, R., *Monopolization and Abuse of a Dominant Position* (The Hague: Martinus Nijhoff, 1970).

[230] The most vocal promoters of the theory of contestable markets being Baumol, W.J., Panzar, J., and Willig, R., *Contestable Markets and the Theory of Industry Structure* (San Diego: Harcourt Brace Jovanovich, 1982). See also Bork, R.H., *The Antitrust Paradox: A Policy at War with Itself* (New York: Free Press, 1993).

[231] See Albors-Llorens, A., 'The Role of Objective Justification and Efficiencies in the Application of Article 82 EC' (2007) 48 *CML Rev* 1727–61; Lowenthal, P.J., 'The Defence of "Objective Justification" in the Application of Article 82' (2005) 28 *World Competition* 455–77; also Vickers, J., 'Abuse of Market Power' (2005) 115:504 *Economic J* F244–F261.

[232] For the existence of special responsibility, see Case 322/81 *NV Nederlandsche Banden Industrie Michelin v Commission of the European Communities* [1983] ECR 3461, para 57; Case T-51/89 *Tetra*

d. Competition rules—state aid

The *de minimis* principle is even more solidly embedded in state aid law than in Article 101 TFEU, since it is instituted through a formal Regulation.[233] Further, the Commission practice of Notices, Communications, block and individual exemptions, has prompted several authors to talk of a 'rule of reason' in the application of Article 107(1).[234]

More importantly, however, the Court has offered states a powerful instrument for sidestepping the application of the state aid rules altogether: the *Altmark* judgment.[235] The net effect of the *Altmark* rules is that money transfers to undertakings entrusted with a mission of general interest do not qualify *at all* as being aids; this is so provided four conditions are met, cumulatively: first, the recipient undertaking must actually have public service obligations to discharge, and the obligations must be clearly defined. Secondly, the parameters on the basis of which the compensation is calculated must be established in advance in an objective and transparent manner. Thirdly, the compensation cannot exceed what is necessary to cover all or part of the costs incurred in the discharge of the public service obligations, taking into account the relevant receipts and a reasonable profit. Finally, where the undertaking which is to discharge public service obligations is not chosen pursuant to a public procurement procedure, which would allow for the selection of the tenderer capable of providing those services at the least cost to the community, the level of compensation needed must be determined on the basis of an analysis of the costs which a typical undertaking, well run and adequately provided with means of transport, would have incurred.[236]

This is quite distinct from being exempted by virtue of either Articles 107(2) and (3) or Article 106(2) TFEU; the difference lies not only at the conceptual/theoretical level, but also at the practical/procedural one: such fund transfers need not be notified to the Commission. The four *Altmark* conditions have subsequently been softened by the General Court in *BUPA*.[237]

e. General assessment of the mitigating factors

The techniques used and the doctrines developed in the various areas of the law may correspond to different legal necessities and economic realities, but they can all

---

Pak Rausing SA v Commission of the European Communities [1990] ECR II-309, para 23; Case T-111/96 ITT *Promedia NV v Commission of the European Communities* [1998] ECR II-2937, para 138.

[233] Commission Regulation 69/2001/EC on the application of Articles 87 and 88 of the EC Treaty to *de minimis* aid [2001] OJ L10/30.

[234] Bartosch, A., 'Is There a Need for a Rule of Reason in European State Aid Law?: Or How to Arrive at a Coherent Concept of Material Selectivity?' (2010) 47 *CML Rev* 729–52.

[235] Case C-280/00 *Altmark* [2003] ECR I-7747; for this judgment and all its implications, see the discussion under subheading B(5)d.

[236] The excerpt reproduced here resumes recitals 89–93 of the Court's judgment and is taken from the Commission's '*Altmark* decision', Rec 4, for which see below in the following paragraphs.

[237] Case T-289/03 *BUPA* [2008] ECR II-81.

influence the economic/non-economic service dilemma. The remoteness doctrine may allow states to keep their less mercantilist regulations away from EU scrutiny. The rule of reason, the contestability theory, the doctrine of oligopolistic interdependence, and other notions in the field of competition law may offer precious instruments in order to moderate the impact of the relevant rules on economic sectors which had previously been considered as non-economic.

From a normative point of view, all the instruments discussed above serve the same function: they fend off the EU rules, thus mitigating their impact on the regulatory freedom of states and the contractual autonomy of undertakings. They operate *ex ante*, when the respective scope of action of the EU and its member states is defined. In this, they are different from exceptions, which operate *ex post*, once it has been determined that the EU rules are, in principle, applicable. Such a distinction, however, is not always completely clear in relation to the competition rules.

5. Exceptions—general

All four categories of rules examined here are subject to exceptions, express or judge-made. This is not the place to develop a general theory of exceptions to the Treaty rules. It is, however, useful to examine briefly how such exceptions may be used in order to draw the line between economic and non-economic activities.

a. Free movement

The express exceptions of Articles 36, 45(3), and 52 TFEU to the free movement rules exclude from the scope of the free movement rules measures which are justified on public policy, security, and health grounds. Therefore, state measures connected to the core state functions, irrespective of whether they qualify as economic or not, are excluded from the Treaty rule by virtue of an express exception. Although express exceptions have on the whole been interpreted in a restrictive way by the Court, public health has been considerably expanded in the last years.[238] Therefore, even if the provision of social healthcare services has qualified as an economic activity, restrictions thereto have been upheld on public health grounds.

Moreover, among the overriding reasons of public interest (ORPIs) admitted by the Court as valid reasons for curbing the Treaty provisions on free movement, the 'financial balance' justification offers yet another ground for upholding national measures which are necessary for maintaining economically non-viable activities, such as healthcare, social security, and the like.[239]

---

[238] For the developments relevant to this ground, see ch 4.

[239] In general, for judge-made exceptions to the free movement of services, including services of a non-economic nature, see Fernandez Martin, J.M., and O'Leary, S., 'Judicial exceptions to the free provision of services' in Andenas, M., and Roth W.H. (eds), *Services and Free Movement in EU Law* (Oxford: OUP, 2002) 163–95.

b. Public procurement

For the exceptions, exclusions, and gradations applicable to the procurement regime, reference should be made to the developments discussed above.[240]

c. Competition rules—private conduct

Article 101(3) TFEU formally introduces exceptions to the application of Article 101(1) TFEU. These, however, to the extent that they are intended to cover conduct already falling under Article 101(1) are of little help in the distinction between economic and non-economic activities.

More interesting for the purposes of the present study is the broad 'rule of reason' approach developed by the Court, encompassing not only considerations of economic welfare, but more generally, reasons of general interest. This rule of reason approach does not operate within Article 101(3) TFEU, but in the framework of Article 101(1) TFEU and technically results in Article 101 TFEU being inapplicable as a whole. Therefore, it should have been dealt with in the previous section, together with other 'mitigating factors'. The reason why it is presented here is because of the nature of the reasons which are taken into account: they would qualify as ORPIs under free movement law.

This broad 'rule of reason' approach has been launched by the Court in *Wouters*.[241] In this case, concerning a Dutch rule precluding lawyers from founding integrated firms with accountants, the Court, having found that all the usual conditions for the application of the competition rules were present, held that some agreements or decisions of associations of undertakings may fall outside Article 101(1) TFEU, in view of their 'context':[242] the objective of securing the sound administration of justice and of protecting consumers could justify restrictions to competition, flowing from the organization and the qualifications requirements that a decision of the Association may include. Further on, in the same judgment, the Court found that exactly the same reasons could justify an eventual violation of the free movement rules concerning establishment and services. In other words, the Court held that the ORPIs related to professional ethics, etc—already recognized as such since the *Van Binsbergen* case[243]—which serve to *justify* restrictions to free movement also serve to *exclude* altogether the application of the competition rules.

This remarkable judgment stood isolated for some time, until the Full Court confirmed it and expanded on it in *Meca-Medina*, a case in which the International Olympic Committee's rules on doping had been held to qualify as a decision of an association of undertakings. The Court confirmed that in the framework of Article 101(1), the context of the collusion needs to be taken into account, referring in

---

[240] See the discussion in subsection B(4)b.
[241] Case C-309/99 *Wouters* [2002] ECR I-1577.
[242] Ibid, para 97.
[243] Case 33/74 *van Binsbergen* [1974] ECR 1299.

particular to the objectives of the conduct examined: in this case, it was 'the need to safeguard equal chances for athletes, athletes' health, the integrity and objectivity of competitive sport and ethical values in sport'.[244] The Court further explained that the concomitant restrictive effects should be tested as to whether they are 'inherent' (ie necessary) and proportionate to the objectives pursued.[245]

The above cases support the idea that, not only do the ORPIs recognized under free movement law also apply as a rule of reason in the framework of Article 101(1), but also that they are subject to the well-known conditions of necessity and proportionality.

d. State aid rules

Article 107(2) deems state aid which either has a social character or compensates for natural disasters to be compatible with the common market.[246] Article 107(3) foresees categories of aids which may be approved by the Commission, on an individual basis: a. for areas facing special difficulties, b. for the promotion of projects of European interest,[247] c. for certain economic activities or areas, d. for culture and heritage, and e. other exceptions specified by the Council on a proposal from the Commission. Moreover, the Commission, upon delegation from the Council,[248] has adopted block exemption regulations (BERs) concerning aid to small and medium-sized enterprises (SMEs),[249] training aid,[250] aid for employment,[251] and national regional investment aid.[252] Therefore, states do have the opportunity to fund activities which are not viable in strictly commercial terms and get individual exemptions.

6. Services of general economic interest as an exception: Article 106(2) TFEU

Article 106(2) TFEU is yet another exception to the Treaty rules.[253] By the same token, however, it has historically been the first and still is the only Treaty provision

---

[244] Case C-519/04P *Meca-Medina* [2006] ECR I-6991, para 43.

[245] Ibid, para 42.

[246] There is also a third ground, which, however, is likely to be repealed after 2014: aid justified by the unification of Germany.

[247] A possibility mostly used to curb the effects of the 2008 financial crisis; see in more detail, Gebski, S., 'Competition First? Application of State Aid Rules in the Banking Sector' (2009) 6 *Competition L Rev* 89–115.

[248] Council Regulation 994/98/EC on the application of Articles 92 and 93 of the Treaty establishing the European Community to certain categories of horizontal State aid [1998] OJ L142/1.

[249] Commission Regulation 70/2001/EC on the application of Articles 87 and 88 of the EC Treaty to State aid to small and medium-sized enterprises [2001] OJ L10/33.

[250] Commission Regulation 68/2001/EC on the application of Articles 87 and 88 of the EC Treaty to training aid [2001] OJ L10/20.

[251] Commission Regulation 2204/2002/EC on the application of Articles 87 and 88 of the EC Treaty to State aid for employment [2002] OJ L 337/3.

[252] Commission Regulation 1628/2006/EC on the application of Articles 87 and 88 of the Treaty to national regional investment aid [2006] OJ L302/29.

[253] The text of Article 106(2) is as follows: 'Undertakings entrusted with the operation of services of general economic interest or having the character of a revenue-producing monopoly shall be subject to

introducing a material rule in favour of activities which, while being of an economic nature, should not be fully subject to market forces. This is why it is examined separately here. Despite the fact that Article 106 TFEU is located within the Treaty rules on competition, it has been constantly understood by the Court—in accordance with its wording—to offer an exception to all Treaty rules.

a. Free movement

The Court has held that Article 106(2) TFEU may justify restrictions to Article 37 TFEU, on the prohibition of commercial monopolies in relation to the free movement of goods.[254] Further, the Court held that restrictions to Article 56 TFEU may also be justified by virtue of Article 106(2) TFEU. This was expressly stated for the first time in *Corsica Ferries France*, concerning specific mooring arrangements for vessels entering Italian ports.[255] However, in this case, the Court held the Italian measure to be justified not only on the basis of the public service mission at stake, under Article 106(2) TFEU, but also on the need to preserve public security, presumably under Article 52 TFEU. More recently, the Court confirmed beyond any doubt that Article 106(2) TFEU may be used as a valid justification for violations of the rules on services in *Deutsche Post*.[256] It held that, in view of the specific mission accomplished by the incumbent monopolist, an alleged violation of Articles 56 *junto* 102 TFEU could be justified by Article 106(2) TFEU.

b. Public procurement

Given that public procurement rules and principles specifically apply to 'public' services, not provided within normal market conditions, Article 106(2) should, in principle, not allow for exceptions to them. Indeed, the special nature of the activity is already taken into account when an entity qualifies as a 'contracting authority', thus making the procurement rules applicable in the first place. It would seem redundant, or even counter-productive, that this same element be considered again in order to set aside the procurement rules.

There is, however, an isolated case where this has happened. In *Ambulanz Glöckner*, the Court was asked to rule on the application of Article 106(2) TFEU in relation to ambulance service authorizations being awarded and not tendered.[257] The Court accepted the argument that emergency transport services, which require costly investments in equipment and qualified personnel may only be financially

---

the rules contained in the Treaties, in particular to the rules on competition, in so far as the application of such rules does not obstruct the performance, in law or in fact, of the particular tasks assigned to them. The development of trade must not be affected to such an extent as would be contrary to the interests of the Union.'

[254] Case C-157/94 *Commission v Netherlands (electricity import exclusivity)* [1997] ECR I-5699.
[255] Case C-266/96 *Corsica Ferries France* [1998] ECR I-3949.
[256] Joined cases C-147 & 148/97 *Deutsche Post* [2000] ECR I-825.
[257] Case C-455/99 *Glöckner* [2001] ECR I-8089.

viable if the same entity also enjoys special rights to non-emergency transport.[258] Implicitly the Court accepted that, in exceptional circumstances, not only is it impossible to have competition *in* the market, but also competition *for* the market—and thus competition is *altogether excluded*.

Glöckner, however, is the only case in which Article 106(2) has been successfully pleaded in order to avoid the application of the procurement rules. It should be noted that it was decided before the public procurement principles had been fleshed out by the Court; it is, therefore, likely to remain no more than an isolated occurrence. More recently, in *Commission v Germany (old-age insurance)*,[259] the Court confirmed that no activity, as such, justifies that the procurement rules and principles be left without application. Therefore, it is highly unlikely that the *Glöckner* carve-out will be applied in the future.

c. *Competition rules—private conduct*

Article 106(2) was clearly intended to justify exceptions to the competition rules and, accordingly, this is the area in which it has been most often applied.

In a number of cases, the Court has positively applied Article 106(2) TFEU, holding that an exclusive or special right was required for the undertaking in question to perform the universal services under economically acceptable conditions.[260] This body of case law was initiated with the judgment in *Corbeau*, where the Court made clear that the *effet utile* of Article 102 TFEU did not preclude member states from attributing exclusive rights, to the extent 'necessary to ensure the performance of the particular tasks assigned to the undertakings possessed of the exclusive rights [sic]'.[261]

Corbeau was considered to be a breakthrough case: not only did it put a brake to the liberalization/deregulation frenzy of its era, but it also legitimized the award of exclusive rights further than was strictly necessary: the holder of the exclusive rights was entitled to 'have the benefit of economically acceptable conditions'.[262] It introduced, however, an important limitation: 'the exclusion of competition is not justified as regards specific services dissociable from the service of general interest which meet special needs of economic operators and which call for certain additional services not offered by the [holder of the exclusive rights]'.[263] This

---

[258] Ibid, para 61.

[259] Case C-271/08 *Commission v Germany (old-age insurance)* [2010] nyr.

[260] In all these cases, the Court accepted the argument that the exclusive right protected the undertaking in question against the risk of cream-skimming, leaving them with the least profitable services. See Case C-320/91 *Corbeau* [1993] ECR I-2533; Case C-393/92 *Almelo* [1994] ECR I-1477; Case C-67/96 *Albany* [1999] ECR I-5751; Joined cases C-147 & 148/97 *Deutsche Post* [2000] ECR I-825; Case C-244/94 *FFSA* [1995] ECR I-4013.

[261] Case C-320/91 *Corbeau*, n 260, para 14.

[262] Ibid, para 16; in later Commission texts, it was explained that this included not only return on capital, but also reasonable benefit (see December 2005/842 [2005] OJ L312/67, as well as the Community Framework for State Aid in the Form of Public Service Compensation [2005] OJ C297/4).

[263] Ibid, para 19.

'severability' test was expressed in quite restrictive terms in the case, though its actual application was left to the national court.

The *Corbeau* conditions have been further eased, to the benefit of member states, in *Glöckner*, in two ways. *First*, in this case, concerning emergency and non-emergency ambulance services, the Court itself applied the severability test in quite a relaxed way: it was easily satisfied that the two kinds of services were not severable and that both could be reserved to the benefit of same undertaking.[264] *Secondly*, the Court, for the first time, admitted that the SGI justifying the award of special/exclusive rights is not just any (rudimentary or minimal) service, but may be characterized by 'quality and reliability'.[265]

d. Competition law—state aid

Since the state aid rules do provide for both activity- and area-specific exceptions (Articles 107(2) and (3) TFEU), for which the Commission may issue block exemption regulations and since the Council may create further exceptions to Article 107(1) TFEU, the utility of Article 106(2) TFEU is not altogether clear in the area of state aids. This notwithstanding, the Court in *FFSA*, concerning a tax break in favour of the French La Poste, held Article 106(2) TFEU to offer a valid ground for exception to the application of Article 107 TFEU.[266] This was confirmed by subsequent judgments[267] and has been officially acknowledged by the Commission in its Community Framework for State Aid.[268] According to this last document, state aid under Article 106(2) TFEU need be notified and may be declared compatible by the Commission.

The need for notification is one important point which differentiates Article 106 (2) TFEU from the *Altmark* case law. In contrast, it has been put forward that the Article 106(2) TFEU exception is more lenient than *Altmark* in that it does not need to meet the fourth *Altmark* condition, ie the efficient cost criterion.[269] It should be noted that given the approach of the General Court in *BUPA*, this distinction may be of limited importance. In any case, both these grounds for not applying the state aid rules are further distinguished from the Articles 107(2) and (3) TFEU exceptions, to the extent that the more refined economic approach introduced by the 2005 State Aid Action Plan only applies to the latter.[270]

---

[264] Case C-455/99 *Glöckner* [2001] ECR I-8089, para 60.
[265] Ibid, para 61.
[266] Case T-106/95 *FFSA* [1997] ECR II-229, para 178.
[267] Case T-46/97 *Sociedade Independente de Comunicação (SIC) SA v Commission of the European Communities* [2000] ECR II-2125; Case C-332/98 *French Republic v Commission of the European Communities (CELF)* [2000] ECR I-4833; Joined cases C-83/01 P, 93 & 94/01 P *Chronopost SA, La Poste and French Republic v Union française de l'express (Ufex), DHL International, Federal express international (France) SNC and CRIE SA* [2003] ECR I-4777.
[268] Framework, 2005, n 262.
[269] See Fiedziuk, N., 'Towards a More Refined Economic Approach to Services of General Economic Interest' (2010) 16 *Eur P L* 271–88, at 277.
[270] Ibid.

e. *General assessment of Article 106(2)*[271]

It has been demonstrated that Article 106(2) has come to be applied in all four sectors under review. It has been shown that its application in the field of public procurement is superfluous, if not counter-productive, and should remain marginal. Further, to the extent that the 'financial equilibrium' ORPI is developed within free movement law, it is unclear what role is left, if any, for Article 106(2) TFEU. Thirdly, in the field of state aid, where non-economic considerations may be taken into account already in the context of the Treaty-based exceptions (Articles 107(2) and (3) TFEU), and where the *Altmark exclusion* operates broadly along the same lines as Article 106(2) TFEU *exception*, the functions left for Article 106(2) TFEU remain elusive. Even in the area primarily contemplated by Article 106(2) TFEU, that of competition law, its usefulness could be questioned, especially in view of the existence of other mitigating factors and the recognition of a broader rule of reason, in *Wouters* and *Meca-Medina*.[272]

These considerations have led G. Davies to comment that Article 106 'is a messy article, full of ambiguities, which has become redundant, and is now positively malignant'; and in a more dramatic way, that 'this leaves Article [106] as an unnecessary Cassandra, promising protection from threats that do not exist, slandering economic law with the implication that it takes no account of the public interest, and trying to recreate old divisions between the economic and the social. The Treaty, and society, would be better if it was gone'.[273] Provocative as they might be, these comments seem to accord with preceding analysis.[274] They tend to ignore, however, the historical and declaratory role played by Article 106 TFEU. It should be remembered that the first and, for many years, only, reference to SGEIs—and to the fact that they may have a role to play in the application of the Treaty rules—was to be found in (what is now) Article 106. If anything, this reference has created a conceptual tool (SGEIs) that armed the Commission, and the IGC negotiating the successive Treaty modifications. For instance, it has served as a guide to the Commission's legislative ventures in the area of network industries and the concept of universal service, as well as in its political explorations through the various neighbouring concepts: SGI, SGEI and SSGI. It has also offered a solid instrument to the Court to keep under control the liberalization frenzy of the

---

[271] The analysis here is broadly based on Davies, G., 'What does Article 86 actually do?' in Krajewski, M., Neergard, U., and van de Gronden, J. (eds), *The Changing Legal Framework for Services of General Interest* (The Hague: TMC Asser Press, 2009) 51–67.

[272] See the analysis under subheading B(5)c.

[273] Davies, G., 2009, n 271, at 51 and 67, respectively.

[274] See, however, for a fundamentally different assessment, Sauter, W., 'Services of General Economic Interest and Universal Service in EU law' (2008) 33 *EL Rev* 176–93, at 174, where he states: 'as before, Art 86(2) [now 106(2)] remains key'. Along the same lines, see Neergaard, U., 'Services of general (economic) interest: what aims and values count?' in Neergaard, U., Nielsen, R., and Roseberry, L. (eds), *Integrating Welfare Functions into EU Law* (Copenhagen: DJØF Publishing, 2009) 191–224, at 206, where she finds that 'in any event, Article 86(2) [now 106(2)] will remain of central importance'.

1990s. The provision provided negotiators and stakeholders with a sound legal argument for insisting on the inclusion of SGEIs in the Charter of Fundamental Rights and the Treaty of Lisbon.

It is true that now, after the entry into force of the Treaty of Lisbon, with Article 16, Protocol No. 26 and the Charter having binding force, Article 106(2) may be the source of more problems than it resolves. Until such time, however, as the new provisions are interpreted by the Court and applied by the Commission, Article 106(2) offers welcome, no matter how imperfect, legal predictability.

C. Conclusion

Three points emerge from the analysis above.

First, from an institutional point of view, the analysis has shown that a clear antagonistic relationship may be identified between the Commission on the one hand, and the member states on the other. Indeed, it has been observed that, starting with the 1996 Communication on SGIs, the Commission has steadily moved the borders between the economic and the non-economic sphere in favour of the former. It was also noted that liberalization of the network-based industries and the effort, coordinated at the EU level, to secure 'universal service' have awakened consciousness of the importance of SGIs and of the need to adopt a coherent regulatory approach toward them. This explains an apparent contradiction: the more the process of liberalization advances and the Commission pushes, through soft law, the expansion of the scope of application of the Treaty rules, the more the member states tend to recognize an EU competence in this field to act also through hard law. In other words, the Commission's activity in this field increases awareness of the problems raised and offers conceptual tools (mainly the distinction between SGI and NESGI) which allow for the adoption of more binding texts and puts the pressure on member states to 'repatriate' from the Commission to the Council (and the European Parliament) competences which traditionally belong to member states. In this game the Court has acted as a referee and, although verbally promoting an expansive vision of the EU (and its own) competences, materially, it has regularly upheld member states' choices in respect of the organization of SGI. It is interesting to note, however, that the Court's activity is perceived unevenly by public opinion and the media: while judgments like *Viking* and *Laval* attract great attention (essentially as being over-intrusive), pronouncements of equal importance which recognize member states' leeway to organize their social sphere, such as *Glöckner, Altmark* or *BUPA*, only receive limited coverage. Against this background, the effects of the triple constitutionalization of SGIs in the Lisbon Treaty, in particular of the clear reserve in favour of member states in relation to NESGIs (Protocol No. 26) and the express competence of the EU in relation to SGEIs (Article 14(2) TFEU) still need to materialize.

Secondly, from a normative perspective, the above reinstatement of SGIs at the EU level makes clear that SGIs will, henceforth, be a policy component to be taken into account in all EU decision making. Irrespective of whether a 'streamlining' obligation results as legally binding from the Lisbon Treaty,[275] the triple constitutionalization of SGIs and the political and doctrinal debate around it, have made it clear that SGIs are a constant feature of the political debate. For one thing, if the EU is to achieve any level of substantial cohesion between its different member states and regions, for the economy to develop as a level playing field, SGIs must be given an important role. Moreover, in a framework of high unemployment and ageing populations, in which the EU's impact is felt outside the mere economic sphere, the EU's capacity to take account of the citizen's needs is a condition for its credibility as a political entity. In this sense, sustainable solutions securing the provision of SGIs appear as a condition for further EU integration. EU action in the field of SGIs may, further, be a means of forging new bonds of solidarity operating in a non-national framework; in this sense, SGI regulation could become a core element of strengthening European citizenship and Europe as a polity.[276]

Thirdly, however, the first two considerations should not mask the fact that the core competence for the provision of SGIs still lies with member states.

Indeed, EU rules result in a rationalization of the way SGIs are operated: by asking why such or such a service need qualify as a SG(E)I, by examining alternative ways for its provision (in the framework of the proportionality test), by demanding that all SGIs satisfy some core conditions, by requiring the cost to be calculated and itemized in an objective manner, by requiring that *ex ante* cost calculation methods are developed and that entities offering SGIs should do so in an economically sound manner, by instituting the public procurement rules and transforming them into generally applicable principles (based on non-discrimination), the EU creates a framework whereby member states are 'forced' to rationalize century long practices, often dictated by ill-defined interests and regulatory capture. In this sense, EU law acts as a means of improving national governance of SGIs.

But there is also a flip side to this. EU law tends to reason in terms of *services* of general interest and to examine the merits of each one of them individually. Member states, on the other hand, are not running mere services (healthcare, educational, etc), but *systems*. The shift of attention from *systems* (at the national

---

[275] Idea put forward, inter alia, by Wernicke, S., 'Taking stock: the EU institutions and services of general economic interest' in Krajewski, M., Neergard, U., and van de Gronden, J. (eds), *The Changing Legal Framework for Services of General Interest* (The Hague: TMC Asser Press, 2009) 69–79; see also Wernicke, S., 'Services of general economic interest in European law: solidarity embedded in the Economic Constitution' in van de Gronden, J. (ed), *EU and WTO Law on Services: Limits to the Realization of General Interest Policies within the Services Markets?* (Alphen aan den Rijn: Kluwer Law International, 2009) 121–37.

[276] See, inter alia, Dougan, M., 'The spatial restructuring of national welfare states within the EU: the contribution of Union citizenship and the relevance of the Treaty of Lisbon' in Neergaard, U., Roseberry, L., and Nielsen, R. (eds), *Integrating Welfare Functions into EU law: From Rome to Lisbon* (Copenhagen: DJØF Publishing, 2009) 147–87; and in a more general manner, on the relationship between SGIs and citizenship, see Swiatkowski, A.M., 'EU citizenship and the rights of access for welfare state: a comparison with welfare rights guaranteed by the Council of Europe as seen from the perspective of a new member state' in Neergaard, U., Roseberry, L., and Nielsen, R. (eds), *Integrating Welfare Functions into EU Law: From Rome to Lisbon* (Copenhagen: DJØF Publishing, 2009) 123–46.

level) to *services* (at the EU level) without any effort to integrate the latter into the former may prove a powerful means of deconstructing national systems. By itself this is not a catastrophic consequence, as long as the faltering national *systems* are gradually replaced by a supra- or infra- national framework for the provision of well-articulated *services* of general interest. But will such a replacement take place?

3

Restrictions

Regulation is not an end in itself; it is only desirable to the extent that it is necessary for the achievement of a further end. The discussion in chapter 1 has indicated several reasons justifying regulation.[1] In addition to those reasons, there is yet another which is specific to the EU context: the need to eliminate restrictions to the operation of the internal market. This is achieved through regulation at the EU—and not the member state—level. Accordingly the identification of restrictions to the free movement of services within the EU, generated by national measures, becomes a fundamental aspect of understanding the EU's regulatory activity in the field (A). Once the legal basis of the 'right to regulate' is thus grounded, it becomes crucial to explore the main qualitative characteristics of restrictions (B), in order to assess, at a later stage, the regulatory means that are best suited to tackle them.

A. Restrictions: the criteria

1. Theoretical foundations

Restrictions are identified by the Court in the course of litigation proceedings; such proceedings are either initiated by private parties before national courts (Article 267 TFEU), or brought directly before the European Court by the Commission (Article 258 TFEU). Either way, the identification of restrictions operates *reactively (ex post)*, after the regulations concerned have produced their restrictive effects. During the last two decades, however, the obligation of notification of technical measures, imposed on national authorities by Directive 98/34[2] and extended by Article 15(7) of the Services Directive,[3] has allowed for a *proactive (ex ante)* examination of restrictions; in this framework, the burden to locate and eliminate restrictions has been shifted from the Court to the Commission.

---

[1] It is worth recalling that these reasons vary depending on whether one follows a Public Interest, a Private Interest or an Institutionalist approach, but no matter the vision adopted, the need for (more or less) regulation is a common ground.

[2] European Parliament and Council Directive 98/34/EC laying down a procedure for the provision of information in the field of technical standards and regulations [1998] OJ L204/37; this Directive repealed the Council Directive 83/189/EEC laying down a procedure for the provision of information in the field of technical standards and regulations [1989] OJ L43/56; its scope was extended by the European Parliament and Council Directive 98/48/EC [1998] OJ L217/18 to cover information society services.

[3] European Parliament and Council Directive 2006/123/EC on services in the internal market [2006] OJ L376/36.

In identifying restrictions to free movement, and irrespective of their diverging agendas, the Commission and Court are guided by the same constitutional and institutional constraints: they need to develop a coherent test in order to enhance legal certainty, while at the same time, respecting the basic competence divide between the EU and its member states (a). Indeed, these problems took a long gestation period and some vacillation to overcome (b)—but it seems that, now, the criteria to characterize a measure as a restriction to the free movement of services are crystallizing (c).

a. The stakes

i. Vertical competence share—subsidiarity

Economic activity is, in principle, regulated at the national level. An increasing number of rules, however, especially in the area of services, stem from multilateral (eg the GATS), plurilateral (eg the WTO public procurement agreement), or bilateral international agreements, as well as from the rules and standards derived from the application of such agreements;[4] other less formalized regulatory processes also play their role (eg the Basel rules on banking supervision). Such rules, however, are only seldom directly applicable, and are typically mediated through regulations internal to each signatory state. Technically, therefore, the states remain the masters of economic regulation.

This notwithstanding, EU member states' regulation should respect the objective of free movement within the EU.[5] As soon as any piece of national regulation raises obstacles to free movement, the issue becomes 'EU relevant' and the member state's competence is put into question. The state concerned may be required to alter its regulation or, at least, by virtue of the supremacy of EU law, to refrain from applying it. In cases where the above is not possible or is judged insufficient, the EU may choose to regulate instead, provided an adequate legal basis is to be found in the Treaty. In this way, the EU amends national rules and pre-empts member states from future regulation in the same field.

In other words, the identification of a restriction is the first logical step for a competence shift, away from the member states and in favour of the EU. Therefore, the identification of a restriction to free movement has clear constitutional implications within the EU.[6] In the words of J. Snell and M. Andenas:[7]

---

[4] See Bernstein, S., and Hannah, E., 'Non-State Global Standard Setting and the WTO: Legitimacy and the Need for Regulatory Space' (2008) 11 *J of Int Economic L* 575–608.

[5] This is true both for policy areas which fall within the EU competences and for areas which lie outside the scope of the EU powers, such as education (see eg Case C-274/05 *Commission v Greece (university degrees)* [2008] ECR I-7969 and Case C-318/05 *Commission v Germany (school fees)* [2007] ECR I-6957) or taxation (see eg Case C-153/08 *Commission v Spain (gambling tax)* [2009] ECR I-9735).

[6] The same can hardly be said in respect to other international organizations, including the WTO, since these are typically confined to negative integration measures and may not adopt legislation replacing and pre-empting that of signatory states.

[7] Snell, J. and Andenas, M., 'Exploring the outer limits: restrictions on the free movement' in Andenas, M., and Roth, W.H. (eds), *Services and Free Movement in EU Law* (Oxford: OUP, 2002) 69–139, 83; see also Snell, J., 'Who's Got the Power? Free Movement and Allocation of Competences in EC Law' (2003) 22 *YEL* 323–51.

'[w]hen the Court decides that a Member State measure constitutes a *prima facie* restriction on the freedom, it allocates the competence to regulate to the Community and, thus, supports, the centralization argument. If a national measure is held to be within the scope of the free provisions, its abolition or harmonization becomes necessary for the establishment of the internal market and the Community gains the competence to act.

Furthermore, the measure is seen as a restriction and thus harmonization becomes a natural, not merely a possible, policy option ... Thus, national regulation is seen only as a temporary stopgap solution pending Community action.'

Therefore, the identification of restrictions to free movement, while being a technical preliminary to the judicial resolution of disputes, is also inherently connected to the constitutional operation of the EU and the vertical allocation of powers.[8] Thus, in addition to the technical question concerning the way in which the principle of subsidiarity should apply in this area of EU law, other, more political issues are also raised.

ii. Extent of harmonization—regulatory competition

Federal systems, as well as the EU, entail regulatory competition.[9] This has its pros and cons, but is an inescapable feature of any system bringing together different legal orders.[10] Regulatory competition is the starting point and, depending on the vision adopted, often the 'default' basis on which such systems are meant to operate. Harmonization, on the other hand, is the end of the 'regulatory trip': it replaces regulatory competition and diversity with homogeneity and legal certainty. Regulatory competition ends where harmonization starts and, indeed, the former often leads to the latter.

Neither of these two regulatory options is inherently good or bad. Depending on the viewpoint adopted, both regulatory competition and harmonization constitute at the same time both the problem and the solution. It is clear, however, that the way restrictions are defined plays a decisive role in defining the mixture between the two. If mere differences between national regulations automatically qualify as restrictions, then regulatory competition is seen as a problem and harmonization will dominate the regulatory scene. If, on the other hand, different regulations are tolerated (even encouraged) and are generally made to work together, through coordination, mutual recognition, administrative cooperation, or other means,

---

[8] See also Weiler, J.H.H., 'The constitution of the common market place: text and context in the evolution of the free movement of goods' in Craig, P., and de Búrca, G. (eds), *The Evolution of EU Law* (Oxford: OUP, 1999) 349–76; van Gerven, W., 'Constitutional aspects of the European Court's case-law on Articles 30 and 36 EC as compared with the U.S. Dormant Commerce Clause' in Dony, M., and de Walsche, A. (eds), *Mélanges en Hommage à Michel Waelbroeck, Vol. II* (Bruxelles: Bruylant, 1999) 1629–44.

[9] For a brief presentation of the essentials of 'regulatory competition' and of the relevant literature, see the discussion in ch 1.

[10] See Reich, N., 'Competition between Legal Orders: A New Paradigm of Law (1992) 29 *CML Rev* 861–96; Barnard, C., and Deakin, S., 'Market access and regulatory competition' in Barnard, C., and Scott, J. (eds), *The Law of the Single European Market: Unpacking the Premises* (Oxford/Portland: Hart Publishing, 2002) 197–224, also available as Jean Monnet Working Paper No. 9/2001, at <http://www.jeanmonnetprogram.org/papers/01/012701.html> (last accessed on 7 November 2011); Snell, J., 2003, n 7.

then harmonization will be less extensive and regulatory competition shall continue to play a decisive role.

iii. Regulatory identity of the EU—the extent of regulatory substitution

A further issue, connected to the previous one, is that the definition of 'restrictions' has a direct bearing on the kind of regulatory activity undertaken by the EU. Indeed, if any national measure having some effect on trade were to qualify as a restriction—and is to be eventually harmonized—then the EU would be transformed into a super-state, substituting its own rules to those of its members. Such an approach raises all sorts of problems, not least in terms of the legitimacy and efficiency of the EU's actions. These problems are exacerbated whenever—as most often happens—the identification of a restriction is not followed by a measure of positive integration: the EU judiciary second-guesses the regulatory choices of elected national legislatures, without, nonetheless, a substitute regulation being adopted at the EU level.

If, on the other hand, 'restrictions' were confined to openly discriminatory measures and to measures whose aim is clearly protectionist, such a vision would neglect the complexity of regulation and would allow for an important amount of national undercover protectionism to persist, thus significantly undermining the single market project.

iv. Promotion of legal certainty—floodgates

A very wide definition of 'restrictions' essentially constitutes a call to litigate. Litigation hardly serves legal certainty, especially in the EU context.

First, a wide definition would encourage individuals who feel they can resist any national measure which is unfavourable to their plans. At the same time, a wide definition would considerably limit the regulatory options available to the national or regional regulator. The regulator, however, is supposed to be pursuing the general (or at least majoritorian) interest, while the individuals their own. A situation where the regulator is stripped of all its discretion and is under a constant obligation to observe individual interests runs against the very purpose of regulation. It may also be economically counter-productive, politically unacceptable, and anti-democratic.

Secondly, a wide definition of restrictions, covering all measures with some impact on trade even if they pursue a valid objective, would necessarily call for a wide application of the principle of proportionality. Nonetheless, this principle is by nature quite imprecise and flexible, counter-productive for legal certainty.[11]

Thirdly, the first two issues become all the more salient in a context where the control of national regulatory measures is not confined to a single judge—as is the case for constitutionality control at the national level—but to all sorts of jurisdictions (civil, criminal, administrative), of all levels (from stand-alone judges to supreme national jurisdictions), in 27 member states (as a national measure

---

[11] For a more detailed discussion of the content and the limits of proportionality, see ch 4.

affecting exports may be judged for its compatibility with EU law by the courts of the importing state). The occasional, often erratic, directions given by the CJEU do not necessarily enhance or clarify this background.

b. Evolution—benchmark judgments

The definition of restrictions to trade in services has been—and still is, despite the adoption of the Services Directive—an issue for the CJEU. Despite being a late-starter in the Court's case law, services have, in some respects, paved the way for judicial developments in other fields of the law. Therefore, while it is true that the first ever judgment of the Court on services was *Sacchi*, delivered as late as 1974, it was only a few months later in *Van Binsbergen* that the Court set the foundations of the principle of mutual recognition;[12] no less than five years before the judgment in *Cassis de Dijon* and the launch of the principle of mutual recognition by the relevant Commission Communication.[13] It was also with its 1991 judgments in *Säger* and the *Dutch TV* cases that the Court explicitly recognized that it is not only in the field of goods that non-discriminatory measures may violate EU law;[14] a few years later, the Court confirmed this approach in relation to services while bringing its services case law into alignment with its case law in the field of establishment and workers.[15]

Several authors have been tempted to present the Court's free movement case law in an evolutionary perspective. J. Weiler, for instance, distinguishes five broad periods:[16] a. the heroic, foundational period, when the Court set the grand principles with judgments such as *Dassonville, Van Binsbergen*, etc;[17] b. the consolidation period, starting with *Cassis de Dijon*,[18] when the excesses of the previous approach have been tempered essentially through the principle of mutual recognition and the development of overriding reasons of public interest (ORPIs); c. the legislative period, boosted by the Single European Act, the 1985 'new approach',

---

[12] Case 155/73 *Giuseppe Sacchi* [1974] ECR 409; Case 33/74 *Johannes Hervicus Maria van Binsbergen v Bestuur van de Bedrijfsvereniging voor de Metaalnijverheid* [1974] ECR 1299.

[13] Case 120/78 *Rewe-Zentral AG v Bundesmonopolverwaltung für Branntwein (Cassis de Dijon)* [1979] ECR 649. See also the *Cassis de Dijon* interpretative Communication [1980] OJ C256/2.

[14] Case C-76/90 *Säger v Dennemeyer & Co. Ltd* [1991] ECR I-4221; Case C-288/89 *Stichting Collectieve Antennevoorziening Gouda v Commissariaat voor de Media* [1991] ECR I-4007 and Case C-353/89 *Commission v Netherlands (Mediawet)* [1991] ECR I-4069.

[15] See, for services, Case C-384/93 *Alpine Investments v Minister van Financiën* [1995] ECR I-1141; for establishment, Case C-55/94 *Reinhard Gebhard v Consiglio dell' Ordine degli Avvocati e Procuratori di Milano* [1995] ECR I-4165; for workers, Case C-415/93 *Union royale belge des sociétés de football association ASBL v Jean-Marc Bosman, Royal club liégeois SA v Jean-Marc Bosman and others and Union des associations européennes de football (UEFA) v Jean-Marc Bosman* [1995] ECR I-4921. On the convergence of freedoms, see, among many, Hatzopoulos, V., 'Trente ans après les arrêts fondamentaux de 1974, les quatre libertés: quatre?' in Demaret, P., Govaere, I., and Hanf, D. (eds), *30 Years of European Legal Studies at the College of Europe—30 ans d'études juridiques européennes au Collège d'Europe: Liber Professorum 1973/74–2003/04* (Brussels: Peter Lang, 2005) 185–201; and more recently, Tryfonidou, A., 'Further Steps on the Road to Convergence Among the Market Freedoms' (2010) 35 *EL Rev* 36–56.'

[16] Weiler, J.H.H., 1999, n 8.

[17] Case 8/74 *Procureur du Roi v Dassonville* [1974] ECR 837; Case 33/74 *van Binsbergen*, n 12.

[18] Case 120/78 *Cassis de Dijon*, n 13.

and, more globally, the '1992 programme'; d. the self-restraint period, starting with *Keck*; and e. the ongoing adjustment period, where the Court's more moderate approach is being tested in practice, while being horizontally applied in other free movement areas.

Looking more specifically at the field of services, A. Biondi distinguishes two main periods: a period of foundation and consolidation leading up to *Säger, Alpine Investments*, etc,[19] and a period of rationalization, marked by *Deliège, Viacom II*, and *Mobistar*.[20] L. Gormley, in a more pragmatic way, builds his reasoning around the *Keck* rupture.[21]

With the focus remaining on services, one can more precisely distinguish four waves in the Court's case law:[22] i. a first wave, extending roughly until the mid-1980s, in which the principle of mutual recognition is developed (*Van Binsbergen*, etc);[23] ii. a second wave extending to the early 1990s, where the Court does censor measures which are not openly discriminatory, but without expressly stating so (*Webb, Commission v Germany*);[24] iii. the 'big bang' period, starting with the 1991 judgments (*Säger, Dutch TV*)[25] and expanding with the 1995 ones (*Alpine Investments* in parallel with *Gebhard* and *Bosman*);[26] iv. and a fourth, ongoing wave of case law marked by two opposed tendencies: on the one hand, the expansion of the scope of the Treaty rules to services previously excluded (healthcare, social, etc), and on the other hand, the rationalization of this expansive trend, through the adoption of the concept of solidarity (*Albany*),[27] the attribution of a greater role to fundamental rights (*Schmidberger, Omega*),[28] and the introduction of some 'restricting restrictions' logic (*Mobistar, Viacom II*).[29]

---

[19] Case C-76/90 *Säger*, n 14, Case C-384/93 *Alpine Investments*, n 15.

[20] Case C-134/03 *Viacom Outdoor Srl v Giotto Immobilier SARL (Viacom II)* [2005] ECR I-1167; Joined cases C-51/96 & C-191/97 *Christelle Deliège v Ligue Francophone de Judo et Disciplines Associés ASBL, Ligue Belge de judo ASBL, Union Européenne de Judo and Francois Pacquée* [2000] ECR I-2549; Joined cases C-544 & 545/03 *Mobistar SA v Commune de Fleron and Belgacom Mobile SA v Commune de Schaerbeek* [2005] ECR I-7723. See also Biondi, A., 'Recurring cycles in the internal market: some reflections on the free movement of services' in Arnull, A., Eeckhout, P., and Tridimas, T. (eds), *Continuity and Change in EU Law* (Oxford: OUP, 2008) 229–42.

[21] Gormley, L., 'The definition of measures having equivalent effect' in Arnull, A., Eeckhout, P., and Tridimas, T. (eds), *Continuity and Change in EU Law* (Oxford: OUP, 2008) 189–205.

[22] Classification already proposed in Hatzopoulos, V., and Do, U., 'Overview of the Case Law of the ECJ in the Field of Free Movement of Services 2000–2005' (2006) 4 *CML Rev* 923–91.

[23] Case 155/73 *Sacchi* [1974] ECR 409; Case 33/74 *van Binsbergen* [1974] ECR 1299.

[24] Case 279/80 *Criminal proceedings against Alfred John Webb* [1981] ECR 3305; Case 205/84 *Commission v Germany (insurance)* [1986] ECR 3755.

[25] Case C-76/90 *Säger* [1991] ECR I-4221; Case C-288/89 *Gouda* [1991] ECR I-4007 and Case C-353/89 *Commission v Netherlands (Mediawet)* [1991] ECR I-4069.

[26] See, for services, Case C-384/93 *Alpine Investments* [1995] ECR I-1141; for establishment, Case C-55/94 *Gebhard* [1995] ECR I-4165; for workers, Case C-415/93 *Bosman* [1995] ECR I-4921.

[27] Case C-67/96 *Albany International BV v Stichting Bedrijfspensioenfonds Textielindustrie* [1999] ECR I-5751.

[28] Case C-112/00 *Eugen Schmidberger, Internationale Transporte und Planzüge v Republik Österreich* [2003] ECR I-5659; Case C-36/02 *Omega Spielhallen-und Automatenaufstellungs-GmbH v Oberbürgermeisterin der Bundesstadt Bonn* [2004] ECR I-9609.

[29] Joined cases C-544 & 545/03 *Mobistar*, n 20; Case C-134/03 *Viacom II*, n 20; 'restricting restrictions' is the title of a highly articulate article by Barnard, C., 'Restricting Restrictions: Lessons for the EU from the US?' (2009) 68 *Cambridge LJ* 575–606.

Varied as the proposed classifications and categorizations of its case law may be, there are a number of CJEU judgments the importance of which is undisputed, in that they shaped the entire body of case law in the field of the free movement of services. There now follows a brief examination of these cases.

The first such judgment is *Van Binsbergen*, concerning the obligation of 'legal representatives' to be resident in the country where they are to represent clients. In this case, the Court reached three conclusions: *first*, that Article 56 TFEU has direct effect. *Secondly*, it was held that 'the restrictions to be abolished pursuant to Articles 59 and 60 [now Articles 56 and 57 TFEU] include all requirements imposed on the person providing the service . . . which do not apply to persons established within the national territory *or which may prevent or otherwise obstruct the activities of the person providing the service*'.[30] Although the measure in question, essentially a residence requirement, could easily qualify as indirectly discriminatory, the Court instead chose to make this general and potentially far-reaching statement. *Thirdly*, the Court elaborated the wide definition of Article 56 TFEU restrictions by recognizing, well before *Cassis de Dijon*, the member states' ability to protect ORPIs:[31]

'Taking into account the particular nature of the services to be provided, specific requirements imposed on the person providing the service cannot be considered incompatible with the treaty where they have as their purpose the application of professional rules *justified by the general good* . . . which are binding upon any person established in the state in which the service is provided [*non-discrimination*] where the person providing the service would escape from the ambit of those rules being established in another member state [*mutual recognition*]'.

Everything which, a few years later, would revolutionize the free movement of goods, through *Cassis de Dijon*, had been already present in this early decision of the Court. It was the fact that the market for services was still relatively immature, and the resulting lack of interest from the Commission, which account for the fact that in the end, *Cassis* and not *Van Binsbergen* became the flagship judgment for the completion of the internal market. The elements on which the Court based its reasoning have been used in subsequent judgments, such as *Van Wesemael, Webb*, and *Commission v Germany*.[32]

A second landmark moment in the Court's case law materialized in 1991, with its decisions in the *Tourist Guide* cases,[33] the *Greek* and *Dutch TV* cases,[34] and most

---

[30] Case 33/74 *van Binsbergen*, n 12, para 10 (emphasis added).

[31] Ibid, para 12 (emphasis and square brackets added).

[32] Joined cases 110 & 111/78 *Ministère public and 'Chambre syndicale des agents artistiques et impresario de Belgique' ASBL v Willy van Wesemael and others* [1979] ECR 35; Case 279/80 *Webb* [1981] ECR 3305; Case 205/84 *Commission v Germany (insurance)* [1986] ECR 3755; Case 220/83 *Commission v France (co-insurance)* [1986] ECR 3663; Case 252/83 *Commission v Denmark (co-insurance)* [1986] ECR 3713; Case 206/84 *Commission v Ireland (co-insurance)* [1986] ECR 3817.

[33] Case C-154/89 *Commission v France (tour guides)* [1991] ECR I-659; Case C-180/89 *Commission v Italy (tourist guides)* [1991] ECR I-709; Case C-198/89 *Commission v Greece (tourist guides)* [1991] ECR I-727.

[34] Case C-260/89 *ERT v DEP and Sotirios Kouvelas* [1991] ECR I-2925; Case C-288/89 *Gouda* [1991] ECR I-4007; Case C-353/89 *Commission v The Netherlands (Mediawet)* [1991] ECR I-4069.

importantly, *Säger*.[35] In these cases, the Court set out clearly that Article 56 TFEU applies to both discriminatory and non-discriminatory measures. Rejecting voices which viewed the Court's approach as based on a broad definition of discrimination,[36] the Court stated that:[37]

'Article 59 of the Treaty [now Article 56 TFEU] requires not only the elimination of all discrimination against a person providing services on the ground of his nationality but also the abolition of any restriction, even if it applies without distinction to national providers of services and to those of other Member States, when it is liable to prohibit or otherwise impede the activities of a provider of services established in another Member State where he lawfully provides similar services.'[38]

As if this were not clear enough, the Court further held that 'a Member State may not make the provision of services in its territory subject to compliance with all the conditions required for establishment'.

The Court confirmed this expansionist approach in its judgment in *Alpine Investments*.[39] This judgment is important in at least three respects. *First*, it confirms that the above expansive approach to 'restrictions' is also followed when examining measures imposed by the exporting—as opposed to the importing—state; in this respect, services are distinguished from the *Groenveld* case law on goods, which only covers discriminatory measures affecting exports.[40] There are signs, however, that the *Groenveld* case law is being progressively reviewed.[41] *Secondly*, despite the fact that the measure at stake concerned the prohibition of cold-calling (undoubtedly a selling arrangement under the *Keck* case law) the Court in *Alpine Investments* refused to transpose to the field of services the distinction between selling arrangements and other requirements, inaugurated a couple of years earlier in the area of goods.[42] It is now accepted, despite early arguments to

---

[35] Case C-76/90 *Säger* [1991] ECR I-4221.

[36] Prominently, Marenco, G., 'Pour une interprétation traditionnelle de la notion de mesure d'effet équivalent à une restriction quantitative' (1984) 19 *CDE* 291–364; and Marenco, G., 'The Notion of Restriction on the Freedom of Establishment and Provision of Services in the Case-law of the Court' (1991) 11 *YEL* 111–50. For further bibliographic references concerning the concept of discrimination in EU free movement law, see the developments in subsection A(1)c(ii).

[37] Case C-76/90 *Säger*, n 35.

[38] Ibid, para 12.

[39] Case C-384/93 *Alpine Investments* [1995] ECR I-1141; see also commentary in Hatzopoulos, V., 'Annotation: Case C-384/93 *Alpine Investments* [1995] ECR I- 1141' (1995) 32 *CML Rev* 1427–45.

[40] Case 15/79 *P.B. Groenveld BV v Produktschap voor Vee en Vlees* [1979] ECR 3409; constantly confirmed thereafter, see eg Case 155/80 *Summary proceedings against Sergius Oebel* [1981] ECR 1993; Case 172/82 *Syndicat national des fabricants raffineurs d'huile de graissage and others v Groupement d'intérêt économique 'Inter-Huiles' and others* [1983] ECR 555; Case C-47/90 *Etablissements Delhaize frères and Compagnie Le Lion SA v Promalvin SA and AGE Bodegas Unidas SA* [1992] ECR I-3669.

[41] Case C-205/07 *Lodewijk Gysbrechts and Santurel Inter BVBA* [2008] ECR I-9947. See also annotated by Roth, W.H., 'Annotation: Case C- 205/07 *Gysbrechts* [2008] ECR I-9947' (2010) 47 *CML Rev* 509–20.

[42] An alternative reading of the two cases is offered by Snell, J., and Andenas, M., 'Exploring the outer limits: restrictions on the free movement' in Andenas, M., and Roth, W.H. (eds), *Services and Free Movement in EU Law* (Oxford: OUP, 2002) 69–139, at 109; see also Snell, J., *Goods and Services in EU Law* (Oxford: OUP, 2002) 92–9. These authors think that the two judgments combine in that they coherently fix the respective competences of the importing and the exporting states: the former

the contrary,[43] that a mechanical transposition of *Keck* in the field of services is not on the Court's agenda.[44] *Thirdly*, the Court held the Treaty rules on services to cover not only future but also prospective services, likely to materialize later on.

In a comment of *Alpine Investments* in 1995, it had been observed that the judgment 'can be seen either as a cornerstone case in the field of the free movement of services or as case limited to its facts'.[45] The former has proven to be true, since in that very same year, the expansive approach of this judgment was expressly transposed to the field of establishment and free movement of workers.[46] *Alpine Investments* itself was quoted by the Court in at least 20 subsequent judgments of the Court and in many more AG opinions.

The *fourth* grand moment in the Court's case law was initiated with the 1999 judgment in *Köhll*, complemented a couple of years later in *Smits and Peerbooms* and *Vanbraekel*.[47] In these judgments, followed by many more, the Court established that the Treaty covers all services offered for remuneration—even if indirect or insufficient[48]—irrespective of whether they are provided by non-profit organizations or in the framework of a social healthcare system. In other words, the Court turns a blind eye to national arrangements in the social field and considers that the default rule is the application of the Treaty rules—subject to certain important qualifications and exceptions. These cases have given rise to important litigation in the field of healthcare and pensions.[49] They were furthered by the controversial judgments of the Court in *Viking* and *Laval*.[50]

Last but not least, contrary to the seminal decisions outlined above, and their grand pronouncements, there is a fifth trend that emerges in a discrete and piecemeal way. In numerous judgments during the last decade, the Court has

may, in principle, impose compliance with its selling, marketing, etc regulations but may not affect the substance of the good/service provided (*Keck*), while the latter is responsible for the substance of the good/service but may not 'export' its own selling/marketing, etc arrangements (*Alpine Investments*); this is a sensible reading which, however, does not invalidate the fact that in *Alpine Investments* the Court openly rejects the application of *Keck*. J. Snell himself further in his writings concedes that the judgments in *Bosman* and *Gebhard* do not fit in this coherent reading.

[43] See eg Oliver, P., 'Goods and services: two freedoms compared' in Dony, M., and de Walsche, A. (eds), *Mélanges en Hommage à Michel Waelbroeck, Vol. II* (Bruxelles: Bruylant, 1999) 1377–405 and da Cruz Vilaça, J.L., 'On the application of *Keck* in the field of free provision of services' in Andenas, M., and Roth, W.H. (eds), *Services and Free Movement in EU Law* (Oxford: OUP, 2002).

[44] This idea was already expressed in Hatzopoulos, V., 1995, n 39.

[45] Ibid, at 1445.

[46] See, for services, Case C-384/93 *Alpine Investments* [1995] ECR I-1141; for establishment, Case C-55/94 *Gebhard* [1995] ECR I-4165; for workers, Case C-415/93 *Bosman* [1995] ECR I-4921.

[47] Case C-157/99 *B.S.M. Geraets-Smits v Stichting Ziekenfonds VGZ and H.T.M. Peerbooms v Stichting CZ Groep Zorgverzekeringen* [2001] ECR I-5473; Case C-368/98 *Abdon Vanbraekel and others v Alliance nationale des mutualités chrétiennes (ANMC)* [2001] ECR I-5363.

[48] For the issue of remuneration, see the analysis in ch 1.

[49] Further on the way the Court deals with healthcare and for the relevant literature see the discussion in ch 5.

[50] Case C-438/05 *International Transport Workers' Federation and Finnish Seamen's Union v Viking Line ABP and OÜ Viking Line Eesti* [2007] ECR I-10779; Case C-341/05 *Laval un Partneri Ltd v Svenska Byggnadsarbetareförbundet, Svenska Byggnadsarbetareförbundets avdelning 1, Byggettan and Svenska Elektrikerförbundet* [2007] ECR I-11767. Further on these cases and for the relevant literature, see the discussion in ch 5.

declined to apply the Treaty rules on services, signalling its will to show self-restraint and limit their scope. To achieve this in the healthcare and pension cases the Court had recourse to the principle of solidarity, to Article 106(2), to other express exceptions of the Treaty (including a disputable invocation of public health), and to ORPIs.[51] In the sports cases, the Court found that measures inherently connected to the exercise of sporting activities do not come under the Treaty even if they restrict the fundamental freedoms.[52] Finally, in *Mobistar* and *Viacom II*, it was held that the measure at stake applied without distinction and had an imperceptible—if not non-existent—effect on inter-state trade[53]; hence, it could not qualify as restriction.

c. Proposed criteria

The turmoil of the case law described above, combined with the high economic, institutional, and constitutional stakes that the definition of restrictions to free movement entails, do not make for easy normative classifications. Indeed, the legal literature on the notion of restrictions to free movement amounts to several hundred articles,[54] none of which fully agrees with any other on the proposed criteria. Some of the contributions are so authoritative and so highly articulate that it is difficult to argue against them or even add to them, were it not for a simple update.[55] Instead of adding yet another analysis of the entire body of case law and doctrine, a meta-analysis of the various criteria, as developed by the Court and discussed by legal doctrine, will follow.

i. General background

As explained above, the wider the concept of restriction to free movement, the narrower the scope for national regulations: instead of being seen as opportunities for the rational choice of the most appropriate regulatory framework, or as the means of international specialization, national regulatory measures are considered,

---

[51] For all these, see the discussion in ch 2.

[52] See, inter alia, Joined cases C-51/96 & C-191/97 *Deliège* [2000] ECR I-2549 and Case C-313/02 *David Meca-Medina and Igor Majcen v Commission of the European Communities* [2004] ECR I-3291; for these cases see among many, Spaventa, E., 'The outer limits of the Treaty free movement provisions: some reflections on the significance of *Keck*, remoteness, and *Deliège*' in Barnard, C., and Odudu, O. (eds), *The Outer Limits of EU Law* (Oxford/Portland: Hart Publishing, 2009) 245–69.

[53] Joined cases C-544 & 545/03 *Mobistar* [2005] ECR I-7723; Case C-134/03 *Viacom II* [2005] ECR I-1167; see Spaventa, E., 2009, n 52.

[54] According to the Eur-Lex database, *Keck* alone accounts for almost 100 comments (<http://eur-lex.europa.eu/Notice.do?val=197884:cs&lang=en&list=197884:cs,190296:cs,190295:cs,&pos=1&page=1&nbl=3&pgs=10&hwords=Keck->) (last accessed on 7 November 2011).

[55] See, among the most authoritative ones, Joliet, R., 'The Free Circulation of Goods: The *Keck and Mithouard* Decision and the New Directions in the Case Law' (1995) 1 *Columbia J of Eur L* 436–51; Gormley, L., 'Reasoning Renounced? The Remarkable Judgment in *Keck & Mithouard*' (1994) 5 *EBL Rev* 63–7; Reich, N., 'The "November Revolution" of the European Court of Justice: *Keck, Meng* and *Audi* Revisited' (1994) 31 *CML Rev* 459–2; Chalmers, D., 'Repackaging the Internal Market: The Ramifications of the *Keck* Judgment' (1994) 19 *EL Rev* 385–403; Barnard, C., 'Fitting the Remaining pieces into the Goods and Persons Jigsaw?' (2001) 26 *EL Rev* 35–59.

from this perspective, as mere obstacles to the realization of a fundamental objective of the EU Treaty. However, in areas where harmonization has for various reasons not occurred (eg due to the absence of an appropriate legal basis or of the necessary political will), the default is regulatory diversity and it should be accepted as such. Regulatory diversity should only be resisted when it counters the attainment of the common objectives. The next question would be to determine the common objectives covered by the wider 'internal market' goal; is it only free trade, or to further the achievement of fully liberalized national markets? While the former objective seems to flow from Article 3(3) TEU, the latter is not altogether outside the scope of EU law (especially if one looks at the extensive harmonization of financial services, network-based industries, etc). In legal terms, it is crucial to determine whether the 'problem' to be dealt with is merely *discrimination* (and the ensuing protectionism) or rather *regulatory diversity*.

Even the more ethnocentric intergovernmentalists agree, nowadays, that the principle of non-discrimination alone cannot provide for the effective functioning of commercial agreements, let alone of a truly internal market. This can be verified by the fact that the WTO agreements and bilateral investment treaties provide, in addition to the 'national treatment' (namely, non-discrimination) clause, for a right to 'market access', covering non-discriminatory measures.[56] It therefore comes as no surprise that in the EU framework, discrimination was abandoned early on as a criterion for restrictions. Or was it?

In the field of goods, *Dassonville* and subsequent case law clearly go beyond discrimination, both verbally and substantively. *Keck* and its progeny, however, mark the partial return to the criterion of discrimination. But when it comes to services, it has been observed that 'there is *no need* for a *Keck* judgment because the Court has never attributed the "restriction prohibition" approach such a wide scope as in the free movement of goods area'.[57] Indeed, the formula introduced in *Säger* and constantly used thereafter by the Court states that Article 56 TFEU 'requires not only the elimination of all discrimination against a person providing services on the ground of his nationality but also the abolition of any restriction...'.[58] Therefore, it may be said that discrimination remains the primary criterion, failing which, the restriction test becomes applicable.[59]

The above legal and other material differences may account for the fact that, despite the best efforts deployed by numerous authors in recent years to forge a

---

[56] Adlung, R., and Molinuevo, M., 'Bilateralism in Services Trade: Is There Fire Behind the (Bit-) Smoke?' (2008) 11 *J of Int Economic L* 365–409.

[57] Roth, W.H., 'The ECJ's case law on freedom to provide services: is *Keck* relevant?' in Andenas, M., and Roth, W.H. (eds), *Services and Free Movement in EU Law* (Oxford: OUP, 2002) 1–24, 7 (emphasis in the original).

[58] Case C-76/90 *Säger* [1991] ECR I-4221, para 12; systematically repeated thereafter, see eg Case C-164/99 *Portugaia Construções Lda* [2002] ECR I-787, para 16; Case C-168/04 *Commission v Austria (posted workers)* [2006] ECR I-9041, para 36; Case C-389/05 *Commission v France (bovine insemination)* [2008] ECR I-5337, para 57.

[59] Although this finding may be weakened in view of more recent case law; see eg Case C-341/05 *Laval* [2007] ECR I-11767.

single theory covering all four freedoms,[60] the Court has never fully acknowledged such a theory; instead, it has occasionally resisted it.[61] This, in turn, means that general findings on the principles governing free movement need be qualified to accurately reflect the situation pertaining specifically to services.

Moreover, since 'language disguises thought',[62] the language used with regard to the various freedoms, and especially in the field of services, needs to be examined in some depth, in order to uncover the words' proper meaning.

ii. Import restrictions

General presentation It has been stated above that international trade agreements typically contain two main liberalizing rules: 'national treatment' and 'market access'. These two rules are flexible enough and, if construed expansively, suffice to remove all restrictions to trade. In most international trade agreements, however, where the adoption of measures of positive integration is not an option, these rules are given a more limited scope, in order to avoid too glaring regulatory gaps.

The two rules can also be found in EU law; the prohibition of discriminations is a general principle of law[63]—considered thus as a floor of rights

---

[60] It is true that most authors agree to the fact that there are several good reasons for a unified approach, rather than to the existence of a unified approach as such. See eg Poiares-Maduro, M., 'Harmony and Dissonance in Free Movement' (2002) 4 *CYEL* 315–41. There is also extensive discussion of this issue in Andenas, M., and Roth, W.H. (eds), *Services and Free Movement in EU Law* (Oxford: OUP, 2002). See more specifically in this volume, Snell, J., and Andenas, M., 'Exploring the outer limits: restrictions on the free movement' 69–139; Jarass, H., 'A unified approach to the fundamental freedoms' 141–61; Hansen, J.L., 'Full circle: is there a difference between the freedom of establishment and the freedom to provide services?' 197–209; Roth, W.H., 'The ECJ's case law on freedom to provide services: is *Keck* relevant?' 1–23; da Cruz Vilaça, J.L., 'On the application of *Keck* in the field of free provision of services' 25–39. See also Snell, J., *Goods and Services in EU Law* (Oxford: OUP, 2002) 22–4; Hatzopoulos, V., 'Trente ans après les arrêts fondamentaux de 1974, les quatre libertés: quatre?' in Demaret, P., Govaere, I., and Hanf, D. (eds), *30 Years of European Legal Studies at the College of Europe—30 ans d'études juridiques européennes au Collège d'Europe: Liber Professorum 1973/74–2003/04* (Brussels: Peter Lang, 2005) 185–201; more recently, see Spaventa, E., 2009, n 52; Tryfonidou, A., 'Further Steps on the Road to Convergence Among the Market Freedoms' (2010) 35 *EL Rev* 36–56.

[61] Supported by quite influential authors, see eg Oliver, P., 'Goods and services: two freedoms compared' in Dony, M., and de Walsche, A. (eds), *Mélanges en Hommage à Michel Waelbroeck, Vol. II* (Bruxelles: Bruylant, 1999) 1377–405; and more recently Oliver, P., 'Of Trailers and Jet-Skis: Is the Case Law on Article 34 TFEU Hurtling in a New Direction' (2010) 33 *Fordham Int'l LJ* 1423–71.

[62] The full quotation by L. Wittgenstein is 'Language disguises the thought; so that from the external form of the clothes one cannot infer the form of the thought they clothe, because the external form of the clothes is constructed with quite another object than to let the form of the body be recognized' in *Tractatus Logico-Philosophicus* (London: Routledge, 2001 [1921]).

[63] Here the terms 'non-discrimination' and 'equal treatment' are being used as synonymous, as indeed, by the Court in several of its judgments, see Case 810/79 *Überschär* [1980] ECR 2747 and more recently, Case C-123/08 *Wolzenburg* [2009] ECR I-9621, para 50; Tridimas highlights the distinction often drawn by legal doctrine between, on the one hand, the general principle of equal treatment which stems from natural law and underlies all EU action and, on the other, the principle of non-discrimination which need be put to work by specific acts of secondary legislation (see Tridimas, T., *The General Principles of EU Law*, 2nd edn (Oxford: OUP, 2006) 64). See also recently, Fallon, M., and Martin, D., 'Dessine-moi une discrimination' (2010) 170 *Journal de Droit Européen* 165–73), who argued on the basis of the EU Charter of Fundamental Rights, whose provisions are 'not clearly made in the case law of the Community judicature which seems to use the terms equality and non-discrimination as interchangeable'.

for free movers—while provisions on all four freedoms invariably refer to 'restrictions'.[64] The CJEU, for its part, has demonstrated a consistent preference for the language of 'restrictions', ever since *Dassonville* and *Van Binsbergen*.[65] This notwithstanding, some of the most influential writers today advance the idea that free movement should be secured through a broad rule of non-discrimination and no more.[66] To explain this apparent contradiction, it is necessary to look into the actual content of the concept of discrimination and of those other criteria which may trigger the application of the free movement rules.

It would seem that there are as many definitions of discrimination as there are authors writing about it.[67] From the various classifications and in the face of terminological confusion,[68] four broad types of discriminatory measures can be identified. Traditionally, authors distinguish between discrimination which is 'formal', 'direct', 'open', 'in law' and discrimination which features as 'informal', 'indirect', 'covert', 'in fact'. It is true that each one of the four adjectives used is slightly different from the previous, and various combinations thereof are possible (such as eg discrimination which is formal but indirect, ie based on a proxy to nationality). A further issue, which is central to the very definition of discrimination and which further complicates the qualification of measures as being discriminatory or not, is that of identifying the circumstances in which two (or more) service providers/recipients are in the same or in a different situation. In this respect, the Court's case law is very limited and quite erratic. In most cases, it assumes that free

---

[64] Article 45 TFEU on workers merely talks about the abolishment of discriminations, but both the Court's case law interpreting it and the legislative acts issued on its basis acknowledge that its objectives go further.

[65] Case 8/74 *Dassonville* [1974] ECR 837 and Case 33/74 *van Binsbergen* [1974] ECR 1299.

[66] This idea was famously promoted in Marenco, G., 'Pour une interprétation traditionnelle de la notion de mesure d'effet équivalent à une restriction quantitative' (1984) 19 *CDE* 291–364; and Marenco, G., 'The Notion of Restriction on the Freedom of Establishment and Provision of Services in the Case-law of the Court' (1991) 11 *YEL* 111–50; also followed to a large extent by Defalque, L. 'Le concept de discrimination en matière de libre circulation des marchandises' (1987) 23 *CDE* 487–510. This was later contested by several authors, eg Daniele, L., 'Non Discriminatory Restrictions to the Free Movement of Persons' (1997) 22 *EL Rev* 191–200; Toner, H., 'Non-discriminatory Obstacles to the Exercise of Treaty Rights—Articles 39, 43, 19 and 18 EC' (2004) 23 *YEL* 275–302; Hatzopoulos, V., 2005, n 60; Wilsher, D., 'Does *Keck* Discrimination Make Any Sense? An Assessment of the Non-discrimination Principle in the European Single Market' (2008) 33 *EL Rev* 3–22. The broad criterion of discrimination has regained support in these last years; see prominently Barnard, C., 'Restricting Restrictions: Lessons for the EU from the US?' (2009) 68 *Cambridge LJ* 575–606 and Snell, J., 'The Notion of Market Access: A Concept or a Slogan?' (2010) 47 *CML Rev* 437–72. Even today, however, many authoritative authors refuse to follow the slippery road of discrimination, see prominently Gormley, L., *EU Law of Free Movement of Goods and Customs Union* (Oxford: OUP, 2009) and Oliver, P., et al, *Oliver on Free Movement of Goods in the European Union* (Oxford: Hart Publishing, 2010).

[67] On top of the articles cited in n 66, see also Garrone, P., 'La discrimination indirecte en Droit Communautaire: vers une théorie générale' (1994) 30 *RTDE* 427–49; Bernard, N., 'Discrimination and Free Movement in EC Law' (1996) 45 *Intl & Comparative L Q* 82–108; Hilson, C., 'Discrimination in Community Free Movement Law' (1999) 24 *EL Rev* 445–62; Eeckhout, P., 'After *Keck and Mithouard*: free movement of goods in the EC, market access and non-discrimination' in Cottier, T., and Mavroidis, P. (eds), *Regulatory Barriers and the Principle of Non-discrimination in World Trade Law* (Michigan: University of Michigan Press, 2000) 190–206; and more recently Fallon, M., and Martin, D., 2010, n 63.

[68] For which, see Hilson, C., 1999, n 67, at 448–51.

movers are on the same footing as nationals of the member state concerned. It is only exceptionally, often to justify an otherwise discriminatory measure, that the Court looks to the context in order to ascertain whether the general presumption of similarity holds true. In particular, it is highly unclear whether the similarity/difference should be appreciated at the legal or the material level. If the former solution seems plausible in the field of taxation, an area by nature formalistic,[69] it is more questionable whether such an approach is appropriate in other areas, such as labour law.[70]

This is the reason why in the paragraphs which follow, instead of adding yet more terms, the focus is on the criterion on which national regulation disfavours free movers, if at all. On this basis, a classification can be made as follows:

a. National measures that formally introduce distinctions, based directly on nationality.

b. National measures that formally introduce distinctions, based on criteria other than nationality, such as residence or the place of establishment.

c. National measures that introduce no formal distinctions at all, but whose requirements are likely to be met more easily by nationals/persons established within the national territory, rather than by free movers. Examples of such measures are the requirements of prior presence or experience within the national territory, possession of given inputs within national territory, and locally acquired professional qualifications

d. National measures that introduce no formal distinctions at all, and give no indication that they protect nationals as against free movers. Free movers, however, are handicapped by the fact that they already comply with similar requirements in their home state. These are also known as 'double burdens'.

e. National measures that introduce no formal distinctions at all, and there is no indication that they protect nationals as against free movers. There is no indication of 'double burdens' either; instead, these measures restrict the commercial freedom of all the operators active in the relevant market (eg opening-hour rules or use restrictions).

From this analysis, categories (a) to (c) are based on some kind of discrimination, while categories (d) and (e), although affecting trade opportunities may not, on a proper use of the word, qualify as discriminatory.

Discriminatory measures

Since non-discrimination on the basis of nationality is a general principle of EU law having horizontal application (expressed in its various forms in Articles 8, 10, 18,

---

[69] See eg Westen, P., 'The Empty Idea of Equality' (1982) 95 *Harvard L Rev* 537–596.

[70] For which see the analysis on *Laval*, below; for a more general discussion of the appropriateness of discrimination as a criterion for the applicability of the internal market rules see Wilsher, D., 'Does *Keck* Discrimination Make Any Sense? An Assessment of the Non-discrimination Principle within the European Single Market' (2008) 33 *EL Rev* 3–22.

and 19 TFEU), measures of type (a) above are illegal per se, irrespective of there being protectionist intent; in principle, they cannot be justified, unless upheld for some valid reason, subject to a strict proportionality test (indeed, there are very few reasons which could make the nationals/goods/services of one member state more fit than those of the others).[71]

Measures described under (b) and (c) are not per se illegal and may be justified by the nature of the activity concerned (eg the need of direct and immediate contact with the service recipient, eg in the case of lawyers), or by the nature of the measure (eg taxation). Especially for measures of type (c), it may not be overly burdensome for the free mover to conform to. Intent, therefore, has a role to play. In EU law, however, contrary to what happens in the US under the Dormant Commerce Clause,[72] such intent is not taken into account at the qualification but rather at the justification stage. If the measure serves some ORPI and the restriction introduced is proportional to the interest, then it will be upheld.[73]

Double burdens

It is submitted here that measures classified under (d) above should not be considered as discriminatory. Double burdens are the result of regulatory diversity and the legislative expression of national preferences. It is difficult to see how or why the existence of divergent national rules and the absence of harmonization would amount to discrimination.[74] In such circumstances, the problem is not the very existence of national rules—indeed, the absence of such rules would be inconceivable in the absence of EU harmonization. The problem with double burdens is the failure of the host state authorities to take into account similar conditions fulfilled in the home member state. The problem, therefore, lies not so much with national legislation (which could, occasionally, become more recognition-friendly), but with the administrative practice of the host member state. And the name of the problem is not discrimination but lack of mutual recognition. Mutual recognition is a value per se within the EU legal order, and as it has been extensively argued elsewhere by the author,[75] a general principle of EU law. The

---

[71] As to the question whether this 'valid reason' is strictly limited to the reasons expressly enumerated in the Treaty, or may extend to judge-made justifications, see the discussion in ch 4.

[72] For which see Barnard, C., 2009, n 66; van Gerven, W., 'Constitutional aspects of the European Court's case-law on Articles 30 and 36 EC as compared with the U.S. Dormant Commerce Clause' in Dony, M., and de Walsche, A. (eds), *Mélanges en Hommage à Michel Waelbroeck, Vol. II* (Bruxelles: Bruylant, 1999) 1629–44.

[73] For the function and the conditions of ORPI, see ch 4.

[74] In the same sense, see Poiares-Maduro, M., 'Harmony and Dissonance in Free Movement' (2002) 4 *CYEL* 315–41, at 63–4; *contra* Barnard, C., 2009, n 66, and Snell, J., 2010, n 66; the authors promoting a wide concept of discrimination also find support in some CJEU cases on the free movement of persons, such as Case C-237/94 *John O' Flynn v Adjudication Officer* [1996] ECR I-2617, para 18, where the Court held that 'conditions imposed by national law must be regarded as indirectly discriminatory where, although applicable irrespective of nationality, they affect essentially migrant workers, or the great majority of those affected are migrant workers, where they are indistinctly applicable but can more easily be satisfied by national workers than by migrant workers or where there is a risk that they may operate to the particular detriment of migrant workers' (references omitted).

[75] Hatzopoulos, V., 'Mutual recognition in the field of services' in Lianos, I., and Odudu, O. (eds), *Regulating Trade in Services in the EU and the WTO: Trust, Distrust and Economic Integration*

failure of the host state's authorities to fulfil their mutual recognition obligations is reproachable per se. The member state concerned may, nevertheless, justify its failure to fulfil its obligations stemming from mutual recognition, by proving that the home and host states' rules are not close enough and cannot be mutually recognized.[76]

By labelling such failure as 'discrimination', the true nature of the problem is concealed. By the same token, the margin left to the host member state is seriously undermined: as soon as the label of 'discrimination' is used, the risk that the justification test will be strictly applied becomes all the more likely.

An illustration of this is offered by the Court's judgment in *Laval*.[77] This case concerned the legality of industrial action pursued by Swedish trade unions against Laval, an employer of posted workers from Latvia. The second question answered by the Court concerned the failure of the trade unions to take into account the obligations to which Laval was subject under the collective agreements already concluded in Latvia, and thus the existence of a 'double burden' for the undertaking. In this respect, the Court held that discrimination may also arise through 'the application of the same rule to different situations'[78] and held that:

'national rules ... which fail to take into account, irrespective of their content, collective agreements to which undertakings that post workers to Sweden are already bound in the Member State in which they are established, give rise to discrimination against such undertakings, in so far as under those national rules they are treated in the same way as national undertakings which have not concluded a collective agreement.'[79]

Under this test, it would seem that all instances where the host member state fails to mutually recognize conditions already fulfilled in the home state will qualify as discriminatory. This is a harsh conclusion since, as explained above, mutual recognition is an open-ended process, the outcome of which is not granted.[80] The Court's approach becomes even stricter in the *Laval* case itself where, in a reversal of previous case law, the strict distinction between express Treaty exceptions and ORPI is revived, and it is further held that only the former may justify discriminations.[81] To strip the Court's findings from the factual background, in *Laval* (and other judgments along its lines), the Court held that failure of mutual recognition—which may be due to all sorts of reasons, including the fundamental

(Cambridge: CUP, forthcoming); and well before that, see Hatzopoulos, V., *Le principe communautaire d'équivalence et de reconnaissance mutuelle dans la libre prestation de services* (Athènes/Bruxelles: Sakkoulas/Bruylant, 1999) at 110–25.

[76] For the principle of mutual recognition and its operation, see the analysis in ch 5.
[77] Case C-341/05 *Laval* [2007] ECR I-11767.
[78] Ibid, para 115.
[79] Ibid, para 116.
[80] It is true that in *Laval*, the Swedish trade unions did not pay any attention to the obligations which Laval had undertaken in Latvia, but it is generally difficult to probe each instance of failure of mutual recognition to check whether the problem was 'qualitative' (ie whether the host state authorities did not take pains to consider the content of the home legislation at all) or 'quantitative' (ie whether they found that the measures were not comparable as to the level of protection and the security offered).
[81] Case C-341/05 *Laval*, n 77, paras 117–119.

incompatibility between national measures—may only be justified by reasons connected to public policy, public security, or public health; this is a remarkable outcome.

Instead of manipulating concepts already sufficiently complex (discrimination, ORPIs, and their relation to express exceptions), the Court could have reached the same result by holding that failure to mutually recognize the burdens already imposed by the home state is a restriction to free movement, unless justified. The reason which the host state could invoke for justifying such a failure would lie on the fact that the home state rules do not guarantee sufficient protection of some ORPI;[82] instead, under the *Laval* line of argument, the host member state is completely deprived of access to ORPI.

Market access

There is no way that measures under (e) above may qualify as discriminatory or even protectionist. Should this mean that they are altogether outside the scope of the free movement rules? Those who think that a broad concept of discrimination should be the sole criterion for the application of the free movement rules oppose the extension of the freedoms to cover such measures.[83] To the extent that there is no EU harmonization in a given field, member states should be free to maintain their regulatory preferences, without the deregulatory pressure of (foreign or national) economic agents, mediated through CJEU judgments. The same position is also taken by those who value regulatory competition, since they oppose, in principle, any process that leads to regulatory uniformity and restricts choice (although they greatly value market access, since the lack thereof restricts the operator's choice of regulatory environment).

Nonetheless, as stated above, the Treaty provisions on free movement (negative integration) are based on the concept of restriction, rather than merely on discrimination.[84] At the same time, the positive integration provisions, giving the EU harmonization powers, clearly supersede the mere liberalization of trade and envision a 'single' or 'internal' market. Unsurprisingly, then, the Court's case law is also—ostensibly at least—not based on discrimination.

Probably the most vocal opponent of a discrimination test has been AG F.G. Jacobs. In his famous opinion in *Leclerc-Siplec*, he persuasively argued as follows:[85]

'The central concern of the Treaty provisions on the free movement of goods is to prevent unjustified obstacles to trade between Member States. If an obstacle to inter-State trade exists, it cannot cease to exist simply because an identical obstacle affects domestic trade [. . .] If a Member State imposes a substantial barrier on access to the market for certain products—for example, by providing that they may be sold only in a very limited number of

---

[82] Indeed, this was the line followed by the Court in the recent gambling case law. For which see ch 5.
[83] See, inter alia, the works cited in subsection A(1)c(ii).
[84] With the exception of rules on workers (Art 43 TFEU).
[85] Case C-412/93 *Société d'Importation Edouard Leclerc-Siplec v TF1 Publicité SA and M6 Publicité SA* [1995] ECR I-179, para 39–41 (AG).

establishments—and a manufacturer of those products in another Member State suffers economic loss as a result, he will derive little consolation from the knowledge that a similar loss is sustained by his competitors in the Member State which imposes the restriction.

Equally, from the point of view of the Treaty's concern to establish a single market, discrimination is not a helpful criterion: from that point of view, the fact that a Member State imposes similar restrictions on the marketing of domestic goods is simply irrelevant. The adverse effect on the Community market is in no way alleviated; nor is the adverse effect on the economies of the other Member States, and so on the Community economy... A discrimination test is therefore inconsistent as a matter of principle with the aims of the Treaty.

There is one guiding principle which seems to provide an appropriate test: that principle is that all undertakings which engage in a legitimate economic activity in a Member State should have unfettered access to the whole of the Community market, unless there is a valid reason for denying them full access to a part of that market.'

Market access as a criterion for applying the free movement rules to non-discriminatory and non-protectionist measures had been put forward by several authors before this opinion, and even before the judgment in *Keck*.[86] It was formally introduced into judicial reasoning in the *Keck* judgment, where the Court justified the reversal of its previous case law, in relation to selling arrangements, by stating that 'the application of such [non discriminatory] rules [. . .] is not by nature such as to prevent their access to the market or to impede access any more than it impedes the access of domestic products'.[87] In this way, the Court, alongside measures directly affecting goods' composition, seemed to be using two criteria for the application of the free movement rules to national measures (concerning selling arrangements): market access and discriminatory effect. With hindsight, however, it can be observed that in practice it is the discriminatory effect test which has proven most significant.[88]

It has further been observed that 'the term "prevention of market access" sounds straightforward, but is anything but'.[89] Indeed, market access as a criterion of applying or not the free movement rules suffers from two major uncertainties.

The first one is of a more *qualitative nature*, and concerns the distinction between measures affecting *access to* and those influencing the *exercise of* an economic activity. Such a distinction, favoured by some AGs but resisted by others,[90] appears rather questionable, both as a general tool applicable to all four

---

[86] White, E.L., 'In Search of the Limits to Article 30 of the EEC Treaty' (1989) 26 *CML Rev* 235–80; Steiner, J., 'Drawing the Line: Uses and Abuses of Article 30 EEC' (1992) 29 *CML Rev* 749–74.

[87] Joined Cases C-267 & 268/91 *Criminal proceedings against Bernard Keck and Daniel Mithouard* [1993] ECR I-6097, para 17.

[88] Snell, J., 'The Notion of Market Access: A Concept or a Slogan?' (2010) 47 *CML Rev* 437–72.

[89] Ibid, at 447.

[90] See eg in favour of the distinction, AG Lenz in C-415/93 *Bosman* [1995] ECR I-4921, para 205 (AG), AG Gulmann in Case C-275/92 *Her Majesty's Customs and Excise v Schindler* [1994] ECR I-1039, para 56 (AG), and AG Fenelly in Case C-190/98 *Volker Graf v Filzmoser Maschinenbau GmbH* [2000] ECR I-493, para 32 (AG); against such a distinction, see eg AG Alber in Case C-176/96 *Jyri Lehtonen and Castors Canada Dry Namur-Braine ASBL v Fédération royale belge des sociétés de basket-ball ASBL (FRBSB)* [2000] ECR I-2681, para 48 (AG).

freedoms and, also, particularly with respect to services.[91] As a general normative device, the distinction between access and exercise is criticized on three grounds.[92] *First*, in terms of its normative justification, it is observed that restrictions on exercise also affect access, to the extent that they reduce profitability and incentives to move to other member states. The Court itself has held that '[t]he manner in which an activity is pursued is liable also to affect access to that activity'.[93] In practical terms, moreover, the qualification of a measure as affecting access to or exercise of a given activity depends on the eye of the beholder: as the *Viking* and *Laval* cases very eloquently illustrate, the measures that the trade unions viewed as conditions for the *exercise* of the activities in question, in fact led the service providers concerned to give up altogether their plans to *access* the relevant market. As a consequence, *secondly*, the distinction can be criticized as overly formalistic and difficult to apply in practice. *Thirdly*, several provisions of the TFEU, such as Article 49(2) TFEU, seem to favour an identical treatment of both access and exercise conditions.

The adequacy of the distinction between access and exercise appears particularly questionable in the field of the free movement of services. Three series of arguments can be advanced against it.[94]

First, unlike goods, which embody some objective value determined by their fabric, material, incorporated technology, and other intrinsic qualities, immaterial services have no intrinsic value: the conditions under which they shall be provided (*exercise*) also determine their content, and, therefore, their value and capacity/ propensity to *access* any given market. Thus, for example, restaurant services, in addition to the value of raw materials, incorporate the value of the location, the time when the service is offered (eg late night dinner), there being music, etc. *Secondly*, since service providers remain in principle subject to the exercise requirements imposed by their home state, the imposition on them of any additional exercise requirements, even non-discriminatory ones, affects their capacity/propensity to access the market of another member state; the situation is different for a good which has been exported to the receiving member state and is, henceforth, exclusively subject to the selling arrangements (= *exercise*) regulations of that state.[95]

---

[91] It should be noted that economists often use two indexes akin to the above legal distinction, in order to measure the impact of regulation on services: the 'entry barriers' and the 'ease of doing business' indexes, see eg Monteagudo, J., and Diexr, A., 'Economic Performance and Competition in Services in the Euro Area: Policy Lessons in Times of Crisis' *European Economy Occasional Papers* (2009) 53, EU Commission/DG Economic and Financial Affairs, available at <http://ec.europa.eu/ economy_finance/publications/publication15841_en.pdf> (last accessed on 7 November 2011) 19–20; economists are, however, constrained to proceed by proxies, an option which should be resisted by lawyers.

[92] Snell, J., 2010, n 88, at 443–6.

[93] Case C-464/02 *Commission v Denmark (motor vehicles)* [2005] ECR I-7929, para 37.

[94] Hatzopoulos, V., 'Recent Developments of the Case Law of the ECJ in the Field of Services' (2000) 37 *CML Rev* 43–82, 68–9; and more extensively, Hatzopoulos, V., *Le principe communautaire d'équivalence et de reconnaissance mutuelle dans la libre prestation de services* (Athènes/Bruxelles: Sakkoulas/Bruylant, 1999) at 233–49.

[95] Hence, for example, if member state A allows advertising only with price indication, while member state B specifically forbids the indication of prices, the printed material and website of a service provider established in the former will, without further ado, be in breach of the laws of the latter.

Therefore, any distinction between measures affecting access and those affecting exercise, whereby the latter would be caught by the free movement rules only when discriminatory, would lead to different results in the field of goods and in that of services, as it would be the source of double burdens for the latter. Last but not least, *thirdly*, concerns about both *access* and *exercise* focus on the provider; Article 56 TFEU, however, also takes into account the recipient's position.

The second uncertainty posed by the market access criterion, is of a more *quantitative nature*, and has to do with the degree of hindrance imposed by the measure in question. Unless one is to scrutinize all national measures—an option which the Court expressly abandoned from *Keck* onwards—then some kind of criterion distinguishing measures which significantly affect market access from those which do not, needs to be found. In this respect, AG F.G. Jacobs in his opinion in *Leclerc-Siplec* thought that 'the appropriate test . . . is whether there is a substantial restriction on that access. That would of course amount to introducing a *de minimis* test into Article 30'.[96] His proposal ran against well-established case law which refused the application of a *de minimis* rule to the free movement provisions (as opposed to competition rules). It is, therefore, not surprising that the Court was unwilling to follow him, at least not immediately. Indeed, 'instead of concentrating on the significance of a hindrance, the Court originally chose to focus on its directness'.[97] The criterion of directness has occasionally surfaced in the Court's case law, especially after *Keck* and *Alpine Investments*, in relation to goods,[98] workers,[99] and capital.[100] This has led some commentators to talk of a 'third way' (between the all inclusive *Dassonville* formula and the over-formalistic *Keck* readjustment).[101] With some delay, this 'third way' has been also transposed to the area of services with *Mobistar*.[102]

The directness criterion, however, has its own problems:[103] a. directness is a matter of degree and, therefore, difficult to apply—and even to distinguish from

---

[96] Case C-412/93 *Leclerc-Siplec* [1995] ECR I-179, para 39–41, para 42 (AG).

[97] Snell, J., 2010, n 88, at 451.

[98] Case C-69/88 *H. Krantz GmbH & Co. v Ontvanger der Directe Belastingen and Netherlands State* [1990] ECR I-583; Case C-93/92 *CMC Motorradcenter GmbH v Pelin Baskiciogullari* [1993] ECR I-5009; Case C-379/92 *Criminal Proceedings against Matteo Peralta* [1994] ECR I-3453; Case C-96/94 *Centro Servizi Spediporto Srl v Spedizioni Marittima del Golfo Srl* [1995] ECR I-2883; Case C-266/96 *Corsica Ferries France SA v Gruppo Antichi del porto di Genova Coop. arl, Gruppo Ormeggiatori del Golfo di La Spezia Coop. arl and Ministero dei Transporti e della Navigazione* [1998] ECR I-3949; Case C-67/97 *Criminal proceedings against Ditlev Bluhme* [1998] ECR I-8033; Case 134/94 *Esso Española SA v Comunidad Autónoma de Canarias* [1995] ECR I-4223; Case C-44/98 *BASF AG v Präsident des Deutschen Patentamts* [1999] ECR I-6269; Case C-190/98 *Volker Graf v Filzmoser Maschinenbau GmbH* [2000] ECR I-493; in this respect, see Rigaux, A., 'Nouvel épisode de la difficile qualification des mesures d'effet équivalent: le sort des abeilles brunes de Laeso' (1999) 9:3 *Europe* 7–8. See also Picod, F., 'La nouvelle approche de la Cour de justice en matière d'entraves aux échanges' (1998) 34 RTDE 169–89 and Toner, H., 'Non-discriminatory Obstacles to the Exercise of Treaty Rights—Articles 39, 43, 19 and 18 EC' (2004) 23 *YEL* 275–302.

[99] Case C-190/98 *Graf* [2000] ECR I-493.

[100] Case C-412/97 *ED Srl v Italo Fenocchio* [1999] ECR I-3845.

[101] See n 98.

[102] Joined cases C-544 & 545/03 *Mobistar* [2005] ECR I-7723.

[103] Snell, J., 2010, n 88.

the significance criterion; b. it is no less formal a concept than the distinction between exercise and access, and therefore no more helpful in practical terms; c. it runs counter to the foundations of the internal market, set in *Dassonville*, whereby both direct and indirect hindrances are problematic; d. most importantly, directness has been tried and failed as a criterion for the application of the US Dormant Commerce Clause.[104]

In its most recent case law, however, the Court's position has shifted and it seems to be embracing a *de minimis* approach. As a counterpart, the Court openly acknowledges 'market access' as a criterion for the application of the free movement rules. This trend may be illustrated by four recent cases, three in the field of goods[105] and one in services.[106] The goods cases all concerned use restrictions, imposed on motorbike trailers, jet-skis, and dark windshield films for cars, while the services case examined an obligation to contract on some types of motor insurance. In every case, the measures did not discriminate in any way on the basis of nationality, establishment, or other grounds; all national measures imposed restrictions on the *use of goods* or the *exercise* of the service activity—no formal restrictions on *access* to the market. This notwithstanding, in all four cases the Court concluded that there was a restriction. The restriction was not direct, but followed from the fact that the regulations in question a. negatively affected demand from consumers (goods cases)[107] or b. imposed significant additional costs and could lead to a revision of the business strategy (services case). It would seem, therefore, that with these judgments, the Court is turning away from both the directness criterion and the formal divide between *access* and *exercise*, at least in the field of services.[108]

As an alternative, the Court makes explicit use, for the first time, of a significance test (*de minimis*). For instance, in the *Italian trailers* case, the Court, after setting out clearly that three series of measures may qualify as restrictions—namely,

---

[104] *Southern Pacific Co v Arizona* 325 US 761 (1945); for more details and further references, see Snell, J., 2010, n 87.

[105] Case C-110/05 *Commission v Italy (trailers)* [2009] ECR I-519, Case C-142/05 *Åklagaren v Percy Mickelsson and Joakim Roos* [2009] ECR I-4273, para 28, and Case C-265/06 *Commission v Portugal (windshield films)* [2008] ECR I-2245; see on these cases, Horsley, T., 'Annotation: Case C-110/05, *Commission v Italy (trailers)* [2009] nyr' (2009) 46 *CML Rev* 2001–19; Derlén, M., and Lindholm, J., 'Article 28 EC and Rules on Use: A Step towards a Workable Doctrine on Measures Having Equivalent Effect to Quantitative Restrictions' (2010) 16 *Columbia J of Eur L* 191–231; Barnard, C., 'Trailing a New Approach to Free Movement of Goods?' (2009) 68 *Cambridge LJ* 288–90; Spaventa, E., 'Leaving *Keck* behind? The Free Movement of Goods after the Rulings in *Commission v Italy* and *Mickelsson and Roos*' (2009) 15 *EL Rev* 914–32; Gormley, L., 'Free Movement of Goods and their Use—What Is the Use of It?' (2010) 33 *Fordham Int'l LJ* 1589–628; Oliver, P., 'Of Trailers and Jet-Skis: Is the Case law on Article 34 TFEU Hurtling in a New Direction' (2010) 33 *Fordham Int'l LJ* 1423–71; De Sadeleer, N., 'L'examen, au regard de l'article 28 CE, des règles nationales régissant les modalités d'utilisation de certains produits' (2009) 162 *Journal du droit européen* 247–50; Rigaux, A., 'Définition des mésures d'effet équivalent' (2009) 19:4 *Europe* 20–2.

[106] Case C-518/06 *Commission v Italy (motor insurance)* [2009] ECR I-3491.

[107] In Case C-110/05 *Commission v Italy (trailers)*, n 105, the Court held in para 37 that the measure in question 'prevents a demand from existing in the market at issue for such trailers and therefore hinders their importation'.

[108] For the distinction between goods and services in this respect, see the analysis in subsection B(3).

discriminatory rules, product rules, and rules restricting market access[109]—observed that the Italian measure exerted 'a considerable influence on the behaviour of consumers which, in its turn, affects the access of that product to the market of that Member State'.[110] In a more explicit way, in *Mickelsson and Roos*, the Court held use restrictions to violate Article 34 TFEU where they 'have the effect of preventing users of personal watercraft from using them for the specific and inherent purposes for which they were intended or of *greatly* restricting their use'.[111]

Concerning services, the *Italian insurance* case is not the first using the 'market access' criterion to qualify a genuinely non-discriminatory measure as a restriction to the free provision of services, but it is more explicit than previous cases. Indeed, it may be said that the first services case in which 'market access' features explicitly as a criterion for the violation of free movement, was *Alpine Investment*, but this concerned an export restriction.[112] Subsequently, in other cases, the Court has found various regulations concerning the *exercise* of an activity to restrict *access* to the relevant market. In *Commission v Greece (online games)*, the Court found that a restriction in the use of computer games limited by volume their access to the Greek market, while at the same time restricted the establishment of traders as well as the occasional service provision.[113] In *Commission v Belgium (construction contractors)*, the Court found that the obligation of construction undertakings having recourse to foreign contracting parties to withhold 15 per cent of their dues until the end of the work and to be jointly liable for their tax debts, 'while it does not deprive service providers who are not registered and not established in Belgium of the ability to supply their services there, . . . [it] does make access to the Belgian market difficult for them'.[114] Similarly, in *Cipolla*, the Court found that the imposition of minimal fees for lawyers in Italy 'is liable to render access to the Italian legal services market more difficult for lawyers established in a[nother] Member State', since it deprives such lawyers of 'the possibility, by requesting fees lower than those set by the scale, of competing more effectively with lawyers established on a stable basis in the Member State concerned and who therefore have greater opportunities for winning clients than lawyers established abroad'.[115]

In the *Italian insurance* case, however, the Court became more explicit in at least three ways. *First*, the Court drew a clear distinction—thus clarifying prima facie contradictory case law—whereby 'the fact that other Member States apply less strict, or more commercially favourable rules to providers of similar services established in their territory' does not in itself amount to a restriction; however,

---

[109] Case C-110/05 *Commission v Italy (trailers)*, n 105, paras 34 and, more importantly, 37.
[110] Ibid, para 56.
[111] C-142/05 *Mickelsson and Roos*, n 105, para 28 (emphasis added).
[112] For detailed discussion on these, see further below, in this subheading.
[113] Case C-65/05 *Commission v Greece (online games)* [2006] ECR I-10341; it is true that the Court's reasoning in relation to services is somewhat elusive.
[114] Case C-433/04 *Commission v Belgium (construction contractors)* [2006] ECR I-653, para 31.
[115] Joined Cases C-94 & 202/04 *Federico Cipolla v Rosaria Fazari, née Portolese, and Stefano Macrino and Claudia Capoparte v Roberto Meloni* [2006] ECR I-11421, paras 58–9.

'the concept of restriction covers measures taken by a Member State which, although applicable without distinction, affect access to the market for undertakings from other Member States and thereby hinder intra-Community trade'.[116] *Secondly*, the Court was more explicit in terms of the criteria used in order to decide whether market access is affected: the fact that access is not formally impeded (eg by denying authorization) is irrelevant;[117] what counts is that the service provider is either faced with 'a *substantial* interference to the freedom to contract'[118] leading him 'in terms of organisation and investment, to *significant* additional costs',[119] or to 're-think their business policy and strategy', thus changing the characteristics of the services offered.[120] *Thirdly*, the Court, through the use of adjectives such as 'substantial', 'significant' (italicized in the quotations above), 'considerable', etc, seems to be adopting a *de minimis* approach.

This approach has been criticized since the substantiality of a restriction, like its directness, is a subjective concept and, thus, *de minimis* in combination with 'market access may simply provide a sophisticated-sounding garb that conceals decisions based on intuition'.[121] In contrast, it is submitted here that even if the above approach is not immediately conducive to legal certainty—although this is likely to follow with time—it offers at least a credible narrative and a valid explanation of why the free movement rules should prevail over national regulatory choices.[122]

Summing up
In view of the case law discussed above, most commentators find that in the field of goods, three types of national measures qualify as restrictions: a. those that discriminate, in the broad sense, b. those that impose specific product requirements, and c. those that hinder market access.[123] In the field of services, where there is no such thing as 'product requirements', the following five-pronged classification is proposed:

a. Measures that discriminate formally (introduce distinctions) and directly (on the basis of nationality) are always illegal, unless 'saved' by express Treaty exceptions;

b. Measures that discriminate formally (introduce distinctions) but indirectly (on the basis of criteria other than nationality) as well as

---

[116] Case C-518/06 *Commission v Italy (motor insurance)*, n 106, paras 63 and 64.
[117] Ibid, para 65.
[118] Ibid, para 66.
[119] Ibid, para 68.
[120] Ibid, para 69.
[121] Snell, J., 2010, n 88, at 469.
[122] For the various internal market narratives, see Lianos, I., 'Shifting Narratives in the European Internal Market: Efficient Restrictions of Trade and the Nature of "Economic" Integration' (2010) 21 *Eur Business L Rev* 705–60.
[123] In this sense, eg Snell, J., 2010, n 88; Derlén, M. and Lindholm, J., 2010, n 105; Doukas, D., 'Untying the Market Access Knot: Advertising Restrictions and the Free Movement of Goods and Services' (2007) 9 *CYEL* 177–215.

c. Measures that discriminate informally (do not introduce distinctions) but have the effect of favouring national service providers, are in principle illegal, but may be justified both by express exceptions and ORPI;

d. Measures that do not discriminate but impose double burdens on foreign service providers are in principle illegal. Since double burdens are the result of a failure of mutual recognition, such measures may be justified not only on the basis of express exceptions and ORPI, but also by demonstrating that the failure of mutual recognition is not due to the host state's failings;

e. Measures that neither discriminate nor impose double burdens are not illegal unless they 'greatly' affect market access; if substantial effect is proven by the party invoking the Treaty rules, the measures may, nonetheless, be justified either by express exceptions or by ORPI.

From these five categories of measures, (a), (b), and (c) may be classified as discriminatory, while (d) and (e) are non-discriminatory. The fact that measures under (b) and (c) do qualify as discriminatory, greatly obscures the issue of their justification.[124]

iii. Export restrictions

The exportation of services is the objective of any modern (service) economy. Export restrictions are, therefore, rare and mostly unintended. This explains why the Court's case law in this respect is scarce. *Alpine Investments* is the first clear judgment on this issue and, indeed, still remains the most important.

In *Alpine Investments* and consistently thereafter, the Court has applied to export restrictions the same criteria as those followed in relation to import restrictions. The Court has, therefore, refused to transpose in the area of services the import/export measures dichotomy adopted in the field of goods. Export restrictions affecting goods are the object of a specific Treaty provision, Article 35 TFEU, and, ever since the judgment in *Groenveld*,[125] the Court has constantly interpreted this provision as prohibiting only national measures which discriminate 'between domestic and export trade in such a way as to provide a particular advantage for national production or for the domestic market'—mere restrictions do not fall within its scope. Or, to use AG Trnstenjak's words,[126]

'[t]he *Groenveld* test comprises three interdependent conditions: first, the object or effect of the measure is the restriction specifically of patterns of exports; secondly, the measure gives rise to a difference in treatment between the domestic trade of a Member State and its export trade; thirdly, by virtue of the measure, a particular advantage is provided for national production or for the domestic market of the State in question, at the expense of the trade or production of other Member States.'

---

[124] For further detail on this issue, see the discussion in ch 4.
[125] Case 15/79 *Groenveld BV* [1979] ECR 3409.
[126] Case C-205/07 *Gysbrechts* [2008] ECR I-9947, para 33 (AG).

This minimalistic reading of Article 35 TFEU has been criticized by several commentators[127] and by several AGs of the Court.[128] In *Peralta*,[129] the Court seemed to transpose the *Groenveld* case law to the field of services. A few months later, however, and without distinguishing or overturning this earlier judgment, the Court in *Alpine Investments* leaned the other way and adopted a unitary approach, whereby Article 56 TFEU is also violated by measures imposing unjustified restrictions to exports, without looking for discrimination. This case concerned a Dutch provision prohibiting all undertakings established in the Netherlands from using cold-calling as a means of promoting sales of financial services. The Court held in its judgment that Article 56 TFEU 'covers not only restrictions laid down by the State of destination but also those laid down by the State of origin. As the Court has frequently held, the right freely to provide services may be relied on by an undertaking as against the State in which it is established, if the services are provided for persons established in another Member State'.[130]

Some commentators initially found *Alpine Investments* puzzling and considered *Peralta* to state the applicable law.[131] The case law which ensued, nonetheless, both in the field of services[132] and in that of workers[133] made clear that *Alpine Investments* was intended to be a judgment of principle, whereas the judgment in *Peralta* constituted no more than an uneasy answer to an extremely tenuous preliminary question.

Indeed, the unitary approach of both imports and exports measures, introduced by *Alpine Investments*, has since been hailed on many accounts. *First*, on the basis that discrimination is not an appropriate test for free movement, in relation to both imports and exports; especially so in the field of services, where the service providers remain, in principle, subject to their home state rules. *Secondly*, in terms of coherence of the applicable rules. There is no valid reason to differentiate where the Treaty does not: while for goods there are two different Treaty provisions dealing respectively with imports and exports, Article 56 TFEU offers a solid textual ground for a common, all-encompassing approach.[134] *Thirdly*, a powerful argument has been made from a combined reading of *Alpine Investments* and *Keck*, in contrast to the more usual trend of examining the two as opposing each

---

[127] Mattera, A., *Le marché unique Européen: ses règles, son fonctionnement* (Paris: Jupiter, 1990); Oliver, P., 'Some Further Reflections on the Scope of Articles 28–30 (ex 30–36) EC' (1999) 36 *CML Rev* 783–806.

[128] See Case 155/80 *Oebel* [1981] ECR 1993 (AG); Case C-47/90 *Delhaize* [1992] ECR I-3669 (AG); Case C-384/93 *Alpine Investments* [1995] ECR I-1141; more recently, Case C-205/07 *Gysbrechts* [2008] ECR I-9947 (AG).

[129] Case C-379/92 *Peralta* [1994] ECR I-3453.

[130] Case C-384/93 *Alpine Investments*, n 128, para 30.

[131] Bernard, N., 'Discrimination and Free Movement in EC Law' (1996) 45 *Intl & Comparative L Q* 82–108, at 107; Daniele, L., 'Non Discriminatory Restrictions to the Free Movement of Persons' (1997) 22 *EL Rev* 191–200, at 198.

[132] Case C-381/93 *Commission v France (maritime transport)* [1994] ECR I-5145.

[133] Case C-415/93 *Bosman* [1995] ECR I-4921.

[134] For these arguments see already Hatzopoulos, V., 'Annotation: Case C-384/93 *Alpine Investments* [1995] ECR I-1141' (1995) 32 *CML Rev* 1427–45.

other. So far as the allocation of competences is concerned, unless there is some discrimination, 'the home country controls the product rules, while the host country deals with selling arrangements'.[135]

These reasons, together with the fact that a unitary approach has been adopted in relation to the other personal freedoms, has led some commentators to suggest that the time was ripe for the Court to change its case law on Article 35 TFEU concerning goods and to adopt common criteria, covering all freedoms, in respect of both imports and exports measures.[136]

A step—albeit a timid one—towards such a unitary approach was made by the Court in the *Gysbrechts* case.[137] This concerned the Belgian regulation concerning distance (and internet) sales and imposed 'overprotective' payment conditions.[138] Such conditions would create a competitive disadvantage for Belgian traders and a disincentive for them to sell outside their territory. The parallel with the measure in *Alpine Investments* is startling. The Belgian regulation was in no way discriminatory, nor did it fulfil the other two conditions set out by *Groenveld*. AG Trstenjak proposed a radical overhaul of the three *Groenveld* conditions in favour of a restriction-based approach, moderated by a *de minimis* principle.[139] The Court, instead, preferred to stick to *Groenveld*, while offering a highly flexible interpretation thereof: in place of insisting on the three-conditions-test, as systemized by AG Trstenjak, the Court found that it was enough that the measure in question gave rise to some de facto discrimination.[140] The measure in question was, accordingly, decreed a violation of Article 35 TFEU, a result which the Court would have reached by following the AG's approach. Given that discrimination, especially de facto, is an open-ended concept and that double burdens are considered by many authors to introduce discrimination,[141] it becomes apparent that the tendency is towards—and definitely, not against—extending the approach inaugurated by *Alpine Investments* for services to the free movement of goods.

---

[135] Snell, J., and Andenas, M., 'Exploring the outer limits: restrictions on the free movement' in Andenas, M., and Roth, W.H. (eds), *Services and Free Movement in EU Law* (Oxford: OUP, 2002) 69–139, 109; see also Snell, J., *Goods and Services in EU Law* (Oxford: OUP, 2002) 92–4; the distinction between product and marketing regulations, however, is not as relevant in the field of services—its normative value is also contested in the field of goods, see under 'ii. Import restrictions'.

[136] See Oliver, P., 1999, n 127, where also reference is made to Roth, W.H., 'Wettbewerb der Mitgliedstaaten oder Wettbewerb der Hersteller? Plädoyer für eine Neubestimmung des Art. 34 EGV' (1995) 159 *Zeitschrift für das gesamte Handelsrecht und Wirtschaftsrecht* 78–95.

[137] Case C-205/07 *Gysbrechts* [2008] ECR I-9947; see also Roth, W.H., 'Annotation: Case C-205/07 *Gysbrechts* [2008] ECR I-9947' (2010) 47 *CML Rev* 509–20.

[138] 'Overprotective' in the sense that they went beyond the protection offered by the relevant EU Directive (European Parliament and Council Directive 97/7/EC on the protection of consumers in respect of distance contracts [1997] OJ L144/19).

[139] In other words, broadly moving along the lines described in the previous pages in relation to import restrictions.

[140] Roth, W.H., 'Annotation: Case C-205/07 *Gysbrechts* [2008] ECR I-9947' (2010) 47 *CML Rev* 509–20, at 514.

[141] See the discussion under subheading A(1)c(ii), especially under title 'double burdens'.

iv. Reverse discrimination

Introduction

The logical corollary of the idea expressed in *Groenveld*, that export measures are only caught when discriminatory, is that reverse discrimination is not caught at all by the free movement rules. It has been observed that:[142]

'an argument that a home state rule, in discriminating between home produced goods and imports, is prejudicing one's ability to compete on the home market, is simply the reverse side of the argument that the same home rule, which applies equally to goods destined for the home market and to those destined for export, is hindering one's ability to export. If the Court is respecting home state autonomy to regulate its own domestic goods in the context of Article 29 [now Article 35 TFEU] and exports, then it must inevitably take the same line as far as the purely internal, home market is concerned in relation to Article 28 [now Article 34 TFEU]'.

For many years, therefore, reverse discrimination was not caught by any free movement rules. The classic example in the field of goods is *Mathot*, concerning the obligation imposed by the Belgian legislature on butter producers to put their name and address on packaging.[143] As for personal freedoms, the typical example is *Saunders*, where the British Government was allowed to enforce against a British national an undertaking, offered in the course of criminal proceedings, not to enter British territory for a given period of time—a measure which would certainly qualify as a restriction to the free movement of workers, had Mrs Saunders not been British.[144] Similarly, in *Dzodzi*, the Court held that the expulsion of the Tongolese widow of a Belgian national from Belgium was a purely internal issue, irrelevant to free movement.[145]

Over the last two decades, however, the situation has greatly evolved, especially in the field of personal freedoms.[146] For one thing, as was explained in the previous section, the *Groenveld* laissez-faire logic, already under review in the field of goods, has never been extended to the other freedoms. *Secondly*, several judgments based on the free movement of persons, seem to embrace purely internal situations and to

---

[142] Hilson, C., 'Discrimination in Community Free Movement Law' (1999) 24 *EL Rev* 445–62, at 460.

[143] Case 98/86 *Ministère Public v Mathot* [1987] ECR 809; before that, see Joined Cases 314–316/81 & 83/82 *Procureur de la République and Comité national de défense contre l'alcoolisme v Alex Waterkeyn and others, Procureur de la République v Jean Cayard and others* [1982] ECR 4337 and Case 355/85 *Mr Driancourt, Commissioner of Police, Thouars, carrying out the duties of Public Prosecutor v Michel Cognet* [1986] ECR 3231, where it was explicitly ruled that a measure which violates free movement rules does not apply to imported goods but may, nevertheless, continue to apply to domestic ones.

[144] Case 175/78 *The Queen v Vera Ann Saunders* [1979] ECR 1129.

[145] Joined Cases C-297/88 and 197/89 *Massam Dzodzi v Belgian State* [1990] ECR I-3763; in this case, the Court did, nonetheless, give a preliminary ruling, to the extent that the regulatory content of the national rule applicable *a quo* was determined by reference to a EU Directive.

[146] For an up-to-date and exhaustive presentation of the relevant case law and doctrine, see Tryfonidou, A., *Reverse Discrimination in EC Law* (Alphen aan den Rijn: Kluwer Law International, 2009).

deal with reverse discrimination.[147] In *Surinder Singh*, the Court found that the residence restrictions imposed by the British authorities on the Indian spouse of a British national who had previously worked and lived in Ireland, violated the rules on free movement of workers.[148] More remarkably, in *Carpenter*, the Court held that residence restrictions imposed on the Filipino spouse of a British national who lived and worked in Britain—but occasionally offered services across borders—were in breach of the rules on services.[149] Thirdly, the citizenship judgments followed.[150] In *D'Hoop* and constantly thereafter, the Court held that 'Union citizenship is destined to be the fundamental status of nationals of the Member States, enabling those who find themselves in the same situation to enjoy within the scope *ratione materiae* of the Treaty the same treatment in law irrespective of their nationality' and that 'it would be incompatible with the right of freedom of movement were a citizen, in the Member State of which he is a national, to receive treatment less favourable than he would enjoy if he had not availed himself of the opportunities offered by the Treaty in relation to freedom of movement'.[151]

The Court, however, has stopped short of completely eliminating the 'reverse discrimination barrier' and of applying EU law in purely internal situations. In the *Government of the French Community* case, flying on the face of AG Sharpston's opinion, the Court held that 'Community law clearly cannot be applied to . . . purely internal situations' and made it clear that 'the Court has on several occasions held that citizenship of the Union is not intended to extend the material scope of the Treaty to internal situations which have no link with Community law'.[152]

In a similar vein, the Court has never admitted openly that the rules on services should apply to purely internal situations. Whenever there is some—even fine—connections with free movement, however, the Court opposes reverse discrimination, following one of the three techniques below.

---

[147] This tendency has been initiated in the field of goods, see Joined cases C-321–324/94 *Criminal proceedings against Jacques Pistre, Michèle Barthes, Yves Milha, and Didier Oberti* [1997] ECR I-2343; but it has been limited shortly thereafter, see Case C-448/98 *Guimont* [2000] ECR I-10663, and has not been pursued in a way parallel to that of the personal freedoms.

[148] Case C-370/90 *The Queen v Immigration Appeal Tribunal and Surinder Singh, ex parte Secretary of State for Home Department* [1992] ECR I-4265.

[149] Case C-60/00 *Mary Carpenter v Secretary of State for the Home Department* [2002] ECR I-6279.

[150] For an account of these judgments and their importance see Tryfonidou, A., 'Reverse Discrimination in Purely Internal Situations: An Incogruity in a Citizen's Europe' (2008) 35 LIEI 43–67.

[151] Case C-224/98 *Marie-Nathalie D'Hoop v Office national de l'emploi* [2002] ECR I-6191, paras 28 and 30, respectively.

[152] Case C-212/06 *Government of the French Community and Walloon Government v Flemish Government* [2008] ECR I-1683, paras 38 and 39 respectively; it has to be noted, however, that even in this case the Court did go on to deliver judgment on the basis that this may be useful for the referring court if the latter is under an obligation, under national law, to avoid reverse discriminations; for a critique of this case, see Dautricourt, C., and Thomas, S., 'Reverse Discrimination and Free Movement of Persons under Community Law: All for Ulysses, Nothing for Penelope?' (2009) 34 *EL Rev* 433–54; see also the passionate opinion of AG Sharpston in Case C-34/09 *Gerardo Ruiz Zambrano v ONEM* [2011] nyr.

Extending the Court's preliminary jurisdiction

In a series of recent judgments, delivered in the framework of preliminary proceedings, the Court acknowledged that the situation submitted to it was purely internal. Instead of declining its jurisdiction to reply, however, the Court did offer the interpretation required to the extent that 'such a reply might be useful to [the referring Court] if its national law were to require that a... national must be allowed to enjoy the same rights as those which a national of another Member State would derive from Community law in the same situation'.[153] Therefore, the Court does not itself rule on the applicability of its judgment, but does, nonetheless, offer an interpretation of the EU rule referred to it. This approach sits uneasily with well-established case law according to which the Court refuses its preliminary jurisdiction in situations where the application of EU law is purely hypothetical—here, the hypothetical character remains to be ascertained by the referring tribunal.[154] Such a tribunal, however, has no choice but to apply the judgment delivered to it, for at least three reasons. *First*, if the referring tribunal were to find that the answer given to it is irrelevant to the facts of the pending case, this would expose to criticism its prior decision to delay the national procedure and refer to the CJEU in the first place. *Secondly*, from the CJEU's formula quoted above, it seems that the only situation in which the interpretation of EU law could be irrelevant is where the internal legal order accepts reverse discrimination. However, even if situations of reverse discrimination could, under certain circumstances, be tolerated, it is highly unlikely that a tribunal would solemnly declare so and, therefore, refuse to follow the CJEU's preliminary ruling; such a statement would probably run against national constitutional law. For these reasons, the referring Court is likely to hold the CJEU judgment to be relevant and, therefore, *thirdly*, to find itself under the legal obligation, stemming from Article 267 TFEU, to apply it to the facts of the case—even if the situation is purely an internal one. Therefore, it may be observed that by abandoning the '*Saunders* orthodoxy', whereby the Court refused to apply internal market rules in the absence of an apparent intra-state dimension, and by delivering preliminary rulings at the disposal of the referring tribunals, the Court in fact pushes such tribunals to apply EU law to purely internal situations and to combat reverse discrimination.[155]

---

[153] See eg Case C-6/01 *Associação Nacional de Operadores de Máquinas Recreativas (Anomar) and others v Estado português* [2003] ECR I-8621, para 41; Case C-380/05 *Centro Europa 7 Srl v Ministero delle Comunicazioni e Autorità per le garanzie nelle comunicazioni and Direzione generale per le concessioni e le autorizzazioni del Ministero delle Comunicazioni* [2008] ECR I-349, para 69; Joined cases C-94 & 202/04 *Cipolla* [2006] ECR I-11421, para 30; Case C-451/03 *Servizi Ausiliari Dottori Commercialisti Srl v Giuseppe Calafiori* [2006] ECR I-2941, para 29.

[154] On the preliminary references of the Court, see, among an extremely rich literature, Davies, G., 'Abstractness and concreteness in the preliminary reference procedure: implications for the division of powers and effective market regulation' in Shuibhne, N.N. (ed), *Regulating the Internal Market* (Cheltenham/Northampton: Edward Edgar Publishing, 2006) 210–44; and much earlier, Hatzopoulos, V., 'De l'arrêt *Foglia v Novello* à l'arrêt *TWD Textilwerke*: la jurisprudence de la Cour de justice relative à l'admissibilité des renvois préjudiciels' (1994) 3 *Revue du Marché Unique Européen* 195–219.

[155] It should be noted, however, that there are some cases which do not follow this tendency. See eg Case C-104/08 (ord) *Marc André Kurt v Bürgermeister der Stadt Wels* [2008] ECR I-97, where the

Are services extra-territorial by nature?

Further to the Court's broad approach to preliminary references, some relatively recent judgments seem to suggest that certain categories of services are inherently and by nature extra-territorial. Hence, the Court applies Article 56 TFEU in such cases, without ever identifying any specific trans-border service movement.[156]

The *first* category of services in which this seems to hold true is transport. In many transport cases, the Court takes for granted that Article 56 TFEU applies alongside the sector-specific rules, and only at a subsequent stage does it examine whether in fact services provided to or from other member states are more severely affected.[157] The existence of some trans-border element does not constitute a prerequisite to the application of Article 56 TFEU, therefore, but one of the considerations inherent in its application.

A *second* category of services in which the Court applies Article 56 TFEU without insisting on the existence of some trans-border element is advertising services. In *Gourmet*,[158] a case in which a Swedish undertaking opposed the total ban imposed by Swedish law on the advertising of alcoholic beverages, the Court held that 'even if [the prohibition] is non discriminatory, [it] has a particular effect on the cross-border supply of advertising space, *given the international nature of the advertising market* in the category of products to which the prohibition relates, and thereby constitutes a restriction on the freedom to provide services within the meaning of Article 59 [Article 56 TFEU]'.[159] It is also worth recalling that in *Carpenter* the Court found Article 56 TFEU to be applicable because a 'significant proportion of Mr Carpenter's business consists of providing services, for remuneration, to advertisers established in other Member States'.[160]

The *third* category of services deemed to be transnational are TV broadcasting and telecommunications services. Hence, in *De Coster*,[161] which concerned a municipal tax imposed on parabolic antennae, the Court dealt dismissively with the matter, simply recalling that 'it is settled case-law that the transmission, and broadcasting, of television signals comes within the rules of the Treaty relating to

Court repeated its traditional view according to which reverse discrimination is perfectly tolerable under EU law.

[156] These developments are taken from Hatzopoulos, V., and Do, U., 'Overview of the Case Law of the ECJ in the Field of Free Movement of Services 2000–2005' (2006) 4 *CML Rev* 923–91.

[157] See Case C-381/93 *Commission v France (maritime transport)* [1994] ECR I-5145; Case C-295/00 *Commission v Italy (disembarkation/embarkation tax)* [2002] ECR I-1737; Joined cases C-430 & 431/99 *Inspecteur van de Belastingdienst Douane, district Rotterdam v Sea-Land Service Inc and Nedlloyd Lijnen BV* [2002] ECR I-5235; Case C-435/00 *Geha Naftiliaki EPE and others v NPDD Limeniko Tameio DOD/SOU and Elliniko Dimosio* [2002] ECR I-10615.

[158] Case C-405/98 *Konsumentombudsmannnen (KO) v Gourmet International Products AB (GIP)* [2001] ECR I-1795.

[159] Ibid, para 39 (emphasis added).

[160] Case C-60/00 *Carpenter*, n 149, para 29. It is true that in Case C-134/03 *Viacom II* [2005] ECR I-1167, concerning a municipal tax imposed on billboard advertising, the Court declined the application of Art 56, but that was more because of the lack of any substantially restrictive effect of the contested measure, rather than because of the lack of any trans-border element.

[161] Case C-17/00 *François De Coster v Collège des bourgmestre et échevins de Watermael-Boitsfort* [2001] ECR I-9445. See also Wennerås, P., 'The *De Coster* Case: Reflections on Tax and Proportionality' (2002) 29 *LIEI* 219–30.

the provision of services' and did not feel compelled to enquire any further into the facts of the case, before applying Article 56 TFEU.[162] More interestingly, in *Mobistar*,[163] which concerned a municipal tax imposed on GSM retransmission pylons, the Court referred to *De Coster* and took for granted that Article 56 TFEU applied to telecommunication services. In the end, however, the Court found no violation of the provision, because all owners of pylons were affected in the same way, irrespective of their nationality, and all telecommunications services were affected similarly, irrespective of whether they were national or cross-border.[164] This is a striking example of the Court 'internalizing' the existence of a trans-border element: it is no longer used as a precondition for the applicability of the free movement of services rules, but rather, as a consideration 'internal' to the said rules, directing the Court's assessment of the existence of a violation.[165]

No need for extra-territoriality when EU legislation exists in the field?
In the field of public procurement, the Court applies the Treaty rules together with, or instead of, the Public Procurement Directives.[166] Long before that, the Court had already decided that the Directive rules apply to wholly internal situations.[167] The reason given for this is that detailed secondary legislation in the field does not merely aim to abolish all discrimination based on nationality, but also—and essentially—to create a level playing field for all European companies to compete unfettered by national regulatory regimes.[168] The fact that principles enshrined in secondary legislation apply irrespective of the presence of a transnational element has been clearly confirmed more recently, in relation to the Data Protection Directive,[169] in *Österreichischer Rundfunk*.[170] Here again, the Directive rules are deemed 'whatever the nationality or residence of natural persons, [to] respect their fundamental rights and freedoms' and therefore, 'the protection principles must apply to all processing of personal data by any person whose activities are governed by Community law'.[171]

---

[162] Case C-17/00 *De Coster*, n 161, para 28.
[163] Joined cases C-544 & 545/03 *Mobistar* [2005] ECR I-7723.
[164] Ibid, paras 32–33.
[165] This seems to constitute a shift from previous case law, in particular Case C-108/96 *Criminal proceedings against Dennis Mac Quen, Derek Pouton, Carla Godts, Youssef Antoun and Grandvision Belgium SA, being civilly liable, intervener: Union professionnelle belge des médecins spécialistes en ophtalmologie et chirurgie oculaire* [2001] ECR I-837. Further on the *De Coster* and *Mobistar* judgments, see the analysis under subheading A(1)c(ii).
[166] See the discussion in ch 2.
[167] Case C-243/89 *Commission v Danemark (Storbaelt)* [1993] ECR I-3353.
[168] Ibid, para 33.
[169] European Parliament and Council Directive 95/46/EC on the protection of individuals with regard to the processing of personal data and on the free movement of such data [1995] OJ L281/31.
[170] Joined cases C-465/00, C-138/01 and C-139/01 *Rechnungshof v Österreichischer Rundfunk and Others and Christa Neukomm and Joseph Lauermann v Österreichischer Rundfunk* [2003] ECR I-4989, para 42. See also Keppenne, J.P., and Van Raepenbusch, S., 'Les principaux développements de la jurisprudence de la Cour de Justice et du Tribunal de Première Instance, Année 2003' (2004) 40 *CDE* 439–513, who also make this point.
[171] Directive 95/46, n 167, Preamble Rec 2 and 12.

The applicability of secondary law to purely internal situations may not appear too exciting a development, especially in areas of advanced EU harmonization, but it becomes more so when, by extrapolation from secondary legislation, the Treaty provisions also become applicable in purely internal situations. This, indeed, has happened in the field of public procurement. The development of the Court's 'transparency' case law[172] had an unintended consequence: Article 56 TFEU (and the transparency principle thereby ensuing) became applicable in all the situations which could have been brought under the scope of the Public Procurement Directives, including purely internal situations. This has become clear in *Coname* and *Parking Brixen*, and was also recently confirmed in *ANAV v AMTAB*.[173]

The three tendencies discussed above account for the growing application of the Treaty rules on services to purely internal situations. This, in turn, leads to an important limitation of instances of reverse discrimination. Reverse discrimination in the area of services, therefore, without being formally outlawed, is nonetheless on its way to extinction. As explained above, this development is consistent with the *Alpine Investments* case law and the idea that export restrictions may violate Article 56 TFEU even when they are non-discriminatory.

2. Quantitative data[174]

It is one thing to set an analytical framework, at the normative level, for how the Court should decide cases before it to make sense of existing case law and guarantee consistency for future cases. It is yet a different exercise—and an instructive one— to stick to the tests actually followed by the Court and try to identify the major trends running through them. Indeed, if the Court's words do have some value, this should not be neglected in the effort to summarize and rationalize the sheer mass of its case law. The presentation of quantitative data, which is attempted here—for the first time to the knowledge of the present author[175]—will attempt to test the criteria described above, in the light of the actual Court's decisions and not their tentative analyses by legal doctrine; the focus of the exercise is on the free movement of services case law.

From the measures brought before the CJEU, the vast majority is found to be in violation of the Treaty provisions on the free provision of services—it is a different question[176] whether the measure is eventually upheld by virtue of some express

---

172 Presented in some detail in ch 5.

173 Case C-231/03 *Consorzio Aziende Metano (Coname) v Comune di Cingia de' Botti* [2005] ECR I-7287 Case C-458/03 *Parking Brixen GmBH v Gemeinde Brixen and Stadtwerke Brixen AG* [2005] ECR I-8585; Case C-410/04 *Associazione Nazionale Autotrasporto Viaggiatori (ANAV) v Comune di Bari and AMTAB Servizio SpA* [2006] ECR I-3303.

174 Based on personal research (jointly with Diane Grisel; see ch 1) on the totality of the Court's case law up to June 2009.

175 The most analytical presentation of restrictions to the free provision of services is, to the author's knowledge, the Commission Communication COM (2000) 888 final, 'An Internal Market Strategy for Services', which, however, is essentially based on consultations with national officials and other parties, rather than on statistical analysis of the Court's case law.

176 For the answer to which, see the developments in ch 4.

Table 3.1. Measures not violating Article 56 TFEU

Measure accepted as introducing no discrimination or restriction	11
Measure accepted in principle, subject to scrutiny by referring court	1
Measure concerning the organization of sport	4
Measure having too remote or insignificant an effect	2
Person claiming protection not connected with service provider (*Grogan*)	1
Total	**19**

exception or ORPI. Indeed, from over 466 measures brought before the Court during the study period,[177] only 19 were found not to violate prima facie the Treaty rules on services. Of these 19 cases, in 11 the Court explicitly ruled out the existence of some discrimination or restriction,[178] while in another it cleared the measure in principle but referred it back to the national court to control its actual effects.[179] In two cases, the Court found that the measures had too remote[180] or too insignificant[181] an effect on services provision, while in *Grogan*, it refused to apply the rules on services altogether, judging that the dissemination of information on an economic activity (abortion) by a voluntary association could not itself qualify as an economic activity.[182] The remaining four measures, which were held by the Court to be outside the scope of Article 56 TFEU, were inherently connected to the exercise of some sport.[183] (See Table 3.1)

Except for these 19 cases, all other measures brought before the Court have been found to violate prima facie Article 56 TFEU. As explained above, violation may occur through measures which are discriminatory in law or in fact, measures which impose double burdens or measures which substantially limit market access. Given

---

[177] The actual number of cases identified during the study period is 283; the number of measures is higher than that of cases, as several cases examine more than one national measure.

[178] Case 90/76 *S.r.l. Ufficio Henry van Ameyde v S.r.l. Ufficio centrale italiano di assistenza assicurativa automobilisti in circolazione internazionale* (UCI) [1977] ECR 1091; Case 15/78 *Société générale alsacienne de banquet SA v Koestler* [1978] ECR 1971; Case 52/79 *Procureur du Roi v Debauve* [1980] ECR 833; Case 251/83 *Eberhard Haug-Adrion v Frankfurter Versicherungs-AG* [1984] ECR 4277; Case C-379/92 *Peralta* [1994] ECR I-3453; Case C-94/99 *ARGE Gewässerschutz v Bundesministerium für Lond-und Fortwirtschaft* [2000] ECR I-11037; Case C-68/99 *Commission v Germany (insurance)* [2001] ECR I-1865; Joined cases C-49–50, 52–54, 68–71/98 *Finalarte Sociedade de Construçáo Civil Lda and others* [2001] ECR I-7831; Case C-56/01 *Patricia Inizan v Caisse primaire d'assurance maladie des Hauts-de-Seine* [2003] ECR I-12403; Case C-412/04 *Commission v Italy (below thresholds)* [2008] ECR I-619; Case C-324/07 *Coditel Brabant SA v Commune d'Uccle and Region de Bruxelles-Capitale* [2008] ECR I-8457.

[179] Case 31/87 *Gebroeders Beentjes BV v Netherlands* [1988] ECR 4635.

[180] Joined cases C-544 & 545/03 *Mobistar* [2005] ECR I-7723.

[181] Case C-134/03 *Viacom II* [2005] ECR I-1167.

[182] Case C-159/90 *The Society for the Protection of Unborn Children Ireland Ltd (SPUC) v Stephan Grogan and others* [1991] ECR 4685.

[183] Case 36/74 *Walrave and Koch v International Cycliste Association Union* [1974] ECR 1405; Case 13/76 *Gaetano Donà v Mario Mantero* [1976] ECR 1333; Joined cases C-51/96 & C-191/97 *Deliège* [2000] ECR I-2549 and Case C-313/02 *Meca-Medina* [2004] ECR I-3291.

that the definition of discrimination is highly contested and that virtually every author adopts a different approach,[184] the classification below will be based on the (often tenuous) qualifications made by the Court in its reasoning. The Court's use of the term 'discrimination' and its qualification as direct/indirect lacks coherence. In the tables shown, the classification used is the one to which the judgments' wording (though not always the substance) makes reference: cases where the term discrimination, with or without some qualification, is used, as well as cases where the Court while not using the 'discrimination' word bases its judgment on some unjustified difference of treatment, are recorded as discriminatory.

In 114 cases, the Court has identified some kind of discrimination, while in the remaining 333, the Court considered that the Treaty rules were violated merely by restrictive measures; in addition, there are several borderline situations.

Within the category of discriminatory measures, instances of direct discrimination are less numerous—and in decline—compared to indirect. From a total of 46 cases of direct discrimination 25 cases, the majority belonging to the early years of the internal market are based on nationality.[185] Another 21 cases of direct discrimination are based on residence/establishment.[186] Alongside these, there are 21 cases of indirect discrimination based on nationality,[187] 13 on establishment[188] and 18 on the place of residence of the parties or of execution of the contract (total 52).[189] Moreover, there are another 11 cases where the imposition of 'double burdens' has been judged by the Court to constitute discrimination.[190] (See Table 3.2)

---

[184] For which, see the analysis in subsection A(1)c(ii).

[185] Such as in Case 36/74 *Walrave and Koch*, n 183; Case 118/75 *Lynne Watson and Alessandro Belmann* [1976] ECR 1185; Case 13/76 *Donà*, n 183; Case 90/76 *van Ameyde*, n 178; Case 52/79 *Debauve*, n 178; Case 168/85 *Commission v Italy (insurance)* [1986] ECR 2945.

[186] Such as eg Case 15/78 *Koestler*, n 178; Case 52/79 *Debauve*, n 178; Case 62/79 *SA Coditel v Ciné Vog Films* [1980] ECR 881; Case 352/85 *Bond van Adverteerders and others v Netherlands* [1988] ECR 2085; Case 427/85 *Commission v Germany (lawyer's services)* [1988] ECR 1123.

[187] Such as eg Case 13/76 *Donà*, n 183; Case 31/87 *Gebroeders Beentjes BV*, n 179 above; Case 3/88 *Commission v Italy (data processing)* [1989] ECR 4035; Case C-272/91 *Commission v Italy (Lottomatica)* [1994] ECR I-1409; Case C-18/93 *Corsica Ferries Italia Srl v Corpo dei Piloti del Porto di Genova* [1994] ECR 1783.

[188] Such as eg Case 76/81 *SA Transporoute et travaux v Ministère des travaux publics* [1982] ECR 417; Case C-113/89 *Rush Portuguesa v Office nationale d'immigration* [1990] ECR I-1417; Case C-154/89 *Commission v France (tourist guides)* [1991] ECR I-659; Case C-180/89 *Commission v Italy (tourist guides)* [1991] ECR I-709; Case C-198/89 *Commission v Greece (tourist guides)* [1991] ECR I-727; Case C-375/92 *Commission v Spain (tourist guides)* [1994] ECR I-923; Case C-211/91 *Commission v Belgium (cable TV)* [1992] ECR I-235.

[189] Such as eg in Case 186/87 *Cowan v Le Trésor Public* [1989] ECR 195; Case C-49/89 *Corsica Ferries France v Direction générale des douanes françaises* [1989] ECR 4441; Case C-45/93 *Commission v Spain (museums)* [1994] ECR I-911; Case C-381/93 *Commission v France (maritime transport)* [1994] ECR I-5145; Case C-274/96 *Criminal proceedings against Horst Otto Bickel and Ulrich Franz* [1998] ECR I-7637.

[190] See already in Case 16/78 *Criminal proceedings against Michel Choquet* [1978] ECR 2293, Joined cases 110 & 111/78 *Van Wesemael* [1979] ECR 35, Case 279/80 *Webb* [1981] ECR 3305, Joined Cases 62 & 63/81 *Seco v EVI* [1982] ECR 223, Case 76/81 *Transporoute*, n 188, and Case 168/85 *Commission v Italy (insurance)*, n 185.

Table 3.2. Discriminatory violations of Article 56 TFEU

Direct based on nationality	25
Indirect based on nationality	21
Indirect based on residence or place of execution of contract	18
Direct based on the place of residence/establishment	21
Indirect based on the place of establishment	13
Other form of indirect discrimination	5
Double burdens	11
Total	114

The above 'double burdens' cases mark the uneasy borderline between discriminatory and non-discriminatory measures: in addition to the 11 cases that the Court has 'classified' under the former category, there are another 19 which have been qualified by the Court as introducing mere restrictions.[191] It is not always easy to follow the Court's reasoning in these cases, nor to understand when the imposition of 'double burdens' would amount to discrimination and when not. (See Table 3.3)

In at least 69 cases, the Court qualifies as merely restrictive measures that impose some additional burden to the foreign service provider,[192] while in another 15, it censors measures which make the foreign provider miss out on some economic opportunity.[193] Further, in another 36 cases, the Court finds that there is some

---

[191] Case C-104/91 *Colegio Oficial de Agentes de la Propriedad Immobiliaria v José Luis Aguirre Borrell and others* [1992] ECR I-3003; C-319/92 *Salomone Haim v Kassenzahnärztliche Vereinigung Nordrhein* [1994] ECR I-425; C-375/92 *Commission v Spain (tourist guides)*, n 188; Case C-340/89 *Vlassopoulou v Ministerium für Justiz, Bundes- und Europaangelengheiten Baden- Württemberg* [1991] ECR I-2357; Case C-43/93 *Vander Elst v Office des Migrations Internationales* [1994] ECR I-3803 and the majority of the other posted workers cases but for *Viking* and *Laval*; Case C-114/97 *Commission v Spain (private security)* [1998] ECR I-6717 and the other private security cases etc.

[192] See eg the tourist guide cases cited in n 188 above; Case C-76/90 *Säger* [1991] ECR I-4221, Case C-43/93 *Vander Elst*, n 191 above, and the other posted workers cases; Case C-222/95 *Société Civile Immobilière Parodi v Banque H. Albert de Bary et Cie* [1997] ECR I-3895; Case C-410/96 *Criminal proceedings against André Ambry* [1998] ECR I-7875; Case C-124/97 *Markku Juhani Läärä, Cotswold Microsystems Ltd and Oy Transatlantic Software Ltd v Kihlakunnasyyttäjä (Jyväskylä) and Suomen valtio* [1999] ECR I-6067, Case C-67/98 *Questore di Verona v Diego Zenatti* [1999] ECR I-7289 and the other gambling cases; Case C-114/97 *Commission v Spain (private security)*, n 191.

[193] In the advertising cases, eg Case C-288/89 *Gouda* [1991] ECR I-4007; C-353/89 *Commission v The Netherlands (Mediawet)* [1991] ECR I-4069; C-384/93 *Alpine Investments* [1995] ECR I-1141; Case C-34–36/95 *Konsumentombudsmannen v de Agostini and TV-Shop* [1997] ECR I-3843; Case C-6/98 *Arbeitsgemeinschaft Deutscher Rundfunkanstalten v PRO Sieben Media AG* [1999] ECR I-7599; Case C-405/98 *Gourmet* [2001] ECR I-1795; Case C-294/00 *Deutsche Paracelsus Schulen für Naturheilverfahren GmbH v Kurt Gräbner* [2002] ECR I-6515; Case C-262/02 *Commission v France (alcohol tv advertising)* [2004] ECR I-6569; Case C-429/02 *Bacardi France SAS, formerly Bacardi-Martini SAS v Télévision Française 1 SA (TF1), Groupe Jean-Claude Darmon SA and Girosport SARL* [2004] ECR I-6613.

Table 3.3. Non-discriminatory violations of Article 56 TFEU

Double burdens	19
Additional burdens for provider	69
Additional burdens or missed advantage for recipient	36
Missed opportunity for provider	15
Access completely prohibited	96
Other reasons—indeterminate	98
Total	**333**

extra burden for the recipient of trans-border services.[194] All these cases could—if stretched according to the analysis by G. Marenco[195]—fall within a broad definition of (quasi-)discrimination.

Discrimination and 'double burdens' aside, there are 15 cases where the Court identifies some restriction without any reference, or even allusion, to any kind of discrimination; most of these cases would require strong determination, or even imagination, to say that somehow discrimination is the criterion followed.[196] The majority of these cases could also be brought under a broad 'market access' logic; indeed, in many of these cases—both (quasi-)discriminatory and non discriminatory—the Court refers itself more or less explicitly to a 'market access' criterion. There is, moreover, a body of 96 cases, which can only be explained by the fact that the measures at stake completely prohibit access to the relevant service activity and where discrimination does not seem at all to be the test followed by the Court.[197]

---

[194] Case C-55/93 *Criminal proceedings against Johannes Gerrit Cornelis van Schaik* [1994] ECR I-4837; Case C-118/96 *Safir v Skattemyndigheten i Dalarnas Län* [1998] ECR I-1897; C-410/96 *Ambry*, n 192 above; Case C-158/96 *Raymond Köhll v Union des Caisses de Maladie* [1998] ECR I-1931 and all the ensuing healthcare cases; Case C-17/00 *De Coster* [2001] ECR I-9445; Case C-136/00 *Rolf Dieter Danner* [2002] ECR I-8147; Case C-435/00 *Geha* [2002] ECR I-10615; Case C-290/04 *FKP Scorpio Konzertproduktionen GmbH v Finanzamt Hamburg-Eimsbüttel* [2006] ECR I-9461; C-433/04 *Commission v Belgium (constructing works)* [2006] ECR I-653.

[195] Marenco, G., 'Pour une interprétation traditionnelle de la notion de mesure d'effet équivalent à une restriction quantitative' (1984) 19 *CDE* 291–364.

[196] Case C-23/93 *TV10 SA v Commissariaat voor de Media* [1984] ECR I-4795; Case C-55/94 *Gebhard* [1995] ECR I-4165; Case C-3/95 *Reisebüro Broede v Gerd Sandker* [1996] ECR I-6511; Case C-398/95 *SETTG v Ypourgos Ergasias* [1997] ECR I-3091; Case C-118/96 *Safir*, n 194 above; Case C-348/96 *Criminal proceedings against Donatella Calfa* [1999] ECR I-11; Joined cases C-51/96 & C-191/97 *Deliège* [2000] ECR I-2549; Case C-309/99 *J.C.J. Wouters, J.W. Savelbergh and Price Waterhouse Belastingadviseurs BV v Algemene Raad van de Nederlandse Orde van Advocaten, intervener: Raad van de Balies van de Europese Gemeenschap* [2002] ECR I-1577; Case C-60/00 *Carpenter* [2002] ECR I-6279.

[197] Case 52/79 *Debauve* [1980] ECR 833; Case 220/83 *Commission v France (co-insurance)* [1986] ECR 3663; Case 292/86 *Gullung v Conseil de l'ordre des avocats du barreau de Colmar* [1988] ECR 111; Case 352/85 *Bond van Adverteerders and others v Netherlands* [1988] ECR 2085; Case 147/86 *Commission v Greece (private schools)* [1988] ECR 1637; Case 38/87 *Commission v Greece (architects,*

These quantitative findings show that the judicial reality is far more complex than the normative analysis in the first part of this chapter would suggest. It is, indeed, this complexity—and incoherence—which makes the normative exercise all the more valuable. The data provided confirm the precepts on which the previous analysis has been based. They make clear that the Court does look beyond discrimination, both verbally and materially; the outer limits of discrimination, however, are difficult to trace. They also show that 'double burdens'—and the correlative failure of member states to mutually recognize attributes already certified by the host state—are rarely tolerated by the Court. There is some uneasiness here, as in some occasions 'double burdens' are deemed to constitute discrimination and in others not.[198] (Substantial) limitation of 'market access' constitutes yet a third reason for the Court's intervention.

The fact, however, that most cases of 'double burdens' and 'market access' (especially the ones concerning mere restrictions, not outright prohibitions) are characterized by the Court as 'missed opportunities' or as imposing 'additional costs' or 'other restrictions', demonstrates the limitations of any classification attempt. Indeed, any normative effort—including the one attempted above—may be seen as a straightjacket, incapable of fully containing judicial reality. It is, then, worth looking into the actual types of measures that have been qualified as restrictions by the Court.

B. Restrictions: the characteristics

1. Origin of restrictions

It has already been briefly noted that in the field of services, much more than in goods, restrictive measures can have a non-state origin.[199] In principle, Article 56 TFEU—like all other internal market rules—should only apply to public, not private, measures. Since, however, non-state measures can seriously undermine the free provision of services, the Court stretched the scope of Article 56 TFEU to cover such measures.[200]

The fact that scrutiny of private measures under Article 56 TFEU remains an exception is confirmed by numerical data. Out of the 283 cases judged by the Court, only 28 had a non-state origin. 'Only' is a misleading word when compared with the case law on other freedoms, where the number of non-state measures examined by the Court is confined to single-digits. The difference can easily be explained by breaking down these 28 measures based on their origin:

---

civil engineers etc) [1988] ECR 4415; Case C-260/89 *ERT* [1991] ECR I-2925; Case C-275/92 *Schindler* [1994] ECR I-1039.

[198] It has been submitted above that the latter approach is the most accurate, but it will be explained in ch 4, why the distinction is not of fundamental importance.

[199] See the discussion in ch 1.

[200] The intellectual process leading to this inclusion and the critiques which may be attached to it are discussed more thoroughly in ch 6.

Table 3.4. Origin of restrictions to Article 56 TFEU   No. of cases

State measures	Legislative measures		170
	Administrative measures	Regulatory measures	10
		Individual measures	46
		Administrative practice	5
	National case law		2
	Other		22
Non-state measures	Insurance and pension funds		11
	Professional orders—associations		3
	Collective agreements—trade union action		9
	Sport regulation		5
Total			283

a. 11 measures or decisions stem from pensions and insurance funds, while b. another three measures stem from professional orders and associations; yet c. another five measures come from sports associations or organizations. More strikingly, d. nine restrictive measures are the result of collective agreements and/or action by the trade unions. It is clear that, sports apart, the other three categories of measures are likely to be more burdensome to the occasional service provider than to those wishing to establish themselves in another member state.

So far as state-imposed restrictions are concerned, it is interesting to note that the vast majority of restrictive measures are enshrined in legislation, and are only rarely administrative measures. Indeed, out of 233 state-imposed restrictions, 170 stem directly from a legislative text, while another 46 constitute individual administrative measures taken for the execution of legislation.[201] Only 10 restrictions originate in general administrative measures and half as many in administrative practice (see Table 3.4). This should not mask the fact that, very often, unfriendly administrative practices supplement unlawful legislative choices. In any case the fact remains that, according to these findings, protection of the regulatory objectives of member states (or, depending on the case, of the corporatist interests of well-organized interest groups) is deeply embedded in national legal orders and is not connected to purely opportunistic or corporatist behaviours. This, in turn, means that administrative cooperation, hailed elsewhere in this book as one of the main imports of the Services Directive,[202] and constitutionalized by Article 197 TFEU, may not produce any spectacular outcomes on its own. On the contrary, the dismantlement

---

[201] It should not be forgotten that on several occasions, even though the Court seems to be judging on the compatibility of a law with the Treaty, behind that law lies some national constitutional provision which the Court prefers not to discuss openly; see eg Case C-274/05 *Commission v Greece (diplomas)* [2008] ECR I-7969.

[202] An analysis of which can be found in ch 6.

of well-embedded restrictions may not be automatic, but needs to be gradual, adequately reasoned, and regularly monitored. The iterative self- and peer-evaluation processes foreseen in the Services Directive may prove useful to this end.

2. Impact: access v. exercise

a. *Generally on the distinction*

Among the various restrictive measures identified during the relevant period, it may be worthwhile to draw a dividing line between measures affecting *access* to, and those affecting the *exercise* of service activities. The distinction between the two categories is a very fine one and may be contested in many ways.[203] This notwithstanding, the access/exercise divide can prove useful in analytical terms, more so than the classification proposed by the Commission in its 2000 Communication 'Strategy for the Internal Market in Services'.[204] In this Communication, which helped set the scene for the Bolkestein proposal, the Commission had identified six categories of restrictions to the provision of services, in chronological order: establishment, use of inputs, promotion, distribution, sales, after-sale services. Such classification, interesting as it may be in descriptive terms, is hardly useful from a normative point of view. In quantitative terms, the first three categories stand for over 80 per cent of the restrictive measures identified. More importantly, the six-prong classification does not seem to have borne any legal consequence, neither at the legislative nor at the judicial level.

Given its innate vagueness, if the distinction between measures affecting access, on the one hand, and exercise, on the other, is to have any sense, the dividing line has to be drawn in a quite rigid and inflexible manner: by 'access measures' reference is made to those which in a direct manner forbid or render more difficult taking up and offering a service activity in the market of another member state (or indeed receiving a service from another member state), while all other measures are deemed to be 'exercise measures'. Following such a strict, if artificial, distinction, it was found that since the origins of the EEC, out of 466 restrictive measures tested under Article 56 TFEU,[205] 289 impede access, while another 177 affect the exercise of service activities.

Measures impeding access to service activities, although more numerous, are easier to list and to classify in a coherent manner. Measures affecting the exercise of services, on the other hand, are of a much wider variety, as they draw inspiration from the diverse modalities of service provision.

---

[203] For more on the normative problems raised by this distinction, see in subsection A(1)c(i), under the title 'Market access'.

[204] COM (2000) 888 final.

[205] This number corresponds to measures tested under the Treaty rule itself, not acts of secondary legislation. There are many more measures than cases actually tried before the CJEU, because several judgments, especially the ones initiated by the Commission against member states, bear on more than one restrictive measure.

b. Access restrictions

Measures impeding access to services can be brought under seven broad categories (see Table 3.5). *First* of all, there are *absolute prohibitions* of certain service activities: advertising of given products,[206] lotteries,[207] electronic games,[208] violent games etc;[209] all these make a total of seven restrictions.

A *second* category of measures relates to *nationality/residence requirements*. These may take various forms, such as requirements concerning the nationality of the shareholders of a service undertaking,[210] the location of its seat,[211] the establishment of a subsidiary or an office in the host state territory,[212] the need for a foreign service provider to designate a local representative or to act together with a local counterpart,[213] or nationality rules for sport.[214] At least 53 measures among those brought before the Court can be included in this category.

A *third* category, linked to the previous one, consists of *establishment/cabinet rules*: single cabinet rules,[215] prohibition to open a cabinet or to dispose of some fixed infrastructure,[216] or territorial exclusivity.[217] Six measures incorporate such restrictions.

A *fourth* category, connected to the previous one, concerns measures introducing restrictions as to the *corporate structure* of the service provider: they may impose a specific legal form, minimal capital requirements, minimal employee numbers,[218] or a non-profit objective.[219] They total nine measures.

---

[206] Case C-405/98 *Gourmet* [2001] ECR I-1795.
[207] Case C-275/92 *Schindler* [1994] ECR I-1039.
[208] Case C-65/05 *Commission v Greece (online games)* [2006] ECR I-10341.
[209] Case C-36/02 *Omega* [2004] ECR I-9609.
[210] Case 168/85 *Commission v Italy (insurance)* [1986] ECR 2945; Case 147/86 *Commission v Greece (private schools)* [1988] ECR 1637; Case 38/87 *Commission v Greece (architects, civil engineers etc)* [1988] ECR 4415; Case C-58/90 *Commission v Italy (health-care auxiliaries)* [1991] ECR I-4193; Case C-279/89 *Commission v UK (fisheries)* [1992] ECR I-5785; Case C-375/92 *Commission v Spain (tourist guides)* [1994] ECR I-923.
[211] See eg Case C-101/94 *Commission v Italy (foreign securities)* [1996] ECR 2691; Case C-355/98 *Commission v Belgium (private security firms)* [2000] ECR I-1221; Case C-279/00 *Commission v Italy (recruitment agencies)* [2002] ECR I-1425.
[212] Case C-355/98 *Commission v Belgium (private security firms)*, n 211 above; Case C-234/03 *Contse SA, Vivisol Srl and Oxigen Salud SA v Instituto Nacional de Gestion Sanitaria (Ingesa), formerly Instituto Nacional de la Salud (Insalud)* [2005] ECR I-9315.
[213] Case 427/85 *Commission v Germany (lawyer's services)* [1988] ECR 1123; Case C-294/89 *Commission v France (lawyers)* [1991] ECR I-3591; Case C-478/01 *Commission v Luxembourg (patent agents)* [2003] ECR I-2351; Case C-319/06 *Commission v Luxembourg (posting of workers)* [2008] ECR I-4323; Case C-564/07 *Commission v Austria (professional indemnity insurance)* [2009] ECR I-100.
[214] Case 36/74 *Walrave and Koch* [1974] ECR 1405; C-51/96 & C-191/97 *Deliège* [2000] ECR I-2549.
[215] Case C-96/85 *Commission v France (insurance)* [1986] ECR 1475.
[216] Case C-55/94 *Gebhard* [1995] ECR I-4165; Case 145/99 *Commission v Italy (lawyers)* [2002] ECR I-2235; Case C-298/99 *Commission v Italy (architects)* [2002] ECR I-3129.
[217] Case 427/85 *Commission v Germany (lawyer's services)* [1988] ECR 1123; C-294/89 *Commission v France (lawyers)*, n 213.
[218] See eg Case C-439/99 *Commission v Italy (trade fairs)* [2002] ECR I-305; Case C-171/02 *Commission v Portugal (private securities)* [2004] ECR I-5645; Case C-514/03 *Commission v Spain (private security)* [2006] ECR I-963; Joined cases C-338, 359 & 360/04 *Criminal proceedings against Massimiliano Placanica, Christian Palazzese and Angelo Sorricchio* [2007] ECR I-1891; as well as the other ECJ orders issued the same date with *Placanica* on the same issues.
[219] Case C-439/99 *Commission v Italy (trade fairs)*, n 218.

In a *fifth* category, measures where the *personal capacities* of the service provider are in question can be included: professional qualifications,[220] as well as (more rarely) honourability requirements.[221] There were 18 such cases in total.

A *sixth* residual category may be said to encompass all *other measures* restricting access to service activities: the grant of exclusive or special rights to already established service providers,[222] the existence of closed or otherwise regulated professions,[223] authorization or other selection procedures under a *numerous clausus* system,[224] and registration requirements;[225] a total of 89 restrictions may be brought in this group of measures.

A *seventh* category of measures comprises those imposing restrictions on the *physical presence* (entry/residence) of the service provider[226] and, more importantly, on that of the service recipient[227] (or their family)[228] in the host state.

Finally, in the broader category of measures restricting access to a service activity, the totality of the *public procurement* case law dealt with under Article 56 TFEU (ie not the typical public procurement case law which bears exclusively on the interpretation of the relevant Directives) should be added. Due to the special nature of the tendering procedure, such measures, irrespective of whether they formally restrict the access of foreign service providers to the domestic market or merely regulate the conditions for

---

[220] Such issues are examined in 17 cases: see eg Case 71/76 *Jean Thieffry v Conseil de l'ordre des avocats à la cour de Paris* [1977] ECR 765; Case 115/78 *J. Knoors v Secretary of State for Economic Affairs* [1979] ECR 399; Case 222/86 *Union nationale des entraîneurs et cadres techniques professionnels du football (Unectef) v Georges Heylens and others* [1987] ECR 4097; Case C-340/89 *Vlassopoulou* [1991] ECR I-2357; Case C-19/92 *Dieter Kraus v Land Baden-Württemberg* [1993] ECR I-1663; Case C-319/92 *Salomone Haim v Kassenzahnärztliche Vereinigung Nordrhein* [1994] ECR I-425; Case C-164/94 *Georgios Aranitis v Land Berlin* [1996] ECR I-135; Case C-234/97 *Fernandez Bobadilla v Museo Prado* [1999] ECR I-4773; Case C-285/01 *Isabel Burbaud v Ministère de l'Emploi et de la Solidarité* [2003] ECR I-8219.

[221] Case 292/86 *Gullung* [1988] ECR 111.

[222] See eg Case 90/76 *van Ameyde* [1977] ECR 1091; Case C-260/89 *ERT* [1991] ECR I-2925; Joined cases C-358 & 416/93 *Criminal proceedings against Aldo Bordessa, Mari Mellado, and Barbero Maestre* [1995] ECR I-361; Case C-55/93 *Van Schaick* [1994] ECR I-4837; Case C-55/96 *Job Centre coop. arl* [1997] ECR I-7119; Case C-163/96 *Criminal proceedings against Silvano Raso and others* [1998] ECR I-533; Case C-266/96 *Corsica Ferries France* [1998] ECR I-3949.

[223] See eg Case C-3/95 *Sandker* [1996] ECR I-6511; Case C-294/00 *Grabner* [2002] ECR I-6515; Case C-389/05 *Commission v France (bovine insemination)* [2005] ECR I-5337.

[224] Case C-243/01 *Criminal proceedings against Piergiorgio Gambelli and others* [2003] ECR I-13031; Joined cases C-338, 359 & 360/04 *Placanica*, n 218.

[225] See eg Case C-355/98 *Commission v Belgium (private security firms)* [1996] ECR I-2691, and all the other private security cases; Joined cases C-369 & 376/96 *Criminal proceedings against Jean-Claude Arblade and Arblade & Fils SARL and Bernard Leloup, Serge Leloup and Sofrage SARL* [1999] ECR I-8453; Case C-358/98 *Commission v Italy (disinfection and sanitation services)* [2000] ECR I-1255; Case C-264/99 *Commission v Italy (road haulage)* [2000] ECR I-4417; Case C-58/98 *Josef Corsten* [2000] ECR I-7919; Joined cases C-49-50, 52-54, 68-71/98 *Finalarte* [2001] ECR I-7831; Case C-390/99 *Canal Satélite Digital SL v Administración General del Estado* [2002] ECR I-607; Case C-215/01 *Bruno Schnitzer* [2003] ECR I-14847.

[226] Case 48/75 *Procureur du Roi v Royer* [1976] ECR. 497; Case 118/75 *Watson and Belmann* [1976] ECR 1185.

[227] Case C-348/96 *Calfa* [1999] ECR I-11; Case C-215/03 *Salah Oulane v Minister voor Vreemdelingenzaken en Integratie* [2005] ECR I-1215.

[228] Case C-60/00 *Carpenter* [2002] ECR I-6279, Case C-200/02 *Kunqian Catherine Zhu and Man Lavette Chen v Secretary of State for the Home Department* [2004] ECR I-9925.

Table 3.5. Measures restricting access to the provision of services

Kind of restriction	Sub-category of restriction	Cases per restriction	No. of cases
Absolute prohibitions			7
Nationality/residence requirements	Nationality requirement for exercising some activity or gaining shareholding	9	53
	Residence—legal seat requirement	11	
	Establishment/subsidiary on national territory	16	
	Local representative or need to act together with local professional	6	
	Nationality rules for sports	2	
	Other	9	
Establishment and cabinet rules	Single practice rules	1	6
	Prohibition to open cabinet or dispose infrastructure	3	
	Territorial exclusivity	2	
Corporate structure of service provider	Specific legal form—minimal capital/ personnel requirements	8	9
	Non-profit objective	1	
Personal capacities	Professional qualifications	17	18
	Honourability requirements	1	
Other restrictions	Exclusive or special rights granted to local providers	21	89
	Closed and regulated professions	7	
	Authorization—*numerus clausus* selection	36	
	Registration requirement—ID card, etc	20	
	Other	5	
Restrictions to physical presence	On service provider	6	8
	On service recipient	2	
Public procurement restrictions			24
Other			75
Total			**289**

service provision, aim to—and do in effect—exclude from the tenders concerned those providers who are not in a position to comply with them. Therefore, even if technically some of the measures concerned regulate the exercise, it is more useful to account for them under the broader category of measures restricting access to the domestic market. A total of 24 cases may be brought under this category.

c. Exercise restrictions

Measures restricting the exercise of a service activity (see Table 3.6) are more diverse and, therefore, more difficult to account for.

The *first* category can cover measures which *limit the professional freedom* of service providers by forbidding integrated collaborations with other professionals,[229] prescribing some specific type of contractual relationship,[230] or imposing other administrative restrictions to the way the service provider is constituted or run.[231] Five measures fall within this category. A further two measures concern limitations imposed on access to property.[232]

A *second* category concerns measures restricting *advertising*, publicity or other means of communication. Such cases concern both advertising as an autonomous service activity (for goods or services)[233] and advertising as a means for non-established service providers to penetrate a new market.[234] There were 12 cases in total.

A *third* category consists of measures which make the access of service providers to *credit, insurance*, and *financial institutions* in the host state more difficult or costly, and/or do not take into account similar guarantee, credit, or insurance arrangements already undertaken in the home state.[235] Eight restrictions of this kind have been identified.

A much more important category includes, *fourthly*, measures which *refuse to recipients of non-domestic services advantages* which they would have been entitled to, had they received the same service domestically. The typical example—with no less than 33 occurrences—is where the expenses for receiving a service abroad (pensions, insurance, education, etc) may not be deducted from revenue, for *tax* calculation purposes.[236] Another body of restrictions, recognized by the Court

---

[229] Case C-309/99 *Wouters* [2002] ECR I-1577.

[230] Case C-398/95 *SETTG* [1997] ECR I-3091; Case C-255/04 *Commission v France (licence to performing artists)* [2006] ECR I-5251.

[231] Case C-439/99 *Commission v Italy (trade fairs)* [2002] ECR I-305; Case C-287/03 *Commission v Belgium (customer loyalty programmes)* [2005] ECR 3761.

[232] Case 63/86 *Commission v Italy (social housing)* [1988] ECR 29; Case 305/87 *Commission v Greece (immovable property)* [1989] ECR 1461.

[233] See eg Case 52/79 *Debauve* [1980] ECR 833; Case 352/85 *Bond van Adverteeders* [1988] ECR 2085; Case C-288/89 *Gouda* [1991] ECR I-4007; Case C-353/89 *Commission v The Netherlands (Mediawet)* [1991] ECR I-4069; Joined cases C-34–36/95 *de Agostini* [1997] ECR I-3843; Case C-6/98 *PRO Sieben* [1999] ECR I-7599; Case C-262/02 *Commission v France (alcohol tv advertising)* [2004] ECR I-6569; Case C-492/02 *Bacardi* [2004] ECR I-6613.

[234] See eg Case C-384/93 *Alpine Investments* [1995] ECR I-1141; Case C-294/00 *Grabner* [2002] ECR I-6515.

[235] See eg Case C-410/96 *Ambry* [1998] ECR I-7875; Case C-279/00 *Commission v Italy (recruitment agencies)* [2002] ECR I-1425; Case C-356/08 *Commission v Austria (doctors' bank accounts)* [2009] ECR I-108; Case C-451/99 *Cura Anlagen GmbH v Auto Service Leasing GmbH (ASL)* [2002] ECR I-3193; Case C-355/00 *Freskot AE v Elliniko Dimosio* [2003] ECR I-5263; Case C-350/07 *Kattner Stahlbau GmbH v Maschinenbau-und Metall-Berufsgenossenschaft* [2009] ECR I-1513.

[236] See eg Case C-118/96 *Safir* [1998] ECR I-1897; Case C-294/97 *Eurowings Luftverkehrs AG v Finanzamt Dortmund-Unna* [1999] ECR I-7447; Case C-55/98 *Skatteministeriet v Bent Vestergaard* [1999] ECR I-7641; Case C-17/00 *De Coster* [2001] ECR I-9445; and more recently, see Case C-522/04 *Commission v Belgium (occupational pension schemes)* [2007] ECR I-5701; Case C-76/05 *Herbert Schwarz and Marga Gootjes-Schwarz v Finanzamt Bergisch Gladbach* [2007] ECR I-6849; Case C-318/05 *Commission v Germany (school fees)* [2007] ECR I-6957.

Table 3.6. Measures restricting exercise of service activities

Kind of restriction	Sub-category of restriction	Cases per restriction	No. of cases
Limits to professional freedom	Forbidding collaboration with other professionals	1	5
	Prescribing type of contractual relationship	2	
	Other administrative restrictions	2	
Making access to property, etc more difficult		2	2
Making credit, insurance, etc more difficult—failure to MR		8	8
Advertising, publicity, etc restrictions		12	12
Home state refusing certain advantages to *recipients* of foreign services	Refusing tax exemptions and other tax advantages	33	49
	Refusal to reimburse service expenses if obtained abroad—or prior authorization	14	
	Other	2	
Host state refusing certain advantages to foreign *recipients* on nationality/ residence		3	3
Procedural advantages for established service providers	*Cautio judicatum solvi* or other deposit	5	9
	Language choice dependent on nationality	1	
	Tax calculation period different depending on location of revenues	1	
	Other	2	
Criminal law differences based on place of establishment	Different sanctions	4	5
	Different incriminations	1	
SGEI obligations	Obligation to contract	1	4
	Price restrictions	3	
Special areas (horizontal)	TV broadcasting, etc	10	41
	Transport	8	
	Posted workers	23	
Other			39
Total			**177**

during this last 15 years, relates to refund refusal for services—essentially healthcare—received abroad;[237] another 14 measures come under this heading. Other measures to discourage recipients from looking abroad for services include the refusal of an insurance bonus when the insurer is in another member state[238] and the refusal to take into account expenses incurred in another member state as a consequence of legal requirements there (eg representation by a local lawyer).[239]

Fifthly, service recipients' freedom to receive services in other member states may also be restricted by *measures of the host state* (as opposed to measures of their home state which were the subject of the fourth category). Measures which make some kind of benefit conditional on nationality or long-term residence fall within this category: eg indemnity for aggression,[240] free access to museums,[241] access to some other social advantage, such as a minimal subsistence fee, etc.[242] The relevant case law (three measures) has been revolutionized and expanded, in the last 10 years, by the 'citizenship' case law.[243]

A *sixth* category consists of purely *procedural advantages* restricted to domestic/established service providers, to the exclusion of providers who have an occasional presence. The various national measures requiring a *cautio judicatum solvi* or other deposit or guarantee as a condition for access to justice constitute the typical example (five measures);[244] the same is true of the measure making the choice

---

[237] See Case C-158/96 *Köhll* [1998] ECR I-1931; Case C-157/99 *Smits and Peerbooms* [2001] ECR I-5473; Case C-368/98 *Vanbraekel* [2001] ECR I-5363; Case C-385/99 *V.G. Müller-Fauré v Onderlige Waarborgmaatschappij oz Zorgverzekeringen UA and E.E.M. van Riet v Orderlinge Waarborgmaatschappij oz Zorgverzekeringen UA* [2003] ECR I-4509; Case C-372/04 *The Queen, on the application of Yvonne Watts v Bedford Primary Care Trust and Secretary of State for Health* [2006] ECR I-4325; Case C-496/01 *Commission v France (medical laboratories)* [2004] ECR I-2351; Case C-56/01 *Inizan* [2003] ECR I-12403; Case C-326/00 *Idryma Koinonikon Asfaliseon (IKA) v Vasileios Ioannidis* [2003] ECR I-1703; Case C-444/05 *Aikaterini Stamatelaki v NPDD Organismos Asfaliseos Eleftheron Epangelmation (OAEE)* [2007] ECR I-3185; Case C-156/01 *R.P. van der Duin v Onderlinge Waarborgmaatschappij ANOZ Zorgverzekeringen UA and Onderlinge Waarborgmaatschappij ANOZ Zorgverzekeringen UA v T.W. van Wegberg-van Brederode* [2003] ECR I-7045; Case C-193/03 *Bosch* [2004] ECR I-9911; Case C-173/09 *Georgi Ivanov Elchinov v Natsionalna zdravnoosiguritelna kasa* [2010] nyr.

[238] Case 251/83 *Haug Audrion* [1984] ECR 4277.

[239] Case C-289/02 *AMOK Verlags GmbH v A & R Gastronomie GmbH* [2003] ECR I-15059.

[240] Case 186/87 *Cowan* [1989] ECR 195.

[241] Case C-45/93 *Commission v Spain (museums)* [1994] ECR I-911; Case C-388/01 *Commission v Italy (museums)* [2003] ECR I-721.

[242] Case C-456/02 *Michel Trojani v Centre Public d'aide sociale des Bruxelles (CPAS)* [2004] ECR I-7573.

[243] On which see Epinay, A., 'The Scope of Article 12 EC: Some Remarks on the Influence of European Citizenship' (2007) 13 *ELJ* 611–22; on a more sceptical tone, see Katrougalos, G., 'The (Dim) Perspectives of the European Social Citizenship' 5/07 Jean Monnet Working Paper, also available at <http://centers.law.nyu.edu/jeanmonnet/papers/07/070501.html> (last accessed on 8 November 2011); and Besson, S., and Utzinger, A., 'Introduction: Future Challenges of European Citizenship: Facing a Wide-Open Pandora's Box' (2007) 13 *ELJ* 573–90.

[244] See eg Case C-20/92 *Anthony Hubbard v Peter Hamburger* [1993] ECR I-3777; Case C-323/95 *David Charles Hayes and Jeannette Karen Hayes v Kronenberger GmbH* [1997] ECR I-1711; Case C-263/99 *Commission v Italy (transport consultants)* [2001] ECR I-4195; Case C-279/00 *Commission v Italy (recruitment agencies)* [2002] ECR I-1425.

of language in a judicial procedure dependent on the parties' nationality.[245] An unjustified procedural disadvantage was also inflicted by a measure which made the tax calculation period longer for revenue gained by activities in other member states, as compared to that gained domestically.[246]

Linked to the above, *seventhly*, there are *criminal law measures* which impose discriminatory or disproportionate sanctions on foreign service providers or recipients (four cases);[247] a measure which imposes different criminal offences depending on the place of establishment of the service providers should also be added to this.[248]

Finally, in an *eighth* category, measures typically (but not necessarily) associated with the provision of some *service of general interest* (SGEI) or, at least, some service closely connected to the general interest could be included. Such measures comprise the obligation to contract and to offer services,[249] as well as price restrictions.[250]

Alongside these eight categories of restrictive measures affecting the exercise of the freedom to provide services, there are another three which may more easily be presented by reference to the specific area of the law they affect rather than by their restrictive content. The reason is not only that these measures correspond to complex legal categories or services, but they are also regulated by specific secondary EU legislation. Such measures concern a. TV broadcasting and cultural obligations, etc (10 measures), b. transport (8 measures), and c. posted workers (23 measures).

3. Comment

Although the distinction between access and exercise restrictions is questionable in legal terms, especially in the field of services, for analytical purposes it does retain some interest. Indeed, *access* restrictions, with the exception of absolute prohibitions, are generally seen as more harmful than *exercise* restrictions. This is so both because of their object (they overtly or covertly exclude providers from other member states and, hence, incorporate some form of discrimination) or their effect (they offer territorial protection to established service providers). Such exclusion, moreover, is more absolute for service providers than for goods' manufacturers: the latter may see their low quality goods being banned from the market of a given member state, but they can still export their high-end products. It is much more difficult to trace a similar dichotomy when it comes to services; national measures

---

[245] Case C-274/96 *Bickel and Franz* [1998] ECR I-7637.

[246] Joined cases C-155 & 157/08 *X and E.H.A. Passenheim-van Schoot v Staatssecretaris van Financiën* [2009] ECR I-5093.

[247] See Joined cases C-338, 359 & 360/04 *Placanica* [2007] ECR I-1891; and the related Orders of the Court.

[248] Case C-153/00 *Criminal proceedings against Paul der Weduwe* [2002] ECR I-11319.

[249] Case C-518/06 *Commission v Italy (motor insurance)* [2009] ECR I-3491.

[250] Case C-96/94 *Centro Servizi Spediporto Srl v Spedizioni Marittima del Golfo Srl* [1995] ECR I-2883; Case C-263/99 *Commission v Italy (transport consultants)* [2001] ECR I-4195; Joined cases C-94 & 202/04 *Cipolla* [2006] ECR I-11421; Case C-451/03 *Calafiori* [2006] ECR I-2941.

pursuing quality do not concern services but the providers themselves, thus fully banning non-compliant ones from the member state concerned. Furthermore, it can be argued that access restrictions are (indirectly) promoted or (directly) enacted by participants *in* a market in order to keep *out* potential newcomers.

Exercise restrictions, on the other hand, tend to be non-discriminatory (at least on their face) and objectively justified by some reason linked to the general interest. Indeed, they are promoted or enacted by the market participants, to regulate their own presence *in* the market, and not specifically to keep others *out* of it. Protectionist *intent* is, therefore more difficult—if not impossible—to establish. Instead, emphasis should be placed on the *effects* of such measures.

Indeed, the great variety of measures restricting the exercise of service activities, summarily presented above, leads to two observations.

First, exercise restrictions are much more diverse and imaginative than access restrictions. In contrast to goods, the characteristics of which (composition, technical characteristics, etc) are taken into account by national measures impeding *access*, the characteristics of services (risk, social impact, etc) are essentially taken into account by *exercise* regulations. But for complete prohibitions, *access* regulations in services typically concern the provider, not the service; the services' characteristics are taken into account and regulated at the level of *exercise* conditions. In other words, the access/exercise divide covers very different measures, depending on whether such measures concern services or goods. Exercise rules for the former cover all services characteristics, while for the latter they concern only the conditions of their commercialization; hence, exercise rules are of central importance for service providers, while they may only incidentally impact on the sales of goods. Moreover, the sheer variety of restrictive measures shows that any attempt to proceed on the basis of formal and watertight distinctions, along the lines of the *Keck* logic, is inappropriate in the field of services, as it would leave the door open to imaginative rule-making to the detriment of non-established service providers.

Secondly, it follows from the brief presentation above that many of the exercise-related restrictive measures are genuinely non-discriminatory; all the same, this does not render them less restrictive. Here again, the inaccuracies of a mechanical transposition of principles from the goods case law become obvious. In particular, the 'market access' v. 'product characteristics' dichotomy does not seem appropriate to services. The same is true for the three-prong test promoted by most authors in the wake of the 'use restriction' case law, according to which, Article 34 TFEU is breached by a. all openly discriminatory rules, b. product rules when discriminatory in law or in fact (or is it that they impose double burdens?), and c. indistinctly applicable rules whenever they limit market access (or have discriminatory effect).[251] As pointed out above, the reality of service provision regulation seems to merge types (b) and (c) to create a broad all-encompassing category of exercise restrictions.

---

[251] For this three-prong test, see the discussion in subsection A(1)c(i), under the subheading 'Market access'.

If access and exercise restrictions are, then, equally problematic for the free provision of services and both need be tackled irrespective of there being any discrimination, the further question raised is whether the two categories are equally difficult to deal with.

From a regulatory point of view, access restrictions seem more difficult to circumvent than exercise restrictions, if no recourse to 'hard' law is to be taken: mutual recognition and/or reference to standards are likely to be of limited help to the excluded service provider—with the notable exception of recognition of professional qualifications. Similarly, codes of conduct and other means of self-regulation are not going to take excluded service providers any further, as these are drafted by the participants in a given market for use by them—as against 'outsiders'.

The situation is different for exercise restrictions. SGEI apart, most other restrictions are likely to yield before an extensive—if imaginative—application of the principle of mutual recognition.[252] Self-regulation and the use of standards may also be of use in this area. Cooperation between member state authorities, the exchange of information, and the use of standardized forms of contracts, all feature as means available to enhance the abolition of exercise restrictions.

In this respect, tax obstacles raised by the home state should not be forgotten. Taxation, however, being a. a highly technical area, b. directly linked to national sovereignty, and c. already extensively regulated at the international level largely through bilateral agreements, is unlikely to yield to such horizontal means of integration (mutual recognition and soft law) and will require more focused—and robust—regulatory interventions.[253]

Absolute prohibitions also constitute quite a delicate issue. In the early gambling cases, the Court has shown great deference towards member states' choices, but in subsequent cases it has stepped up the proportionality control—and has strengthened it with a 'coherence' control.[254] The recent cases on use restrictions further show that total prohibitions are not fully immune from EU law,[255] especially where no moral issues are involved. The position seems to be pretty much the same under the GATS, following the Appeal Body's opinion in *US/Gambling*.[256]

---

[252] For the application of the mutual recognition principle in the field of services, see ch 6.

[253] See in this respect, for indirect taxation, Genschel, P., 'Why No Mutual Recognition of VAT? Regulation, Taxation and the Integration of the EU's Internal Market for Goods' (2007) 14 *J of Eur Public Policy* 743761; and for direct taxation, Cordewener, A., Kofler, G., and van Thiel, S., 'The Clash between European Freedoms and National Direct Tax Law: Public Interest Defences Available to the Member States' (2009) 46 *CML Rev* 1951–2000.

[254] For which, see the discussion in ch 4.

[255] Case C-110/05 *Commission v Italy (trailers)* [2009] ECR I-519; Case C-142/05 *Åklagaren v Percy Mickelsson and Joakim Roos* [2009] ECR I-4273, para 28; see on these cases, Horsley, T., 'Annotation: Case C-110/05, *Commission v Italy (trailers)* [2009] nyr' (2009) 46 *CML Rev* 2001–19; Derlén, M., and Lindholm, J., 'Article 28 EC and Rules on Use: A Step Towards a Workable Doctrine on Measures Having Equivalent Effect to Quantitative Restrictions' (2010) 16 *Columbia J of Eur L* 191–231.

[256] *US/Gambling*, DS 285, adopted on 20 April 2005.

C. Conclusion

All in all, the three basic criteria of 'restrictions' identified, at the normative level, in the first part of the present chapter are only partly confirmed by the statistical data provided above. *Access* restrictions are largely censored by the Court without much ado. Therefore, the fact that in its recent free movement case law (concerning goods), the Court spelled out market access as a criterion is a welcome development, as it provides a name to a well-established practice;[257] though it is hardly an innovation, at least in the field of services. So far as *exercise* restrictions are concerned, the Court does not seem to base its reasoning expressly on the theoretical distinction between discriminatory and non-discriminatory measures, drawn above. It is true that the Court strikes down any form of ostensible discrimination—both direct and indirect—extending, at times, as far as double burdens. Double burdens, however, are also struck down on their own, without any discrimination element. Further, when the Court examines other (non-discriminatory) exercise restrictions, it does not seem to be paying any attention as to whether such measures relate to the service itself or to the way it is provided (a distinction altogether more problematic in the field of services than in goods).

In view of this, the idea that the concept of 'restrictions' in all four freedoms tends towards a unitary definition[258] is only partly confirmed, as the immaterial, volatile and flexible nature of services makes the relevant area less susceptible to normative classification than the fields of manufactured goods or persons.

---

[257] Case C-110/05 *Commission v Italy (trailers)* [2009] ECR I-519; Case C-142/05 *Åklagaren v Percy Mickelsson and Joakim Roos* [2009] ECR I-4273, para 28; and Case C-265/06 *Commission v Portugal (windshield films)* [2008] ECR I-2245.

[258] For which, see A(1)c(i).

4

Justifications

In the previous chapter it was observed that the overwhelming majority of restrictive measures brought to the attention of the Court are prima facie found to violate the Treaty rules on services. This, however, does not lead the Court to systematically strike down all national measures. That is because many of the measures with protective effects pursue at the same time legitimate interests. Nevertheless, the existence of a legitimate interest does not automatically lead to the absolution of the national measure in question, but is subject to the principle of proportionality. The Court follows a two-prong test, first inquiring into the *interest* pursued (A), and then examining whether the restrictive *measure* is justified (B).

A. Identifying the grounds for justifications: the interests protected

The Treaty itself recognizes several grounds for exceptions: public policy, public security, and public health, as well as the exercise of official authority (1). Alongside these, the Court has had to add a highly significant body of judge-made justifications, essentially—but not exclusively—in the form of 'overriding reasons of public interest' (ORPIs) (2). The Services Directive, for its part, introduced legislative exceptions for the first time (3).

1. Treaty-based justifications

Article 52 TFEU establishes three grounds which may justify restrictions to the Treaty rules on establishment and services—even when discriminatory: public policy, public security, and public health. Moreover, Article 51 TFEU foresees that the Treaty provisions do not apply 'to activities which are connected, even occasionally, with the exercise of official authority'. Article 62 TFEU makes these provisions specifically applicable to services.

The official authority exception, established in Article 51 TFEU, is of virtually no relevance to the provision of services. From a legal point of view, the Court has considerably restricted the scope of this exception to cover only activities (as opposed to entire professions or positions) which genuinely involve the exercise of public power.[1] From a practical point of view, it is difficult to imagine situations where an *occasional* service provider from another member state would pretend to get involved in the exercise of official authority. This explains why there is not a single services case in which this derogation has been successfully invoked by a member state. This situation, however, could change in the future, as services traditionally carried out by the state are increasingly entrusted to private service providers: private security services have repeatedly been examined by the Court in recent years, while private prisons could be another area in which the free provision of services clashes with the exercise of official authority.[2] Tax collection could also yield to private initiative.

As for the three grounds enumerated in Article 52 TFEU, these have traditionally been interpreted in a very restrictive manner.

In particular, the application of the *public security* exception has been considerably constrained by Directive 64/221 on public order, now embodied in the Directive 2004/38 (the Citizenship Directive).[3] This explains why, since the establishment of the EEC, public security has successfully served as a justification in only 16 services cases.[4] The Court's tight-handed approach has guided member states to plead 'around' this express Treaty provision. Thus, when, for instance, the Spanish Government was trying to justify the restrictions to the establishment and operation of private security firms in its territory, instead of pleading an Article 52 TFEU argument (public security), the member state put forward an ORPI of complying with the requirements connected to terrorism.[5] Similarly, the Dutch Government, in its own effort to justify restrictions to private security firms, invoked the need to foster trust of the public towards private security agents.[6]

Public policy has also been applied quite restrictively by the Court: it only accounts for 14 measures accepted. One of the major trends in this regard has

---

[1] See, eg the early judgments in Case 2/74 *Jean Reyners v Belgian State* [1974] ECR 631, concerning the profession of lawyers; see also Case C-306/89 *Commission v Greece (travel agents, etc)* [1991] ECR I-5863; Case C-272/91 *Commission v Italy (Lottomatica)* [1994] ECR I-1409; Case C-263/99 *Commission v Italy (transport consultants)* [2001] ECR I-4195; as well as the long series of cases on private security services (Case C-114/97 *Commission v Spain (private security)* [1998] ECR I-6717; Case C-355/98 *Commission v Belgium (private security firms)* [2000] ECR I-1221; Case C-189/03 *Commission v Netherlands (private security firms)* [2004] ECR I-5645; Case C-514/03 *Commission v Spain (private security)* [2006] ECR I-963). The Court's restrictive stance in relation to the concept of official authority has been furthered by two judgments delivered by the Court while this book was under print, in Case C-52/08 *Commission v Portugal (notaries)* [2011] ECR nyr and Case C-53/08 *Commission v Austria (notaries)* [2011] ECR nyr.

[2] The attribution of such services and the choice of providers, however, are likely to be channelled through the rules on public procurement and would only incidentally come to be judged directly under the Treaty rules; see in this respect the analysis in ch 5.

[3] European Parliament and Council Directive 2004/38 (EC) on the right of citizens of the Union and their family members to move and reside freely within the territory of the Member States amending Regulation (EEC) No 1612/68 and repealing Directives 64/221/EEC, 68/360/EEC, 72/194/EEC, 73/148/EEC, 75/34/EEC, 75/35/EEC, 90/364/EEC, 90/365/EEC and 93/96/EEC [2004] OJ L158/77.

[4] As explained in ch 1 above, the quantitative data gathered covers case law issued from 1 January 1958 to 30 June 2009.

[5] Case C-514/03 *Commission v Spain (private security)*, n 1.

[6] Case C-189/03 *Commission v Netherlands (private security firms)*, n 1.

been the identification of public morality as a distinct ground from public policy. In *Schindler* and the other gambling/gaming cases, the Court held public morality to lie outside the scope of Articles 36 and 52 TFEU exceptions; it is unclear, however, if it qualified as yet another ORPI.[7] In any event, the moral, religious, and cultural aspects of gambling activities were all seen as factors justifying extensive discretion to the national authorities. The confines of the 'public policy' exception were further blurred in *Commission v Greece (online games)*, where it was held that public morality, policy, and security are 'considerations, which must be taken together, concern[ing] the protection of the recipients of the service and, more generally, of consumers, as well as the maintenance of order in society, and those objectives are amongst those which may be regarded as overriding reasons relating to the public interest'.[8]

Following these tendencies, public policy and public security are both quite restrictively invoked—and even more restrictively admitted—as grounds for the justification of measures that are in breach of the freedom to provide services.

The scope of the *public health* exception, on the other hand, has been considerably expanded by the Court during recent years. The public health circumstances which justify restrictions to the free movement of persons were described in Directive 64/221, and subsequently in Directive 2004/38, in a very confined way. Hence no case has ever reached the CJEU in which this ground was invoked to justify measures restricting the access of suffering persons to the territory of another member state. Moreover, the Court has cut short the effort of member states to resist the entry—physical or virtual—of foreign health professionals, on the ground that they could constitute a threat for public health.[9]

The few cases in which public health had been used with some success concerned the justification of restrictions to the advertising of harmful goods, such as tobacco or alcohol,[10] and more recently, restrictions to services advertising.[11]

An unexpected development in the use of public health as a means of justifying restrictive measures occurred with the patient mobility cases, starting in 2001.[12] In these cases, the member states tried to justify their exit and entry restrictions on patients, invoking various grounds. The Court accepted that maintaining the financial balance of social security systems did constitute an ORPI. Further, it held that the objective of ensuring 'a balanced medical and hospital service open to

---

[7] For all these cases and the public morality derogation, see the discussion in subsection A(2)b.

[8] Case C-65/05 *Commission v Greece (online games)* [2006] ECR I-10341, para 33.

[9] Case C-158/96 *Raymond Köhll v Union des Caisses de Maladie* [1998] ECR I-1931; Case C-157/99 *B.S.M. Geraets-Smits v Stichting Ziekenfonds VGZ and H.T.M. Peerbooms v Stichting CZ Groep Zorgverzekeringen* [2001] ECR I-5473.

[10] Case 96/85 *Commission v France (doctors and dentists)* [1986] ECR 1475; Case C-405/98 *Konsumentombudsmannnen (KO) v Gourmet International Products AB (GIP)* [2001] ECR I-1795.

[11] Case C-294/00 *Deutsche Paracelsus Schulen für Naturheilverfahren GmbH v Gräbner* [2002] ECR I-6515; Case C-500/06 *Corporación Dermoestética SA v To Me Group Advertising Media* [2008] ECR I-5785.

[12] See eg C-157/99 *Smits and Peerbooms*, n 9; Case C-368/98 *Abdon Vanbraekel and others v Alliance nationale des mutualités chrétiennes (ANMC)* [2001] ECR I-5363.

all', as well as the 'maintenance of treatment capacity or medical competence on national territory' are both essential for public health, and even for the survival of the population, and do fall under Article 52 TFEU derogations.

It has been noted by several authors that reference to Article 52 TFEU was not at all necessary in these judgments.[13] *For one thing*, both the consideration of a balanced medical/hospital service and that of treatment capacity are intrinsically linked to the financial means dedicated to them—they need not be considered as separate issues. *Secondly*, there is no apparent reason why these should be read as falling within Article 52, rather than as constituting independent additional ORPIs.[14] The Court's position was made yet more complex when, in *Hartlauer*, it was held that 'two objectives may . . . be covered by . . . [Article 52] derogation in so far as they contribute to achieving a high level of protection of health, namely the objective of maintaining a balanced high-quality medical or hospital service open to all and the objective of preventing the risk of serious harm to the financial balance of the social security system'.[15] This statement clearly goes against the principle that public health should be construed in a restrictive manner. It also counters the idea put forward by the Court in its early healthcare judgments, where it distinguished between the provision of healthcare, on the one hand, and the question of paying for it, on the other; while the latter is linked to the financial equilibrium of the social security system, the maintenance of treatment capacity, etc has to do with the former.

The Court's reversal is understandable, however, given that reference to Article 52 TFEU allows for the justification of discriminatory measures, while the introduction of a new ORPI would not.[16] Therefore, by making use of Article 52 TFEU, the Court is spared from inconclusive discussions, at later stages of its reasoning, such as whether resident and non-resident patients are in a comparable situation (a discussion that the Court has had problems circumventing in the field of direct taxation).[17] In view of this, and of the increased number of cases concerning patients' rights, this part of Article 52 TFEU is the most used of all (17 cases), particularly over the last 10 years (see Table 4.1).

---

[13] See eg Hatzopoulos, V., 'Killing National Health and Insurance Systems but Healing Patients? The European Market for Health Care Services after the Judgments of the ECJ in *Vanbraekel* and *Peerbooms*' (2002) 36 *CML Rev* 683–729, at 725–6.

[14] Ibid.

[15] Case C-169/07 *Hartlauer Handelsgesellschaft mbH v Wiener Landesregierung and Oberösterreichische Landesregierung* [2009] ECR I-1721, para 47.

[16] For the question whether ORPIs may justify discriminatory national measures, see subheading A(2)a.

[17] See eg the ease with which the Court alludes to Article 52 TFEU in Case C-73/08 *Nicolas Bressol and others and Céline Chaverot and others v Gouvernement de la Communauté française* [2010] nyr, para 62, in order to justify a measure limiting the number of non-resident students in Belgian universities, without having discussed whether resident and non-resident students are in comparable situations: 'it follows from the case-law that a difference in treatment based indirectly on nationality may be justified by the objective of maintaining a balanced high-quality medical service open to all, in so far as it contributes to achieving a high level of protection of health'.

Table 4.1. Treaty exceptions to the free movement of services in the CJEU case law

	Express exceptions	No. of cases
1.	Exercise of official authority	0
2.	Public policy	14
3.	Public order	16
4.	Public health	17
	Total	47

2. Judge-made justifications

The idea that national measures restricting free movement may be allowed to stand, provided they are 'reasonable' is as old as the foundational judgments of the CJEU in the area. As early as *Dassonville*, the Court, after expressing the very broad definition of measures of equivalent effect to a quantitative restriction, conceded that 'in the absence of Community system guaranteeing [an objective in the general interest], if a Member State takes measures to prevent unfair practices in this connection, it is however subject to the condition that these measures should be *reasonable*'.[18] A few months later, the same idea was expressed more explicitly in relation to services, in *Van Binsbergen*.[19] The Court qualified a Dutch measure as a restriction to Article 56 TFEU because it imposed a residence requirement for the exercise of the activity of legal representation. It then went on to state that:[20]

'taking into account the particular nature of the services to be provided, specific requirements imposed on the person providing the service cannot be considered incompatible with the Treaty where they have as their purpose the application of... rules justified by the general interest... which are binding upon any person established in the State'.

The same idea was broadly expressed in *Van Wesemael*,[21] in relation to services, before being definitively articulated in a peremptory way by *Cassis de Dijon*.[22] After a gestation period, the *Dutch TV* cases made it clear that exceptions to both goods and services—and indeed to all free movement rules—operate along the same lines.[23] This and subsequent case law also made clear that early variations in terminology between the various freedoms did not bear any substantial

---

[18] Case 8/74 *Procureur du Roi v Dassonville* [1974] ECR 837, para 79.

[19] Case 33/74 *Johannes Hervicus Maria van Binsbergen v Bestuur van de Bedrijfsvereniging voor de Metaalnijverheid* [1974] ECR 1299.

[20] Ibid, para 12.

[21] Joined cases 110 & 111/78 *Ministère public and 'Chambre syndicale des agents artistiques et impresario de Belgique' ASBL v Willy van Wesemael and others* [1979] ECR 35.

[22] Case 120/78 *Rewe-Zentral AG v Bundesmonopolverwaltung für Branntwein (Cassis de Dijon)* [1979] ECR 649.

[23] Case C-288/89 *Stichting Collectieve Antennevoorziening Gouda v Commissariaat voor de Media* [1991] ECR I-4007; Case C-353/89 *Commission v Netherlands (Mediawet)* [1991] ECR I-4069.

differences.[24] It therefore became possible to talk about 'overriding reasons of public interest' as judge-made grounds that serve to justify national measures restricting any free movement rules.

Several early judgments seemed to imply that ORPIs, unlike the express Treaty derogations, are not mere justifications saving *ex post* restrictive measures; rather, the existence of some ORPI would be taken into account at the qualification stage, therefore avoiding the label of 'restriction' at the first place (*ex ante*).[25] Such a vision, however, has been negated by subsequent case law, which clearly treats ORPI 'justifications' in parallel with the express Treaty exceptions.[26] The recent case law on gambling even suggests the contrary, since the Court holds it 'necessary to consider to what extent the restriction at issue in the main proceedings may be *allowed* as a derogation expressly provided for by [the Treaty], or *justified*, in accordance with the case-law of the Court, by overriding reasons in the public interest'.[27] Therefore the discussion concerning the relationship between ORPIs and the exceptions expressly provided by the Treaty is still inconclusive.

A further characteristic that ORPIs share with express Treaty exceptions is that they may only be successfully invoked by member states subject to the principle of proportionality; or at least, that is what the Court consistently repeats. On closer inspection, however, this affirmation calls for some qualification, as the application of proportionality control is not always consistent and tends to be lenient in relation to specific grounds of general interest.

a. Overriding reasons of public interest: subject to a strict proportionality review

ORPIs are judge-made exceptions to the free movement rules. They have been 'invented' by the Court in *Van Binsbergen* and, more explicitly, in *Cassis de Dijon* and their number and variety have constantly developed ever since.[28] Their legal

---

[24] The terms used are 'mandatory requirements' for goods, as opposed to 'overriding reasons in the public interest' (ORPI) mostly used in the field of personal freedoms; on terminology and on the convergence of justifications in the different freedoms case law, see Hatzopoulos, V., 'Exigences essentielles, impératives ou impérieuses: une théorie, des théories ou pas de théorie du tout?' (1998) 2 *RTDE* 191–236.

[25] Mattera, A., *Le Marché Unique Européen: ses règles, son fonctionnement* (Paris: Jupiter, 1990), at 274–5; also Hatzopoulos, V., 1998, n 24.

[26] For this evolution and the relevant case law, see Martin, D., '"Discriminations", "entraves" et "raisons impérieuses" dans le traité CE: trois concepts en quête d'identité, (partie 1e) (1998) 34 *CDE* 261–318, at 294–9.

[27] See eg Case C-42/07 *Liga Portuguesa de Futebol Profissional and Bwin International Ltd v Departamento de Jogos da Santa Casa da Misericórdia de Lisboa* [2009] ECR I-7633, para 55 and in most other gambling cases.

[28] Article 4(8) of the Services Directive (Directive 2006/123) now offers an authoritative list of ORPIs recognized in the field of services: public policy; public security; public safety; public health; preserving the financial equilibrium of the social security system; the protection of consumers, recipients of services and workers; fairness of trade transactions; combating fraud; the protection of the environment and the urban environment; the health of animals; intellectual property; the conservation of the national historic and artistic heritage; social policy objectives and cultural policy objectives.

nature and their interplay with the internal market rules have occupied legal doctrine quite extensively.[29] Three remarks need be made here.

First of all, ORPIs have been enumerated for the first time in a binding document in Article 4(8) of the Services Directive. This Article states that '"overriding reasons relating to the public interest" means reasons recognised as such in the case law of the Court of Justice, including the following grounds'.[30] Therefore, enumeration is only indicative– and by no means exhaustive; at the same time, the core characteristic of ORPIs, that they are judge-made, is not at all abandoned or ignored, but, by contrast, appears confirmed by the Directive's text.

Secondly, the fact that ORPIs constitute an open-ended list, which, indeed, grows day by day, is the price to pay for the extremely wide notion of restriction followed by the Court: the broader the notion of restriction followed by the Court, the longer the list of ORPIs invoked by the member states in order to justify their measures.

Thirdly, the Court is generally ready to accept as valid almost any ORPI presented by the member states. It is at a subsequent stage, when examining the necessity and proportionality of the measures concerned, that the CJEU exerts its substantial control.[31] The only reasons which have not been accepted as 'overriding' are those which directly or indirectly serve (micro)economic objectives,[32] as well as those which have as their main *raison d'être* the inefficiencies of national administrations. Moreover, the Court has held that ORPIs, just like the express exceptions foreseen in the Treaty, may not serve to exclude an entire economic activity from the Treaty rules.[33] These limitations apart, the Court is extremely open to the objectives put forward by the member states. Indeed, the list contained in the Services Directive is not only indicative but also very comprehensive, as it groups under more general headings several overriding reasons recognized by the Court. Along the same broad lines of the Services Directive, but with some additional detail, the quantitative data in Table 4.2 has been obtained from a review of the Court's Services case law.[34]

Table 4.2 requires some qualifications.

First, the table records ORPIs which have been proposed by the member states and have been acknowledged as such by the Court, either explicitly or implicitly. An implicit recognition of an ORPI is done when the Court, without plainly recognizing the proposed interest as being 'overriding', does nonetheless enter into the examination of the necessity and the proportionality of the measure concerned.

---

[29] See, among many, Fernandez Martin, J.M., and O'Leary, S., 'Judicial exceptions to the free provision of services' in Andenas, M., and Roth, W.H. (eds), *Services and Free Movement in EU Law* (Oxford: OUP, 2002) 163–95; Hatzopoulos, V., 1998, n 24.

[30] For which see, n 28.

[31] See Hatzopoulos, V., 1998, n 24; Barnard, C., 'Restricting Restrictions: Lessons for the EU from the US?' (2009) 68 *Cambridge LJ* 575–606.

[32] For the invocation of ORPIs of an economic nature, see the analysis further below.

[33] Concerning ORPIs, see Case C-211/91 *Commission v Belgium (cable TV)* [1992] ECR I-235 and Case C-257/05 *Commission v Austria (boiler inspectors)* [2006] ECR I-134; concerning Treaty exceptions, see Case C-114/97 *Commission v Spain (private security)* [1998] ECR I-6717 and Case C-355/98 *Commission v Belgium (private security)* [2000] ECR I-1221.

[34] Based on personal research (jointly with Diane Grisel) on the Court's case law up to June 2009. For more information on data collection, see ch 1.

Table 4.2. ORPIs accepted by the CJEU in the field of services

	ORPIs broad categories	Sub-categories	No. of cases	Total
1.	Environment	Natural	4	5
		Urban	1	
2.	Social	Social order	5	48
		Financial equilibrium of social services system	10	
		Respect of the essential characteristics of the social services system	1	
		Protection of workers/employment conditions	22	
		Regulate the access of third country nationals on the labour market	5	
		Prevent social dumping	2	
		Prevent undeclared labour	1	
		Social policy objectives (other than the protection of workers)	1	
		Social protection of the victims of road accidents	1	
3.	Morality/Public morals	(mostly used as a reason to allow member state greater flexibility—not as an ORPI; but as in *Commission v Greece (online games)*[35])	1	1
4.	Fairness of transactions/ Fraud	Fairness of commercial transactions	4	16
		Prevention of fraud/Protection of reputation/credibility	12	
5.	Protection	Of service recipients	13	51
		Of consumers	23	
		From the propensity of spending	9	
		Of citizens/the public in general (including from terrorism)	2	
		Of creditors	2	
		Navigation security	1	
		Of confidential information	1	
6.	Quality	Of craftsmen work	2	16
		Of providers qualifications	3	
		Professional/disciplinary rules, etc	10	

(continued)

[35] Case C-65/05 *Commission v Greece (online games)* [2006] ECR I-10341.

Table 4.2. Continued

ORPIs broad categories	Sub-categories	No. of cases	Total
	Ease of communication between providers/recipients (patients)/authorities	1	
7. Intellectual property		1	1
8. Historic and cultural heritage/Cultural policy/ Pluralism	Protection of historic/cultural heritage	3	19
	Cultural policy	9	
	Protection of ethnic-cultural minority	1	
	Pluralism	6	
9. Organization of educational system	Promotion of research, education, etc	3	4
	Guarantee a high level of higher education	1	
10. Operation of justice	Smoothness of procedures	5	7
	Determination of competent jurisdiction if claims raised	1	
	Protection of rights stemming from EU law	1	
11. Public service mission	Without reference to Article 106(2)	2	6
	With reference to Article 106(2)	4	
12. Fundamental rights		8	8
13. Tax ORPIs	Fiscal balance (impossibility to tax non-residents)	3	46
	Fight against tax evasion/fraud	6	
	Efficiency of fiscal control	13	
	Coherence of fiscal system	14	
	Smooth operation of the system of imposition at the source	4	
	Balanced distribution of the power to raise tax	1	
	Territoriality principle	5	

Secondly, measures justified by the desire of member states to prevent situations of abuse of rights (*fraude à la loi* or *abus de droit*),[36] have not been counted, as the Court is quite inconsistent in this respect: in some cases such measures are accepted as ORPIs,[37] while in others they are

[36] For which see Sørensen, E., 'Abuse of Rights in Community Law: A Principle of Substance or Merely Rhetoric?' (2006) 43 *CML Rev* 423–59.

[37] See eg Case C-113/89 *Rush Portuguesa v Office nationale d' immigration* [1990] ECR I-1417; Case C-148/91 *Vereniging Veronica Omroep Organisatie v Commissariat voor de Media* [1993] ECR I-487; Case C-23/93 *TV10 SA v Commissariat voor de Media* [1984] ECR I-4795; Case C-244/04

not.[38] Moreover, the need to prevent abuse of rights situations stems primarily from the EU—not the national—legal order.[39]

Thirdly, the tax ORPIs, not listed in the Services Directive, are treated as a separate category altogether. Indeed, their exclusion from the Services Directive seems to confirm the widespread idea that tax law is an area where the internal market rules apply as in a 'parallel universe', subject to the same broad principles but to distinct technical rules.[40]

Fourthly, public safety, an ORPI listed on its own in the Services Directive, has been included in the general category of 'protection'.

Subject to these qualifications, a few substantive observations should be made.

i. Table 4.2 offers clear indications as to the main rationales driving member states to invoke ORPIs: protection (of consumers or service recipients) and quality of services, social considerations, cultural (and more general identity) reasons, tax. By the same token, it offers clear guidance as to the fields in which regulatory action (in the broad sense) may be required by the EU in order to achieve further integration in services' trade.

Four main axes requiring EU action can easily be identified: protection, quality, social considerations, and cultural policy/pluralism. The capacity of the EU to intervene in each one of these areas is uneven. *Protection* of the recipients of services could be achieved through a Directive instituting special rules for providers' liability, in a similar way to Directive 85/374.[41] Self-regulation may also play an important role in this respect. The same is true concerning the promotion of *quality* at the EU level. The difference between the two axes is that any regulatory (or self-regulatory) activity in respect of quality can only be sector-specific, as opposed to a liability regime which could be devised in a purely horizontal manner. The regulation of *social issues* seems a much more delicate mission, both for political and for

Commission v Germany (work visa regime) [2006] ECR I-885; Case C-168/04 *Commission v Austria (posted workers)* [2006] ECR I-9041.

[38] Case 145/99 *Commission v Italy (lawyers)* [2002] ECR I-2235; Case C-171/02 *Commission v Portugal (private securities)* [2004] ECR I-5645.

[39] See in this respect de la Feira, R., 'Prohibition of Abuse of (Community) Law: The Creation of a New General Principle of EC Law through Tax' (2008) 45 *CML Rev* 395–441; Sørensen, E., 2006, n 36 above; see also de la Feria, R., and Vogenauer, S. (eds), *Prohibition of Abuse of Law: A New General Principle of EU Law* (Oxford/Portland: Hart Publishing, 2011).

[40] See Banks, K., 'The Application of the Fundamental Freedoms to Member State Tax Measures: Guarding against Protectionism or Second-guessing National Policy Choices?' EUI RSCAS Working Paper No. 2007/31, also available at <http://cadmus.iue.it/dspace/bitstream/1814/7685/1/RSCAS_2007_31.pdf> (last accessed on November 8, 2011); Snell, J., 'Non-discriminatory Tax Obstacles in Community Law' (2007) 56 *Intl & Comparative L Q* 339–70; Bizioli, G., Balancing the Fundamental Freedoms and Tax Sovereignty: Some Thoughts on Recent ECJ Case Law on Direct Taxation (2008) 3 *European Taxation* 133–40; Demaret, P., 'The non-discrimination principle and the removal of fiscal barriers to intra-Community trade' in Cottier, T., and Mavroidis, P. (eds), *Regulatory Barriers and the Principle of Non-discrimination in World Trade Law* (Michigan: University of Michigan Press, 2000) 171–89.

[41] Council Directive 85/374/EEC on the approximation of the laws, regulations and administrative provisions of the Member States concerning liability for defective products [1985] OJ L210/29; for a brief discussion of the consumer protection aspects related to service provision, see the developments in the introduction of ch 5.

legal reasons. Lastly, *cultural policy and pluralism* are by nature less prone to common regulation at a European level.

ii. There are some areas in which regulatory activity already in place—or in the process of being adopted—will have direct impact on member state autonomy. The various Regulations adopted in recent years in the area of private international law, as well as the very important—as yet unfinished—effort to introduce a European Civil Code,[42] are both likely to make national initiatives redundant in the areas of fairness of transactions and combat of fraud, as well as in the area of the administration of justice.

iii. This enumeration raises, once again, the question of whether there is really a purpose in distinguishing between Treaty and judge-made exceptions.[43] The Court is ambivalent in this respect. In several cases—such as the health cases quoted above—it tends to blur any distinction between the two sets of justifications.[44] According to this trend, 'the freedom to provide services may...be limited by national rules justified by the reasons mentioned in Article 56(1) of the EC Treaty, read together with Article 66, or for overriding requirements of the general interest'.[45] In several cases, ORPIs are applied without even qualifying whether the national measure is discriminatory or not,[46] while in others they justify measures specifically qualified as discriminatory.[47] In certain cases, on the other hand, the Court clearly distinguishes between exceptions included in the Treaty and the judge-made ones, by stating that only the former may justify discriminatory measures.[48] This restrictive turn in the Court's jurisprudence has been confirmed by recent case law.[49]

This latter position may be grounded on two types of arguments, one based on legal and one on policy considerations. In legal terms, since Articles 51, 52, and 55 TFEU constitute exceptions to the fundamental Treaty freedoms, they should be applied restrictively. However, it would constitute an oxymoron to interpret these restrictively while, at the same time, attaining the same end result (the justification of discriminatory measures) through the 'back-door' of judge-made justifications. Moreover, since non-discrimination is a general principle of EU law it may only be derogated from by virtue of some express Treaty provision. From a policy point of

---

[42] For the latest available text, see The Study Group on a European Civil Code and The Research Group on EC Private Law (Acquis Group) *Principles, Definitions and Model Rules of European Private Law: Draft Common Frame of Reference (DCFR), Full Edition*, 6 vols (Munich: Sellier European Law Publishers, 2009); see also von Bar, C., 'A Common Frame of Reference for European Private Law: Academic Efforts and Political Realities' (2008) 12 *Electronic J of Comparative L*, available at <http://www.ejcl.org/121/art121-27.pdf> (last accessed on November 8, 2011).

[43] See Hatzopoulos, V., 'Exigences essentielles, impératives ou impérieuses: une théorie, des théories ou pas de théorie du tout?' (1998) 2 *RTDE* 191–236.

[44] See the discussion in subsection A(1).

[45] Case C-262/02 *Commission v France (alcohol tv advertising)* [2004] ECR I-6569, para 23.

[46] See eg Case C-250/95, *Futura Participations SA & Singer v Administration des Contributions (Luxembourg)* [1997] ECR I-2471; Case C-118/96 *Safir v Skattemyndigheten i Dalarnas Län* [1998] ECR I-1897; Case C-158/96 *Köhll* [1998] ECR I-1931.

[47] See eg Case C-204/90 *Hans-Martin Bachmann v Belgium* [1992] ECR I-249.

[48] Case C-341/05 *Laval un Partneri Ltd v Svenska Byggnadsarbetareförbundet, Svenska Byggnadsarbetareförbundets avdelning 1, Byggettan and Svenska Elektrikerförbundet* [2007] ECR I-11767, para 117.

[49] See eg Case C-219/08 *Commission v Belgium (posted workers)* [2009] ECR I-9213; Case C-153/08 *Commission v Spain (gambling tax)* [2009] ECR I-9735.

view, since ORPIs have been recognized—in *Van Binsbergen, Cassis de Dijon* and thereafter—as a palliative for the fact that *non-discriminatory* measures may be held to contravene free movement rules, it is only such measures which should be liable to be upheld by virtue of ORPIs. Seen from the reverse perspective, measures which discriminate against imported goods or services are innately against the very idea of an internal market and may only exceptionally be justified. Non-discriminatory measures, on the other hand, cause less harm to the functioning of the internal market and hence they may be perfectly justified whenever they pursue some ORPI.[50]

It is submitted, however, that the above distinction between express Treaty exceptions and ORPIs, although historically grounded, is no longer appropriate; or, if it were to apply, it should only concern formally discriminatory measures on the basis of nationality.[51] At least three arguments may be put forward in favour of such an approach, one descriptive and three prescriptive. *First*, there is a vast body of case law which negates such a distinction.[52] *Secondly*, the experience gained from over 50 years of CJEU case law shows that there are many perfectly valid general interest objectives, other than those foreseen by the Treaty, which are occasionally pursued by broadly discriminatory measures. On such occasions, the Court juggles with the unclear boundaries of the concept of discrimination in order to reach the desired outcome; it does so at the expense of legal certainty and coherence. *Thirdly*, these unclear boundaries make the distinction between express exceptions and ORPIs all the more artificial: since there is no single definition of discrimination, at the end of the day, the justification or not of a national measure depends on the discretion of the Court. This outcome, again, can hardly be said to promote legal certainty.

iv. A final point which needs be highlighted, although it does not directly ensue from Table 4.2, is the recognition of economic ORPIs. In this respect, the Court's case law is far from clear, since the Court constantly states that 'purely economic considerations' may not qualify as ORPIs, while at the same time, in practice, it does grant member states the possibility to pursue economic aims. It has been rightly observed that the Court 'has [a.] either interpreted the concept of restriction narrowly to avoid the issue of justification altogether or [b.] linked the economic aims to other public interest considerations, or [c.] simply denied or ignored the economic nature of the objectives'.[53] Further, it may be said that occasionally [d.]

---

[50] For a fuller presentation of arguments against the assimilation of judge-made exceptions/ justifications with the Treaty exceptions, see Spaventa, E., 'On Discrimination and the Theory of Mandatory Requirements' (2000) 3 *CYEL* 457–7.

[51] A proposal already put forward by Hatzopoulos, V., 'Annotation: Case C-250/95, *Futura Participations SA & Singer v Administration des Contributions (Luxembourg)*' [1997] ECR I-2471 (1998) 35 *CML Rev* 493–518. The idea there is mainly that the definition of restrictions should be based on a very broad test of discrimination—or, indeed, mere restrictions, while the availability of ORPIs as justifications should only be ruled out in cases of formal discriminations on the basis of nationality.

[52] See eg above n 45 to 47.

[53] Snell, J., 'Economic aims as justifications for restrictions to free movement' in Schrauwen, A. (ed), *Rule of Reason: Rethinking Another Classic of European Legal Doctrine* (Groningen: Europa Law Publishing, 2005) 37–56, at 37.

the Court has ignored other public interest reasons and refused altogether to accept an ORPI by qualifying it as purely economic.

The first trend may be illustrated by the Court's judgment in *Sodemare*,[54] where the activity of running old-people's homes was found to be altogether outside the scope of free movement rules; *Smits and Peerbooms* and more recent healthcare case law represent the second trend, whereby the maintenance of treatment capacity and of the financial balance of the social healthcare systems are combined with the objective of protecting public health; an example of the third trend can be found in the judgments in *Köhll* and *Decker* where the Court 'accepted an economic aim while claiming it was not doing so';[55] the fourth trend, finally, is reflected in the Court's judgment in *SETTG*, where the 'maintenance of industrial peace in an economically sensitive sector as a means of bringing a collective labour dispute' was stripped of its social character and seen as a purely economic objective.[56]

J. Snell tries to explain this apparent incoherence by opposing 'purely' economic objectives, which must be refused, to economic objectives closely connected to some genuine general interest goal, which should be accepted.[57] Such a distinction, Snell argues, falls in line with the logic of Article 106(2), which 'permits the pursuit of general interest aims through the fulfilment of intermediate economic objectives'.[58] The test proposed, however, is highly subjective, since it is easy to claim— but difficult to prove or disprove—that savings accrued to the state or to a given sector of the economy will be used for some purpose of general interest. A more subtle explanation would be that the Court is willing to recognize as ORPIs economic objectives of a structural, but not of a conjectural nature;[59] or to use more economic terms, 'macro-' measures are to be accepted, but not 'micro-'.[60] Thus, the financial balance of a social security scheme,[61] the coherence of a tax system,[62] or the balance between sports' clubs[63] are valid reasons justifying restrictions to the fundamental Treaty provisions, while other more specific economic objectives are not.

---

[54] Case C-70/95 *Sodemare SA and others v Regione Lombardia* [1997] ECR I-3395.

[55] In both these cases, the Court recalled the principle that 'aims of a purely economic nature cannot justify a barrier' to fundamental freedoms recognized by the Treaty. It further stated, however, that 'the risk of seriously undermining the financial balance of the social security system may constitute an overriding reason in the general interest capable of justifying a barrier of that kind'. See Case 99/78 *Weingut Gustav Decker KG v Hauptzollamt Landau* [1979] ECR 101, para 39 and Case C-158/96 *Köhll*, n 45, para 44.

[56] Case C-398/95 *Syndesmos ton en Elladi Touristikon kai Taxidiotikon Grafeion v Ypourgos Ergasias* [1997] ECR I-3091, para 23.

[57] Snell, J., 2005, n 52, at 48.

[58] Ibid, at 51.

[59] Hatzopoulos, V., 'Recent Developments in the Case Law of the ECJ in the Field of Services' (2000) 37 *CML Rev* 43–82, at 79.

[60] This distinction was originally made by Demaret, P., in his course 'Les quatre libertés' in the College of Europe, taught for over 20 years, until 2003.

[61] As in Case C-158/96 *Köhll* [1998] ECR I-1931.

[62] As in Case C-204/90 *Bachmann* [1992] ECR I-249.

[63] As in Case C-415/93 *Union royale belge des sociétés de football association ASBL v Jean-Marc Bosman, Royal club liégeois SA v Jean-Marc Bosman and others and Union des associations européennes de football (UEFA) v Jean-Marc Bosman* [1995] ECR I-4921.

b. Evading a strict proportionality review: solidarity and morality

Solidarity and morality are worth a special mention. It is submitted here that measures dictated by solidarity or connected to public morality are subject to a minimal proportionality control, if at all. Therefore, in these two areas member states are given a remarkable margin to manoeuvre.

Public morality has been an issue before the CJEU in four broad areas: pornographic goods,[64] prostitution,[65] gambling and gaming,[66] and other activities which could offend human life and dignity.[67]

The scene had already been set in the very early cases, concerning pornographic goods, where the Court a. held that 'it is for every member state to determine in accordance with its own scale of values and in the form selected by it the requirements of public morality in its territory' and b. refused to exercise any proportionality control of the national measure.[68] Pornographic goods, however, may be different from the other areas enumerated above, to the extent that a. they are not based on personal contact and, therefore, may not be adapted to the personality, age, etc of the user and b. public morality does figure in Article 36 TFEU in relation to *goods*, but not in the other derogatory free movement provisions.

This textual difference explains why in *Adoui and Cornuaille*, the first prostitution case, the question of justification was purely dealt with under the heading of public order (Directive 64/221)[69]—thus allowing much less discretion to the member state concerned.[70] In the *Grogan* case, concerning abortion, the Court showed its deference towards national preferences, by finding that the rules on services did not apply, invoking a purely technical ground. The special function of morality has been solemnly recognized no earlier than in *Schindler* and the subsequent gambling and gaming case law.[71] In these cases, the Court acknowledged that 'it is not possible to disregard the moral, religious or cultural aspects of lotteries' and concluded that 'those particular factors justify national authorities having a sufficient degree of latitude . . . in the light of the specific social and cultural

---

[64] Case 34/79 *Regina v Maurice Donald Henn and John Frederick Ernest Darby* [1979] ECR 3795; Case 121/85 *Conegate Limited v HM Customs & Excise* [1986] ECR 1007.

[65] Joined cases 115 & 116/81 *Rezguia Adoui v Belgian State and City of Liège, and Dominique Cornuaille v Belgian State* [1982] ECR 1665; Case C-268/99 *Aldona Malgorzata Jany and Others v Staatssecretaris van Justitie* [2001] ECR I-8615.

[66] For the relevant case law, see in more detail the analysis in ch 5.

[67] Case C-159/90 *The Society for the Protection of Unborn Children Ireland Ltd (SPUC) v Stephan Grogan and others* [1991] ECR 4685; Case C-36/02 *Omega Spielhallen-und Automatenaufstellungs-GmbH v Oberburgermeisterin der Bundesstadt Bonn* [2004] ECR I-9609.

[68] Case 37/49 *Henn & Darby*, n 64, para 15; subsequently, in Case 121/85 *Conegate*, n 64 above, the Court did censor the national measure at stake, but on grounds of discrimination, not due to the lack of proportionality.

[69] Council Directive 64/221/EEC on the coordination of special measures concerning the movement and residence of foreign nationals which are justified on grounds of public policy, public security or public health [1964] OJ L56/850, English Spec Ed, Series I Chapter 1963–4, 117.

[70] This did not matter much, as, in this case, a clearly discriminatory practice of the Belgian authorities was in question.

[71] For which, see ch 5.

features of each member state'.[72] Moreover, in *Omega*, the Court made clear that there are no common conceptions of moral, religious, or cultural considerations, and therefore, no general criterion for assessing the proportionality of national measures. It further went out of its way to state that 'the need for, and proportionality of, the provisions adopted are not excluded merely because one Member State has chosen a system of protection different from that adopted by another State'.[73]

The relevant case law shows that so long as the ground of public morality put forward by member states is genuine and not clearly protectionist, it will be accepted provided that the issue is not exhaustively harmonized by some EU measure.[74] The Court, contrary to its traditional outlook on other general interest grounds, openly refuses to enter the slippery path of proportionality evaluation of member states' moral choices. Instead, the Court limits its control to the existence of discrimination or 'incoherence': whenever the morally reprehensible activity is tolerated or,[75] even, openly promoted,[76] or offered by nationals of the state concerned, only then will the national measure in question be struck down by the Court.

From this case law, three remarks follow. *First*, irrespective of whether an express exception to this effect exists in the Treaty, the Court shows exceptional deference to national moral standards.[77] *Secondly*, in relation to the free movement of persons and services (where no express Treaty derogation exists in relation to public morality), the Court does not opt for a wide interpretation of the public policy exception; rather it acknowledges public morality as a distinct ground granting discretion to member states. *Thirdly*, it would seem that this ground, at least in the field of services, does not operate as a typical justification to restrictions, for the lack of proper proportionality review. Measures addressing issues of public morality are always allowed, and the Court only censors them when found discriminatory. Needless to say, this leaves to member states considerable room for manoeuvre.

Solidarity is the second ground in relation to which the member states are given wide discretion to issue measures detrimental to free movement. The criteria which the Court uses in order to identify solidarity have been briefly described in previous

---

[72] Case C-275/92 *Her Majesty's Customs and Excise v Schindler* [1994] ECR I-1039, paras 60 and 61.

[73] C-36/02 *Omega*, n 66. See also Ackermann, T., 'Annotation: Case C-36/02 *Omega Spielhallen-und Automatenaufstellungs-GmbH v Oberbürgermeisterin der Bundesstadt Bonn*' (2005) 42 *CML Rev* 1107–20.

[74] Case C-1/96 *The Queen v Minister of Agriculture, Fisheries and Food, ex p Compassion in World Farming Ltd* [1998] ECR I-1251, para 47.

[75] See eg Case 121/85 *Conegate*, n 64, Joined cases 115 & 116/81 *Adoui and Cornuaille*, n 65.

[76] See eg Case C-67/98 *Questore di Verona v Diego Zenatti* [1999] ECR I-7289; Joined cases C-338 & 359 & 360/04 *Criminal proceedings against Massimiliano Placanica, Christian Palazzese, and Angelo Sorricchio* [2007] ECR I-1891.

[77] This trend was identified by legal writers a long time ago and is being constantly confirmed by subsequent judgments. See Catchpole, L., and Barav, A., 'The Public Morality Exception and the Free Movement of Goods: Justification of a Dual Standard in National Legislation?' (1980) 7 *Legal Issues of Economic Integration* 1–21; see also Hetsch, P., 'Émergence de valeurs morales dans la jurisprudence de la CJCE' (1982) 18 *RTDE* 511–25; the complete lack of proportionality control in this field, however, has been strongly criticized, see eg Fernandez Martin, J.M., and O'Leary, S., 2002, n 29.

discussions.[78] It is recalled that solidarity has been developed as a ground for giving member states a free hand, primarily in the field of competition, and to a lesser extent, in relation to free movement. It is also recalled that it may operate *ex ante*, thus bringing the activity in question outside the scope of the Treaty rules[79] or, on the contrary, *ex post*, as yet another ORPI.[80] The same ambivalence is also present in relation to the effects of solidarity on the application of competition rules.[81] What is clear, however, is that, as with public morality, the contours of solidarity are not questioned by the Court. Member states are entirely free to define the scope of social services and the extent to which solidarity applies to them.[82] What the Court examines, however, is whether the concrete manifestations of solidarity are such as to exclude all market forces—and thus the application of the economic rules of the Treaty—or whether some room is left for the (partial) application of the rules. Hence, if proportionality does play a role in controlling the scope of the solidarity exception, this does not happen at the level of defining the concept of solidarity and the *broad areas* covered by it, but rather, at the (much more practical) level of drawing the line between *activities* which are excluded from, or subject to, the Treaty rules.

c. The riddle of fundamental rights

The protection of fundamental rights in the EU legal order is an issue which has occupied legal literature for several decades.[83] There are several reasons today, however, which bring fundamental rights to the fore and make it necessary to examine the way they may affect the free movement rules. At the constitutional level, the entry into force of the Lisbon Treaty endows the EU, for the first time, with a legally binding Charter of Fundamental Rights; at the same time, EU accession to the ECHR is forthcoming.[84] At the judicial level, the CJEU during

---

[78] See the discussion in ch 2.

[79] In this sense, see Case C-70/95 *Sodemare SA and others v Regione Lombardia* [1997] ECR I-3395.

[80] In this sense, see eg Case C-157/99 *Smits and Peerbooms* [2001] ECR I-5473, and all the recent case law concerning free movement of patients.

[81] Hervey, T., '"Social solidarity": a buttress against internal market law?' in Shaw, J. (ed), *Social Law and Policy in an Evolving EU* (Oxford: Hart Publishing, 2000) 31–47, also available at <http://aei.pitt.edu/2294/1/002338_1.PDF> (last accessed on 9 November 2011); the author observes that in Case C-67/96 *Albany International BV v Stichting Bedrijfspensioenfonds Textielindustrie* [1999] ECR I-5751, the Court found that the activity in question did not present 'enough' solidarity characteristics to fall altogether outside the scope of the Treaty, but could, nonetheless, justify an exception under Art 106(2) TFEU.

[82] Subject to manifest error control exercised by the Commission and/or the Court, see the observations in ch 2.

[83] See, among many, von Bogdandy, A., 'The European Union as a human rights organisation? Human rights and the core of the European Union' (2000) 37 *CML Rev* 1307–38; Lenaerts, K., 'Respect for Fundamental Rights as a Constitutional Principle of the European Union' (2000) 6 *Columbia J of Eur L* 1–25; Weuwahl, N. and Rosas, A. (eds), *The EU and Human Rights* (The Hague: Martinus Nijhoff, 1995); Tridimas, T., *The General Principles of EU Law* (Oxford: OUP, 2006) ch 7, where numerous references to further bibliography can be found.

[84] Krüger, H.K., 'Why the EU Should Accede to the European Convention of Human Rights' Euractiv article (2002, updated in 2010), available at <http://www.euractiv.com/en/future-eu/eu-accede-european-convention-human-rights/article-117174> (last accessed on 8 November 2011);

the last 15 years has actively engaged in an ongoing dialogue with the ECtHR[85] and has occasionally paid fundamental rights even heavier reliance than the latter's case law would account for.[86] For these reasons, fundamental rights are expected to play an ever-increasing role in the years to come, not least in relation to the economic freedoms. Indeed, such a tendency is already visible.

The relationship between the protection of fundamental rights and the internal market rules was openly acknowledged by the Court for the first time in *ERT*:[87] the Greek ban on private television ran against the EU rules on services and any reference by the member state to public policy and other justificatory grounds should be appraised 'having regard to all the rules of Community law, including freedom of expression, as embodied in Article 10 of the European Convention on Human Rights, as a general principle of law the observance of which is ensured by the Court'.[88] Thereafter, fundamental rights were used by the Court 'as a sword' on several occasions, often in a controversial manner.[89] In *Carpenter*, the right to family life, supposedly embedded in the EU free movement rules and protected by Article 8 ECHR grounded a violation of Article 56 TFEU.[90] More questionably still, in *Karner*, a ban on advertising which was found by the Court not to fall under either the rules on goods or on services, was nonetheless tested by the Court for its compatibility with the right of freedom of expression enshrined in Article 10 ECHR.[91] In *Mangold*, a judgment which has provoked even greater controversy, the Court recognized (on unclear foundations) and enforced a general principle of non-discrimination on grounds of age; this principle was even found to be applicable a. between individuals, b. before the expiration of the transposition period of

more extensively, see Pernice, I., and Kanitz, R., 'Fundamental Rights and Multilevel Constitutionalism in Europe' Walter Hallstein Institut Working Paper No. 7/04, also available at <www.whi-berlin. de/documents/whi-paper0704.pdf> (last accessed on 8 November 2011).

[85] See eg the Court's judgment in Case C-84/95 *Bosphorus Hava Yollari Turizm ve Ticaret AS v Minister for Transport, Energy and Communications and others* [1996] ECR I-3953 and the ECtHR judgment in *Bosphorus International*, Application No. 45036/98, judgment delivered on 30 June 2005. For commentary on these cases, see Douglas-Scott, S., 'Annotation: Case *Bosphorus Hava Yollari Turizm Ve Ticaret Anonim Sirketi v. Ireland*' (2006) 43 *CML Rev* 243–54. See also Douglas-Scott, S., 'A Tale of Two Courts; Luxembourg, Strasbourg and the Growing European Human Rights Acquis' (2006) 43 *CML Rev* 629–65; on a more sceptical note concerning the relationship between the two legal orders—and the two Courts—see Greer, S., and Williams, A., 'Human Rights in the Council of Europe and the EU: Towards "Individual", "Constitutional" or "Institutional" Justice?' (2009) 15 *EL Rev* 462–81.

[86] Notably in the *Kadi* line of cases, where the Court reviews UN Security Council Resolutions for their compatibility with fundamental rights, a solution which was not granted under the ECtHR jurisprudence (Joined cases 402 & 415/05P *Yassin Abdullah Kadi and Al Barakaat International Foundation v Council of the European Union and Commission of the European Communities* [2008] ECR I-6351; see also AG opinion in the case).

[87] Case C-260/89 *ERT v DEP and Sotirios Kouvelas* [1991] ECR I-2925.

[88] Ibid, para 44.

[89] For the use of this terminology and a more detailed discussion in this respect, see Hatzopoulos, V., and Do, U., 'Overview of the Case Law of the ECJ in the Field of Free Movement of Services 2000–2005' (2006) 43 *CML Rev* 923–91.

[90] Case C-60/00 *Mary Carpenter v Secretary of the State for the Home Department* [2002] ECR I-6279.

[91] Case C-71/02 *Herbert Karner Industrie-Auktionen GmbH v Troostwijk GmbH* [2004] ECR I-3025.

the Directive setting rules on age discrimination.[92] This approach was confirmed by the Grand Chamber in *Kücükdeveci*.[93]

More important for the purposes of the present analysis, however, are the cases in which the protection of fundamental rights is invoked by the member states 'as a shield', against the application of the free movement rules, rather than 'as a sword'.[94] The first such occasion arose in *Grogan*, where the right to life (of the unborn) was weighed against the right to provide medical (abortion) services.[95] The Court, using a legal technicality, managed not to enter into the substance of the question.

Twelve years later, however, in *Schmidberger*, the Court could not avoid ruling on the opposition between fundamental rights and free movement rules.[96] On the basis of its earlier *Strawberries* judgment,[97] the CJEU held that Austria's failure to prohibit a demonstration blocking an important transit motorway, through which goods could be transported, constituted a violation of the free movement of goods. The respondent member state sought to justify its decision by reference to the freedoms of expression and of assembly, protected by Articles 10 and 11 ECHR, respectively. The Court recalled that the free movement of goods was one of the 'fundamental principles' of the Treaty, subject, nonetheless, to exceptions.[98] Articles 10 and 11 ECHR, too, tolerated exceptions.[99] It held, therefore, that 'the interests involved must be weighed having regard to all the circumstances of the case in order to determine whether a fair balance was struck between those interests'.[100] This balancing exercise amounts, in actual fact, to a proportionality control, whereby the restrictions imposed on free movement are evaluated against the aim of protecting the relevant fundamental rights; in this respect, national authorities enjoy a wide margin of discretion.[101] This notwithstanding, the Court, after an extensive proportionality review (occupying no less than 12 paragraphs of

---

[92] Case C-144/04 *Werner Mangold v Rüdiger Helm* [2005] ECR I-9981.

[93] Case C-555/07 *Seda Kücükdeveci v Swedex GmbH & Co. KG* [2010] nyr.

[94] For the terminology, see again Hatzopoulos, V. and Do, U., 2006, n 89; generally on the relationship between fundamental rights and Treaty freedoms, see De Witte, B., 'Balancing of economic law and human rights by the European Court of Justice' in Dupuy, P.-M., Francioni, F., and Petersmann, E.-U. (eds), *Human Rights in International Investment Law and Arbitration* (Oxford: OUP, 2009) 197–207; Avbelj, M., 'The European Court of Justice and the Question of Value Choices—Fundamental Human Rights as an Exception to the Freedom of Movement of Goods', Jean Monnet Paper No. 6/04, also available at <http://centers.law.nyu.edu/jeanmonnet/papers/04/040601.pdf> (last accessed on 8 November 2011); also Morijn, J., 'Balancing Fundamental Rights and Common Market Freedoms in Union Law: *Schmidberger* and *Omega* in the Light of the European Constitution' (2006) 12 *ELJ* 15–40; Tridimas, T., *The General Principles of EU Law* (Oxford: OUP, 2006), at 337–41.

[95] Case C-159/90 *Grogan* [1991] ECR 4685.

[96] Case C-112/00 *Eugen Schmidberger, Internationale Transporte und Planzüge v Republik Österreich* [2003] ECR I-5659.

[97] Case C-265/95 *Commission v France (strawberries)* [1997] ECR I-6959; in this judgment, the Court held the member state to be responsible for (allowing) the unlawful acts of private parties (demonstrating in the highways and destroying strawberries from Spain).

[98] Case C-112/00 *Schmidberger*, n 96, para 78.

[99] Ibid, para 79.

[100] Ibid, para 81.

[101] Ibid, para 82.

the judgment) judged the national measure (administrative permission to demonstrate) compatible with the free movement requirements.[102]

By contrast, proportionality control of any form was virtually absent in the second judgment in which a fundamental right was invoked against a fundamental freedom. In *Omega*, the German restriction on the provision of leasing services was aimed at protecting human dignity, a value given constitutional status under German law.[103] If the status of human dignity as a broadly accepted fundamental right (or principle) is uncontroversial, the highly restrictive content given to it under German law is something of a peculiarity. The Court, nonetheless, stated that 'the specific circumstances which may justify recourse to the concept of public policy may vary from one country to another and from one era to another. The competent national authorities must therefore be allowed a margin of discretion within the limits imposed by the Treaty'.[104] At this point, one could expect a proportionality review to follow, along the lines of *Schmidberger*. Instead, the Court held that 'it is not indispensable in that respect for the restrictive measure issued by the authorities of a Member State to correspond to a conception shared by all Member States as regards the precise way in which the fundamental right or legitimate interest in question is to be protected'.[105] Consequently, the national measure was upheld.

In *Viking* and *Laval*,[106] where the right to collective action was used against the freedom of establishment and the free provision of services, the Court reasoned pretty much along the terms of *Schmidberger*. It recognized that the right to industrial action is a fundamental right protected, as such, under EU law, but not an absolute one. Similarly, the free movement rules constitute the 'fundamental freedoms' of the EU, themselves subject to exceptions. The balancing exercise which followed was based on an evaluation of proportionality, clearly less extensive than in *Schmidberger*, and the outcome was the opposite: industrial action carried out in the cases in question was held to be disproportionate to the aim pursued, and therefore, in breach of the Treaty freedoms. A further, not insignificant, difference is that in *Omega*, the Court analysed the measure pursuing the fundamental right as falling within the 'public policy' express Treaty exception, it thus being irrelevant whether the contested measure introduced some kind of discrimination.[107] In *Laval*, on the other hand, the Court clearly held that 'none of the considerations referred... constitute grounds of public policy, public security or public health within the meaning of Article 46 EC [now Article 52 TFEU], applied in conjunction with Article 55 EC [now Article 62 TFEU]' and held 'that discrimination such as that in the case in the main proceedings cannot be justified'.[108] This in turn

[102] For more on the proportionality control of national measures, see under subheading B(2)a.
[103] Case C-36/02 *Omega* [2004] ECR I-9609.
[104] Ibid, para 31.
[105] Ibid, para 37.
[106] Case C-438/05 *International Transport Workers' Federation and Finnish Seamen's Union v Viking Line ABP and OÜ Viking Line Eesti* [2007] ECR I-10779 and Case C-341/05 *Laval*, n 48.
[107] Case C-36/02 *Omega*, n 103, para 29.
[108] Case C-341/05 *Laval*, n 48, para 119.

would seem to imply that respect for fundamental rights en bloc does not qualify as such as a ground of public policy; rather the specific content of each individual right is to be taken into account.[109]

These cases are not easy to reconcile, since they seem to answer two basic questions in inconsistent, if opposing, manners.

First, it is not clear whether the pursuance of fundamental rights a. is linked to public policy and public security, b. operates as yet another ORPI, or iii. constitutes a third independent ground justifying restrictions to the free movement rules.[110] Option (a) is conceptually incoherent since fundamental rights are individual and bottom up, typically protecting persons against top-down measures adopted for the protection of public policy and security, on account of the collective (general) interest. Option (b) is no less problematic, since, as the Court's case law stands in view of the *Laval* judgment, it would mean that measures serving some fundamental right would only be accepted if non discriminatory. Option (c) has the problem of creating new, ill-defined, legal categories, with uncertain legal effects.[111]

Secondly, it is even less clear what kind of a proportionality control is to be applied to restrictive measures pursuing some fundamental right. In all cases discussed above, the Court states that the control should be limited.[112] Indeed, in *Omega*, it skipped proportionality control altogether. In contrast, in *Schmidberger* and *Laval*, the CJEU engaged in an extensive evaluation of proportionality, and in the end decided in favour of and against the member state, respectively. One way of reconciling the difference in approach between *Omega* and the other two cases is to distinguish between common and 'un-common' fundamental rights:[113] for the former, the Court, based on member states' constitutional traditions, as well as the ECtHR's jurisprudence, feels comfortable to proceed itself to the required proportionality review; for the latter, on the other hand, it finds it more appropriate to leave the proportionality review to the national judges who are more familiar with the technicalities of protecting the right at stake. A more satisfactory explanation (which combines with, rather than contradicts, the previous one) is that what determines the Court's approach is the absolute or relative character of the fundamental right concerned: human dignity (as in *Omega*) is an absolute right, the technicalities of which may be freely determined at the member state level, while the freedom of expression, of assembly (as in *Schmidberger*), and of collective action

---

[109] For a discussion of the relationship between fundamental rights and fundamental freedoms in *Laval*, see Hinajeros, A., '*Laval* and *Viking*: The Right to Collective Action versus EU Fundamental Freedoms' (2008) 8 *Human Rights L Rev* 714–29; also Novitz, T., 'A Human Rights Analysis for the *Viking* and *Laval* Judgments' (2008) 10 *CYEL* 541–62.

[110] These three positions seem to be supported by Case C-36/02 *Omega*, n 103, Case C-341/05 *Laval*, n 48, and Case C-112/00 *Schmidberger* [2003] ECR I-5659, respectively.

[111] For a discussion of these options and their shortfalls, see Morijn, J., 2006, n 94.

[112] See Biondi, A., 'Free Trade, a Mountain Road and the Right to Protest: European Economic Freedoms and Fundamental Individual Rights' (2004) *Eur Human Rights L Rev* 51–61, where the author refers to a 'reasonableness' control.

[113] See Morijn, J., 2006, n 94, at 34–7.

(as in *Laval*) are all rights subject to exceptions, and therefore allow for a robust proportionality control to be carried out by the CJEU.[114]

A further source of uncertainty lies with the way the two Courts, in Luxembourg and in Strasbourg, will develop their respective jurisprudence in the years to come. Indeed, if in *Bosphorus* the ECtHR seemed to give a positive 'peer review' to the CJEU in relation to the right to property, the opposite seems to be the case in relation to the right of collective action. Indeed, almost a year after the CJEU's judgments in *Viking* and *Laval*, the Strasbourg Court in *Demir and Baykara v Turkey*, reversed its previous case law (on which the CJEU had partly based its reasoning in *Viking* and *Laval*) and held that 'the right to bargain collectively with the employer has, in principle, become one of the essential elements of the "right to form and to join trade unions for the protection of [one's] interests" set forth in Article 11 of the Convention' which may only suffer interference that is strictly necessary in a democratic society.[115] The fact that the newly discovered scope of Article 11 ECHR allows for very limited exceptions was confirmed in a Chamber judgment of 2009 in case *Enerji Yapi-yol Sen v Turkey*.[116] It is highly unlikely that the unfettered realization of one of the EU freedoms qualifies, in the eyes of the ECtHR, as a strict necessity in a democratic society. It has been observed, in this respect, that:

'it is difficult then to see how the ECtHR could avoid upholding Article 11 and the right to collective bargaining and to strike over the business freedoms contained in what are now Articles 49 and 56 of the TFEU. And so issues would bat to and fro between the two courts in a titanic battle of the juristocrats, each vying for supremacy in the European legal order, one determined to impale trade union rights on the long lance of economic freedom and the other subordinating economic freedom to the modest demands of human rights and constitutionalism'.[117]

Fundamental rights are expected to play an increased role in EU litigation in the years to come, as EU action is, henceforth, formally bound to respect the EU Charter of Fundamental Rights. If the relationship between fundamental rights and fundamental EU freedoms is currently still something of a riddle, further clarifications are on their way.

3. Legislative justifications

Sector-specific Regulations and Directives implementing the free provision of services (eg the various transport Regulations[118] or the Audiovisual Media Servces

---

[114] Such an explanation is supported by C-36/02 *Omega*, n 103 (AG), para 53.
[115] ECtHR *Demir and Baykara v Turkey*, Application No. 34503/97 [2008], para 154.
[116] ECtHR *Enerji Yapi-Yol Sen v Turkey*, Application No. 68959/01 [2009].
[117] Ewing, K.D. and Hendy, J., 'The Dramatic Implications of Demir and Baykara' (2010) 39 *Int LJ* 2–51, 42; also available (as draft) at <http://www.law.utoronto.ca/documents/conferences2/StrikeSymposium09_Ewing-Hendy.pdf> (last accessed on 9 November 2011).
[118] For a detailed presentation of these Regulations, see ch 6, under subheading A(1).

Directive)[119] include derogations and exceptions to their rules. This is not the place to look into the sector-specific rules and exceptions.[120] What need to be examined, however, are the general/horizontal legislative justifications of restrictions to the free provision of services, recognized by the Services Directive.[121]

The Services Directive had the initial ambition of generalizing the application of the country of origin principle (CoOP)—and foresaw exceptions thereto. During the political negotiation leading to the adoption of the text, the CoOP was dropped and replaced by the modest principle of 'freedom to provide services'.[122] As it now stands, Article 16(1) of the Directive provides that 'Member States shall respect the right of providers to provide services in a Member State other than that in which they are established'. However, immediately afterwards, in the same paragraph, it is stated that this principle does not rule out restrictive measures which are non-discriminatory, as long as they are necessary and proportional for the attainment of some objective of public policy, public security, public health, or the protection of the environment.[123] If this were not clear enough, Article 16(3) reiterates that these same reasons may justify the adoption of restrictive measures by the host state.[124]

The fact that Article 16 of the Directive expressly provides for exceptions to the free provision of services for the four reasons mentioned above (public policy, order, health, and the environment) raises two issues. *First*, the Directive uses the three Treaty-based grounds for exception together with one which is judge-made. This is not only a conceptual shift (already identified several years ago in the Court's case law),[125] but also has substantive implications. According to the Court's case law, Treaty-based derogations may justify both discriminatory and non-discriminatory measures. Article 16 of the Directive, on the other hand, may serve to uphold only non-discriminatory measures. Therefore, the question is raised whether it is possible for the Directive, a text of secondary legislation, to limit the justificatory potential of the Treaty's three grounds that expressly allow for the justification of discriminatory measures.

[119] European Parliament and Council Directive 2007/65/EC amending Council Directive 89/552/EEC on the coordination of certain provisions laid down by law, regulation or administrative action in Member States concerning the pursuit of television broadcasting activities [2007] OJ L332/27.

[120] For this, see the discussion in ch 6.

[121] European Parliament and Council Directive 2006/123/EC on services in the internal market [2006] OJ L376/36.

[122] For a more detailed presentation of the Services Directive and relevant literature, see ch 6.

[123] It is worth noting that the 'public policy' ground seems much more comprehensive in the English versions, than in French, where reference is made to '*ordre public*'.

[124] It is difficult to understand why the European Parliament insisted on both provisions being inserted in Art 16, since they seem to set the same rule and create confusion. The view that Arts 16(1) and (3) of the Directive stand for the same rule is confirmed in Commission's *Handbook on the Implementation of the Services Directive* (October 2007) 48, where the two provisions are dealt with indistinctly together; the Handbook is available online at <http://ec.europa.eu/internal_market/services/services-dir/index_en.htm> (last accessed on 9 November 2011).

[125] On the relationship between Treaty-based and judge-made exceptions, see the analysis under subheading A(2)a.

Secondly, and more importantly, the four reasons listed in Article 16 of the Services Directive as justifying restrictions to the free provision of services are different from the more inclusive category of 'overriding reasons relating to the public interest', defined in Article 4(8) of the Directive and used in other parts of it (especially concerning the establishment of service providers). Should this mean that within the scope of the Directive, Member States may invoke only these four grounds to justify restrictions of a non-discriminatory nature to the free provision of services, while the other judge-made 'overriding reasons' become inapplicable? Such an interpretation would be valid only if the Directive fully harmonized all other overriding reasons raised by the free provision of services—but this is certainly not the case. As will be explained in chapter 6, the Directive is more about coordination and the exchange of information than about harmonization. Even where harmonization does occur, it remains minimal and concerns elements peripheral to service provision: the promotion of self-regulation, professional insurance, points of single contact, use of standard-form documents, etc. Except for consumer protection, which may be indirectly fostered by the exchange of information and administrative cooperation foreseen in the Directive, no other ORPI is directly served by the terms of the Directive. Indeed, no harmonization of ORPIs whatsoever (optional, minimum, partial, or other)[126] is undertaken by the Services Directive. The states' competence to pursue the ORPIs they value stems directly from their responsibility towards their citizens and may not be set aside unless the EU legal order pre-empts them, by legislating in the same field[127]—and it remains to be ascertained whether EU legislation has fully covered the 'regulatory space' or whether residual national competence remains.[128] In more legalistic terms, ORPIs, being a judge-made invention, stem from the interpretation of the Treaty rules themselves. The fact that ORPIs should always be protected, if need be by national legislation restrictive of free movement, is a principle embedded in the Treaty; for some, it may even qualify as a general principle of EU law.[129] It is not

[126] For the different kinds of harmonization, see Slot, P.J., 'Harmonisation' (1996) 21 *EL Rev* 378–97; and more recently, Vos, E., 'Differentiation, harmonisation and governance' in de Witte, B., Hanf, D., and Vos, E. (eds), *The Many Faces of Differentiation in EU Law* (Antwerpen: Intersentia, 2001) 145–79; Weatherill, S., 'Harmonisation: How Much, How Little?' (2005) 16 *EBLR* 533–45.

[127] For an exhaustive discussion of the effects of minimum—or incomplete—harmonization on member states' competence to regulate in the same fields, see Dougan, M., 'Minimum Harmonization and the Internal Market' (2000) 37 *CML Rev* 853–85, where more references are to be found, some developing the argument opposite to the one made here.

[128] Also referred to as 'exhaustion' in Slot, P.J., 1996, n 126 above, at 391; also Vos, E., n 126 above, at 149; see also Weatherill, S., 'Beyond pre-emption? Shared competence and constitutional change in the EC' in O'Keeffe, D., and Twomey, P. (eds), *Legal Issues of the Maastricht Treaty* (London: Chancery, 1994) 23–5; in relation to the theory of exhaustion, it is interesting to note Case C-441/02 *Commission v Germany (posted workers)* [2006] ECR I-3449 and Case C-168/04 *Commission v Austria (posted workers)* [2006] ECR I-9041. There, the Court's reasoning was based on the premise that the area in question has not been harmonized at all, since Directive 96/71 (European Parliament and Council Directive 96/71/EC concerning the posting of workers in the framework of the provision of services [1997] OJ L18/1) concerns other aspects of posting. The Directive is not even mentioned in the judgments.

[129] Hatzopoulos, V., 'Exigences essentielles, impératives ou impérieuses: une théorie, des théories ou pas de théorie du tout?' (1998) 2 *RTDE* 191–236.

possible to change such a rule/principle by means of a simple text of secondary legislation; and it is even more so where the text is of a merely prescriptive nature and does not purport to establish any kind of harmonization of the interests at stake.

Indeed, the fact that the Services Directive is not a harmonization Directive distinguishes it from situations previously brought to the CJEU, where the issue of residual powers left to member states to regulate ORPIs on top of EU rules was considered. In *Buet*, the Court found that the Doorstep Selling Directive[130] was not protective enough of consumers' interests and that France was entitled to adopt a complete ban for certain kinds of products (educational material).[131] In the same vein, *di Pinto* added that France could adopt more restrictive measures enhancing consumer protection above the level provided for by the same Directive (but could not extend the scope *ratione personae* of the Directive).[132] This approach corresponds to the one adopted a few years earlier in *Campus Oil*, with the difference that at stake there was not consumer protection (an ORPI) but public policy (an express exception): the Court found that the Community legislation in place did not 'sufficiently' guarantee supplies of petroleum products and permitted the Irish restrictive measures.[133]

In recent years, however, the Court has shown the reverse tendency, of treating minimum harmonization as full, and not allowing for more restrictive national measures, even where such possibility seems to be allowed from the text of the Directive. This tendency may be observed in the field of electronic communications,[134] consumer protection,[135] and (posted) worker's protection.[136] These recent judgments may have nourished doubts as to the validity of the position presented above, that member states retain the competence to regulate ORPIs until/unless completely pre-empted by EU harmonization.[137]

All the above situations, however, are different from the Services Directive, since the latter does not purport to harmonize ORPIs *at all* and may only incidentally enhance their protection. In this respect, the recent judgment of the Grand Chamber in *Commission v Italy (trailers)*, where the Court somewhat restates the

---

[130] Council Directive 85/577/EEC to protect the consumer in respect of contracts negotiated away from business premises [1985] OJ L372/31.

[131] Case 382/87 *R. Buet and Educational Business Services (EBS) v Ministère public* [1989] ECR 1235.

[132] Case C-361/89 *Criminal proceedings against Patrice Di Pinto* [1991] ECR I-1189.

[133] Case 72/83 *Campus Oil Limited and others v Minister for Industry and Energy and others* [1984] ECR 2727.

[134] Case C-500/06 *Dermoestética* [2008] ECR I-5785; but in the opposite direction, where the Television without Frontiers (TVWF) Directive (Directive 89/552/EEC [1989] OJ L298/23) was considered to introduce partial harmonization allowing for member states' regulation, see Case C-222/07 *Union de Televisiones Comerciales Asociadas* [2009] ECR I-1407.

[135] Case C-205/07 *Lodewijk Gysbrechts and Santurel Inter BVBA* [2008] ECR I-9947; see also Roth, W.H., 'Annotation: Case C-205/07 *Gysbrechts* [2008] ECR I-9947' (2010) 47 *CML Rev* 509–20.

[136] Case C-346/06 *Dirk Rüffert v Land Niedersachsen* [2008] ECR I-1989.

[137] See eg Gschwandtner, S., 'National Private Law Rules as Restrictions to Market Freedoms' EUI Law Working Paper No. 22/2009, also available at <http://cadmus.eui.eu/dspace/bitstream/1814/13114/1/LAW_2009_22.pdf> (last accessed on 9 November 2011).

principles applicable to free movement,[138] may provide a useful reference. The Italian ban on the use of motorcycle trailers having been qualified as a restriction to Article 34 TFEU, the question was raised whether such a ban could be upheld by the objective of promoting road safety, an area in which there is already EU legislation. The Court held that 'in the absence of *fully* harmonising provisions at Community level, it is for the Member States to decide upon the level at which they wish to ensure road safety in their territory'.[139]

It is submitted, therefore, that Article 16 of the Services Directive, despite only mentioning four exception grounds to the free movement principle, may not prevent member states from protecting ORPIs as they deem fit.[140] If this is correct, Article 16 of the Directive, both for the principle it poses (ie free provision of services) and for the exceptions it allows (ORPIs subject to the well-known conditions of necessity and proportionality), is no more than a mere restatement of the Court's case law in the field.[141]

Article 17 of the Directive has the suggestive title '*Additional* derogations from the freedom to provide services'. This provision is difficult to understand after the abandonment of the country of origin principle (CoOP).[142] Article 17 made sense when it served to exclude from the far-reaching CoOP some activities judged sensible or inappropriate for that type of regulation. Now that Article 16 is restricted to restating the Court's case law—subject to express exceptions—it is legally unclear what Article 17 stands for. In other words, will it be possible for member states to claim some exception under Article 17, and in the affirmative, where from? From the Court's case law interpreting the Treaty rules, as codified by Article 16 of the Directive?[143]

---

[138] For the relevant discussion, see the detailed discussion in ch 3.

[139] Case C-110/05 *Commission v Italy (trailers)* [2009] ECR I-519, para 61.

[140] See, in the same sense, Snell, J., 'Freedom to provide services in the case law and in the Services Directive: problems, solutions and institutions' in Neergaard, U., Nielsen, R., and Roseberry, L. (eds), *The Services Directive: Consequences for the Welfare State and the European Social Model* (Copenhagen: DJOF, 2008) 171–98; also Lemaire, C., 'La Directive, la liberté d'établissement et la libre prestation de services: confirmations, innovations' (2007) 17:2 *Europe* 15–26, at 21; Hatzopoulos, V., 'Assessing the Services Directive 2006/123/EC' (2008) 10 *CYEL* 215–61; *contra* Barnard, C., 'Unravelling the Services Directive' (2008) 45 *CML Rev* 323–94; Bergamini, E., 'Freedom of establishment under the Services Directive' in Neergaard, U., Nielsen, R., and Roseberry, L. (eds), *The Services Directive: Consequences for the Welfare State and the European Social Model* (Copenhagen: DJOF, 2008) 149–69, at 165, as well as the Commission's *Handbook on Implementation of the Services Directive*, n 124 above, at 49 and fn 107, where it is stated that the enumeration of reasons for exceptions in Art 16 'excludes Member States from invoking other public interest objectives'.

[141] This finding is, of course, contested by those who disagree with the general argument made here. See, in particular, the authors cited in n 140.

[142] For which see ch 6, subsection A(6); see also Hatzopoulos, V., 'Assessing the Services Directive, 2006/123/EC' (2008) 10 *CYEL* 215–61.

[143] The question is a rhetorical one, since the answer is clearly negative. The only perceptible impact that Art 17 could have lies at the political level: it may be seen as suggesting that the EU legislature, arguably the bearer of direct legitimacy, questions the—often poorly motivated—choices made by the Court. This argument is made by Snell, J., 'Free movement of services and the Services Directive: the legitimacy of the case law' in van de Gronden, J. (ed), *EU and WTO Law on Services, Limits to the Realization of General Interest Policies within the Services Markets?* (Austin: Kluwer Law International, 2009) 31–54. In the end, however, the author admits that what is needed in view of the legislator's

Article 18 of the Directive foresees the possibility of 'case-by-case derogations' in respect of individual service providers, in order to secure the safety of services. According to this provision, member states may adopt restrictive measures following the mutual assistance procedure introduced in Article 35 of the Directive. Such measures may only be adopted provided that there is no EU harmonization in the field concerned and that they have some added value in relation to the rules applicable in the provider's home state. Again, this provision made sense in the original draft of the Directive, but much less so now: since member states are authorized by Articles 16(1) and (3) to introduce restrictions for the protection of public policy, security, health, and the environment, it is only in exceptional circumstances of rogue service providers that they are likely to have recourse to the more restrictive and technical rule of Article 18.

All in all, legislative exceptions to the free provision of services would make sense when inserted into a text advancing service provision beyond the established CJEU case law. This is true for exceptions foreseen in sector-specific legislative texts, eg in the field of financial services, electronic communications, network-based industries, or the draft Patients' Rights Directive.[144] These texts specify the conditions for the application of the general Treaty rules in specific areas, therefore extending their material scope; to this extent, they may also be subject to specific exceptions. The Services Directive, on the other hand, being a horizontal text, does not open up new areas to service provision. Its main added value, which would have justified horizontal exceptions, would lie in the consecration of the CoOP. Since the CoOP has been dropped from the Directive, the ill-defined horizontal exceptions are legally obsolete and, as such, constitute no more than a source of complication and legal uncertainty.

B. Justifying and evaluating justifications: the measures adopted

1. Justifying justifications

It is now well-established case law that free movement qualifies as an EU fundamental freedom.[145] This, however, has not prevented the Court, while interpreting restrictively the express Treaty provisions, from recognizing an indeterminate number of exceptions, as they have been presented above. This apparent contradiction calls for a satisfactory justification.

So long as the proposal that ORPIs operate *ex ante* and prevent a given measure from qualifying as a restriction was supported by case law, the idea was convincingly

---

reservations is not a reversal of well-established case law, but rather a more adequate motivation for the Court's judgments.

[144] For a thorough presentation of all these texts, see the developments in ch 5.

[145] See already in Case 222/86 *Union nationale des entraîneurs et cadres techniques professionnels du football (Unectef) v Georges Heylens and others* [1987] ECR 4097, paras 12, 14 and 15; and more recently Case C-438/05 *Viking* [2007] ECR I-10779, paras 45, 51; Case C-341/05 *Laval* [2007] ECR I-11767, paras 93 and 103.

put forward that they are not exceptions, but rather a manifestation of residual competences left to member states.[146] Nowadays, however, such an idea seems no longer supported by case law. A second explanation of the existence of ORPIs within the EU legal order is put forward in terms of a 'rule of reason' consisting in the 'recognition by the Court, on essentially equitable grounds, that certain interests or values are deserving of judicial protection at the Community level pending the intervention of the Community legislator'.[147]

In this author's view,[148] expressed several years ago:

'[a] necessary side-effect of the Court's recognizing that non discriminatory measures may violate of EC law, has been the institution, by the Court, of a mechanism allowing for such measures to be upheld when pursuing legitimate objectives. The principle of equivalence and mutual recognition—the cornerstone criterion for establishing whether a non discriminatory measure is nevertheless restrictive—and the theory of mandatory requirements were born by one and the same judgment of the Court in Case *Cassis de Dijon*; they are inextricably connected'.[149]

According to the vision above, the recognition of ORPIs is the price to pay for bypassing the criterion of discrimination as the sole ground of restriction of the free movement rules. In that contribution it was even proposed that ORPIs should be treated as corresponding to a functional general principle of law, whereby the application of the Treaty freedoms should not be allowed to prejudice other equally valuable objectives.[150] Support for such a vision was gathered i. from the close links between ORPIs and the general principle of mutual recognition (itself a general principle of law),[151] ii. the fact that the same logic was followed across different freedoms despite the textual, factual, and terminological differences, and iii. that ORPIs put forward by the member states are also taken into account by the EU legislature in areas such as the regulation of financial services and network-bound industries.[152] If such a proposal is somehow far-fetched, it remains, nonetheless, the case that ORPIs have now gained legislative recognition by the Services Directive and may, under certain circumstances, justify exceptions to the free provision of services (especially by established service providers).

---

[146] Mattera, A., *Le Marché Unique Européen: ses règles, son fonctionnement* (Paris: Jupiter, 1990), at 274–5.

[147] Gormley, L., *Prohibiting Restrictions on Trade within the EEC* (Amsterdam: Elsevier, 1985) 51–7; and Gormley, L., 'The genesis of the rule of reason in the free movement of goods' in Schrauwen, A. (ed), *Rule of Reason: Rethinking Another Classic of EC Legal Doctrine* (Groningen: Europa Law Publishing, 2005) 21–33.

[148] Inspired by Marenco, J., 'The Notion of Restriction on the Freedom of Establishment and Provision of Services in the Case-law of the Court' (1991) 11 *YEL* 111–50, as well as Bernard, N., 'Discrimination and Free Movement in EC Law' (1996) 45 *Int & Comparative L Q* 82–108.

[149] Hatzopoulos, V., 'Annotation: Case C-250/95, *Futura Participations SA & Singer v Administration des Contributions (Luxembourg)*' [1997] ECR I-2471 (1998) 35 *CML Rev* 493–518, at 500–1.

[150] A position which is not fundamentally different from that of L. Gormley, 1985, n 147.

[151] Hatzopoulos, V., *Le principe communautaire d'équivalence et de reconnaissance mutuelle dans la libre prestation de services* (Athènes/Bruxelles: Sakkoulas/Bruylant, 1999) 117–8.

[152] Hatzopoulos, V., 'Exigences essentielles, impératives ou impérieuses: une théorie, des théories ou pas de théorie du tout?' (1998) 2 *RTDE* 191–236, at 235.

2. Evaluating justifications: from proportionality to coherence

'If it is accepted that free movement is exhausted in the obligation of Member States to treat imported products or services on an equal footing with domestic ones, discrimination is the touchstone of integration. But if it is accepted that free movement goes beyond equal treatment and requires freedom of access to the market, then any obstacle to free access becomes an unlawful impediment unless objectively justified. Under the second model, proportionality is elevated to the principal criterion for determining the dividing line between lawful and unlawful barriers to trade.'[153]

Since discrimination is by no means considered to be the only criterion for determining barriers to trade in services[154], this statement underlines the role of proportionality in defining the scope of application of the free movement rules.

a. Proportionality as a two- or three-prong test

Proportionality is a well-established legal principle developed in the course of the twentieth century, underpinned by the principles of liberal democracy. It has been developed by the judiciary in order to protect individuals against the surge of administrative discretion. It is a principle common to all legal orders, and a general principle of EU law.[155]

Proportionality constitutes an extremely flexible principle granting important judicial discretion. Indeed, such flexibility is clearly manifest within the EU, since the standard used by the Court when judging on the proportionality of some *EU* measure is the 'manifestly inappropriate test', as opposed to the 'less restrictive alternative test' used when *national* measures are at stake.[156]

In the latter series of cases, relevant for the purposes of the present study, there is disagreement between authors as to whether the test followed is a two- or a three-prong one. The view which finds wider support in the wording of the Court's judgments is that the principle of proportionality comprises two criteria: one examining *suitability* and one addressing *necessity*.[157] The oft-repeated *Gebhard* formula supports such a view, since it states that, in order to be justified, restrictive measures 'must be suitable for securing the attainment of the objective which they pursue; and they must not go beyond what is necessary in order to attain it'.[158]

If proportionality were to be limited to these two criteria, there would be no major objections to the application of this principle, since both tests have a certain

---

[153] Tridimas, T., 2006, n 82, at 196.

[154] For this discussion, see in detail the developments in ch 3.

[155] Tridimas, T., 2006, n 83, at 136–7. The importance of the proportionality principle in the EU legal order is illustrated by the fact that T. Tridimas dedicates three entire chapters of his book (chs 3, 4 and 5) to the principle, as opposed to single chapters for every other general principle; see also Emiliou, N., *The Principle of Proportionality in European Law* (London: Kluwer Law International, 1996).

[156] Ibid, at 138.

[157] Ibid, at 139, where further references to the relevant case law can be found.

[158] Case C-55/94 *Reinhard Gebhard v Consiglio dell' Ordine degli Avvocati e Procuratori di Milano* [1995] ECR I-4165, para 37.

degree of objectivity. The 'suitability' test entails an objective means-to-an-end analysis, deciding whether the measure in question is appropriate for achieving the claimed objective. The 'necessity' test is a bit more complex, as it takes into account a. the nature of the activity or service, b. the consequences of an eventual failure by the service provider, and c. the alternative means of protection available to state authorities.[159] At any rate, what is weighed is the national measure at stake as against alternative ways in which that state could attain the objective pursued.[160]

Several authors, however, inspired by the German version of proportionality, suggest that either as part of the 'necessity' test or as a stand-alone criterion, the Court occasionally proceeds to the examination of another question, that of proportionality *stricto sensu*.[161] Such a test would mean that a measure 'although it is recognized to be the most suitable and necessary as compared with other possible measures, must nonetheless be abandoned, or replaced by a less efficient measure, because of considerable adverse consequences for other third party interests, of a private or a public nature'.[162] In other words, the true proportionality test supposes that the Court 'inventarizes the interests to be weighed and determines whether they are legitimate and which of them do have to be taken into account and, moreover... establishes a hierarchy between those interests'.[163] Thus the weighing exercise is not internal to the national legal order and to the quality of regulation of the member state concerned, but rather external, since it openly opposes the national objective with the EU (free movement) objective.

Indeed, in the Court's case law there are some occasions where the very objective pursued by the member state is discredited. *Säger*, one of the foundational judgments in the field of services, offers a clear example. The German law which required patent agents to hold a licence was found altogether disproportionate, in view of the simple nature of the service provided and of the limited consequences of the eventual failure of the service provider. The Court found that the German regulatory choice was not only paternalistic, but, in view of the objective of free provision of services, also protectionist.[164]

Most strikingly, the Court has applied the strict proportionality test to the various posted workers cases concerning wages. Thus, in cases *Mazzoleni* and *Portugaia Construções*, the Court acknowledged that the application of host state

---

[159] For the identification of these three elements of proportionality, see Hatzopoulos, V., 1998, n 24; there, the existence of some judicial remedy—and more generally of a '*droit au juge*' is considered as a further element of the proportionality test. This element is not analysed here.

[160] See Snell, J., *Goods and Services in EC Law* (Oxford: OUP, 2002) 196–200.

[161] de Búrca, G., 'The Principle of Proportionality and its Applications in EC Law' (1993) 13 *YEL* 105–50; Tomuschat, C., 'Le principe de proportionnalité: *Quis iudicabit?* (1997) 13 *CDE* 97–102; Snell, J., and Andenas, M., 'Exploring the outer limits: restrictions on the free movement' in Andenas, M., and Roth, W.H. (eds), *Services and Free Movement in EU Law* (Oxford: OUP, 2002) 69–139.

[162] van Gerven, W., 'Constitutional aspects of the European Court's case-law on Articles 30 and 36 EC as compared with the U.S. Dormant Commerce Clause' in Dony, M., and de Walsche, A. (eds), *Mélanges en Hommage à Michel Waelbroeck, Vol. II* (Bruxelles: Bruylant, 1999) 1629–44, at 1636.

[163] Ibid, at 1638.

[164] Case C-76/90 *Säger v Dennemeyer & Co. Ltd* [1991] ECR I-4221.

wages to posted workers was, in principle, a valid objective.[165] However, it went on to state that 'there may be circumstances in which the application of such rules would be neither *necessary* nor *proportionate* to the objective pursued'.[166] The proportionality test would require the weighing of the objective of the avoidance of social dumping against the burden incurred by the service provider for complying with the national regulation. In other words, an objective valued at the national level would be put on the scales against an objective valued at the EU level; and the Court would be called upon to put its weight on the one or the other side of the scales. This 'true' proportionality approach[167] was solemnly confirmed in *Schmidberger* and, in an even clearer manner, in the *Viking* and *Laval* cases. In identical terms, in these more recent cases, the Court held that the protection of fundamental rights, such as the right to industrial action, pursued by the contested national measures 'must be reconciled with the requirements relating to rights protected under the Treaty and in accordance with the principle of proportionality'.[168] And in both *Laval* and *Viking*, the Court, on the basis of the proportionality test, gave prevalence to the free movement objective.[169]

It is clear that if such 'external' proportionality were to constitute the decisive criterion for qualifying restrictions/justifications to the free movement rules, it would fundamentally alter the way the EU and its member states operate.[170] At the horizontal level, such a development would shift the power from legislatures to judges applying EU law, since the latter would become the final arbiters of the costs and benefits of regulation. At the vertical level, such a development would shift power from the member states to the CJEU, since it would be entitled, on the basis of an unclear weighing exercise, to strike down national choices. Such weighing would put at stake often heterogeneous interests (eg the right to industrial action v. the right to post workers in the EU), or even incommensurable interests (eg the risk to human life v. a demanding authorization procedure); the choice of precedence in such controversial cases would be more akin to a political action than to adjudication.[171] Moreover, the CJEU, being one of the most strongly EU-minded institutions, would be prone to give precedence to EU, rather than national, objectives. Even if this were not to materialize, the situation would raise salient issues of legitimacy and democratic representation in the Court's actions. If such a broad test

---

[165] Case C-165/98 *Criminal proceedings against André Mazzoleni and Inter Surveillance Assistance SARL* [2001] ECR I-2189; Case C-164/99 *Portugaia Construções Ldª* [2002] ECR I-787.

[166] Case C-165/98 *Mazzoleni*, n 165, para 30 (emphasis added).

[167] Also referred to as 'true proportionality' in Snell, J., 2002, n 160, at 200–12.

[168] Case C-341/05 *Laval* [2007] ECR I-11767, para 94; Case C-438/05 *Viking* [2007] ECR I-10779, para 46.

[169] The outcome of these cases should, nonetheless, be contrasted to the judgment in Case C-112/00 *Schmidberger* [2003] ECR I-5659, where prevalence was given to the protection of the fundamental rights of expression and of assembly; more generally, on the issue of fundamental rights, see the discussion under subheading A(2)c.

[170] See Snell, J., *Goods and Services in EC Law* (Oxford: OUP, 2002), at 200–06.

[171] Further on the issue of proportionality in the *Viking* and *Laval* cases see Hös, N., 'The Principle of Proportionality in the *Viking* and *Laval* Cases: An Appropriate Standard of Judicial Review?' EUI Working Paper No. 2009/06, also available at <http://cadmus.eui.eu/dspace/bitstream/1814/11259/1/LAW_2009_06.pdf> (last accessed on 9 November 2011).

of proportionality were to be systematically followed by the Court, it would inevitably be the source of reactions, both at the scientific[172] as well as at the civil society level.[173]

b. Consistency and coherence as an alternative to 'true' proportionality

In the recent case law of the Court, a much more reasonable trend can be observed, which appears as an alternative to the appreciation of proportionality *stricto sensu*. Progressively, through a series of seemingly technical judgments, mainly in the field of services, the Court seems to be completing the two-pronged proportionality test by adding, next to *suitability* and *necessity*, a third test, one examining *consistency* and *coherence*.[174] This test was spelled out for the first time in *Gambelli*,[175] one of the Italian betting cases, where the Court held that, in order for the national restrictive measures to be accepted, they should be 'suitable for achieving those objectives [invoked by the Italian government], inasmuch as they must serve to limit betting activities in a consistent and systematic manner'.[176] Since Italy was pursuing an otherwise expansive policy concerning gambling, it was on this ground that this, and several other gambling and gaming cases, were decided against member states.[177] It is also on this ground that the following measures were struck down: a restriction on the establishment of dental clinics in Austria, since operators already established on national territory were free to set up new group practices comparable to clinics;[178] an advertising ban of chirurgical treatments on national television, while similar advertising was allowed on local television;[179] a stopover tax on transiting crafts and vessels as a means of protecting the environment in Sardegna, since only non-residents were subject to it.[180] It was, on the other hand,

---

[172] Opposing a broad proportionality control, see in the US framework, Regan, D., 'Judicial Review of Member-State Regulation of Trade within a Federal or Quasi-federal system: Protectionism and Balancing, Da Capo' (2001) 99 *Michigan L Rev* 1853–902; and for the EU, Chalmers, D., 'The Single Market: from prima donna to journeyman' in Shaw, J., and More, G. (eds), *New Legal Dynamics of the European Union* (Oxford: Clarendon, 1995) 55–72, at 68, who talks of an 'impossible balancing act'.

[173] See eg Scharpf, F., 'The Only Solution Is to Refuse to Comply with ECJ Rulings' 4:1 (2009) *Social Europe Journal* (06/04/2009), available at <http://www.social-europe.eu/2009/04/interview-the-only-solution-is-to-refuse-to-comply-with-ecj-rulings/> (last accessed on 9 November 2011), calling for civil disobedience to the Court's case law, precisely after the *Viking* and *Laval* judgments (n 168).

[174] On this test, see Mathisen, G., 'Consistency and Coherence as Conditions for Justification of Member State Measures Restricting Free Movement' (2010) 47 *CML Rev* 1021–48; although most of the analysis proposed there on the function of this test is not agreed to by the present author.

[175] Case C-243/01 *Criminal proceedings against Piergiorgio Gambelli and others* [2003] ECR I-13031.

[176] Ibid, para 67.

[177] See, notably, Joined cases C-338, 359 & 360/04 *Placanica* [2007] ECR I-1891; as well as the series of Orders pertaining to the same set of facts in Case (ord) C-395/05 *Antonello D'Antonio and others* [2007] ECR I-24, Case (ord) C-466/05 *Gianluca Damonte* [2007] ECR I-27, Case (ord) C-191/06 *Aniello Gallo and Gianluca Damonte* [2007] ECR I-30; see also Case C-153/08 *Commission v Spain (gambling tax)* [2009] ECR I-9735.

[178] Case C-169/07 *Hartlauer* [2009] ECR I-1721.

[179] Case C-500/06 *Dermoestética* [2008] ECR I-5785.

[180] Case C-169/08 *Presidente del Consiglio dei Ministri v Regione Sardegna* [2009] ECR I-10821.

exactly because this requirement was satisfied that the Court upheld the bet-taking monopoly of the Santa Casa de Misericordia in Portugal,[181] the requirement that pharmacies be operated only by qualified pharmacists in Germany,[182] and the geographical restrictions on the establishment of pharmacies in Spain.[183]

Although in *Gambelli* the Court seemed to examine the consistency and coherence of the national measures as part of the 'suitability' test, in subsequent case law, the test gained more independence. This begs the question whether, in addition to the traditional proportionality control, a new additional and independent test is put forward by the Court. The answer seems to be that the test is new but integrated in the proportionality review, as its third prong. Indeed, after the Court has examined i. the nature of the measure (= *suitability*) and ii. its *necessity* in order to attain the claimed objective, it then goes on to evaluate iii. its *coherence* and *consistency*.

Coherence is an internal test and looks into the very content of the measure under scrutiny, essentially asking the question 'does it make sense?' or 'is it logical?'. It looks into the restrictive measure and enquires whether the restriction is a standalone rule or, whether, on the contrary, it forms part of a coherent system. In *Hartlauer*, the very legislation which prohibited the establishment of new dental clinics nonetheless allowed for the establishment of group practices (which did not differ greatly from clinics).[184] Similarly, in *Dermoestetica* the very same piece of legislation which prohibited advertising in national media, allowed it in local ones.[185] None of the measures satisfied the requirement of coherence.

Consistency, on the other hand, is an external test and refers to the way the contemplated measure relates to other policies affecting the same legitimate objective. In the gambling cases, there was no consistency between the criminalization of bet-taking, on the one hand, and the expansive betting policy pursued in all other respects, on the other. Two antagonistic policy objectives—controlling bet-taking while increasing gambling revenues—opposed each other, in such a way that was 'inconsistent' in relation to the other.

The difference is, therefore, that coherence looks into the various aspects of the protective policy (as expressed in one or several related regulatory instruments), while consistency looks at the way the protective policy combines with other related (or, indeed, antagonistic) policies.

It is submitted that this approach is extremely helpful, in many respects. For one thing, it offers an alternative third prong to the proportionality test, one which is internal—not external—to the legal order in question. To this extent, it does not present all the disadvantages of the 'true' proportionality test, as highlighted above. Moreover, the consistency/coherence test has added value, since it amounts to a

---

[181] Case C-42/07 *Liga Portuguesa de Futebol Profissional and Bwin International Ltd v Departamento de Jogos da Santa Casa da Misericórdia de Lisboa* [2009] ECR I-7633.
[182] Joined cases C-171 & 172/07 *Apothekerkammer des Saarlandes and others and Helga Neumann-Seiwert v Saarland and Ministerium für Justiz, Gesundheit und Soziales* [2009] ECR I-4171.
[183] Joined cases C-570 & 571/07 *José Manuel Blanco Pérez, María del Pilar Chao Gómez v Consejería de Salud y Servicios Sanitarios and Principado de Asturias* [2010] nyr.
[184] Case C-169/07 *Hartlauer* [2009] ECR I-1721.
[185] Case C-500/06 *Dermoestética* [2008] ECR I-5785.

'hypocrisy test'[186] that unveils latent protectionism; in that sense, it usefully completes the suitability and necessity tests.[187] Moreover, this test is less abstract than those of suitability and necessity, in that it does not merely measure the national rule as against its proclaimed objectives, but looks into it and positions it within the general regulatory framework in force in the member state concerned. Hence, it appears more objective and its outcomes are more foreseeable. Further, the consistency/coherence test helps identify the contradictions within national legislation and/or administrative practice, often due to no more than the poor quality of administration. In this way, the new test, when it does not serve as a 'hypocrisy test', functions at least as an 'efficiency test'.[188] Indeed, the identification of contradictory or else inconsistent regulation is a major challenge for all legal orders, and an objective pursued in the framework of the various regulatory reform initiatives.[189] The consistency/coherence test adds national jurisdictions to the other monitoring mechanisms, at least as regards measures touching on the internal market.

---

[186] To use the expression of AG Mengozzi in Joined cases C-316/07, C-409–410/07 & C-358-360/07 *Markus Stoß, Avalon Service-Online-Dienste GmbH and Olaf Amadeus Wilhelm Happel v Wetteraukreis and Kulpa Automatenservice Asperg GmbH, SOBO Sport & Entertainment GmbH and Andreas Kunert v Land Baden-Württemberg* [2010] nyr (AG), para 50; see also Mathisen, G., 'Consistency and Coherence as Conditions for Justification of Member State Measures Restricting Free Movement' (2010) 47 *CML Rev* 1021–48, at 1034.

[187] The idea that the proportionality test should be limited to the internal legal order and refrain from taking into account outside values in the sense of 'real' proportionality exposed before, is strongly supported by the language recently used by the Court, see eg in *Markus Stoß*, n 186, para 91, where the Court states that 'the need for and proportionality of the measures thus adopted having to be assessed *solely in relation to the objectives* thus pursued *and the level of protection* which *the national authorities* concerned seek to ensure' (emphasis added); exactly the same idea is also to be found in Case C-46/08 *Carmen Media Group Ltd v Land Schleswig Holstein and Inneminister des Landes Schleswig-Holstein* [2010] nyr, para 46.

[188] A counter-argument may be made, however, that this test systematically penalizes new—or indeed innovative—legislation which may be contradicted by pre-existing legislation, in force or deadwood.

[189] For which, see briefly the analysis in ch 8.

5

Judge-made Regulation in the Field of Services

The economic importance of services has only come to be fully recognized in the last 20–30 years. Extensive studies of the way services are produced and traded—and therefore, of the means of imposing restrictions on them—have only appeared over the same period. What is more, the multi-faceted, often intermediary, nature of services makes them difficult to regulate. These are some of the reasons which explain the relative scarcity of regulatory texts in the field of services, especially when compared with goods. Indeed, as will be shown in the following chapter, regulation in the field of services has been case-specific, with the first horizontal text, the Services Directive, only appearing in 2006, after an intensive and painful gestation period.

In the face of regulatory inertia, and in response to increasing pressure from the market, the Court took on responsibility for actively implementing the Treaty rules on the free provision of services. While the first, foundational judgments in the field are almost concomitant with those on goods—*Van Binsbergen* and *Walrave* follow only a few months on from *Dassonville*—it is in the early 1990s that the services case law took off and developed exponentially.[1] The judgments in *Gouda* and *Säger*[2] have prompted a very rich—and constantly sustained—wave of case law. Indeed, the CJEU has gone from deciding 40 cases in the five-year period between 1995–1999 (an average of eight cases per year) to deciding over 140 cases based on Article 56 TFEU between 2000–2005 (more than 23 per year, on average).[3] This number has been further raised to 137 for the period 2006–10 (an average of 27,4 cases per year—actually 2010 alone accounts for 50 cases!). Moreover, an important proportion of the judgments in question have been delivered by the Full Court or the Grand Chamber, often with the participation of several member states. Hence, today the legal rules applicable to the free provision of services in the EU can not be explored without an extensive examination of the case law. Such a study is necessary not only to trace the evolution of the application of the various rules

---

[1] Case 33/74 *Johannes Hervicus Maria van Binsbergen v Bestuur van de Bedrijfsvereniging voor de Metaalnijverheid* [1974] ECR 1299; Case 36/74 *B.N.O. Walrave and L.J.N. Koch v Association Union cycliste internationale, Koninklijke Nederlandsche Wielren Unie and Federación Española Ciclismo* [1974] ECR 1405; Case 8/74 *Procureur du Roi v Dassonville* [1974] ECR 837.

[2] Case C-288/89 *Stichting Collectieve Antennevoorziening Gouda v Commissariaat voor de Media* [1991] ECR I-4007; Case C-76/90 *Säger v Dennemeyer & Co Ltd* [1991] ECR I-4221.

[3] See Hatzopoulos, V., and Do, U., 'Overview of the Case Law of the ECJ in the Field of Free Movement of Services 2000–2005' (2006) 43 *CML Rev* 923–91, at 923.

and principles,[4] but also to determine the precise content of the legal rules applicable in this field of EU law.

This is the object of the present chapter. Looking into the Court's case law, one may identify several broad service categories (A), in which the numerous CJEU judgments build up an important body of regulatory principles and, even, introduce specific rules. Although the process is gradual and, at times, erratic, the ensuing judge-made 'regulation' is often as detailed as regulation through legislation. Indeed, judge-made rules in some areas serve as a substitute to legislation (B), while in others they complete the legislation in place (C); taxation being a special case (D). The positivist sector-specific presentation is followed by some more horizontal and normative considerations concerning the role of secondary legislation and the fields in which it could develop in the near future (E).

A. Categories of services concerned

Looking first at categories of services, a basic tripartite distinction can be drawn depending on whether the services concerned are purely business services, purely consumer services, or mixed services. Such a distinction could be useful from a regulatory point of view, since both the *needs* and the *means* may differ at the two ends of this scale, namely in business as opposed to private services.

Thus undertakings, the recipients of business services, may enjoy important market power—especially if they belong to manufacturing industries[5]—and often have access to information comparable to that of the service providers. Information asymmetries, therefore, one of the main drivers of service regulation, are missing in this category of services. By the same token, any form of paternalism seems unjustified for this category. More radically, it could even be submitted that regulation pursuing safety, health, and consumer protection (SHEC) objectives is not needed for business services: businesses should be left to choose the level of quality and, correlatively, cost which they deem appropriate for their clients/consumers. Moreover, undertakings, either individually or through their representative bodies, are often involved with the making and implementation of regulation, since they 'talk directly to power'. From this point of view, there seems to be no need to have recourse to formal legal regulation: incentives, default clauses, and other alternative means of regulation (in the broad sense) achieve the same results.[6]

Personal services, on the other hand, put at stake the personal, even intimate, needs of their recipients (healthcare and aesthetic services being prime examples). Personal services are often linked to some public service or other special obligation of the state towards its citizens (healthcare is again a good example, network-based

---

[4] On these, see the discussion in chs 2–4.

[5] It is worth remembering that most big industries are in the manufacturing sector, while, on the other hand, most service providing undertakings are SMEs; for more detail, see the discussion in ch 1.

[6] For such 'alternative' means of regulation, see the analysis in ch 7.

Table 5.1. CJEU's case law classified according to the service recipients

Type of service—on the basis of the recipient	No. of cases
Purely business services	34
Mixed services—business and private	205
Purely private services	61
Total	300

services also fall into this category). In any event, individual service recipients need to be protected *qua* consumers.

This theoretical construct, however, collapses when it encounters the reality of the Court's case law. Indeed, only 34 cases may be classified as involving purely business services, 61 cases as involving purely consumer services, while the vast majority of cases (205) concerns services which are offered without distinction to businesses and consumers alike.[7] (See Table 5.1)

The data in Table 5.1 may be read in two ways, depending on whether the glass is seen as half-empty or half-full. If services addressed to businesses are taken in isolation, their relatively small number suggests that there is no point, as yet, to look for a distinct regulatory pattern for them; the EU's efforts should concentrate in promoting free movement of such services in order to foster the competitiveness of EU businesses. Indeed, the finding may support the Commission's efforts to advance the liberalization of business services.[8] If, on the other hand, services oriented to businesses alone are counted together with 'mixed' services which are also accessible to the general public, then this broad category corresponds to 243 cases from a total of 300. The relatively low number of personal services traded across borders may be explained by several facts, for example: a. such services are often offered by the state to its citizens, thus impinging upon normal trade patterns, b. they correspond to immediate or repetitive consumer demand, which is typically met locally, c. they are based on long-standing trust relations and/or habits, and d. their providers are typically small or medium undertakings lacking the means and/or ambition of crossing national—or even the regional—borders.

It should also be noted that it is in personal services where the service recipient's initiatives are the most pronounced. While overall the recipient's position has only rarely been taken into account in the Court's case law, it was most often considered in the field of personal services, mainly in healthcare, education, and general tourism.

---

[7] The fact that these numbers amount to more than the actual number of cases (namely, 283) is explained by the fact that some cases concern more than one service activity.

[8] Communication COM (2003) 747 final, 'The Competitiveness of Business-related Services and their Contribution to the Performance of European Enterprises'; and Communication COM (2004) 83 final, 'Report on Competition in Professional Services'.

It follows that the average 'user' of the Treaty freedom of trade in services is the provider (as opposed to the recipient) of purely business or mixed services (as opposed to purely personal services). This, in turn, may be explained by the fact that a. businesses are more likely to rationalize their demand for services on the basis of economic efficiency, rather than on the basis of sentimental attachment, proximity, habit, or other more subjective factors; and b. that undertakings offering such services are more likely to be larger in size and have a transnational presence, than providers of personal services.

This, in turn, means that any effort to further increase trade in services within the EU should *supply-wise* focus on the needs of SMEs and their difficulties in trading across borders, while *demand-wise* make information more readily available to tentative recipients concerning the quality and cost of services provided in other member states. The country of origin principle (CoOP) would have satisfied the former requirement.[9] Despite the demise of the CoOP, the Services Directive does go some way in satisfying the latter requirement, since it will help with the dissemination of information and electronic filing. Moreover, a more sustained application of the public procurement rules would offer further opportunities to big service providers.

If, therefore, the above three-prong classification of services (purely business services, purely personal services, mixed services) is not immediately useful in the sense that it does not lead, as yet, to different regulatory patterns, it does, nonetheless, offer some hints as to the broader objectives of future regulation. Further directions may be deduced by looking individually into the various service activities. Indeed, by further detailing the above tripartite division of services, Table 5.2 offers interesting information as to the kinds of services which are/are not traded within the EU.

The first, and probably most striking observation, is that the services which have mostly occupied the Court are those excluded from the scope of the Services Directive. Indeed, it may seem somewhat paradoxical that, while trying to foster trade in services, the Services Directive does not cover the services most frequently contested before the CJEU. This paradox can be partly explained by the fact that, as it will be explained below, some of the areas had already been exhaustively 'regulated' by the Court's case law.

Secondly, in view of the limited success of the 'horizontal' approach followed by the Commission in proposing the Services Directive, it is likely that in the future a more focused vertical—or, at least, multi-sector—approach may be followed. The data in Table 5.2 gives an indication as to the sectors which should be dealt with.

Thirdly, a striking feature of the data presented is that the Court has intervened extensively, not only in areas where secondary legislation is completely lacking (B), but also, and most importantly, in areas with pre-existing legislation (C).

---

[9] For the CoOP see ch 6, A(6); see also Hatzopoulos, V., 'Assessing the Services Directive, 2006/123/EC' (2008) 10 *CYEL* 215–61.

Table 5.2. Business/mixed/private services—detailed table

	Kind of service	No. of cases	Total/ category
Purely business services	Advertising, advertising boards, etc	8	
	HR management, recruitment, workers' documentation, etc	7	
	Certification—Trials—Quality controls	3	
	Commercial agents	1	
	Debt recovery	1	
	Organization of events	1	
	Interim placement of workers—posted workers[10]	**11**	
	Research activities	2	
			34
Mixed services	Counsel, legal, tax, accountancy	15	
	Insurance	18	
	Patent renewal services—Patent agents	4	
	Sales and leasing services	9	
	Real estate (agencies)	3	
	Travel (agencies)	2	
	Fairs, expositions, etc	1	
	Architect—Construction—Demolition—Public works	29	
	Engineer services—technical	2	
	Craftsmanship	2	
	Equipment installation and maintenance	7	
	Information services (journalism, internet, press agencies)	1	
	Hotel and catering services	1	
	Training services (vocational training, seminars, etc)	9	
	Distribution/exploitation of commercial centre	5	
	Electricity and gas services	**3**	
	Transport services	**24**	
	Telecom and audio-visual services	**25**	

(continued)

[10] In this table, market service activities excluded from the scope of the Services Directive are marked in bold.

Table 5.2. Continued

	Kind of service	No. of cases	Total/ category
	Financial services	15	
	Private security services	7	
	Independent artists and journalists	3	
	Public service concessions	6	
	Logistics services	1	
	Docking services	1	
	Fishing services	1	
	Veterinary/artificial insemination services	2	
	Geologist services	1	
	Informatics services	2	
	Postal services	2	
	Transport consultants	1	
	Public parkings	1	
	Waste management (public)	1	
	Cleaning, cleansing, desinfection services	1	
			205
Private services	Entertainment, theme parks, games (excluding gaming), shows	4	
	Tourist guides and tourist services in general	13	
	Healthcare services	21	
	Sports	5	
	Gaming and gambling	12	
	Medical analyses	1	
	Driving schools	3	
	Personal services (hairdressers, etc)	1	
	Concession of fishing pond	1	
			61
	Grand total		300

B. Judge-made regulation as a substitute to legislation

1. Gambling/gaming

Gambling, betting, and, more generally, gaming have actively occupied the Court in the last 15 years. The opportunities for online gaming offered by technology are only expected to increase the pressure on national regulatory regimes and to multiply the legal issues raised. Although the situation in member states is quite varied, convergence may be observed as to the existence of a. access and exercise restrictions, justified by the need to curb fraud and to secure revenues for the public purse, and b. special tax arrangements for the proceedings, both for service providers and for winning consumers.[11]

In relation to the latter (tax issues), the Court has been quite straightforward. Any differential tax treatment for games' proceedings based on the place of establishment of the organizer constitutes a restriction to the free provision of services, if not blunt discrimination; justifying arguments about tax coherence, fiscal evasion, and the financing of benevolent activities did not convince the Court.[12]

In relation to the restrictions imposed on access to the activity, the Court's position evolved in three phases. In the *Schindler, Zenatti*, and *Läärä* cases[13] the Court held gambling and gaming to constitute services within the meaning of Article 56 TFEU, but was strikingly indulgent towards member states: it readily accepted justifications stemming from all sorts of overriding reasons of public interest (ORPIs), without enquiring into the measures proportionality or even their discriminatory nature.[14] In the subsequent *Anomar, Gambelli, Placanica*, and *Commission v Greece (online games)*[15] cases, the Court was more insistent on the proportionality of the restrictive measures, and required that they form part of a coherent set of regulations.[16] In view of the member states' piecemeal regulation in

---

[11] See the Final Report of the Swiss Institute of Comparative Law, *Study of Gambling Services in the Internal Market of the EU* (2006), commissioned by the Commission, available at <http://ec.europa.eu/internal_market/services/docs/gambling/study1_en.pdf> (last accessed 9 November 2011); see also Littler, A. and Fijnaut, C., *The Regulation of Gambling, European and National Perspectives* (Leiden: Martinus Nijhoff, 2007); and for general commentaries of the recent case law also Doukas, D., and Anderson, J., 'Commercial Gambling without Frontiers: When the ECJ Throws, the Dice is Loaded' (2008) 27 *YEL* 237–76 and Della Sala, V., 'Stakes and States: Gambling and the Single Market' (2010) 17 *JEPP* 1024–38.

[12] See Case C-42/02 *Diana Elisabeth Lindman* [2003] ECR I-13519 and Case C-153/08 *Commission v Spain (gambling tax)* [2009] ECR I-9735; in the latter, the case for discrimination is more expressly spelled out.

[13] Case C-275/92 *Her Majesty's Customs and Excise v Schindler* [1994] ECR I-1039; Case C-124/97 *Markku Juhani Läärä, Cotswold Microsystems Ltd and Oy Transatlantic Software Ltd v Kihlakunnasyyttäjä (Jyväskylä) and Suomen valtio* [1999] ECR I-6067; Case C-67/98 *Questore di Verona v Diego Zenatti* [1999] ECR I-7289; for all these cases, see Allen, B., 'Ladies and Gentlemen, No More Bets Please' (2000) 27 *LIEI* 201–6.

[14] See Hatzopoulos, V., 'Annotation: Case C-275/92 *Her Majesty's Customs and Excise v Schindler*' [1994] ECR I-1039 (1995) 32 *CML Rev* 841–55 and Straetmans, G., 'Annotation: Case C-124/97, Läärä, Judgment of the Court of 21 September 1999 and Case C-67/98, Zenatti, Judgment of the Court of 21 October 1999' (2000) 37 *CML Rev* 991–1005.

[15] Case C-6/01 *Associação Nacional de Operadores de Máquinas Recreativas (Anomar) and others v Estado português* [2003] ECR I-8621; Case C-243/01 *Criminal proceedings against Piergiorgio Gambelli and others* [2003] ECR I-13031; Joined Cases C-338, 359 & 360/04 *Criminal proceedings against Massimiliano Placanica, Christian Palazzese, and Angelo Sorricchio* [2007] ECR I-1891. *Placanica* is a Grand Chamber judgment; on the same date, another three Orders of the Court with similar content were published (Case C-191/06 (ord) *Aniello Gallo and Gianluca Damonte* [2007] ECR I-30, Case C-395/05 (ord) *Antonello D'Antonio and others* [2007] ECR I-24, Case C-466/05 (ord) *Gianluca Damonte* [2007] ECR I-27); Case C-65/05 *Commission v Greece (online games)* [2006] ECR I-10341.

[16] For the 'coherence' requirement in the Court's case law, see ch 4 above.

the area, this case law had a profoundly liberalizing potential; at the same time, however, it generated fears that the liberalizing effect could be overstressed and member states could be compelled to open up to activities which they wished to exclude from their territory. These concerns, albeit at first nourished by the Court's case law on use-restrictions of jet-skis, side-cars, and dark window-shield films,[17] have, in the end, been relieved by the (Grand Chamber) judgment in *Liga Portuguesa de Futebol*.[18] In this case, the Court accepted that moral considerations combined with the risk of fraud may justify not only an exclusive right (restriction to the freedom of establishment), but also an absolute prohibition of online gambling (restriction to the free provision of services) from other member states. Thus it was held that the fact that the gaming company in question held a licence in one member state did not preclude the host member state from imposing its own authorization requirements, especially since 'because of the lack of direct contact between consumer and operator, games of chance accessible via the internet involve different and more substantial risks of fraud by operators against consumers compared with the traditional markets for such games'.[19] By the same token, the Court acknowledged the fact that the same service may be subject to different rules depending on its mode of delivery (establishment/mode 3 v. trans-border supply/ mode 1).[20] In a more general way, this shift of the Court's case law highlights the limitations of mutual recognition in relation to socially/morally sensible activities.

This more lenient approach of the Court towards member states has been confirmed in a series of recent judgments,[21] where the Court has repeatedly stated that 'the Member States are free to set the objectives of their policy on betting and gambling according to their own scale of values and, where appropriate, to define in detail the level of protection sought'.[22] Such discretion, however, is not absolute, but subject to the principle of proportionality. From the three prongs of the proportionality test proposed in the previous chapter, namely, a. suitability, b. necessity, and c. consistency and coherence, it is the last prong that occupies a dominant role in this sensitive area.[23] Even the 'hypocrisy test',[24] clearly spelled out

---

[17] See Case C-110/05 *Commission v Italy (trailers)* [2009] ECR I-519; Case C-142/05 *Åklagaren v Percy Mickelsson and Joakim Roos* [2009] ECR I-4273; and Case C-265/06 *Commission v Portuguese Republic* [2008] ECR I-2245. See also commentary by Horsley, T., 'Annotation: Case C-110/05, Commission v Italy (trailers) [2009] nyr' (2009) 46 *CML Rev* 2001–19; see also Derlén, M., and Lindholm, J., 'Article 28 EC and Rules on Use: A Step Towards a Workable Doctrine on Measures Having Equivalent Effect to Quantitative Restrictions' (2010) 16 *Columbia J of Eur L* 191–231.

[18] Case C-42/07 *Liga Portuguesa de Futebol Profissional and Bwin International Ltd v Departamento de Jogos da Santa Casa da Misericórdia de Lisboa* [2009] ECR I-7633.

[19] Ibid, para 70, repeated in subsequent case law.

[20] On the different modes of services delivery, see the discussion in ch 2.

[21] Case C-203/08 *Sporting Exchange Ltd v Minister van Justitie (Betfair)* [2010] nyr; Case C-258/08 *Ladbrokes Betting & Gaming Ltd and Ladbrokes International Ltd v Stichting de Nationale Sporttotalisator* [2010] nyr; Case C-58/09 *Leo-Libera GmbH v Finanzamt Buchholz in der Nordheide* [2010] nyr.

[22] See eg C-203/08 *Sporting Exchange (Betfair)*, n 21, para 28; Case C-64/08 *Criminal proceedings against Ernst Engelmann* [2010] nyr, para 50.

[23] For the reasons why this criterion is particularly suitable for application in sensitive areas, see the developments in ch 4, B(2)b.

[24] To use the expression of Joined cases C-316/07, 358/07, 359/07, 360/07, 409/07 & 410/07 *Markus Stoß, Avalon Service-Online-Dienste GmbH and Olaf Amadeus Wilhelm Happel v Wetteraukreis*

in the early *Gambelli* and *Placanica* judgments, was watered down by the Court in subsequent gaming cases, where it was held that 'national legislation . . . can be regarded as limiting betting activities in a consistent and systematic manner even where the holder(s) of an exclusive licence are entitled to make what they are offering on the market attractive by introducing new games and by means of advertising'.[25]

Even under such a lenient test, however, in subsequent cases the Court managed to strike down several member state restrictions to gambling/gaming, placing emphasis on the material findings of the referring courts.[26]

Whenever a member state decides to grant exclusive rights (in the form of a single licence or other means) to an entity which is not under the direct control of that state (as was the case in *Liga Portuguesa and Bwin*), it may not do so in an arbitrary way, but needs to respect the public procurement and transparency principles:

'[w]ithout necessarily implying an obligation to launch an invitation to tender, that obligation of transparency requires the concession-granting authority to ensure, for the benefit of any potential concessionaire, a degree of advertising sufficient to enable the service concession to be opened up to competition and the impartiality of the procurement procedures to be reviewed'.[27]

This is all the more so, whenever the number of authorizations to be granted is much higher than just one, as was the case in *Placanica*.[28] According to the Italian legislation, the activity in question required a government licence, from which (mostly non-Italian) undertakings quoted in the stock market were altogether excluded. The Court did not restrain itself to submitting that such blanket exclusion was disproportionate to the objective of protecting consumers. It further held that whenever operators have been unlawfully excluded from the award of licences (which were determinate in number), 'it is for the national legal order to lay down detailed procedural rules to ensure the protection of the rights which those operators derive by direct effect of Community law' and that 'appropriate courses of action could be the revocation and redistribution of the old licences or the award by *public tender* of an adequate number of new licences'.[29] This reflects an idea implemented in the regulated industries (telecommunications, energy, etc) and

---

and Kulpa Automatenservice Asperg GmbH, SOBO Sport & Entertainment GmbH and Andreas Kunert v Land Baden-Württemberg [2010] nyr (AG), para 50; more on this 'hypocrisy test' see in ch 4, B(2)b.

[25] Case C-258/08 *Ladbrokes*, n 21, para 38 and operative part.

[26] Case C-64/08 *Engelmann*, n 22; Case C-409/06 *Winner Wetten GmbH v Bürgermeisterin der Stadt Bergheim* [2010] nyr; Joined cases C-447/08 & 448/08 *Criminal proceedings against Otto Sjöberg & Anders Gerdin* [2010] nyr; Joined cases C-316/07, 358/07, 359/07, 360/07, 409/07 & 410/07 *Markus Stoß*, n 24; Case C-46/08 *Carmen Media Group Ltd v Land Schleswig-Holstein and Innenminister des Landes Schleswig-Holstein* [2010] nyr; for a comprehensive presentation of this recent case law, see Bernard, E., 'La Cour de justice précise les règles du jeu' (2010) 20:11 *Europe* 7–11.

[27] Case C-203/08 *Sporting Exchange (Betfair)*, n 21, para 41.

[28] Joined cases C-338, 359 & 360/04 *Placanica* [2007] ECR I-1891.

[29] Ibid, para 63 (emphasis added).

which had for some time been put forward by the Commission in a more general scale, concerning access to essential facilities:[30] whenever some scarce resource is to be distributed between competitors, it should be done through public tendering procedures, following basic procurement principles (ie non-discrimination and equal treatment, transparency, proportionality, and mutual recognition).[31] This very idea is also represented in Article 12 of the Services Directive, according to which 'where the number of authorisations available for a given activity is limited because of the scarcity of available natural resources or technical capacity, Member States shall apply a selection procedure to potential candidates which provides full guarantees of impartiality and transparency'. This provision however, seems to address mainly the problem of scarce resources, not limitations imposed by regulatory choice. Therefore, the principle of *Placanica/Betfair/Engelmann* seems to be furthered and completed by the rule in Article 12 of the Services Directive.

More gaming cases are in the pipeline, a result of both expansive policies by multi-national firms[32] and the Commission's determination to rationalize the market.[33] In view of the bulk of case law, both delivered and forthcoming, and of the financial interests at stake, and given that gaming and gambling were expressly excluded both from the E-commerce Directive and from the Services Directive,[34] it comes as no surprise that the Commission has been urged by the other institutions to initiate a dialogue with the aim of reaching political agreement on the legal status of gambling in Europe.[35] Thus gaming is an area in which EU regulatory activity is to be expected in the foreseeable future; indeed, in October 2010, the Commissioner in charge of the Internal Market Agenda announced that a forthcoming Green Paper in the field will be adopted.[36] In view of the percularities of the area, however, the activity of the EU is likely to take the form of

---

[30] On the doctrine of essential facilities see Hatzopoulos, V., 'The Evolution of the Essential Facilities Doctrine' in Amato, G., and Elhermann, C.-D (eds), *EC Competition Law: A Critical View* (Oxford/Portland: Hart Publishing, 2007) 317–58.

[31] See the discussion under subheading C(4).

[32] See eg pending Case C-212/08 *Société Zeturf Limited v Premier ministre, Ministre de l'Agriculture et de la Pêche, Ministre de l'Intérieur, de l'Outre-mer et des Collectivités territoriales, Ministre de l'Economie, de l'Industrie et de l'Emploi* [2008] OJ C197/12, also pending Case C-347/09 *Criminal proceedings against Jochen Dickinger and Franz Oemer* [2009] OJ C 282/26.

[33] The Commission has initiated proceedings against several member states, among which are France, Sweden, and Greece; see Kilsby, J., 'EU Commission Turns Up Heat on Europe's Gambling Monopolies' *Gambling Compliance*, 28 June 2008, available at <http://www.gamblingcompliance.com/node/7734> (last accessed on 9 November 2011).

[34] European Parliament and Council Directive 2000/31/EC on certain legal aspects of information society services, in particular electronic commerce, in the Internal Market ('Directive on electronic commerce') [2000] OJ L178/1; and European Parliament and Council Directive 2006/123/EC on services in the internal market [2006] OJ L376/36, respectively.

[35] See 'Commission Urged to clarify gambling's EU Legal Status' *Euractiv* (04/03/2009), available at <http://www.euractiv.com/en/sports/commission-urged-clarify-gambling-eu-legal-status/article-179946> (last accessed on 9 November 2011).

[36] See also Speech of the internal market Commissioner M. Barnier, 'Jeux en ligne: une réalité à reconnaître, pour davantage la connaître et mieux la réguler', 12/10/2010, available at <http://ec.europa.eu/internal_market/services/docs/gambling/conference12102010/speechmb.pdf> (last accessed on 9 November 2011).

minimal harmonization, at best, or of some soft law/coordinating instrument; anything more ambitious would face considerable opposition in the Council.

2. Private security services

Another field in which EU regulation could prove helpful is private security services. The case law of the Court in the field has been on the rise over the last decade[37] and a brief overview of the cases decided shows that the requirements imposed by the different member states on security firms are fairly similar: total exclusion of foreign undertakings, nationality requirements for owners, directors, and/or staff, special registration requirements, individual authorization for every staff member, special ID cards, performance bonds, etc.[38] More often than not, several of the above requirements are imposed cumulatively.

Given that both the interests to be protected and the means to protect them are largely common to all member states, it should not be difficult to agree on a basic harmonizing text concerning the constitution of private security companies and leading to a form of 'European passport' for such activity. Basic operational rules could also be agreed at the EU level, while supervision would necessarily lie with the authorities of the state, where private security firms operate. The need for EU action in this field seems all the more compelling since the Commission has already acknowledged that private companies may be involved with security-related research, in view of contributing to safeguarding the EU Area of Freedom, Security, and Justice (AFSJ).[39]

Regulatory action in the field could be facilitated, or indeed prepared, by the Confederation of European Security Services (CoEES), founded in 1989 as an umbrella organization for national private security associations. Indeed, one of the main objectives of CoEES is 'to increase the quality level of the entire industry, including through standardisation of regulations'.[40] Following a 'softer' path of regulation,[41] the CoEES could set voluntary standards and a system of certification, compliance with which would enable private security firms to operate without restrictions throughout the EU.

---

[37] See Hatzopoulos, V., and Do, U., 'Overview of the Case Law of the ECJ in the Field of Free Movement of Services 2000–2005' (2006) 43 *CML Rev* 923–91.

[38] See, in particular, Case C-114/97 *Commission v Spain (private security)* [1998] ECR I-6717; Case C-355/98 *Commission v Belgium (private security)* [2000] ECR I-1221; Case C-283/99 *Commission v Italy (private security)* [2001] ECR I-4363; Case C-189/03 *Commission v Netherlands (private security)* [2004] ECR I-5645; Case C-514/03 *Commission v Spain (private security)* [2006] ECR I-963.

[39] Communication COM (2007) 511 final, 'Public–Private Dialogue in Security Research and Innovation'; for a brief critical comment, see Bigo, D., and Jeansdesboz, J., 'The EU and the European Security Industry: Questioning the "Public–Private Dialogue"' CEPS/INEX Policy Brief 5/2010, available at <http://www.ceps.be/book/eu-and-european-security-industry-questioning-'public-private-dialogue'> (last accessed on 9 November 2011).

[40] See <http://www.coess.org/?CategoryID=175> (last accessed 9 November 2011).

[41] See the discussion in ch 7.

3. Tourist guides

Tourist guides is another field in which there is some important case law.[42] Judicial activity in the area, however, has slowed down in recent years and, to the knowledge of the author, no major Commission initiative is forthcoming. This may be explained by the fact that, following the Court's judgments, member states banned outright discriminations, while, on the other hand, the Commission was unwilling to push in an area which touches upon the states' cultural heritage and, by implication, national identity. Furthermore, some form of self-regulation takes place at the level of the European Federation of Tourist Guide Associations (Fédération Européenne des Guides, FEG), based in Paris.[43] This body has established a very basic Quality Charter and Code of Conduct, as well as some basic training principles. What is more, the implementation of the Services Directive by the member states has led to considerable adjustments to the rules of establishment and service provision by tourist guides.[44]

C. Judge-made regulation as a top-up to legislation

1. Healthcare services[45]

In order to make possible the limited movement of capital, at a time when the relevant Treaty freedom was completely idle, the CJEU held that current payments for services received in another member state should be free of any restriction. By the same token the Court recognized that medical patients, students, and tourists moving to another member state are service recipients, in the sense of Article 56 TFEU.[46]

---

[42] Case C-154/89 *Commission v France (tourist guides)* [1991] ECR I-659; Case C-180/89 *Commission v Italy (tourist guides)* [1991] ECR I-709; Case C-198/89 *Commission v Greece (tourist guides)* [1991] ECR I-727; Case C-375/92 *Commission v Spain (tourist guides)* [1994] ECR I-923.

[43] See <http://www.feg-touristguides.com/about-feg.html> (last accessed on 9 November 2011).

[44] See Commission Communication 'Towards a Better Functioning Single Market for Services—Building on the Results of the Mutual Evaluation Process of the Services Directive' COM(2011) 20 final, accompanied by the Commission Working Paper SEC(2011) 102 final.

[45] This part draws substantially on the author's previous writings concerning healthcare. See in particular, Hatzopoulos, V., 'Assessing the Services Directive, 2006/123/EC' (2008) 10 *CYEL* 215–61; Hatzopoulos, V., 'Killing National Health and Insurance Systems but *Healing* Patients? The European Market for Health Care Services after the Judgments of the CJEU in *Vanbraekel* and *Peerbooms*' (2002) 36 *CML Rev* (2002) 683–729; Hatzopoulos, V., 'Health law and policy: the impact of the EU' in de Búrca, G. (ed), *EU Law and the Welfare State: In Search of Solidarity* (Oxford: OUP, 2005) 123–60; Hatzopoulos, V., 'Services of general interest in healthcare: an exercise in deconstruction?', in Neergaard, U., Roseberry, L., and Nielsen, R. (eds), *Integrating Welfare Functions into EU law: From Rome to Lisbon* (Copenhagen: DJØF Publishing, 2009) 225–52; Hatzopoulos, V., 'Financing National Health Care in a Transnational Environment: The Impact of the EC Internal Market' (2009) 26 *Wisconsin Int L J* 761–804.

[46] Joined cases 286/82 & 26/83 *Luisi and Carbone v Ministero del Tesoro* [1984] ECR 377; the same conclusion was also reached by the Court in Case C-159/90 *The Society for the Protection of Unborn Children Ireland Ltd (SPUC) v Stephan Grogan and others* [1991] ECR 4685. In the latter case,

In *Decker* and *Köhll*,[47] the CJEU made clear that the Treaty rules on free movement of goods and services, respectively, apply even when the relevant services are offered in the framework of a publicly funded healthcare system. Consequently, the Court held that the competent healthcare funds could not make the refunding of medical expenses incurred by their patients in another member state conditional upon the funds' prior authorization. What was less clear, however, was whether this case law also covered a. national healthcare systems which offer benefits-in-kind rather than a simple refund, b. complex healthcare services which may only be delivered within a hospital infrastructure, c. full refund of expenses incurred by the patients in another member state, when they had not received previous authorization from their fund. A further question which remained unanswered was d. whether the system of previous authorization itself, provided for in Regulation 1408/71[48] and applied (with variations) by all member states, is contrary to Article 56 TFEU.

In relation to these topics, the CJEU gave negative answers to questions (b), (c), and (d), in cases *Peerbooms*[49] and *Vanbraekel*.[50] Despite the fact that the final outcome of these cases seems to restrict the scope of Article 56 TFEU, the reasoning of the CJEU is particularly wide. It proceeds on the assumption that healthcare services, provided in the framework of social insurance systems or by national healthcare systems, are services like any other. Only overriding reasons of public interest (ORPIs), such as maintaining the financial balance of the social security scheme and ensuring the sound planning of national healthcare facilities, may justify restrictions to the fundamental freedom to receive services. The expansive interpretation of the Treaty rules on the free movement of services in the healthcare sector was confirmed one year later, in the *Müller-Fauré* judgment and was further clarified in *Watts*.[51] In the latter case, the CJEU clearly answered in the affirmative question (a) above,[52] thus extending the scope of Article 56 TFEU to healthcare systems that offer benefits-in-kind. In this same decision, it was also made clear that the healthcare fund of a member state is obliged to authorize its

---

however, the Court avoided applying the relevant Treaty rules, as it was unable to identify any consideration for the services offered.

[47] Case C-120/95 *Nicolas Decker v Caisse de maladie des employés privés* [1998] ECR I-1831 and Case C-158/96 *Raymond Köhll v Union des Caisses de Maladie* [1998] ECR I-1931.

[48] Council Regulation 1408/71/EEC on the application of social security schemes to employed persons and their families moving within the Community [1971] OJ L149/2, codified and replaced by European Parliament and Council Regulation 592/2008/EC amending Council Regulation (EEC) No 1408/71 on the application of social security schemes to employed persons, to self-employed persons and to members of their families moving within the Community [2008] OJ L177/1.

[49] Case C-157/99 *B.S.M. Geraets-Smits v Stichting Ziekenfonds VGZ and H.T.M. Peerbooms v Stichting CZ Groep Zorgverzekeringen* [2001] ECR I-5473.

[50] Case C-368/98 *Abdon Vanbraekel and others v Alliance nationale des mutualités chrétiennes (ANMC)* [2001] ECR I-5363.

[51] Case C-385/99 *V.G. Müller-Fauré v Onderlinge Waarborgmaatschappij oz Zorgverzekeringen UA and E.E.M. van Riet v Orderlinge Waarborgmaatschappij oz Zorgverzekeringen UA* [2003] ECR I-4509; Case C-372/04 *The Queen, on the application of Yvonne Watts v Bedford Primary Care Trust and Secretary of State for Health* [2006] ECR I-4325.

[52] Although a positive answer could already be assumed from the previous CJEU judgments.

patients to receive treatment in another EU country, whenever such treatment may not be offered to them without undue delay in their state of origin.

This case law, lengthy, highly technical, and politically controversial, has been presented in detail by several authors and the replication of such commentary would serve no purpose here.[53] In summary, alongside urgent treatment provided by virtue of the European Health Insurance Card (formerly document E111), patients from any member state moving abroad, may:

a. receive outpatient treatment[54] in any other member state and obtain a refund from their home state, at the tariffs applicable in the latter; no prior authorization is necessary for the refund to be obtained, since the relevant right stems directly from Article 56 TFEU;

b. receive any kind of treatment in other member states under the same conditions (tariffs, refund, indemnity, etc—but for the duration) as patients of the host state, provided they have obtained prior authorization (document E112) by their home institution, according to Article 22 of Regulation 1408/71 (now Article 20 of Regulation 883/2004);[55]

c. force the delivery of the above authorization (for receiving treatment abroad) whenever the treatment objectively necessary for their medical condition[56] is not available in their home state or is not available within a reasonable period, taking into consideration the specific needs of each particular patient;[57] this is also a right directly stemming from Article 56 TFEU.

It should be added that these rights benefit all people insured with the competent institution of a member state, irrespectively of whether the home state[58] i. operates a refund system, like the one followed (principally) in France, Germany, and Luxembourg,[59] ii. operates a benefits-in-kind system through physicians and

---

[53] See on top of the articles cited in n. 45 above, Davies, G., 'Welfare as a Service' (2002) 29 *LIEI* 27–40; Cabral, P., 'The Internal Market and the Right to Cross-border Medical Care' (2004) 29 *EL Rev* 673–85; and Van der Mei, A.P., 'Cross-border Access to Medical Care: Non-hospital Care and Waiting Lists' (2004) 31 *LIEI* 57–67; van der Mei, A.P., 'Cross-border Access to Health Care within the EU: Some Reflections on *Geraets-Smits and Peerbooms* and *Vanbraekel*' (2002) 9 *Maastricht J of Eur and Comparative Law* 189–213. More recently, see Dawes, A., 'Bonjour Herr Doctor: National Healthcare Systems, the Internal Market and Cross-Border Medical Care within the EU' (2006) 33 *LIEI* 167–82. For a full account of the relationships between the EU and health law, see Hervey, T., and McHale, J., *Health Law and the European Union* (Cambridge: CUP, 2004).

[54] In-patient treatment has been restrictively defined, see Case C-8/02 *Ludwig Leichtle v Bundesanstalt für Arbeit* [2004] ECR I-2641.

[55] European Parliament and Council Regulation 883/2004/EC on the coordination of social security systems [2004] OJ L166/1, which is in force since May 2010.

[56] For the objective assessment of the necessity of the treatment, independently from national preferences, see Case C-368/98 *Vanbraekel*, n 50.

[57] Case C-385/99 *Müller-Fauré*, n 51, and Case C-372/04 *Watts*, n 51.

[58] The three-prong classification which follows is simplistic, for the sake of argument, and does not account for the special characteristics of each one of the national systems.

[59] See Case C-158/96 *Köhll* [1998] ECR I-1931; Case C-56/01 *Patricia Inizan v Caisse primaire d'assurance maladie des Hauts-de-Seine* [2003] ECR I-12403; Case C-193/03 *Betriebskrankenkasse der Robert Bosch GmbH v Bundesrepublik Deutschland* [2004] ECR I-9911.

hospitals, as is the case in the Netherlands,[60] or iii. offers benefits-in-kind via essentially public institutions, as is the case in the UK and Italy.[61]

These principles, set out in the foundational judgments mentioned above, have been further clarified in a long series of subsequent cases. These include *Inizan*, where the Court set the conditions which national authorization procedures should satisfy in order to conform with Article 56 TFEU;[62] *van der Duin*, where the Court set the rules for determining which is the 'competent institution' in so-called 'zig-zag' situations where the national of member state A lives permanently in member state B but receives services in the former;[63] *IKA v Ioannidis*, where the Court made clear that pensioners may receive hospital treatment abroad while on a visit there without prior authorization, even if their condition was already known and did not really constitute an emergency;[64] *Leichte*, where the CJEU held that physiotherapy and rehabilitation services do not constitute hospital services for which patients need authorization from their fund, even though they are offered within an organized and dedicated infrastructure;[65] *Bosch*, where the Court upheld as compatible with Regulation 1408/71 the national practice of reimbursing, without prior authorization, all expenses incurred abroad, below a given amount;[66] *Acereda Herrera*, where the Court submitted that the refund administered pursuant to a Regulation 1408/71 authorization need not cover travel expenses if such expenses are not covered for patients moving within national territory;[67] *Stamatelaki*, where the Court made it clear that a public fund may also be liable to pay for treatment received in a private clinic in another member state;[68] *Elchinov*, where the Court noted that, while member states are free to determine the list of treatments covered/ not covered by the competent institutions, such lists are to be interpreted in a flexible manner in order to include similar treatments offered in other member states;[69] and *Commission v Spain (healthcare services)*, where the Court confirmed the right to the so called '*Vanbraekel* supplement' available whenever treatment received in another member state is 'cheaper' than the cost of the same treatment at home, but limited the scope of such right by excluding urgent treatments (since, by definition, in emergencies the patient's choice may not be affected by the lack of

---

[60] Case C-157/99 *Smits and Peerbooms* [2001] ECR I-5473; Case C-368/98 *Vanbraekel*, n 50 above, and Case C-385/99 *Müller-Fauré*, n 51 above.

[61] Case C-372/04 *Watts*, n 51.

[62] Case C-56/01 *Inizan*, n 59.

[63] Case C-156/01 *R.P. van der Duin v Onderlinge Waarborgmaatschappij ANOZ Zorgverzekeringen UA and Onderlinge Waarborgmaatschappij ANOZ Zorgverzekeringen UA v T.W. van Wegberg-van Brederode* [2003] ECR I-7045.

[64] Case C-326/00 *Idryma Koinonikon Asfaliseon (IKA) v Vasileios Ioannidis* [2003] ECR I-1703 and Hatzopoulos, V., 'Annotation: Case C-326/00 *Ioannidis v IKA* [2003] ECR I-1703' (2003) 40 *CML Rev* 1251–68.

[65] Case C-8/02 *Leichtle* [2004] ECR I-2641.

[66] Case C-193/03 *Bosch*, n 59.

[67] Case C-466/04 *Manuel Acereda Herrera v Servicio Cántabro de Salud* [2006] ECR I-5341.

[68] Case C-444/05 *Aikaterini Stamatelaki v NPDD Organismos Asfaliseos Eleftheron Epangelmation (OAEE)* [2007] ECR I-3185.

[69] Case C-173/09 *Georgi Ivanov Elchinov v Natsionalna zdravnoosiguritelna kasa* [2010] nyr.

such supplement);[70] *Commission v France (Major Medical Equipment)* where the Court accepted that a prior authorization may be required not only in relation to treatments necessitating a hospital infrastructure, but also by outpatient treatments requiring the use of very important/expensive equipment.[71]

As a consequence of this case law, mobility of patients across the EU countries is greatly facilitated. This, however, has not led, up until now, to opening the floodgates of 'peripatetic' patients picking and choosing healthcare services in various member states.[72] This notwithstanding, it cannot be denied that the case law in the field reflects an intense 'dialogue' among the national/insurance health systems of the various member states. This dialogue has the aim of enhancing their effective cooperation and correcting the weaknesses of each individual system in order to avoid the phenomena of a mass exit of patients. This very dialogue entails competition amongst national/insurance health systems, pushing them to rationalize and promote efficiency. In order, however, to avoid the risk that such competition develops downwards spirals, and with the objective of making such ground-breaking principles more accessible to the average EU citizen, the Commission has tried to push through legislation in the area. Strikingly enough, the European Parliament, a few months after insisting that healthcare be removed from scope of the Services Directive,[73] in a report of 10 May 2007 'invite[d] the Commission to submit to it, a proposal to reintroduce health services into Directive 2006/123/EC, and a proposal to codify European Court of Justice rulings on European patients' rights'.[74] The ensuing Resolution, however, only addressed the need for codification.[75] It did not take much more to 'force' the Commission's hand to contemplate fresh legislation in the field.

The impact assessment carried out in turn by the Commission envisaged the following four options:[76] a. take no action at all, b. provide guidance on cross-border mobility avoiding any regulatory action, c. establish a general legal framework for health services, through a coordinating Directive, d. create a detailed harmonized framework for the provision of healthcare. According to the econometric proxy used by the Commission, option (a) would lead to 195,000 extra 'mobile' patients, option (b) to 270,000 new patients, option (c) to 780,000 new

---

[70] Case C-211/08 *Commission v Spain (healthcare services)* [2010] nyr.

[71] Case C-512/08 *Commission v France (major medical equipment)* [2010] nyr.

[72] See Hervey, T., and McHale, J., *Health Law and the EU* (Cambridge: CUP, 2004) 143–4.

[73] For the reasons which motivated the European Parliament's position, see one of the reports submitted to it, by Baeten, R., 'The Proposal for a Directive on Services in the Internal Market applied to Healthcare Services' presented at the European Parliament's public audience, 11 November 2004, available at <http://www.europarl.europa.eu/hearings/20041111/imco/baeten_en.pdf> (last accessed on 9 November 2011).

[74] Report A6-0173/2007 FINAL, on the impact and consequences of the exclusion of health services from the Directive on services in the internal market (Rapporteur: Vergnaud, B.), 10 May 2007, para 71.

[75] Resolution INI/2006/2275, Impact and consequences of the exclusion of Health Services from the Directive on Services in the Internal Market.

[76] Commission Staff Working Document SEC (2008) 2163, Accompanying document to the proposal for a Directive of the European Parliament and of the Council on the application of patients' rights in cross-border healthcare.

patients, same as option (d); therefore, option (c) was withheld.[77] On the basis of Article 95 EC (Article 114 TFEU), a draft Directive on 'patients' rights' has been proposed.[78] This draft was heavily amended by the European Parliament and the Council,[79] and although it has not been a top priority for any of the 2010 (Spanish and Belgian) Presidencies, serious advances have been marked and the text was eventually adopted on 9 March 2011.[80] The final content of the Patients' Rights Directive may not be discussed here.[81] What is important, for the present purposes, is the fact that, under the pressure of a long and ground-breaking body of case law, the EU has duly assessed and acknowledged the need for regulatory action in the field of healthcare; the ball is now in the politicians' court.

2. Professional qualifications

The recognition of professional qualifications is extensively organized by secondary legislation.[82] The scope of such legislation as it stands, however, is limited in two inter-related ways. First, the relevant Directive is restricted to the mere recognition of professional rights and does not extend to full academic recognition. As a consequence, secondly, only 'regulated professions' come under the scope of the Directive, while the vast majority of unregulated professions remain untouched by any text of secondary law.

By contrast, access to non-regulated professions, according to the internal market orthodoxy, should be entirely free for service providers from other member states—after all, if these professions are not regulated, it is because they do not endanger general public interest. In practice, however, professionals are left to their own devices to face the administrative intricacies of member states. This explains that alongside the Court's judgments concerning the timely transposition,[83] the correct implementation,[84] and the interpretation of the relevant

---

[77] For a very interesting economic analysis of the EU market for healthcare services and for the estimated impact of the draft Directive, see Dziworski, W., 'Internal Market for Healthcare Services—Economic Aspects' Paper delivered in the Conference *Internal Market and Domestic Legitimacy*, 24–25 March 2009, College of Europe, Warsaw/Natolin, on file with the author.

[78] Proposal for a Directive COM (2008) 414 final on the application of patients' rights in cross-border healthcare; such proposal has been able to benefit from the hindsight offered by Hervey, T., and Trubek, L., 'Freedom to Provide Health Care Services in the EU: An Opportunity for "Hybrid Governance"' (2007) 13 *Columbia J of Eur L* 623–47.

[79] For the last available draft, see Interinstitutional file 2008/142(COD), 13 September 2010.

[80] Directive 2011/24/EU of the European Council and of the Council on the application of patients' rights in cross-border healthcare [2011] OJ L88/45; the final version of the Directive also had Art 168 TFEU as its legal basis, a change which is also reflected in its content, since, next to patient mobility, it also seeks to promote health care quality.

[81] For the reasons that a) the content is quite technical and requires special developments and b) the Directive has been adopted after the period covered by the present book, i.e. until December 2010; for an assessment of the early draft, see Hervey, T., 'Co-operation between health care authorities in the proposed Directive on Patients' Rights in cross-border healthcare' in Van de Gronden, J., Szyszczak, E., Neergaard, U., and Krajewski, M. (eds), *Health Care and EU Law* (The Hague: Asser Press, 2011) 159–87.

[82] European Parliament and Council Directive 2005/36/EC on the recognition of professional qualifications [2005] OJ L255/22, codifying and replacing over a dozen of pre-existing texts. For the history and content of this piece of legislation, see the discussion under sub-heading A4, in ch 6.

[83] See eg Case C-365/83 *Commission v Greece (Directive 89/48)* [1995] ECR I-499.

[84] See eg Case C-274/05 *Commission v Greece (university degrees)* [2008] ECR I-7969.

Directives,[85] an important body of case law has developed to cover cases which either predate or fall outside their scope. As early as 1977 the Court held that the requirement of specific qualifications, lawful as it may be, does, nonetheless, constitute a restriction to the free movement of persons and has to be eased by all available means (even in the absence of the recognition Directives foreseen by the Treaty).[86] The Court also held that it was unlawful to deny access to a profession to a person 'solely by reason of the fact that the person concerned does not possess the national diploma corresponding to the diploma which he holds'.[87] In *Heylens*, the Court recognized that 'freedom of movement of workers is one of the fundamental objectives of the Treaty' and has set out the oft repeated principle that:

'the procedure for the recognition of equivalence must enable the national authorities to assure themselves on an objective basis, that the foreign diploma certifies that its holder has knowledge and qualifications which are, if not identical, at least equivalent to those certified by the national diploma. That assessment of the equivalence of the foreign diploma must be effected exclusively in the light of the level of the knowledge and qualifications which its holder can be assumed to possess in the light of that diploma, having regard to the nature and duration of the studies and practical training which the diploma certifies that he has carried out.'[88]

Further, in *Vlassopoulou*, the Court held that even where the above comparison reveals only partial equivalence, the host member state may not altogether ban access to the corresponding profession, but '*is entitled to require the person concerned to show that he has acquired the knowledge and qualifications which are lacking*'.[89]

Even after the adoption of the Article 53 TFEU Directives on mutual recognition of diplomas and of the General System, the Treaty rules continue to apply, in order to cover access to non-regulated professions,[90] professions which for any reason evade the material scope of the mutual recognition Directives,[91] to people who have not as yet acquired a full professional qualification in the state of their

---

[85] See eg Case C-102/02 *Ingeborg Beuttenmüller v Land Baden-Württemberg* [2004] ECR I-5405 and Case C-141/04 *Michail Peros v Techniko Epimelitirio Ellados* [2005] ECR I-7163, concerning the direct effect of the Directive; Case C-285/01 *Isabel Burbaud v Ministère de l'Emploi et de la Solidarité* [2003] ECR I-8219 and Case C-313/01 *Christine Morgenbesser v Consiglio dell'Ordine degli avvocati di Genova* [2003] ECR I-13467, concerning its material scope; Case C-164/94 *Georgios Aranitis v Land Berlin* [1996] ECR I-135 and Case C-234/97 *Fernandez Bobadilla v Museo Prado* [1999] ECR I-4773 for the concept of 'regulated profession'.

[86] Case 11/77 *Patrick v Ministère des Affaires Culturelles* [1977] ECR 1199.

[87] Case 71/76 *Jean Thieffry v Conseil de l'ordre des avocats à la cour de Paris* [1977] ECR 765.

[88] Case 222/86 *Union nationale des entraîneurs et cadres techniques professionnels du football (Unectef) v Georges Heylens and others* [1987] ECR 4097, para 13.

[89] Case C-340/89 *Vlassopoulou v Ministerium für Justiz, Bundes- und Europaangelengheiten Baden-Württemberg* [1991] ECR I-2357, para 19.

[90] See eg Case C-164/94 *Georgios Aranitis v Land Berlin* [1996] ECR I-135 for the profession of geologist.

[91] See eg Case C-31/00 *Conseil national de l'ordre des architectes v Nicolas Dreessen* [2002] ECR I-663 for an architecture degree delivered outside the scope of the 'architects' Directive (Council Directive 85/384/EEC on the mutual recognition of diplomas, certificates and other evidence of formal qualifications in architecture, including measures to facilitate the effective exercise of the right of establishment and freedom to provide services [1985] L223/15).

studies,[92] or to the right of universities from one member state to provide educational services in the territories of others.[93] Under the Treaty rules, however, the procedure to be followed is less circumscribed by EU law and its final outcome appears more uncertain than under the recognition directives. This is so despite the rule in *Vlassopoulou* implying that recognition should always be granted except for rare cases of extreme lack of equivalence between the diploma invoked and the profession aimed at.

Moreover, as the Court's judgment in *Burbaud* made plain, despite the enactment and generalization of the General Systems of recognition, important obstacles still remain in relation to access to public sector employment.[94] In this case, the Court opted for a very wide (and disputable) interpretation of the concept of a 'regulated profession', as covering employment in the public sector following an entry competition.

The fact that an important number of cases remain outside the scope of the mutual recognition Directives together with the judicial acrobatics which the Court has had recourse to in order to accommodate the concept of 'regulated profession' constitute, it is here submitted, good enough reasons to review the EU policy in relation to mutual recognition granting access to professional activities abroad. Directive 2005/36, following the pattern inaugurated 16 years earlier by the First General System Directive, only concerns the 'professional qualifications', as opposed to 'diplomas'. As mentioned above, this means that only professional rights attached to a given diploma are taken into account and not the level of studies that such a diploma stands for. This, in turn, means that the Directive's scope is limited by reference to the unclear criterion of 'regulated activity'. Historically this may be explained by the fact that back in 1989 the EU, then called the EEC, lacked any explicit competence in the field of education. Therefore, the Commission, prompted by the Court's judgments in *Blaizot* and *Gravier*, based its proposal on what has now become Article 53 TFEU.[95] The Commission's proposal was quite ambitious in respect of the horizontal technique put into place (the General System), but rather modest in respect of its material scope: while Article 53 TFEU has always offered a legal basis for issuing 'directives for the mutual recognition of diplomas, certificates and other evidence of formal qualifications',[96] the Directive's scope has been restricted to 'professional qualifications'—not the

---

[92] See eg Case C-313/01 *Morgenbesser*, n 85, and Case C-345/08 *Krzysztof Peśla v Justizministerium Mecklenburg-Vorpommern* [2009] nyr, concerning legal trainees.

[93] See eg Case C-153/02 *Valentina Neri v European School of Economics (ESE Insight World Education System Ltd)* [2003] ECR I-13555; it has to be noted, however, that while in this judgment the Court based its reasoning on the Treaty rules on establishment, the same conclusions were reached in Case C-365/83 *Commission v Greece (Directive 89/48)* [1995] ECR I-499, by interpreting the First General System Directive (Council Directive 89/48/EEC on a general system for the recognition of higher-education diplomas awarded on completion of professional education and training of at least three years' duration [1989] OJ L19/16).

[94] Case C-285/01 *Burbaud*, n 85.

[95] Case 24/86 *Vincent Blaizot v University of Liège and others* [1988] ECR 379 and Case 293/83 *Françoise Gravier v City of Liège* [1985] ECR 593.

[96] In the same sense, see Garben, S., 'The Bologna Process: From a European Law Perspective' (2010) 16 *ELJ* 186–210, also available as EUI Working Paper No. 2008/12 at <http://cadmus.eui.eu/

actual diplomas on which such qualifications rely—and has, thus, been limited by the concept of 'regulated activity'.[97]

Since 1989, however, EU law has greatly evolved. *For one thing*, starting with Maastricht, every subsequent Treaty has invariably strengthened the EU's competence in the field of education and training (while acknowledging member states' primacy). *Secondly*, the Court's case law on the far-reaching consequences stemming directly from the Treaty provisions on free movement has been considerably fleshed out since 1989.[98] *Thirdly*, the European Credit and Accumulation System (ECTS) has been put into place, laying the foundations for the substantive comparison between study cycles.[99] *Fourthly*, the Bologna process, initiated in 1998/99, is expressly aimed at achieving the 'harmonisation of the architecture of the European Higher Education system'.[100] *Moreover*, Directive 2005/36 foresees five different levels of diplomas, certificates, etc, therefore comparing like with like, making equivalence more likely and enhancing recognition. Last but not least, Article 165 TFEU stating that 'the Union shall contribute to the development of quality education ... while fully respecting the responsibility of the Member States for the content of teaching and the organization of education systems' does not seem to impede EU action in the field of academic recognition, to the extent that access to the workplace depends upon such recognition. For instance, the possibility of using Article 53 TFEU for legislating in the field of academic recognition has been (implicitly) admitted by the Court in *Erasmus*.[101] It could be argued that Article 53 TFEU constitutes *lex specialis* compared to the blanket competence reserve of Article 165 TFEU and should prevail; furthermore, a comparison could be drawn with healthcare, where the existence of an equivalent competence reserve (Article 168 TFEU) has not prevented the Commission from proposing legislation in this field, despite the lack of any specific legal basis comparable to Article 53 TFEU.[102]

In view of all these developments, it is here proposed that the next step in the field of facilitating professionals' mobility should be the adoption of measures for

dspace/handle/1814/8406> (last accessed on 9 November 2011), who cites Davies, H., 'Higher Education in the Internal Market', UACES European Studies Online Essays, unavailable online.

[97] The resulting antinomy is that access to regulated activities—which, by definition, are highly sensitive—is regulated at the EU level, while member states maintain their stranglehold on professions whose exercise is innocuous and does not justify any regulation; see Garben, S., 2010, n 96, at 192.

[98] The reading of any basic—but recent—textbook of EU law testifies to such a development. See eg Chalmers, D., Davies, G., and Monti, G., *European Union Law: Cases and Materials* (Cambridge: CUP, 2010), at 846 *et seq*.

[99] The ECTS is not formally an EU system and has not been put into place by any regulatory act; for more information on the ECTS, see <http://ec.europa.eu/education/lifelong-learning-policy/doc48_en.htm> (last accessed on 9 November 2011).

[100] The Bologna process has been initiated outside the EU institutional setting, but has eventually been signed up by most member states as well as non-member states; see Sorbonne joint declaration, by the competent ministers of France, Germany, Italy, and the UK, 25/05/1998, available at <http://www.bologna-berlin2003.de/pdf/Sorbonne_declaration.pdf> (last accessed on 9 November 2011); more generally on the Bologna Process, see <http://www.ond.vlaanderen.be/hogeronderwijs/Bologna> (last accessed 9 November 2011); see also Garben, S., 2010, n 96.

[101] Case 242/87 *Commission v Council (Erasmus)* [1989] ECR 1425.

[102] See the discussion under subheading C1.

the academic—as opposed to merely the professional—recognition of diplomas. In this way, the unhappy criterion of 'regulated profession' and the lacunae it creates to the General System will disappear.[103]

3. Posted workers[104]

The starting point in the Court's case law concerning posted workers are cases *Evi v Seco*, *Rush Portuguesa*, and *Vander Elst*.[105] The first concerned a French undertaking using third-country nationals in railway repairs in Luxembourg, the second dealt with a Portuguese undertaking deploying Portuguese nationals (at a time when they did not yet benefit from free movement) in railway construction in France, and the third involved a Belgian undertaking having its Moroccan workers employed in construction (demolition) works in France. Read together, these three cases broadly settled the issue of posted workers, introducing three key principles: a. a service provider may move from one member state to another with his own personnel, irrespective of their nationality, without having to satisfy supplementary administrative requirements linked either to immigration or to labour market regulations; b. a service provider may, nonetheless, be required to comply with the legislation (collective agreements, arbitral sentences, etc) of the host state concerning minimum remuneration and other working conditions and all national measures reasonably suited to enforcing/monitoring such a requirement are acceptable;[106] c. a service provider may not be required to comply with all the social security obligations and associated formalities for workers who are already covered in the provider's (home) state of establishment, unless such burdens actually add up to the protection of workers. These basic principles, especially in relation to minimum pay, were later 'codified' by Directive 96/71.[107] The Directive also provided for the

---

[103] It is worth mentioning that the Commission in its Green Paper on 'Modernising the Professional Qualifications Directive' COM(2011) 367 final, circulated while the present book was in press, shied away from proposing such a drastic extension of the Directives scope; what it did do, however, is that it mooted the idea that 'the notion of "regulated education" could encompass all training recognised by a Member State which is relevant to a profession and not only the training which is explicitly geared towards a specific profession' (see question 8 of the Green Paper).

[104] This part is essentially based on parts of the author's previous writings. See Hatzopoulos, V., 'Liberalising Trade in Services: Creating New Migration Opportunities' (2010) 146 *Tidskrift utgiven av Juridiska Föreningen i Finland* 39–68.

[105] Joined cases 62/81 and 63/81 *Société anonyme de droit français Seco and Société anonyme de droit français Desquenne & Giral v Etablissement d'assurance contre la vieillesse et l'invalidité* [1982] ECR I-223; Case C-113/89 *Rush Portuguesa v Office nationale d'immigration* [1990] ECR I-1417; Case C-43/93 *Vander Elst v Office des Migrations Internationales* [1994] ECR I-3803.

[106] For the importance of minimal pay agreements as a means to combat poverty see Funk, L., and Lesch, H., 'Minimum Wage Regulations in Selected European Countries' (2006) 41 *Intereconomics* 78–92.

[107] European Parliament and Council Directive 96/71/EC concerning the posting of workers in the framework of the provision of services [1996] OJ L18/1; the word 'codified' is an oversimplification in this context, as the exact content of the Directive and the extent to which it restricts or expands the scope of application of previous case law has been hotly debated by legal scholars, see eg Davies, P., 'Posted Workers: Single Market or Protection of National Labour Law Systems?' (1997) 34 *CML Rev* 571–602 and Meyer, F., 'Libre circulation des travailleurs et libre prestation de services, à propos de la directive "détachement du travailleur"' (1998) 12 *Revue Internationale de Droit Economique* 57–73.

designation of one or more 'liaison offices' and for cooperation between the competent national authorities, in order to facilitate the free provision of services when it involves the posting of workers.

All three principles outlined above were consequently confirmed in *Arblade and Leloup*.[108] This case concerned two French undertakings who had been employing their own personnel (the nationality of which is not specified in the Court's judgment) in Silo constructions in Belgium and had infringed Belgian regulations which, among other things, a. imposed minimum pay, b. necessitated the drawing-up, keeping, and retaining of social documents for each of the workers employed, and c. required the payment of supplementary social security contributions for each worker, in the form of '*timbres intempéries*' and '*timbres fidélité*'. According to the principles above, the Court accepted that there was indeed an infringement as regards regulation (a) above, but not (b) and (c). It is also worth noting that, following the adoption of Directive 96/71 and while the above judgments were still pending, on February 1999, the Commission tabled a draft Directive on the posting of workers who are third-country nationals (TCNs) for the provision of cross-border services,[109] but this initiative did not receive the support of member states and was eventually dropped from the Commission's agenda.

It is in the last 10 years, however, that developments in the area of posted workers have been spectacular; in at least two respects. For one thing, the Court has cut down on national administrative requirements concerning entry and working conditions of TCNs (a). More importantly, the Court has somewhat curbed the principle that posted workers should be fully subject to working and pay conditions of the host country (b). While the former development makes it easier for TCNs to integrate into the EU job market, the latter confers on them (or gives them back) a clear competitive advantage over workers from the receiving state.

a. Softening up administrative requirements for entry and work

As early as the case of *Vander Elst*,[110] the Court had held that it was enough for TCNs legally resident and employed in Belgium and temporarily posted to France to comply only with the migration requirements of the former state and that no individual work permits could be required by the French authorities. Similarly, in *Commission v Luxembourg (posted workers I)*,[111] the rule at stake required all service providers deploying non-EU personnel in Luxembourg either to have their personnel obtain an individual work permit or, alternatively, have a collective work permit issued for them. This rule only concerned the right to work and applied on top of any entry requirements to which workers were already subject. The Court found that the objectives of the legislation in question (namely, the social welfare of non-

---

[108] Joined cases C-369 & 376/96 *Criminal proceedings against Jean-Claude Arblade and Arblade & Fils SARL and Bernard Leloup, Serge Leloup, and Sofrage SARL* [1999] ECR I-8453.
[109] Communication COM (1999) 3 final on the posting of workers who are third-country nationals for the provision of cross-border services [1999] OJ C67/12.
[110] Case C-43/93 *Vander Elst*, n 105.
[111] Case C-445/03 *Commission v Luxembourg (posted workers I)* [2004] ECR I-10191.

EU workers and the stability of the Luxembourg labour market) could be equally well attained through a system of simple declaration, instead of an authorization requirement. It was further found that, being unnecessary to the attainment of the above objectives, the measure in question unduly restricted the service provider's freedom of movement. It thus becomes clear that TCNs may work in a member state without the required working permit, so long as such work is provided in the framework of an employment contract with an undertaking based in any other member state.

In *Commission v Germany (posted workers)*,[112] the regulation at stake required foreign workers to possess an entry and work visa, which was only delivered to posted workers, provided (among other things) that they were already employed with the posting firm for at least a year. The Court found this requirement—and the visa regime, in general—in breach of Article 56 TFEU, in that it was disproportionate to the pursued objectives. It also ruled that a declaration obligation imposed on the posting undertaking would suffice for the protection of the reasons invoked by Germany. A similar requirement was in question in *Commission v Austria (posted workers)*,[113] which burdened posted workers instead of posting undertakings, and was also condemned. In *Commission v Luxembourg (posted workers II)*,[114] the Court went as far as to hold that a mere notification obligation, which should be accomplished at any time before the first day of work, violated Article 56 TFEU, because it contained 'ambiguities' that could 'dissuade undertakings wishing to post workers to Luxembourg from exercising their freedom to provide services'.[115]

b. *Wage and social rights portability*

i. Inroads to the full applicability of host state legislation
Concerning minimum pay, the Court has shown clear signs of departure from the full and automatic application of the host state legislation. In *Mazzoleni*,[116] the question arose whether the personnel of a French security company occasionally deployed in sites in Belgium should be paid at the higher tariffs applicable there. The Court held that the application of the host country legislation may be, under certain circumstances, neither *necessary* nor *proportionate*.[117] The necessity test requires the host state authorities to verify whether their national legislation is needed to ensure an 'equivalent' level of remuneration for workers, taking into

---

[112] Case C-341/02 *Commission v Germany (posted workers)* [2005] ECR I-2733.
[113] Case C-168/04 *Commission v Austria (posted workers)* [2006] ECR I-9041; in this case, the impossibility of regularizing the papers of posted workers already on the spot was also condemned.
[114] Case C-319/06 *Commission v Luxembourg (posted workers II)* [2008] ECR I-4323.
[115] Ibid, para 81. In the more recent Case C-219/08 *Commission v Belgium (posted workers)* [2010] nyr, however, the Court was ready to accept the obligation of posting service providers to submit declarations concerning the status of their posted workers.
[116] Case C-165/98 *Criminal proceedings against André Mazzoleni and Inter Surveillance Assistance SARL* [2001] ECR I-2189.
[117] Ibid, para 30 (emphasis added).

account fiscal and social charges applicable in the states concerned.[118] Even if the necessity test is satisfied, the application of the host state legislation may still be countered, if it entails disproportionate administrative burdens for the service provider or inequalities between its employees (proportionality test).[119] A few months later, in *Portugaia Construções*,[120] the Court held that the host state's collective agreement on salaries could be applied only if it contributed in a 'significant way' to the employees' social protection.[121] Therefore, the previously sacrosanct principle of respect to host state minimum pay requirements becomes conditional on a. significantly increasing the employees' revenue and b. not disproportionably burdening the employer.[122] The same principles broadly apply in relation to social security contributions in the host state (*Finalarte*).[123]

ii. Portability of home state legislation?

It is, however, with its infamous judgments in *Laval*, *Viking*, and *Rüffert*,[124] that the Court administered a decisive blow to the applicability of host state minimum wages and rules of social protection and opened the way for some kind of regime portability for posted workers. These judgments are extremely important in many respects and have aroused excitement among trade unions, practitioners, and academic writers.[125] It is not the place here to provide yet another comprehensive analysis of these cases; rather, the focus will be on the issue of minimum wages.

---

[118] Ibid, para 35.

[119] Ibid, para 36.

[120] Case C-164/99 *Portugaia Construções Ld²* [2002] ECR I-787.

[121] Ibid, para 29.

[122] This is a peculiar proportionality test: usually, the restrictive measure is appraised as against a less restrictive one, while here the competing interests themselves are compared.

[123] Joined cases C-49-50, 52-54, 68-71/98 *Finalarte Sociedade de Construçâo Civil Lda and others* [2001] ECR I-7831.

[124] Case C-341/05 *Laval un Partneri Ltd v Svenska Byggnadsarbetareförbundet, Svenska Byggnadsarbetareförbundets avdelning 1, Byggettan and Svenska Elektrikerförbundet* [2007] ECR I-11767; Case C-438/05 *International Transport Workers' Federation and Finnish Seamen's Union v Viking Line ABP and OÜ Viking Line Eesti* [2007] ECR I-10779; Case C-346/06 *Dirk Rüffert v Land Niedersachsen* [2008] ECR I-1989.

[125] For the latter, see, among many, Cremers, J., Dolvik, J.E., and Bosch, G., 'Posting of Workers in the Single Market: Attempts to Prevent Social Dumping and Regime Competition in the EU?' (2007) 38 *Ind Relations J* 524–41; Malmberg, J., and Sigeman, T., 'Industrial Actions and EU Economic Freedoms: The Autonomous Collective Bargaining Model Curtailed by the ECJ' (2008) 45 *CML Rev* 1115–46; Ronmar, M., 'Free Movement of Services vs National Labour Law and Industrial Relations Systems: Understanding the *Laval* Case from a Swedish and Nordic Perspective' (2008) 10 *CYEL* 493–521; Ashiagbor, D., 'Collective Labor Rights and the European Social Model' (2009) 3 *J of L and Ethics of Human Rights* 222–66; Barnard, C., '*Viking* and *Laval*: An Introduction' (2008) 10 *CYEL* 463–92; Dashwood, A., '*Viking* and *Laval*: Issues of Horizontal Direct Effect' (2008) 10 *CYEL* 525–40; Deakin, S., 'Regulatory Competition after Laval' (2008) 10 *CYEL* 581–609; Sciarra, S., '*Viking* and *Laval*: Collective Labour Rights and Market Freedoms in the Enlarged EU' (2008) 10 *CYEL* 563–80; Woolfson, C., and Sommers, J., 'Labour Mobility in Construction: European Implications of the *Laval un Partneri* Dispute with Swedish Labour' (2006) 12 *Eur J of Industrial Relations* 49–68; Hös, N., 'The Principle of Proportionality in the *Viking* and *Laval* Cases: An Appropriate Standard of Judicial Review? EUI Working Paper No. 2009/6, also available at <http://cadmus.eui.eu/bitstream/handle/1814/11259/LAW_2009_06.pdf?sequence = 1> (last accessed on 9 November 2011); Novitz, T., 'A Human Rights Analysis for the *Viking* and *Laval* Judgments' (2008) 10 *CYEL* 541–62; Joerges, C., and Rödl, F., 'Informal Politics, Formalised Law

In *Laval* and *Viking*, the main question raised was that of the legality of industrial action undertaken by trade unions in high-wage countries (Sweden and Finland, respectively), in order to impose their own wage requirements on low-wage posted workers (from Latvia and Estonia, respectively), at a time when such workers enjoyed no right to work on their own. In *Viking*, the question was only debated under the perspective of Article 56 TFEU, while in *Laval*, Directive 96/71 was also held to be applicable.[126] The Court held, for the first time, that industrial action is a fundamental right which trade unions possess in order to protect the interests of their members. The right, however, should be exercised in accordance with the Treaty fundamental freedoms (such as the freedom of establishment and the free provision of services) and only be the source of restrictions which are proportionate to the aims pursued. It is this proportionality test which has a sting in the tail, since for its application, it is necessary to take into account the level of protection afforded to workers in their home state and compare it with the protection level for which trade unions are fighting. Only 'if it were established that the jobs or conditions of employment at issue were... jeopardised or under serious threat' would the exercise of the right to strike be justified in view of the internal market requirements. This seems to be a much weaker test than the usual equivalence test followed by the Court: what is required is not that the protection offered by the home state is equivalent or, at least, comparable to that offered by the host state legislation; it is enough that the workers' condition is not 'under serious threat'.[127]

Failure to take into account the level of protection guaranteed under home state legislation is not merely a hindrance to the enjoyment of the fundamental freedoms, but an outright discrimination: it is one of the rare situations where discrimination lies in the application of the same rules to different situations, the difference here being that foreign service providers are already subject to their home rules on workers' protection. In other words, the failure to apply the principle of mutual recognition (of social and other charges) amounts, in this case, to discrimination![128] Such discrimination may only be upheld by virtue of some express Treaty exception and not by ORPIs.[129]

---

and the "Social Deficit" of European Integration: Reflections after the Judgments of the CJEU in *Viking* and *Laval*' (2009) 15 *ELJ* 1–19; see also Blanpain, R., and Swiatkofski, A.M. (eds), *The Laval and Viking Cases: Freedom of Services and Establishment v Industrial Conflict in the European Economic Area and Russia* (Alphen aan den Rijn: Kluwer Law International, 2009).

[126] This aspect of the judgment alone is open to considerable criticism, since it seems to recognize that the rules of a Directive are relevant in a dispute between private parties (the posting undertakings on one hand and the trade unions on the other). In other words, the Directive is given horizontal direct effect; see in particular, Dashwood, A., 2008, n 125, and Deakin, S., 2008, n 125.

[127] Which, of course, raises the subsequent question of when a threat can be considered 'serious' enough.

[128] See eg Case C-341/05 *Viking*, n 124, para 72 and Case C-438/05 *Laval*, n 124, para 116; this finding has been discussed—and criticized—in ch 3.

[129] Case C-438/05 *Laval*, n 124, para 116; this observation has also been discussed—and criticized—in ch 4. It is worth noting that this distinction as to the causes which may justify discriminatory and non-discriminatory measures had generally been eclipsed from the recent case law of the Court, only to make an impressive comeback in the case under consideration.

The need to take into account the level of protection already offered by the legislation of the home state has been confirmed in very strong words in the Court's case law. In *Viking*, without further ado, the Court found the general Flag of Convenience (FOC)[130] policy pursued by the ITF (International Transport Worker's Federation) to fall foul of the Treaty provisions, because it was applied 'irrespective of whether or not that owner's exercise of its right of freedom of establishment is liable to have a harmful effect on the work or conditions of employment of its employees'.[131] Similarly, in *Laval*, the *Lex Britannia*[132] was condemned since it failed 'to take into account, irrespective of their content, collective agreements to which undertakings that post workers to Sweden are already bound in the Member State in which they are established'.[133] Further, in *Commission v Austria (posted workers)* the Court held the requirement that Austrian wage and employment conditions be routinely observed to be in breach of Article 56 TFEU, since it 'does not take account of the measures for the protection of workers by which the undertaking intending to carry out the posting is bound in the Member State of origin'.[134]

At the same time, the Posted Workers Directive, which was supposed to make sure that basic employment regulations of the host state apply to all workers posted there,[135] was seriously undermined by the Court in *Laval*, and even more so, in the subsequent *Rüffert* and *Commission v Luxembourg* cases,[136] in four ways. *First*, the scope of measures which the host member state may impose on posted workers has been drastically circumscribed: it cannot apply measures which a. have not been agreed upon following some of the procedures described in the Directive,[137] b. which are of no general territorial application,[138] c. which do not fix the actual

---

[130] According to the definition given in the ITF's website 'a flag of convenience ship is one that flies the flag of a country other than the country of ownership. Cheap registration fees, low or no taxes and freedom to employ cheap labour are the motivating factors behind a shipowner's decision to "flag out" '; see <http://www.itfglobal.org/flags-convenience/sub-page.cfm> (last accessed 9 November 2011).

[131] C-341/05 *Viking*, n 124, para 89.

[132] A section in the Swedish Co-Determination Act (the country's key collective labour law) allowing trade unions to disregard collective agreements to which undertakings have agreed in other states.

[133] C-438/05 *Laval*, n 124, para 116.

[134] Case C-168/04 *Commission v Austria (posted workers)* [2006] ECR I-9041, para 49.

[135] Directive 96/71 [1996] OJ L18/1. The Posted Workers Directive in fact creates an exception to the general private international law rules, as enshrined in the Rome Convention, now turned into European Parliament and Council Regulation 593/2008/EC on the law applicable to contractual obligations (Rome I) [2008] OJ L177/6, according to which, unless otherwise agreed, workers in temporary postings remain subject to their home state rules; see for a full argument about the Regulation, the Posted Workers Directive, and the judgments under consideration, Deakin, S., 2008, n 125, at 590–5.

[136] Case C-346/06 *Rüffert*, n 124; Case C-319/06 *Commission v Luxembourg (posted workers II)* [2008] ECR I-4323; the former case concerned the obligation imposed by a German Lander that all employees or subcontractors of undertakings executing works within its territory receive pay above the national minimum, while the latter concerned several aspects of the Luxembourg legislation, including a system of automatic indexation of wages above the national minimum. Both were found incompatible with the Posted Workers Directive (Directive 96/71, n 135).

[137] Case C-438/05 *Laval*, n 124, paras 63, 67, 70 and 71.

[138] Case C-346/06 *Rüffert*, n 124, para 29.

level of pay but limit themselves to setting criteria for its calculation,[139] or d. which prescribe wages above the bare minimum.[140] At any rate, the list of issues enumerated in the Directive, and about which the host state may apply its own legislation, is an exhaustive one.[141] *Secondly*, the possibility of the host state to impose measures justified by public order considerations is also seriously limited: the concept of public order stems from EU law—it is not left to the individual states to determine—and subject to restrictive interpretation.[142] *Thirdly*, contrary to a clear statement in Recital 17 and Article 3(7), whereby the Directive's terms 'shall not prevent application of terms and conditions which are more favourable to workers', the Court finds that member states cannot be allowed 'to make the provision of services in [their] territory conditional upon the observance of terms and conditions of employment which go beyond the mandatory rules for minimum protection'.[143] By transforming the 'floor' into a 'ceiling',[144] the Court not only flies in the face of the express Directive's provisions, but also against 'the widely accepted understanding of other social policy directives and regulations, which neither seek to set out uniform laws nor even a level playing field, but to establish a floor of rights above which regulatory competition is possible'.[145] *Fourthly* and most significantly, the Court in the most recent *Commission v Luxembourg (posted workers II)* case discretely opens the way for using the Directive against its very objective, in order to pre-empt the host state from imposing its own measures to posted workers; it was held that for issues which are subject to a minimum harmonization and are, as a matter of law, secured by all member states, the host member state may not impose its own (more demanding) conditions.[146] It is true that in the judgment under consideration, the minimum harmonization contemplated by the Court was organized by a different Directive (Directive 91/533);[147] the same can be said, however, for the Posted Workers Directive (even if it ends up as a self-defeating harmonization measure).

Therefore, the Court has transformed what was initially thought of as a guarantee against social dumping and as a safe haven from the application of the CoOP to quite the opposite: to a presumption of regime portability. Such portability stems from Articles 49 and 56 TFEU and may, on some occasions, be orchestrated by virtue of the very Directive which was supposed to counter it.

---

[139] Ibid, para 24.

[140] Ibid, para 33; Case C-319/06 *Commission v Luxembourg*, n 136, paras 45–55.

[141] Case C-319/06 *Commission v Luxembourg*, n 136, para 26.

[142] Ibid, paras 30–31.

[143] Case C-438/05 *Laval*, n 137, para 80; Case C-346/06 *Rüffert*, n 124, para 33.

[144] This point is made, among others, by Malmberg, J., and Sigeman, T., 'Industrial Actions and EU Economic Freedoms: The Autonomous Collective Bargaining Model Curtailed by the ECJ' (2008) 45 *CML Rev* 1115–46, at 1145.

[145] Excerpt taken from Deakin, S., 'Regulatory Competition after Laval' (2008) 10 *CYEL* 581–609, at 597 (fn omitted).

[146] C-319/06 *Commission v Luxembourg*, n 136, paras 38–44.

[147] Council Directive 91/533/EEC on an employer's obligation to inform employees of the conditions applicable to the contract or employment relationship [1991] OJ L288/32.

4. Public procurement[148]

The ways in which public authorities, and more generally authorities disposing of public money, purchase goods, services, and works have been regulated at the EU level since the early 1970s.[149] The Court's case law applying the Directives was already significant and steadily growing in the 1980s and, even more so, in the 1990s. It is over the last decade, however, that the Court has considerably widened the scope of application of the rules contained therein, by enriching it with two additional dimensions.[150]

a. *Extending the scope of public procurement rules: the transparency case law*

The Court has held that, alongside the specific and technical rules of the Public Procurement Directives, a series of general principles apply in all circumstances where public money is put into the market. The Court began by holding, in the case of *Commission v France (Nord Pas de Calais)*[151] that, in addition to the Directive's technical rules, a general principle of non-discrimination should also be respected in any award procedure. More importantly, in a series of judgments starting with *Telaustria*,[152] a case concerning a concession in the field of telecommunications, the Court submitted that the same principle also applies to concession contracts (and presumably any other type of contract which involves public funding and is not covered by the Procurement Directives). Subsequently, *Coname*[153] concerned the direct award in Italy of a contract for the service covering the maintenance, operation, and monitoring of the methane gas network. In its judgment, the Court explained that the principle of non-discrimination carries with it a further requirement of transparency, satisfied by adequate publicity. This trend was further pursued some months later in *Parking Brixen*,[154] another Italian

---

[148] This part is essentially based on the author's previous writings. See eg Hatzopoulos, V., 'Public procurement and state aid in national healthcare systems', in Mossialos, E., Permanand, G., Baeten, R., and Hervey, T. (eds.), *Health Systems Governance in Europe: The Role of EU Law and Policy* (Cambridge: CUP, 2010) 381–420 and Hatzopoulos, V., and Stergiou, H., 'Public procurement law and health care: from theory to practice' in Van de Gronden, J., Krajewski, M., Neergaard, U., and Szyszczak, E. (eds), *Health Care and EU Law* (The Hague, Asser Press, 2011).

[149] Starting with Council Directive 71/305/EEC concerning the coordination of procedures for the award of public works contracts [1971] OJ L185/5 and Council Directive 77/62/EEC coordinating procedures for the award of public supply contracts [1977] OJ L13/1; it was not until the adoption of the Council Directive 92/50/EEC (relating to the coordination of procedures for the award of public service contracts [1992] OJ L209/1) that special rules were adopted for the purchase of services.

[150] For an early assessment of the relevant case law, see Bovis, C., 'Developing Public Procurement Regulation: Jurisprudence an its Influence on Law Making' (2006) 43 *CML Rev* 461–95.

[151] Case C-225/98 *Commission v France (Nord Pas de Calais)* [2000] ECR I-7445.

[152] Case C-324/98 *Telaustria Verlags GmbH and Telefonadress GmbH v Telekom Austria AG, joined party: Herold Business Data AG* [2000] ECR I-10745.

[153] Case C-231/03 *Consorzio Aziende Metano (Coname) v Comune di Cingia de'Botti* [2005] ECR I-7287.

[154] Case C-458/03 *Parking Brixen GmbH v Gemeinde Brixen and Stadtwerke Brixen AG* [2005] ECR I-8585.

case concerning the construction and management of a public parking lot. The Court found that 'a complete lack of any call for competition in the case of the award of a public service concession does not comply with the requirements of Articles 43 EC and 49 EC [now Articles 49 and 56 TFEU] *any more than with the principles of equal treatment, non-discrimination and transparency*'.[155] The same principle was confirmed some days later in *Contse*,[156] concerning the award of a contract for the supply of home oxygen equipment in Spain.

Picking up on the momentum created by these judgments, the Commission has come up with an interpretative Communication 'on the community law applicable to contract awards not or not fully subject to the provisions of the public procurement directives' (the so called *de minimis* Communication).[157] This Communication covers a. contracts below the thresholds for the application of the Procurement Directives and b. those which are covered by the Directives but are listed in Annex IIB of the general procurement Directive and in Annex XVIIB of the utilities Directive and are, thus, excluded from the technical procurement rules.

This Communication did not cover concession contracts and Public Private Partnerships (PPPs), for a larger consultation process had been initiated by the Commission's White Paper of 2004, followed by a Communication of November 2005;[158] the final outcome of the process was a 2008 interpretative Communication on Institutionalized Public Private Partnerships (IPPPs).[159]

The *de minimis* Communication (like the Communication concerning IPPPs) basically explains the way in which the principles set out by the Court's jurisprudence should be put to work. The four principles pursued are: a. non-discrimination (based on nationality) and equal treatment (also on a purely national basis), b. transparency, c. proportionality, and d. mutual recognition (hereinafter: the 'procurement principles'). According to the Communication, the obligations accruing to contracting entities under the general Treaty rules are proportionate to the interest that the contract at stake presents for parties in other member states. The procurement principles should be respected throughout all four aspects of the award procedure: advertising prior to the tender, content of the tender documents, publicity of the award decision, and judicial protection.

Without scrutinizing the Communication in detail, it is worth making two remarks. *First*, the subject matter of the Communication is for the most part already regulated in the Public Procurement Directives (eg service contracts referred to in Annex IIB of the general procurement Directive and in Annex XVIIB of the utilities Directive): the Procurement Directives themselves set minimal requirements concerning the technical specifications used in the tenders, as well as the

---

[155] Ibid, para 48 (emphasis added).
[156] Case C-234/03 *Contse SA, Vivisol Srl and Oxigen Salud SA v Instituto Nacional de Gestion Sanitaria (Ingesa), formerly Instituto Nacional de la Salud (Insalud)* [2005] ECR I-9315.
[157] OJ [2006] C179/2.
[158] Communication COM (2005) 569 final on Public-Private Partnerships and Community Law on Public Procurement and Concessions.
[159] Communication C (2007) 6661 on the application of Community law on Public Procurement and Concessions to Institutionalised Public–Private Partnerships (IPPP).

publicity of the contract's award, while the 'procedures Directive' is fully applicable to these services. This first remark leads to the *second* one: since the legislator specifically decided to treat services included in the above Annexes in a particular way, is it politically admissible and legally sound for the Commission to impose more stringent obligations through a soft law text? The Commission's position, nonetheless, was confirmed by the Court in the landmark case *Commission v Ireland (An Post)*, concerning the management and distribution of pension benefits, a social service listed in Annex IIB of Directive 2004/18.[160] While the Court admitted that the award of such activity was subject to the general requirements of the transparency case law (notably prior advertising), it limited, nonetheless, the scope of application of such requirements: the Court considered that service contracts come within the scope of Treaty provisions on free movement only when these contracts present 'certain cross-border interest' to an undertaking located in another member state. It held that these provisions are breached if such an undertaking 'was unable to express its interest in that contract because it did not have access to adequate information before the contract was awarded'. The Court seems to focus on the likelihood that a company established in another member state would have been interested in making an offer, had it been properly informed about the public contract through any form of advertisement. In the framework of an action against a member state, it is for the Commission to show that the criterion of 'certain cross-border interest' is fulfilled.[161] In the case of *An Post*, the CJEU found that the Commission had not provided adequate evidence and the Commission's application was dismissed.[162] It is unclear how this finding will affect the onus of proof in disputes between tenderers and the contracting authority (ie not involving the Commission). The ruling in *SECAP* explains further the exact meaning of 'certain cross-border interest':[163] 'in view of its particular characteristics, a given contract is likely to be of certain cross-border interest and therefore, attract operators from other Member States'.[164] This depends, amongst other things, on 'the estimated value [of the contract] in conjunction with its technical complexity or the fact that the works are to be located in a place which is likely to attract the interest of foreign operators'.[165]

b. Substituting the public procurement rules for other Treaty rules

The Court recognized the public procurement principles as not only stemming directly from the Treaty, but also as overarching in any circumstance where public

---

[160] Case C-507/03 *Commission v Ireland (An Post)* [2007] ECR I-9777.

[161] Ibid, para 33: 'According to settled case law, it is the Commission's responsibility to provide the Court with the evidence necessary to enable it to establish that an obligation has not been fulfilled and, in so doing, the Commission may not rely on any presumption.'

[162] The CJEU applied the same reasoning to contracts whose value falls below the thresholds of the Directive in Case C-412/04 *Commission v Italy (below thresholds)* [2008] ECR I-619.

[163] Joined cases C-147–148/06 *SECAP SpA and Santorso Soc. coop. arl v Comune di Torino* [2008] ECR I-3565.

[164] Ibid, para 24.

[165] Ibid.

money is at stake. Further, it has established that under some circumstances, public procurement principles may make up for the non-application of other EU rules.

As noted above, in *Placanica*, the Court held that if a member state were to limit the number of authorizations given for a certain activity, these should be given out in accordance to competitive and transparent procedures.[166] Article 12 of the Services Directive foresees similar requirements for the attribution of authorizations over the exploitation of scarce resources. In other words, whenever the proper functioning of, and competition within, the internal market is impaired, the restriction should be compensated for by the application of the public procurement rules. The idea being that whenever competition *in* the market is restricted, it should be compensated by competition *for* the market.

If the above 'substitution' seems fair, in that it substitutes an internal market rule ('free movement is being restricted . . . ') with another internal market rule ('. . . but public procurement principles are followed'), the Court later devised a much more radical substitution in *Altmark*.[167] In this and subsequent judgments the Court has held state aid rules to be inapplicable where the funds given to some undertaking correspond to the cost of provision of some service of general interest (SGI) entrusted to the said undertaking. This holds true, according to the Court, when four conditions are fulfilled. The four *Altmark* conditions have been fleshed out by the so-called '*Altmark* package'[168] and tend to ensure that the sums paid do not exceed what is actually needed for the provision of the SGI.

First, the recipient undertaking must actually have public service obligations entrusted to it, and these obligations must be clearly defined. *Secondly*, the parameters on the basis of which the compensation is calculated must be established in advance in an objective and transparent manner. *Thirdly*, the compensation cannot exceed what is necessary to cover all or part of the costs incurred in the discharge of the public service obligations, taking into account the relevant receipts and a reasonable profit. *Finally*, where the undertaking, which is to discharge public service obligations in a specific case, is not chosen pursuant to a public procurement procedure (which would allow for the selection of the tenderer capable of acting at the lowest cost to the community), the level of compensation needed must be

---

[166] See the analysis under subheading B(1).

[167] Case C-280/00 *Altmark Trans GmbH and Regierungspräsidium Magdeburg v Nahverkehrsgesellschaft Altmark GmbH, and Oberbundesanwalt beim Bundesverwaltungsgericht* [2003] ECR I-7747. For detailed commentary on the case, see the discussion in ch 2.

[168] Also known as the 'Monti-Kroes' package and consists of one Directive, one Commission Decision and one Communication. More specifically, these are Commission Directive 80/723/EEC on the transparency of financial relations between Member States and public undertakings [1980] OJ L195/35; Commission Decision 2005/842/EC on the application of Article 86(2) of the EC Treaty to State aid in the form of public service compensation granted to certain undertakings entrusted with the operation of services of general economic interest [2005] OJ L312/67; and Communication, 'Community Framework for State Aid in the Form of Public Service Compensation' [2005] OJ C297/4. While this book was under print the Commission published a Communication (COM (2011) 46 final) and launched a consultation in view of reviewing the above legislative and semi-legislative package, see the dedicated Commission webpage at <http://ec.europa.eu/competition/state_aid/legislation/sgei.html> (last accessed 14 December 2011).

determined on the basis of an analysis of the costs, which a typical undertaking, well run and adequately provided with means of transport, would have incurred.[169]

From the very wording of the fourth condition, it follows that the *default setting* for the attribution and finance of some public service obligation is through public procurement. Only in exceptional circumstances, in which this is not the case, prices should be determined according to hypothetical market conditions. More than the wording, the substantive content of this fourth condition suggests that the application of the procurement rules will be the means to avoid the applicability of state aid rules. For one thing, it will be very difficult to prove what the costs of 'a typical undertaking, well run and adequately provided with means of transport' would have been in a hypothetical market (what is 'well run' and what qualifies as 'adequate' means of transport?). Most importantly, for most SGIs, there is no market other than the one emerging under the impact of EU law. Hence, it will be virtually impossible to simulate such conditions in order to ascertain what the cost structure of a 'well run typical undertaking' would be.[170] The most reliable way to benefit from the Court's judgment in *Altmark* and evade the application of the rules on state aid would be to attribute public service contracts (and the related funding) following public tenders; these, in turn, would have to be organized according to the procurement procedures.[171]

c. Applying the public procurement rules to all kinds of services

The developments above show that public procurement rules are expected to play an ever-increasing role in the functioning of the internal market, especially as the provision of services in general, and of services of general economic interest (SGEIs) in particular, is increasingly entrusted to private entities. In this respect, it is worth noting that after having implied in *Ambulanz Glöckner*[172] that, because of their character of general interest, urgent transport contracts could be awarded on the basis of prior authorization, without a tender procedure, more recently, in *Commission v Germany (old-age insurance)*,[173] the Court loudly rejected the German argument according to which some activities evade, by their proper nature, the application of public procurement rules.[174] This, in the face of the criticisms from

---

[169] Commission Decision 2005/842, n 168, Preamble Rec 4.

[170] For the difficulties of these conditions, see further in Idot, L., 'Les services d'intérêt général économique et les règles de concurrence' in Louis, J.V., and Rodriguez, S. (eds), *Les services d'intérêt économique général et l'UE* (Brussels: Bruylant, 2006) 39–63.

[171] Since the fourth condition is the most hard to fulfil, national authorities often start the examination of any given measure from this condition and immediately dismiss the applicability of the *Altmark* criteria; see eg Decision No. 346, Case K3K-175/2006, *Elena Avtotransport* of the Bulgarian Commission for the Protection of Competition, 2 November 2006. For commentary on the case, see Fessenko, D., 'The Bulgarian NCA cleared a State aid in the form of compensation for public transportation services under national State aid rules (*Elena Avtotransport*)', 02/11/2006 *e-Competitions* No. 13146.

[172] Case C-475/99 *Firma Ambulanz Glöckner v Landkreis Südwestpfalz* [2001] ECR I-8089.

[173] Case C-271/08 *Commission v Germany (old-age insurance)* [2010] nyr.

[174] Ibid, paras 45–50.

several stakeholders[175] and authors as to the appropriateness of the application of public procurement rules on social services.[176] In this respect, a. the lack of flexibility of the procurement rules, especially in relation to the role of non-profit social organizations, b. the transformation of partnership relationships into competitive ones, c. the restriction of cooperation between local authorities, resulting from the restrictive concept of 'in-house contracting' followed by the EU, d. the negative effect on establishing long-term trust relationships with suppliers and other partners, e. the possible disruption to the continuity of public service, f. increased transaction costs, and g. delays, are just some of the arguments put forward against the general application of public procurement rules in the field of core social services.

The fact that the case law above is likely to trigger fresh legislative initiatives in the field of public procurement is confirmed by the Commission's 2010 Single Market Act.[177] There, the Commission undertakes to submit proposals for simplifying and rendering more flexible the procurement procedures (proposal 17), for setting the rules for services concessions (proposal 18), and for supporting social, ethical, and environmental objectives (proposal 36).[178]

D. Taxation issues

From the case law presented in chapter 3 (especially in part B), it seems that direct taxation issues (impositions, exemptions, advantages, credits, etc) reach the courts quite often. Even more numerous are the cases relative to VAT. It is certainly not the place here to discuss this extremely rich and technical area of case law.[179] A few

---

[175] See eg Commission Report, 'Social Services of General Interest: Feedback Report to the 2006 Questionnaire of the Social Protection Committee', available at <http://ec.europa.eu/employment_social/social_protection/docs/feedback_report_en.pdf> (last accessed on 9 November 2011) 10–12; see also (on an earlier set of replies from the member states), Maucher, M., 'Analysis of the Replies of All European Union Member States' Governments to the Questionnaire of the Social Protection Committee Preparing the Communication on Social and Health Services of General Interest' (2005), available at <http://www.soziale-dienste-in-europa.de/Anlage25573/auswertung-antworten-ms-mitteilung-sgdai-ed.pdf> (last accessed on 9 November 2011).

[176] See, very briefly, Hatzopoulos, V., 'Public procurement and state aid in national healthcare systems' in Mossialos, E., Permanand, G., Baeten, R., and Hervey, T. (eds), *Health Systems Governance in Europe: The Role of EU law and Policy* (Cambridge: CUP, 2010) 381–420, at 407–8; for a lengthy and passionate discussion, see McCrudden, C., *Buying Social Justice. Equality: Government Procurement and Legal Change* (Oxford: OUP, 2007), where the author suggests that public procurement rules may (or indeed must) be used for the pursuance of social objectives, a direction taken up by the Court in this precise case; for the same ideas, see Barnard, C., 'Procurement law to enforce labour standards' in Davidov, G., and Langille, B. (eds), *The Idea of Labour Law* (Oxford: OUP, 2011).

[177] Communication COM (2010) 608 final, 'Towards a Single Market Act for a Highly Competitive Social Market Economy 50 Proposals for Improving Our Work, Business and Exchanges with One Another'.

[178] Indeed, while this book was in production the Commission published proposals COM (2011) 895 final and COM (2011) 896 final, to amend Directives 2004/17 and 2004/18 respectively, as well as a new draft Directive on concession contracts (COM (2011) 897 final).

[179] For which see, among many, a. in relation to direct taxation, Harris, P., and Oliver, D., International Commercial Taxation (Cambridge: CUP, 2010), Lang, M., Pistone, P., Schuch, J., and

thoughts shall be offered, however, concerning ongoing and forthcoming initiatives in this area.

1. Direct taxation

Direct taxation is a very complex area, not least because the EU lacks any legislative competence and the applicable rules stem from both national and international law. This, in turn, leads the CJEU occasionally to superimpose 'corrections', by means of unclear (and often contradictory) judgments. Two remarks should be made in this respect.

First, as far as the taxation of (first and, especially, second pillar) pension and insurance policies is concerned, problems arise from the differences between national insurance systems. In view of controlling public expenditure, member states are increasingly forced to reduce public pension benefits and encourage their citizens to take out supplementary pensions in the market. In order to offer incentives to their citizens, member states are likely to adopt the so called ET system (contributions Exempt, pensions payments Taxed), rather than the reverse TE system (contributions Taxed, pensions payment Exempt).[180] This, however, results in an oxymoron: whenever the citizen of member state A takes insurance with a company in member state B, the exemption offered by the former state will benefit the public purse of the latter, since the tax is withheld at the source of the revenue, that is by the tax authorities of the insurance company (member state B).[181] Coordination between member states may be necessary in order to resolve this problem.

Secondly, and more generally, the Court has always been more cautious with taxation issues than with any other category of impediments to the internal market. If the 'coherence of the tax system' excuse, introduced in *Bachmann and Commission v Belgium*,[182] has been progressively emptied of much of its

---

Staringer, C. (eds), *Introduction to European Tax Law: Direct Taxation* (Wien: Spiramus Press, 2008); Cordewener, A., Kofler, G., and Van Thiel, S., 'The Clash between European Freedoms and National Direct Tax Law: Public Interest Defences Available to the Member States' (2009) 46 *CML Rev* 1951–2000; Snell, J., 'Non-discriminatory Tax Obstacles in Community Law' (2007) 56 *Int & Comparative L Q* 339–70; Kingston, S., 'A Light in the Darkness: Recent Developments in the ECJ's Direct Tax Jurisprudence' (2007) 44 *CML Rev* 1321–59; Banks, K., 'The Application of the Fundamental Freedoms to Member State Tax Measures: Guarding against Protectionism or Second-guessing National Policy Choices?' EUI RSCAS Working Paper No. 2007/31, also available at <http://cadmus.iue.it/dspace/bitstream/1814/7685/1/RSCAS_2007_31.pdf> (last accessed on 9 November 2011); b. in relation to the VAT: Bernaerts, Y., *The 2010 VAT Directive and the Case Law of the Court of Justice of the EU* (Louvain la Neuve: Anthemis, 2010); de la Feria, R., *The EU VAT System and the Internal Market* (Amsterdam: IBDF, 2009); Terra, B., and Kajus, J., *A Guide to the European VAT Directives* (Amsterdam: IBFD, 2008); Voyez, J. (ed), *VAT in Europe* (Croydon: Tolley Publishing, 2000).

[180] The ET system is also recommended by the European Commission. See Communication COM (2001) 214 final, 'The Elimination of Tax Obstacles to the Cross-Border Provision of Occupational Pensions' [2001] OJ C165/4.

[181] This oxymoron is very clearly explained in Cordewener, A., 'Annotation: Case C-136/00, *Rolf Dieter Danner*, Judgment of the Court of Justice (Fifth Chamber) of 3 October 2002, [2002] ECR I-8147' (2003) 40 *CML Rev* 965–81.

[182] Case C-204/90 *Bachmann v Belgium* [1992] ECR I-249; Case C-300/90 *Commission v Belgium (insurance)* [1992] ECR I-305.

content[183] in recent years, two new overriding reasons have gained in importance, allowing for restrictive fiscal measures.[184] National anti-avoidance measures, to the extent that they are necessary (not just handy) in order to counter abusive or fraudulent constructs allowing for tax evasion, are allowed by the Court. More importantly, however, the Court has been close to nourishing a 'sovereignty' argument by recognizing as ORPI 'the balanced allocation of tax jurisdiction': starting with case *D*, the Court accepted that bilateral tax treaties are based on an inherent balance which should be left untouched by the internal market rules, even if this results in allowing member state A to discriminate between citizens of member states B and C.[185] This trend has been followed in subsequent cases and has raised serious concerns with EU lawyers (less so with tax lawyers).[186]

The Commission in its 2010 Internal Market Act promises to 'take steps to improve coordination of national tax policies, notably by proposing a Directive introducing a common consolidated corporate tax base (CCCTB) in 2011'.[187] This may be one of the first steps, but not a significant one, towards converging tax systems and eliminating tax-related obstacles to free movement.[188] The well-known reluctance of several member states to proceed with direct tax harmonization combined with the mounting mutual distrust nourished by the financial and the ensuing EMU crisis, make any substantive approximation of tax legislation unlikely in the foreseeable future.[189]

---

[183] See Vanistendael, F., 'Cohesion: The Phoenix Rising from His Ashes' (2005) 14 *Eur Community Tax Rev* 208–21; but note that the cohesion justification has been accepted once again in the recent Case C-157/07 *Krankenheim- Ruhesitz* [2008] ECR I-8061, para 43.

[184] For a comprehensive statement of these, see Case C-446/03 *Marks & Spencer plc v David Halsey (Her Majesty's Inspector of Taxes)* [2005] ECR I-10837. The Court mentioned that these grounds should be 'taken together', an unclear expression generating controversy.

[185] This is a highly disputable outcome; see Case C-376/03 *D v Inspecteur van de Belastingdienst/ Particulieren/Ondernemingen buitenland te Heerlen* [2005] ECR I-5821.

[186] For a thorough—and critical in this respect—analysis of the relevant case law of the Court see Cordewener, A., Kofler, G., and van Thiel, S., 'The Clash between European Freedoms and National Direct Tax Law: Public Interest Defences Available to the Member States' (2009) 46 *CML Rev* 1951–2000.

[187] COM (2010) 608 final, n 177, proposal No. 19. On CCCTB, a Workshop has been organized by the Commission on 20 October 2010. A summary record by the chair of the Workshop is available at <http://ec.europa.eu/taxation_customs/resources/documents/taxation/company_tax/common_tax_base/summ-record-ccctb-workshop_20-10-2010.pdf> (last accessed on 9 November 2011).

[188] For previous efforts in this direction, see Council Directive 90/434/EEC on the common system of taxation applicable to mergers, divisions, transfers of assets and exchanges of shares concerning companies of different Member States [1990] OJ L225/1; Council Directive 90/435/ EEC on the common system of taxation applicable in the case of parent companies and subsidiaries of different Member States [1990] OJ L225/6; Convention 90/436/EEC: Convention on the elimination of double taxation in connection with the adjustment of profits of associated enterprises [1990] OJ L225/10; Council Directive 2003/48/EC on taxation of savings income in the form of interest payments [2003] OJ L157/38; and Council Directive 2003/49/EC on a common system of taxation applicable to interest and royalty payments made between associated companies of different Member States [2003] OJ L157/49.

[189] This finding is likely to change in view of the imminent, at the time of publishing this book, adoption of the 'EU Fiscal Treaty' agreed by the European Council (minus the UK), on 8–9 December 2011; such a development did not seem likely at the time of writing.

2. Indirect taxation—VAT

VAT was established as far back as 1967 to become the only indirect tax applicable throughout the EU.[190] A uniform VAT coverage was established in 1977 through the 6th VAT Directive which remained the core legislative instrument in this field for almost 30 years and has been amended over 30 times.[191] All VAT Directives were codified and repealed by Directive 2006/112, also called 'the recast VAT Directive'.[192] VAT rules for services have been reshuffled with effect from January 2010, in order to better accommodate increasing trade patterns and diversifying modes of delivery.[193]

VAT is a tax conceived to accommodate trade in goods, where there are several intermediaries: intended to be neutral, independent of the number of intermediate transactions, it is collected 'fractionally' at each transaction. It is a consumption tax and, as such, it is charged at the place of consumption. This guideline of taxation at the place of consumption is also followed, in principle, in the area of services.[194] Services, however, are different from goods, so far as VAT is concerned, in at least two ways: a. intermediaries are rare, if non-existent and b. it is often difficult to establish the place of consumption. These characteristics are all the more true with electronic and other forms of 'modern' services.[195] Further, VAT, as an indirect tax, is different from most other impediments to the free provision of services, since it can not be subject to the principle of mutual recognition.[196] This has led the Commission to amend 'the VAT Directive'[197] in relation to the place of supply of services.[198] The new rules, in force since January 2010, introduce a basic distinction between intermediary and final services: the former (B2B services) are taxed at the customer's place of establishment, while the latter (B2C services) are taxed

---

[190] First Council Directive 67/227/EEC on the harmonization of legislation of Member States concerning turnover taxes [1967] OJ 71/1301.

[191] Sixth Council Directive 77/388/EEC on the harmonization of the laws of the Member States relating to turnover taxes—Common system of value added tax: uniform basis of assessment [1977] OJ L145/1.

[192] Council Directive 2006/112/EC on the common system of value added tax [2006] OJ L347/1, with effect as of January 2007.

[193] Council Directive 2008/8/EC amending Directive 2006/112/EC as regards the place of supply of services [2008] OJ L44/11.

[194] The question of which VAT rate is charged is a different (yet very important issue). Pending the transition from the 'destination'-based system to an 'origin'-based system, as the Commission has proposed, the following compromise has been put forward. An 'origin'-based system applies for sales to private persons, while for transactions between taxable persons it is still a 'destination'-based VAT system.

[195] Ivinson, J., 'Why the EU VAT and E-Commerce Directive Does Not Work' (2003) 14 *Int Tax Rev* 27–31.

[196] See Genschel, P., 'Why No Mutual Recognition of VAT? Regulation, Taxation and the Integration of the EU's Internal Market for Goods' (2007) 14 *JEPP* 743–61.

[197] Directive 2006/112, n 192, which has already been modified eight times.

[198] Council Directive 2008/8 amending Directive 2006/112/EC as regards the place of supply of services [2008] OJ L44/11.

at the supplier's establishment.[199] Further, a series of case-specific rules have been introduced: a. B2C services provided by an intermediary are taxed at the location where the main transaction (not the one with the intermediary) is taxable; b. all services connected to immovable property are taxable where such property is located; c. transport services are taxable according to the distances covered or at the place of departure, while ancillary services (eg loading) are taxed at the member states where they are physically carried out; d. this last criterion is also followed for cultural, artistic, and educational services, as well as for hotel, catering etc (unless such services are offered in a plane or train, in which case they are taxable at the place of departure); e. e-services provided by providers outside the EU are taxable in the place where the consumer resides or has a permanent address, while f. broadcasting, telecommunication services etc offered by non-resident providers are taxable at the place where the final customer effectively receives the service; more and more technical rules are spelled out in the Directive. Further developments are expected in the field of VAT, since in its 2010 Single Market Act, the Commission proposes to 'publish a new VAT strategy in 2011'.[200]

E. Assessment—future regulatory needs

The presentation above[201] of the various categories of restrictions imposed to the free provision of services and of justifications thereto calls for several comments.

1. The role of secondary legislation

From the developments above, it may be observed that, the existence of secondary legislation in several areas of law notwithstanding, the CJEU's intervention remains crucial. All the judgments discussed interpret and apply the Treaty rules alone, or alongside some text of secondary law; the numerous cases confined to the interpretation of secondary legislation have not been presented here. There are numerous cases, therefore, where the Court, despite the existence of secondary legislation, has had direct recourse to the Treaty rules, in order to judge on the compatibility of national measures[202] with the free provision of services: this was the case with 24 measures on public procurement, 24 measures on posted workers, 17 measures on the mutual recognition of diplomas, 12 measures on advertising and commercial communication, 10 measures on broadcasting and 8 measures on transport. Two

---

[199] This distinction corresponds to a large extent to the distinction made in ch 5, between business services and personal services.

[200] Communication COM (2010) 608 final, 'Towards a Single Market Act for a Highly Competitive Social Market Economy 50 Proposals for Improving Our Work, Business and Exchanges with One Another', proposal 20.

[201] See the discussions in ch 3 and 4, as well as the analysis in the current chapter.

[202] In the following discussion reference is made to 'measures' rather than 'cases', as one case may examine the compatibility of more than one national measure with EU law.

observations flow from this, one in relation to the role of secondary law in the integration process and one in relation to the quality of secondary law.

As to the role of secondary law as a means of furthering EU integration, the data above seem to infirm the simplistic analysis according to which negative integration (by means of case law) opens the way for positive integration (by means of secondary legislation). Indeed, it would seem that positive integration triggers further negative integration in an ever-sustainable cycle. The existence of some text of secondary legislation makes the rules more accessible to private parties, which, in turn, become prone to litigate on them. In most areas, moreover, regulation has not ceased to evolve. It is difficult to decide whether such a dynamic (or unstable) regulatory framework should be read as a sign of weakness (ie unsuccessful experimentalism) or as a sign of success and dynamic spill-over of the rules put in place. A further factor which should be taken into account is the rapid evolution characterizing the sectors regulated: technology has progressed at an unprecedented pace in the area of electronic communications and audio-visual services and the same is true for transport. As for financial and insurance services, technological progress has played a role, but more important has been the impact of the globalization of the markets in the last 20 years and the creation and recognition of new risks.

Whatever the causes of these successive waves of regulation in these fields, the fact remains that this regulation clearly entails extensive harmonization. The Court, nonetheless, still has recourse to primary law in order to complete the (real or perceived) lacunae of secondary legislation, typically ending up by expanding its scope of application; the public procurement case law is the most striking example in this respect. On other occasions, however, where secondary legislation is itself judged unsatisfactory, the Court's case law restricts rather than extends its scope of application; the case law on posted workers illustrates this tendency well. Thus the ball is back on the legislator's side of the court, in order for it to legislate as a supplement or counter to the judge-made rules. Indeed, if the Services Directive can be seen as a codification of previous case law, occasions on which the legislature 'takes back' or restricts rights recognized by the Court are not unknown.[203]

An approximate test of the quality of any given piece of secondary legislation may be offered by the number of occasions in which the Court had to interpret the

---

[203] Several modifications of Regulation 1408/71 [1971] OJ L149/2 have had the objective of 'correcting' previous interpretations by the CJEU. For instance, Council Regulation 1390/81/EEC extending to self-employed persons and members of their families Regulation (EEC) No 1408/71 on the application of social security schemes to employed persons and their families moving within the Community [1981] OJ L143/1 and Council Regulation 2793/81/EEC amending Regulation (EEC) No 1408/71 on the application of social security schemes to employed persons and their families moving within the Community and Regulation (EEC) No 574/72 fixing the procedure for implementing Regulation (EEC) No 1408/71 [1981] OJ L275/1 amended Regulation 1408/71 in order to reverse the Court's judgment in the *Pierik* cases (Case 117/77 *Bestuur van het Algemeen Ziekenfonds Drenthe-Platteland v G. Pierik (Pierik I)* [1978] ECR 825 and, on the same facts, Case 182/78 *Bestuur van het Algemeen Ziekenfonds Drenthe-Platteland v G. Pierik (Pierik II)* [1979] ECR 1977). Moreover, the Posted Workers Directive (Directive 96/71 [1996] OJ L18/1) was aimed at circumscribing the effects of the Court's judgments in Joined cases 62 & 63/81 *Seco v EVI* [1982] ECR 223 and Case C-43/93 *Vander Elst* [1994] ECR I-3803.

terms of a text of secondary legislation alone, compared to the number of judgments in which the Court had recourse to the primary law, in order to elaborate or 'correct' secondary legislation.

A brief overview of the relevant case law confirms the generally perceived impressions about the quality of legislation. Public procurement has been regulated at the EU level since the 1970s and has been subject to several modifications, culminating in the 2004 Directives.[204] Despite the economic stakes and the different national traditions in the area, in the process of successive amendments, member states have come to reduce the heat in negotiations and eventually reached elaborate and operational texts. The fact that the Public Procurement Directives constitute successful legislative texts is confirmed by numerical data: for 24 measures which had to be decided in conjunction with the Treaty provisions, there are 92 CJEU cases on the interpretation of the Directives without recourse to the Treaty.

At the opposite end, the Posted Workers Directive, the product of an uneasy political compromise, has been interpreted together with the relevant Treaty rules in 24 distinct measures, but has never led to a judgment on its own!

Other texts of secondary legislation score somewhere in between: the mutual recognition of diplomas Directives (now codified in Directive 2005/36) have been interpreted (and occasionally applied) together with the Treaty rules 17 times, but have also triggered a 55-strong body of case law on their own; transport Directives and Regulations have been interpreted 8 times together with the Treaty rules and 13 times on their own in relation to services (they have been interpreted many more times in relation to the freedom of establishment). TV broadcasting has been brought before the CJEU at least 10 times, while the TV without frontiers Directive—now reshaped into the Audiovisual Media Services (AVMS) Directive—has been applied at least 17 times on its own.

This analysis may be an unsurprising indication of the fact that first-generation legislative texts, especially when they are the result of intense political compromise, tend to be more dysfunctional; nonetheless, they become more effective on the basis of successive amendments. The procedure (purely technocratic/comitology as opposed to open public consultation, etc) followed for such amendments has not been found to exert decisive impact. What does seem to matter, though, is the general framework in which member states are called to negotiate: it is one thing to discuss on the basis of a blank page and something else altogether to negotiate against a pre-existing bad text—in the former situation, member states may prefer to keep their domestic regulation or negotiate fiercely around it, while in the latter

---

[204] European Parliament and Council Directive 2004/17/EC coordinating the procurement procedures of entities operating in the water, energy, transport and postal services sectors [2004] OJ L134/1 and European Parliament and Council Directive 2004/18/EC on the coordination of procedures for the award of public works contracts, public supply contracts and public service contracts [2004] OJ L134/114.

their only option is to improve the existing common text. Indeed, if the above holds true, it could serve as a basis for a 'time-differential theory' on the effectiveness of EU secondary legislation: if the implementation of a legislative text proves to be unsatisfactory, a second-generation, more efficient legislation is likely to see the light of day. This finding could also ground the idea that, in view of furthering integration, bad secondary legislation is better than no legislation at all, since it is bound to evolve and become more efficient—or, indeed, disappear.[205]

Finally, this finding could sound a note of optimism on the added value of the Services Directive. Given the imperfections of its text and its apparent departures from the Treaty rules,[206] the Services Directive will certainly give rise to intense litigation on the basis of the Treaty. It may be, however, that the technocratic revisions of the Directive, written in its final Articles, will lead to a much more manageable text in the foreseeable future.

2. What next? Need for further action?

The analysis above makes it possible to present some thoughts on the directions that forthcoming regulation could follow in the area of services.

First, the difficulties in negotiating the Services Directive and the numerous exclusions, exceptions, and derogations that it had to suffer in order to go through the law-making process show that any truly horizontal ambition will have to wait. Indeed, it has been adequately explained that one of the reasons the Directive met with such strong opposition was the fact that it affected so many different interests; it was impossible to play one interest against the other, rather all interests turned against the Directive.[207] Further, as stems from the brief analysis above, despite all the 'rounding' effects the negotiations brought, the Services Directive *is* expected to have some cross-cutting effects. Thus, future regulatory actions are more likely not to have a horizontal scope of application and instead, be more targeted. 'Targeted' does not necessarily mean sector-specific. Indeed, some sector-specific legislative instruments are in the pipeline (healthcare services), while others, which may require specific legislative intervention, have been identified above (namely private security services and gambling). Alongside these, however, some horizontal-thematic action may be required.

---

[205] It is a different question whether such a legislative scheme is desirable from an efficiency point of view.

[206] See the discussion in ch 6, under subheading B(2).

[207] De Witte, B., 'Setting the Scene: How did Services get to Bolkenstein and Why?' EUI Law Working Paper No. 2007/20, 9, also available at http://cadmus.iue.it/dspace/bitstream/1814/6929/1/LAW_2007_20.pdf (last accessed on 10 November 2011); see also Crespy, A., 'When "Bolkestein" is Trapped by the French Anti-Liberal Discourse: A Discursive-Institutionalist Account of Preference Formation in the Realm of European Union Multi-Level Politics' (2010) 17 *J of Europ Pub Pol* 1253–70.[0]

a. Reshaping the General Systems of diploma recognition

Reshaping the General Systems for the mutual recognition of diplomas, in order to integrate the Bologna *acquis*, may be a way forward. See in this respect the extensive discussion above.[208]

b. Circumscribing the definition of SGEI

EU action may also prove useful in the area of SGEIs. As explained already,[209] the legal qualification of a service as being of general economic interest carries important legal consequences: i. it may evade the application of the internal market rules, ii. it may elude the application of the competition rules and the rules on state aid, but iii. it may be subject to the rules on public procurement. To date, each member state unilaterally defines which services do qualify as SGEIs and which do not, subject to the Commission and the Courts' control for 'manifest error'.[210] Different definitions of the scope of SGEI, legitimate as they may be, lead nevertheless to important divergences in the application of the EU rules.[211] Such divergences run counter to EU integration, both at the practical/legal and at the psychological/political level. This explains the Commission's ongoing efforts to define the outer boundaries of SGEIs through Communications and other means of soft law,[212] as well as the emergence of proposals for (binding) secondary legislation. Much more importantly, it underpins the introduction, in the Lisbon Treaty, of Article 14 TFEU, specifically giving competence to the EU to legislate in this field.[213]

It should be remembered that the adoption of a binding horizontal text, however, could not possibly provide catch-all definitions and classifications; at best, it could designate the outer limits of member states' discretion and offer some criteria/indicators for defining SGEIs at the national level. The eventual adoption of such a text would not elude the need for concrete coordination between the member states. To date, such coordination has been top-down, orchestrated by the successive Commission Communications and other consultation processes. However, in the future, Open Method of Communication (OMC)-type processes could be forthcoming in this area.

---

[208] Under subheading C(2).

[209] See the discussion in ch 2.

[210] Case T-289/03 *British United Provident Association Ltd (BUPA), BUPA Insurance Ltd and BUPA Ireland Ltd v Commission of the European Communities* [2005] ECR II-741, para 166; see also ibid, para 168, where it is stated that 'the control which the Community institutions are authorised to exercise over the use of the discretion of the Member State in determining SGEIs is limited to ascertaining whether there is a manifest error of assessment'.

[211] In this sense, see also Neergaard, U., 'Services of general economic interest: the nature of the beast' in Krajewski, M., Neergard, U., and van de Gronden, J. (eds), *The Changing Legal Framework for Services of General Interest* (The Hague: TMC Asser Press, 2009) 17–50.

[212] For a presentation of those means, see the developments in ch 2.

[213] Although most commentators contended that the possibility already existed even before entry into force of the Lisbon Treaty. For more exhaustive analysis on the issue of SGEIs, see ch 2.

c. Enhancing mutual recognition

A further direction in which the EU could deploy regulatory means would be towards enhancing mutual recognition. Furthering mutual recognition in the field of services could help both the access to and the exercise of service activities.[214] So far as access is concerned, mutual recognition may be seen as the intellectual foundation and the step before the country of origin principle (CoOP).[215] CoOP could further be analysed as 'forced' (as opposed to *simple* and *managed*) mutual recognition, whereby the host state is obliged to accept providers from other member states without being able to require compliance with locally applicable regulatory standards. In view of the extensive mutual recognition obligations imposed on member states by the Court, it has been suggested that, at the end of the day, the main difference between an extensive application of the principle of mutual recognition and that of the CoOP, is nothing other than the onus of proof.[216] In mutual recognition, it is still for the service providers to prove that they satisfy the regulatory standards of the host state, while in the framework of CoOP, it is up to the host authorities to prove that the application of their standards is necessary. This notwithstanding, it is clear that mutual recognition has been—and still is—a useful tool, facilitating market access for service providers.

The statistics above[217] have shown that mutual recognition may also facilitate the *exercise* of service activities. It could offer a credible solution to most cases where the existence of deposit guarantees, insurance contracts, credit opening, etc already undertaken in the home state are not duly taken into account by the host state authorities. It could, further, facilitate these situations where foreign services providers are refused some kind of a procedural advantage.

The obligations imposed by mutual recognition, however, are more procedural than substantive. It introduces an obligation of means, not of result. National authorities should, in all circumstances, have in place the necessary procedures to evaluate the qualifications, experience, etc that the service provider already has. If, however, such qualifications are fundamentally different from the ones required by the host state, the competent authorities are not obliged to conclude any kind of recognition. It becomes clear, therefore, that enhancing substantive mutual recognition in the field of services should be one of the forthcoming tasks of the EU. The ways in which mutual recognition in this area may become more efficient will be further explored below.[218]

---

[214] For an early evaluation of the role of mutual recognition in the field of services, see Hatzopoulos, V., *Le principe communautaire d'équivalence et de reconnaissance mutuelle dans la libre prestation de services* (Athènes/Bruxelles: Sakkoulas/Bruylant, 1999); for further, more recent thoughts, see Hatzopoulos, V., 'Mutual recognition in the field of services' in Lianos, I., and Odudu, O. (eds), *Regulating Trade in Services in the EU and the WTO: Trust, Distrust and Economic Integration* (Cambridge: CUP, forthcoming).

[215] For a brief analysis of the CoOP see in ch 6, under A(6)a.

[216] See the developments concerning the CoOP in ch 6.

[217] See the analysis in ch 2–4, as well as in the present chapter.

[218] See the discussion in ch 6.

d. Other measures

Further, there are some more practical measures whereby the EU could facilitate services provision. The obligation of registration with professional bodies, Chambers of Commerce, etc is being dealt with by the Services Directive (Directive 2006/123) and the 'Service Provision' Chapter of the Mutual Recognition Directive (Directive 2005/36). The relevant rules, however, do provide for exceptions and do allow for member state discretion. A way around the resulting obstacles could be the creation of European-wide registries, on a profession-specific basis, entry to which would be automatically valid in all member states. Alternatively, the national professional bodies and chambers could be encouraged to enter into mutual recognition agreements, in order to make sure that registrations in one are automatically recognized by all the others. Further, and in an even more practical direction, the adoption of standard-form guarantee letters, to be issued by banks and other financial and credit institutions, could facilitate their recognition by national authorities.

6

Regulation through Legislation

Ever since the publication of the General Programmes of 1962,[1] regulating the internal market for services has been a riddle for the EU. In its effort to open up trade in services, the EU legislature has tried and erred—with occasional successes—in various ways. Traditionally, a basic distinction is drawn between, on the one hand, sector-specific and, on the other hand, horizontal legislation. Helpful as it may be, this distinction is neither accurate nor historically precise. Instead, an effort will be made below to describe the basic regulatory blocks adopted by the EU legislature (A), and then subject them to more appropriate normative classifications (B).

A. Content of EU legislation on services—a positivist approach

Chapter 1 explained that the concept of 'services', both in economic terms and within the EU Treaty, is riddled with a fundamental ambivalence: it refers to both the human activity of offering services (personal approach) and to services themselves (product approach).[2] Accordingly, legislative acts concerning the free movement of services may be classified into two broad categories: rules on the free movement of persons (providers and recipients of services), on the one hand, and rules concerning the various determinants (access and exercise conditions, liability rules, etc) of the service itself, on the other. This latter category contains various rules on personal qualifications, conduct, and the like, but is clearly distinguishable from the rules governing the right of entry and stay within the territory of another member state. Entry and stay rules, put in place since the early days of the EEC, were for the most part codified in Directive 2004/38 (the Citizenship Directive).[3]

---

[1] General Programme for the abolition of restrictions on freedom to provide services [1962] OJ 2/32; OJ Spec Ed Series II Volume IX p 3. The General Programmes were non-binding declaratory documents adopted as soon as the 'transition period' for the common market ended (in 1960) and constituting a 'roadmap' of the actions to be followed for achieving free movement within the market; their implementation has partially failed because of the requirement of unanimity in the Council and the Luxembourg Compromise, but many of the ideas expressed therein have materialized as part of the 1985 Action Plan leading to the completion of the internal market by 1992.

[2] See ch 1, subsection A(1)b.

[3] European Parliament and Council Directive 2004/38/EC on the right of citizens of the Union and their family members to move and reside freely within the territory of the Member States [2004] OJ L158/77.

In parallel, an extremely rich body of case law has developed in the last decade, in which it is recognized that additional citizenship rights stem directly from the relevant Treaty provision, Article 20 TFEU. These developments, exciting as they are, cannot be presented in the present work.[4] The focus, therefore, will be on regulatory measures which affect service provision as such, to the exclusion of those affecting the free movement of persons.

The EU's approach in relation to service provision can be characterized as neither systematic nor coherent. At different times, different regulatory approaches have been followed in different areas, with different objectives. Some regulatory blocks are sector-specific (such as transport, the other network industries, financial services), while others are more horizontal (such as the mutual recognition of professional qualifications), typically with a relatively limited scope. It is only with the adoption of the Services Directive that a truly horizontal approach was adopted in the field of services.[5] In what follows, however, the different regulatory measures adopted by the EU in the field of services are not discussed on the basis of their horizontal/vertical nature, but rather on the basis of the regulatory technique followed.

From this perspective, six plus one broad categories may be distinguished. The 'plus-one' category covers legislation in the field of consumer protection. This is an autonomous area of EU competence, where the EU has legislated independently from any effort to liberalize trade in services. Indeed, Title XV TFEU, consisting of a single Article (169), gives the Union shared competence in the field. This separate legal basis nothwithstanding, consumer protection is a policy area which is of fundamental importance for the further development of services. Indeed, many important legislative texts, both horizontal and vertical, are already applicable in this field.

Horizontal measures on consumer protection comprise the Doorstep Selling Directive and the Distance Selling Directive,[6] as well as the e-commerce

---

[4] For a comprehensive and up-to-date presentation see Barnard, C., *The Substantive Law of the EU*, 3rd edn (Oxford: OUP, 2010) 417–8; see also, inter alia, Dougan, M., 'Expanding the frontiers of EU citizenship by dismantling the territorial boundaries of the national welfare states?' in Barnard, C., and Odudu, O. (eds), *The Outer Limits of EU Law* (Oxford/Portland: Hart Publishing, 2009) 119–65 and by the same author, 'The spatial restructuring of national welfare states within the EU: The contribution of Union citizenship and the relevance of the Treaty of Lisbon', in Neergaard, U., Roseberry, L., and Nielsen, R. (eds), *Integrating Welfare Functions into EU Law—From Rome to Lisbon* (Copenhagen: DJOF, 2009) 147–87; O'Leary, S., 'Developing an Ever Closer Union between the Peoples of Europe? A Reappraisal of the Case Law of the Court of Justice on the Free Movement of Persons and EU Citizenship' (2008) 27 *YEL* 167–93; Epinay, A., 'The Scope of Article 12 EC: Some Remarks on the Influence of European Citizenship' (2007) 13 *ELJ* 611–22; Jacobs, F., 'Citizenship of the EU—A Legal Analysis' (2007) 13 *ELJ* 591–610; Kostakopoulou, D., 'EU Citizenship: Writing the Future' (2007) 13 *ELJ* 623–46.

[5] European Parliament and Council Directive 2006/123/EC on services in the internal market [2006] OJ L376/36 (the Services Directive). It should be noted that the 'truly' horizontal character of the Services Directive (SD) is questioned in view of the numerous exclusions from its scope.

[6] Council Directive 85/577/EEC to protect the consumer in respect of contracts negotiated away from business premises [1985] OJ L372/31; and European Parliament and Council Directive 97/7/EC on the protection of consumers in respect of distance contracts [1997] OJ L144/19, respectively; the latter has been modified a couple of times, in particular by Directive 2002/65/EC [2002] OJ L271/16, which adopted special rules for the provision of financial services.

Directive.[7] The broad common principle underlying these Directives is that extensive information should be made available to consumers before (and after) the conclusion of a contract; accompanied, where possible, by the right to withdraw from a contract within a given period of time.[8] Moreover, the Unfair Terms in Consumer Contracts Directive[9] and, in a more indirect way, the Unfair Commercial Practices Directive[10] determine to a large extent what terms and conditions may be imposed on consumers. According to the former text, such terms should be brought to the consumer's attention in a clear manner, should not be abusive, and, in case of doubt, should be interpreted in the consumer's favour. This framework is under revision, since the Commission has proposed to rationalize and codify several of the above-mentioned texts in a single Directive.[11] A lacuna in protection, however, can be identified in the area of services, since the Producer Liability Directive and the Guarantees Directive,[12] both of fundamental importance for the protection of consumers from defective or otherwise unsatisfactory *goods*, are of limited importance, if any, to *services* recipients.

In addition to the horizontal texts discussed above, there are various sector-specific rules for consumer protection. Thus several provisions (or, indeed, entire Directives) within the regulatory packages for transport, for financial services, and for the network-based services are dedicated to consumer protection.[13] Alongside

[7] European Parliament and Council Directive 2000/31/EC on certain legal aspects of information society services, in particular electronic commerce, in the Internal Market (Directive on electronic commerce) [2000] L178/1.

[8] For the application of this right to e-commerce activities, see Case C-205/07 *Lodewijk Gysbrechts and Santurel Inter BVBA* [2008] ECR I-9947.

[9] Council Directive 93/13/EEC on unfair terms in consumer contracts [1993] OJ L95/29; for this Directive, see Nebbia, P., *Unfair Contract Terms in European Law: A Study in Comparative and EC Law* (Oxford/Portland: Hart Publishing, 2007); see also the individual contributions contained in Collins, H., *Standard Contract Terms in Europe: A Basis for and a Challenge to European Contract Law* (Alphen ann den Rijn: Kluwer Law International, 2008); Rott, P., 'Minimum Harmonisation for the Completion of the Internal Market? The Example of Consumer Sales Law' (2003) 40 *CML Rev* 1107–35.

[10] European Parliament and Council Directive 2005/29/EC concerning unfair business-to-consumer commercial practices in the internal market ('Unfair Commercial Practices Directive') [2005] OJ L149/22; for this Directive, see Weatherill, S., and Bernitz, U., *The Regulation of Unfair Commercial Practices under EC Directive 2005/29* (Oxford/Portland: Hart Publishing, 2007); and Howells, G., Micklitz, H.W., and Wilhelmsson, T., *European Fair Trading Law: The Unfair Commercial Practices Directive* (Aldershot/Burlington: Ashgate, 2006).

[11] Directive Proposal COM (2008) 614 final, 'on consumer rights'; the Commission has also launched a public consultation; all relevant documents, including the Commission's proposal, are available in <http://ec.europa.eu/consumers/rights/cons_acquis_en.htm> (last accessed on 10 November 2011). While this book was under print this proposal has been adopted into Directive 2011/83/EU of the European Parliament and of the Council of 25 October 2011 on consumer rights, amending Council Directive 93/13/EEC and Directive 1999/44/EC of the European Parliament and of the Council and repealing Council Directive 85/577/EEC and Directive 97/7/EC of the European Parliament and of the Council [2011] OJ L 304/64.

[12] Council Directive 85/374/EEC on the approximation of the laws, regulations and administrative provisions of the Member States concerning liability for defective products [1985] OJ L210/29; European Parliament and Council Directive 1999/44/EC on certain aspects of the sale of consumer goods and associated guarantees [1999] OJ L171/12.

[13] These are briefly presented in the relevant subheading below.

those, there are a few other sector-specific rules, concerning Consumer Credit, Package Tours, and Time Sharing.[14]

Finally, the Services Directive imposes extremely broad information obligations on service providers (especially important if the service provision in question does not fall under any of the distance or e-commerce Directives), the institution of extra-judicial means of dispute resolution (already foreseen in the e-commerce Directive), the adoption of codes of conduct (again already foreseen in the e-commerce Directive), and labels in order to promote quality. Moreover, by organizing mutual assistance between national authorities and by putting in place the internal market information (IMI) system, the Services Directive seeks to ensure that 'crook' service providers are not allowed to prosper to the detriment of consumers in other member states. Consumer protection and the regulatory techniques used in this respect cannot be studied further here, although consumer issues will occasionally surface in the developments which follow.[15]

This specific category aside, EU measures aimed at the liberalization of trade in services concern one of the following broad sectors: i. transport, ii. recognition of professional qualifications and of working experience, iii. liberalization of basic financial services, iv. liberalization of network-bound industry sectors, v. baseline rules for IT services, and vi. general (horizontal) rules facilitating the provision of services. Each one of the above categories calls for some brief analysis.

1. Transport policy: towards a common policy?

Even in the founding Treaties, transport policy was set apart from the other policies concerning services. Title IV of the Rome Treaty, consisting of Articles 74–84, was dedicated to transport. Later, as the Amsterdam Treaty 'communitarized' the part of the third pillar concerning 'Visas, Asylum and Immigration policy' and included the relevant provisions in the EC Treaty under Title IV, Transport had to move to Title V and Articles 70–80. After the Treaty of Lisbon amendments, Transport provisions are now included in Title VI TFEU (Articles 90–100). Apart from this relocation and renumbering, however, very little has changed over the years in these provisions, and the legal bases they offer. For instance, the founding Treaties required qualified majority voting in the Council (after the expiry of phase b of a

[14] Council Directive 87/102/EEC for the approximation of the laws, regulations and administrative provisions of the Member States concerning consumer credit [1987] OJ L42/48; Council Directive 90/314/EEC on package travel, package holidays and package tours [1990] OJ L158/59; European Parliament and Council Directive 94/47/EC on the protection of purchasers in respect of certain aspects of contracts relating to the purchase of the right to use immovable properties on a timeshare basis [1994] OJ L280/83, respectively.

[15] For a brief, but insightful, analysis of the interaction between consumer protection and service provision see Micklitz, H.W., 'Regulatory strategies on services contracts in EC law' in Caffagi, F., and Muir-Watt, H. (eds), *The Regulatory Function of European Private Law* (Cheltenham/Northampton: Edward Elgar Publishing, 2009) 16–61. More generally for consumer protection under EU law, see Weatherill, S., *EU Consumer Law and Policy* (Cheltenham/Northampton: Edward Elgar Publishing, 2005) and Micklitz, H.W., Reich, N., and Rott, P., *Understanding EU Consumer Law* (Antwerpen: Intersentia, 2009).

12-year transitional period, namely eight years) and consultation with the EP. Qualified majority is still the rule, while consultation with the EP has been transformed into co-decision by the Treaty of Maastricht (now Article 91(1) TFEU), which also added the requirement of consultation with the then instituted Committee of the Regions (now Article 91(1) TFEU). Alternative legal bases providing for unanimity in the Council (Article 91(2) TFEU), for the exclusion of the EP (Article 95(3) TFEU), or for the adoption of Commission decisions (Articles 95(4) and 96(2) TFEU) have been used very rarely.

Moreover, a clear 'hierarchical' relation between general rules on services and the specific rules on Transport was introduced in the Rome Treaty, with Article 51(1) (now 58(1) TFEU) stating that '[f]reedom to provide services in the field of transport shall be governed by the provisions of the title relating to transport'. The Court, for its part, held as early as 1985 that this clause prevents Articles 56 and 57 TFEU (then 59 and 60 EC) from having direct effects in the field of transport.[16] From this, it follows that transport liberalization can only be achieved by means of secondary legislative measures, adopted by virtue of Title VI of the TFEU. Indeed, the Council eventually pushed through a lengthy, technical, and complex body of legislation, after it was prompted by a CJEU judgment condemning its failure to act (Article 265 TFEU).[17]

EU legislation in the field of transport covers all four modes of transport: rail, road, waterborne, and air. A brief overview of the Europa webpage for each of these modes shows that the core objectives pursued by the EU are the following: a. the opening up of markets and the securing of competition, b. the homogenization of market conditions and the creation of a level playing field, c. protection, and d. the respect of public service obligations. Since an exhaustive presentation of the entire legislative block on transport is impossible in the present study, the four core objectives above will be illustrated by indicative references to road haulage.[18]

a. Opening up of markets and securing competition

The 'liberalization' of road haulage has called for four kinds of measure. *First*, a common professional permit was established through Directives, completed by a common driver's licence.[19] The permit and licence thus obtained in the home

---

[16] Case 13/83 *European Parliament v Council (transport policy)* [1985] ECR 1513, para 63. However, in this very case (para 74), and more clearly in subsequent cases, the Court held that the general Treaty principles, such as the principle of non-discrimination on the basis of nationality, do apply even in the absence of secondary legislation, see eg Case C-251/04 *Commission v Greece (towage services)* [2007] ECR I-67.

[17] Case 13/83 *European Parliament v Council (transport policy)* [1985] ECR 1513.

[18] Road haulage is selected because a. it is by far the most important means of transportation and distribution of goods and b. it is only marginally affected—if at all—by public service obligations.

[19] Council Directive 89/438/EEC amending Directives 74/561/EEC, 74/562/EEC and 77/796/EEC [1989] OJ L212/101, repealed by Council Directive 96/26/EC on admission to the occupation of road haulage operator and road passenger transport operator and mutual recognition of diplomas, certificates and other evidence of formal qualifications intended to facilitate for these operators the right to freedom of establishment in national and international transport operations [1996] OJ L124/1; see

member state of the driver are subject to automatic mutual recognition in all other member states. *Secondly*, the opening up of member states' markets to road haulage: initially, the right to cross other member states' territories for the purpose of completing an international transportation was recognized,[20] followed by the right to (limited) road cabotage (transportation within other member states' territories).[21] *Thirdly*, the complete liberalization of transport fees from state supervision was achieved,[22] as well as the prohibition of all discrimination on the basis of establishment.[23] *Fourthly*, the application of Article 101(1) TFEU on concerted practices was specifically adapted to the field of road transport, in order on the one hand to exclude from the scope of this Treaty provision 'technical agreements', and to establish a group exemption for specific agreements between small undertakings, on the other.[24]

b. *Homogenization of market conditions and creation of a level playing field*

In view of the importance of transport infrastructure, both rolling (trucks, containers, trailers, etc) and fixed (motorways, regional roads, hubs, etc), and of the existence of serious externalities (negative effects for third parties), the creation of a single market called for the creation of a level playing field, whereby the cost structures of transport companies across the EU would be set against a common background. Here again, three categories of measures were adopted: i. Directives on common technical specifications and their mutual recognition;[25] ii. Directives harmonizing the cost of the use of infrastructure: vehicle taxes,[26] petrol taxes,[27]

---

also European Parliament and Council Directive 2006/126 (EC) on driving licences (Recast) [2006] OJ L403/18.

[20] Council Regulation 881/92/EEC on access to the market in the carriage of goods by road within the Community to or from the territory of a Member State or passing across the territory of one or more Member States [1992] OJ L95/1.

[21] Council Regulation 3118/93/EEC laying down the conditions under which non-resident carriers may operate national road haulage services within a Member State [1993] OJ L279/1.

[22] Council Regulation 4058/89/EEC on the fixing of rates for the carriage of goods by road between Member States [1989] OJ L390/1.

[23] Council Regulation 11/60/EEC concerning the abolition of discrimination in transport rates and conditions [1960] OJ 52/1121; OJ Spec Ed Series I Chapter 1959–1962 p 60.

[24] Council Regulation 1017/68/EEC applying rules of competition to transport by rail, road and inland waterway [1968] OJ L175/1; OJ Spec Ed Series I Chapter 1968(I) p 302. This Regulation has lost much of its importance since the entry into force of the Council Regulation 1/2003/EC on the implementation of the rules on competition laid down in Articles 81 and 82 of the Treaty [2003] OJ L1/1, which 'decentralizes' the application of Art 101(3).

[25] Council Directive 70/156/EEC on the approximation of the laws of the Member States relating to the type-approval of motor vehicles and their trailers [1970] OJ L42/1; OJ Spec Ed Series I Chapter 1970(I) p 96; see also Council Directive 96/53/EC laying down for certain road vehicles circulating within the Community the maximum authorized dimensions in national and international traffic and the maximum authorized weights in international traffic [1996] OJ L235/59.

[26] Council Directive 93/89/EEC on the application by Member States of taxes on certain vehicles used for the carriage of goods by road and tolls and charges for the use of certain infrastructures [1993] OJ L279/32.

[27] Council Directive 92/81/EEC on the harmonization of the structures of excise duties on mineral oils [1992] OJ L316/12 and Council Directive 92/82/EEC on the approximation of the rates of excise

and toll charges[28] are subject to minimal harmonization; iii. Regulations 'internalizing' and harmonizing customs controls,[29] while facilitating international transport conventions.[30]

c. Protection

This objective aims at the protection of three distinct subjects: workers, passengers/ third parties, and the environment.

i. The effort to protect workers and avoid social dumping as well as 'race to the bottom' practices necessitated the adoption of specific rules on driving and resting times. In this respect, Regulation 3820/85 was adopted long before a general agreement (in the form of Directive 93/104) on working time could be reached.[31] Such measures primarily aim at workers' social protection, but they also contribute to the creation of a level playing field.[32]

ii. Transport is an intrinsically dangerous activity and the source of many injuries and deaths. In addition to worsening traffic conditions, the transport of dangerous or toxic substances in irregular containers or trailers may create additional dangers. This has led to the adoption of common rules on the transportation and control of dangerous substances.[33] Safety measures have also been taken in the field of waterbound or air transport.[34] Where passengers are involved, their minimal rights (and obligations) have been harmonized, as well.[35]

---

duties on mineral oils [1992] OJ L316/19, as well as Council Directive 2003/96/EC restructuring the Community framework for the taxation of energy products and electricity [2003] OJ L283/51.

[28] See Directive 93/89, n 26; also European Parliament and Council Directive 1999/62/EC on the charging of heavy goods vehicles for the use of certain infrastructures [1999] OJ L187/42.

[29] Council Regulation 4060/89/EEC on the elimination of controls performed at the frontiers of Member States in the field of road and inland waterway transport [1989] OJ L390/1.

[30] Council Regulation 719/91/EEC on the use in the Community of TIR carnets and ATA carnets as transit documents [1991] OJ L78/6.

[31] Council Regulation 3820/85/EEC on the harmonization of certain social legislation relating to road transport [1985] OJ L370/1, repealed and replaced by European Parliament and Council Regulation 561/2006/EC on the harmonisation of certain social legislation relating to road transport [2006] OJ L102/1; Council Directive 93/104/EC concerning certain aspects of the organization of working time [1993] OJ L307/18. Regulation 3820/85 has been completed by the European Parliament and Council Directive 2002/15/EC on the organisation of the working time of persons performing mobile road transport activities [2002] OJ L80/35, regulating working time specifically in the field of road transport.

[32] See subsection A(1)b.

[33] Council Directive 94/55/EC on the approximation of the laws of the Member States with regard to the transport of dangerous goods by road [1994] OJ L319/7; Council Directive 95/50/EC on uniform procedures for checks on the transport of dangerous goods by road [1995] OJ L249/35; see also Council Directive 96/35/EC on the appointment and vocational qualification of safety advisers for the transport of dangerous goods by road, rail and inland waterway [1996] OJ L145/10.

[34] See eg European Parliament and Council Regulation 2111/2005/EC on the establishment of a Community list of air carriers subject to an operating ban within the Community and on informing air transport passengers of the identity of the operating air carrier [2005] OJ L344/15.

[35] See eg European Parliament and Council Regulation 261/2004/EC establishing common rules on compensation and assistance to passengers in the event of denied boarding and of cancellation or

iii. For the protection of the environment, in the field of road transport the EU has adopted rules defining tolerable levels of sound[36] and gas emissions,[37] while it is continuously adopting anti-pollution standards.[38]

d. Public service obligations

Regulation 1191/69 concerning the accomplishment of public service obligations in the field of land (rail, road, and inland waterways) transport was the first—and for many years the only—legal text dealing with the notion of public service at the EU level.[39] The Regulation requires member states to 'terminate all obligations inherent in the concept of a public service',[40] except for the ones that 'are essential in order to ensure the provision of adequate transport services'.[41] These remaining public service obligations may consist of: i. the obligation to operate, ii. the obligation to carry, and iii. tariff obligations.[42] Undertakings bearing such obligations should receive compensation calculated on the basis of principles set out in the Regulation. The Regulation has been extensively used by the member states, especially in the field of rail transport (essentially for passengers) and in that of suburban coach services.[43] It is this very Regulation which gave rise to the dispute in the *Altmark* case, where the Court spelled out the links between this Regulation, Article 106(2) TFEU on undertakings entrusted with some mission of general interest, and Article 107 TFEU on state aids.[44]

---

long delay of flights [2004] OJ L46/1; European Parliament and Council Regulation 1371/2007/EC on rail passengers' rights and obligations [2007] OJ L315/14; see also the Regulation Proposal COM (2008) 816 final, 'concerning the rights of passengers when travelling by sea and inland waterway', approved on second reading by the Council in October 2010; and Regulation Proposal COM (2008) 817, 'on the rights of passengers in bus and coach transport'.

[36] Council Directive 77/212/EEC amending Directive 70/157/EEC relating to the permissible sound level and the exhaust system of motor vehicles [1977] OJ L66/33.

[37] Council Directive 70/220/EEC on the approximation of the laws of the Member States relating to measures to be taken against air pollution by gases from positive-ignition engines of motor vehicles [1970] OJ L76/1; OJ Spec Ed Series I Chapter 1970(I) p 171. This Directive has been modified 21 times since its adoption. It is completed by Council Directive 88/77/EEC on the approximation of the laws of the Member States relating to the measures to be taken against the emission of gaseous pollutants from diesel engines for use in vehicles [1977] OJ L36/33.

[38] See eg European Parliament and Council Regulation 715/2007/EC on type approval of motor vehicles with respect to emissions from light passenger and commercial vehicles (Euro 5 and Euro 6) and on access to vehicle repair and maintenance information [2007] OJ L171/1.

[39] Council Regulation 1191/69/EEC on action by Member States concerning the obligations inherent in the concept of a public service in transport by rail, road and inland waterway [1969] OJ L156/1; OJ Spec Ed Series I Chapter 1969(I) p 276.

[40] Ibid, Art 1(1).

[41] Ibid, Art 1(2).

[42] Ibid, Art 2(2).

[43] By contrast, this Regulation has rarely been used for road haulage. This explains why road haulage has been completely excluded from the scope of European Parliament and Council Regulation 1370/2007 on public passenger transport services by rail and by road [2007] OJ L315/1, replacing Regulation 1191/69 (n 39) as from December 2019, according to the transitional period provided for in Art 8.

[44] Case C-280/00 *Altmark Trans GmbH and Regierungspräsidium Magdeburg v Nahverkehrsgesellschaft Altmark GmbH, and Oberbundesanwalt beim Bundesverwaltungsgericht* [2003] ECR I-7747.

At a broader level, the EU also pursues a wider vision of transport policy, whereby it seeks to promote intermodality and create transport corridors throughout Europe. Moreover, it increasingly contemplates the use of IT and other modern technologies to ensure better fleet management and the availability of information. Last but not least, the internalization of transport externalities has become a recurring topic in the recent political discussions in this area.[45] The latter issues are mainly policy objectives and are explored and pursued through means of Green and White Papers, Communications, public consultations, and action plans.[46]

All in all, EU policy in the field of transport, an area in which the EU has dominated the regulatory scene and is unfettered by the principle of subsidiarity, is not as straightforward as one would anticipate: it is supposed to be a 'common' policy but it is, in fact, pregnant with exceptions, exemptions, derogations, and 'rolling' transitional periods. The transport market is, in theory, already liberalized but important regulatory steps still need to be taken, while older texts must be constantly adapted and revisited to keep up with technological developments—in road haulage alone, there are at least 200 important binding legal instruments altogether, while at least 40 significant modifications and/or new texts have been adopted since 2000. Furthermore, it should not be overlooked that EU regulatory initiatives in the field developed against a strong background of self-regulation (involving agreements between operators, for example in the field of rail, the Worldwide Organization of Cooperation for Railway Companies (Union International des Chemins de Fer (UIC) 1922)), and international cooperation (through the Convention on International Carriage by Rail (Convention pour le Transport International Ferrovaire (COTIF) 1893)). This background was not always easy to overcome and replace. Indeed, pre-existing international rules such as these have been used to question EU action in this field.[47]

For more on this case, see the discussion in ch 2. On the interpretation of Regulation 1191/69 (n 39), see also, more recently, Case C-504/07 *Associação Nacional de Transportadores Rodoviários de Pesados de Passageiros (Antrop) and Others v Conselho de Ministros, Companhia Carris de Ferro de Lisboa SA (Carris) and Sociedade de Transportes Colectivos do Porto SA (STCP)* [2009] ECR I-3867.

[45] Externalities are unintended side-effects (positive or negative) of a given activity: in the case of transport there are mainly negative externalities, such as traffic congestion, pollution, traffic accidents, etc. Externalities may be 'internalized' where the entity causing them is made to bear their cost eg by having to comply with stricter environmental standards, by participating in the cost of maintenance and/or expansion of the motorways or to the building of smaller roads for regional traffic, etc.

[46] See eg Communication COM (2000) 364 final, 'Towards a Safer and More Competitive High-quality Road Transport System in the Community'; White Paper COM (2001) 370 final, 'European Transport Policy for 2010: Time to Decide'; Communication COM (2007) 606 final, 'The EU's Freight Transport Agenda: Boosting the Efficiency, Integration and Sustainability of Freight Transport in Europe'; Communication COM (2008) 433 final, 'Greening Transport'; Communication COM (2008) 886 final, 'Action Plan for the Deployment of Intelligent Transport Systems in Europe'; Communication COM (2009) 279 final, 'A Sustainable Future for Transport: Towards an Integrated, Technology-led and User Friendly System'; see also the various strategy documents available at the dedicated Commission webpage at <http://ec.europa.eu/transport/strategies/2009_future_of_transport_en.htm> (last accessed 10 November 2011).

[47] Micklitz, H.W., 'Regulatory strategies on services contracts in EC law' in Caffagi, F., and Muir-Watt, H. (eds), *The Regulatory Function of European Private Law* (Cheltenham/Northampton: Edward Elgar Publishing, 2009) 16–61.

From a regulatory point of view, the technique used in the field of transport policy is a mixture of the following: a. exhaustive—and yet piecemeal—harmonization (essentially through Regulations), b. minimal harmonization combined with mutual recognition (through Directives), and c. coordination and steering through soft law. So far as mutual recognition is concerned, it should be noted that it is essentially based on substantial prior harmonization. Its effects are virtually automatic: access to the markets of other member states is, in principle, guaranteed to operators who comply with the Directives' rules. Finally, with respect to soft law, it should be added that it is increasingly used as a means to pursue transport policy. This is confirmed by the publication and the content of the recent Communication on 'A Sustainable Future for Transport', which will constitute the primary reference text for several years to come.[48]

2. Financial services: from a decentralized to a central 'passport'

Together with transport, financial services (in a broad sense, including banking, insurance, and investment services) were the first two categories of services to which classical economists recognized some value. Apart from this historical link, transport and financial services share at least three characteristics. For one thing, they are valuable not only as final consumer services, but also occupy an important role as intermediate services—the lubricant of modern economies. Moreover, since Breton Woods (and in different forms thereafter, culminating in the Basel rules and the G 10 recommendations adopted as a response to the 2008 financial crunch),[49] financial services are subject to international regulation. Thirdly, their liberalization under the Treaties is subject to the liberalization of capital movements[50] and, since those were denied direct applicability,[51] the liberalization of financial services had to wait until all restrictions to capital movement were abolished.[52]

---

[48] Communication COM (2009) 279 final, 'A Sustainable Future for Transport: Towards an Integrated, Technology-led and User Friendly System'.

[49] For the Basel Committee on Banking Supervision and the Basel rules (Basel I, II, and III), see the official site of the Bank for International Settlements, which hosts the secretariat of the Committee at <http://www.bis.org/bcbs/index.htm> (last accessed on 10 November 2011); see, however, on a rather critical tone Lall, R., 'Why Basel II Failed and Why Basel III is Doomed' Global Economic Governance Working Paper No. 2009/52, University College, Oxford, available at http://www. globaleconomicgovernance.org/wp-content/uploads/GEG-Working-paper-Ranjit-Lall.pdf (last accessed on 10 November 2011).

[50] Article 58(2) TFEU.

[51] Case 203/80 *Criminal proceedings against Guerrino Casati* [1981] ECR 2595. There is a parallel between this case and, in the field of transport, Case 13/83 *European Parliament v Council* (*transport policy*) [1985] ECR 1513.

[52] This was achieved with the Council Directive 88/361/EEC for the implementation of Article 67 of the Treaty [1988] OJ L178/5. Ever since, however, the Court has readily applied the Treaty rules as a complementary framework to the Directive rules. See, as the first occasion, Case C-416/93 *Criminal proceedings against Aldo Bordessa, Vicente Marí Mellado and Concepción Barbero Maestre* [1995] ECR I-361.

These three reasons explain why the EU was fast to adopt its first measures concerning banking and insurance services already in the early 1970s.[53] However, it was not until the late 1980s and early 1990s, that an important leap forward was made, with the Second Banking Directive,[54] the Life and Non-life Assurance Directives,[55] and the Investment Services Directive.[56] The relevant legislation has developed in three stages.

a. Phase one: Decentralized passports—home country control

Thanks to these texts, the market for financial services started seriously to open up, through the institution of a European 'passport'. The system established, very similar in all three sectors, is based on a fundamental division of competences between the home state and the host states. On the one hand, the home state is responsible for delivering the authorization, which, like a 'passport', allows the undertaking to open up branches or offer services in all other member states. The home state is also responsible for making sure that the authorization conditions continue to be met, and to withdraw the authorization when they cease to; and it enjoys the competence to supervise and monitor. The host state, on the other hand, is given only subsidiary powers, which boil down to the following: a. the right to be informed about prospective operations of foreign undertakings in its territory,[57] b. the right to impose its own deontological rules, rules on opening hours, publicity,

---

[53] See eg Council Directive 73/183/EEC on the abolition of restrictions on freedom of establishment and freedom to provide services in respect of self-employed activities of banks and other financial institutions [1973] OJ L194/1 and the First Banking Directive (Council Directive 77/780/EEC on the coordination of the laws, regulations and administrative provisions relating to the taking up and pursuit of the business of credit institutions [1977] OJ L322/30). In the field of insurance, see for instance, Council Directive 73/239/EEC on the coordination of laws, regulations and administrative provisions relating to the taking-up and pursuit of the business of direct insurance other than life assurance [1973] OJ L228/3 and Council Directive 77/92/EEC on measures to facilitate the effective exercise of freedom of establishment and freedom to provide services in respect of the activities of insurance agents and brokers (ex ISIC Group 630) and, in particular, transitional measures in respect of those activities [1977] OJ L26/14.

[54] Council Directive 89/646/EEC on the coordination of laws, regulations and administrative provisions relating to the taking up and pursuit of the business of credit institutions and amending Directive 77/780/EEC [1989] OJ L386/1.

[55] Council Directive 92/96/EEC on the coordination of laws, regulations and administrative provisions relating to direct life assurance (third life assurance Directive) [1992] OJ L360/1. Council Directive 92/49/EEC on the coordination of laws, regulations and administrative provisions relating to direct insurance other than life assurance and amending Directives 73/239/EEC and 88/357/EEC (third non-life insurance Directive) [1992] OJ L228/1.

[56] Council Directive 93/22 on investment services in the securities field [1993] OJ L141/27.

[57] There are some procedural differences, concerning the time limits and content of notifications, depending on whether the foreign undertaking intends to open up a branch or merely to offer services on the host state's territory, but in either case the host state may not oppose such plan. The situation is completely different when the foreign undertaking wishes to establish a subsidiary in the host state, in which case the new legal person needs a fresh authorization delivered by the host state authorities; this distinction is being questioned as to its compatibility with the Court's case law according to which all forms of establishment should be treated in the same way, see eg Case 270/83 *Commission v France (avoir fiscal)* [1986] ECR 273; among several writers, see van Gerven, W., 'The Second Banking Directive and the Case Law of the Court of Justice' (1990) 10 *YEL* 57–70.

etc rules on foreign undertakings, and c. the right to 'punish'[58] or 'penalize'[59] irregularities that breach national rules in the general interest. Even in this case, however, the host state regulators need first to ask the undertaking to rectify the breach and then give the home regulators an opportunity to react,[60] except in cases of urgency. Because of the predominant role of the home state, this system is also known as the 'home country control'.[61]

In order to facilitate the recognition of such 'passports' and to enhance the effectiveness of the 'home country control', two major aspects concerning their issuance have been regulated at EU level. *First*, the Directives set out that the home state, responsible for delivering the passport, is the one in which the undertaking has both its registered and its head office.[62] This rule is intended to preclude regulatory shopping, by means of letterbox offices; it may be, however, that it is ill-suited to accommodate the exponential increase in online services. *Secondly*, the above-mentioned Directives (on their own or as completed by other Directives) introduce harmonized regulatory standards for three key authorization conditions: a. capital adequacy must be secured through a minimal solvency ratio and limitations on authorized 'big risks';[63] b. common rules are set concerning the definition of 'own funds', and the consolidation of results of undertakings of the same group;[64] c. common publicity rules are set.[65]

---

[58] Second Banking Directive, n 54, Art 21(5).

[59] Council Directive 93/22/EEC on investment services in the securities field [1993] OJ L141/27 (the Investment Services Directive), Art 19(6).

[60] See eg Second Banking Directive, n 54, Arts 21(2) and (3) and Investment Services Directive, n 59, Arts 19(3) and (4). For a detailed analysis of the powers of the host state in relation to the protection of the general good, see Tison, M., 'Unravelling the general good exception: the case of financial services' in Andenas, M., and Roth, W.H. (eds), *Services and Free Movement in EU Law* (Oxford: OUP, 2002) 321–81.

[61] For a first definition of the 'home country control' system, see White Paper COM (1985) 310 final, 'Completing the Internal Market', paras 102–3. For an excellent presentation of the content, the function and the limits of the 'home country control' system in the area of financial services, see Lomnicka, E., 'The home country control principle in the Financial Services Directives and the case law' in Andenas, M., and Roth, W.H. (eds), *Services and Free Movement in EU Law* (Oxford: OUP, 2002) 295–319. For a comparative and evolutionary perspective of this system in different areas of EC law and in relation to the CoOP see Hatzopoulos, V., 'Assessing the Services Directive, 2006/123/EC' (2008) 10 *CYEL* 215–61.

[62] This requirement is clearly spelled out in Art 1 of the Investment Services Directive (n 59), while it is also made out, though in a more 'cryptic' way (Art 1 by reference to Directive 77/780) in the Second Banking Directive (n 54); see in this respect Lomnicka, n 61, at 298, in particular fn 21.

[63] See, in the field of banking, Council Directive 89/647/EEC on a solvency ratio for credit institutions [1989] OJ L386/14 and Council Directive 92/121/EEC on the monitoring and control of large exposures of credit institutions [1993] OJ L29/1, respectively; both Directives, together with the Second Banking Directive (n 54) have been repealed and replaced by European Parliament and Council Directive 2000/12/EC relating to taking up and pursuit of the business of credit institutions [2000] OJ L126/1.

[64] See, in the field of banking, Council Directive 89/299/EEC on the own funds of credit institutions [1989] OJ L124/16, and Council Directive 92/30/EEC on the supervision of credit institutions on a consolidated basis [1992] OJ L110/52, also repealed and replaced by Directive 2000/12, n 63.

[65] See, in the field of banking, Council Directive 86/635/EEC on the annual accounts and consolidated accounts of banks and other financial institutions [1986] OJ L372/1, as amended by European Parliament and Council Directive 2003/51/EC [2003] OJ L178/16; and European Parlia-

All these Directives only introduced minimal harmonization[66] and aimed at avoiding any risk of a 'Delaware effect' taking place within the EU, whereby corporations would migrate to the member state imposing the lower standards.[67] Although member states are, in theory, free to introduce stricter rules for domestic undertakings, this has rarely been the case in practice: regulatory competition, national constitutional requirements prohibiting reverse discrimination, and Article 56 TFEU, as interpreted in *Alpine Investments*, have stood in the way of stricter requirements.[68] What did happen, though, was the maintenance of divergent regulatory standards from one member state to the other. These surviving differences were due to the combined effect of the latitude left by the Directives to the member states and of the fact that many issues were left out of them altogether.

Thus, although free movement was in principle[69] secured on the basis of the 'passports', true harmonization of licensing and supervision conditions has never been accomplished. This, in turn, has had three adverse consequences. For one thing undertakings were not allowed to 'go global' but had to adapt to the divergent national requirements, therefore forbearing effective economies of scale. Moreover,

ment and Council Directive 2006/46/EC [2006] OJ L224/1; see also Council Directive 89/117/EEC on the obligations of branches established in a Member State of credit institutions and financial institutions having their head offices outside that Member State regarding the publication of annual accounting documents [1989] OJ L44/40.

[66] See eg Second Banking Directive, n 54, Preamble Rec 9 and Investment Services Directive, n 59, Preamble Rec 27; other Directives, such as Council Directive 85/611/EEC on the coordination of laws, regulations and administrative provisions relating to undertakings for collective investments in transferable securities [1985] OJ L375/3 explicitly mention the minimal character of the harmonized rules put into place in their operative part (Art 1(7)); this Directive has now been repealed and replaced by the MiFiD, for which see n 73.

[67] For the concept of the 'Delaware effect' in particular, and of regulatory competition in general, see Griffin, P., 'The Delaware Effect: Keeping the Tiger in Its Cage—The European Experience of Mutual Recognition in Financial Services' (2001) 7 *Columbia J of Eur L* 337–54; Davies, G., 'The Legal Framework of Regulatory Competition', SSRN online paper (2006), available at <http://papers.ssrn.com/sol3/papers.cfm?abstract_id=903138> (last accessed on 9 November 2011); Barnard, C., and Deakin, S., 'Market access and regulatory competition' in Barnard, C. and Scott, J. (eds), *The Law of the Single European Market, Unpacking the Premises* (Oxford/Portland: Hart Publishing, 2002) 197–224, also available as Jean Monnet Working Paper No. 9/2001, at <http://www.jeanmonnetprogram.org/papers/01/012701.html> accessed on 10 November 2011); much earlier, see Ogus, A., 'Competition between National Legal Systems: A Contribution of Economic Analysis to Comparative Law' (1999) 48 *Int & Comparative L Q* 405–18; this author distinguishes between 'homogeneous legal products' in which it is unlikely that there be a significant variation of preferences between market actors in different jurisdictions, such as 'facilitating' rules for contracts, corporations, property, and 'heterogeneous legal products' which are 'interventionist' in nature, in the sense that they protect defined interests (consumers, employees, tenants, etc) at the expense of others, thereby having a social cost: regulatory competition is expected to be fiercer in this latter category, while in the former, some kind of convergence is likely to be achieved.

[68] Case C-384/93 *Alpine Investments v Minister van Financiën* [1995] ECR I-1141; for commentary, see Hatzopoulos, V., 'Annotation: Case C-384/93 *Alpine Investments* [1995] ECR I-1141' (1995) 32 *CML Rev* 1427–45. In this case, it was held that member states may not impose on undertakings established in their territories measures which would restrict, even potentially, their capacity to provide services in other member states.

[69] Subject to the different notification requirements, which in practice have proven to be more than mere 'procedural' requirements; see Lomnicka, E., 2002, n 61, at 303 and Tison, M., 2002, n 60.

there were important variations in consumer protection.[70] In the field of investment services, *thirdly*, national regulatory divergences had the effect of increasing the cost of the various 'products' put into the market.[71]

b. Phase two: Centralized passports—unified conditions for authorizations

These reasons led the EU legislature to modify its regulatory pattern. This change of track was signalled with the 1999 Financial Services Action Plan, which announced the amendment of several texts and the adoption of new ones.[72] The single most important outcome of this Action Plan was the Markets in Financial Instruments Directive 2004/39 (MiFiD).[73] This Directive, replacing the Investment Services Directive, is no longer a 'minimum', but rather a 'full' harmonization legal text, establishing 'a comprehensive regulatory regime governing the execution of transactions in financial instruments'.[74] Despite technically modifying only the Investment Services Directives,[75] several of the MiFiD rules also apply to banks, when they offer the relevant investment services.[76] Under the MiFiD, the authorization, monitoring, and surveillance of undertakings are still tasks for the home state authorities; whatever is controlled by the home state is fully recognized in other member states. The fundamental difference with the previous system is that under the MiFiD, the recognition organized is not 'mutual'. In other words, national authorities who grant authorizations are bound strictly to apply the precise rules of the Directive—not divergent national rules. Therefore, member states are not called to recognize 'mutually' their respective legislations, but the proper application of the common regulatory framework by the authorities of the home state.

In order to make sure that the framework thus agreed is properly implemented at the national level, the MiFiD contains an entire chapter (Chapter II, Articles

[70] See MiFiD, n 73 below, Preamble Rec 3: 'it is necessary to provide for the degree of harmonization needed to offer investors a high level of protection and to allow investment firms to provide services throughout the Community'.

[71] See London Economics/PriceWaterhouseCoopers/Oxford Economic Forecasting, *Quantification of the Macro-Economic Impact of Integration of EU Financial Markets, Final Report to the EC/DG Market* (London, 2002), available at <http://ec.europa.eu/internal_market/securities/studies_en.htm> (last accessed on 11 November 2011).

[72] Communication COM (1999) 232 final, 'Financial Services: Implementing the Framework for Financial Markets: Action Plan'.

[73] European Parliament and Council Directive 2004/39/EC on markets in financial instruments [2004] OJ L145/1. The MiFiD itself was further modified by European Parliament and Council Directive 2006/31/EC [2006] OJ L114/60, European Parliament and Council Directive 2007/44/EC [2007] OJ L247/1, and European Parliament and Council Directive 2008/10/EC [2008] OJ L76/33.

[74] MiFiD, n 73, Preamble Rec 5; see Moloney, N., 'Law-making in EC financial market regulation after the Financial Services Action Plan' in Weatherill, S. (ed), *Better Regulation* (Oxford/Portland: Hart Publishing, 2007) 321–67; see also Catà Becker, L., 'Monitor and Manage: MiFID and Power in the Regulation of EU Financial Markets' (2008) 27 *YEL* 349–86.

[75] According to its title, the MiFiD (n 73) amends Directive 85/611 (n 66), Council Directive 93/6/EEC on the capital adequacy of investments firms and credit institutions [1993] OJ L141/1, and Directive 2000/12 [2000] OJ L126/1. The MiFiD also repeals Directive 93/22 [1993] OJ L141/27.

[76] MiFiD, n 73, Art 1(2).

56–62), bearing the title 'Cooperation between competent authorities of different member states', whereby the obligation to cooperate, exchange information, and take specific measures to comply with the Directive's rules is expounded; national 'contact points' deemed to facilitate the Directive's application are also designated. Thus, the MiFiD is more about the decentralized application of a centrally agreed set of rules, than about real mutual recognition. In this sense, it constitutes a clear departure from the previous system;[77] by the same token, the regulation pattern for financial services is brought closer to that of other genuinely common policies, such as transport, in which the core conditions for the pursuance of the activity are agreed at the EU level.

It is worth noting that this shift in paradigm is connected—in terms of both time and content—with a significant innovation in the regulatory process in the field of financial services: the Lamfalussy process. Based on the Lamfalussy Report published on 15 February 2001,[78] a new regulatory process was formally instituted by the Stockholm European Council[79] and it was further revisited by the Commission in 2007.[80] The MiFiD has been one (probably the most important) of the first four regulatory acts[81] to be adopted under this new process.[82]

c. Phase three: The crisis aftermath—centralizing supervision

While the adoption of the measures in the 1999 Action Plan was supposed to lead to a 'regulatory pause' with the focus being on implementation and monitoring, the 2008 financial crisis has prompted fresh measures, for both short-term crisis management and medium-to-long-term responses.[83] Measures in the latter

---

[77] It should not be overlooked, however, that even in the 'old' system, full harmonization was not completely absent, see eg the Admissions Directive (Council Directive 79/279/EEC coordinating the conditions for the admission of securities to official stock exchange listing [1979] OJ L66/21), or the Listing Particulars Directive (Council Directive 82/121/EEC on information to be published on a regular basis by companies the shares of which have been admitted to official stock-exchange listing [1982] OJ L48/26).

[78] Available at <http://ec.europa.eu/internal_market/securities/docs/lamfalussy/wisemen/final-report-wise-men_en.pdf> (last accessed on 12 November 2011); see also Staff Working Paper SEC (2004) 1459, 'The Application of the Lamfalussy Process to EU Securities Market Legislation: A Preliminary Assessment by the Commission Services'.

[79] Presidency Conclusions, Stockholm European Council, 23–24 March 2001, Annex I, also available at <http://ue.eu.int/ueDocs/cms_Data/docs/pressData/en/ec/00100-r1.%20ann-r1.en1.html> (last accessed on 11 November 2011).

[80] Communication COM (2007) 727 final, 'Review of the Lamfalussy Process: Strengthening Supervisory Convergence'.

[81] The other three being: European Parliament and Council Directive 2003/6/EC on insider dealing and market manipulation (market abuse) [2003] OJ L96/16; European Parliament and Council Directive 2003/71/EC on the prospectus to be published when securities are offered to the public or admitted to trading and amending Directive 2001/34/EC [2003] OJ L345/64; and European Parliament and Council Directive 2004/109/EC on the harmonisation of transparency requirements in relation to information about issuers whose securities are admitted to trading on a regulated market and amending Directive 2001/34/EC [2004] OJ L390/38.

[82] For an official assessment of the process, see Staff Working Paper, SEC (2004) 1459, n 78.

[83] For the former category, see Quaglia, L., Eastwood R., and Holmes, P., 'The Financial Turmoil and EU Policy Cooperation 2007–8' (2009) 47 *JCMS* Annual Review 1–25; and the entire special issue of the *JCMS*; for the latter, see, among many, Quaglia, L., 'The "Old" and "New" Politics of

category further strengthen the EU's impact on the organization of financial services, both from a substantial and from an institutional point of view.

Substantive modifications include the amendment of the Deposit Guarantee Scheme Directive (to increase the minimum level of coverage and the reduction of payment time)[84] and of the Capital Requirement Directive (liquidity risk management; higher capital on trading book and securitization; sound remuneration practices).[85] There was also the adoption of the Regulation on Credit Rating Agencies (CRAs)[86] and the draft Directive on the Alternative Investment Fund Managers (AIFMs).[87] More controversial than the substantive modifications have been the institutional reforms, which have led to instituting the European System of Financial Supervision (ESFS). This system consists of a. three European Supervisory Authorities, namely the European Banking Authority (EBA, to be based in London), the European Securities and Markets Autority (ESMA, to be based in Paris) and the European Insurance and Occupational Pensions Authority (EIOPA, to be based in Frankfurt), b. a joint committee of the European Supervisory Authorities, and c. the European Systemic Risk Board (ESRB, to be based in Frankfurt).[88] The three Supervisory Authorities are to succeed the three corresponding Committees of Supervisors instituted by Commission decisions to participate in the Lamfalussy Process,[89] but will enjoy much more extensive powers of coordination between the national supervisory authorities and, in extreme cases, powers of adopting decisions addressed to individual financial institutions.

In view of this, a clear regulatory pattern has emerged in the field of financial services. Under the initial passport system, member states were responsible both for

---

Financial Services Regulation in the EU' Observatoire Social Européen Research Paper 2010/2, also available at <http://www.ose.be/files/publication/OSEPaperSeries/Quaglia_2010_OSEResearch-Paper2_0410.pdf> (last accessed on 11 November 2011); see also Moloney, N., 'EU Financial Market Regulation after the Global Financial Crisis: "More Europe" or More Risks?' (2010) 47 *CML Rev* 1317–83.

[84] European Parliament and Council Directive 2009/14/EC on deposit-guarantee schemes as regards the coverage level and the payout delay [2009] OJ L68/3.

[85] European Parliament and Council Directive 2009/111/EC as regards banks affiliated to central institutions, certain own funds items, large exposures, supervisory arrangements, and crisis management [2009] OJ L302/97.

[86] European Parliament and Council Regulation 1060/2009/EC on credit rating agencies [2009] OJ L302/1.

[87] Directive Proposal COM (2009) 207 final, 'Alternative Investment Fund Managers and amending Directives 2004/39/EC and 2009/ . . . /EC'.

[88] See COD (2009) 143; for some brief comments on this new institutional framework, see <http://euobserver.com/9/30866/?rk=1>; and <http://www.euractiv.com/en/financial-services/eu-passes-historic-agreement-bank-supervision-news-498050?utm_source=EurActiv + Newsletter&utm_campaign=2f8b62c414-my_google_analytics_key&utm_medium=email> (both last accessed on 11 November 2011).

[89] Commission Decision 2009/78/EC establishing the Committee of European Banking Supervisors [2009] OJ L25/23; Commission Decision 2009/79/EC establishing the Committee of European Insurance and Occupational Pensions Supervisors [2009] OJ L25/28; and Commission Decision 2009/77/EC establishing the Committee of European Securities Regulators [2009] OJ L25/18. These will be replacing the corresponding level 3 Lamfalussy Committees, namely the Committee of European Banking Supervisors (CEBS), the Committee of European Insurance and Occupational Pensions Supervisors (CEIOPS), and the Committee of European Securities Regulators (CESR).

granting the authorizations (the home state) and for supervising (share between the home and host states) the credit institutions. The MiFiD substantially extended harmonization concerning the authorization conditions, while the post-crisis reforms substantially centralize supervision. In both respects—authorization and supervision—the tendency is clearly towards progressive centralization.

3. Professional qualifications: from sectoral harmonization to horizontal mutual recognition

The recognition of professional—and indirectly academic—qualifications is key to the free movement of professionals. Such recognition is paramount both for the establishment of workers and service providers (Article 49 TFEU) and for the occasional service provision (Article 56 TFEU) on the territory of other member states. This was understood by the founding fathers of the Communities and is the reason for the insertion of a specific legal basis in Article 57 of the Rome EEC Treaty (now Article 53(1) TFEU), allowing the Council to 'issue Directives for the mutual recognition of diplomas, certificates and other evidence of formal qualifications'. By virtue of this provision, three blocks of regulatory acts have been adopted.

a. Long-lived transitional measures

A long series of 'transitional' measures were issued in the late 1960s and early 1970s, concerning various manufacturing and distribution activities.[90] These early Directives were 'transitional', in the sense that they were supposed to apply, pending harmonization of the conditions for the exercise of the relevant activities. They established an imperfect system of mutual recognition of (essentially) professional experience, which was planned to operate as a means of opening up access to other member states' professional markets. The fact that no prior harmonization had been attempted, and that the Directives were adopted at a time when the direct

---

[90] Council Directive 64/222/EEC in respect of activities in wholesale trade and activities of intermediaries in commerce, industry and small craft industries [1964] OJ L56/857; OJ Spec Ed Series I Chapter 1963–1964 p 120; Council Directive 64/427/EEC in respect of activities of self-employed persons in manufacturing and processing industries falling within ISIC Major Groups 23–40 [1964] OJ L117/1863; OJ Spec Ed Series I Chapter 1963–1964 p 148; Council Directive 68/364/ EEC in respect of activities of self-employed persons in retail trade [1968] OJ L260/6; OJ Spec Ed Series I Chapter 1968(II) p 501; Council Directive 68/366/EEC in respect of activities of self-employed persons in the food manufacturing and beverage industries [1968] OJ L260/12; OJ Spec Ed Series I Chapter 1968(II) p 509; Council Directive 68/368/EEC in respect of activities of self-employed persons in the personal services sector [1968] OJ L260/19; OJ Spec Ed Series I Chapter 1968(II) p 517; Council Directive 70/523/EEC in respect of activities of self-employed persons in the wholesale coal trade and in respect of activities of intermediaries in the coal trade [1970] OJ L267/18; OJ Spec Ed Series I Chapter 1970(III) p 835; Council Directive 74/556/EEC relating to activities, trade in and distribution of toxic products and activities entailing the professional use of such products including activities of intermediaries [1974] OJ L307/1; Council Directive 75/368/EEC in respect of various activities and, in particular, transitional measures in respect of those activities [1975] OJ L167/22; and Council Directive 75/369/EEC in respect of itinerant activities and, in particular, transitional measures in respect of those activities [1975] OJ L167/29.

effect of the relevant Treaty provisions had not yet been recognized[91] both help explain the limited effectiveness of these Directives and the very few occasions they have reached the Court.[92] Nevertheless, the harmonization towards which these measures were supposed to be 'transitional' never materialized. They were only repealed in 1999, 35 years after the first one was adopted.[93] The activities governed by these 'transitional' Directives are now covered by the 'Second General System' of mutual recognition, which will be described in detail in the paragraphs which follow.

b. Sector-specific recognition based on harmonization

An effort was made in the 1970s and mid-1980s to harmonize the conditions for access to several professions. A total of six medical professions and the profession of architect were the object of the endeavour. The regulatory approach followed typically consists of pairs of Directives, of which the first Directive effects a minimal harmonization of the content/duration of the relevant study cycles, while the second organizes a system of quasi-automatic recognition of the ensuing professional titles in all member states.[94] The architect's Directive does both in a single text.[95] In addition, two Directives were adopted in order to facilitate the provision of services and the establishment of lawyers, but they exclusively concern qualified lawyers, not those who are simply university graduates.[96]

---

[91] As it eventually happened in 1974, with Case 2/74 *Jean Reyners v Belgian State* [1974] ECR 631, in the field of establishment, and Case 33/74 *Johannes Hervicus Maria van Binsbergen v Bestuur van de Bedrijfsvereniging voor de Metaalnijverheid* [1974] ECR 1299, in the field of services.

[92] Until they were eventually repealed, in 1999, only two of the above Directives had been brought before the CJEU: Directive 64/427 (n 90) was interpreted in Case 115/78 *J. Knoors v Staatssecretaris van Economische Zaken* [1979] ECR 399, Case 130/88 *C.C. van den Bijl v Staatssecretaris van Economische Zaken* [1989] ECR 3039, Joined cases C-193 & C-194/97 *Manuel de Castro Freitas and Raymond Escallier v Ministre des Classes moyennes et du Tourisme* [1998] ECR I-6747, and Case C-58/98 *Josef Corsten* [2000] ECR I-7919; Directive 68/368 (n 90) was interpreted in Case 20/87 *Ministère public v André Gauchard* [1987] ECR 4879 and Case 204/87 *Criminal proceedings against Guy Bekaert* [1988] ECR 2029.

[93] European Parliament and Council Directive 1999/42/EC establishing a mechanism for the recognition of qualifications in respect of the professional activities covered by the Directives on liberalization and transitional measures and supplementing the general systems for the recognition of qualifications [1999] OJ L201/77.

[94] For medical doctors, Council Directive 75/362/EEC [1975] OJ L167/1 and Council Directive 75/363/EEC [1975] OJ L167/14, replaced by Council Directive 93/16/EC to facilitate the free movement of doctors and the mutual recognition of their diplomas, certificates and other evidence of formal qualifications [1993] OJ L165/1; for nurses, Council Directive 77/452/EEC [1977] OJ L176/1 and Council Directive 77/453/EEC [1977] OJ L176/8; for dentists, Council Directive 78/686/EEC [1978] OJ L233/1 and Council Directive 78/687/EEC [1978] OJ L233/10; for veterinaries, Council Directive 78/1026/EEC [1978] OJ L362/1 and Council Directive 78/1027/EEC [1978] OJ L362/7; for midwives, Council Directive 80/154/EEC [1980] OJ L33/1 and Council Directive 80/155/EEC [1980] OJ L33/8; for pharmacists, Council Directive 85/432/EEC [1985] OJ L253/34 and Council Directive 85/433/EEC [1985] OJ L253/37.

[95] Council Directive 85/384/EEC on the mutual recognition of diplomas, certificates and other evidence of formal qualifications in architecture, including measures to facilitate the effective exercise of the right of establishment and freedom to provide services [1985] OJ L223/15.

[96] Council Directive 77/249/EEC to facilitate the effective excercise by lawyers of freedom to provide services [1977] OJ L78/17 and European Parliament and Council Directive 98/5/EC to

This approach, in addition to the fact that it only concerns a few 'bourgeois' professions, has the very important drawback of entailing long negotiations in areas ripe with cultural, ideological, and other prejudices and prone to corporatist control. Further, this detailed sector-specific approach may be a source of rigidity and run counter to the principle of subsidiarity, formally introduced in the EU legal order with the Treaty of Maastricht.[97] This regulatory approach seemed outdated as early as 1985, after the adoption of the horizontal 'new approach' for internal market legislation.[98] The new approach is based on *Cassis de Dijon* as fleshed out by the CJEU in its early 'professional qualification' case law,[99] where it univocally established that member states are expected to give due consideration to the actual knowledge testified by the different diplomas, certificates, and other qualifications and are not allowed to hide behind formal differences in the educational or vocational training systems. Building on this case law and putting into practice the experience acquired from the 'new approach' in the area of goods, the Commission put forward a genuinely original method for the mutual recognition of professional qualifications, also known as the 'General System', to which the analysis now turns.

c. The General Systems: mutual recognition helped by procedural harmonization

The approach followed in the General Systems is entirely novel in that it remains completely agnostic about the content of the different study cycles. Instead, this third legislative block is based on the rights enjoyed by the interested professionals in the state of qualification (home state) and follows a backward-looking reasoning: thus any person who enjoys the right to access a certain profession in

facilitate practice of the profession of lawyer on a permanent basis in a Member State other than that in which the qualification was obtained [1998] OJ L77/36; holders of law degrees wishing to practise in another member state, may do so either according to the terms of the General System (European Parliament and Council Directive 2005/36/EC on the recognition of professional qualifications [2005] OJ L255/22, see eg Case C-118/09 *Robert Koller* [2010] ECR nyr) or by virtue of the general Treaty rules on establishment (see eg Case C-313/01 *Christine Morgenbesser v Consiglio dell'Ordine degli avvocati di Genova* [2003] ECR I-13467; and Case C-345/08 *Krzysztof Pesla v Justizministerium Mecklenburg-Vorpommern* [2009] ECR nyr).

[97] See, among many, Cass, D.Z., 'The World that Saves Maastricht? The Principle of Subsidiarity and the Division of Powers within the European Community' (1992) 29 *CML Rev* 1107–36; and more recently, Schutze, R., 'Subsidiarity after Lisbon: Reinforcing the Safeguards of Federalism' (2009) 68 *Cambridge LJ* 525–36.

[98] Based on minimal harmonization (often through standardization) and mutual recognition, see Council Resolution on a new approach concerning technical harmonisation and standardisation [1985] OJ C136/1.

[99] Case 71/76 *Jean Thieffry v Conseil de l'ordre des avocats à la cour de Paris* [1977] ECR 765; Case 115/78 *Knoors*, n 92; Case 222/86 *Union nationale des entraîneurs et cadres techniques professionnels du football (Unectef) v Georges Heylens and others* [1987] ECR 4097; Case C-340/89 *Vlassopoulou v Ministerium für Justiz, Bundes-und Europaangelengheiten Baden-Württemberg* [1991] ECR I-2357; Case C-19/92 *Dieter Kraus v Land Baden-Württemberg* [1993] ECR I-1663; Case C-319/92 *Salomone Haim v Kassenzahnärztliche Vereinigung Nordrhein* [1994] ECR I-425; Case C-164/94 *Georgios Aranitis v Land Berlin* [1996] ECR I-135.

one (home) member state should be able do so in all other (host) member states.[100] The latter may only impose compensatory measures, in the form of either an apprenticeship period or an aptitude exam, strictly restricted to two circumstances: either when the duration and/or content of the study cycle followed is considerably different, or when the tasks that the interested parties will have to perform (in the exercise of the profession) in the host state are fundamentally different from those they were expected to perform in the home state. National educational systems remain, accordingly, unaffected.[101] But even with regard to professional requirements, substantive rules are not at all harmonized. Instead, only a layer of harmonized procedural/technical rules is superimposed on pre-existing national procedures, with a view to facilitating mutual recognition and to limiting member states' arbitrariness. The price to pay for such 'superficial' harmonization is that, contrary to the system of quasi-automatic recognition instituted by the 'paired' Directives on medical professions[102] and by the architect's Directive,[103] under the General System, recognition is not automatic: it is subject to substantive evaluation by the host state authorities, who may impose compensatory measures thus delaying the access of foreign professionals in the host state.

For the General System to apply, the critical condition is that the profession concerned is somehow regulated in the host member state. If it is not, then access to it should be unfettered, and need not be subject to the Directive's mechanism; indeed, any restriction imposed on professionals from other member states wishing to exercise a non-regulated profession would directly violate Articles 49 and/or 56 TFEU.[104]

---

[100] The *Cassis de Dijon* logic is easily discernible behind this basic statement; see Case 120/78 *Rewe-Zentral AG v Bundesmonopolverwaltung für Branntwein (Cassis de Dijon)* [1979] ECR 649. See also Graham, R., 'Mutual recognition and country of origin in the case law of the ECJ' in Blanpain, R. (ed), *Freedom of Services in the EU, Labour and Social Security Law: The Bolkestein Initiative* (The Hague: Kluwer Law International, 2006) 37–50.

[101] At least in theory; in practice, the spill-over effects of the general system may be extremely far-reaching. For example, Greece has had to recognize the validity of degrees delivered by foreign universities established within its territory, in the face of long-standing case law of the Greek *Conseil d'Etat* holding such practice to be contrary to the Constitutional requirement of 'public and free' higher education. See Case C-274/05 *Commission v Greece (university degrees)* [2008] ECR I-7969 and Case C-465/08 (ord), *Commission v Greece (opticians II)* [2009] ECR I-116. Italy has had to do the same, although there the prohibition of private tuition stemmed from a law (it did not enjoy constitutional status); see Case C-153/02 *Valentina Neri v European School of Economics (ESE Insight World Education System Ltd)* [2003] ECR I-13555.

[102] See n 94.

[103] See n 95.

[104] In practice, however, in view of the administrative practices of member states, it is often more difficult to gain access to an unregulated profession, rather than to be able to benefit from the procedural safeguards of the General System. This explains why in the recent case law of the Court the concept of a regulated profession is construed in a broad manner, also covering professions regulated by collective agreements (not by statute), see Case C-234/97 *Fernandez Bobadilla v Museo Prado* [1999] ECR I-4773; more boldly, in Case C-285/01 *Isabel Burbaud v Ministère de l'Emploi et de la Solidarité* [2003] ECR I-8219, the Court held that the existence of a recruitment procedure in order to exercise a specific profession in the public sector renders this very profession 'regulated'.

The first General System covered only degrees and diplomas issued after at least three years of studies.[105] It was completed by the second General System[106] which concerns studies of lesser duration. The scope of the second system appears broader, in that it absorbs the 'transitory' Directives,[107] and, at the same time, extends recognition beyond study cycles and vocational training to pure professional experience.[108]

All of these Directives were amended and consolidated by Directive 2005/36.[109] In a text of no fewer than 121 pages (including numerous Annexes), the sector-specific harmonization of the 'bourgeois' professions is accompanied by the (more rationalized and detailed) General Systems. Five levels of education are distinguished, from simple 'attestations of competence' acquired through training courses or general primary and/or secondary education to diplomas certifying at least four years of post-secondary education. The equivalence of the corresponding levels of education in every member state is also organized.

Beyond refining the pre-existing systems of mutual recognition, the consolidating Directive introduces two important novel features. Title II on the 'Free provision of services' provides—subject to exceptions—that professionals legally established in one member state may occasionally exercise their activity in other member states subject to a requirement of prior declaration, without the need for the recognition of any qualifications; while Title V sets out in some detail the conditions for '[a]dministrative cooperation and responsibility for implementation'. Indeed, in order to secure the efficient implementation of the Directive and to overlook national authorities, the Commission has set up a coordinator's group.[110]

From the point of the regulatory technique used, Directive 2005/36, like the Services Directive (Directive 2006/123),[111] could be qualified as a 'horizontal hybrid'. 'Horizontal' because, although it is mainly intended to help service providers to establish themselves in other member states, it also contains specific rules for the occasional service provider. 'Hybrid', because in a single text one can find rules on harmonization, pure mutual recognition, administrative cooperation, and more.[112]

---

[105] Council Directive 89/48/EEC on a general system for the recognition of higher-education diplomas awarded on completion of professional education and training of at least three years' duration [1989] OJ L19/16.

[106] Council Directive 92/51/EEC on a second general system for the recognition of professional education and training [1992] OJ L30/40, modified several times.

[107] For which, see within the present subsection, under 'Long-lived transitional measures'.

[108] European Parliament and Council Directive 1999/42/EC establishing a mechanism for the recognition of qualifications in respect of the professional activities covered by the Directives on liberalisation and transitional measures and supplementing the general systems for the recognition of qualifications [1999] OJ L201/77.

[109] European Parliament and Council Directive 2005/36/EC on the recognition of professional qualifications [2005] OJ L255/22.

[110] Commission Decision 2007/172/EC, Setting up the group for coordinators for the recognition of professional qualifications [2007] OJ L 79/38.

[111] For which, see the discussion in subsection A(7).

[112] For the concept of hybrid regulation, see Hervey, T., and Trubek, L., 'Freedom to Provide Health Care Services in the EU: An Opportunity for "Hybrid Governance"' (2007) 13 *Columbia J of Eur L* 623–47; This hybrid character is likely to be strengthened in view of the projections made in the Green Paper 'Modernising The Professional Qualifications Directive (Com (2011) 367 final), published while this book was in production.

4. Network industries: sector-specific liberalization rules

a. General characteristics

A network 'is a set of points (or nodes) and interconnecting lines (or edges) organised with the object of transmitting flows of energy (electricity, heat), information (sound, data, pictures) or material (water, freight, passengers). ... Some networks are one-way, like gas, cable TV and water delivery, while others are two-way, such as passengers transportation or telephone'.[113] From an economic point of view, two-way networks are different from one-way ones, in that they often develop 'network externalities':[114] the network's value to its users increases together with the number of users and, unless interconnected, big networks (with many subscribers) are much more valuable than smaller ones.

'Network industries are characterised by the delivery of products or services to final customers via a "network infrastructure" linking upstream supply with downstream customers.'[115] Typically, network infrastructures have limited capacity. Moreover, they are expensive to build and difficult (or impossible) to duplicate. In this sense, they constitute 'natural monopolies', in that the cost structure is such, that no combination of undertakings may operate as cost efficiently as a single supplier.[116] This characteristic is further strengthened by network externalities, where they exist.

---

[113] European Commission, DG for economic and financial affairs, *European Economy: Liberalization of Network Industries: Economic Implications and Main Policy Issues* (Brussels, 1999), at 81.

[114] The terms 'network externalities' account for the simple idea that irrespective of the intrinsic value of any given network (eg a telecommunications network), or standard (eg Microsoft Windows operating system), every new subscriber of the network/standard adds up to its value, since it expands the number of people able to communicate on this same network/standard; network externalities may be countered by interconnection obligations. On network externalities see, among many, Lemley, M., and McGowan, D., 'Legal Implications of Network Economic Effects' (1998) 86 *California L Rev* 479–611, at 483; Lopatka, J., and Page, W., 'Microsoft, Monopolization and Network Externalities: Some Uses and Abuses of Economic Theory in Antitrust Decision Making' (1995) 40 *Antitrust Bulletin* 317–70. See also Economides, N., 'The Economics of Networks' (1996) 16 *Int J of Ind Organization* 673–99, also available at <http://www.stern.nyu.edu/networks/top.html> (last accessed on 11 November 2011); Economides, N., and White, L., 'One-way networks, two-way networks, compatibility and anti-trust' in Gabel, D., and Weiman, D. (eds), *Opening Networks to Competition: The Regulation and Pricing of Access* (Amsterdam: Kluwer Academic Press, 1996) 9–29; also, Economides, N., and White, L., 'Networks and Compatibility: Implications for Anti-trust' (1994) 38 *Eur Economic Rev* 651–62.

[115] European Commission, 1999, n 113, at 21.

[116] This happens when the marginal cost of production is steadily decreasing (typically after significant investment in infrastructure): each undertaking is inclined to produce as much as possible to keep reducing marginal and, ultimately, average total cost. This, however, may be impossible because of a. scarcity of (one of) the resources or other physical constraint (such as limited transport capacity), and b. demand which is not infinite. Therefore, if more undertakings have to share the market in question, each one of them will be producing less than its full capacity, at a higher total cost than under monopoly conditions. Hence, a monopoly is socially preferable; see Baumol, W.J., Bailey, E.E., and Willig, E.D., 'Weak Invisible Hand Theorems on the Sustainability of Multiproduct Natural Monopoly' (1977) 67 *American Economic Rev* 350–65; see also Waterson, M., *Regulation of the Firm and Natural Monopoly* (Cambridge, Massachussetts: Blackwell, 1988).

Very often, network infrastructures are used to deliver goods or services satisfying the basic needs of a population, to which everyone should have access; these uses correspond to the concept of 'public service'. Some of the goods and services offered are of particular importance to the state, for strategic, socio-economic, and political reasons. These three broad characteristics (namely, the existence of natural monopoly, the provision of 'public service' and the economic/political significance of network industries) explain why these industries are regulated in all countries.[117] Regulation is further justified by two additional factors which, without being specific to network industries, are especially unacceptable in the area (for the reasons mentioned above): market failures and information asymmetry.

For all these reasons, since World War II states have been intervening in network industries in four possible ways: a. by participating in or controlling the undertakings' ownership, b. by granting legal monopolies to specific undertakings, c. by extensively regulating the status, powers, and operation of the undertakings involved, or, at least, d. by setting strict standards for the goods/services offered. Nonetheless, government intervention into industries has three standard risks: a. imperfect knowledge of cost and demand conditions, b. capture by interest groups and political influence, and c. limited commitment ability.[118] Indeed, all these dangers have materialized to varying degrees in every state and have often given rise to dissatisfaction about the quality and/or price of the output provided.

Public dissatisfaction, combined with technical innovation (allowing alternative infrastructures) and new consumption patterns (a turning to quality/custom goods and services) all call into question the states' regulatory regimes. This trend was furthered at the EU level by spill-over effects of the completion of the internal market (the realization that legal monopolies may constitute a restriction to the free movement rules),[119] and by the progressive application of competition rules on public actions in cases such as *Van Eycke, Meng*, and *Reiff*, to name just a few.[120] Fiscal austerity imposed by the Maastricht convergence criteria as well as the need for investments and the pressure from potential market entrants constituted the final impetus that led to the era of 'deregulation'.

The first area in which these factors were of decisive importance was telecommunications. The Commission, inspired by the American experience with the Open Network Provision[121] and almost concomitantly with the first competitive

[117] Further on these three reasons, see Geradin, D., 'The Liberalization of Network Industries in the EU: Where Do We Come and Where We Go?' Paper prepared for the Finnish Presidency, 20 September 2006, also available at <http://www.vnk.fi/hankkeet/talousneuvosto/tyo-kokoukset/globalisaatioselvitys-9-2006/artikkelit/Geradin_06-09-20.pdf> (last accessed on 11 November 2011).

[118] See European Commission, 1999, n 113, at 71.

[119] Case C-260/89 *ERT v DEP and Sotirios Kouvelas* [1991] ECR I-2925.

[120] For this line of case law, see the discussion in ch 2; see also Buendia Sierra, J.L., *Exclusive Rights and State Monopolies under EC Law: Article 86 (former Article 90) of the EC Treaty* (Oxford: OUP, 2000); and, more recently, Szyszczak, E., 'Competition and the liberalised market' in Shuibhne, N.N. (ed), *Regulating the Internal Market* (Cheltenham/Northampton: Edward Elgar Publishing, 2006) 87–104; and in a more provocative tone, Davies, G., 'Article 86 EC, the EC's Economic Approach to Competition Law, and the General Interest' (2009) 5 *Eur Competition J* 549–84.

[121] Hatzopoulos, V., 'L'"open network provision" moyen de la dérégulation' (1994) 30 *RTDE* 63–99.

experiments in the UK (the licensing of Mercury Telecommunications as a second voice operator), presented its landmark 1987 Green Paper on telecommunications,[122] followed by three subsequent packages of legislation. This process culminated in the 2002 'Telecom package', consisting of one framework Directive and four 'targeted' Directives on access, authorizations, universal service, and data protection, respectively.[123] In addition, the Commission, grounded on the support of various authors,[124] went as far as proposing the establishment of a common European electronic communications market authority.[125]

In the same vein, the Commission has come up with legislative packages in the field of electricity and gas, rail transport, and postal services.

b. Regulatory approach

Despite the common characteristics shared by all network industries (briefly mentioned above), they differ from one another in many important respects, such as GDP share, intensity of labour, capital investment, profitability, network characteristics, rate of evolution of technologies, and the existence of common technical standards.[126] Accordingly, the liberalization of network industries in the

---

[122] Green Paper COM (1987) 290 final, 'Towards a Dynamic European Economy: Green Paper on the Development of the Common Market for Telecommunications Services and Equipment'.

[123] Framework Directive (European Parliament and Council Directive 2002/21/EC on a common regulatory framework for electronic communications networks and services [2002] OJ L108/33); Access Directive (European Parliament and Council Directive 2002/19/EC on access to, and interconnection of electronic communications networks and associated facilities [2002] OJ L108/7); Authorization Directive (European Parliament and Council Directive 2002/20/EC on the authorization of electronic communications networks and services [2002] OJ L108/21); Universal Service Directive (European Parliament and Council Directive 2002/22/EC on universal service and users' rights relating to electronic communications networks and services [2002] OJ L108/51); Directive on privacy and electronic communications (European Parliament and Council Directive 2002/58/EC concerning the processing of personal data and the protection of privacy in the electronic communications sector [2002] OJ L201/37); on this package see, among many, Bavasso, A., 'Electronic Communications: A New Paradigm for European Regulation' (2004) 41 *CML Rev* 87–118; for an overall and recent assessment of the relevant policy see Galanis, T., *Droit de la concurrence et régulation sectorielle: l'exemple des communications électroniques* (Bruxelles/Athènes: Sakkoulas/Bruylant, 2010); for a more critical approach, see Mouline, A., 'Libéralisation des services de télécommunications en Europe: Emergence d'une structure oligopolistique dominée par les opérateurs historiques?' in Potvin-Solis, L. (ed), *La libéralisation des services d'intérêt économique général en réseau en Europe* (Bruxelles: Bruylant, 2010) 401–18.

[124] See eg Stoffaës, C., 'Towards European Regulation of Network Industries' Discussion Group Report, Initiative for Public Utility Services in Europe, Paris, 2003, also available at <http://www.archives.diplomatie.gouv.fr/europe/pdf/rapportstoffaes.gb.pdf> (last accessed on 11 November 2011); see also European Commission, DG for economic and financial affairs, *European Economy: Liberalization of Network Industries: Economic Implications and Main Policy Issues* (Brussels, 1999), containing a study by the Université des Sciences Sociales de Toulouse, entitled 'Network industries and public service'.

[125] European Parliament and Council Regulation 1211/2009/EC establishing the Body of European Regulators for Electronic Communications (BEREC) and the Office [2009] OJ L337/1; for this authority, see briefly in subsection A(4)b(iv); see also in the developments in ch 7.

[126] European Commission, 1999, n 113, at 67.

EU has been qualified as 'recent, gradual, uneven, complex'.[127] It is, however, feasible to trace common basic features across these EU policies.[128]

The Commission itself, since its 2002 Communication,[129] conducts a periodic horizontal evaluation of all network industries providing SGEIs, which effectively means all network industries.[130]

From an economic perspective, the common trends underpinning EU policy in all network industries can be explained under a six-step approach.[131] Step one asks whether the network sector is characterized by natural monopoly; in the affirmative, competition *for* the market should be organized, instead of competition *in* the market. Step two consists of identifying the restrictions to free movement, and of trying to establish transparency and a level playing field through unbundling obligations; step three defines universal or public service obligations in the industry in question, while step four regulates its financing; step five defines access rules and tackles interconnection conditions and prices; step six, finally, is concerned with cross-border issues in the EU.

From a legal perspective, EU policy in the network industries may be seen as entailing five components: i. liberalization, ii. regulation, iii. the application of competition rules, iv. the establishment of sector-specific authorities, and v. the introduction of atypical forms of regulation.[132]

i. Liberalization—removal of exclusive rights

The first component calls for liberalization and the removal of exclusive rights. In this respect, the approach adopted has been progressive and cautious. For instance, in telecommunications, at first only value-added services were liberalized, to be followed later by mobile and satellite telephony, and only at a third stage was competition generalized to cover fixed telephony. Similarly, in the field of energy, competition was introduced gradually, to cover only industrial users and only up to

---

[127] Pelkmans, J., 'Making EU Network Markets Competitive' (2001) 17 *Oxford Rev of Economic Policy*, 432–56, also available at <http://people.pwf.cam.ac.uk/mb65/library/pelkmans.2001.pdf> (last accessed on 11 November 2011).

[128] Ibid; see also Geradin, D., n 117; Geradin, D., 'L'ouverture à la concurrence des entreprises de réseau: Analyse des principaux enjeux du processus de libéralisation' (1999) 35 *CDE* 13–48; Slot, P.J., and Skudder, A., 'Common Features of Community Law in the Network-Bound Sectors' (2001) 48 *CML Rev* 87–129; Arnbak, J., 'Multi-utility regulation: yet another convergence?' in Mansell, R., Samarajiva, R., and Mahan, A. (eds), *Networking Knowledge for Information Societies: Institutions and Intervention* (Delft: Delft University Press, 2002) 141–7, also available at <http://lirne.net/resources/netknowledge/arnbak.pdf> (last accessed on 11 November 2011).

[129] COM (2002) 331 final, 'on the horizontal evaluation of services of general economic interest (SGEIs)'.

[130] See for the most recent one, European Commission DG Economic and Financial Affairs, *European Economy: Evaluation of the Performance of Network Industries Providing Services of General Economic Interest* (Brussels, 2007), at 1.

[131] Pelkmans, J., 2001, n 127, at 437–41.

[132] Géradin, D., 2006, n 117.

a certain percentage of total production; only the third energy package[133] substantially liberalizes generation, distribution (storage, for gas), and supply, while it provides for an independent transmission operator subject to strict (ownership) unbundling obligations. Another example of this gradual approach to liberalization can be found in the area of postal services. In particular, the weight of parcels exclusively reserved to incumbents has been gradually reduced from 2 kg for printed matters and 10 kg for packages, to 50 g for printed matters and the full liberalization of packages.[134] The field of rail transport was a similar case, where freight transport was at first partially liberalized by the first railway package and then fully liberalized by the second railway package. Only the third railway package aimed to liberalize passenger transport, and again, it was limited to international movement, which means that rail cabotage issues were not explored.[135]

---

[133] The main Directives in each package comprise a. in the field of electricity, European Parliament and Council Directive 96/92/EC concerning common rules for the internal market in electricity [1996] OJ L27/20; European Parliament and Council Directive 2003/54/EC concerning common rules for the internal market in electricity [2003] OJ L176/37; European Parliament and Council Directive 2009/72/EC concerning common rules for the internal market in electricity [2009] OJ L211/55; b. in the field of gas, European Parliament and Council Directive 98/30/EC concerning common rules for the internal market in natural gas [1998] OJ L204/1; European Parliament and Council Directive 2003/55/EC concerning common rules for the internal market in natural gas [2003] OJ L176/57; European Parliament and Council Directive 2009/73/EC concerning common rules for the internal market in natural gas [2009] OJ L221/94.

[134] European Parliament and Council Directive 97/67/EC on common rules for the development of the internal market of Community postal services and the improvement of quality of service [1997] OJ L15/14; modified by European Parliament and Council Directive 2002/39/EC with regard to the further opening to competition of Community postal services [2002] OJ L176/21.

[135] In fact, there are four packages: *a. Package 'zero'*: Council Directive 91/440/EEC on the development of the Community's railways [1991] OJ L237/25; Council Directive 95/18/EC on the licensing of railway undertakings [1995] OJ L143/70; Council Directive 95/19/EC on the allocation of railway infrastructure capacity and the charging of infrastructure fees [1995] OJ L143/75; Council Directive 96/48/EC on the interoperability of the trans-European high-speed rail system [1996] OJ L235/6; and European Parliament and Council Directive 2001/16/EC on the interoperability of the trans-European conventional rail system [2001] OJ L110/1; *b. First package*: European Parliament and Council Directive 2001/13/EC on the licensing of railway undertakings [2001] OJ L75/26; and European Parliament and Council Directive 2001/14/EC on the allocation of railway infrastructure capacity and the levying of charges for the use of railway infrastructure and safety certification [2001] OJ L75/29; *c. Second package*: Railway Safety Directive (European Parliament and Council Directive 2004/49/EC on safety in the Community's railways and amending Council Directive 95/18/EC on the licensing of railway undertakings and Directive 2001/14/EC on the allocation of railway infrastructure capacity and the levying of charges for the use of railway infrastructure and safety certification [2004] OJ L164/44); European Parliament and Council Directive 2004/50/EC amending Council Directive 96/48/EC on the interoperability of the trans-European high-speed rail system and Directive 2001/16/EC of the European Parliament and of the Council on the interoperability of the trans-European conventional rail system [2004] OJ L164/114; and the Agency Regulation (European Parliament and Council Regulation 881/2004/EC establishing a European Railway Agency [2004] OJ L164/1); *d. Third package:* European Parliament and Council Directive 2007/58/EC amending Council Directive 91/440/EEC on the development of the Community's railways and Directive 2001/14/EC on the allocation of railway infrastructure capacity and the levying of charges for the use of railway infrastructure [2007] OJ L315/44; European Parliament and Council Directive 2007/59/EC on the certification of train drivers operating locomotives and trains on the railway system in the Community [2007] OJ L315/51; European Parliament and Council Regulation 1370/2007/EC on public passenger transport services by rail and by road and repealing Regulations 1191/69 and 1107/70 [2007] OJ L315/1; European Parliament and Council Regulation 1371/2007/EC on rail passengers'

ii. Fresh regulation

The second component of EU policy in network industries consists of the enactment of a new regulatory framework, aimed at establishing a level playing field between incumbents and new entrants. Regulation in this area, essentially grounded on a general (Article 114 and occasionally, Article 106(3) TFEU) or a specific legal basis (Article 91(1) TFEU for transport issues), pursues four objectives. *First*, the unbundling of activities reserved from competition is mandated, in order to secure cost transparency; unbundling may by limited to accounting, but may go as far as breaking down the incumbent undertaking into various entities. *Secondly*, access, interconnection, and 'must carry' obligations are organized; pricing and standard setting mechanisms may also be appropriate for this purpose. *Thirdly*, universal or public service obligations are defined and the means for their financing are determined. *Lastly*, independent regulatory authorities are established in order to oversee the operation of the newly created markets.

iii. Application of the competition rules

The third component of EU policy in network industries is the application of competition law rules, which is necessary to support the process of opening the market. Since the CJEU judgment in *Telefónica*,[136] it is clear that the Treaty competition rules apply to cases covered by sector-specific regulation and stand at a hierarchically higher level than the latter. Encouraged by this judgment, which has been confirmed ever since, the Commission has actively intervened to overrule national regulatory authorities that misapplied sector-specific legislation.[137] Moreover, the Court's judgment in *Altmark*,[138] a case entailing the application of

rights and obligations [2007] OJ L315/14; and the new Agency Regulation (European Parliament and Council Regulation 1335/2008/EC establishing a European Railway Agency [2008] OJ L354/51).

[136] Case C-79/00 *Telefónica de España SA v Administración General del Estado* [2001] ECR I-10057; in this case, the Court held that the Royal Decree transposing into Spanish law the 'interconnection/Open Network Provision (ONP)' Directive (European Parliament and Council Directive 97/33/EC on interconnection in Telecommunications with regard to ensuring universal service and interoperability through application of the principles of Open Network Provision (ONP) [1997] OJ L199/32) was legal, despite the fact that it exceeded the terms of the Directive. In fact, the Decree gave to the National Regulatory Authority (NRA) not only the right to encourage and support but also to *impose* on the incumbent the conclusion of interconnection agreements. Hence, it could be said that the Court found that, next to the specific ONP requirements stemming from the Directive, other more general competition rules founded the right of intervention of the NRA.

[137] See eg Commission Decision 2003/707/EC *Deutsche Telekom AG* [2003] OJ L263/9; here, the Commission held that the high access fees charged by the incumbent monopolist to its competitors for access to its local telecommunications network constituted a violation of Art 106 TFEU; this, despite the fact that the access tariffs had been approved by the NRA as being compatible with the applicable ONP Directives; appeals against this decision have been dismissed both by the CFI and by the Court, see Case C-280/08 P *Deutsche Telekom AG v European Commission, Vodafone D2 GmbH, formerly Vodafone AG & Co. KG, formerly Arcor AG & Co. KG and Others* [2010] ECR nyr.

[138] Case C-280/00 *Altmark* [2003] ECR I-7747; for this case see among many Merola, M., and Medina, C., 'De l'arrêt Ferring à l'arrêt Altmark: continuité ou revirement dans l'approche du financement des services publics' (2003) 39 *CDE* 639–94; see also the developments in ch 2.

Regulation 1191/69 for public service[139] in transport, shows that Treaty rules on state aids are also applicable to cases where sector-specific regulation is involved.

Inspired by this development, many authors put forward the idea that progressively, as competition consolidates in the network industries, competition law rules should become fully operational and sector-specific regulation should cease to exist.[140] Proponents of such a unified regime make three sets of arguments, of a temporal, substantive, and procedural nature. From a *temporal* perspective, they submit that after a while the duality is not necessary and, thus, could not be justified in view of the 'better governance' principles. From a *substantive* point of view, they maintain that a unified regime: a. would avoid diverging rules and rulings, which could be adopted by different authorities (sector-specific national regulatory authorities (NRAs) and national competition authorities (NCAs)) at the national level,[141] b. would do away with diverging sector-specific rules in the different member states and secure a unified application of competition rules, thus creating a truly internal market, c. would limit the risk of capture to which sector-specific authorities are exposed, to the extent that, in accomplishing their tasks, they rely heavily on expertise (and experts) from the market players and that, eventually, their self-interest runs parallel to that of the regulatees. From a *procedural* point of view, the unified regime possesses two, interconnected advantages: competence conflicts between national authorities would be eliminated, while the risk of divergent solutions depending on the procedure followed would be diminished.

The counter-arguments to this idea are not less convincing.[142] From a *temporal* point of view, the opponents of a unified regime point out that, with the exception of telecommunications, all other sectors will not be truly competitive any time soon. From a *substantive* point of view, the following counter-arguments can be put forward: a. sector-specific authorities have specific market knowledge that the NCAs and the courts lack; b. the former intervene *ex ante*, in a structural manner, which may be much more efficient than the *ex post* behavioural control exercised by virtue of the general competition rules (this counter-argument does not take into account the *ex ante* merger control); c. the safeguard of public service obligations is better protected by NRAs than by NCAs; and d. multiple overseers (NRAs, NCAs, courts) reduce the scope for capture. Finally, from a *procedural* point of view the separation of tasks is regarded as creating a more focused remit for each overseer.[143]

---

[139] Council Regulation 1191/69/EEC on action by Member States concerning the obligations inherent in the concept of a public service in transport by rail, road and inland waterway [1959] OJ L156/1; OJ Spec Ed Series I Chapter 1969(I) p 276.

[140] See recently Galanis, T., *Droit de la concurrence et régulation sectorielle: l'exemple des communications électroniques* (Bruxelles/Athènes: Sakkoulas/Bruylant, 2010); also Madiega, T., *Interaction between EC Competition Law and Sector-Specific Regulation in Converging Electronic Communications Markets* EUI PhD Thesis (Florence, 2007).

[141] For the NRAs, see the discussion under subheading A(4)b(iv).

[142] For an extensive discussion of the arguments both for and against the abolition of sector-specific legislation, see the works cited in n 140.

[143] European Commission, DG for economic and financial affairs, *European Economy: Liberalization of Network Industries: Economic Implications and Main Policy Issues* (Brussels, 1999), at 131.

iv. Institution of sector-specific authorities

The fourth characteristic of EU policy in network industries is the institution of sector-specific authorities to oversee the smooth functioning of the markets.[144] These authorities are instituted either at the national level, known as national regulatory authorities (NRAs), or at the EU level, taking the form of an Agency.[145] Other hybrid solutions are also followed.

NRAs

All sector-specific Directives foresee the institution of some entity enjoying independence both from central government and from the incumbents, to oversee the market. Although this entity need not have legal personality of its own and can take the form of a firmly separate office within a ministry, most member states have opted for the institution of autonomous bodies, characterized by some degree of independence. These NRAs perform a quadruple role. *First,* they act as sector-specific regulators. Under this hat, they set up rules concerning access, tariffs, selection criteria, etc; they also issue authorizations to market participants and other individual decisions. *Secondly,* NRAs perform a quasi-judicial role, providing mediation or other means of extra-judicial conflict resolution. *Thirdly,* they have a control function, in parallel with central state authorities and with the NCA of each member state. *Fourthly,* they play a significant role in exchanging information, by taking part in transnational networks of high-ranking officials.[146]

EU Agencies

Given the flexibility allowed by the sector-specific Directives to member states and their NRAs, the level of coordination achieved between NRAs may not be sufficient, especially in areas where safety and security are paramount. This explains the creation of Agencies. The European Maritime Safety Agency (EMSA) was created in an attempt to prevent environmental disasters at sea, following the wrecks of the *Erika* (1999) and the *Prestige* (2002);[147] the establishment of the European Aviation Safety Agency (EASA) ensures cooperation between national civil aviation admin-

---

[144] Some of these governance methods, briefly presented here in relation to network-bound industries, are further discussed in ch 8.

[145] Geradin, D., and Petit, N., 'The Development of Agencies at EU and National Levels: Conceptual Analysis and Proposals for Reform' (2004) 23 *YEL* 137–97; also Stoffaës, C., 'Towards European Regulation of Network Industries' Discussion Group Report, Initiative for Public Utility Services in Europe, Paris, 2003, also available at <http://www.archives.diplomatie.gouv.fr/europe/pdf/rapportstoffaes.gb.pdf> (last accessed on 11 November 2011).

[146] On this aspect and, more generally on the 'reflexive' function of NRAs, see Brousseau, E., and Glachant, J.M., 'The Institutional Economics of Reflexive Governance in the Area of Utility Regulation', EUI/RSCAS Working Paper No. 2010/90, available at <http://cadmus.eui.eu/bitstream/handle/1814/15168/RSCAS_2010_90.pdf?sequence=1> (last accessed on 11 November 2011).

[147] European Parliament and Council Regulation 1406/02/EC establishing a European Maritime Safety Agency [2002] OJ L208/1, amended by the European Parliament and Council Regulation 1644/2003/EC [2003] OJ L 245/10, European Parliament and Council Regulation 724/04/EC [2004] OJ L129/1, and European Parliament and Council Regulation 1891/06/EC [2006] OJ L 394/1. The Agency was established in December 2002.

istrations;[148] the European Rail Safety Agency (ERSA) was set up in the framework of the second railway package and is responsible for the harmonization of rail safety standards and the interoperability of the rail network and rolling stock.[149]

A step further in the creation of a single regulatory framework in the network industries field is signalled by the recent Regulation for the Body of European Regulators for Electronic Communications (BEREC).[150] This Agency replaces the European Regulators Group (ERG) and shall also take over competences from the European Network Security Agency (ENISA), whose mandate comes to an end in March 2012;[151] it shall 'complement at the European level the regulatory tasks performed at the national level by the regulatory authorities' and will have limited decision-making powers.[152]

Other forms of cooperation

There are at least three other forms of cooperation that take place in the network industries.[153]

First, operators in each industry often come together through the establishment of associations. This can happen either spontaneously, or on request of the Commission (or one of the forums and groups set up by it). These associations may be 'integrated' in the sense that they bring together all the participants in a given market (for instance, the Madrid and Florence forums in the field of energy) or 'horizontal' in the sense that they bring together operators active at a given level of the economic process (such as the Gas Transmission Europe (GTE) and the European Transmission System Operators (ETSO) associations).[154] These forums are useful for purposes of exchange of information and coordination, but the lack of any institutional backbone accounts for their limited capacity to deal with controversial issues. This leads to their either remaining idle or being transformed into

---

[148] European Parliament and Council Regulation 1592/02/EC on common rules in the field of civil aviation and establishing a European Aviation Safety Agency [2002] OJ L240/1, amended several times and replaced by European Parliament and Council Regulation 216/08/EC on common rules in the field of civil aviation and establishing a European Aviation Safety Agency [2008] OJ L79/1, itself amended by Regulation 690/2009/EC [2009] OJ L199/6; the Agency became operational in September 2003.

[149] European Parliament and Council 2004/49/EC on safety on the Community's railways (Railway Safety Directive) [2004] OJ L164/44), amended by Directive 2008/57/EC [2008] OJ L191/1 and Directive 2008/110/EC [2008] OJ L345/62.

[150] European Parliament and Council Regulation 1211/2009/EC establishing the Body of European Regulators for Electronic Communications (BEREC) and the Office [2009] OJ L337/1.

[151] ENISA was set up by European Parliament and Council Regulation 460/2004/EC establishing the European Network and Information Security Agency [2004] OJ L77/1 and its mandate has been extended once by European Parliament and Council Regulation 1007/08/EC [2008] OJ L293/1.

[152] Regulation Proposal COM (2007) 699 final, 'on establishing the European electronic communications market authority'.

[153] Stoffaës, C., 2003, n 124, at 14–18.

[154] GTE was set up in 2000, at the request of the Commission and the Madrid Forum. This organization brings together natural gas transmission network operators, including those that are part of integrated gas groups; ETSO was also set up in 2000, at the request of the Commission and the Florence Forum. The members of this body are high-voltage electricity transporters and include the transmission entities in integrated electricity groups.

more institutionalized forms of cooperation: the Florence Forum was turned into the Electricity Committee by Regulation 1228/2003.[155]

A *second* form of cooperation is among national regulators, through the creation of associations and/or networks. These may be informal, in the sense that their creation was 'spontaneous', such as the Council of European Energy Regulators (CEER, set up by virtue of a Memorandum of Understanding signed by several national regulatory authorities), the European Committee for Postal Regulation (CERP), and the Telecommunications Independent Regulators Group (IRG). Associations of national regulators can also be formally created by the Commission or by Community legislation. For example, Commission Decision 2002/627 established the European Regulators Group (ERG, now replaced by the BEREC) for electronic communications, to work alongside the IRG previously established by the operators.[156] Similarly, in the energy field, Commission Decision 2003/796 established the European Regulatory Group for Electricity and Gas (ERGEG), to work alongside the CEER.[157] The ERGEG became the Agency for the Cooperation of Energy Regulators (ACER) through Regulation 713/2009.[158] The latter brings together representatives from the national regulators, but also has its own administrative board and personnel. Its tasks will not be limited to coordinating the national regulatory frameworks of the member states, but also to complete them[159] through the issuance of individual regulatory decisions.[160] More recently still, the European Regulators Group for Postal Services was established through a Commission's Decision, to take over and expand the tasks of the CERP.[161]

Thirdly, there are groups initiated and chaired by the Commission, according to the various comitology settings. Many Directives provide for the creation of specialized committees to assist the Commission in specific areas, such as in the electricity and gas sectors.[162] One of the best-known committees is the Communications Committee (CoCom), established by a Framework Directive.[163]

---

[155] European Parliament and Council Regulation 1228/2003/EC on conditions for access to the network of cross-border exchanges in electricity [2003] OJ L176/1, Art 13.

[156] Commission Decision 2002/627/EC establishing the European Regulators Group for Electronic Communications Networks and Services [2002] OJ L200/38.

[157] Commission Decision 2003/796/EC on establishing the European Regulators Group for Electricity and Gas [2003] OJ L296/34; actually, the CEER prepares the EGREG's meetings and the two together are called 'the European Energy Regulators'; see their common website at <http://www.energy-regulators.eu/portal/page/portal/EER_HOME> (last accessed on 11 November 2011).

[158] European Parliament and Council Regulation 713/2009/EC establishing an Agency for the Cooperation of Energy Regulators [2009] OJ L211/1.

[159] Ibid, Preamble Rec 6.

[160] Ibid, Preamble Rec 3.

[161] Commission Decision 2010/C 217/07 establishing the European Regulators Group for Postal Services [2010] OJ C217/7.

[162] In the electricity sector, see Art 13 of Regulation 1228/2003, n 155, now repealed by the European Parliament and Council Regulation 714/2009/EC on conditions for access to the network for cross-border exchanges in electricity [2009] OJ L211/15, which also provides for the creation of a committee in Art 23; in the gas sector, see Art 30 of European Parliament and Council Directive 2003/55/EC concerning common rules for the internal market in natural gas [2003] OJ L176/57, now repealed by European Parliament and Council Directive 2009/73/EC concerning common rules for the internal market in natural gas [2009] OJ L221/94, which also provides for a committee, in Art 51.

[163] The COCOM was established by Arts 22 and Preamble Rec 34 of the Framework Directive (European Parliament and Council Directive 2002/21/EC on a common regulatory framework for

v. Atypical forms of regulation

The final characteristic of the network industries, alongside the emergence of new 'atypical' actors, is the use of 'atypical' forms of regulation. 'This embraced closer monitoring by the Commission through scoreboards, utilising traditional enforcement techniques under Article [Article 258 TFEU], but relying also upon peer pressure and the use of individual litigation to ensure that the Member States met their duties.'[164] In addition, 'a number of regulatory techniques which tend towards the soft side of regulation'[165] have been employed: the instruments of Commission Communications,[166] Green and White papers, notices, press releases, non-papers, and speeches of the Commissioners have all been used abundantly. 'The new forms of economic governance have had the effect of steering the Member States, as well as the various non-state actors involved, towards ideas of convergence on economic policies, conventionally seen as unsuitable, unthinkable and untouchable by Community law making processes.'[167]

5. IT Directives: internal market clauses

Technically connected to the EU policies on network industries, but distinct from them from a regulatory point of view, are the so-called 'information technology (IT) Directives'.

The oldest of these texts is the 'Television Without Frontiers' (TVWF) Directive, adopted as far back as in 1989 and amended in 1997.[168] It was further amended to become the Audiovisual Media Services (AVMS) Directive.[169] The following factors made the reforms necessary: a. technological developments and the 'convergence' of technologies affecting not only the technical means employed

---

electronic communications networks and services [2002] OJ L108/33). It replaced the ONP Committee and the Licensing Committee which were instituted under the 1998 regulatory package for telecommunications. The COCOM assists the Commission in carrying out its executive powers under the new regulatory framework and the European Parliament and Council Regulation 733/2002/EC on the implementation of the.eu Top Level Domain [2002] OJ L113/1. COCOM's first meeting was held on 10 July 2002. In practice, there are at least two meetings every quarter; see <http://ec.europa.eu/information_society/policy/ecomm/committees_working_groups/index_en.htm#cocom> (last accessed on 11 November 2011).

[164] Szyszczak, E., 'Competition and the liberalised market' in Shuibhne, N.N. (ed), *Regulating the Internal Market* (Cheltenham/Northampton: Edward Elgar Publishing, 2006) 87–104, at 89.

[165] Ibid, at 92.

[166] Especially in the field of telecommunications, the Notice on the application of the competition rules to access agreements in the telecommunications sector ([1998] OJ C265/2) has been of extreme importance for market players.

[167] Szyszczak, E., 2006, n 164.

[168] Council Directive 89/552/EEC on the coordination of certain provisions laid down by law, regulation or administrative action in Member States concerning the pursuit of television broadcasting activities [1989] OJ L298/23; modified by the European Parliament and Council Directive 97/36/EC [1997] OJ L202/60.

[169] European Parliament and Council Directive 2007/65/EC amending Council Directive 89/552/EEC on the coordination of certain provisions laid down by law, regulation or administrative action in Member States concerning the pursuit of television broadcasting activities [2007] OJ L332/27.

but also the very regulatory objective of the TVWF Directive,[170] b. the need to adopt more flexible advertising rules, and c. the need to strengthen member states' defence against circumvention practices.[171]

Following a lengthy consultation period initiated in 2003,[172] the Commission came up with a draft Directive in 2005,[173] which was finally adopted two years later. The AVMS Directive is interesting (and controversial) in many ways. From a regulatory point of view, and without even touching on the substance of the Directive,[174] there are three innovations that merit attention. *First*, the home country control principle—a victim of its own success—is restricted in order to avoid abuse: nationality rules for broadcasters become stricter and technology tuned,[175] while broadcasters may have to comply with rules of 'general public interest' in a 'host' state, whenever their services are specifically targeted at this 'host' state.[176] *Secondly*, the Directive explicitly applies the principle of 'graduated' regulation, in the sense 'that different levels of regulation, and levels of detail in regulatory requirements will apply to different electronic media'.[177] A neat distinction is drawn between 'linear' (prescheduled) and 'non-linear' (interactive) broadcasts, the former being subject to full force regulation, the latter only to minimum rules concerning among other topics, the protection of minors, the prohibition of

---

[170] Such convergence having implications both for broadcasters and for regulators, see Geach, N., 'Converging Regulation for Convergent Media: An Overview of the AVMS' (2008) 1 *J of Information L and Technology* 1–19, also available at <http://go.warwick.ac.uk/jilt/2008_1/geach> (last accessed on 11 November 2011); see also Valcke, P., Stevens, D., Lievens, E., and Werkers, E., 'AVMS in the EU, Next Generation Approach or Old Wine in New Barrels?' (2008) 71 *Communications and Strategies* 103–18; Valcke, P., and Stevens, D., 'Graduated Regulation of "Regulatable" Content and the European AVMS Directive: One Small Step for the Industry and One Giant Leap for the Legislator?' (2007) 24 *Telematics and Informatics* 285–302, also available at <http://law.kuleuven.be/icri/publications/948ti2007.pdf> (last accessed on 11 November 2011).

[171] See Dehousse, F., and Van Hecke, K., 'Towards an Audiovisual Media Directive: An Analysis of the Commission Proposal' (2005) 58 *Studia Diplomatica* 139–51, also available at <http://aei.pitt.edu/9087/01/060606-AudioVis.directive.pdf> (last accessed on 11 November 2011).

[172] Report COM (2002) 778 final, 'on the application of Directive 89/552/EEC "Television without Frontiers"'; the Commission's intention to revise the TVWF Directive (n 168) was further substantiated later in the same year with Communication COM (2003) 784 final, 'on the future of European regulatory audiovisual policy'.

[173] Directive Proposal COM (2005) 646 final, 'amending Council Directive 89/552/EEC on the coordination of certain provisions laid down by law, regulation or administrative action in Member States concerning the pursuit of television broadcasting activities'.

[174] For which see the discussion and bibliography in ch 5; see also Nenova, M.B., 'The New AVMS Directive: Television *Without* Frontiers, Television *Without* Cultural Diversity' (2007) 44 *CML Rev* 1689–725.

[175] AVMS Directive (consolidated version), n 168, Art 2.

[176] Ibid, Art 3.

[177] See Valcke, P., and Stevens, D., 2007, n 170, at 291. EU legislation providing for divergent levels of regulation is not a novelty; see de Witte, B., Hanf, D., and Vos, E. *The Many Faces of Differentiation in EU Law* (Antwerp/Oxford/New York: Intersentia, 2001); also de Búrca, G., 'Differentiation within the core: the case of the Internal Market' in de Búrca, G., and Scott, J. (eds), *Constitutional Change in the EU: From Uniformity to Flexibility?* (Oxford/Portland: Hart Publishing, 2000) 133–72. Differentiation has also been constitutionalized through the adoption of the second and third Pillar with the Maastricht Treaty, but has been formally abandoned with the Lisbon Treaty. Usually, however, differentiation occurs in a 'vertical' manner, between different member states. It is less common to have such important regulatory gaps 'horizontally', ie between different matters regulated by the same regulatory instrument.

hate speech, and of surreptitious advertising. *Thirdly*, this is the first Directive, to the author's knowledge, in which the Commission recommends the use of co- and self-regulation as means for its transposition into national law.[178]

Alongside this 'media' Directive are the two e-Directives, adopted during the dot-com bubble era, with the aim of encouraging the emergence of pan-European providers of electronic services (e-services) that would be in a position to compete on the international scene. The first text concerns the provision of electronic signatures,[179] while the second is more concerned with content and e-commerce in general.[180]

E-services, in contrast to the vast majority of mainstream services, do not require physical contact between the provider and the recipient, being by nature provided at a distance. Typically, they are provided without any movement of physical persons, through the use of networks.[181] This unique characteristic of e-services provision has two consequences for the way they should be regulated. For one thing, since service providers need not move to, or be established, even momentarily, in the state where the service is provided, they enjoy greater flexibility in choosing the country of their establishment. This, in turn, makes it easier for them to practice regulatory arbitrage and, thus, puts member states under strong regulatory competition.[182] Thus, the adoption of harmonized minimal regulatory standards is necessary to avoid downward spirals generated by such competition. On the other hand, since service providers do not, in principle, physically move in any other member state, it seems logical that they be subject exclusively to their home state regulation and control. These two characteristics have been incorporated in the texts mentioned above, and have resulted in the so called 'internal market clauses' (IMCs).

IMCs take the form of a quid pro quo: home state authorities make sure that service providers established in their territory satisfy the minimum coordinated rules and, in return, host state authorities cannot exclude such 'compliant' service

---

[178] AVMS Directive (consolidated version), n 168, Art 3(7). See also Preamble Rec 36, reading as follows: 'Without prejudice to Member States' formal obligations regarding transposition, this Directive encourages the use of co-regulation and self-regulation. This should neither oblige Member States to set up co- and/or self-regulatory regimes nor disrupt or jeopardise current co- or self-regulatory initiatives which are already in place within Member States and which are working effectively; the margin left to member states themselves to define and pick the form of co- or self-regulation is remarkable'; on this very issue, see Prosser, T., 'Self-regulation, Co-regulation and the AVMS Directive' (2008) 31 *J of Consumer Policy* 99–113, at 106 *et seq*; see also Craufurd-Smit, R., 'EC media regulation in a converging environment' in Shuibhne, N.N. (ed), *Regulating the Internal Market* (Cheltenham/Northampton: Edward Edgar Publishing, 2006) 105–43, at 127–30.

[179] E-signature Directive (European Parliament and Council Directive 1999/93/EC on a Community framework for electronic signatures [2000] OJ L13/12).

[180] E-commerce Directive (European Parliament and Council Directive 2000/31/EC on certain legal aspects of information society services, in particular electronic commerce, in the Internal Market [2000] OJ L178/1).

[181] Electronic services correspond perfectly to GATS mode 1. They also fall under Art 56 TFEU: although this was never seriously disputed, the Court only had the occasion to recognize that expressly, in the cases concerning the Dutch TV (Case C-288/89 *Stichting Collectieve Antennevoorziening Gouda v Commissariaat voor de Media* [1991] ECR I-4007 and Case C-353/89 *Commission v Netherlands (tv programmes)* [1991] ECR I-4069).

[182] For regulatory competition in the field of services, see the discussion in ch 1.

providers, for any reason falling within the coordinated field. IMCs are based on strict 'nationality' requirements intended to restrict arbitrary or otherwise abusive 'regulatory shopping' by service providers; the trend is for such requirements to become increasingly strict, as can be witnessed in the AVMS Directive.[183] The clauses also provide for minimal harmonization, essentially linked to the general interest. In the AVMS Directive, especially in relation to 'linear' services, harmonization goes beyond the general interest *stricto sensu*, but still qualifies as minimal in the sense that member states are free to impose stricter rules on broadcasters established in their territories. Alongside general interest objectives, IMCs provide for cases of general exclusions and specific derogations, subject to the monitoring of the Commission.

From a regulatory point of view, the IMCs follow the logic of 'home country control' and function very much in the way of a 'passport', like those granted to undertakings in the financial sector.[184] Thus, it has been observed that 'the purpose of the IMC is twofold: an extended application of the mutual recognition principle and the application of the law of the country of origin'.[185] However, it is submitted here that the IMC is different from the 'passport' system, in at least three respects.[186] For one thing, home country control is a logical—almost undisputed—choice in the case of media and e-undertakings who never move away from home, while this choice is not as patently obvious in relation to financial institutions. *Secondly*, the European 'passport' equates to an authorization, valid throughout the EU, delivered by the competent home authorities, who have made sure that the coordinated conditions are met. The e-Directives, in contrast, specifically state that the relevant activities should be open, with no prior authorization system.[187] This, in turn, raises the issue of the responsibility borne by the home state: it may not authorize in advance but should, nevertheless, make sure that service providers established on its territory comply with the relevant provisions of the Directives.[188] *Thirdly*, in contrast to 'passports' which are delivered following partial or, recently, exhaustive[189] harmonization, the IMC is only based on minimal harmonization linked to the protection of the general interest. It relies, therefore, to a greater extent on home state legislation and on trust of home authorities. By the same token, it

---

[183] European Parliament and Council Directive 2010/13/EU on the coordination of certain provisions laid down by law, regulation or administrative action in Member States concerning the provision of audiovisual media services (Audiovisual Media Services Directive) [2010] OJ L95/1.

[184] See the analysis under subheading A(2).

[185] Van Huffel, M., 'The legal framework for financial services and the Internet' in Shuibhne, N.N. (ed), *Regulating the Internal Market* (Cheltenham/Northampton: Edward Edgar Publishing, 2006) 144–80, at 157.

[186] Van Huffel (ibid) observes that the rights stemming from the e-commerce Directive (n 180) may serve as a 'second chance passport' and open the way for the provision of online financial services to providers who do not qualify for a 'real passport' under the relevant Directives.

[187] E-commerce Directive (n 180) Art 4(1); E-signature Directive (n 179) Art 3(1); the AVMS Directive (n 168) does not mention anything about the need of a prior authorization and leaves the choice to the member states.

[188] On this issue, see van Huffel, M., n 185, at 151.

[189] This is the case with the MiFiD (European Parliament and Council Directive 2004/39EC on markets in financial instruments [2004] OJ L145/1) and subsequent legislation. See also the discussion in subsection A(2).

corresponds to a regulatory technique whereby 'competition [between legal orders] works as a substitute for harmonisation'.[190]

6. The Services Directive: regulatory reform and administrative cooperation

Undisputedly, the single most important attempt to regulate the free provision of services in the EU is the 'Services Directive' (SD).[191] It is arguably also the text of secondary legislation that has aroused the strongest feelings among European citizens, let alone the stakeholders directly affected. In the views of some, it is also the main cause of the defeat of the EU Constitutional Treaty in referenda in France and the Netherlands.[192]

The SD first appeared as a highly ambitious draft,[193] aimed at a comprehensive and horizontal application of the home country control principle, revamped as the 'country of origin principle' (CoOP).

The CoOP would not only cover the authorization and basic supervision of undertakings—as in the 'passport' system—but also the conditions of their every-day operation. Furthermore, dispute resolution would be governed by the rules of the country of origin of the service provider. The leap forward would not be merely quantitative, but essentially qualitative: under the CoOP, service providers com-plying with the regulatory requirements of one member state would no longer need to worry about the regulations and procedural requirements of all other member states. All service providers, and especially SMEs, would benefit from facilitated entry into new markets, as information-gathering and compliance costs would be drastically reduced.[194]

The second way in which the CoOP would be different from the pre-existing home country control would be its horizontal scope—covering all service activities, with some important exceptions.

The draft was placed at the top of the Commission's legislative agenda and was endorsed by the Council at its first reading. However, trade unions strongly objected, the media entered the debate and diffused streams of—occasionally deliberately but mostly ignorantly—false information, which, in turn, provoked public disquiet. The confusion between the 'polish plumber', the SD, the then

[190] Van Huffel, M., 2006, n 185, at 176.

[191] European Parliament and Council Directive 2006/123/EC on services in the internal market [2006] OJ L376/36. Crespy, A., 'When "Bolkestein" Is Trapped by the French Anti-Liberal Dis-course: A Discursive-Institutionalist Account of Preference Formation in the Realm of European Union Multi-level Politics' (2010) 17 *J Europ Public Policy* 1253–70.

[192] See eg Milner, H., 'YES to the Europe I Want; NO to This One; Some Reflections on France's Rejection of the EU Constitution' (2006) 39 *Political Sciences and Politics* 257–60; Ivaldi, G., 'Beyond France's 2005 Referendum on the European Constitutional Treaty: Second-Order Model, Anti-Establishment Attitudes and the End of the Alternative European Utopia' (2006) 29 *WEP* 47–69, also available at <http://hal-unice.archives-ouvertes.fr/docs/00/09/02/33/PDF/Ivaldi_WEP2006.pdf> (last accessed on 11 November 2011).

[193] Directive Proposal COM (2004) 2 final, 'on services in the internal market'.

[194] This perspective was particularly appealing to the UK. See House of Lords, Completing the Internal Market in Services, Report with Evidence, 6th Report of Session 2005–6, 63–74.

Commissioner Bolkestein, Frankenstein, other mythical creatures, and the failed EU Constitutional Treaty is still present in the minds of many Europeans.[195] The European Parliament could not remain unmoved by the strong passions expressed; it, therefore, came forward with over 300 amendments, most of which were incorporated.[196] The final text of the Directive is a retreat from the 2004 draft.[197] The single most important amendment is the abandonment of the CoOP in favour of the imprecise 'free provision of services' principle.[198] The next most important is the significant increase in the number of activities excluded from the scope of the Directive.

The precise content of the Directive, as it now stands, and the way in which it will affect the free provision of services within the EU has been extensively debated.[199] What most commentators agree on, however, is that the 'free provision of services principle', enshrined in Article 16 of the SD, will hardly have any practical effect, other than to give rise to fresh litigation.[200] Many authors also question the 'horizontal' character of the final Directive, after all the exclusions, exceptions, and derogations it suffered.[201]

---

[195] Political scientists are still analysing the reasons for the rejection of the Constitutional Treaty and deciphering the role played by the SD; see n 192.

[196] On this story and the reasons behind it, see de Witte, B., 'Setting the Scene: How Did Services Get to Bolkestein and Why?' EUI Law Working Paper No. 2007/70, also available at <http://cadmus.iue.it/dspace/bitstream/1814/6929/1/LAW_2007_20.pdf> (last accessed on 11 November 2011); also Flower, J., 'Negotiating European Legislation: The Services Directive' (2006–7) 9 *CYEL* 217–38.

[197] Directive 2006/123 (n 191); for an evaluation of the legislative outcome see Chang, M., Hanf, D., and Pelkmans, J., 'The Services Directive: Trojan Horse or White Knight?' (2010) 32 *European Integration* 97–114; Klamert, M., 'Of Empty Glasses and Double Burdens: Approaches to Regulating the Services Market *à propos* the Implementation of the Services Directive' (2010) 37 *LIEI* 111–32; Kostoris Padoa-Schioppa, F., 'Dominant Losers: A Comment on the Services Directive from an Economic Perspective' (2007) 14 *JEPP* 735–42.

[198] Directive 2006/123 (n 191), Art 16.

[199] The various aspects of the Directive 2006/123 (n 191) have been analysed in detail by several authors; two edited volumes in English, one predating and one post-dating the adoption of the Directive, bring together some of the most important ones: see Blanpain, R. (ed), *Freedom of Services in the EU, Labour and Social Security Law: The Bolkestein Initiative* (The Hague: Kluwer Law International, 2006) and Neergaard, U., Nielsen, R., and Roseberry, L. (eds), *The Services Directive, Consequences for the Welfare State and the European Social Model* (Copenhagen: DJOF, 2008). See also, for an *ex post* assessment of the text finally adopted, Barnard, C., 'Unravelling the Services Directive' (2008) 45 *CML Rev* 323–94; Griller, S., 'The new services directive of the EU: hopes and expectations from the angle of (further) completion of the internal market' in Koeck, H.F. and Karollus, M.M. (eds), *The New Services Directive of the EU, FIDE XXIII Congress 2008, Volume III* (Vienna: Congress Publications, 2008); Hatzopoulos, V., 'Legal aspects in establishing the internal market for services', in Pelkmans, J., Hanf, D., and Chang, M. (eds), *The EU Internal Market in Comparative Perspective, Economic, Political and Legal Analyses* (Brussels: Peter Lang, 2008) 139–89; Hatzopoulos, V., 'Assessing the Services Directive, 2006/123/EC' (2008) 10 *CYEL* 215–61; and more in detail, Hatzopoulos, V., 'Que reste-t-il de la directive sur les services?' (2008) 44 *CDE* 299–355; see also, for the 'official version' of the way in which the Directive should be implemented, Commission of the EC, *Handbook for the Application of the Services Directive* (Brussels, 2007).

[200] See Barnard, C., 2008, n 199 and Griller, S., 2008, n 199, Do, U., 'La proposition de directive relative aux services dans le marché intérieur . . . définitivement hors service?' (2006) *Revue de Droit de l'Union Européenne* 1–20; Pellegrino, P., 'Directive sur les services dans le marché intérieur, Un accouchement dans la douleur' (2007) *Revue du Marché Unique Européen* 14–21.

[201] Manin, P., '"Conclusions" sur la Directive 2006/123/CE' (2007) 17:6 *Europe* 29–30, at 29.

Despite all this, after the dust has settled, and once it has been established that the Directive is clearly not the important catch-all instrument which would definitively liberalize services within the EU, it becomes apparent that, nonetheless, the SD does have some added value. Its value is twofold, both substantive and procedural.[202]

a. Substance

From a substantive point of view, the Directive is likely to help service provision in three ways.

i. Clear rules on the establishment of service providers

Chapter III of the Directive (Articles 9–15) codifies the Court's case law in relation to the establishment of service providers. Such codification is very welcome for the following reasons. *First*, the codification of the case law in the text of a Directive— and its subsequent transcription into national law—does away with the casuistic character of the principles developed by the Court and brings them closer to both service providers and to member states' administrations. *Secondly*, the principles shift from being *ex post* remedies for service providers into *ex ante* obligations for national administrations. *Thirdly*, the Directive goes beyond the mere expression of principles and offers practical details about their application, something the Court may only rarely do. *Fourthly*, the discretionary powers of the member states are circumscribed, as the states are subject to obligations to report, both to one another and to the Commission, the restrictions they maintain (Article 39 SD).

ii. Rules in favour of service recipients

The Directive innovates by introducing rules benefiting service recipients. In Section 2 of Chapter IV, consisting of three articles, the Directive prohibits restrictions imposed by the home state (Article 19), condemns discriminatory measures that the host state could adopt (Article 20), and offers assistance for services recipients (Article 21). Such rights are available in relation to all the services covered by the Directive, even if they are excluded from the 'free provision of services' (Article 16 of the Directive), notably in relation to SGEIs.

iii. Limited harmonization

The Directive contains several potentially harmonizing rules, which represent three different modes of harmonization: de jure, de facto, and self-induced. *De jure* harmonization is advanced, in a peripheral and marginal manner by Chapter V of the SD, entitled 'Quality of services'. This part consists of six long Articles, and provides for common measures, essentially aimed at compensating for the informa-

---

[202] Indeed, it has been calculated that the full implementation of the SD, as it now stands, could increase trade in commercial services by 45 per cent and Foreign Direct Investment (FDI) by 25 per cent, bringing an increase of between 0.5 per cent and 1.5 per cent increase in GDP. See Communication COM (2010) 2020 final, 'Europe 2020: A Strategy for Smart, Sustainable and Inclusive Growth', at 20).

tion asymmetries which often exist in services markets. *De facto* harmonization, more importantly, is achieved through Chapter II of the SD, entitled 'administrative simplification'. This part harmonizes formalities, documents, and procedures preparatory to the exercise of service activities. Single contact points shall be established (Article 6), harmonized forms and documents may be used (Article 5 (2)), and predetermined information shall be at the disposition of service providers (Article 7). Thirdly, *self-induced* harmonization is promoted not only through the use of voluntary quality policies, placing emphasis on certification, evaluation, labels, and quality charters (Article 26), but also through the promotion of European codes of conduct (Article 37).

b. Procedure

Contrary to the SD's poor substantive content, its procedural arrangements are both innovative and powerful. The Directive is impregnated with modern methods of governance and embodies a new drafting style directly inspired by the Commission's Report on Better Lawmaking and the European Governance White Paper.[203] The SD's procedural arrangements are essentially orientated towards achieving administrative simplification at member state level and enhancing—if not imposing—administrative cooperation between national authorities.[204] These two objectives are examined in turn below.

i. Administrative simplification at the national level
Administrative simplification is one of the SD's main objectives. In this respect, the techniques followed by the SD are quite original for a text of *hard* law—but already well established as a means of fostering *soft* cooperation among states.

For some time now, and quite intensively since the launch of the Lisbon Agenda in 2000, the Commission has been working on the issue of administrative simplification. Building on the experience acquired by the OECD in this field,[205] the Commission intended to promote the exchange of best practice and benchmarking, and it has also devised several indicators to measure the performance of national administrations. Up until now, however, all these efforts have remained largely 'esoteric' to the Commission and have only taken the form of working documents, internal reports, and recommendations.[206] Only in 2007 did

---

[203] Commission Report to the European Council COM (1997) 626 final; see also the Commission's webpage on this issue at <http://ec.europa.eu/governance/better_regulation/impact_en.htm> (last accessed on 11 November 2011); White Paper COM (2001) 428 final, 'European Governance'; for these initiatives and for 'better regulation' in general, see the developments in ch 9.

[204] There are also some important provisions aimed at the periodical modification of the Directive itself, following a process of reporting and consultation, for which see Hatzopoulos, V., 'Assessing the Services Directive, 2006/123/EC' (2008) 10 *CYEL* 215–61, at 260; for these procedures, see the analysis in subsection B(1)d(i).

[205] Several general reports, as well as national reports are available at <http://www.oecd.org/topic/ 0,3373,en_2649_37421_1_1_1_1_37421,00.html> (last accessed on 11 November 2011).

[206] The Commission pursues administrative simplification not only at the Member States level, but also concerning its own legislative acts and proposals: see Communication COM (2005) 535 final,

the Commission launch the 'CUT 25' Action Programme, aimed at reducing the national administrative burden by 25 per cent by the year 2012.[207] In the framework of this action plan, the Commission has proposed several legislative measures since January 2007.

Well before these texts were even proposed by the Commission, the SD was the first text of a horizontal nature to put forward binding rules on administrative simplification. Chapter II of the SD introduces three basic rules on the subject.

a. Article 5 requires member states to evaluate their requirements concerning access to, and exercise of, service activities. Should these prove not to be 'sufficiently simple', member states have to simplify them. The fact that the 'sufficiently simple' criterion is vague and that the responsibility for evaluating it falls to the very member state concerned means that Article 5 should be seen more as a political self-commitment rather than a legal norm.

b. Articles 6–8 form a coherent set of rules with the potential to revolutionize the establishment of service providers in other member states. Identified as a 'best practice' during the first phase of the 2000 Lisbon Strategy, 'one-stop shops' are made into a legal obligation. Hence, member states are to establish single points of contact, for service providers, with twofold responsibilities. *First*, these points should provide all the information foreseen in Article 7 of the Directive.[208] *Secondly*, and more importantly, they should accomplish, on behalf of service providers, all the necessary formalities and procedures granting access to the service activity concerned. This is a way around national bureaucracy that brings with it its own dynamics for substantive simplification: when a part of the national administration (the single point of contact) is responsible for coping with the formalities of all other administrative authorities, a strong incentive is given for an overall reduction in red tape. The creation of these single points of contact should considerably diminish the burden of establishment, both in terms of information collection and of setup fixed costs; SMEs are expected to be the main beneficiaries. The role of single points of contact is all the more important after the abandonment of the CoOP, since the 'free provision of services' principle allows the host member state to require compliance with its own requirements.[209]

'Implementing the Community Lisbon Programme: A Strategy for the Simplification of the Regulatory Environment', as well as the Report COM (2006) 690 final, 'on the strategy for the simplification of the regulatory environment'.

[207] Communication COM (2007) 23 final, 'Action Programme for Reducing Administrative Burdens in the European Union'.

[208] Such information concerns the procedures and requirements in order to access and exercise service activities, the contact details of the competent authorities, the means for accessing public registers and databases, the means of redress available and the contact details of the relevant professional associations or organisations.

[209] However, member states have no real incentive to offer their best services to providers from other member states, at considerable cost. Therefore, some monitoring system, either by the Commission or through peer-review, should secure the effective functioning of single points of contact.

c. The SD also makes use of the available technology and mentions that all information provided by the single points of contact should be available by electronic means at a distance and should be regularly updated (Article 7). What is more, all procedures and formalities that are necessary for the exercise of a service activity should be made available for completion online (Article 8).

ii. Administrative cooperation between Member State authorities

In contrast to Chapter II (on administrative simplification), the importance of Chapter VI on 'administrative cooperation' has clearly been reduced with the abandonment of the CoOP, since competence sharing and mutual help between home and host state authorities has now become less crucial. However, it would be wrong to dismiss altogether nine (out of 45) provisions of the SD. Hence, it is noteworthy that the creation of one or more 'liaison points' in every member state, responsible for the exchange of information between national authorities, will certainly help the application of the SD (Article 28). In addition, a 'European Network of Member States' authorities' has been created to run an alert mechanism, whenever it 'becomes aware of serious specific acts or circumstances relating to a service activity that could cause serious damage to the health or safety of persons or to the environment' (Article 32). The establishment of an electronic internal market information (IMI) exchange system (Article 34(1)) and several rules on the respective competences of the home and host State, complete the rules on cooperation.

From the analysis above, it becomes clear that the SD may not be chiefly concerned with direct services liberalization; instead, it seems primarily and decisively to affect the way in which member states' administrations operate. It is a—in fact the first—EU text of hard law aimed at regulatory reform at the member state level. The creation of liaison points combined with the establishment of the European Network that operates the alert mechanism will increase the flows of information exchanged. This, in turn, will allow detailed comparisons to take place and will put national authorities under pressure to revise unsatisfactory practices in their territory. This trend will be further reinforced by the obligation to screen for burdensome sets of requirements and by periodic reporting and peer-evaluation.

The detailed competence share between national authorities (Articles 28–31), combined with the broad duty of cooperation stemming directly from Article 4(3) TEU,[210] will put national administrative authorities under strain. An effort simply to work together with others will not be enough; instead, positive results in favour of the European citizen, both as a service provider and a recipient, will be required.

---

[210] See eg Case C-326/00 *Idryma Koinonikon Asfaliseon (IKA) v Vasileios oannidis* [2003] ECR I-1703, and for a thorough presentation of this case, Hatzopoulos, V., 'Annotation: Case C-326/00 *Ioannidis v IKA* [2003] ECR I-1703' (2003) 40 *CML Rev* 1251–68; also Case C-476/01 *Criminal proceedings against Felix Kapper* [2004] ECR I-5205 and Case C-215/03 *Salah Oulane v Minister voor Vreemdelingenzaken en Integratie* [2005] ECR I-1215; for this general trend in the Court's case law, see Hatzopoulos, V., 2008, n 199, at 234–6.

This, in turn, will prompt national administrations out of their insularity and will force them to find commonly acceptable solutions.

In particular, the use of unified documents (Article 5(2) SD)—if it materializes—will inevitably lead to convergence of the conditions for their issuance and review, and more generally to a cross-fertilization between administrative cultures. More importantly, the creation of single points of contact (Article 6) and the electronic filing of documents (Article 8) is set to change fundamentally the administrative structures—and possibly the very political configuration—of member states. Public officials, being the mouth and hands of the state, exercise power over citizens: they can rebuff, ask for more documents, make observations, impose conditions, and, occasionally, ask for bribes.[211] As soon as this 'vertical' relation gives way to a 'horizontal' one, between officials of different administrations (namely, between those serving in the single points of contact and those competent to issue the necessary authorizations and documents), the power relation is transformed into a mere bureaucratic one: what was the basis of power now becomes the source of burden. By the same token, officials, faced with the difficulty and/or absurdity of administrative requirements and procedures, get a clear idea of how simplification can be achieved; in this way, simplification ceases to be an external and abstract requirement preached by 'good governance' officials and becomes an internal, realistic commodity with specific content. Therefore, there is a double incentive—both psychological and practical—for administrative simplification. Administrative simplification, in turn, means fewer officials and, possibly, fewer administrative structures.

More strikingly still, it cannot be discounted that single points of contact will have an effect on the political configuration of member states—especially federal or strongly decentralized ones. A fundamental contradiction becomes apparent from the very terms of the Directive. This is vividly captured in Recital 59, which states:

'The authorisation should as a general rule enable the provider to have access to the service activity, or to exercise that activity, throughout the national territory, unless a territorial limit is justified by an overriding reason relating to the public interest.... This provision should not affect regional or local competences for the granting of authorisations within the Member States.'

As if this were not clear enough, Recital 60 explains the following at length:

'This Directive, and in particular the provisions concerning authorisation schemes and the territorial scope of an authorisation, should not interfere with the division of regional or local competences within the Member States, including regional and local self-government and the use of official languages.'

The requirement that authorizations have general territorial validity is expressed in Article 10(4) of the SD, while the idea that local competences should not be

---

[211] The 'visual' of a public official looking down, from behind his desk, with disdain over sweaty citizens trying to get their case through, was presented in a very lively way by G. Davies, in the Conference 'Services Liberalisation in the EU and the WTO', organized by the Europainstitut, Jean Monnet Center of Excellence, Economic University of Wien, Wien, 5–6 March 2009.

affected is to be found in Article 10(7). It is worth asking how these two rules will be applied in federal or strongly decentralized member states, where the competence for delivering authorizations lies with local authorities. Such authorizations cannot possibly be valid throughout the entire national territory without infringing the competences of similar authorities of other territorial entities. It remains to be seen whether the proper functioning of a federal or strongly decentralized state could feature as an overriding reason in the sense of Recital 59 and Article 10(4) of the Directive. It is even less clear how Article 10(7) of the Directive will be applied in practice, given that it is expected not to 'call into question the allocation of the competences, at local or regional level, of the Member States' authorities granting authorisations'. These uncertainties are far from theoretical and have already troubled the officials in several member states, when they undertook to transpose the Directive.[212]

c. *Tentative assessment of the impact of the Services Directive*

This tentative assessment of the SD tries to bring together the findings of the three previous chapters (on restrictions, justifications, and judicial regulation of services) and to feed them into the content of the SD, as outlined above. Indeed, the SD was intended to codify and develop the Court's case law both in defining restrictions and in allowing derogations thereto, while exercising a horizontal scope of application. It is clear from the above that the prospects of the SD revolutionizing service provision are quite dim. This notwithstanding, the elements identified in the previous chapters, in particular the quantitative data gathered, shows that there is still some space for improvement through the application of the SD.

Although the distinction between measures limiting access and those restricting the exercise of service activities is essentially formulated by legal commentary rather than hard law,[213] the SD does to some extent follow the same logic: Chapter III deals with 'establishment', while Chapter IV with 'service provision'. 'Establishment' broadly corresponds to 'access', whenever such 'access' is more than occasional and purely temporary. Indeed, from the case law cited in the previous chapters, it becomes clear that the vast majority of access restrictions are related to the conditions for the establishment of the service provider in the host member state. Such restrictions are henceforth regulated by the SD in quite a detailed and clear way. Indeed, the inclusion in the Directive of the 'black list' of absolutely prohibited requirements (Article 14) together with the clear rules on authorizations (Articles 9–13) are expected to eliminate many of the 'access' restrictions so far imposed on foreign service providers. The abolition of several of the 'grey list'

---

[212] Eg Roig, E., 'Intricate Aspects of the Scope [of the services directive] in Spain' paper delivered at the EIPA/ECR Seminar on *The Services Directive: The Challenge of Implementation And Management at Sub-State Level*, Barcelona 19–20 April 2010, states that within the federal system of Spain, the authorizations delivered by one community are not valid within others and that a system of automatic mutual recognition of such communal decisions has been put into place in order for authorizations to cover the entirety of the national territory, in accordance with the SD.

[213] See the discussion in ch 3.

measures (Article 15), depending on the quality of member states' screening and the intensity of the Commission's review, will further this trend.

Access to occasional and/or temporary service provision, which is not directly regulated by Chapter III of the SD is, nonetheless, considerably facilitated by Chapter I of Directive 2005/36 on the mutual recognition of diplomas (the General System). According to Article 5 of this Directive 'Member States shall not restrict, for any reason relating to professional qualifications, the free provision of services in another Member State ... where the service provider moves to the territory of the host Member State to pursue, on a temporary and occasional basis'. This obligation is further qualified by conditions and exceptions, but the principle is there that the occasional provision of services does not require any formal recognition of professional qualifications.

To the extent that the rules of the relevant provisions of the SD and of the General System have been legislated into national law, litigation in respect of 'market access' of service providers—established or temporary—should reduce in the years to come. The legislature, for its part, should pause for a few years, use the data provided by the member states and by the Commission, by virtue, respectively, of their screening and monitoring obligations under the two Directives, and, eventually, evaluate the need for adjustments.

The opposite seems true for measures restricting 'exercise'. As already suggested,[214] this category is much more varied and case-specific. This may have been one of the reasons why the (Bolkestein) draft SD aimed to deal with 'exercise' restrictions by virtue of the blanket CoOP. Since this principle was abandoned, however, in favour of the 'freedom to provide services' principle, member states enjoy the same freedom as before to introduce restrictive measures: it is enough that such measures be justified, non-discriminatory, and proportional. It is, as yet, unclear, whether the reasons justifying such restrictive measures are limited to the four expressly enumerated in Article 16 of the Directive (public policy, public security, public health, and protection of the environment) or whether the full body of 'overriding reasons of general interest' is available to member states.[215] This issue alone is expected to be the source of considerable litigation. Litigation will be prompted further by the important exceptions to and exclusions from the Directive's scope, especially so since some of them may be seen as retreats from pre-established case law. Indeed, it remains to be seen whether the deliberate choice of the legislature to exclude these sectors/activities from the Directive's scope will reflect on the Court's approach towards these same sectors/activities.[216]

There is, nonetheless, in the SD a set of rules which will—discretely but certainly—have some impact on temporary service provision. The numerical data above show that an important proportion of restrictions to temporary service

---

[214] See the discussion in ch 3.

[215] See the discussion in ch 4.

[216] See Snell, J., 'Freedom to provide services in the case law and in the services directive: problems, solutions and institutions' in Neergaard, U., Nielsen, R, and Roseberry, L. (eds), *The Services Directive: Consequences for the Welfare State and the European Social Model* (Copenhagen: DJOF, 2008) 171–97.

provision is not imposed on providers themselves, but on service recipients. The SD does take those into account. In a short Section consisting of three articles, the Directive prohibits restrictions imposed by the home state (Article 19), condemns discriminatory measures liable to be adopted by the host state (Article 20), and offers 'assistance to recipients' (Article 21). To be more precise, the recipient's home state may neither impose any authorization or declaration requirement nor put limits on the financial aid to which the recipient is entitled, just because the latter opted to receive a given service in another member state. Clearly, the principles established in *Köhll, Smits and Peerbooms*, and *Vanbraekel* underpin Article 19 of the SD. Similarly, the Court's judgments in *Trojani, Collins*, and *Bidar*,[217] seem to transcend Article 20 which prevents the host state from introducing any discriminatory measure against foreign service recipients. It has to be noted that—unlike Article 16 of the SD—SGEIs are not excluded from the scope of these two provisions. Hence, they may be invoked by nationals of one member state in order to secure access to services with a social character in other member states. The final provision on service recipients aims to make information accessible to recipients and to build up confidence in services offered in other member states: electronic means of communication, single points of contact, simple guides, etc are all available to the service recipients in their home state.

B. Regulatory technique of legislative instruments— a normative approach

The above brief presentation of the six different legislative categories shows that no single means or method exists for the regulation of services. Rather, a very wide palette of regulatory techniques is followed, ranging from unification to mere exchange of information and soft coordination.[218]

From a dynamic point of view, a twin evolution can be identified: a gradual diminution of the extent/degree of harmonization, combined with increasing reliance on home state regulation. This partial replacement of harmonization with mutual recognition, on the one hand, reduces regulation but, on the other, entails a different kind of regulation: mutual recognition needs to be organized or 'managed'[219] through texts of secondary legislation, in order for it to become more efficient. Mutual recognition, the cornerstone of the 1985 'new approach'

---

[217] Case C-456/02 *Michel Trojani v Centre Public d' aide sociale des Bruxelles* (CPAS) [2004] ECR I-7573; Case C-138/02 *Brian Francis Collins v Secretary of State for Work and Pensions* [2004] ECR I-2703; Case C-209/03 *Bidar* [2005] ECR I-2119; See in general, on the 'social sensibility' of the CJEU, Hatzopoulos, V., 'A (More) Social Europe: A Political Crossroad or a Legal One-Way? Dialogues between Luxembourg and Lisbon' (2005) 42 *CML Rev* 1599–635.

[218] For an early effort of classification see Knill, C., and Lenschow, A., 'Modes of Regulation in the Governance of the EU: Towards a Comprehensive Evaluation?' (2003) 7 European Integration online Papers (EIoP) No. 1, available at <http://eiop.or.at/eiop/texte/2003-001a.htm> (last accessed on 11 November 2011).

[219] The term is introduced in Nicolaidis, K., 'Trusting the Poles? Constructing Europe through Mutual Recognition' (2007) 15 *JEPP* 682–98.

for the completion of the internal market,[220] can hardly qualify as 'new' or 'modern', more than 25 years after it made its entry in the EU legal order. However, it still posits problems, especially in the area of services regulation; hence the recent revival of academic study in this area.[221] The objective of identifying the optimal means to regulate services has been further nourished by the goal of 'better' governance, as put forward by the 2001 Commission Communication and the relevant literature;[222] at the same time, 'new' governance techniques have, in actual fact, been increasingly used in different fields touching upon service provision. In the pages that follow, the evolution of the classic community method (CCM) and the various facets of harmonization will be examined, in a horizontal, yet analytical, way. The attention then focuses on the normative role of mutual recognition in the field of services and the way in which it intertwines with harmonization is also examined.

1. Harmonization

Although it is not necessary here to define in detail what the CCM entails,[223] it is beyond doubt that, in the field of the internal market, it essentially leads to harmonization through the use of Directives, Regulations, and Decisions. Indeed, in the early years of the realization of the internal market, harmonization was almost seen as an objective of its own.[224] This changed with *Cassis de Dijon* and the 'new approach', but harmonization has never ceased to be an objective of the internal market. The

---

[220] Council Resolution concerning a new approach on technical harmonization and standardization [1985] OJ C136/1; Council Resolution concerning a global approach for conformity evaluation [1990] OJ C10/1. The system put into place has been reinvigorated recently by the European Parliament and Council Regulation 764/2008/EC laying down procedures relating to the application of certain national technical rules to products lawfully marketed in another Member State [2008] OJ L218/21; see also European Parliament and Council Regulation 765/2008/EC setting out the requirements for accreditation and market surveillance relating to the marketing of products [2008] OJ L218/30, and Commission Decision 768/2008/EC on a common framework for the marketing of products, and repealing Council Decision 93/465/EEC [2008] OJ L218/82.

[221] See the discussion under subheading B(2), where also references to the relevant literature are to be found.

[222] See the discussion in ch 9, where relevant literature is cited.

[223] For an excellent empirical and normative analysis of the way the CCM has operated, see Craig, P., 'Democracy and Rulemaking within the EC: An Empirical and Normative Assessment' (2002) 8 *ELJ* 105–30; Dehousse, R., 'La méthode communautaire a-t-elle encore un avenir?' in Rey, J.J. and Walebroeck, M. (eds), *Mélanges en l'honneur à J. v Louis* (Bruxelles: Editions de l'Université Libre de Bruxelles, 2003) 95–107; Manin, P., 'La "méthode communautaire": changement et permanence' in Blanquet, M. (ed), *Mélanges en honneur à Guy Isaac: Cinquante ans de droit communautaire* (Toulouse: Presses Universitaires Sciences Sociales Toulouse, 2004) 213–37[0]; more specifically on the way the CCM relates to new modes of governance, see see Zeitlin, J., 'Is the Open Method of Coordination an Alternative to the Community Method?' available at <http://eucenter.wisc.edu/OMC/Papers/JZ_Community_Method.pdf> (last accessed on 11 November 2011); for an up-to-date critical analysis see Dehousse, R. (ed), *The Community Method: Obstinate or Obsolete?* (Basingstoke: Palgrave Macmillan, 2011).

[224] For the different kinds of harmonization, see Slot, P.J., 'Harmonisation' (1996) 21 *EL Rev* 378–97; and more recently, Vos, E., 'Differentiation, harmonisation and governance' in de Witte, B., Hanf, D., and Vos, E. (eds), *The Many Faces of Differentiation in EU Law* (Antwerpen: Intersentia, 2001) 145–79.

brief overview in the first part of the present chapter shows that harmonization underpins, either as an objective or, at least, as a means, the entirety of EU legislation in the area of services. In this respect, several questions need to be answered.

a. Is harmonization old-fashioned—destined to disappear?

i. Harmonization is at the heart of common policies, such as road haulage. The gradual liberalization of road haulage was essentially based on extensive harmonization and managed—even forced—mutual recognition. Even in such a policy field, however, where harmonization plays the pivotal role, it is neither complete nor exhaustive. It was explained above that a. the various legislative instruments were adopted over a significant time span, one building on and completing the other; b. they foresee very important exclusions, exceptions, derogations, and transitional periods, c. they have been under constant review. Therefore, even 'old-fashioned' harmonization can be quite open-ended and flexible and might not necessarily lead to unification of the law of member states.

It is true that harmonization has been in stark retreat in some of the areas described in the first part of the present chapter. One of the most striking examples is the recognition of professional qualifications. While for the six medical professions—and to a lesser extent for architects—extensive harmonization of study cycles has been deemed necessary, the General Systems leave the national study systems entirely intact and only harmonize the conditions for the imposition of compensatory measures. It is also true that the IT Directives (namely the AVMS, the e-commerce and the e-signature Directives) based as they are on the IMC, bring about very little harmonization; and that the SD constitutes an original regulatory attempt entailing almost no harmonization at all.

This trend shifts, however, when attention turns to the other fields examined above. In the process of liberalizing the network industries, harmonization has been restricted essentially to the delimitation of a core of SGIs (or universal service) and the definition of a few other basic characteristics (types of services or share of the market liberalized); the limited extent of harmonization reflects the very important structural differences that still exist in the regulated markets of member states. This diversity, reinforced by technological change, has prompted several 'generations' of regulatory texts (four in the telecoms and rail sector, three for electricity and gas, two for postal services). Thus, harmonization has not been decreasing in this field but has, on the contrary, been increasing.

More striking is the evolution of regulation in the field of financial services (including bank, insurance, and investment services). The initial 'passport' system was grounded on minimal harmonization of the basic rules on own funds, accounting, and publicity, complemented by an extensive application of the principle of mutual recognition. The MiFiD, however, radically changes this paradigm, as it entails full harmonization of the main conditions leading to the authorization of financial institutions, while the post-crisis measures also centralize supervision in the field.

ii. Hence, the idea that harmonization will gradually disappear and give way to other more 'modern' methods of regulation does not seem to be supported by the actual practice of the institutions. There are, nevertheless, two general trends which may be identified in the way harmonization will henceforth operate. For one thing, both examples above show that harmonization might no more be the first, but rather the last regulatory technique employed. Indeed, in both the field of network industries and in that of financial services, extensive harmonization was only resorted to after it became clear that lighter regulatory techniques (partial harmonization in the network industries, combination of light harmonization and mutual recognition in the financial services) would not deliver the desired outcomes. Full harmonization, therefore, appears to be the last resort for the achievement of the regulatory objective; it is employed once other 'lighter' techniques have been tried and failed. The second point, connected to the first, relates to the procedure leading to harmonization: it increasingly follows a bottom up/participatory pattern, rather than a top down one. In the network industries, the need for further harmonization was not unilaterally decided by the Commission. Rather, the need for and the content of such harmonization was the subject of consultation at various levels: a. between the sector-specific NRAs and national actors (incumbents and new entrants), b. among the NRAs themselves, operating in European networks, c. between the NRAs and the Directive-specific committees, d. between the NRAs, Directive-specific committees, and other self-regulatory bodies, e. between all these actors and the Commission. This participatory pattern has been fully institutionalized in the area of financial services with the Lamfalussy process: one of the first regulatory texts to be adopted according to this process was the MiFiD.

b. Full or partial harmonization?

The analysis above also answers this second question. Harmonization is likely to be limited to the absolutely necessary areas and leave member states free to pursue their regulatory objectives in all other areas. This approach, consistent with the principle of subsidiarity, is expected to be strengthened by the entry into force of the Lisbon Treaty: the right of national parliaments to question the legislative initiatives of the Commission (Article 69 TFEU), as well as the possibility opened to member states to resist (at least at the political level) European legislation which runs counter to their national identity (Article 4§2 TFEU) constitute factors which may further restrict the harmonizing fervour of the Commission.

Furthermore, harmonization is more likely to be minimal, in the sense that it only sets the floor of minimum common rules, allowing member states to pursue the regulatory objectives they deem important. Only when regulatory competition thus developed ends up prejudging either the individual policies of member states or the common policy objectives, will harmonization be pushed further.

c. Harmonization and technology: neutrality v. promotion of standards

One of the drawbacks of harmonization, already identified before the 'new approach' was launched, is that it can stifle technological development. Indeed, as long as harmonization was vertical and detailed, any goods or services not produced according to the harmonized procedures would not benefit from free movement. This changed with the 'new approach' in at least three ways. *First*, horizontal legislative instruments cannot be detailed and therefore, tend to describe the desired outcome—especially in terms of safety, health, environmental, and consumer (SHEC) protection—rather than the process itself. Hence any process, old or innovative, is good provided it secures the prescribed level of protection. *Secondly*, whenever standards are used, they are adopted by the European standardization bodies (European Committee for Standardization (CEN), European Committee for Electro-technical Standardization (CENELEC), European Telecommunications Standards Institute (ETSI) with the participation of the industry itself and their revision is a technical—not political—exercise. *Thirdly*, standards are rarely mandatory; instead, they are typically accompanied by an 'equivalence clause', whereby any technique securing an equivalent outcome is admitted. In this sense, 'new approach' Directives are more 'technologically neutral' than old-fashioned vertical Directives; by the same token, they need not be amended often.

Moreover, the EU legislature has deliberately chosen to adopt technologically neutral Directives most often in areas where technology is of paramount significance and the regulatory choice of standards might bias rational market choices. Hence, the TVWF Directive applied to 'broadcasts transmitted across frontiers by means of various technologies';[225] more explicitly, the e-signature Directive—in a field where technical solutions are booming—states that 'rapid technological development and the global character of the Internet necessitate an approach which is open to various technologies'.[226] The latest amendment of the TVWF Directive and its transformation into the AVMS Directive, however, marks a departure from this idea of neutrality: depending on the technique used for transmission (one-way or interactive), different sets of rules apply to service providers.[227] Therefore, the relationship between harmonization and technical evolution may be described in three propositions: i. horizontal harmonization tends to be technology-neutral; ii. this changes, however, as soon as new technology gets crystallized or whenever regulation needs to become more detailed; iii. even technology-neutral legislation needs periodic revision, since new technology brings with it new opportunities and new challenges.

d. Revision/report procedures

Linked to points i–iii in the previous paragraph is the inclusion, in an increasing number of EU legislative texts, of 'rendez-vous' clauses, allowing for their periodic revision.

---

[225] Directive 89/552/EEC [1989] OJ L298/23 (TVWF Directive), Preamble Rec 3.
[226] Directive 1999/93/EC [2000] OJ L13/12 (e-signature Directive), Preamble Rec 8.
[227] It is true, however, that the Dir does not distinguish further between the various techniques for one-way or interactive transmission.

i. Description

Such provisions may be as simple as imposing an obligation on the Commission to submit to the EP and the Council a Report concerning the application of the Directive together with any necessary proposals.[228] Such a report is typically required two years after the lapse of the transposition period and the proposals contained therein may lead to further legislative adaptations. A typical example of such a clause can be found in the 'Citizenship Directive'.[229] A more complex 'rendez-vous' clause is found in the Professional Qualifications Directive.[230] Here, member states have to report regularly (every two years) to the Commission which, in turn, has to report in longer intervals (every five years), presumably to the EP and the Council, on the state of implementation of the Directive. Moreover, the Commission is also under a duty to follow comitology procedures and to connect, through the publication of reasoned reports, the Committee in question with 'experts from the professional groups concerned'.[231]

In addition to the above, several other examples of 'rendez-vous' clauses could be mentioned. The most complete 'rendez-vous' clause is set out in the Services Directive, which actually contains two! As part of the mutual evaluation instituted by the Directive, the Commission receives the screening results from all the member states, circulates them among peers, receives feedback from them, feeds the results into comitology, and presents a summary report to the EP and the Council, 'accompanied where appropriate by proposals for additional initia-tives'.[232] As if this were not enough, Article 41 bears the title 'review clause' and foresees that at the end of 2011 and every three years thereafter, the Commission shall present to the EP and the Council a comprehensive Report on the application of the Directive. 'It shall also consider the need for additional measures for matters excluded from the scope of application of this Directive. It shall be accompanied, where appropriate, by proposals for the amendment of the directive with a view to completing the Internal Market for services'. It is to be noted that in the Profes-sional Qualifications Directive, the Commission may adduce additional informa-tion through national contact points to fulfil its reporting duties.[233] In the Services Directive, not only does the Commission overlook the functioning of national 'points of single contact',[234] but also organizes the European Network to operate the alert mechanism.[235]

---

[228] Directive 2006/123/EC [2006] OJ L376/36 (Services Directive), Arts 39(4) and 41.

[229] Directive 2004/38/EC [2004] OJ L158/77 (Citizenship Directive), Art 39.

[230] Directive 2005/36/EC on the recognition of professional qualifications [2005] OJ L255/22, Arts 59–60.

[231] Articles 58–59; it is true that, contrary to the Citizenship Directive (n 229 above), Directive 2005/36 (n 230) does not explicitly foresee the possibility for the Commission to propose amend-ments, but see under subheading B(1)d(ii).

[232] Services Directive, n 228 above, Art 39.

[233] Directive 2005/36, n 230, Art 57.

[234] In the course of evaluating the member state's performance in implementing the Services Directive.

[235] Services Directive, n 228, Art 32.

ii. Comment

It is unclear how the express empowering provisions found in the text of the Service Directive and, in a less detailed manner, in the Citizenship Directive (absent in the Professional Qualifications Directive) add to the inalienable right of the Commission to propose legislation or amendments thereto. It is clear, however, that the mere fact that legislative texts are subject to reporting—especially when such reporting is periodic—has its own significance, both from a procedural and from a substantive point of view. So far as procedure is concerned, 'rendez-vous' clauses have at least two positive effects. *First*, similar to 'sunset clauses' which are well known under US law,[236] 'rendez-vous' clauses make sure that legislation which becomes unsuitable or obsolete does not remain in force indefinitely. This, in turn, means that no legal gaps are involuntarily left in areas where the legislator is slow to repeal and replace unfit legislative acts. It also means that no confusing deadwood legislation will muddle legal certainty when fresh legislative acts are adopted without explicitly repealing all previous measures. Both outcomes reflect problems which the Commission tried to deal with in its 2001 'Governance' White Paper.[237] *Secondly*, the 'rendez-vous' clauses entail a depoliticization of the decision-making process: it is one thing to put to the fore fresh legislation, and a different matter entirely to amend existing legislation, following an institutionalized process of exchanging information and extensive reporting. In the latter case, the Commission needs no political mandate whatsoever, no extensive consultation with stakeholders and/or civil society, and less investment of political capital for putting forward its ideas. Indeed, any new draft legislation needs to go through the EP, but the EP's role in areas which have been regularly monitored and reported by the Commission may not be as decisive as it is when fresh legislation is discussed. In general it may be said that amendments to existing legislation, being of a more technical nature, favour the role of the Commission over that of the European Parliament and of the Council (member states are likely to battle against new legislation encroaching on their competences, but less likely to resist amendments to make already existing legislation more efficient).[238]

From a substantive point of view, 'rendez-vous' clauses ensure some degree of reflexivity and adaptability of the legislative instruments. Further, they set the conditions for amendments which specifically address the shortcomings of existing legislation. Therefore, they are orientated towards a constant improvement of the quality of EU legislation. This is true especially in the fields where reporting is not only based on official documents stemming from member states' governments, but

---

[236] A 'sunset clause' is a provision in a statute or regulation that terminates or repeals all or portions of the law after a specific date, unless further legislative action is taken to extend it. In the US, a 12-member 'Sunset Committee' is convened equally from the Senate and the House of Representatives and reviews the action of Agencies scheduled for review in the sunset law or in the Agency's enabling law, or indeed the action of any other Agency the Committee deems fit; the Committee may recommend: a. the continuation without modification, b. the continuation with modification, or c. the termination of the operation of the Agencies.

[237] For which, see the discussion in ch 9.

[238] The idea that it is easier to amend an existing text rather than negotiating one from scratch is discussed in some detail in ch 5.

also from NRAs or other networks directly involved in the implementation of the Directives concerned.

e. Implementation

i. The implementation of EU legislation is entrusted to member states. Two tendencies, however, can be identified in recent years, which are especially relevant for services. *First*, implementation monitoring has become more pressing, in at least three ways. Article 258 proceedings are consistently pursued by the Commission and, after a first hesitant period, the imposition of fines by virtue of Article 260 TFEU has now become commonplace; this tendency is likely to be pushed further by virtue of the possibility opened by Article 260(3) TFEU, that the Commission demands and the Court imposes fines even in its first judgment against member states failing to notify implementation measures. Moreover, compliance has ceased being a purely judicial issue and has partially transformed into a political one. Scoreboards of performing and underperforming states are published twice a year and are compared against the objective of reducing compliance failure to below 1 per cent,[239] infringement proceedings are analysed per state and per sector, reasons for the compliance deficit are put forward, and strategies for the future are discussed. The very fact that states are ranked against their own implementation results and compared to one another, and that their failures become the object of analysis and discussion among their peers increases the pressure to conform. In this way, hard compliance monitoring is combined with peer review and naming and shaming. Further, the SOLVIT network seeks to de-dramatize non-compliance and to resolve concrete, and yet simple, implementation deadlocks.[240]

ii. In recent years, however, a slightly different trend can be identified concerning implementation. Indeed, it can be said that implementation is being hesitantly raised from the national to the EU level. This is happening in two ways: *indirectly*, through the institution of national contact points (by the Professional Qualification, the IT, or the Services Directive) or NRAs (in the network industries) and their operation as pan-European networks; *directly*, through the creation of agencies.[241] Typically, agencies possess no direct powers to implement the various EU policies or to compel states to that effect. Their various research, dissemination, and coordination functions, however, do act as facilitators for member state compliance.[242]

---

[239] For the latest one, published in September 2010, see <http://ec.europa.eu/internal_market/score/index_en.htm> (last accessed on 12 November 2011).

[240] Details on SOLVIT are gives in subsection B(2)c.

[241] On the role of agencies, see the Communication COM (2002) 718 final, 'on the operating framework for the European Regulatory Agencies'.

[242] More details on agencies active in the field of services are presented in ch 8, where also references to the relevant literature are to be found.

2. Mutual recognition (MR)[243]

a. *Why services are different from goods concerning MR*

The fact that MR is not extensively organized by the EU, nor 'imposed' by the CJEU (and national courts and authorities) in the field of services in so extensive a manner as in the field of goods, is not purely haphazard. Indeed, the 'new approach' of legislation inaugurated in 1985 and based on MR,[244] the issuance of Directives describing minimal safety and security standards and EU labelling (enhancing MR), and the obligation of transparency in respect of technical standards (forcing 'pre-emptive' MR) are all restricted to the area of goods.

At least five reasons might account for the discrepancy.

i. Decentralized and/or non-state origin of the measures

Goods are generally affected by regulations guaranteeing safety, health, environment and consumer (SHEC) protection.[245] These rules are typically decided by the state—alone or in collaboration with the industry. Self-regulation and the use of voluntary standards is also an option, although rarely followed in matters endangering SHEC. SHEC regulations tend to cover the entire territory for which they are decided; it is rare that the level of SHEC protection varies within a single member state. Service regulations, on the other hand, tend to be much more diversified and their objectives appear much more complex than merely SHEC: cohesion and social policy, redistribution, protection of labour, a high level of 'public service', disciplinary organization of the professions, to name but a few. The content of such regulations very often varies within a single state. Moreover, depending on the constitutional settings of the state, such regulations may be adopted by sub-state units (federated states, municipalities etc) or even by non-state entities, such as trade unions, professional associations, etc.

Therefore, it should come as no surprise that the 'stretching' of the free movement rules to cover 'private' measures started with Article 56 TFEU on services.[246] Even today, the Court is much readier to scrutinize non-state measures under the rules on services (and persons) than under the rules on goods.[247] It is now

---

[243] This section draws heavily on Hatzopoulos, V., 'Mutual recognition in the field of services' in Lianos, I., and Odudu, O. (eds), *Regulating Trade in Services in the EU and the WTO: Trust, Distrust and Economic Integration* (Cambridge: CUP, forthcoming 2012).

[244] See the discussion under subheadings B(1)a and B(1)b.

[245] The paternity of the acronym 'SHEC' and the term 'SHEC regulations' is attributed to Pelkmans, J., 'Mutual Recognition in Goods: On Promises and Disillusions' (2007) 15 *JEPP* 699–716, at 702. It also appears in previous works of his.

[246] Case 36/74 *B.N.O. Walrave and L.J.N. Koch v Association Union cycliste internationale, Koninklijke Nederlandsche Wielren Unie and Federación Española Ciclismo* [1974] ECR 1405.

[247] See Hatzopoulos, V., 'Trente ans après les arrêts fondamentaux de 1974, les quatre libertés: quatre?' in Demaret, P., Govaere, I., and Hanf, D. (eds), *30 Years of European Legal Studies at the College of Europe—30 ans d'études juridiques européennes au Collège d'Europe: Liber Professorum 1973/74–2003/04* (Brussels: Peter Lang, 2005) 185–201; and more extensively, see Snell, J., *Goods and Services in EC Law* (Oxford: OUP, 2002), at 130–59.

accepted that Article 56 TFEU may be violated by measures adopted by sports' associations or federations,[248] professional associations,[249] insurance funds,[250] trade unions,[251] and even automobile associations.[252]

At least three legal difficulties stem from this state of affairs. For *one* thing, the extent to which the internal market rules can be stretched in order to cover private regulators may have reached its limits.[253] *Secondly*, it becomes difficult to assess the effects of regional and local regulations on intra-community trade and to subject them to the Treaty rules. Even if this hurdle is overcome, *thirdly*, it is extremely complicated to apply MR on numerous divergent national regulations.

ii. Services subject to non-incorporated rules

Services are, to a large extent, tailor-made to suit their recipients' needs. Moreover, it is difficult to define a service 'unit' as well as to identify the ingredients of a service. The active role played by recipients in the production of services leads some authors to talk about 'co-production'.[254] This explains why services regulations rarely concern the service itself; instead, they define the conditions which the service providers should themselves fulfil (such as qualifications, authorizations, entry into registers, deontology rules, provider's liability) or the circumstances

---

[248] Case 36/74 *Walrave and Koch*, n 246 above; Case 13/76 *Gaetano Donà v Mario Mantero* [1976] ECR 1333; Case C-415/93 *Union royale belge des sociétés de football association ASBL v Jean-Marc Bosman, Royal club liégeois SA v Jean-Marc Bosman and others and Union des associations européennes de football (UEFA) v Jean-Marc Bosman* [1995] ECR I-4921; Joined cases C-51/96 & C-191/97 *Christelle Deliège v Ligue Francophone de Judo et Disciplines Associés ASBL, Ligue Belge de judo ASBL, Union Européenne de Judo and Francois Pacquée* [2000] ECR I-2549; Case C-519/04P *David Meca-Medina and Igor Macjen v Commission of the European Communities* [2006] ECR I-6991.

[249] Case 292/86 *Claude Gullung v Conseil de l'ordre des avocats du barreau de Colmar* [1988] ECR 111; Case C-309/99 *J.C.J. Wouters, J.W. Savelbergh and Price Waterhouse Belastingadviseurs BV v Algemene Raad van de Nederlandse Orde van Advocaten, intervener: Raad van de Balies van de Europese Gemeenschap* [2002] ECR I-1577; Case C-506/04 *Graham J. Wilson v Ordre des avocats du barreau de Luxembourg* [2006] ECR I-8613; Joined cases C-94 & 202/04 *Federico Cipolla v Rosaria Fazari, née Portolese and Stefano Macrino and Claudio Capopart v Roberto Meloni* [2006] ECR I-11421.

[250] See, among several cases, Case C-158/96 *Raymond Kohll v Union des caisses de maladie* [1998] ECR I-1931; Case C-157/99 *B.S.M. Geraets-Smits v Stichting Ziekenfonds VGZ and H.T.M. Peerbooms v Stichting CZ Groep Zorgverzekeringen* [2001] ECR I-5437 and all the recent case law concerning the free movement of patients.

[251] Case C-438/05 *International Transport Workers' Federation and Finnish Seamen's Union v Viking Line ABP and OÜ Viking Line Eesti* [2007] ECR I-10779; Case C-341/05 *Laval un Partneri Ltd v Svenska Byggnadsarbetareförbundet, Svenska Byggnadsarbetareförbundets avdelning 1, Byggettan and Svenska Elektrikerförbundet* [2007] ECR I-11767.

[252] Case C-49/07 *Motosykletistiki Omospondia Ellados NPID (MOTOE) v Elliniko Dimosio* [2008] ECR I-4863.

[253] As the academic debate about the recent judgments in Case C-438/05, *Viking* (n 251) and Case C-341/05, *Laval* (n 251) has shown; see eg Cremers, J., Dolvik, J.E., and Bosch, G., 'Posting of Workers in the Single Market: Attempts to Prevent Social Dumping and Regime Competition in the EU?' (2007) 38 *Ind Relations J* 524–41; Malmberg, J., and Sigeman, T., 'Industrial actions and EU Economic Freedoms: The Autonomous Collective Bargaining Model Curtailed by the ECJ' (2008) 45 *CML Rev* 1115–46; for a fuller presentation of the academic commentary of these cases, see the analysis in ch 5.

[254] Rubalcaba, L., 'Historical and anthropological origin of the service economy' in Rubalcaba, L. (ed), *The New Service Economy: Challenges and Policy Implications for Europe* (Cheltenham/Northampton: Edward Elgar Publishing, 2007) 14–42; see also the discussion in ch 1.

under which the providers may offer their services (namely opening hours and days, location, price fixing, access subject to a devolution system). In other words, services regulations are essentially non-incorporated, in the sense that they concern the *process*, but they are not necessarily reflected in the actual *content* of a service. Therefore, in principle, non-incorporated regulations exhaust their effects within the providers' home country, while incorporated ones produce externalities also felt in the host state.[255] This, in turn, means that goods/services produced according to incorporated rules securing lower standards of (consumer, environment, etc) protection might be resisted by consumers in the host state.[256] Non-incorporated regulations, on the other hand, will meet much lower resistance from consumers in the host state—and therefore local non-incorporated rules will be faced with greater pressure from the dynamics of regulatory competition.[257] If the host state is to safeguard its own standards of non-incorporated rules, it specifically needs to adopt acts of an essentially protective nature. Such rules are unlikely to yield to the effect of MR—or if they do, the protective measures of the host state are given extra-territorial effect, since they are complied with in the home state.

iii. No prior notification system of rules on services

The fact that most service-related measures are non-incorporated and that they are of a non-technical nature accounts for the lack of any system of prior notification of such rules. In the field of goods, Directive 98/34[258] requires that all 'technical specifications', 'technical rules', or 'other requirements' affecting the production, commercialization or, even, use of goods[259] be notified to the Commission prior to their entry into force. This notification requirement is reinforced by a standstill period, during which member states cannot enact the measure in question, and which allows the Commission to initiate legislation, thus pre-empting national initiatives. Moreover, the Court has held that national measures that have not been duly notified are unenforceable.[260] The prior notification procedure is acknowl-

---

[255] For the distinction between incorporated and non-incorporated regulations and the risk of race to the bottom, see Scharpf, F., 'Introduction: The Problem-solving Capacity of Multi-level Governance' (1997) 4 *JEPP* 520–38; see also, more recently, Davies, G., 'Process and Production Method-based Trade Restrictions in the EU' (2008) 10 *CYEL* 69–97; see, however, for a critical review of the distinction and of its legal consequence, Howse, R., and Regan, D., 'The Product/Process Distinction: An Illusory Basis for Disciplining Unilateralism' (2000) 11 *Eur J of Int L* 249–89.

[256] In the history of regulatory competition, in addition to stories of races to the bottom (also known as the 'Delaware effect'), there are also stories of races to the top (also known as the 'California effect', after this state managed to impose its own higher standards of anti-pollution rules on the entire US).

[257] Eg an imported vehicle with high CO_2 emissions or insufficient security devices is likely to raise more reactions than imported software programmed by an overtime worker.

[258] European Parliament and Council Directive 98/34/EC laying down a procedure for the provision of information in the field of technical standards and regulations [1998] OJ L204/37; this Directive repealed Council Directive 83/189/EEC [1989] OJ L59/1; its scope was further extended by Council Directive 98/48/EC [1998] OJ L217/18) to cover information society services.

[259] The Directive also covers measures concerning 'use' which affect the provision of services, see Case C-267/03 *Criminal proceedings against Lars Erik Staffan Lindberg* [2005] ECR I-3245.

[260] Case C-194/94 *CIA Security International SA v Signalson SA and Securitel SPRL* [1996] ECR I-2201; see in this respect, Slot, P.J., 'Annotation: Case C-194/94 *CIA Security c/Signalson* [1996] ECR

edged as one of the great successes of the internal market strategy, as almost 900 measures are notified each year to the Commission.[261] The most common outcome of such notifications is that an equivalence clause is inserted into the national measures, according to which goods are admitted into the market which satisfy the prescribed rules 'or equivalent'. In this way, a system of 'pre-emptive recognition' is introduced into national legislation by virtue of the notification Directive. This system only covers goods and—after the 1998 extension—information society services,[262] which have a clearly pronounced technical aspect.

In the field of services, the Services Directive establishes for the first time a prior notification obligation of national measures affecting services. This system, however, is much more limited in scope and intensity than the system for goods. *First*, it only concerns measures affecting the *establishment* of service providers, not the occasional *service provision*. *Secondly*, the measures which need to be notified are enumerated in Article 15(7) of the Directive, presumably in an exhaustive way.[263] *Thirdly*, member states are not subject to any standstill obligation, while the Commission's powers are limited to issuing individual decisions requiring the modification or repeal of the measures in question—but no general legislative powers are given. Last but not least, because of the more 'relaxed' nature of the notification obligation, it is contestable whether the *CIA Security* doctrine of inopposability of non-notified measures will be extended to the Services Directive system.[264]

iv. Absence of extensive standardization/certification

The limited role that technical rules play in the field of services has a further consequence in the way these rules are regulated.

In the field of goods, when technical standards or other requirements are too remote to subsume to MR, the regulator has an option: either to harmonize or to proceed by means of standardization. This second option has been used extensively since the introduction of the 'new approach' in 1985.[265] The Commission gives a mandate to the CEN, CENELEC, or the ETSI, depending on the technological area, for the adoption of standards. The latter are non-binding, unless introduced

---

I-2201' (1996) 33 *CML Rev* 1035–50 and Coppel, J., 'Horizontal effect of directives, Case C-194/94 *CIA Security International v Signalson*' (1997) 26 *Ind L J* 69–73; see also Dougan, M., 'The "Disguised" Vertical Effect of Directives?' (2000) 59 *Cambridge LJ* 586–612.

[261] Pelkmans, J., 'Mutual Recognition in Goods: On Promises and Disillusions' (2007) 15 *JEPP* 699–716, at 707.

[262] Information society services are defined, in Art 1(2)a of the Directive as 'any service normally provided for remuneration, at a distance, by electronic means and at the individual request of a recipient of services'.

[263] These are: a. quantitative or territorial restrictions, b. specific legal form requirements, c. shareholding requirements, d. restrictions on the mutual recognition of qualifications, e. double cabinet restrictions, f. minimum numbers of employees, g. price fixing, and h. tying in obligations.

[264] Case C-194/94, *CIA Security International SA v Signalson SA and Securitel SPRL*, n 260.

[265] See the discussion in subsection 2(B)1(a); for a more detailed presentation of the new approach, see Hatzopoulos, V., *Le principe communautaire d'équivalence et de reconnaissance mutuelle dans la libre prestation de services* (Athènes/Bruxelles: Sakkoulas/Bruylant, 1999), at 419–35. This book constitutes an improved version of the author's PhD thesis, supported in 1997 at the University of Strasbourg.

into some text of hard law, such as a Directive.[266] Therefore, standardization entails some degree of harmonization, de facto or de jure (depending on the binding/non-binding nature of the norms adopted), with the participation of industry representatives in standardization bodies.[267]

In the field of services, however, things are quite different. For reasons already explained above, rules affecting services are not of a technical, but a broader (social, environmental) nature. It is, therefore, both technically impossible and politically undesirable to have recourse to standardization in order to reduce disparities. Moreover, the industry involved has less incentive to participate in non-technical standardization. Indeed, standards are in the interests of industry to the extent that they open up new markets. As already mentioned, spontaneous resistance to alien technical (incorporated) standards is much higher than resistance to non-incorporated standards; thus, industry is keener on standardization of the former rather than the latter. It is even empirically proven that very often industry pushes for the adoption of technical standards, while it resists non-technical (social, environmental, etc) ones.[268]

Therefore, the system of the adoption of standards and the certification of conformity of goods, carried out under the supervision of national accreditation authorities, is not transposable as such to the area of services. It is interesting to note, in this respect, that the Commission has only issued two horizontal standardization mandates to the attention of CEN (M/340 of 8 October 2003 and M/371 of 16 July 2005), which have largely remained without effect: from a total of 13,466 CEN publications, only 36 standards (adopted or under adoption) primarily concern services, none of which is published in the OJ (therefore acquiring binding effect). The areas in which these standards have been adopted are maintenance, transport, tourism, real estate, customer services, energy, installation management, translation, and incineration, to mention the most important.[269]

This shortage of standards has been highlighted by the Commission in its EUROPE 2020 Strategy (COM (2010) 2020) and is likely to change to the extent that the Commission's recent Communication on 'a strategic vision for European standards' (COM (2011) 311 final) gets positively implemented.

---

[266] On standards in the EU, see Boy, L., 'Normes' (1998) 12 *Revue Internationale de Droit Economique* 115–46; Graz, J.C., 'Quand les normes font loi: Topologie intégrée et processus différenciés de la normalisation internationale' (2004) 35 *Etudes Internationales* 233–60, also available at <http://www.erudit.org/revue/ei/2004/v35/n2/009036ar.html> (last accessed on 12 November 2011).

[267] On the accountability of standard-setting bodies, see Kerwer, D., 'Rules that Many Use: Standards and Global Regulation' (2005) 18 *Governance* 611–32.

[268] Graz, J.C., 2004, n 266.

[269] According to a simple search at the relevant CEN webpage, at <http://esearch.cen.eu/> (last accessed on 12 November 2011). It is true that this number should increase in the near future by virtue of the implementation of mandate M/371 (see <http://www.cen.eu/cen/Services/Business/Value/Pages/default.aspx>, last accessed on 12 November 2011). It is also worth mentioning the CHESSS initiative (CENs Horizontal European Service Standardisation Strategy), launched in 2007 and concluded in 2009 which has allowed to identify more sectors which could be subject to standardization (<http://www.cen.eu/cen/Services/Business/Value/CHESSS/Pages/default.aspx>, last accessed on 12 November 2011).

v. Sensitive political stakes

It has already been stated that services regulations are more often of a social, environmental, etc nature, rather than of a purely technical/SHEC one. Beyond the practical consequences presented above, this also bears its own intrinsic difficulty with respect to MR. Especially in the social field, there is no point in enquiring into the equivalence of different measures, without having regard to the more general policy in which they are integrated. Alas, it is much more complicated to judge the equivalence of *policies* than of *measures*; and this for at least three reasons. *First*, it is often difficult to grasp the precise content and objectives of various policies. *Secondly*, even if this first step has been completed successfully, it is difficult to judge the respective value of different policies: it is a political and highly ideological task. *Thirdly*, there is the pressing issue of legitimacy: which supranational institution is in a position to second-guess policies decided by national representative bodies? [270]

This difficulty acquires extra weight if read against the distinction between incorporated and non-incorporated measures. Through the former, the host state regulates the effects of goods or services in its own territory. Through the latter, however, the host state imposes its own views upon other states, whose providers need to comply with the host state's regulation in order to have access to its market. This introduces a strong element of extra-territoriality which runs counter to the very logic of MR.[271]

The difficulties of bridging divergent political traditions can best be illustrated by reference to SGIs. It has proven impossible for 'service public' countries, on the one hand, and common law countries, on the other,[272] to establish any common ground, or indeed any equivalence between their respective systems. This has led the Commission to intervene, in various ways: by means of sector-specific Directives (in the field of telecommunications) by dedicated Directive chapters (in other network industries, such as postal services or energy), by means of horizontal instruments of soft law (the 1996, 2000 and 2007 Communications), or by means of launching public consultations, resulting in White and Green Papers.[273] In this sense, SGIs constitute an illustration of the limitations of MR in the field of services.

---

[270] On the more general question of the mismatch between international trade, on one hand, and social regulation at the national level, on the other, see Maduro, M.P., 'Is there any such thing as free or fair trade?' in de Búrca, G., and Scott, J. (eds), *The EU and the WTO, Legal and Constitutional Issues* (Oxford/Portland: Hart Publishing, 2001) 259–82.

[271] Ibid.

[272] For these two concepts and their evolution under EU law, see Harlow, C., 'Public service, market ideology and citizenship' in Freedland, M., and Sciarra, S. (eds), *Public Services and Citizenship in European Law: Public and Labour Law Perspectives* (Oxford: Clarendon Press, 1998) 48–56; see also in the same edited volume, Amato, G., 'Citizenship and public services: some general reflections' 145–56.

[273] See in particular Communication 'Services of General Interest' [1996] OJ C281/3; Communication 'Services of General Interest in Europe' [2001] OJ C17/4; Green Book COM (2003) 270 final, 'on services of general interest'; White Book COM (2004) 374 final, 'on services of general interest'; Commission Communication COM (2007) 725 final, 'Services of General Interest Including Social

b. How MR is organized in the field of services

For all the reasons above, the use of MR in the field of services is not self-evident. Judicial or else 'pure' MR is limited, since the policy objectives of divergent national measures go way beyond pure SHEC preoccupations, making it difficult to find underlying points of convergence. Moreover, the difficulty in identifying 'technical rules' and the lack of standards in the area of services makes the transposition of the 'new approach', as such, difficult. This notwithstanding, the preceding analysis shows that there has been considerable evolution in the way that MR is managed in the field of services. This evolution results in MR being increasingly based on thinner harmonization and, as upshot result, its effects becoming increasingly uncertain.

A simple comparison of MR patterns demonstrates this evolution.[274]

In transport policy, the issuance of permits and licences is harmonized in extensive detail. The national documents issued following the harmonized rules are, in return, automatically recognized in all other states. The same is true for the six medical professions and for the profession of architects, where MR has been organized on the basis of prior harmonization of relevant study programmes.[275] Similarly, as has been explained above, the MiFiD fully harmonizes the conditions for the delivery of authorizations to financial institutions and such authorizations are fully recognized in all other member states. In all these examples, the host member states retain some powers to question the entitlement issued by the home state, but such powers are either residual or exceptional, or both.

This system is different from the one put in place by the old 'passport' Directives for banks, insurance, and investment services, whereby only certain aspects of the authorization of financial institutions were harmonized and, in return, the powers held by the host member states were more pronounced.

The e-Directives, introducing the so-called internal market clause (IMC), mark an evolution compared to 'passports', to the extent that the IMC makes the home state authorities responsible not only for the authorization but also for the supervision of service providers, and presupposes heavy doses of mutual trust.

Compared with the above 'passport' and IMC systems, the country of origin principle (CoOP) put forward by the draft Directive constituted a regulatory advance, in at least three respects. *First* and foremost, because it was deemed to govern not only the authorization and operation conditions of the service activity but also to determine the applicable law, in case of a dispute. Hence, the entirety of the service provision (authorization, operation, conflict resolution) was to be covered by the CoOP. This difference also justifies the evolution of terminology

Services of General Interest: A New European Commitment'; for all these texts and the relevant literature, see the discussion in ch 2.

[274] This evalution is already traced in the more descriptive part A of the present chapter.

[275] The difference being that for the medical professions, harmonization is technically 'prior', in the sense that one Directive harmonizes and then, the Directive following immediately thereafter recognizes the diplomas issued in conformity with the harmonizing Directive; for architects, there is a single Directive (in two parts), harmonizing and recognizing in the same text.

from 'home country control' mainly used in the field of 'passport' Directives to the more far-reaching CoOP. *Secondly*, the draft Directive had an extremely wide scope, by no means restricted to services offered at a distance. *Thirdly*, the level of harmonization put forward by the draft Directive was so elementary that one could legitimately question whether the very term 'harmonization' is appropriate.[276] These three differences have stood in the way of the CoOP principle flourishing.

Lastly, a far-reaching pattern of MR which has succeeded is that of the general system for diplomas and professional qualifications. Here, the object being recognized (diplomas, study cycles, duration thereof, and so on) is not itself harmonized. Instead, what are harmonized are the conditions for, and the kinds of, compensatory measures which the host state may impose. Recognition itself is, nonetheless, compulsory for the host member states which may only, whenever necessary, impose counterveiling measures.

c. How can MR become more efficient in the field of services?

On the basis of the case law and in order to further accomplish the possibilities thus recognized, managed MR is progressively being established. Depending on the substantial rules adopted, managed MR entails some degree of harmonization. If one looks briefly into the different systems of managed MR, without paying any attention to the substantive rules of each one of them, some basic 'horizontal' means of enhancing MR may be identified. These means may be distinguished in two broad categories: measures which aim to increase member states' trust in MR and measures which aim to enhance the effects of MR.

i. Measures that increase trust in MR
Strict rules on establishment
MR is a catalyst of regulatory competition: it allows undertakings the freedom to choose the regulatory framework (and hence the state) they deem better for their activity, then to distribute their goods and services within the entire common market by virtue of the principle of MR. This freedom of choice, nevertheless, should not allow either a continuous forum shopping nor an arbitrary cherry-picking. Against this background the CJEU has developed its anti-fraud case law. As early as the case of *Van Binsbergen*,[277] the Court held that cases amounting to fraud would be treated under the rules of establishment rather than those on services. Further, in *Säger*, the Court made clear that, in order to benefit from free movement, the service provider should be established in, and compliant with, the rules of one and the same state. This position has been radically

---

[276] For a critical evaluation of the content of the Services Directive, see the analysis in subsection A(6).

[277] See Case 33/74 *Van Binsbergen* 1974] ECR 1299, para 13a; the same idea is also expressed in Case 246/80 *C. Broekmeulen v Huisarts Registratie Commissie* [1981] ECR 2311; Case C-148/91 *Vereniging Veronica Omroep Organisatie v Commissariat voor de Media* [1993] ECR I-485 and Case C-23/93 *TV10 SA v Commissariat voor de Media* [1994] ECR I-4795.

revisited in *VT4*[278] where the Court held that '[t]he Treaty does not prohibit an undertaking from exercising the freedom to provide services, if it does not offer services in the Member State in which it is established'. Henceforth, it is possible to be established in one member state but only provide services to recipients in another member state—and in compliance with the requirements of the latter state.[279]

Such freedom opens the way to abuse. This is the reason why most texts of secondary legislation organizing some kind of MR provide for strict nationality rules: in order to claim the benefits of managed MR, the undertakings should be compliant with the requirements of the member state determined according to these nationality rules. The importance of nationality rules bears a negative correlation to the level of harmonization achieved by every single text of secondary legislation: it is when harmonization is unimportant that the prevention of the arbitrary choice of a legal order becomes important. In view of the fact that most recent EU texts are not harmonization-intensive, it may be that weight should be placed on the determination of the appropriate nationality rules.

Compulsory host state rules
Under certain circumstances, it is not enough that the service provider complies with *some* rules but specifically with the host state rules. In these cases, the provider is left with no choice.

The typical area where the application of the host state rules is important is the social field. Therefore, Directive 96/71 (the Posted Workers Directive) states that the main characteristics of the work relationship shall be governed by the host state regulation.[280] Security is another area in which the host state may legitimately impose its own rules. For instance, Regulation 3118/93 opening up road haulage cabotage foresees that transport undertakings should observe host rules not only on tariffs, transport terms, and working time (social preoccupations), but also concerning the weight and dimensions of the vehicle, the precautions for transporting dangerous products, and so on.

More generally, the derogatory application of compulsory host state *lois de police* in situations where the rules of some other state apply in principle—be it by virtue of some rule of private international law or by virtue or the EU MR principle—is not a legal novelty. In order to increase member states' trust on MR, it could be useful to determine, on a case-specific basis, the sets of compulsory host state rules which should always be respected and could not yield to MR.

---

[278] Case C-56/96 *VT4 Ltd v Vlaamse Gemeenschap* [1997] ECR I-3143, para 22.
[279] See also the Court's judgments in Case C-212/97 *Centros Ltd v Erhvervs-og Selskabsstyrelsen* [1999] ECR I-1459; Case C-208/00 *Überseering BV v Nordic Construction Company Baumanagement GmbH (NCC)* [2002] ECR I-9919; Case C-321/05 *Hans Markus Kofoed v Skatteministeriet* [2007] ECR I-5795. On the totality of the relevant case law see Kjellgren, A., 'The jurisprudence of the ECJ on circumvention, fraud and abuses of Community law' in Andenas, M., and Roth, W.H., *Services and Free Movement in EU Law* (Oxford: OUP, 2001) 245–78.
[280] European Parliament and Council Directive 96/71/EC concerning the posting of workers in the framework of the provision of services [1997] OJ L18/1.

Provisional suspension of MR
MR is based on trust. There are situations, however, in which trust falters. The home member state may fail either at the regulatory level, by adopting measures which are deemed insufficient or inappropriate by the host state; or at the implementation/individual level by failing to monitor or sanction specific providers. In both cases, it is crucial to allow the host state to suspend the effects of MR in order to secure interests judged vital.

Consumer protection—service providers' liability
One of the main grounds invoked by member states in order to restrict the free provision of services is consumer protection. In this respect, EU law is somehow deficient. A Commission initiative to institute a common system of service providers' liability has not prospered,[281] despite its relatively limited ambition: it stopped short of establishing a system of objective liability (as is the case for producer liability[282]) and only referred to a reversal of the onus of proof.

The Services Directive is not much more helpful. Compulsory information to be provided to service recipients (Article 22), mutual assistance between national authorities (Articles 28–31), and the alert mechanism (Article 32) do offer some assurance to consumers, but only in an indirect way. On the other hand, the only provision which explicitly deals with 'Professional liability insurance and guarantees' relegates the issue to each individual member state. Indicative of the impossibility of agreement on common rules concerning providers' liability is the current draft Directive on patients' rights.[283] Despite liability for medical malpractice being of paramount importance for patient's mobility and notwithstanding the fact that patients are particularly vulnerable 'consumers' (because of their medical condition and because of information asymmetries), the Directive only foresees that healthcare services are 'provided according to the legislation of the Member State of treatment' (Article 4(1)).

Therefore, breaking common ground concerning providers' liability could be a means of increasing mutual trust between member states (and their service recipients) and advancing the application of MR.

ii. Measures to render MR more effective
General Systems of MR
In the field of professional qualifications, the General Systems of MR have taken over the previous system of sector-specific rules.[284] Instead of harmonizing the

---

[281] Decision Proposal COM (1992) 482, 'on establishing a third Community action programme to assist disabled people—HELIOS II'.

[282] Directive 85/374/EC on the approximation of the laws, regulations and administrative provisions of the Member States concerning liability for defective products [1985] OJ L210/29.

[283] Directive 2011/24/EU of the European Parliament and the Council On the application of patients' rights in cross-border healthcare [2011] OJ L 88/45.

[284] Directive 89/48/EEC on the first general system of recognition of higher-education diplomas [1989] OJ L 19/16; Directive 92/51/EEC on a second general system for the recognition of professional education and training [1992] OJ L209/25, modified several times; both these Directives have now been repealed and replaced by Directive 2005/36/EC on the recognition of professional qualifications [2005] OJ L255/22.

conditions of training for each individual profession, the General Systems only harmonize the conditions for, and the kinds of, compensatory measures available to the host state. The implementation of these Systems has been a success story. The Court has consistently interpreted their terms extensively,[285] and has covered all cases which do not come within their scope by interpreting the relevant Treaty rules in a way parallel to the Directives. The EU legislature codified the General Systems and expanded their scope in Directive 2005/36.

It may be that issues other than professional qualifications, such as the issuance of authorizations or the entry into registries could also be the subject of some kind of a General System of MR.

Standardization and certification
Standardization and certification in the field of services is likely to develop at a fast pace in the years to come.[286] This will certainly foster the effective application of MR. Moreover, the impact on services of the standards concerning the production, commercialization, and use of goods should not be underestimated.[287]

Administrative cooperation—networking
MR depends largely on good faith and cooperation between national authorities. The very term 'mutual' somehow stresses the proactive stance that national authorities should adopt. Administrative cooperation affects MR on at least three levels. At a *psychological* level, administrative cooperation allows national authorities to get to know one another, both at the personal and at the operational level and to develop trust. At a *practical* level, through administrative cooperation, they become acquaintened with each other's practices, techniques, documents, etc. At an *operational* level, administrative cooperation makes it possible for national authorities to work closer together and resolve situations and problems linked with the cross-border nature of the legal situations they are faced with.

To this end, the creation of points of contact and the establishment of networks are appropriate means. Hence, for example, the General Systems on the recognition of professional qualifications, as well as the e-signature Directive foresee the establishment of national points of contact. Similarly, the network industries Directives provide for the networking of the different national regulatory authorities.[288] It is, however, the Services Directive which is the most innovative text in this respect.[289]

---

[285] See the discussion under subheading 2(A)3.

[286] For the prospects of standardization in the field of services, see in more detail the developments in ch 7.

[287] See eg Case C-267/03 *Criminal proceedings against Lars Errik Staffan Lindberg* [2005] ECR I-3245: a 'technical rule' concerning the use of electronic betting machines had a direct impact on the provision of betting services.

[288] See Geradin, D., and Petit, N., 'The Development of Agencies at EU and National Levels: Conceptual Analysis and Proposals for Reform' (2004) 23 *YEL* 137–97; see also the discussion in subheading 2(A)4 and, more extensively, the analysis in ch 7.

[289] For the procedural arrangements of the Services Directive, see the developments in ch 7.

Exchange of information and of best practices
In addition to the previous point, the system of periodic reporting and peer review offers a triple positive effect. *First,* national authorities are made to question their own practices in order to justify them to their peers. *Secondly,* the peers become familiar both with the measures and with the underlying organizational logic of other member states' administrations. Therefore, when it comes to comparing their own system with those of their peers—in the process of applying MR—national authorities have all the necessary data. *Thirdly,* in the absence of commonly agreed standards, the exchange of best practices which takes place in this framework can be highly beneficial.

Dispute resolution: SOLVIT and the services directive
A final point on how to make MR more efficient is related to dispute resolution. This problem has two interconnected aspects.

First, disputes between the service provider and the authorities of the host (or, occasionally, home) state. In this respect, it has been observed, in relation to the *Bobadilla* case, that a waiting time of 25 months for the preliminary ruling alone, plus the delay of the national judicial procedure, in order to achieve the recognition of her diploma in her own country, is not the benchmark of a properly working internal market.[290] It is not uncommon, in fact, that member states, through protracted litigation, play the card of delayed implementation.

In this respect, the SOLVIT system, put into place by the Commission as a means of extra-judicial settlement of disputes related to the internal market, occupies an increasingly important role.[291] This system consists of a network of online dispute resolution available both to undertakings and to consumers. The 'plaintiffs' contact the SOLVIT point of contact in their country. If the complaint is within the 'tasks' of the SOLVIT network, this contact point registers it within an electronic database and contacts the SOLVIT point in the member state where the problem has occurred. The latter SOLVIT point, together with the authorities of the state concerned, tries to resolve the problem. This system, after a hesitant start, is gaining more and more credibility and the number of disputes settled is growing year after year.[292] There are, however, two limitations to SOLVIT's potential. First, it has limited competence *ratione matieriae*.[293] Moreover, SOLVIT may mediate only between an individual and a state authority, not between two individuals.

---

[290] Atanasiu, I., 'Some reflections on the role of the ECJ in relation to "Social Europe"' in Baquero Cruz, J., and Closa Montero, C. (eds), *European Integration from Rome to Berlin: 1957–2007, History, Law and Politics* (Brussels, etc: PIE-Peter Lang, 2009) 173–84, 182.

[291] Communication COM (2001) 702 final, 'Effective Problem Solving in the Internal Market ("SOLVIT")'.

[292] See the 2010 annual SOLVIT Report at <http://ec.europa.eu/solvit/site/docs/solvit_2010_report_en.pdf> (last accessed on 12 November 2011).

[293] Including recognition of professional qualifications and diplomas; access to education; residence permits; voting rights; social security; employment rights; driving licences; motor vehicle registration; border controls; market access for products; market access for services; establishment as self-employed; public procurement; taxation; free movement of capital or payments.

The *second* aspect of dispute resolution concerns disputes between service providers and their recipients. In this respect, three developments should be highlighted:

i. Regulation 44/2001 (Brussels I) on jurisdiction,[294] provides as the first criterion for special jurisdiction (ie other than the defendant's country of residence) 'the place of the performance of the obligation in question', which, in the case of services is where 'the services were provided or should have been provided' (Article 5). This criterion, however, makes little sense for services provided at a distance (GATS Mode 1), as well as for those where both the provider and the recipient move together to a third state (eg tourist guide cases). It would, therefore, be useful to clarify (possibly by means of soft law) the way in which the Regulation should apply in the various situations of service provision falling under Article 56 TFEU.

ii. We are currently going through a phase of intense activity in the area of the rules applicable and the execution of judgments in trans-border situations. The adoption of the 'Rome I' Regulation on jurisdiction in contractual disputes,[295] on one hand, and Regulations on 'small claims' and 'European injunction',[296] on the other, should develop the resolution of trans-border disputes.

iii. Article 27 of the Services Directive requires service providers to supply their contact details, to respond to complaints in the shortest possible time, and 'to make their best efforts to find a satisfactory solution'.

C. Conclusion

From the above it becomes clear that while harmonization is still an objective of the internal market for services, MR is bound to play an ever-increasing role, either as a precursor or as substitute to harmonization. The forthcoming introduction of standards for services will give a decisive push to the use of MR. MR, however, may not be seen as being panacea by offering solutions in relation to all restrictions to the free movement of services. It has been explained above that MR itself is not a unitary technique, but is subject to graduation and to diversification in the way it applies. What is more, in the absence of EU—de facto or de jure—harmonization MR may not lead to any market opening. It has been observed that MR is more about the availability of procedures, whereby the service providers are enabled/facilitated to prove that they satisfy the requirements of the host state, rather than

---

[294] Council Regulation 44/2001/EC on jurisdiction and the recognition and enforcement of judgments in civil and commercial matters [2001] OJ L16/1.

[295] European Parliament and Council Regulation 593/2008/EC on the law applicable to contractual obligations (Rome I) [2008] OJ L177/6.

[296] European Parliament and Council Regulation 861/2007/EC establishing a European Small Claims Procedure [2007] L199/1; European Parliament and Council Regulation 1896/2006/EC creating a European order for payment procedure [2006] OJ L 399/1.

about actual recognition, which may be impossible in the face of unbridgeable differences. Indeed, in the recent gambling cases the Court has underlined the limits of MR:[297] in areas where the underlying ideological and moral perceptions are completely different, and where the technological and regulatory means put to work by member states are not comparable, MR may not be an option at all.[298]

Since harmonization is often not an option at all, and since MR is not always an effective way of opening up markets, alternative means are increasingly being used for the achievement of free movement objectives. These means may still be regulatory, but voluntary and bottom up rather than hierarchical and top down. Or, they may be non-regulatory. It is to these two categories that the discussion now turns.

---

[297] The case law on gambling is discussed above in ch 5.

[298] See eg Case C-42/07 *Liga Portuguesa de Futebol Profissional and Bwin International Ltd v Departamento de Jogos da Santa Casa da Misericórdia de Lisboa* [2009] ECR I-7633, para 69.

7

Private Regulation

A. Brief introduction to private regulation

The previous chapter highlighted that one peculiarity of service regulation is that it often takes place at a sub-state level and, occasionally, via non-state measures. Indeed, in the field of services, much more than in the field of goods, private regulation plays an important role.

The term 'private regulation' here is understood as a broad category, encompassing both 'co-regulation' and 'self-regulation'. The former refers to situations where private bodies actively participate in the formation or implementation of rules, together with the government and/or stakeholders (such as users, consumers, those affected by externalities, etc). The latter refers to situations where regulatory activities are performed exclusively by regulatees.[1] Moreover, 'contrary

---

[1] The literature on private regulation is not scarce, especially US literature. At the EU level, the area has been 'monopolized' in recent years by Caffagi, F., whose works are very comprehensive and contain extremely rich bibliographic references to previous works; see eg Cafaggi, F., 'Private Regulation in European Private Law' EUI RSCAS Working Paper No. 2009/31, also available at <http://cadmus.eui. eu/dspace/bitstream/1814/12054/3/RSCAS_2009_31.pdf> (last accessed on 13 November 2011); Cafaggi, F., 'Rethinking Private Regulation in the European Regulatory Space' EUI Law Working Paper No. 2006/13, also available at <http://cadmus.eui.eu/dspace/bitstream/1814/4369/1/LAW2006.13.PDF> (last accessed on 13 November 2011); also Caffaggi, F., and Muir-Watt, H., 'The Making of European Private Law: Regulation and Governance Design' European Governance Papers (EUROGOV) No. N-07-02, also available at <http://www.connex-network.org/eurogov/pdf/egp-newgov-N-07 02.pdf> (last accessed on 13 November 2011); Caffaggi, F., 'Le rôle des acteurs privés dans le processus de régulation: participation, autorégulation et régulation privée' (2004) 109 *Révue Française d'administration publique* 22–36; see also Chalmers, D., 'Private Power and Public Authority in European Union Law' (2005–6) 8 *CYEL* 59–94; further see Scott, C., 'Regulating private legislation' in Caffagi, F., and Muir-Watt, H. (eds), *The Regulatory Function of European Private Law* (Cheltenham/Northampton: Edward Elgar Publishing, 2009) 254–68; Rudolph, P., 'The history, variations, impact and future of self-regulation' in Mullerat, R. (ed), *Corporate Social Responsibility: The Corporate Governance of the 21st Century* (The Hague: Kluwer Law International, 2005) 365–84; Black, J., 'Decentering Regulation: Understanding the Role of Regulation and Self-Regulation in a Post Regulatory World' (2001) 54 *Current Legal Problems*, 103–46; Pattberg, P., 'The Institutionalisation of Private Governance: How Business and Non-profit Organizations Agree on Transnational Rules' (2005) 18 *Governance* 589–610; and in a more general way, Prosser, T., *Law and the Regulators* (Oxford: OUP, 1997); see also a more sceptical approach in French by Mazuyer, E., and de la Rosa, S., 'La régulation sociale européenne et l'autorégulation: le défi de la cohérence dans le recours à la *soft law*' (2009) 3–4 *CDE* 295–333.

to co-regulation, self-regulation does not involve a legislative act and is essentially voluntary'.[2]

The development of private regulation, alongside public regulation, is not a new phenomenon, but a cyclical one.[3] It can be explained by at least three factors: a. asymmetric information, especially where the information involved is highly technical and private parties have better access and greater expertise than government agencies, b. the legitimacy of regulatory power, in the sense that regulatee participation increases representation and acceptance of the resulting regulation, c. as a result of the first two factors, increased compliance.

Private regulation is only likely to become more important in the years to come, through the combined effect of the state's withdrawal from important economic sectors and its replacement by private initiative combined with the increasing complexity of many service activities, which can be addressed only by the stakeholders themselves. Moreover, the scarcity of commonly agreed standards in the provision of services leaves more space for self-regulation.

For the positive functions of private regulation to materialize, however, two basic conditions should be fulfilled. First, private regulation should be complied with. Secondly, it should be directed towards serving primarily public—not private—interests.

Compliance with private regulation may stem from various sources, both internal and external to the regulation concerned.[4] Internally, private regulation may be applied by regulatees for one or more of the following reasons: a. they are convinced of its value for promoting their interests; b. even if their personal interest is not directly served, they understand that regulation is beneficial to their profession, corporation, etc and they feel bound by their participation therein (eg lawyers, doctors, etc); c. they fear the market reaction (exit) to their non-compliance; d. they may be bound to comply by contractual clauses. Alongside these 'internal' factors, external action by government may render private regulation binding: a. by adopting 'default rules' which apply whenever private regulation is not complied with, or b. by having breaches of the private rules supported by some kind of administrative or even criminal sanctions, or c. by formally turning private regulation into public. (See Figure 7.1)

More salient than the issue of compliance with private rules is that of their legitimacy. Private regulation entails the appropriation by non-state actors of an essentially public function. Irrespective of ideological preconceptions, such appropriation is inherently dangerous, as private parties are guided by their private interests. This danger may be mitigated, according to C. Scott, by four factors:[5] *interdependence*, in the sense that 'key actors lack the capacity to act alone, and in order to bring actions to fruition they require the cooperation of others';[6]

---

[2] Delimatsis, P., '"Thou Shall Not…(Dis)trust": Codes of Conduct and Harmonization of Professional Standards in the EU' (2010) 47 *CML Rev* 1049–87, 1069.
[3] See Caffagi, F., 2006, n 1, where further references are to be found.
[4] On the issue of compliance see primarily Scott, C., 2009, n 1.
[5] Ibid, at 263–6.
[6] Ibid, at 264.

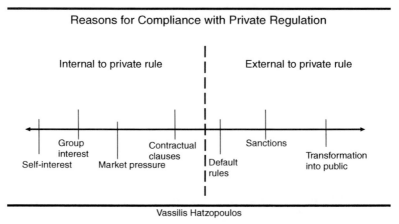

Figure 7.1. Reasons for compliance with private regulation

redundancy, in the sense that if private rules fail the legislative default will cover the vacuum; *competition*, in the sense that failure of a private regulator to produce adequate norms will be met by the norms produced by a competitive regulator; and *community*, in the sense that any private regulating body is accountable to its members and to peer pressure among private regulators. Interdependence, redundancy, competition, and community should in principle prevent private regulators from using regulatory powers to their exclusive interest, but in practice it cannot be discounted that they do privilege private interest at the expense of public. Therefore, some formalization of the self-regulating process needs to take place. Such formalization should consist of three prongs.[7] *First*, the necessary procedural safeguards should be respected in order to make sure that technocratic regulatory bodies act in the general (and not in their self-) interest. *Secondly*, the basic characteristics of public regulatory processes, such as fairness, transparency, accountability, and participation should somehow be transfused into private rule-making.[8] *Thirdly*, legal control should be secured, given that judicial review in its classic form may not be available and that, in purely private regulatory constellations, contractual freedom severely constrains the judicial margin of appreciation.

The considerations above explain why private actors are rarely left to legislate alone; it also explains why it is more precise, instead of talking of 'private regulation', to talk about 'coordinated regulatory processes'.[9]

---

[7] Caffagi, F., 2006, n 1.

[8] The extent to which private regulation may be made to satisfy the above characteristics is being seriously questioned by legal and political scientists; see the rather critical accounts contained in Curtin, D., Mair, P., and Papadopoulos, Y. (eds), *Special Issue on Accountability and European Governance* (2010) 33 *WEP* 929–1164; see also Papadopoulos, Y., 'Problems of democratic accountability in network and multi-level governance' in Conzelmann, T., and Smith, R. (eds), *Multi-Level Governance in the European Union: Taking Stock and Looking Ahead* (Baden Baden: Nomos, 2008) 31–52.

[9] Caffagi, F., 2006, n 1, at 15.

Along the spectrum of coordinated processes or private regulation, several types of regulation can be identified.[10]

    i. *Public regulation*, where private bodies have a right of consultation or, more importantly, participation. A typical EU example of such private participation into public regulation would be the Lamfalussy process.[11]

    ii. *Co-regulation*, which involves the active participation of private regulators at some stage of the regulatory procedure, after the basic regulatory choices have been set. Private actors are typically involved either in detailing and/or in monitoring the general legislative choices. The definition of standards by private bodies, the certification of products and services, the accreditation of certification bodies, the adoption of codes of conduct, the monitoring that such codes are respected, and the imposition of disciplinary sanctions all constitute examples of what co-regulation might entail.

    iii. *Delegated private regulation*, which is based on a formal (typically legislative) act conferring to the private party the right to rule-making. This act necessarily defines the limits of the conferred powers and imposes certain conditions upon the functioning and possibly, the composition of the receiving body. Examples of this technique are to be found in a few texts of secondary legislation in the broader area of the internal market, such as the Market Abuse Directive,[12] whereby, in every member state, the competent authority may choose, instead of exercising its powers itself, to delegate them to other authorities or to undertakings in the market.[13] In a similar vein, Regulation 733/2002, which creates the '.eu' top level domain name, foresees that the registry of this new domain shall be run by a private undertaking, to be chosen following a public tender procedure.[14]

    iv. *Ex post recognized private regulation*, where either the private body itself is retrospectively recognized as enjoying some legislative powers, or the rules it has adopted are given legal value. A variant thereof is the situation where privately produced rules have to be approved by a public authority in order to become effective.

---

[10] Taxonomy borrowed by Caffagi, F., 2006, n 1, at 15–26.

[11] For which see ch 6, subheading A(2).

[12] European Parliament and Council Directive 2003/6/EC on insider dealing and market manipulation (market abuse) [2003] OJ L96/16, Art 12.

[13] Other examples may be found in the Unfair Commercial Practices Directive (European Parliament and Council Directive 2005/29/EC concerning unfair business-to-consumer commercial practices in the internal market and amending Council Directive 84/450/EEC, Directives 97/7/EC, 98/27/EC and 2002/65/EC of the European Parliament and of the Council and Regulation 2006/2004/EC of the European Parliament and of the Council [2005] OJ L149/22), Art 11(1).

[14] European Parliament and Council Regulation 733/2002 (EC) on the implementation of the .eu Top Level Domain [2002] OJ L113/1, Art 3.

Article 155 TFEU, providing for the implementation of agreements reached by the social partners,[15] by means of a Council Decision, introduces a constitutionalized and highly visible instance of *ex post* recognized private regulation.[16] The greater weight placed on corporate social responsibility may be another manifestation of this type of regulatory process.[17]

v. Finally, the possibility of indirect recognition of the enforceability of private acts, through judicial decisions, should not be forgotten.[18]

From the brief presentation above, it becomes clear that private regulation is not unknown to the EU legal order but, on the contrary, is constantly gaining in importance and variety. Private regulation officially entered the EU legal order with the 1985 New Approach to harmonization and the extensive use of standards— voluntary or compulsory—adopted by standardization organizations, typically composed of industry participants. The 'privatization' of internal market regulation promoted through the 'New Approach' has not escaped the attention of legal doctrine, which as early as 1990 was asking: 'what sort of Single Market is being created here? The answer seems to be that it is a market in which business flourishes, relatively free from protective regulation, but the legitimate interests of other social groups are at risk of being ignored'.[19] Despite this criticism, however, in 2005, D. Chalmers 'finds private law making to be a central and expanding feature of most significant fields of Community law'[20]: not only a. in core internal market issues, but also in the fields of b. employment and social law, c. information and communication technologies, d. environment protection, e. financial services, f. consumer protection and unfair consumer practices, g. protection against crime, h. sports' law, and i. professional activities. Indeed, co-regulation and self-regulation

---

[15] The representatives of the European trade unions on the one hand and employers' organizations on the other; see <http://ec.europa.eu/social/main.jsp?catId=329&langId=en> (last accessed 13 November 2011).

[16] For which see, among many, Franssen, E., *Legal Aspects of the European Social Dialogue* (Antwerpen: Intersentia, 2002); Weltz, C., *The European Social Dialogue under Articles 138 and 139 of the EC Treaty: Actors, Processes, Outcomes* (Alphen aan den Rijn: Kluwer Law International, 2008); more briefly, see Smismans, S., 'The European Social Dialogue in the Shadow of Hierarchy' (2008) 28 *J Public L* 161–80; Barnard, C., 'The Social Partners and the Governance Agenda' (2002) 8 *ELJ* 80– 101; and Reale, A., 'Representation of Interests, Participatory Democracy and Lawmaking in the EU: Which Role and Which Rules for the Social Partners?' Jean Monnet Working Paper No. 15/2003, also available at <http://centers.law.nyu.edu/jeanmonnet/papers/03/031501.html> (last accessed on 14 November 2011).

[17] For which see the analysis in subsection B(1)c.

[18] For the criteria developed by different legal orders in order to define whether a regulator is subject to judicial review, see Craig, P., *Administrative Law*, 6th edn (Oxford: OUP, 2008) 893–5; Harlow, C., 'Public service, market ideology and citizenship' in Freedland, M., and Sciarra, S. (eds), *Public Services and Citizenship in European Law: Public and Labour Law Perspectives* (Oxford: Clarendon Press, 1998) 48–56; in the EU context, the question has been indirectly raised in Case C-160/03 *Spain v Eurojust (temporary staff)* [2005] ECR I-2077, as to whether the (rare) regulatory acts adopted by EU Agencies are subject to scrutiny by the CJEU—a question answered in the negative on this occasion.

[19] McGee, A., and Weatherill, S., 'The Evolution of the Single Market, Harmonisation or Liberalisation' (1990) 53 *Modern L Rev* 578–96, 579.

[20] Chalmers, D., 'Private Power and Public Authority in European Union Law' (2005–6) 8 *CYEL* 59–94.

are both formally recognized, quite restrictively, it is true—as means for the accomplishment of the EU's objectives in the 2003 Interinstitutional Agreement on Better Law-making.[21]

From the account above it becomes clear that private regulation plays a particularly important role in the field of services. Indeed, in this area where private regulation, especially in the form of professional and disciplinary rules, has a history as long as public regulation, two current trends are noteworthy. On the one hand, the EU tends to promote private regulation as an alternative to EU regulation (B). At the same time, however, the EU is quite sceptical towards rules spontaneously adopted by private actors (C).

B. Promoting private regulation

1. Direct promotion

As is clear from the illustrations above, the EU does provide some support for private regulation. Such support, however, even after the 2001 White Paper on Governance,[22] appears spasmodic and seems neither to follow any particular pattern, nor be inspired by any clearly defined policy. This notwithstanding, at least four ways of involving private actors into EU decision making in the area of services can be identified.[23]

a. *Codes of conduct*

Codes of conduct and other disciplinary/deontological rules have always played an important role in the regulation of services.[24] They fulfil a double function. First, as market integration instruments: 'they facilitate mobility of service suppliers (mobility enabling function), but at the same time they aim to enhance trust in

---

[21] European Parliament, Council and Commission, Interinstitutional Agreement on Better Law-making [2003] OJ C321/1.

[22] COM (2001) 428 final, 'European Governance'.

[23] The social dialogue Directives—transformed to Decisions by the Lisbon Treaty—are not examined in the present chapter, for three reasons: a. the procedure followed is particular, but the end-result is a fully-fledged EU legislative act; b. both the procedure and the outcomes have been extensively discussed in legal and political science literature (see n 16 above), and c. all accounts agree on the conclusion that this procedure has not as yet, and is not likely, to play any significant role in the functioning of the EU internal market.

[24] A comprehensive definition of codes of conduct, or rather a description of what they do is offered by Delimatsis, P., 2010, n 2, at 1059 and 1064: 'CoC [Codes of Conduct] typically codify traditional virtues that have demarcated a given profession for decades or even centuries and spell out binding obligations adopted by governments, usually going beyond what law prescribes. They comprise rules relating to independence, impartiality, loyalty, professional competence and integrity, trustworthiness, confidentiality, conflict of interest, charging of fees, and professional secrecy. CoC typically include rules about desirable behaviour (value orientation) and rules about prohibited behaviour (compliance orientation). Such rules are typically related to professional conduct, but they may also call for a certain lifestyle in private life. Furthermore, depending on the specifics of the profession, they define the conflicting interests and ideally hierarchize them ... CoC also describe the conduct which the recipients of services are *entitled* to receive from the professionals abiding by the CoC and thus create expectations as to the quality standard for a given service.'

services and service suppliers originating in other Member States (confidence-building function)'.[25] Secondly, they may also exclude foreign service providers in a number of ways including a. reducing consumer's trust in them; b. imposing on them some additional cost (such as professional liability insurance) or burden (such as registration requirement); c. imposing on them legal form restrictions or restrictions concerning multi-disciplinary activities; d. prohibiting effective means of penetrating a new market, such as advertising or price competition; or e. merely by subjecting them to rules in conflict with those applicable in their home state. The potentially restrictive effects of professional rules and codes of conduct was expressly recognized—and justified—by the Court as early as the *Van Binsbergen* case.[26] Indeed, it can be said that the need to respect national professional rules has offered the Court the matrix for inventing its ORPI doctrine.[27]

Recognizing early the role that codes of conduct can play in the area of services, the EU had recourse to such instruments in order to add value to hard legislation and to sustain free movement in the field.[28] Indeed, a brief overview of the EU's legislative activity in the field of services shows that the EU legislature has started paying attention to the (self-)regulatory opportunities offered by codes of conduct long before the publication of the 2001 Governance White Paper.[29] It also demonstrates that it is almost exclusively in the field of services that the EU institutions are interested in codes of conduct. Such interest takes several forms.[30]

First, codes of conduct which already exist at the national level may contribute to the objective pursued by the EU, for example, consumer protection. Such codes should be brought to the attention of consumers,[31] and occasionally represent the object of approximation by some EU instrument.[32] *Secondly*, codes of conduct promoted by member states are seen, in some circumstances, to constitute appropriate means for the transposition into national law of parts of a given Directive.[33]

---

[25] A comprehensive definition of codes of conduct, or rather a description of what they do is offered by Delimatsis, P., 2010, n 2, at 1057.

[26] Case 33/74 *Johannes Hervicus Maria van Binsbergen v Bestuur van de Bedrijfsvereniging voor de Metaalnijverheid* [1974] ECR 1299. It should be also noted that the next service case decided after *Van Binsbergen* directly put at stake some rule of private origin (Case 36/74 *B.N.O. Walrave and L.J.N. Koch v Association Union cycliste internationale, Koninklijke Nederlandsche Wielren Unie and Federación Española Ciclismo* [1974] ECR 1405).

[27] For which see the discussion in ch 4.

[28] More on the use of codes of conduct, Lundblad, C., 'Some legal dimensions of corporate codes of conduct' in Mullerat, R. (ed), *Corporate Social Responsibility: The Corporate Governance of the 21st Century* (The Hague: Kluwer Law International, 2005) 385–400; Doig, A., and Wilson, J., 'The Effectiveness of Codes of Conduct' (2002) 7 *Business Ethics: A European Rev* 140–9.

[29] COM (2001) 428 final, n 22.

[30] The analysis which follows is based on the legislative texts concerning services in which the term 'codes of conduct' appears; the legislation thus identified may not be exhaustive but most important texts are being briefly mentioned.

[31] See eg the Services Directive (European Parliament and Council Directive 2006/123/EC on services in the internal market [2006] OJ L376/36), Art 22(3)b.

[32] See eg the e-commerce Directive (European Parliament and Council Directive 2000/31/EC on certain legal aspects of information society services, in particular electronic commerce, in the Internal Market [2000] OJ L178/1), Art 1(2).

[33] See eg European Parliament and Council Directive 2008/122/EC on the protection of consumers in respect of certain aspects of timeshare, long-term holiday product, resale and exchange

It is more likely, *thirdly*, that the adoption of codes of conduct at the European—and not the national—level is found more appropriate for the implementation of parts of EU Directives.[34] Such codes shall be encouraged by and may need to be notified to the Commission.[35] On a few occasions, the Commission itself may, to some extent, determine the minimal scope and content of the codes. During the whole process of adopting a code of conduct, the existence of international standards and other codes should also be taken into account.[36]

Since codes of conduct themselves constitute 'soft law', it is worth noting that they may be promoted equally by Regulations, Directives, Decisions, as well as by Recommendations, from any of the three legislative bodies of the EU.[37] In a few circumstances, however, codes of conduct may actually be turned into 'hard law', by means of sanctions attached to their violation.[38]

Codes of conduct are typically established and adopted by the members or the representatives of some profession. In this sense, they are the paradigmatic example of pure self-regulation. Nevertheless, on some occasions, the participation of consumers and service recipients is also foreseen, at least by EU legislation.[39]

contracts [2009] OJ L33/10, Preamble Rec 22 and Art 14(1); also Council Directive 2000/78/EC establishing a general framework for equal treatment in employment and occupation [2000] OJ L303/16; European Parliament and Council Directive 95/46/EC on the protection of individuals with regard to the processing of personal data and on the free movement of such data [1995] OJ L281/35, Art 27.

[34] See eg European Parliament and Council Directive 2007/65/EC amending Council Directive 89/552/EEC on the coordination of certain provisions laid down by law, regulation or administrative action in Member States concerning the pursuit of television broadcasting activities [2007] OJ L332/27 (the AVMS Directive), introducing Article 3e in the original TVWF Directive (Council Directive 89/552/EEC) on the coordination of certain provisions laid down by law, regulation or administrative action in Member States concerning the pursuit of television broadcasting activities [1989] OJ L298/23); see also the Services Directive, n 31 above, Preamble recs 100, 113, 114 and Art 37; also the e-commerce Directive, n 32 above, Arts 8(2) and 16.

[35] See, in particular, the Services Directive, n 31, Art 6.

[36] European Parliament and Council Regulation 1107/2006/EC concerning the rights of disabled persons and persons with reduced mobility when travelling by air [2006] OJ L204/1, Art 9; on the effectiveness of international codes of conduct, see Kolk, A., van Tulder, R., and Welters, C., 'International Codes of Conduct and Corporate Social Responsibility: Can Transnational Corporations Regulate Themselves?' (1999) 8 *Transnational Corporations*, 143–80, also available at <http://www.unctad.org/en/docs/iteiit12v8n1_en.pdf#page=151> (last accessed on 14 November 2011).

[37] Indeed, all three of them have issued Recommendations promoting the adoption of codes of conduct; see Commission Recommendation on media literacy in the digital environment for a more competitive audiovisual and content industry and an inclusive knowledge society [2009] OJ L227/9; European Parliament and Council Recommendation on the protection of minors and human dignity and on the right of reply in relation to the competitiveness of the European audiovisual and on-line information services industry [2006] L378/72; Council Recommendation 98/560/EC on the development of the competitiveness of the European audiovisual and information services industry by promoting national frameworks aimed at achieving a comparable and effective level of protection of minors and human dignity [1998] OJ L270/48; and it is in this last recommendation, that the scope and content of the codes to be adopted has been set out in detail.

[38] The only example identified is in the Unfair Commercial Practices Directive (Directive 2005/29/EC [2005] OJ L149/22), Art 6(2)b, where a prohibited 'misleading action' is constituted by the 'non-compliance by the trader with commitments contained in codes of conduct by which the trader has undertaken to be bound'.

[39] See eg Directive 2008/122, n 33, Preamble Rec 22 and Art 14(1); see also Commission Decision 2005/752 (EC) establishing an expert group on electronic commerce [2005] OJ L282/20, Preamble Rec 3 and Art 2; Unfair Commercial Practices Directive, n 38 above, Preamble Rec 20 and Art 10;

The basic aims pursued by codes of conduct are trust-building and consumer protection. Codes of conduct also feature as an adequate means of regulation for the new commercial environment, the internet, which requires flexible and, often, technical, regulation. Furthermore, the Services Directive (SD) contemplated for the first time their use as a means to comply with requirements stemming from EU law in a more general/horizontal manner. Indeed, the SD declares a strong attachment to the adoption of codes of conduct, since it states, in Recital 7 that it is intended to introduce 'a balanced mix of measures involving targeted harmonization, administrative cooperation, the provision on the freedom to provide services and encouragement of the development of codes of conduct on certain issues'; it therefore treats the four (completely heterogeneous) means of furthering service provision as carrying the same weight. Article 37 of the SD further states that codes of conduct developed at EU level should contribute to the achievement of its general objectives; in other words, they should be 'facilitating the provision of services or the establishment of a provider in another Member State'.

b. Standards and quality labels

Very few (voluntary) standards have been developed by the European standardization bodies in the area of services.[40] There are even fewer legislative texts specifically aimed at establishing standards in the area of service provision. In this field, the only binding document which introduces standards, as indicated in its very title, is a Commission Decision in the field of electronic communications (the more comprehensive term for telecommunications).[41]

Even more significantly, there is no binding text focusing specifically on quality labels in the area of services; the only exception is the 2008 Commission Decision, aimed at the protection of children using the internet and other communication technologies, which does foresee the adoption of quality labels.[42]

As a growing number of services today depend on IT and services become increasingly standardized, however, both standards and quality labels are expected to be developed further in the future, in ways parallel to the use of codes of conduct.[43] This is yet another area in which the development of standards is expected to play a crucial role is the protection of the environment.

Universal Service Directive (European Parliament and Council Directive 2002/22/EC on universal service and users' rights relating to electronic communications networks and services [2002] OJ L108/51), Art 33; see also the e-commerce Directive, n 32, Art 16(2).

[40] See the discussion and data provided in ch 6.

[41] Commission Decision establishing a list of standards and/or specifications for electronic communications networks, services and associated facilities and services and replacing all previous versions [2006] OJ L86/11, itself modified by Commission Decision 2008/286 (EC) [2008] OJ L93/24.

[42] European Parliament and Council Decision 1351/2008 (EC) establishing a multiannual Community programme on protecting children using the Internet and other communication technologies [2008] OJ L348/118; this comes as a follow up to European Parliament and Council Decision 276/1999/EC adopting a multiannual Community action plan on promoting safer use of the Internet by combating illegal and harmful content on global networks [1999] OJ L33/1.

[43] See the Commission's recent Communication on 'a strategic vision for European standards' (COM(2011) 311 final).

c. Corporate social responsibility

Corporate social responsibility[44] (CSR) is 'a concept whereby companies integrate social and environmental concerns in their business operations and in their interaction with the stakeholders on a voluntary basis'.[45] Or, to put it more catchily, it 'is the deliberate inclusion of public interest into corporate decision-making, and the honoring of a triple bottom line: People, Planet, Profit'.[46] Definitions tend to be quite general and open-ended, as the precise content and implications of CSR are the object of a more descriptive than of a normative discipline. Indeed, comparative analyses reveal different perceptions on the two sides of the Atlantic;[47] even within Europe itself, the accounts are not unidimensional.[48]

The virtues and shortfalls of CSR in Europe have already been much studied[49] and it is not the place here to reproduce the relevant debate. It is worth noting, however, that the Commission has recognized the opportunities offered by CSR and has tried to give it some guidance. After the 2001 Green Paper on 'Promoting a European Framework for CSR',[50] the Commission issued an early Communication in 2002 and a more ambitious one in 2006, aimed at 'making Europe a pole of excellence on CSR'.[51] The latter Communication sets up the European Alliance for CSR, a European umbrella for new or existing CSR initiatives. Its objectives are: a. raising awareness, improving knowledge on CSR, and reporting on its

---

[44] Also known as corporate responsibility, corporate citizenship, responsible business, sustainable responsible business (SRB), or corporate social performance: see Wood, D., 'Corporate Social Performance Revisited' (1991) 16 *The Academy of Management Rev* 691–718.

[45] Communication COM (2002) 347 final, 'Corporate Social Responsibility: A Business Contribution to Sustainable Development', at 5.

[46] Taken from Wikipedia, <http://en.wikipedia.org/wiki/Corporate_social_responsibility#cite_note-2> (last accessed on 14 November 2011).

[47] Williams, C., and Aguilera, R., 'Corporate social responsibility in a comparative perspective' in Crane, A., McWilliams, A., Matten, D., Moon, J., and Siegel, D. (eds), *The Oxford Handbook of Corporate Social Responsibility* (Oxford: OUP, 2008) 522–31.

[48] Habisch, A., Wegner, M., Schmidpeter, R., and Jonker, J., *Corporate Social Responsibility across Europe* (Berlin/Heidelberg: Springer, 2005); EC, *Corporate Social Responsibility: National Public Policies in the EU* (Luxembourg: EUR-OP, 2004) and more up to date and extensively, EC, *Corporate Social Responsibility: National Public Policies in the EU* (Luxembourg: EUR-OP, 2007).

[49] See more recently, Mullerat, R. (ed), *Corporate Social Responsibility, The Corporate Governance of the 21st Century* (The Hague: Kluwer Law International, 2005); Demirag, I. (ed), *Corporate Social Responsibility, Accountability and Governance: Global Perspectives* (Sheffield: Greenleaf, 2005); for a more empirical approach, see Barth, R., and Wolff, F. (eds), *Corporate Social Responsibility in Europe: Rhetoric and Realities* (Aldershot: Edward Elgar Publishing, 2009); also, from a different perspective, Breitbarth, T., Harris, P., and Aitken, R., 'Corporate Social Responsibility in the EU: A New Trade Barrier?' (2009) 9 *J of Public Affairs*, 239–55; in French, de Cannart d'Hamale, E., de Walsche, E., Hachez, N., and Cools, P., *La responsabilité sociale des enterprises: concept, pratiques et droit* (Bruges: Vanden Broele, 2006); Drai, E., 'Responsabilité sociétale des entreprises: un mouvement créateur de valeur' (2008) 54 *Petites Affiches* 4–8.

[50] COM (2001) 366 final.

[51] Communication COM (2002) 347 final, n 45 above, and Communication COM (2006) 136 final, 'Implementing the Partnership for Growth and Jobs: Making Europe a Pole of Excellence on Corporate Social Responsibility'.

achievements, b. helping to mainstream and develop open coalitions of cooperation, and c. ensuring an hospitable environment for CSR.

The Commission's initiative has been greeted with mixed feelings by the industry, some of whose members reacted negatively to the Commission's intrusion into an issue which is, by its proper definition, a task for the enterprise. The Commission's initiative to offer some bearing (occasionally turning into steering), however, has not been without supporters.[52]

The 2008 financial crisis has curbed the enthusiasm for CSR, despite Commission efforts to underline its importance.[53] Nonetheless, as soon as economic recovery gets underway and given the social mayhem created by the crunch, CSR is expected to play an increasingly important role in the EU.

d. Associations of undertakings

Large undertakings, especially in the network industries, tend to come together and act in concert. This may happen 'spontaneously' as a result of the oligopolistic structure of the market; 'spontaneous' coordination typically relates to prices and is scrutinized under Article 101 TFEU (when it is not all that spontaneous) or Article 102 TFEU (when one undertaking is clearly dominant and leads the others into tacit collusion). Coordination may also concern technical matters, in which case it often gets institutionalized. Indeed, it may be that by institutionalizing technical cooperation in oligopolistic markets, it is intended to ensure the de facto concertation almost always takes place.

It was explained above[54] that associations of undertakings may be set up either spontaneously, or at the request of the Commission, or of one of the forums and groups established by it. These associations may be 'integrated' in the sense that they bring together all the participants in a given market, or 'horizontal' in that they bring together operators active at a given level of the economic process. They are useful for the exchange of information and for coordination purposes, but cannot effectively cope with controversial issues; this is why they either transform into more solid forms of cooperation or disintegrate. However, even if they do disintegrate or otherwise ultimately cease to function, during their effective operation, associations of undertakings have a considerable role to play in the regulation of the internal market.[55]

---

[52] See the responses to the Green Paper (see n 50); see also the academic literature (see n 49) for views that the responsibility for defining the general interest should not be left to corporations alone, but requires the intervention of actors with a more global vision of general interest and a higher degree of legitimacy.

[53] See eg speech by Verheugen, G., 'CSR, Essential for Public Trust in Business' Speech 09/53 delivered in the CSR forum, Brussels, 10 February 2009, also available at <http://europa.eu/rapid/pressReleasesAction.do?reference=SPEECH/09/53&format=PDF&aged=0&language=EN&guiLanguage=en> (last accessed on 14 November 2011). The Commission's attachment to CSR has been confirmed, while this book was under print, by the publication of a Communication on 'a renewed EU strategy 2011–14 for CSR', COM(2011) 681 final.

[54] For a more detailed discussion, see ch 5, under subheading A(5)b.

[55] See in ch 6, for sector-specific bodies and the role played by them.

2. Indirect promotion

The theory of 'default rules' in contract law has been developing in the US literature since the late 1980s.[56] Later on, it was adapted to the context of regulatory activity and has become known as the 'regulatory penalty default' theory.[57] According to the theory, a regulatory agency may adopt rules which are harsher than the ones the regulatees are happy to cope with. In order to avoid the harsher rules, parties may prefer to 'bargain around' the default rule to reach explicit, less onerous policy objectives. 'A "penalty default" rule, in other words, [is] a fallback provision which induces a more powerfully placed or better-informed party to enter into a bargaining process when it otherwise would lack an incentive to do so.'[58] Default rules are particularly valuable in contexts of information asymmetry, since they may give incentives to the informed party to disclose the information it holds.

An example given in the US literature concerns is California Proposition 65, also known as the Safe Drinking Water and Toxic Environment Act 1986.[59] This regulatory text places the burden on businesses to identify and warn those exposed to risk or, alternatively, to reduce exposures below the actionable 'significant risk' threshold. Since it is scientifically elusive to define i. those exposed, and ii. the level of exposure risk, iii. since the kind of warning which should be 'clear and reasonable' is not specified, and iv. since the amounts which may be claimed in case of breach of the Act are significant, many polluters opted for investing in polluting below the set threshold. Further examples from the US environmental regulations involve Acts which are so complicated to comply with or have such severe sanctions that endangering industries prefer to modify their activities or to engage in compensatory initiatives, in order to evade altogether the application of the harsh regulations.[60]

Regulatory experiences with penalty defaults are not unknown in the EU legal order, especially in the social field. Hence, for instance, the European Works Councils Directive[61] establishes a procedure for the establishment of a Works Council (or equivalent), applicable only if direct negotiations fail between transnational companies and their employees, modelled by the Directive itself.

[56] Ayres, I., and Gertner, R., 'Filling Gaps in Incomplete Contracts: An economic Theory of Default Rules' (1989) 99 *Yale LJ* 87–128, also available at <http://digitalcommons.law.yale.edu/cgi/viewcontent.cgi?article=2544&context=fss_papers> (last accessed on 14 November 2011).

[57] Karkkainen, B., 'Information-forcing regulation and environmental governance' in de Búrca, G., and Scott, J. (eds), *Law and New Governance in the EU and the US* (Oxford/Portland: Hart Publishing, 2006) 293–321; see also Kenner, J., 'Regulating working time: beyond subordination?' in Weatherill, S. (ed), *Better Regulation* (Oxford/Portland: Hart Publishing, 2007) 195–217; Hertig, G., and McCaherty, J., 'Legal options: towards better EC company law regulation' in Weatherill, S. (ed), *Better Regulation* (Oxford/Portland: Hart Publishing, 2007) 219–45.

[58] Barnard, C., and Deakin, S., 'In Search of Coherence: Social Policy, The Single Market and Fundamental Rights' (2000) 31 *Ind Relations J* 331–45, at 342.

[59] Available at <http://www.arb.ca.gov/bluebook/bb07/head/hea_d_20_ch_6_6.htm> (last accessed on 14 November 2011).

[60] Karkkainen, B., 2006, n 57, at 298–314.

[61] Council Directive 94/45/EC on the establishment of a European Works Council or a procedure in Community-scale undertakings and Community-scale groups of undertakings for the purposes of informing and consulting employees [1994] OJ L254/64.

Similarly, the Information and Consultation Directive[62] sets out certain minimum requirements for the content and procedures for information and consultation, while, at the same time, it allows member states to authorize the social partners to negotiate different agreements.

Alongside the few occasions in which penalty defaults have been used as such in EU legislation, there are two more general trends in the EU's regulatory activity that could have a similar effect.

First, as discussed in the previous chapter, EU legislation increasingly features as a last resort solution, once other (softer, more indirect) regulatory means have been exhausted or have proved inefficient. At the same time, the EU legislature is all the more eager to promote or, at any rate, tolerate self-regulation, in the form of codes of conduct, labels, CSR, etc. Thus sufficient space is left, and indeed incentives created industries to cover regulatory lacunae through self-regulation in order to render the EU's intervention unnecessary.

Secondly, through their recommendations and opinions and through the indicators chosen and the objectives set in the various OMCs, the EU institutions do give a clear sign of the directions they deem desirable. By the same token, in areas where they have not exercised legislative powers, they set the objectives which should inform the industry's choices.

C. Controlling private regulation

Private regulation comes at a price: it may promote private interests. This raises three kinds of problems. *First* of all, several general questions of representation and legitimacy could be raised.[63] *Secondly*, possible breaches of competition law rules should be guarded against, since private regulation allows—or even requires—private undertakings to come together and propose—or set—the market conditions in which they operate. *Thirdly*, and this is an issue confined to the context of the EU, private regulation does not necessarily favour—and indeed may undermine—the accomplishment of the internal market.

For all three reasons, the EU, its actively encouraging stance notwithstanding, sometimes casts a suspicious eye on private regulation. In the legal system of the EU Treaties, private conduct is subject to scrutiny under competition rules, namely Articles 101 and 102 TFEU. Article 101 may be applied to any kind of professional or industry representative body, since such a body is likely to qualify as an association of undertakings, even if it does not itself exercise any economic activity.[64] A body that brings together industry representatives may be subject to

---

[62] European Parliament and Council Directive 2002/14/EC establishing a general framework for informing and consulting employees in the European Community [2002] OJ L80/29.

[63] For which, see the introduction to the present chapter.

[64] Case C-35/99 *Criminal proceedings against Manuele Arduino, third parties: Diego Dessi, Giovanni Bertolotto and Compagnia Assicuratrice RAS SpA* [2002] ECR I-1529, Case C-309/99 *J.C.J. Wouters, J.W. Savelbergh and Price Waterhouse Belastingadviseurs BV v Algemene Raad van de Nederlandse Orde van Advocaten, intervener: Raad van de Balies van de Europese Gemeenschap* [2002] ECR I-1577.

competition rules, even if it is created by some legislative act and even if its statutes are approved and its members nominated by the competent minister.[65] The test used by the Court, in order to assess whether a private body does fall within the ambit of Articles 101 and 102 TFEU, is whether it is bound to pursue the general interest, or whether, on the contrary, it remains free to pursue its self-interest and that of its members.[66] The existence of a collective body representing industry interests may also trigger the application of Article 102 TFEU, as it constitutes a sign of collective dominance.[67]

Whenever private action does not stand alone, but is somehow combined with state intervention, however, the simple situation above can get complicated. In some occasions, the intertwining of private and public regulatory activity will confer a hybrid 'public' character to the ensuing measures, and increase the intensity of their control by subjecting them not only to competition rules, but also to rules on fundamental internal market freedoms (1). In other occasions, the interaction between the private and public spheres will take the resulting measures altogether outside the scope of the Treaty rules (2).

1. Public involvement increasing the intensity of control over private measures

Private measures which have in some fashion been adopted or enhanced under the influence of public intervention generally possess great impact within the regulatory space. Such hybrid rules, half-private and half-public in nature, are caught by a hybrid legal construct invented by the CJEU: the combination of Articles 101 and 102 TFEU with Articles 4(3) TEU and/or 106 TFEU.[68] Whenever the public character of a measure is clearly dominant, however, the measure will be subject to the internal market rules. Indeed, from a rather complex—and not always coherent—body of case law, one can outline both the treatment of private measures under 'public' (ie internal market) law (a) and the treatment of public measures under 'private' (ie competition) law (b).

a. Private measures under the realm of internal market rules

Purely public measures, adopted by some central or decentralized state authority are, in principle, caught by the internal market rules (essentially Articles 49, 54 and 56 TFEU). The scope *ratione materiae* of these rules, nevertheless, may be extended

---

[65] Case 123/83 *Bureau national interprofessionnel du cognac v Guy Clair (BNIC I)* [1985] ECR 391 and Case 136/86 *Bureau national interprofessionnel du cognac v Yves Aubert (BNIC II)* [1987] ECR 4789.

[66] Ibid, paras 18–21 and 12–13, respectively.

[67] For the concept of collective dominance see recently Mezanotte, F., 'Interpreting the Boundaries of Collective Dominance in Article 102 TFEU' (2010) 21 *EBL Rev* 519–37.

[68] See Slot, P.J., 'The Application of Articles 3(f), 5 and 85 to 94 EEC' (1987) 12 *EL Rev* 179–89; Gyselen, L., 'State Action and the Effectiveness of the Treaty's Competition Provisions' (1989) 26 *CML Rev* 33–60.

to cover measures with a private origin. There are at least three circumstances in which this can occur, corresponding to three different rationales:

   i. The *'organizational rationale'*, according to which internal market rules should cover measures adopted by a private body set up and/or effectively controlled by the state or some emanation thereof.[69]

   ii. The *'object rationale'* calls for an extension of the scope of the above rules to include measures by a private body which are, nevertheless, intended to regulate some activity in a collective manner. Such rules are very common in the field of sports,[70] but are also to be found in other areas, such as legal services,[71] insurance,[72] and road safety.[73]

   iii. The *'effect rationale'*: This category is much more controversial, since it involves measures which, although not intended as such to introduce regulations applicable collectively, in practice produce effects felt collectively. The only example in this category is industrial actions.[74]

---

[69] Case 249/81 *Commission v Ireland (Buy Irish)* [1982] ECR 4005; Case 222/82 *Apple and Pear Development Council v K.J. Lewis Ltd and others* [1983] ECR 4083; Case C-302/88 *Hennen Olie BV v Stichting Interim Centraal Orgaan Voorraadvorming Aardolieprodukten and State of the Netherlands* [1990] ECR I-4625; Case C-325/00 *Commission v Germany (labels of origin)* [2002] ECR I-9977.

[70] See, for the first time, Case 36/74 *B.N.O. Walrave and L.J.N. Koch v Association Union cycliste internationale, Koninklijke Nederlandsche Wielren Unie and Federación Española Ciclismo* [1974] ECR 1405; Case 13/76 *Gaetano Donà v Mario Mantero* [1976] ECR 1333; Case C-415/93 *Union royale belge des sociétés de football association ASBL v Jean-Marc Bosman, Royal club liégeois SA v Jean-Marc Bosman and others and Union des associations européennes de football (UEFA) v Jean-Marc Bosman* [1995] ECR I-492; Joined cases C-51/96 & C-191/97 *Christelle Deliège v Ligue Francophone de Judo et Disciplines Associés ASBL, Ligue Belge de judo ASBL, Union Européenne de Judo and Francois Pacquée* [2000] ECR I-2549; Case C-176/96 *Jyri Lehtonen and Castors Canada Dry Namur-Braine ASBL v Fédération royale belge des sociétés de basket-ball ASBL* (FRBSB) [2000] ECR I-2681; Case C-309/99 *Wouters*, n 64; Case C-519/04P *David Meca-Medina and Igor Macjen v Commission of the European Communities* [2006] ECR I-6991 and other sports cases.

[71] See implicitly already in Case 292/86 *Gullung v Conseil de l'ordre des avocats du barreau de Colmar* [1988] ECR 111; and more explicitly Case C-309/99 *Wouters*, n 63; Case C-506/04 *Graham J. Wilson v Ordre des avocats du barreau de Luxembourg* [2006] ECR I-861; Joined cases C-94 & 202/04 *Federico Cipolla v Rosaria Fazari, née Portolese and Stefano Macrino and Claudio Capopart v Roberto Meloni* [2006] ECR I-11421.

[72] See eg Case 90/76 *S.r.l. Ufficio Henry van Ameyde, S.r.l. Ufficio centrale italiano di assistenza assicurativa automobilisti in circolazione internazionale (UCI)* [1977] ECR 1091.

[73] Case C-49/07 *Motosykletistiki Omospondia Ellados NPID (MOTOE) v Elliniko Dimosio* [2008] ECR I-4863.

[74] Case C-438/05 *International Transport Workers' Federation and Finnish Seamen's Union v Viking Line ABP and OÜ Viking Line Eesti* [2007] ECR I-1077; Case C-341/05 *Laval un Partneri Ltd v Svenska Byggnadsarbetareförbundet, Svenska Byggnadsarbetareförbundets avdelning 1, Byggettan and Svenska Elektrikerförbundet* [2007] ECR I-11767. In both cases, the Court stated that the reason why the trade union's action fell under the internal market rules was because it was 'aimed at regulating in a collective manner' some economic activity. In both cases, nonetheless, industrial action was quite separate from actual regulation and it seems that it was the effects, rather than the object of the action that caused the Court's concern. This is clearer in *Viking* where action by the ITF (International Transport Workers' Federation) against flag of convenience practices did not form part of any specific negotiation process but rather constituted a generalized practice. Indeed, in this judgment, the Court quite boldly held that it was not the regulatory function of the trade unions which prompted the application of the internal market rules (ibid, para 65: 'There is no indication in that case-law [concerning the application of internal market rules on measures of private origin] that could validly

b. Public measures scrutinized under the competition rules

According to the wording and the logic of the TFEU, purely private measures should be caught by the relevant competition rules alone: Articles 101 and 102 TFEU.[75] However, whenever private measures are prompted, encouraged, enhanced, or otherwise directly connected with some public measure, the latter may also be challenged under the competition rules. In such cases, in order to expand the scope of application of Articles 101 and 102 TFEU, the Court either combines them with the general obligation of loyalty stemming from Article 4(3) TEU (ex Article 10 EC) or, in its more recent case law, with the general rule of Article 106(1) TFEU according to which 'Member States shall neither enact nor maintain in force any measure contrary to the rules contained in the Treaties, in particular to those [on competition]'.

After some hesitation, the position of the Court has been stabilized, in this respect, in its benchmark judgments in *Meng, Reiff,* and *Ohra*.[76] In these three judgments, which have been repeatedly quoted by the Court in subsequent cases where the public/private divide was not clear, the CJEU identified three situations in which public measures come under competition rules:[77] 'where a Member State [a.] requires or favours the adoption of agreements, decisions or concerted practices contrary to [Article 101], or [b.] reinforces their effects, or [c.] deprives its own legislation of its official character by delegating to private traders responsibility for taking economic decisions affecting the economic sphere'. A further circumstance where competition rules apply to public measures is d. where such measures render private conduct contrary to Articles 101 and 102 'superfluous'.[78]

Examining the Court's case law, these four categories can be illustrated, qualified, and further classified as follows, on the basis of the intensity of public involvement:

>   i. *Delegation:* corresponds to *Meng/Reiff/Ohra* third scenario, in which the private body legislates alone, on the basis of some kind of delegation from the public authority, in order to adopt rules with the same legal weight as

---

support the view that it applies only to associations or to organisations exercising a regulatory task or having quasi-legislative powers'). For this aspect of the cases, see Barnard, C., '*Viking* and *Laval*: An Introduction' (2008) 10 *CYEL* 463–92; Dashwood, A., '*Viking* and *Laval*: Issues of Horizontal Direct Effect' (2008) 10 *CYEL* 525–40; for a fuller discussion and further references on these cases, see the analysis in ch 5.

[75] It should not be forgotten that alongside Arts 101 and 102 which concern private conduct, Art 107 specifically regulates state action in the field of subsidies (state aids), while Art 106 serves as a passerelle for the application of competition rules to public undertakings.

[76] See Case C-2/91 *Criminal proceedings against Wolf W. Meng* [1993] ECR I-5751; Case C-185/91 *Bundesanstalt für den Güterfernverkehr v Gebrüder Reiff GmbH & Co. KG* [1993] ECR I-5801; Case C-245/91 *Criminal proceedings against Ohra Schadeverzekeringen NV* [1993] ECR I-5851; on these judgments, see the, by now 'classic' article, Reich, N., 'The "November Revolution" of the European Court of Justice: *Keck, Meng* and *Audi* Revisited' (1994) 31 *CML Rev* 459–92.

[77] Ibid, paras 10, 14 and 14, respectively (letters a, b and c have been added by the author).

[78] Case 229/83 *Association des Centres distributeurs Édouard Leclerc and others v SARL 'Au blé vert' and others* [1985] ECR 1, para 15.

those adopted by the delegating agency itself. It is a question of national law whether and under which circumstances such a delegation is valid. Under EU law, however, answering another question appears more critical:[79] whether 'the rules adopted by the professional association remain state measures and are not covered by the Treaty rules applicable to undertakings' or 'the rules adopted by the professional association are attributable to it alone'; only in the latter case, are the competition rules fully applicable. In order for measures adopted by a private body to 'remain state measures', the following criteria are taken into account by the Court: a. the body should not be composed exclusively by representatives of the profession or be nominated by them,[80] b. it should be under a formal duty to serve the general interest, not only that of the represented profession,[81] c. the state should have maintained its right to review the measure before its entry into force,[82] and d. the state bodies are free, in some circumstances, to depart from the measure thus set.[83] The above criteria need not be fulfilled cumulatively, but it is unclear whether the fulfilment of a single criterion would be enough.

  ii. *Ex post validation*: corresponds (partly) to *Meng/Reiff/Ohra* second scenario and refers to private measures, which are subsequently given binding force by the intervention of some public authority.[84] Here again, it is decisive to check whether the public authority is free a. to review the terms of the measure before making it binding and b. to deviate, occasionally, from its content.[85]

 iii. *Sanction*: corresponds to (the remaining part of) *Meng/Reiff/Ohra* second scenario, and refers to the situation where private measures are not formally made into public measures, but where their violation entails some legal sanction imposed by a public authority.[86]

 iv. *Co-regulation (stricto sensu)*: corresponds to *Meng/Reiff/Ohra* first scenario and refers to measures adopted by a private body with the encouragement ('requires or favours') of the public regulatory agencies. This will typically happen with a view to the private measures to completing or implementing some policy goals pursued by public measures.[87]

---

[79] See Case C-309/99 *Wouters* [2002] ECR I-1577, paras 68 and 69.
[80] Ibid, para 61.
[81] Ibid, para 62.
[82] Joined cases C-94 & 202/04 *Cipolla* [2006] ECR I-11421, para 50.
[83] Ibid, para 51.
[84] See eg Case 311/85 *ASBL Vereniging van Vlaamse Reisbureaus v ASBL Sociale Dienst van de Plaatselijke en Gewestelijke Overheidsdiensten* [1987] ECR 3801; Case 136/86 *BNIC II* [1987] ECR 4789; Case C-18/93 *Corsica Ferries Italia Srl v Corpo dei Piloti del Porto di Genova* [1994] ECR 1783; Joined cases C-94 & 202/04 *Cipolla*, n 82.
[85] See the cases cited in n 84.
[86] See eg Case 123/83 *BNIC I* [1985] ECR 391; Case 66/86 *Ahmed Saeed Flugreisen and Silver Line Reisebüro GmbH v Zentrale zur Bekämpfung unlauteren Wettbewerbs e.V.* [1989] ECR 803.
[87] Case 66/86 *Ahmed Saeed Flugreisen*, n 86; Case 90/76 *Van Ameyde* [1977] ECR 1091; Case C-245/91 *Ohra* [1993] ECR I-5851.

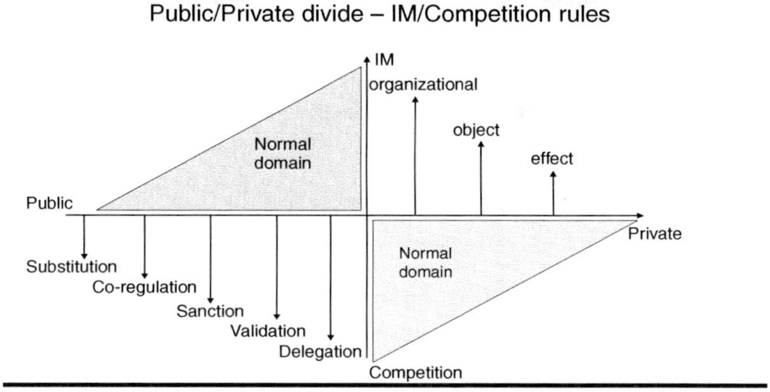

Public/Private divide – IM/Competition rules

Figure 7.2. Public/Private divide—IM/Competition rules

v. *Substitution:* corresponds to the *Leclerc v Au blé vert* situation, where the public measure encourages[88] or obliges the private actors to adopt restrictive measures, or otherwise forecloses the market in a way that the adoption of private measures becomes superfluous.[89] In this case, private measures may be altogether absent—since the decisive element is precisely that they become unnecessary—yet the competition rules may still apply.

The above categories are represented in Figure 7.2.

The way in which the internal market rules interact and complement the competition rules has been lengthily discussed by scholars.[90] More often than not, a measure in breach of competition rules, when it is the result of private action, will also be incompatible with the internal market rules as soon as it is reclassified as public action. This is so because the scope of application of both sets of rules is restricted to economic activities alone and there is no obvious reason why an activity may qualify as being economic under one set of rules and not under

---

[88] Case 66/86 *Ahmed Saeed*, n 86, para 49 and 52.
[89] Case 229/83 *Leclerc v Au blé vert* [1985] ECR 1.
[90] See Idot, L., 'Concurrence et libre circulation: Regards sur les derniers développements' (2005) *Revue des Affaires Eur* 391–409, at 370. For the convergence between the freedoms, see Waelbroeck, M., 'Les rapports entre les règles sur la libre circulation des marchandises et les règles applicables aux entreprises dans la CEE' in Capotorti, F., Ehlermann, C.D., Frowein, J., Jacobs, F., Joliet, R., Koopmans, T., and Kovar, R. (eds), *Du Droit International au Droit de l'intégration: Liber Amicorum Pescatore* (Baden Baden: Nomos, 1987) 181–203; Stuyck, J., 'Libre circulation et concurrence: les deux piliers du Marché commun' in Dony, M., and de Walsche, A. (eds), *Mélanges en hommage à Michel Waelbroeck, Volume II* (Bruxelles: Bruylant, 1999) 1477–98; Mortelmans, K., 'Toward Convergence in the Application of the Rules on Free Movement and on Competition' (2001) 38 *CML Rev* 613–49. See also Baquero-Cruz, J., 'Beyond competition: services of general interest and EC law' in de Búrca, G. (ed), *EU Law and the Welfare State: In Search of Solidarity* (Oxford: OUP, 2005) 169–212, at 179, who seems to embrace the opinion that the qualification of an activity as 'economic' should trigger the applicability of both the rules on the internal market and competition.

the other.[91] As already explained at some length,[92] the ideological question of whether any given activity qualifies as economic is typically broken down to several more technical criteria (namely, the nature of the body involved, the nature of the activity, the object of the measure, the existence of mitigating factors, and the existence of general exceptions or the applicability of Article 106(2)): the combined application thereof determines whether and to what extent the EU rules apply.

2. Public involvement excluding private measures from *any* control

There are situations where the intertwining between public authority and private conduct results in the 'hybrid' measures being altogether excluded from the scope of the Treaty. This happens essentially where the services involved are of a non-economic nature.[93]

Hence, services like police, the army, refuse collection, funeral services, and the like do not, in principle, fall within the ambit of either Article 56 TFEU or the competition rules. Such services may be classified into two broad categories: a. 'social' services which are essentially unmarketable, precisely because they do not embody market values, and b. 'strategic' services which the state would hardly entrust any other entity to pursue.[94] In the former category, the Court has held inter alia that the organization of primary pension schemes[95] and of statutory insurance against accidents at work and occupational diseases,[96] the setting up of a mandatory indemnity system for farmers, [97] and the running of care homes for the elderly,[98] all fall outside the scope of Article 56 TFEU. In the latter category, the Court has submitted that Treaty rules are not applicable inter alia in the coordination of air-traffic control,[99] the operation of a body entrusted with preventive anti-pollution surveillance,[100] and the organization of communal funeral services.[101] However, despite their social character, complementary and

---

[91] In the same sense, see Idot, L., 2005, n 90; *contra* Case C-205/03P *FENIN* [2006] ECR I-6295 (AG), para 51. For a more detailed discussion of this issue, see ch 2.

[92] See the relevant discussion in ch 2.

[93] For the distinction between economic and non-economic services and its legal implications, see extensively the analysis in ch 2.

[94] See Scott, C., 'Services of General Interest in EC Law: Matching Values to Regulatory Technique in the Public and Private Sectors' (2000) 6 *ELJ* 310–25, at 313.

[95] Joined cases C-159 & 160/91 *Christian Poucet v Assurances Générales de France and Caisse Mutuelle Régionale du Languedoc-Roussillon* [1993] ECR I-637.

[96] Case C-350/07 *Kattner Stahlbau GmbH v Maschinenbau-und Metall-Berufsgenossenschaft* [2009] ECR I-1513.

[97] Case C-355/00 *Freskot v Elliniko Dimosio* [2003] ECR I-5263.

[98] Case C-70/95 *Sodemare SA, Anni Azzurri Holding SpA and Anni Azzurri Rezzato Srl v Regione Lombardia* [1997] ECR I-3395. In the meantime, some uncertainty was created by the judgment in Case C-244/94 *Fédération Française des Sociétés d'Assurance, Société Paternelle-Vie, Union des Assurances de Paris-Vie and Caisse d'Assurance et de Prévoyance Mutuelle des Agriculteurs v Ministère de l'Agriculture et de la Pêche* [1995] ECR I-4013.

[99] Case C-364/92 *SAT Fluggesellschaft mbH v Eurocontrol* [1994] ECR I-43.

[100] Case C-343/95 *Diego Calì & Figli Srl v Servizi ecologici porto di Genova SpA (SEPG)* [1997] ECR I-1547.

[101] Case 30/87 *Corinne Bodson. SA Pompes funèbres des régions libérées* [1988] ECR 2479.

voluntary (second and third pillar) pension schemes come within the Treaty rules just like healthcare services. Likewise, public security and public order are not fields exclusively reserved to the state police, but may be partly secured by market forces, ie private security companies.[102]

The distinction between services which do, and those which do not have an economic nature is not an easy one to draw, particularly because it depends on basic political and social choices concerning the role of the state. It is dynamic too, depending both on the way the state accomplishes its mission and on market forces and private entrepreneurship.[103] What is sure, however, is that private measures which relate to this category of services are outside the scope of the Treaty, since the services themselves evade its scope.

D. Conclusion

The EU's ambivalent approach (promoting but controlling) towards private regulation gives rise to a fundamental paradox, eloquently expressed by D. Chalmers:

'Private law making reflects a further decline of the idea of government as bureaucratic domination . . . It is a retreat of the state or, in this case, the European Union. If government is perceived, by contrast, in more functional terms, as the realization of a series of public goods, then private law making represents an extension of government.'[104]

He further explains that private regulation in the current economic climate is an irreversible necessity:

'Government is not only expected to do more quantitatively. It is also expected to do more qualitatively . . . There is an expectation of doing more with less. They have to produce all this, however, against a backdrop of finite political and economic resources . . . Private law making . . . represents a creed of economy of government in which the Union is to deploy its resources more strategically and sensitively, intervening where needs are more acute, whilst coordinating, elsewhere, as broad an array of actors as possible towards as broad and ambitious a set of policy goals as possible.'[105]

Since private regulation is here to stay—and blossom—the question which needs to be answered is whether the mechanisms described above for 'taming' it, in favour of the general (and EU) interest, are sufficient. It is well documented, throughout this book,[106] that the internal market and competition rules pursue primarily economic—as opposed to social or personal—objectives. Therefore, if private regulation is not to be abused, it would seem that these two sets of rules do not offer adequate remedies. Hence, the three objectives already described in the introduction to the

---

[102] See the discussion in ch 5.
[103] See the discussion in ch 2.
[104] Chalmers, D., 'Private Power and Public Authority in European Union Law' (2005–6) 8 *CYEL* 59–94, at 76.
[105] Ibid.
[106] Especially so, in ch 2; but also in ch 4.

present chapter will require some more attention: procedural safeguards, process guarantees, and review procedures. In relation to the first, strict conditions attached to the delegation of powers, whenever delegation formally takes place, could be a way forward. In relation to process requirements, openness, participation, etc are easy to stipulate but much less so to secure, since organized interests are likely to dominate the process. Therefore, weight should be given to the third condition, the review of private regulation. In this respect, contractual freedom, the lack of specific review procedures in private law, the fact that often standardization and other such bodies lack legal personality, and the fact that norms protecting individual rights (such as constitutional, EU, or ECHR endowments) lack horizontal applicability and do not bind private parties, are all factors countering the efficacy of review of private regulation. In this respect, D. Chalmers proposes to make private regulators subject to the EU Charter of Fundamental Rights and entrust National Competition Authorities (NCAs), which are already active in monitoring private conduct and operate as a European network, with the powers to control the respect of the Charter.[107] Radical as this proposal may appear, it has the advantage of being well argued and of strengthening the appeal of private regulation as an alternative to government action. Further ways of making private regulation a more credible solution to the regulatory needs of the EU are still in the pipeline.

[107] Chalmers, D., 2006, n 104 uses the adjective 'ontological'.

8

Non-legislative Means of EU Regulation

Non-regulatory means of coordination have emerged in the last 20 years as a result of two major trends, one at the national and one at the supranational level. At the national level, the last two decades saw states switching from economic interventionism to delegated governance; a trend that has prompted several commentators to talk about the emergence of 'the regulatory State'.[1] At the supranational level, through successive Treaty modifications, the EU has been given competence in additional policy areas, thus generating a greater need for policy coordination and expertise. Patterns of delegation of powers, both in the internal and the external spheres of the EU, have accordingly been considerably altered.

At the same time, however, member states have been reluctant to transfer real regulatory powers to the EU. Therefore, the Classic Community Method (CCM) of EU governance, based on a structured and clearly hierarchized legislative procedure and leading to binding texts of harmonization or, at least, coordination, has proven insufficient to cope with the growing need for coordination.[2] In this context of changing delegation patterns and the increasing need to pursue coordination at the EU level, without surrendering further legislative powers to the EU, non-regulatory means have been developed, spontaneously or following basic institutional premises. These new means can be viewed in the broader context of what has been termed 'network governance' in Europe,[3] which in turn is connected to the broader literature on 'policy networks'.[4]

---

[1] See, for an early account, Majone, G., 'The Regulatory State and Its Legitimacy Problems' (1999) 22 *WEP* 57–78; on the same phenomenon and its impact on governance, see more recently Coen, D., and Thatcher, M., 'Network Governance and Multi-level Delegation: European Networks of Regulatory Agencies' (2008) 28 *J of Public Policy* 49–71.

[2] For the 'Classic Community Method', see Craig, P., 'Democracy and Rulemaking within the EC: An Empirical and Normative Assessment' (2002) 8 *ELJ* 105–30; Dehousse, R., 'La méthode communautaire a-t-elle encore un avenir?' in Rey, J.J., and Waelbroeck, M. (eds), *Mélanges en l'honneur à J. V. Louis* (Bruxelles: Editions de l'Université Libre de Bruxelles, 2003) 95–107; Manin, P., 'La "méthode communautaire": changement et permanence' in Blanquet, M. (ed), *Mélanges en honneur à Guy Isaac: Cinquante ans de droit communautaire* (Toulouse: Presses Universitaires Sciences Sociales Toulouse, 2004) 213–37.

[3] See eg Kassim, H., 'Policy Networks, Networks and EU Policy Making: A Sceptical View' (1994) 17 *WEP* 15–27; Peterson, J., 'Policy Networks and EU Policy Making: A Reply to Kassim' (1995) 18 *WEP* 389–407; Ward, S., and Williams, R., 'From Hierarchy to Networks? Sub-central Government and EU Urban Environment Policy' (1997) 35 *JCMS* 439–64; Schout, A., and Jordan, A., 'Coordinated European Governance: Self-Organizing or Centrally Steered?' (2005) 83 *Public Administration* 201–20; Jönsson, C., and Strömvik, M., 'Negotiations in networks' in Jönsson, C. (ed), *European Union Negotiations: Processes, Networks and Institutions* (London: Routledge, 2005) 13–26.

[4] See, among many, Rhodes, R.A.W., 'Governance and public administration' in Pierre, J. (ed.), *Debating Governance* (Oxford: OUP, 2000) 54–90; Borzel, T., 'What's So Special about Policy

Network governance is characterized by three key elements in the field of regulation:[5] a. the linkage of actors from different institutional levels—national, EU, and international—from both the public and the private sector in a form of sectoral governance; b. a shift of power from previously well-established actors to organizations or individuals whose main role is connecting and coordinating; and c. a change in the mode of governance, away from hierarchy and towards consultation, negotiation, and soft law.

The following can be seen as the major manifestations of network governance in the EU: a. the establishment of deliberative and self-enforcing mechanisms, essentially in the form of the various committees operating under the Commission and the Council auspices (comitology), b. the institutionalization of iterative target-setting and monitoring processes, under the umbrella term of the 'open method of coordination' (OMC), c. the creation of Agencies, and d. the progressive setup of incorporated trans-governmental networks, composed of National Regulatory Authorities (NRAs).

Comitology is a generic term for a wide variety of committees, operating at different levels (of representation, seniority, etc), according to divergent rules (or no rules at all), for different 'principals' (typically the Commission, but also the Council, the various Agencies, and other institutions), and delivering different outcomes. Their operation can either be analysed at an abstract, theoretical level, or in a very precise, empirical manner. The former type of analysis has been undertaken in a highly authoritative way by C. Joerges and J. Neyer and there is not much to be added.[6] As for the latter, an empirical study would require extensive field research, access to documents which are not always publicly available, and numerous interviews, which do not fit within the scope of the present work. Thus comitology, although an important means of non-regulatory coordination, will not be discussed here. In addition, there is no indication in the literature and no practical evidence to the knowledge of the present author, to suggest that comitology in the field of services bears special characteristics, distinguishing it from other areas. In contrast, the other three non-regulatory means were developed to a large extent in the field of services. These non-regulatory alternatives and their impact in the area of services are briefly examined in what follows.

Networks? An Exploration of the Concept and its Usefulness in Studying European Governance', *European Integration Online Papers* 1997 No 16, also available at <http://eiop.or.at/eiop/texte/1997-016a.htm> (last accessed on 14 November 2011).

[5] See Coen, D., and Thatcher, M., 2008, n 1, at 50.

[6] See Joerges, C., and Neyer, J., 'From Intergovernmental Bargaining to Deliberative Political Processes: The Constitutionalisation of Comitology' (1997) 3 *ELJ* 273–99; also, on a more technical note, Lenaerts, K., and Verhoeven, A., 'Towards a Legal Framework for Executive Rule-making in the EU?: The Contribution of the New Comitology Decision' (2000) 37 *CML Rev* 645–86; and more recently, Vos, E., 'The Role of Comitology in European Governance' in Curtin, D.M., and Wessel, R.A. (eds), *Good Governance and the European Union: Reflections on Concepts, Institutions and Substance* (Antwerp: Intersentia, 2005) 107–24.

A. Open Methods of Coordination (OMCs)[7]

While the term 'Open Method of Coordination' only dates back to the 2000 Spring European Council held in Lisbon, the method itself has been around for much longer: a (strong) variant thereof, instituted by the Maastricht Treaty (1992), underpinned the economic coordination which eventually led to and still drives European Monetary Union (EMU), while the European Employment Strategy (EES), introduced by the Amsterdam Treaty (1997), is also based on the method. Nonetheless, it was not until the Lisbon extraordinary summit that the OMC got its name. More specifically, it was designated as the core instrument for the achievement of the so-called Lisbon objectives, namely, the acceleration of the overall EU growth rate and the increase in employment rates under conditions of social cohesion and environmental protection.

The OMC can be analysed as a multi-level process of governance, comprising at least four stages. First, the European Council agrees on the general objectives to be achieved and offers general guidelines. Then, the Council of Ministers selects quantitative and/or qualitative indicators, for the evaluation of national practices. These indicators are chosen following a proposal by the Commission or by other independent bodies and agencies. The third stage is the adoption of measures at the national or regional level (taking local particularities into consideration), aiming at the achievement of the set objectives, and in pursuit of the indicators chosen. These are usually referred to as the 'National Action Plans' or NAPs. The process is completed by mutual evaluation and peer review between member states (occasionally alongside a system of naming and shaming/faming), at the Council level.

Although, for analytical purposes, the OMC is often contrasted with the Classic Community Method (CCM), such a stark opposition does not correspond to reality. As explained throughout this chapter, the reality of EU governance is infinitely more complex and less prone to clear-cut classifications. Instead, it may be seen as a continuum, where different governance instruments and techniques, hard and soft, top down and bottom-up, democratic or technocratic, involving sanctions or not, all complement one another.[8] Indeed, even the most devout supporters of the OMC contend that the OMC is not a way around, but rather an accompaniment to, the CCM.[9] Hence, 'it is not a matter about shifting

---

[7] The developments in this subheading draw on Hatzopoulos, V., 'Why the Open Method of Coordination Is Bad for You: A Letter to the EU' (2007) 13 *ELJ* 259–92.

[8] See among many, Sabel, C., and Zeitlin, J., 'Learning from Difference: The New Architecture of Experimentalist Governance in the EU' (2008) 14 *ELJ* 271–327, also available at <http://eucenter. wisc.edu/OMC/Papers/EUC/zeitlinSabelEUGov.pdf> (last accessed on 14 November 2011).

[9] Zeitlin, J., 'Is the Open Method of Coordination an alternative to the Community Method?' in Dehousse, R. (ed), *The Community Method: Obstinate or Obsolete?* (Basingstoke: Palgrave Macmillan, 2011), also available at <http://eucenter.wisc.edu/OMC/Papers/JZ_Community_Method.pdf> (last accessed on 14 November 2011).

from one governance mode to another and of substituting the [CCM] with the OMC'.[10]

Since its official launch in 2000, the OMC has been used or, at least, proposed as a means of coordination between EU member states in various fields. According to one account, by E. Szyszczak,[11] 13 different OMCs may be said to be in place. She proposes a four-tier classification as follows: a. *developed areas* (with a legal basis within the Treaty): Broad Economic Policy Guidelines (BEPGs) and EES; b. *adjunct areas*: the modernization of social protection, social inclusion, pensions, healthcare; c. *nascent areas*: innovation and R&D, education, information society, environment, immigration, enterprise policy; and d. *unacknowledged areas*: tax. Each of these OMCs differs from the others in several respects: the duration of each cycle of coordination, the type of outcomes, the degree of compliance pressure imposed on the participating states, the stakeholders involved, role of the participating institutions, etc. The Commission itself on its official website identifies six different OMC areas: education, employment, Lisbon Strategy, social policy, vocational training, and youth.[12] These various OMCs may be classified from 'strong' to 'weak' by reference to three criteria: a. the degree of determinacy of the common guidelines, b. the possibility of sanctions, and c. the degree of clarity regarding the roles of the various actors. Hence, it is accurate to state that 'there seem to be as many types of OMCs as there are policy areas'.[13] The term OMCs, in the plural, is a more accurate depiction of reality. There is also a temporal dynamic in all OMCs: they seem to be fluid and ever-evolving, both the European and the national components of the process being subject to change from one cycle to the next. The 2005 'streamlining' of the EES with the BEPGs is the most striking illustration of the overarching fluidity characterizing OMCs. The various OMCs are deemed to be reformed, and further streamlined, under the follow-up to the Lisbon Agenda, the so called 'Europe 2020 Strategy'.[14]

1. OMCs in the field of services

It stems from the above that there is no single definition of the OMC and that, depending on the focus of the criteria used, the term OMC may account for various forms of 'new governance'. Indeed, depending on the criterion deemed essential,

---

[10] Senden, L., 'The OMC and its Patch in the European Regulatory and Constitutional Landscape' EUI RSCAS Working Paper No 2010/61, at 8, also available at <http://cadmus.eui.eu/dspace/bitstream/1814/14436/1/RSCAS_2010_61.pdf> (last accessed on 14 November 2011).

[11] Szyszczak, E., 'Experimental Governance: The Open Method of Coordination' (2006) 12 *ELJ* 486–502, at 494.

[12] See the Europa website at <http://europa.eu/scadplus/glossary/open_method_coordination_en.htm> (last accessed on 14 November 2011).

[13] Borràs, S., and Greve, B., 'Concluding Remarks: New Method or Just Cheap Talk?' (2004) 11 *JEPP* 329–36. See also Zeitlin, J., 'The OMC in question' in Zeitlin, J., and Pochet, P. (eds), *The Open Method of Coordination in Action: The European Employment and Social Inclusion Strategies* (Brussels: Peter Lang, 2005) 19–33, at 20–21.

[14] COM (2010) 2020 final, 'Communication from the Commission Europe 2020: A Strategy for Smart, Sustainable and Inclusive Growth' 27–30.

different processes may qualify as OMCs. Most authors consider the cyclical/ iterative nature of the exercise as its main characteristic; hence, they consider the governance of the EMU to be a form of OMC, enhanced by the possibility of imposing sanctions.[15] Nonetheless, it could be counter-argued that the EMU coordination process cannot qualify as an OMC, given the absence of mutual learning, which is elsewhere deemed an essential part of the OMC.[16]

It is also clear that OMC is essentially used in areas in which the EU lacks substantial powers—therefore, the OMC is unlikely to occupy any dominant role in the regulatory space covered by internal market hard law. Therefore, from the six OMC areas identified by the Commission, only one concerns directly an activity which qualifies as a service: healthcare. Indeed, various Commission Communications mention the OMC as a means for the pursuance of healthcare objectives.[17] It was thought that 'the OMC process, unlike other health care policy initiatives, does not look for trade-offs among the main health care goals of accessibility, quality, and financial sustainability . . . rather, it regards these three broad goals as mutually reinforcing, and seeks to balance them through the idea of increased efficiency'.[18]

Nevertheless, the resulting actions have been of a relatively limited scope. An informal coordination process was initiated under the auspices of the High Level Reflexion Group on Health Services and Medical Care,[19] created by virtue of the 2004 'modernizing' Communication; this group, however, has only been active from 2004 to 2006.[20] In addition, a highly informal healthcare OMC, coordinated by the Social Protection Committee, was initiated, only to be integrated later on as part of the social protection OMC. An empirical assessment of the said OMC, based on documentary evidence, does not account for any spectacular outcomes.

'The European Commission and Council see great benefit in the exchange of policy learning among the member states in respect to these new governance activities, in particular those that are seen as likely to enhance efficiency. However, the EU Institutions do not seem—at

---

[15] See eg Hodson, D., 'Macroeconomic Co-ordination in the Euro Area: The Scope and Limits of the Open Method' (2004) 11 *JEPP* 231–48, also available at <http://eucenter.wisc.edu/OMC/Papers/ EconPolCoord/hodsonJEPP.pdf> (last accessed on 14 November 2011); Hodson, D., and Maher, I., 'Soft Law and Sanctions: Economic Policy Coordination and Reform of the Stability and Growth Pact' (2004) 11 *JEPP* 798–813, also available at <http://eucenter.wisc.edu/OMC/Papers/EconPolCoord/ hodsonMaherJEPP2004.pdf> (last accessed on 14 November 2011); Schelkle, W., 'EU Fiscal Governance: Hard Law in the Shadow of Soft Law?' (2007) 23 *Columbia J of Eur L* 705–31.

[16] This thought is owed to J. Zeitlin and his comments on a draft of my paper above n 7.

[17] See eg Communication COM (2004) 304 final, 'Modernising Social Protection for the Development of High-Quality, Accessible and Sustainable Health Care and Long-Term Care: Support for the National Strategies Using the 'Open Method Of Coordination'; Communication COM (2004) 356 final, 'e-Health—Making Healthcare Better for European Citizens: An Action Plan for a European e-Health Area'; Communication COM (2004) 29 final, 'The Spring Report 2004: Delivering Lisbon'.

[18] Hervey, T., 'The EU's Governance of Health Care and the Welfare Modernization Agenda' (2008) 2 *Regulation and Governance* 103–20, at 107.

[19] See Szyszczak, E., 2006, n 11, at 491–2.

[20] See Hervey, T., 'The EU and the governance of health care' in de Búrca, G., and Scott, J. (eds), *Law and New Governance in the EU and the US* (Oxford/Portland: Hart Publishing, 2006) 179–210, at 206; see also the corresponding (now archived) page at the Commission's website, at <http://ec. europa.eu/health/ph_overview/co_operation/mobility/high_level_hsmc_en.htm> (last accessed on 14 November 2011).

least based on the present documentary evidence—to be interested in using the shared learning function of the OMC to alter existing health care policy paradigms in Europe, through dissemination of new ideologies of health care through social learning among the relevant policy elites.'[21]

Despite the OMC's limited role in the regulation of sector-specific service activities, it occupies a very important role in other policy areas which indirectly affect the provision of services: the OMC is the main instrument used by the EU for its European Employment Strategy and is also actively used in the area of social protection (inclusion and pensions). The way the OMC operates and the results it yields in each of these policy areas has been lengthily discussed by scholars and the relevant discussion may not be replicated here.[22]

At the same time, less formalized OMC-type processes are operating in various areas touching other service activities. The iterative/cyclical logic of the OMC is followed by several sector-specific Directives, as well as by the Services Directive, which often set out periodical evaluations and *rendez-vous* clauses.[23] Similarly, the mutual learning objective of the OMC is pursued both by means of hard law (eg the above-mentioned directives) and by other non-regulatory means, as will be explained in the following paragraphs.

2. Evaluation of OMCs in the field of services

The OMC is the subject of heated debate amongst both lawyers and political scientists.[24] While it is relatively easy to identify the institutional and

---

[21] Hervey, T., 2008, n 18, at 113.

[22] Indeed, the bibliography selected by the EU Center of Excellence of the University of Wisconsin, specifically concerning the OMC as a means of promoting the European Employment Strategy, accounts for more than 70 articles; and the number is comparable for the OMC studies in relation to social exclusion; these come on top of the general articles and books about the OMC; see <http://eucenter.wisc.edu/OMC/open12.html> (last accessed 19 December 2011).

[23] Further, see the discussion in ch 6, under subheading D(1)b(i).

[24] For the OMC, see, among many, the books (in relevance order) by Zeitlin, J., and Pochet, P. (eds), *The Open Method of Coordination in Action: The European Employment and Social Inclusion Strategies* (Brussels: Peter Lang, 2005); Dehousse, R. (ed), *L'Europe sans Bruxelles?: Une analyse de la Methode Ouverte de Coordination* (Paris: L'Harmattan, 2004); Snyder, F. (ed), *The EU and Governance/L'UE et la Gouvernance* (Bruxelles: Bruylant, 2006); de Búrca, G., and Scott, J., *Law and New Governance in the EU and the US* (Oxford/Portland: Hart Publishing, 2006). In periodic literature, see the special issues of *ELJ* (2002:1), *JEPP* (2004:2), *Columbia J of Eur L* (2007:3), dedicated to the OMC and other new methods of governance (individual articles from these issues are only cited when specifically used). See also the following (recent) articles: Senden, L., 2010, n 10; Tholoniat, L., 'The Career of the OMC: Lessons from a "Soft" EU Instrument' (2010) 33 *WEP* 93–117; Büchs, M., 'How Legitimate Is the OMC?' (2008) 46 *JCMS* 765–86; Armstrong, K., Begg, I., and Zeitlin, J., 'The Open Method of Co-ordination and the Governance of the Lisbon Strategy' (2008) 46 *JCMS* 413–50; Citi, M., and Rhodes, M., 'New Modes of Governance in the EU: Common Objectives versus National Preferences' European Governance Papers (EUROGOV) No N-07-01, <http://www.connex-network.org/eurogov/pdf/egp-newgov-N-07-01.pdf> (last accessed on 14 November 2011); Hatzopoulos, V., 2007, n 7; Armstrong, K., and Kilpatrick, C., 'Law, Governance or New Governance?: The Changing Open Method of Coordination' (2007) 13 *Columbia J of Eur L* 649–77. For a more complete bibliography on the OMC see Hatzopoulos, V., 2007, cited above; an even fuller list of bibliographic references is to be found at the website of the Wisconsin/Madison EU Centre of Excellence at <http://eucenter.wisc.edu/OMC/open12.html> (last accessed 14 November 2011).

legal implications of the OMCs, it is much more difficult to assess their effectiveness as a regulatory method. Empirical evidence is difficult to evaluate and accounts are often contradictory.

'Many critics of the OMC take substantive policy change, especially as reflected in new legislation, as the main criterion for assessing its domestic influence.[25] Judged solely on this basis, as they insist, it is hard to show that the OMC has had a major impact outside of certain restricted cases, and even in those it is only one of several factors. But if we consider other types of impact, including not only procedural changes in governance and policy making processes, but also cognitive and discursive shifts, along with changes in issue salience and political agendas, then we may identify deeper and more numerous influences.'[26]

Indeed, despite the scepticism as to the efficiency of the OMC,[27] and the criticisms expressed by several authors,[28] it is suggested that, at least in the field of employment and social inclusion areas, the OMC should be considered as a qualified success, in at least three respects.[29] *First*, substantive policy changes have been induced in the form of a. changes in national policy thinking (cognitive shifts), b. changes in national political agendas (political shifts), and c. changes in specific national policies (programmatic shifts). *Secondly*, procedural shifts in governance and policy making have been produced, in the form of a. better horizontal coordination and cross-sectoral integration of interdependent policy areas, b. improvements in national steering and statistical capacities, c. enhanced vertical coordination, and d. increased involvement of non-state actors in domestic policy making. Mutual learning is the *third* benefit accruing from the OMC.

Such indirect 'achievements', however, may be overshadowed by the EU's failure to manage the EMU efficiently and to ensure compliance with the Stability and Growth Pact, despite the fact that the OMC followed in this field was 'enhanced' by the possibility of imposing sanctions; the Greek and Irish crises are testimonies to such failure. Furthermore, the credibility of the OMC has been unfavourably tested in the field for which it was formally devised, namely the achievement of the Lisbon objectives: it is by no means controversial to observe that at the end of 2010 the European economy was far from being the most competitive of the world and

---

[25] Moravcsik, A., 'The European Constitutional Compromise and the Neofunctionalist Legacy' (2005) 12 *JEPP* 349–86; Kröger, S., 'The End of Democracy as We Know It?: The Legitimacy Deficits of Bureaucratic Social Policy Governance' (2007) 29 *J of Eur Integration* 565–82; Citi, M., and Rhodes, M., 2007, n 24.

[26] Zeitlin, J., 2010, n 9, at 9 (of the electronic version).

[27] See eg Featherstone, K., 'Soft Co-ordination Meets "Hard" Politics: The EU and Pension Reform in Greece' (2005) 12 *JEPP* 733–50; Lodge, M., 'The Importance of Being Modern: International Benchmarking and National Regulatory Innovation' (2005) 12 *JEPP* 649–67.

[28] See works cited in n 27 above; see also Radaelli, C., *The Open Method of Coordination: A New Governance Architecture for the European Union?: Swedish Institute for European Policy Studies (SIEPS) Report No. 1* (Stockholm: SIEPS, 2007); Hatzopoulos, V., 2007, n 7.

[29] Zeitlin, J., 2011, n 9.

that the achievement of this and the other Lisbon objectives have been reported for another 10 years.[30]

B. Agencies

Although the establishment of the first EU agency dates back to the 1970s, it is over the last 20 years that their number has rapidly increased.[31] This administrative phenomenon has extensively occupied writers, both in the legal and the political science literature.[32]

Several reasons account for the emergence of agencies; some are general, while others apply specifically to the EU framework. Among the former, the most prominent reason is that agencies seem to provide an adequate response to doubts expressed about the legitimacy and the feasibility of political systems to operate in technologically complex societies: they offer the prospect of professional management, independent expertise, and depoliticized decisions.[33] This, in turn, has created a wider trend for setting up agencies in national and international administrations, strongly influenced by new public management.[34] Moreover, agencies (mainly executive) have existed for over 100 years in the US,[35] and (for shorter periods of time) in various member states.[36]

---

[30] Communication COM (2010) 2020 final, 'Europe 2020: A Strategy for Smart, Sustainable and Inclusive Growth'.

[31] According to the Commission, a second generation of agencies started their activities in 1994–5, and a third generation (the most endowed) emerged in the early years of the 2000s; see <http://europa.eu/agencies/community_agencies/history/index_en.htm> (last accessed on 14 November 2011).

[32] For the emergence of agencies, see Majone, G., 'The New European Agencies: Regulation by Information' (1997) 4 *JEPP* 262–75; Kreher, A., 'Agencies in the EC: A Step Towards Administrative Integration in Europe' (1997) 4 *JEPP* 225–45; Chiti, E., 'The Emergence of a Community Administration: the Case of European Agencies' (2000) 37 *CML Rev* 309–43; Vos, E., 'Reforming the European Commission: What Role to Play for EU Agencies?' (2000) 47 *CML Rev* 1113–34; Yataganas, X., 'Delegation of Regulatory Authority in the EU, The Relevance of the American Model of Independent Agencies' Jean Monnet Working Paper No 03/2001, also available at <http://centers.law.nyu.edu/jeanmonnet/papers/01/010301.html> (last accessed on 14 November 2011); Majone, G., 'Delegation of Regulatory Powers in a Mixed Polity' (2002) 8 *ELJ* 319–39; Craig, P., 'The Constitutionalisation of Community Administration' (2003) 28 *EL Rev* 840–64; Flinders, M., 'Distributed Public Governance in the EU' (2004) 11 *JEPP* 520–44; Geradin, D., and Petit, N., 'The Development of Agencies at EU and National Levels: Conceptual Analysis and Proposals for Reform' (2004) 23 *YEL* 137–97; Chiti, E., 'An Important Part of the EU's Institutional Machinery: Features, Problems and Perspectives of European Agencies' (2009) 46 *CML Rev* 1395–442; Griller, S., and Orator, A., 'Everything under Control? The Way Forward for Agencies in the Footsteps of the Meroni Doctrine' (2010) 35 *EL Rev* 3–35; see also Communication COM (2002) 718 final, 'The Operating Framework for the European Regulatory Agencies'.

[33] See Majone, G., 2002, n 32.

[34] OECD, *Distributed Public Governance: Agencies, Authorities and Other Government Bodies* (Paris: OECD Publishing, 2002).

[35] The first US agency, the Interstate Commerce Commission (ICC) was set up in 1889; see Yataganas, X., 2001, n 32, at 25; for the role of the agencies in the US, see, among many others, Strauss, P., 'The Place of Agencies in Government: Separation of Powers and the Fourth Branch' (1984) 84 *Columbia L Rev* 573–633.

[36] Barbieri, D., and Ongaro, E., 'EU Agencies: What Is Common and What Is Distinctive Compared with National-Level Public Agencies' (2008) 74 *Int Rev of Administrative Sciences* 368–420.

More specifically, within the EU, many more reasons have supported the creation of agencies. The 'intensification' of internal market coordination (in the field of drugs, intellectual property, and network-based industries, to state but a few), and the diversification of EU competences (especially with the addition of the two intergovernmental pillars and the communautarization of 'Title IV' by the Treaty of Amsterdam) dramatically increased the administrative workload and the expertise required by the Commission for the daily administration of the tasks assigned to it. This increase, combined with the cap on Commission staff—now approximately 26,000 civil servants—has caused a diversion of growth in staff towards (newly created) EU agencies. This would allow the Commission to 'act as an "*administration de mission*" and identify the areas in which action by the Community is necessary, without getting entangled in the daily management of EU policies; agencies, bringing together technical and economic expertise, should deal with the latter'.[37] This, in turn, would allow the Commission to tackle better the 'governance crisis' of the early 2000s, which eventually led to the publication of the 2001 White Paper on Governance.[38]

Compared with traditional means of coordination, agencies were supposed to encourage the coordination of regulatory practices in the member states, while at the same time, to contribute to the efficient and flexible implementation of EU legislation and policies, particularly in areas where technical or scientific considerations are important. Furthermore, they were expected to reduce political transaction costs, organize independent expertise, increase transparency, and enhance credible commitment.[39] Moreover, agencies can be more efficient than the Commission, because they generally constitute smaller organizational entities with more focused expertise, responding more flexibly to complex and emerging issues. In addition, by facilitating networks of national authorities, EU agencies can diffuse regulatory practices and styles.[40] Finally, concerns expressed over the transparency and accountability of agencies[41] are now alleviated, if not dispelled, since the Lisbon Treaty formally 'constitutionalizes' them by extending over them judicial and parliamentary control, as well as an express obligation to grant access to their documents.

Therefore, recent decades have seen EU agencies 'mushroom'. Indeed, according to the official Commission webpage, there are 23 agencies active in the area of

---

[37] Vos, E., 2000, n 32, at 1118 (fn omitted); see also in the same wavelength, Yataganas, X., 2001, n 32, at 6.

[38] COM (2001) 428 final, 'European Governance—A White Paper' [2001] OJ C287/1; see also, Yataganas, X., 2001, n 32, at 6.

[39] Schout, A. and Pereyra, F., 'The Institutionalization of EU Agencies: Agencies as "Mini-Commissions"' (2010) 88 *Public Administration* 1–15.

[40] See, in this sense, Groenleer, M., Versluis, E., and Kaeding, M., 'Regulatory Governance through EU Agencies? The Implementation of Transport Directives' Paper presented at the ECPR Standing Group on Regulatory Governance Conference '(Re)Regulation in the Wake of Neoliberalism: Consequences of Three Decades of Privatization and Market Liberalization', Utrecht, 5–7 June 2008, also available at <http://regulation. upf.edu/utrecht-08-papers/mgroenleer_eversluis.pdf> (last accessed on 15 November 2011), at 6.

[41] See e.g. Vos, E., 2000, n 32, at 1120.

economic policy (what used to be the first pillar), three agencies in the field of police and judicial cooperation, another three in the field of Common Security and Defence Policy (CSDP) and yet another six provisional 'executive agencies', specifically entrusted with management of one or more EU programmes; to all these, another two Euratom agencies should be added.[42] These make a total of 37 agencies, covering all areas of EU activity—the majority of which are, nonetheless, active in the economic sphere. It is precisely the category of 'economic' agencies, which is of interest for the purposes of the present study.[43]

Agencies active in the economic field have been subject to various classifications. The Commission itself distinguishes between executive and regulatory agencies.[44] In so doing, it is effectively re-branding distinctions that had already been proposed by commentators, which differentiated executive from information agencies (the latter further distinguished depending on whether the information provided is or is not part of the official decision-making process).[45] These distinctions accompany a more political one: if the EU policy process is analysed as comprising four stages (agenda setting, policy formulation, policy decision, and policy implementation), agencies are mainly involved in policy implementation and, to a lesser extent, formulation.[46]

---

[42] See <http://europa.eu/agencies/index_en.htm> (last accessed on 15 November 2011). The fact that the agencies are distinguished as above, however, may be a sign that this page has not been updated since the entry into force of the Lisbon Treaty, in December 2009.

[43] This is also the category which has attracted most of the Commission's attention; see SG/8597/01, Commission Report by the Working Group 'Establishing a Framework for Decision-making Regulatory Agencies', available at <http://ec.europa.eu/governance/areas/group6/report_en.pdf> (last accessed on 15 November 2011); Communication COM (2002) 718 final, 'The Operating Framework for the European Regulatory Agencies'; Draft Interinstitutional Agreement COM (2005) 59 final, 'on operating framework of European Regulatory Agencies'; Meta-evaluation on the Community Agency System: Final Report, Commission Services Document, DG Budget (2003); Communication COM (2008) 135 final, 'European Agencies: The Way Forward'; Meta-study on Decentralised Agencies: Cross-cutting Analysis of Evaluation Findings, Euréval, (2008), available at <http://ec.europa.eu/dgs/secretariat_general/evaluation/docs/study_decentralised_agencies_en.pdf> (last accessed on 15 November 2011); Evaluation of the EU decentralized agencies in 2009, Rambol/Euréval/Matrix Report commissioned by the Commission, available at <http://ec.europa.eu/dgs/secretariat_general/evaluation/docs/decentralised_agencies_2009_part4_en.pdf> (last accessed on 15 November 2011).

[44] COM (2002) 718 final, n 43.

[45] See eg de Búrca, G., 'The institutional development of the EU: a constitutional analysis' in Craig, P., and de Búrca, G. (eds), *The Evolution of EU Law* (Oxford: OUP, 1999) 55–82, at 76.

[46] Barbieri, D., and Ongaro, E., 2008, n 36, at 397. A different, more functional distinction may be drawn between agencies which a) provide, coordinate and disseminate information (on their own or by creating and coordinating networks of national experts), b) provide specific services and specific measures necessary for the implementation of EU policies, and c) produce specific information, expertise and services which are the compulsory basis for decision making, but lack decision-making powers of their own (Vos, E., 2000, n 32, at 1120). Alternatively, agencies may be distinguished in a) information, b) implementation, and c) management responsible (Dehousse, R., 2002, n 24, at 7). In a similar vein, agencies may be classified depending on their tasks, which may be focused on a) decision making, b) inspection, c) training, and d) research (Groenleer, M., Versluis, E., and Kaeding, M., 2008, n 40). Yet a different distinction is between agencies which a) contribute to the proper application of the internal market rules by individuals, b) weigh individual against general interest in an effort to implement EU policies touching on social regulation, c) provide scientific information enabling EU institutions to develop sound policy actions in the field of social regulation, or d) are active in the field of social policy (Chiti, E., 2000, n 32, at 316–7). Lastly, agencies have been classified on the

1. Agencies in the field of services

Of the 23 'economic' agencies in place, five are exclusively active in the field of service provision. The same is true for two provisional executive agencies.

Unsurprisingly, agencies have been set up in service areas where highly specialized expert knowledge is crucial; their mandate is typically connected to safety and security issues. What is more, agencies are mostly active in areas in which there is extensive EU secondary legislation. From this point of view, in the field of services, the creation of agencies does not lead to direct competence creep, but is rather intended as a way to rationalize the implementation of technical EU rules, which are already in place. At a second glance, however, it may be observed that the competences given to agencies are not restricted to safety and security, but have broader implications for the provision of services traditionally considered as 'public' services. Under this perspective, agencies in the field of services may be ultimately seen as yet another means by which the EU is striving to coordinate the conditions for the provision of services of general interest (SGIs).

a. General agencies

The first service agencies were created in the field of transport, in which the EU has long held competence. Both the European Aviation Security Agency (EASA) and the European Maritime Safety Agency (EMSA) were founded in 2002.[47] Of the two, the EASA had more extensive competences, since it was given limited regulatory powers; its powers were further extended in its 2008 reshuffling.

In particular, the EASA's mission falls under three headings: i. information gathering and dissemination, in that it offers expert advice to the EU for drafting new legislation and carries out safety analysis and research; ii. implementation and monitoring of safety rules, including inspections in the member states, and iii. regulatory duties, including type certification of aircraft and components, as well as the approval of organizations involved in the design, manufacture, and maintenance of aeronautical products; it also grants authorizations to third country operators. The highpoint in the EASA's certification functions has been the certification of the 'giant' Airbus 308, replacing member states authorizations and, thus, allowing the new Airbus to fly to all suitable EU airports. The regulatory

---

basis of their objectives (or the model they follow): a) agencies serving the operation of the internal market (regulatory model), b) observatories (monitoring model), c) agencies promoting social dialogue at EU level (cooperation model), and d) agencies operating as subcontractors to the European public service (executive model) (Yataganas, X., 2001, n 32, at 29–30).

[47] European Parliament and Council Regulation 1592/2002/EC on common rules in the field of civil aviation and establishing a European Aviation Safety Agency [2002] OJ L240/1, repealed by European Parliament and Council Regulation 216/2008/EC on common rules in the field of civil aviation and establishing a European Aviation Safety Agency, and repealing Council Directive 91/670/EEC, Regulation (EC) No 1592/2002 and Directive 2004/36/EC [2008] OJ L79/1; European Parliament and Council Regulation 1406/2002 establishing a European Maritime Safety Agency [2002] OJ L208/1.

functions of the EASA were extended by the 2008 Regulation and further extension is foreseen in the future. Based in Cologne, the EASA already employs some 500 professionals from across Europe.[48]

The European Maritime Safety Agency (EMSA) was partly created as a response to the maritime disasters of *Erika* (1999) and *Prestige* (2002), in order to enhance maritime safety. Contrary to the EASA, however, it lacks proper regulatory powers and its functions are limited to coordinating national authorities and evaluating classification societies recognized by the EU as well as maritime training centres outside the EU. Like the EASA, the EMSA possesses implementation powers to ensure that EU law in the field is properly applied; it is also entrusted with the duty to gather and share information. One of the main achievements of the EMSA has been the setting up of SafeSeaNet, a system for monitoring all the ships that transport dangerous cargoes, and for standardizing the response to accidents. The EMSA's founding Regulation has been amended three times and a fourth amendment is currently on its way. The EMSA is seated in Lisbon, and has a 50-strong staff.[49]

The European Railway Agency (ERA) was created a couple of years later, by Regulation 881/2004, as part of the second railway package; its mandate was extended in 2008.[50] It has no proper regulatory powers, but falls only a little short of that. It may address recommendations to the Commission, and issue opinions on the Commission's request on various issues, such as technical and operational harmonization (including conditions for mutual acceptance of railway vehicles), safety assessment methods, safety targets, and safety certification conditions. To this end, it also proposes new and updated legislative acts for adoption by the Commission. Further, it has an information dissemination function through networking with national bodies, providing registers and databases, and giving guidance on the implementation of the regulatory framework. The ERA's core activities cover the following areas: a. cross-acceptance of national rules, the checks against these rules, and the relevant authorizations; b. interoperability, both at the technical and the personnel level; c. the European Rail Traffic Management System (ERTMS), set up to create a unique signalling and communication standard throughout Europe; d. safety, to be achieved in various ways (eg by setting targets and monitoring railways against them, by monitoring certification of railways undertakings, infrastructure managers, and train managers, by following and giving opinions on national safety rules, and by keeping public databases of security-related documents); e. economic evaluation, aimed at fostering the competitiveness of railway transportation; and f. consultations with the social partners, whenever agency proposals have an impact on the social environment or the

---

[48] More on the EASA may be found on its website, at <http://easa.europa.eu/what-we-do.php> (last accessed on 15 November 2011).

[49] More on the EMSA may be found on its website, at <http://www.emsa.europa.eu/end173.html> (last accessed on 15 November 2011).

[50] European Parliament and Council Regulation 881/2004/EC establishing a European Railway Agency [2004] OJ L164/1; amended by European Parliament and Council Regulation 1335/2008/EC [2008] OJ L354/51.

working conditions of employees in the industry. The ERA is seated in Valenciennes, France.[51]

The European Network and Information Security Agency (ENISA) was created by Regulation 460/2004 in order to ensure the high level of network and information security necessary in the EU.[52] Its initial mandate was for five years, then extended for another five, now expiring in September 2013. Its powers, however, are much more limited than those given to the transport-related agencies, since they are only confined to information collection and dissemination and to mediating between EU institutions, national authorities, and businesses. Together with the EU institutions and national authorities, ENISA seeks to develop a culture of security for information networks across the EU. It is particularly active in the area of broadband, online banking, e-commerce, and mobile phone security. It is based in Brussels.[53]

The most recently founded agency in the area of services is the Agency for the Cooperation of Energy Regulators (ACER), created by Regulation 713/2009.[54] As explained above,[55] this agency is not entirely new, but rather emerged as a result of the 'agencification' of a pre-existing cooperation structure between NRAs.[56] ACER will complement and coordinate the work of NRAs. Its competences include participation in the creation of European network rules; taking binding individual decisions on terms and conditions for access and operational security for cross-border infrastructure if NRAs cannot agree; giving advice on various energy-related issues to the European institutions; and monitoring and reporting to the European Parliament and the Council. Since it will be competent to adopt binding decisions, ACER will have an Administrative Board, a Regulatory Board, and a Board of Appeal. It is expected that ACER will have a staff of around 50 people and, as of 3 March 2011, it is fully operational in its permanent office in Ljubljana.[57]

Finally, the newly established European Supervisory Authorities (ESA) and the European Systemic Risk Board (ESRB) in the area of financial services should also

[51] More on the ERA may be found on its website, at <http://www.era.europa.eu/Pages/Home.aspx> (last accessed on 15 November 2011).

[52] European Parliament and Council Regulation 460/2004/EC establishing the European Network and Information Security Agency [2004] OJ L77/1; amended by European Parliament and Council Regulation 1007/2008/EC amending Regulation (EC) No 460/2004 establishing the European Network and Information Security Agency as regards its duration [2008] OJ L293/1; amended again while this book was under print, by European Parliament and Council Regulation (EC) 580/2011 [2011] OJ L165/3.

[53] More on the ENISA may be found on its website, at <http://www.enisa.europa.eu/> (last accessed on 15 November 2011).

[54] European Parliament and Council Regulation 713/2009/EC establishing an Agency for the Cooperation of Energy Regulators [2009] OJ L211/1.

[55] See also the discussion in ch 5, especially under subheading A(5)b.

[56] The European Regulatory Group for Electricity and Gas (ERGEG) established by Council Decision 2003/796/EC on establishing the European Regulators Group for Electricity and Gas [2003] OJ L296/34.

[57] More on the ACER may be found on its website, at <http://www.energy-regulator.eu/portal/page/portal/ACER_HOME> (last accessed on 15 November 2011).

be mentioned, although at the time of writing it was not clear whether they would formally qualify as agencies.[58]

b. Executive agencies

Executive agencies came into existence under Regulation 58/2003, which determines the general conditions for the creation and functioning of executive agencies. They have a limited lifespan, which may be extended. At the time of writing, six executive agencies were in operation;[59] two of them directly active in areas which relate to service provision.

The Executive Agency for Health and Consumers (EAHC, formerly the Public Health Executive Agency) was created on 1 January 2005 to support implementation of the EU Public Health Programme. In 2008, the agency's lifetime was prolonged until 31 December 2015, and its tasks expanded to include supporting actions in the field of consumer protection (Consumer Programme) and training for safer food (Better Training for Safer Food initiative).[60] Among the above, the Health Programme is the one most directly related to services provision. This programme constitutes the European Commission's main instrument for implementing the EU health strategy; it aims to improve the level of physical and mental health and wellbeing of EU citizens and reduce health inequalities throughout the Union. In particular, the Programme supports health-promoting and preventive actions that address major health determinants, eg nutrition, physical activity, or smoking. To illustrate, the first Programme of EU action in the field of public health (2003–8) financed over 300 projects and other actions. The programme is implemented in the form of annual work plans, which the European Commission adopts. The EAHC occupies about 40 staff members and is based in Luxembourg.[61]

The Trans-European Transport Network Executive Agency (TEN-T EA) assures the technical and financial implementation and management of the Trans-European Transport Network (TEN-T) programme. Created in 2006, the agency has a mandate until 31 December 2015.[62] Its work of managing key

---

[58] For those and for the scarce literature concerning them, see above in ch 6, subheading A(2).

[59] The Education, Audiovisual, and Culture Executive Agency (EACEA), the European Research Council Executive Agency (ERC Executive Agency), the Executive Agency for Competitiveness and Innovation (EACI), the EAHC, the Research Executive Agency (REA), and the Trans-European Transport Network Executive Agency (TEN-T EA).

[60] Commission Decision 2004/858/EC setting up an executive agency, the 'Executive Agency for the Public Health Programme', for the management of Community action in the field of public health [2004] OJ L369/73, as amended by Commission Decision 2008/544/EC amending Decision 2004/858/EC in order to transform the Executive Agency for the Public Health Programme into the Executive Agency for Health and Consumers [2008] OJ L173/27.

[61] More on the EAHC may be found on its website, at <http://ec.europa.eu/eahc/index.html> (last accessed on 15 November 2011).

[62] Commission Decision 2007/60/EC establishing the Trans-European Transport Network Executive Agency pursuant to Council Regulation [2007] OJ L32/88; amended by Decision 2008/593/EC amending Decision No 2007/60/EC as regards the modification of the tasks and the period of operation of the Trans-European Transport Network Executive Agency [2008] OJ L195/35.

transport infrastructure projects from the 2000–6 and 2007–13 financial perspectives is accomplished in close collaboration with its 'parent', DG MOVE of the Commission. The latter remains responsible for the overall policy, programming, and evaluation of the TEN-T programme. The agency is active in finance, project management, engineering, and legal affairs, and is based in Brussels.[63]

2. Evaluation of agencies in the field of services

'Although EU agencies constitute a mushrooming phenomenon, they have remained weak in terms of their roles and powers and are mainly used to gather information.'[64] 'The controls imposed on them imply that "more EU agencies" does not mean "agencification" (in the sense of autonomous and professionally managed bodies).' 'Apart from better information, the added value is still under discussion.'[65] 'The European Commission and evaluators experience difficulties in defining their "added value" and a discussion on whether they can be abolished is never far away.'[66] 'So far, empirical evidence of this presumably positive impact is lacking and vision and strategy on *how* exactly European agencies are supposed to improve implementation is absent.'[67] These are just a few sceptical notes on the efficacy and efficiency of agencies in the EU.

The more optimistic observers find that 'agencies—especially via their inspection tasks—do play a role in ensuring the application of European legislation, but have to manoeuvre gently between member states, the Commission and related international organizations in order to fulfil this role'.[68]

Stronger than academic scepticism, agencies have also aroused irritation among member states' bodies. It is difficult to imagine any harsher statement coming from the UK Parliament, in respect of one of the best-endowed EU agencies, the EASA:

'We have been concerned by the evidence we have received of the chaos surrounding the establishment of the European Aviation Safety Agency (EASA). It is clear that this organisation is not yet ready to do its job and it is vital that the UK transfers no further responsibilities to it until it has shown itself capable of undertaking its existing responsibilities. The brief history of the founding, planning and implementation of EASA inspires a feeling of despondency about the ability of those minded to make transnational European agencies work either effectively or efficiently. The Commission must examine closely the lamentable history of this half-baked, halfcock project, and apply the lessons learnt to future endeavours. We also hope it will seek to provide evidence of its competence by righting the situation of EASA promptly.'[69]

---

[63] More on the TEN-T EA may be found on its website, at <http://tentea.ec.europa.eu/en/home.htm> (last accessed on 15 November 2011).
[64] Schout, A., and Pereyra, F., 2010, n 39, at 1.
[65] Ibid, at 4.
[66] Ibid, at 1.
[67] Groenleer, M., Versluis, E., and Kaeding, M., 2008, n 40, at 5.
[68] Ibid.
[69] UK House of Commons Select Committee on Transport, Thirteenth Report, Session 2005–6, available at <http://www.parliament.the-stationery-office.com/pa/cm200506/cmselect/cmtran/809/80902.htm> (last accessed on 15 November 2011).

Despite the enthusiasm initially nurtured by the creation and institutionalization of EU agencies, empirical evidence at the time of writing is, at best, ambivalent. Contrary to 'US-type' agencies enjoying wide regulatory powers, EU agencies have developed more into information-gathering and processing bodies, in the service of the Commission as well as the general public.[70] In the rare cases where they have been given regulatory powers, these are very limited. Moreover, most of the agencies suffer from large boards of directors, poor staffing, and limited financial resources. Despite having a distinct legal personality and enjoying formal independence (in the form of administrative and financial autonomy), EU agencies are, nevertheless, subject to, amongst others: a. the Commission's opinion on budget and establishment plans; b. approval of the budget and establishment plan by the European Parliament (EP); c. discharge of the budget by the EP; d. audits by the European Court of Auditors; e. controls by the OLAF (Office de la Lutte Anti-fraude); f. periodical evaluation by the Council and the EP; g. financial and staff regulations.[71]

Two series of reasons may account for the limitations to agency activity in the EU, one political and one legal.

First, from a political point of view, the creation of agencies, the powers, and the resources given to them is the outcome of bargaining between EU institutions and member states.[72] These actors, however, pursue divergent and changing interests. The Commission may be ready to forgo control of routine technical responsibilities, but less willing to delegate authority to agencies, where this would involve a surrender of its existing policy making and enforcement competences; the more so, in policy areas where it already has far-reaching competences (see eg the reluctance of the Commission to follow the German proposal for the creation of an independent European Cartel Office).

Having gained significant legislative powers, the EP is likely to resist delegating broad decision-making authority to agencies, for fear that it would ultimately lose in the administrative process what it has gained in the legislative. Where the EP does agree to delegate decision-making authority to agencies, it tries to maintain direct or indirect oversight and always demands transparency, codification, and judicial review of agency administrative procedures.

Member states are reluctant to delegate powers to European agencies that would threaten the functioning of national bureaucracies. Where they do agree to the establishment of agencies, they are also likely to demand state dominated management boards and to restrict powers to the networking of existing national administrative structures.

Secondly, from a legal point of view, the Court, as early as 1958, prohibited any delegation of powers—other than purely technical—from EU institutions to

---

[70] Schout, A., and Pereyra, F., 2010, n 39, at 4.

[71] Ibid, at 5.

[72] The analysis which follows heavily draws on Keleman, D., 'The Politics of "Eurocratic" Structure and the New European Agencies' (2002) 25 *WEP* 93–118; his views have been confirmed by the more recent and empirical study by Gronnegaard Christensen, J., and Lehmann Nielsen, V., 'Administrative Capacity, Structural Choice and the Creation of EU Agencies' (2010) 17 *JEPP* 176–204.

outside bodies, as this would undermine the 'institutional balance' within the Union.[73] Indeed, such delegation would not only alter the balance set by the Treaty between the institutions, but would also further distance the exercise of power from the member states level, as it would technically amount to the Commission sub-delegating powers given to it by member states.

According to the Commission's unchanged position and to leading authors, the *Meroni* doctrine does stand as a legal obstacle to the creation of 'regulatory independent agencies of the sort found, for instance, in the United States'.[74] This view is increasingly questioned by lawyers and political scientists alike.[75] Some question the applicability of *Meroni* to agencies. For one thing, *Meroni* concerned delegation (in the ECSC framework) to an *outside* body, while agencies are *EU* bodies. Further, *Meroni* concerned sub-delegation of power directly conferred by the states to the High Authority, not the implementation of policies adopted at the EU level and set up by texts of secondary legislation, thus having a primarily EU, not national, origin. Moreover, the doctrine is accused of being anachronistic, for failing to accommodate the development and growing complexity of EU competences and the need for expertise.[76] Other commentators question more generally the validity and scope of the *Meroni* doctrine by noting that such a strict anti-delegation doctrine does not square either with subsequent case law of the Court (in the framework of the EU), or with the ongoing practice of the Commission and Council. Further, they question the value of 'institutional balance' and whether its nature is more descriptive than normative, thus, subject to ongoing adjustments.[77] Others openly make the case for an extensive doctrine in favour of delegation of powers to agencies.[78] Finally, there is a purely political, but nonetheless valid argument, according to which:

'regardless of *Meroni*, it is unlikely that the ECJ would block the establishment of, or substantially limit the authority of an agency that had won the approval of the Parliament, Council and Commission. ECJ's control is likely to come not from limitations it places on delegation to agencies, but from the ongoing controls of agency actions it can provide.'[79]

---

[73] Joined Cases 10/56 *Meroni & Co., Industrie Metallurgiche, società in accomandita semplice v High Authority of the European Coal and Steel Community* [1958] Special English edition 157; on the issue of institutional balance see Prechal, S., 'Institutional balance: a fragile principle with uncertain contents' in Heukels, T., Blokker, N., and Brus, M. (eds), *The European Union after Amsterdam* (The Hague: Kluwer Law International, 1998) 273–94; and more recently, Jacqué, J.P., 'The Principle of Institutional Balance' (2004) 41 *CML Rev* 383–91.

[74] See, prominently, Lenaerts, K., 'Regulating the Regulatory Process: Delegation of Powers in the European Community' (1993) 18 *EL Rev* 23–49, at 40; and more recently Lenaerts, K., and Verhoeven, A., 2000, n 6, at 657.

[75] For a fuller account of the criticisms of the *Meroni* doctrine in relation to agencies, see Yataganas, X., 2001, n 32, at 34–6; see also Dehousse, R., 'Misfits: EU Law and the Transformation of European Governance' Jean Monnet Working Paper 02/2002, also available at <http://centers.law.nyu.edu/jeanmonnet/papers/02/020201.rtf> (last accessed on 15 November 2011), at 7–9; and more recently Griller, S., and Orator, A., 2010, n 32.

[76] For these criticisms, see Dehousse, R., 2004, n 24, at 7–9.

[77] For this line of arguments, see Yataganas, X., 2001, n 32, at 34–6.

[78] See Mashaw, J., 'Prodelegation: Why Administrators Should Make Political Decisions' (1985) 1 *J of L Economics and Organization* 81–100.

[79] Keleman, D., 2002, n 72, at 99.

It has also been held that the *Meroni* limitations could be overcome by some Treaty provision setting the conditions for delegation,[80] but such a proposal was not included in the Lisbon Treaty.

In view of all these considerations, it becomes clear that, despite the fact that agencies have been present in the field of services for some time now, their regulatory potential remains yet to mature and bear fruit. This would require further political commitment from the member states and the Commission and, on the other hand, legal clarification by the CJEU, in order to overcome the *Meroni* uncertainties. It is also clear that new agencies should not be instituted without taking stock of the experience gained so far.

C. Networking

As stated in the introduction to the present chapter, networks—and related scientific literature—have developed in the EU during the last 20 years. Many arguments may be put forward in favour of the development of networks, especially at the EU level. They may be said to compensate for any perceived democratic deficit at the decision-making process, while bypassing the centre. They also help to reduce the implementation deficit, to bridge regional disparities and promote a European identity, to coordinate interaction between unconnected actors, to facilitate information exchange, and, lastly, to help identify financial opportunities.[81]

S. Ward and R. Williams classify networks in three broad categories: a. lobbying and exchange networks, b. policy networks, and c. intergovernmental relations networks.[82]

Networks falling under the first category typically bring together organizations, pressure groups, businesses, and sub-central governments and have as their main aim the exchange of information and the expression of the interests respectively represented by the participants.

Policy networks have been accurately defined as 'webs of relatively stable and ongoing relationships which mobilise and pool dispersed resources so that collective (or parallel) action can be orchestrated toward the solution of a common policy... They are characterised by predominantly *informal* interactions between *public and private* actors with distinctive but *interdependent interests* who strive to solve problems of collective action on a central, *non-hierarchical level*'.[83]

---

[80] Yataganas, X., 2001, n 32.

[81] For a more detailed presentation of the characteristics of networking in the EU, see, among many, Ward, S., and Williams, R., 1997, n 3.

[82] Ibid, at 440–1.

[83] Borzel, T., 'What's So Special about Policy Networks?: An Exploration of the Concept and Its Usefulness in Studying European Governance', European Integration Online Papers 1997 No 16, also available at http://eiop.or.at/eiop/texte/1997-016a.htm (last accessed on 15 November 2011), at 5 (emphasis in the original).

They may be further classified depending on their participation, duration, resources, etc.[84]

The third category of networks, namely intergovernmental relations networks, aiming at the coordination of relations between national regulatory authorities (NRAs) at the transnational level, is particularly relevant in the area of services: in reality, almost all such networks are active in the field of services. Since literature on NRA networks is quite limited, a brief presentation of such networks (1) will make it possible to proceed to a provisional—if premature—evaluation thereof (2).

1. Networks in the field of services

It was explained above that in network industries where competition is more developed, NRAs have been formally organized into networks.[85] In the fields of electronic communications and energy, one can even observe a 'second generation' network, formally organized by some piece of legislation. The European Regulators Group (ERG) formally established by Commission Decision 2002/627 has now been replaced by the Body of European Regulators for Electronic Communications (BEREC).[86] Similarly, the European Regulatory Group for Electricity and Gas (ERGEG) established by Council Decision 2003/796 to work closely with the Council of European Energy Regulators (CEER),[87] was turned into the the Agency for the Cooperation of Energy Regulators (ACER) by Regulation 713/2009.[88] The European Committee for Postal Regulation (ECPR) has been formalized into a European Regulators Group for Postal Services by Decision 2010/C 217/07.[89] Also, the application of Directive 2005/36 (the Professional Qualifications Directive) has prompted the creation of a coordinator's group.[90] (See Table 8.1)

In view of the above, it becomes clear that the creation of transgovernmental networks of NRAs, or other national authorities entrusted with the application of specific directives, is a technique particularly employed in the field of services. Of the 11 networks identified in Table 8.1, the first four are horizontal in nature and also concern non-service activities, the fifth is explicitly dedicated to all services, while the remaining six are openly sector-specific and concern specific services.

---

[84] Ibid.

[85] This trend was presented above in ch 6, in subsection A(4)b.

[86] European Parliament and Council Regulation 1211/2009/EC establishing the Body of European Regulators for Electronic Communications (BEREC) and the Office [2009] OJ L337/1.

[87] Commission Decision 2003/796/EC establishing the European Regulators Group for Electricity and Gas [2003] OJ L296/34; actually the CEER prepares EGREG's meetings and the two together are called the European Energy Regulators. For their common website, see <http://www.energy-regulators. eu/portal/page/portal/EER_HOME> (last accessed on 15 November 2011).

[88] European Parliament and Council Regulation 713/2009/EC establishing an Agency for the Cooperation of Energy Regulators [2009] OJ L211/1.

[89] Commission Decision 2010/C217/07 establishing the European Regulators Group for Postal Services [2010] OJ C217/7.

[90] Commission Decision 2007/172/EC, Setting up the group for coordinators for the recognition of professional qualifications [2007] OJ L 79/38.

Table 8.1. Transgovernmental networks in the field of services

	Area	Name	Instituted	Reshuffled	Legal instrument
1	Competition policy	European Competition Network (ECN)	2003		Regulation 1/2003
2	Data protection	Art 29 Working Party	1995		Directive 95/46/EC
3	Consumer protection	European Consumer Centres Network	2006		Regulation 2006/2004
4	Professional qualifications	Group of coordinators	2007		Commission Decision 2007/172/EC
5	Quality of services	European Network for Alert Mechanism	2006		Directive 2006/123 (Art 32)
6	Electronic communications	European Regulators Group (ERG)—Body of European Regulators for Electronic Communications (BEREC)	2002	2009	Commission Decision 2002/627—Regulation 1211/2009
7	Energy	European Regulatory Group for Electricity and Gas (ERGEG)—Agency for the Cooperation of Energy Regulators (ACER)	2003	2009	Council Decision 2003/796—Regulation 713/09
8	Banking	Committee of European Banking Supervisors (CEBS) To be replaced by the European Banking Authority (EBA)	2003	2010	Commission Decision of 5 November 2003 Political agreement (2010) for the European Supervisory Authorities
9	Insurance	Committee of European Insurance and Occupational Pensions (CEIOPS)	2003		Commission Decision of 5 November 2003 establishing the CEIOPS
10	Securities	Committee of European Securities Regulators (CESR)	2003		Commission Decision of 6 June 2001 establishing the CESR
11	Broadcasting	European Platform of Regulatory Authorities (a network of the EU and Council of Europe states)	1995		Non-profit association under Alsatian law

Of the networks identified, the Data Protection Working Party is the only one which was foreseen *ab initio* from the first steps of the EU's regulatory activity in the area concerned; all the others were introduced in subsequent stages of the legislative process, in order to reinforce existing legislation and to secure better implementation thereof.

So far as the sector-specific networks are concerned, it is easy to observe a temporal parallelism: they were instituted en bloc in 2002–3 and were seriously reinvigorated in 2009. Specifically, the upgrading of the electronic communications and energy regulators' networks in 2009 may be linked to the entry into force of the latest legislative packages in these fields, and also due to the fact that competition was consolidated or seriously strengthened; it was thus realized how crucial trans-national cooperation has become in these fields. In the area of banking, insurance, and securities, the strengthening of the role of NRA networks is certainly connected to the 2008 financial crisis and to the prevalence of a more centralized, continental-style regulation, requiring more effective coordination.[91] Finally, it should be remembered that the transposition period of the Services Directive, enacted in 2006, only expired in December 2009. Therefore, from a temporal point of view, it becomes clear that the development of networks provided for therein is a recent and still ongoing phenomenon, and as such, difficult to evaluate.

2. Evaluation of networks in the field of services

There is a heated academic debate over the efficiency and effectiveness of NRA networks. Some authors see in such networks a very powerful means of coordination, remaining to be fully deployed in the years to come.[92] Others, more sceptical, maintain that, like all other manifestations of network governance, NRA networks will only be as efficient as their 'principals' will allow for.[93]

A unique characteristic of NRA networks is that they operate on the basis of a double delegation: one *vertical*, from the EU, which mandated their creation and which foresees the minimum requirements of their independence, and one *horizontal*, coming from member states executives, who entrust NRAs with specific duties and powers (especially at the implementation level).[94] This double delegation appears as a source of both strengths and weaknesses.

---

[91] Quaglia, L., 'The "Old" and "New" Politics of Financial Services Regulation in the EU' Observatoire Social Européen Research Paper 2010/2, also available at <http://www.ose.be/files/publication/OSEPaperSeries/Quaglia_2010_OSEResearchPaper2_0410.pdf> (last accessed on 15 November 2011).

[92] See eg Eberlein, B., and Newman, A., 'Escaping the International Governance Dilemma?: Incorporated Transgovernmental Networks in the European Union' (2008) 21 *Governance* 25–52.

[93] See eg Coen, D., and Thatcher, M., 2008, n 1.

[94] See Coen, D., and Thatcher, M., 2008, n 1; Eberlein, B., and Newman, A. (2008, n 92, at 32) look at this double delegation from the member state perspective and describe it as follows: 'Incorporated transgovernmental networks exist within a two-level structure of "dual delegation". National governments have simultaneously ceded authority to supranational institutions and sub-state NRAs.'

On the positive side, there are several reasons why NRA networks could feature as efficient coordination mechanisms. For one thing, 'they combine supranational coordination . . . with national delegated authority. Their decisions then simultaneously inform EU policy and actual enforcement on the ground'.[95] Such incorporated transgovernmental networks differ from existing bureaucratic interactions between member state officials in at least four respects.[96] *First*, NRAs, by their very institutional design, enjoy a large degree of autonomy, buffering them from direct political control: leadership appointed by and accountable to the national parliaments, guaranteed budget, control over personnel and appointments, etc. Moreover, empirical research confirms that such NRAs do, in actual fact, enjoy a high degree of autonomy from elected politicians.[97] *Secondly*, the officials involved enjoy a large degree of formal delegation and are not subordinate to bureaucratic chains of command, like other member state officials. *Thirdly*, in their respective fields of competence, NRAs bear formal *authority*, without political recourse to legislatures.[98] *Fourthly*, they have been granted statutory power to control market access, administer fines, and formulate new regulatory rules. Therefore, they have an enhanced role in the field of implementing regulation. *Fifthly*, 'transgovernmental networks share the broader policy universe in a given sector with other actors, including private actors, and they will most likely participate in larger public–private policy networks . . . These regulatory groups organize and interact with sectoral stakeholders as supranational legislation is developed and at the same time devise on-the-ground strategies for implementation'.[99]

On the negative side, the existence of a double delegation from both the national and the supranational level—and hence, the existence of two principals with clearly distinct agendas—may become a source of tension and, finally, weakness of the NRA networks. Indeed, after over 20 years of experience with NRAs in the EU, 'we still observe diverse regulatory principles and different relationships between [NRAs], elected politicians and suppliers'.[100] This increased diversity means that their chances to integrate successfully into a network and operate in any meaningful way are limited. Moreover, such networks, whenever formally created—or precisely because of the lack of a formal act of empowerment—usually lack resources and rights of initiative (they are typically supported by the Commission). 'Such shadows of government potentially limit the innovative scope of European Regulatory Networks in this issue and raise important questions about their ability to evolve

---

[95] Eberlein, B., and Newman, A., 2008, n 92, at 32.

[96] For which, see more extensively the full argument, ibid, at 29–32.

[97] Thatcher, M., 'The Third Force? Independent Regulatory Agencies and Elected Politicians in Europe' (2005) 18 *Governance* 347–73; the two explanations put forward by this author are that either elected politicians used alternative (ie informal and indirect) methods of control, thus limiting 'agency losses', or that they found that the benefits of NRA autonomy and the costs of applying their formal control outweighed agency losses.

[98] Eberlein, B., and Newman, A., 2008, n 92, at 32.

[99] Ibid.

[100] Coen, D., and Thatcher, M., 2008, n 1, at 55, the term 'IRAs' meaning Independent Regulatory Authorities is used in the original, but has been replaced by NRAs in the present for coherence purposes.

into strong regulatory bodies'.[101] Further, such networks are given very broad functions but few powers and resources. Last but not least, 'they face rival venues both for coordination and for more traditional governmental functions of deciding through hierarchy and hard law'.[102] The above weaknesses unavoidably mean that 'if the networks are to have an impact on regulatory governance in Europe, they must either develop informal resources and influence after formal delegation has taken place and/or gain new powers through new delegations in order to evolve into more powerful regulatory bodies'.[103]

The preceding analysis on transnational networks suggests that such networks are more likely to develop in novel and distributive, coordination-type policies, rather than in entrenched and highly redistributive policies.[104] Contrasting this observation with the OMC, which has mainly been deployed in the social field, it could be generally concluded that transnational networks, on the one hand, and the OMC, on the other, are parallel non-regulatory means, coordinating different—if interlocking—policy areas.

The ideas developed above demonstrate that transnational networks may further evolve and become central in the coordination of highly technical policy areas. The fact that, as already mentioned, most transnational networks have had their statutes extended and strengthened in 2009, only reinforces this perspective. A fresh evaluation of the evolution they bring will be necessary in the near future.

---

[101] Ibid, at 50 (fn omitted).
[102] Ibid, at 61.
[103] Ibid, at 51 (fn omitted).
[104] Eberlein, B., and Newman, A., 2008, n 92, at 31.

9

Old v. New Governance in Services: an Outlook

A. New governance and better regulation—taking stock

The regulation of services can be viewed in a new light, given the recent developments of 'new governance' and 'better regulation' in the EU. New governance is a broader concept than better regulation, since it also encompasses non-regulatory means of pursuing policy objectives, but both are interconnected.

The quality of regulation became a central public issue for the first time with the Treaty of Amsterdam,[1] which contained a Protocol setting the principles of good regulation. The 2000 Lisbon Agenda also emphasized the quality of regulation as part of making the EU the most competitive and dynamic knowledge-based economy in the world. As a result, the Mandelkern high-level group was set up, and delivered its report in November 2001.[2] It put forward seven principles for better regulation: necessity, proportionality, subsidiarity, transparency, accountability, accessibility, and simplicity. The Mandelkern recommendations were adopted by the 2001 White Paper on European Governance,[3] which in turn, provided the foundations for the Commission's 2002 Action Plan for simplifying and improving the regulatory environment.[4] This is connected to the 2002 better

---

[1] For some early thoughts on this issue see Timmermans, C., 'How Can One Improve the Quality of Community Legislation?' (1997) 34 *CML Rev* 1229–57; Xanthaki, H., 'The Problem of Quality in EU Legislation: What on Earth Is Really Wrong?' (2001) 38 *CML Rev* 651–76; and more recently Labory, S., and Malgarini, M., 'Regulation in Europe: justified burden or costly failure?' in Galli, G., and Pelkmans, J. (eds) *Regulatory Reform and Competitiveness in Europe, 1: Horizontal Issues* (Cheltenham/Northampton: Edward Elgar Publishing, 2000) 81–126.

[2] Mandelkern Group Report of 13 November 2001, also available at <http://ec.europa.eu/governance/better_regulation/documents/mandelkern_report.pdf> (last accessed on 16 November 2011).

[3] White Paper COM (2001) 428 final, 'European Governance'; see on this White Paper, Joerges, C., Mény, Y., and Weiler, J.H.H. (eds), *Mountain or Molehill?: A Critical Appraisal of the Commission White Paper on Governance*, Jean Monnet Working Paper No. 06/2001, also available at <http://centers.law.nyu.edu/jeanmonnet/papers/01/010601.html> (last accessed on 16 November 2011), where the contributions of Scharpf, F., Telo, M., Héritier, A., Armstrong, K., Magnette, P., Joerges, C., and others are to be found; see also Armstrong, K., 'Rediscovering Civil Society: The EU and the White Paper on Governance' (2002) 8 *ELJ* 102–32; Joerges, C., 'The Commission's White Paper on Governance in the EU: A Symptom of Crisis' (2002) 39 *CML Rev* 441–5; see also in French, Georgakakis, D., and de Lassalle, M., *La "Nouvelle gouvernance Européenne": Genèses et usages politiques d'un Livre Blanc* (Strasbourg: PUS, 2007).

[4] Action Plan COM (2002) 278 final, 'Simplifying and Improving the Regulatory Environment'.

law making Communication, the 2003 Interinstitutional Agreement on Better Law-making, and the 2005 Communication 'Better Regulation for Growth and Jobs in the EU'.[5] Several directions have been pursued thereafter. *First*, Regulatory Impact Assessment (RIA) for prospective legislation was instituted and gradually extended.[6] It is generally seen as the cornerstone of the better regulation approach, both at the EU and at the OECD level; it is henceforth monitored and evaluated, both internally and externally.[7] *Secondly*, a methodology for assessing—and reducing—the administrative costs imposed by legislation has been put into place;[8] it is monitored on a yearly basis.[9] *Thirdly*, the simplification of existing legislation has been set as an objective,[10] projected through three-year rolling plans and monitored through yearly scoreboards.[11] *Fourthly*, the codification and recasting of the existing *acquis* is also monitored.[12] *Fifthly*, EU legislation is evaluated on a yearly basis, to ensure implementation of the principles of subsidiarity and proportionality.[13]

These developments are not exempt from criticism. Indeed the efficiency of RIA as a means for producing better regulation has been seriously questioned.[14] No less contestable is the 'standard cost model', which has been adopted to

[5] See Communication COM (2002) 275 final, 'European Governance: Better Lawmaking, Interinstitutional agreement on better law-making' [2003] OJ C321/1 and Communication COM (2005) 97 final, 'Better Regulation for Growth and Jobs in the European Union', respectively.

[6] Instituted by Communication COM (2002) 276, 'on impact assessment', and thereafter regularly monitored.

[7] For the latest internal Report (for 2009), see Commission Staff Working Document SEC (2009) 1728; for the latest external Report (dating from April 2007), see <http://ec.europa.eu/governance/impact/key_docs/docs/tep_eias_final_report.pdf> (last accessed on 16 November 2011). All impact assessments effectuated by the Commission are to be found at <http://ec.europa.eu/governance/impact/ia_carried_out/cia_2011_en.htm> (last accessed 16 November 2011).

[8] See Staff Working Document SEC (2005) 175, 'minimising administrative costs imposed by legislation', annexed to the Communication COM (2005) 97 final, 'on better regulation for growth and jobs in the EU', and Communication COM (2005) 518 final, 'EU Common Methodology for assessing administrative costs imposed by legislation'.

[9] For the latest report on this issue, see Working Document COM (2009) 16 final, 'Reducing Administrative Burdens in the EU—2008 Progress and 2009 Outlook'; and more recently see MEMO/10/654, 'Reducing Administrative Burdens—Context and Overview of Achievements and Examples', available at <http://ec.europa.eu/enterprise/policies/smart-regulation/administrative-burdens/files/20101207_hlg_memo_en.pdf> (last accessed 16 November 2011)); see also SEC (2009) 1728 'Impact Assessment Board Report for 2009'.

[10] See COM (2002) 278 final, n 4; Communication COM (2003) 71 final, 'Updating and Simplifying the Community Acquis'.

[11] See Working Document COM (2006) 690 final, 'First Progress Report on the Strategy for the Simplification of the Regulatory Environment', having in annex the Simplification Rolling Programme (2006–9); more recently, see Report COM (2009) 17 final, 'Third Progress Report on the Strategy for Simplifying the Regulatory Environment'.

[12] See Communication COM (2001) 645 final, 'Codification of the acquis communautaire'; see also COM (2009) 17 final, n 11.

[13] For the latest report, see Report COM (2009) 504 final, 'on subsidiarity and proportionality'.

[14] See eg Andrews, P., 'Are market failure analysis and impact assessment useful?' in Weatherill, S. (ed), *Better Regulation* (Oxford/Portland: Hart Publishing, 2007) 49–81; and in the same edited volume, Chittenden, F., Ambler, T., and Xiao, D., 'Impact assessment in the EU' 271–86; on the general issue of RIA effectiveness see European Court of Auditors Special Report No 3/2010 'Impact Assessments in the EU Institutions: Do They Support Decision Making?', available at <http://ec.europa.eu/commission_2010-2014/president/news/documents/pdf/20100928coa_impact_report_en.pdf> (last accessed on 16 November 2011).

calculate administrative burden.[15] More importantly, the very idea of 'better' regulation is often unfavourably compared to 'smart' regulation.[16] Essentially, it is questioned for whom regulation should be better, while it is noted that the interests of the regulatees (mainly undertakings) on the one hand, and those of the general public (consumers and taxpayers) on the other, are often contradictory.[17] It is also argued that even between small and big undertakings interests diverge, while it is observed that 'policy makers emphasise process criteria in evaluating regulatory quality, rather than criteria concerning the consequences of regulation'.[18] It is worth noting that the Commission itself in its latest documents has adopted the language of 'smart' regulation to replace 'better'.[19]

Despite terminology—and substantive—differences, it becomes clear that, henceforth, the quality of regulation is an issue in which the Commission invests heavily.[20]

New governance relates to better regulation not only because both concepts have been introduced into the EU legal order through the same official documents, mentioned above, but also because they feed into each other. The term 'new governance' here is used in a broad sense, to encompass 'the use of legal and political authority, wealth and information, to exercise control in the management of relationships and resources in the pursuit of social and economic ends'.[21] In this

---

[15] See among many, Torriti, J., 'The standard cost model: when "better regulation" fights against red tape' in Weatherill, S. (ed), *Better Regulation* (Oxford/Portland: Hart Publishing, 2007) 83–106.

[16] See eg Baldwin, R., 'Better regulation: tensions aboard the Enterprise' in Weatherill, S. (ed), *Better Regulation* (Oxford/Portland: Hart Publishing, 2007) 27–47; on smart regulation, see Baldwin, R., 'Is Better Regulation Smarter Regulation?' (2005) *Public L* 485–511; see also Gunningham, N., and Grabosky, P., *Smart Regulation* (Oxford: OUP, 1998), and the abridged version of the concluding chapter of this book in Gunningham, N., and Sinclair, D., 'Designing smart regulation' in Hutter, B. (ed), *Environmental Regulation* (Oxford: OUP, 1999) 305–34, also available at <http://www.oecd.org/dataoecd/18/39/33947759.pdf> (last accessed on 16 November 2011); smart regulation is based on five regulatory design principles: a) preference for policy mixes incorporating instrument and institutional combinations; b) preference for less interventionist measures; c) escalation up an instrument pyramid to the extent necessary to achieve policy goals; d) empowerment of participants which are in the best place to act as surrogate regulators; and e) maximization of opportunities for win/win outcomes.

[17] See also Weatherill, S., 'The challenge of better regulation' in Weatherill, S. (ed), *Better Regulation* (Oxford/Portland: Hart Publishing, 2007) 1–17, at 3, where it is submitted: 'As a slogan "Better Regulation" invites neither contradiction nor even debate. Who would promote "Worse Regulation"?... But what does "Better Regulation" really mean?'.

[18] Kitching, J., 'Is less more? Better regulation and the small enterprise' in Weatherill, S. (ed), *Better Regulation* (Oxford/Portland: Hart Publishing, 2007) 155–73, at 167.

[19] Communication COM (2010) 543 final, 'Smart Regulation in the EU'.

[20] This is a direction encouraged by the European Parliament Resolution of 9 September 2010 on better lawmaking (P7_TA(2010)0311), available at <http://www.europarl.europa.eu/sides/getDoc.do?pubRef = -//EP//TEXT + TA + P7-TA-2010-0311 + 0 + DOC + XML + V0//EN> (last accessed on 16 November 2011). For all the relevant initiatives, see the Commission's specific webpage on the matter, at <http://ec.europa.eu/governance/better_regulation/index_en.htm> (last accessed on 16 November 2011); for an early assessment of these, see Pelkmans, J., Labory, S., and Majone, G. 'Better EU regulatory quality: assessing current initiatives and new proposals' in Galli, G., and Pelkmans, J. (eds), *Regulatory Reform and Competitiveness in Europe 1, Horizontal Issues* (Cheltenham/Northampton: Edward Elgar Publishing, 2000) 461–531.

[21] Hervey, T., 'The EU and the governance of health care' in de Búrca, G. and Scott, J. (eds), *Law and New Governance in the EU and the US* (Oxford/Portland: Hart Publishing, 2006) 179–210, at

sense, new governance instruments serve many of the objectives as 'better regulation'. In the 2001 White Paper, the Commission considered that taking the following course of action would bring improvements in regulation:[22] a. examining whether regulation is needed and whether it is appropriate at the EU level; b. envisaging the broader solution to any issue, combining formal rules with other non-binding tools; c. choosing the right type of instrument; d. promoting co-regulation; e. completing or reinforcing EU action by activating the OMC procedure; f. developing a culture of evaluation and feedback; and g. ensuring that instruments adopted respect the principles of proportionality and subsidiarity. With the exception of category (c), all other objectives are clearly served by new governance instruments and processes.

Given the breadth of the concept of 'new governance' and the variety and flexibility of the ways in which it operates, it is impossible to list its instruments and processes in any abstract manner; the proper way to approach such a task would be to look into given sectors and explore whether and how new governance manifests itself there.[23] For the purposes of the present study, however, it may be enough to highlight some general aspects.

'The idea of new or experimental governance . . . places considerable emphasis upon the accommodation and promotion of diversity, on the importance of provisionality and revisability . . . and on the goal of policy learning. New governance processes generally encourage or involve the participation of affected actors (stakeholders) rather than merely representative actors, and emphasise transparency . . . as well as ongoing evaluation and review'.[24] The Open Method of Coordination (OMC) is thought to be the paradigmatic—but by no means the only—example of new governance. It is not the place here to discuss the virtues and drawbacks of the OMC or, more generally, of new governance.[25]

---

179. An alternative (and broader) definition is given by de Búrca, G., and Scott, J., 'Introduction' in de Búrca, G., and Scott, J. (eds), *Law and New Governance in the EU and the US* (Oxford/Portland: Hart Publishing, 2006), 1–12, at 2, whereby 'new governance' is defined as 'a range of processes and practices that have a normative dimension but do not operate primarily or at all through the formal mechanism of traditional command-and-control-type legal institutions'.

[22] White Paper COM (2001) 428 final, 'European Governance', at 20–2.

[23] Hence, in bibliography, after several articles which dealt generally with new governance and contrasted it with 'old', a wealth of sector-specific contributions has seen the light, and indeed, it is through those that one may evaluate the advantages and drawbacks of new governance. See eg Hervey, T., 'The EU's Governance of Health Care and the Welfare Modernization Agenda' (2008) 2 *Regulation and Governance* 103–20; Armstrong, K., 'The OMC and Fundamental Rights: A Critical Appraisal' unpublished Paper presented to the seminar 'Fundamental Rights and Reflexive Governance', Columbia Law School, New York (4 November 2005), also available at <http://eucenter.wisc.edu/OMC/Papers/Rights/armstrong.pdf> (last accessed on 16 November 2011); Howarth, W., 'Aspirations and Realities under the Water Framework Directive: Proceduralisation, Participation and Practicalities' (2009) 21 *J of Environmental L* 391–417; Morado Foadi, S., 'The Missing Piece of the Lisbon Jigsaw: Is the Open Method of Coordination Effective in Relation to the European Research Area?' (2008) 14 *ELJ* 635–54; Featherstone, K., 'Soft co-ordination Meets "Hard" Politics: The EU and Pension Reform in Greece' (2005) 12 *JEPP* 733–50.

[24] De Burca, G. and Scott, J, 2006, n 21, at 3.

[25] Alongside the literature focusing on the OMC, cited in ch 8, see more generally, on new governance, Snyder, F. (ed), *The EU and Governance—L'UE et la Gouvernance* (Bruxelles: Bruylant,

What could be of use, however, for the purposes of the present chapter, is to identify the elements of new governance which are already present in the regulation of services. From the description above, the key features which qualify governance as 'new' seem to be the following: *diversity, provisionality, revisability, policy learning, transparency, stakeholder participation, evaluation* and *review*. In previous discussions,[26] while explaining notions, such as 'harmonization' and 'mutual recognition' in the field of services, several of these characteristics have been identified.

First, it is clear that as mutual recognition gains in importance (at the expense of harmonization), *diversity* and *policy learning* are promoted (through regulatory competition); this may also lead to *evaluation and review* of national policies in the light of other member states' policies. The more mutual recognition departs from the existence of prior harmonization and moves towards the home country rule, the more *mutual learning* is involved in the process. Such mutual learning is additionally fostered by means of administrative cooperation and the dissemination of information.

However, this should not be taken to imply that harmonization itself is impermeable to new governance concerns. By contrast, the dominant trend towards minimal harmonization leaves space for *diversity*.[27] Furthermore, the fact that harmonization is only adopted after other methods have been tried (and have failed) also reflects the idea of *policy learning* and—depending on the procedure followed for the adoption of harmonized rules—*stakeholder participation*. In addition, harmonization, even when it is technology-neutral, has to follow technological developments, and this allows for *revisability*.

Moreover, the institution of NRAs in the network-bound sectors and their organization into policy networks clearly serves the *exchange of information*—which has been reliably gathered and processed—as well as *transparency*. The same objectives are served, at a lower level of institutionalization, by the creation of national contact points for the implementation of the various Directives and the networking of such contact points. The obligations imposed on member states to make public, by electronic means or otherwise, their requirements for obtaining authorizations, permits, recognition of diplomas, and the like, further promote the above objectives.

Finally, 'rendez-vous' clauses ensure *revisability*, through institutionalized evaluation and review procedures. Depending on the procedure followed for revision, *stakeholder participation* is more or less ensured.

Locating these characteristics as present in service regulation certainly does not mean that 'better regulation' has been achieved, or that new governance has exhausted its means in this area. It does signify, however, that new governance has imperceptibly yet clearly made its way into the Classic Community Method (CCM),

---

2006); de Búrca, G., and Scott, J., *Law and New Governance in the EU and the US* (Oxford/Portland: Hart Publishing, 2006).

[26] See the developments in ch 6.

[27] Although full harmonization is not altogether abandoned (eg in the field of financial services), as mentioned in ch 6.

far more in the field of service regulation than in other areas of EU law. It also stands for the idea that there is not rupture, but continuity between 'old' and 'new' governance.[28] This transformation has prompted some commentators to speak of intermediate 'new old governance' tools, eg framework Directives.[29]

Indeed, in the new governance literature, there is an ongoing debate as to whether new governance is antagonistic against old (the gap thesis), whether the two are bound to be made to work together (the hybridity thesis), or whether the former is going to transform the latter (the transformation thesis).[30] The analysis above gives more credit to the third thesis. It shows that one of the most tangible effects that 'new governance' and 'better regulation' have had in the field of services, has been the injection into—or, the emasculation of— the CCM with instruments aimed at the realization of new governance objectives. Contrary to the general assumption, new governance does not necessarily translate into soft law, but may alternatively have the effect of rendering the law 'softer', by making it more flexible and evolutive and by entrusting its application to open-ended processes.

B. Future outlook

The discussion under the previous subheading makes clear that regulation, especially in the field of services, is in constant evolution, which in the last 10 years has turned into turmoil. It is, therefore, unwise to put forward projections about the way in which services' regulation may develop in the years to come. Based on the observations above, however, it would be sensible to offer reasoned speculations in relation to the gradual introduction of RIA (1) and to the increased recourse to soft law (2) in the area of services.

1. Evaluation of better regulation and Regulatory Impact Assessment (RIA)

The centrepiece principle of better regulation, actively promoted by the OECD and adopted by most EU member states and the EU itself, is Regulatory Impact

---

[28] See, in this respect, Scott, J., and Trubek, M., 'Mind the Gap: Law and New Approaches to Governance in the EU' (2002) 8 *ELJ* 1–18; Trubek, D., Cortell, P., and Nance, M., 'Soft Law, Hard Law and European Integration: Toward a Theory of Hybridity', Jean Monnet Working Paper No. 02/2005, also available at <http://centers.law.nyu.edu/jeanmonnet/papers/05/050201.pdf> (last accessed on 16 November 2011); more recently, see Trubek, D., and Trubek, L., 'New Governance and Legal Regulation: Complementarity, Rivalry and Transformation' (2007) 23 *Columbia J of Eur L* 539–64; Maher, I., 'Law and the OMC: Towards a New Flexibility in European Policy-Making?' (2004) 2 *J for Comparative Government and Eur Policy* 248–63; Hatzopoulos, V., 'Why the Open Method of Coordination Is Bad for You: A Letter to the EU' (2007) 13 *ELJ* 259–92.

[29] Kilpatrick, C., 'New EU employment governance and constitutionalism' in de Búrca, G., and Scott, J. (eds), *Law and New Governance in the EU and the US* (Oxford/Portland: Hart Publishing, 2006) 121–51, at 122.

[30] For these theses (and their 'code' names used in brackets), see de Búrca, G., and Scott, J., 2006, n 21.

Assessment (RIA).[31] RIA is preparative for and an aid to regulation. There is nothing which distinguishes RIA in relation to services from RIA in other fields of regulation. This notwithstanding, the reason why a book on services should include a reference to RIA is that the economic importance and complexities of services are likely to prompt fresh regulation for the relevant Treaty freedom, more than in any other. Such regulation will develop against the background of the scarce and piecemeal EU regulation already in place.[32] Since RIA is supposed to take into account regulation already in place and to foretell the way it will be affected by proposed fresh regulation, a basic comprehension of RIA's mechanisms and putative outcomes is essential for understanding the way in which regulation in services might develop.

a. RIA as a solution

'By providing a methodological framework of rational policy selection, RIA allows for the outcomes to be assessed against the goals that are set for regulatory systems.'[33] RIA's object is:

'to explain the objectives of the [regulatory] proposal, the risks to be addressed and the options for delivering the objectives. In doing so it should make transparent the expected costs and benefits of the options for the different bodies involved, such as other parts of Government and small businesses, and how compliance with regulatory options would be secured and enforced.'[34]

From a simplistic point of view, RIA can be seen as a cost-benefit analysis presented in a non-technical way, so that officials can use it, independently of their academic and professional background.[35] Although there is not a single method to assess the regulatory impact of proposed regulation, and indeed, practices in different states vary,[36] several common principles emerge from the comparison of the various RIA Guidelines. For example, the latest EU Guidelines on RIA, issued on January 2009,[37]

---

[31] See eg Radaelli, C., de Francesco, F., and Troeger, V., 'Implementation of Regulatory Impact Assessment in Europe', Speech delivered to the ENBR workshop, University of Exeter, 27–28 March 2008, also available at <http://centres.exeter.ac.uk/ceg/research/riacp/documents/Implementationof-RIAENRworkshop.pdf> (last accessed on 16 November 2011), at 3. In the present context, the term RIA is used in a generic way in order to encompass the various means of providing a detailed and systematic appraisal of the potential impacts of a new regulatory instrument, in order to assess whether the instrument will achieve the desired objectives.

[32] Briefly presented in ch 6.

[33] Quotation taken from Kirkpatrick, C., and Parker, D., 'Regulatory Impact Assessment: an overview' in Kirkpatrick, C., and Parker, D. (eds), *Regulatory Impact Assessment: Towards Better Regulation?* (Cheltenham/Northampton: Edward Elgar Publishing, 2007) 1–16, at 3.

[34] UK National Audit Office, *Better Regulation: Making Good Use of Regulatory Impact Assessments*, Report by the Comptroller and Auditor General HC 329, Session 2001–02 (London, 2002) 52.

[35] Andrews, P., 'Are market failure analysis and impact assessment useful?' in Weatherill, S. (ed), *Better Regulation* (Oxford/Portland: Hart Publishing, 2007) 49–81, at 64.

[36] For a recent account of the general developments concerning RIA and of practices followed in various countries, see Kirkpatrick, C., and Parker, D., 2007, n 33.

[37] Commission Guidelines SEC (2009) 92, also available at <http://ec.europa.eu/governance/impact/commission_guidelines/docs/iag_2009_en.pdf> (last accessed on 16 November 2011).

list six main analytical steps: a. definition of the problem, including the question whether the EU is the appropriate level of tackling it; b. description of the various policy objectives; c. identification of the policy options and appreciation under the proportionality perspective; d. assessment of the likely economic, social, and environmental impacts; e. comparison of the different options; and f. specification of core progress indicators and possible monitoring and evaluation arrangements, on a regular basis. These six steps are further analysed in the Annexes to the Guidelines.[38] It should be noted that the Guidelines draw inspiration from the OECD RIA Checklist, which is structured on the basis of 10 steps.[39] The latter largely correspond to experiences in the US, the UK, and other states.[40]

A brief normative analysis of the six steps detailed above demonstrates that the objectives of RIA within the EU are fivefold. Specifically, RIA is intended to: a. 'speak the truth' to the legislator; b. offer solid reasoning for regulatory action; c. provide a forum for stakeholder input; d. highlight trade-offs; and e. structure and proceduralize law making.[41] Moreover, it may constitute a valuable mechanism allowing political 'principals' to exercise control over regulatory bodies ('agents') and to ensure that the latter are not captured by specific regulatee interests.[42] Under a more modest evaluation, RIA is at least believed to provide policy makers with two useful pieces of information: estimation of the societal cost of proposed regulation and identification of those who in reality are likely to bear the cost. In other words, RIA reduces the uncertainty faced by regulators and sheds light on factors they might ignore.[43]

The use of RIA at the EU level can have the following effects: a. to challenge the need for new regulation; b. to improve such new regulation by making it less burdensome and/or more effective; and c. to put into place a mechanism for review, revision, or rescission of the regulation, whenever this is deemed appropriate.[44]

---

[38] Annexes 1–13 are available at <http://ec.europa.eu/governance/impact/commission_guidelines/docs/iag_2009_annex_en.pdf> (last accessed on 16 November 2011).

[39] OECD *Regulatory Impact Analysis: Best Practices in OECD Countries* (Paris: OECD, 1997). These questions are: 1. is the problem correctly defined?; 2. is government action justified?; 3. is regulation the best form of government action?, 4. is there a legal basis for regulation?; 5. what is the appropriate level(s) of government intervention for this regulation?; 6. do the benefits of regulation justify the costs?; 7. is the distribution of effects across society transparent?; 8. is the regulation clear, consistent, comprehensible, and accessible to users?; 9. have all interested parties had the opportunity to present their views?; 10. how will compliance be achieved?.

[40] For a comprehensive bibliographical list, and for official EU, UK, and US sources, see the European Network for Better Regulation website at <http://www.enbr.org/biblio.php> (last accessed on 16 November 2011).

[41] Meuwese, A., 'Inter-institutionalising EU impact assessment' in Weatherill, S. (ed), *Better Regulation* (Oxford/Portland: Hart Publishing, 2007) 287–309, at 298–302.

[42] Radaelli., C., de Francesco, F., and Troeger, V., 2008, n 31, at 6.

[43] Andrews, P., 2007, n 35, at 69.

[44] Chittenden, F., Ambler, T, and Xiao, D., 'Impact assessment in the EU' in Weatherill, S. (ed), *Better Regulation* (Oxford/Portland: Hart Publishing, 2007) 271–86, at 275.

b. RIA as a problem

The efficiency of RIA, however, both in view of the objectives pursued and of the results achieved, can be seriously questioned. Several shortfalls of the RIA have been identified. Some of them are of a normative nature, while others have a material dimension.

i. Normative shortfalls of RIA

From a normative point of view, at least four grounds for critique have been put forward.

Market failure analysis as a necessary prerequisite to RIA. A first line of argument doubts the appropriateness of RIA as a means for determining the necessary regulatory strategies. According to the supporters of this view, before engaging in a RIA, a market failure analysis is necessary. Such analysis should be aimed at establishing whether there is in principle any realistic prospect of regulation improving on the market outcome. RIA is supposed to answer a subsequent question, namely 'whether a specific, proposed intervention addresses the relevant market failure or regulatory failure well enough to yield, if it is implemented, a likelihood of net benefits, given its own costs and the circumstances of the relevant economic market'.[45] According to this argument, the two levels of analysis should be clearly distinguished from each other and the latter should only be pursued whenever the former promises a clearly positive outcome. Under the current trend, however, hopes for achieving better regulation lie essentially with RIA alone. This 'may incentivise regulators to pay less attention to the question whether intervention is sensible and more attention to gathering evidence to establish that a particular intervention will yield net benefits'.[46] In this view, RIA alone may be an expensive and misleading exercise.

RIA unfit to deliver smart regulation. Secondly, RIA's tentative outcomes are often measured against 'smart' regulation's basic postulates: a. preference for policy mixes incorporating a broader range of instruments and institutions; b. preference for less interventionist measures; and c. for measures as binding as required by the policy objective; d. empowerment of participants who are able to act as surrogate regulators; and e. maximization of opportunities for win/win outcomes.[47] There are several reasons why RIA may not achieve the above 'smart' outcomes.[48] For *one* thing, RIA processes are attuned to measuring the effects of traditional top-down regulatory systems and may discourage alternative regulatory strategies involving voluntary and incentive-driven measures. Such measures are, by definition, unsuitable for RIA, as it is extremely difficult to predict their effects, and

---

[45] Argument and quotations from Andrews, P., 2007, n 35, at 49–50.
[46] Ibid, at 50.
[47] For smart regulation, see eg Baldwin, R., 2007, n 16; Baldwin, R., 2005, n 16; see also Gunningham, N., and Grabosky, P., 1998 and 1999, n 16.
[48] Baldwin, R., 2007, n 16, at 34.

therefore, to calculate their costs and benefits.[49] *Secondly*, RIAs tend to concentrate on the effects of any given regulatory instrument rather than identify the cumulative effect of various instruments—especially if some of them cannot by nature be subjected to RIA. In other words, it is not able to cope with too many variables, estimates, and judgments.[50] In this respect, the bureaucratic incentive of officials involved in RIA is an important limiting factor: officials are more likely to favour unidimensional regulatory solutions, allowing for straightforward impact assessment, rather than more complicated regulatory frameworks.[51] 'The consideration of alternatives is liable, accordingly, to be straight-jacketed by existing regulatory frameworks.'[52] *Thirdly*, RIA focuses more on the *ex ante* general design of regulation rather than on the way the various actors and regulatory agencies are likely to cope with such regulation; quality is assessed basically by reference to process criteria, without taking the material consequences of regulation into account.[53] By its very structure, RIA is thus not expected to increase compliance in any substantial way.[54] *Fourthly*, by its proper definition, RIA is a one-shot evaluation method and is, thus, inappropriate for the development of responsive strategies involving escalating degrees of coercion. For the same reason, it is ill-suited to accommodate surrogate regulators and regulatory defaults.[55] *Fifthly*, it can be questioned whether (and why) public officials, whose authority is adduced from traditional top-down regulatory schemes, would have any incentive to trim their own powers, through RIA.

RIA masks an undercover political agenda. A third line of argument has to do with the desirability/necessity of RIA, in at least two situations. *First*, RIA is a welfare maximizing instrument, not a redistributional one. Therefore, it may benefit society as a whole, but it cannot reduce inequalities.[56] In this sense, RIA is not necessary when the regulator's aim is to benefit one group (eg a less advantaged one) over another.[57] This also explains that right-of-centre governments, interested in producing an efficient regulatory environment, are keener on RIA than left-of-centre governments which are more attuned to social objectives.[58] *Secondly*, RIAs are likely to play a marginal role, if at all, whenever government pushes through regulation which is animated by strong ideological reasons, manifesto commitments, or political settlements.[59] In this respect, they might even be seen as subverting democracy.

Doubts as to the suitability of RIA for the EU decision-making process. Fourthly, and most importantly, there is a further series of arguments, questioning the efficiency

---

[49] Ibid. [50] Ibid, at 35.
[51] Ibid. [52] Ibid, at 35–6.
[53] Bihlander, M., 'Better regulation by abdication?: Remarks on parliamentary democracy and governmental lawmaking' in Weatherill, S. (ed), *Better Regulation* (Oxford/Portland: Hart Publishing, 2007) 149–73, at 167.
[54] Baldwin, R., 2007, n 16, at 36.
[55] Ibid, at 36–7.
[56] Ibid, at 56.
[57] Ibid, at 68.
[58] See eg Radaelli, C., de Francesco, F., and Troeger, V., n 31, at 8.
[59] Ibid, at 71; see also Baldwin, R., 2005, n 16.

of RIA in the EU framework. To start with, it is suggested that the complexity of the EU decision-making process will undermine any benefits possibly stemming from RIA.

'The tendency to produce detailed, inflexible regulations is deeply rooted in the EC's political system. With its extreme fragmentation of political power and the distrust between EC policy-makers and the Member State administrations that implement most EC policy, the EC is simply not a polity structured to produce simple, flexible and informal regulation. For one thing, a structure containing a number of very different Member States is almost inevitably going to incorporate elements of the regulatory priorities of each. . . . Over-regulation in this instance is a function of the weakness and permeability of Brussels to Member States' demands, rather than of an overweening excessively regulatory Commission.'[60]

Moreover, whilst RIA is allowed to question the need for new regulation, its conclusions should not go as far as challenging the Commission's prerogative and reconfiguring the EU institutional balance.[61] In addition, unlike national regulatory processes typically involving one main legislator, in the EU, the regulatory power is dispersed amongst the Commission, the European Parliament (EP), and the Council, each having the power to substantially amend the other's proposals. It is therefore not clear how important the amendment proposed should be, in order to justify a fresh RIA—and by which body it should originate.[62] Furthermore, in relation to the previous point, it is noted that each of the above actors pursues its own institutional agenda and has its own operational limitations. For instance, timing RIAs in order to fit into the EP's procedures has not always been easy; more substantially, the impact of RIAs in the highly politicized decision making of the Council is questionable.[63] Last but not least, EU regulation is typically implemented by agencies at the domestic level. In this respect, the 'gold-plating' of European regulation in the process of its transposition into national law (ie the imposition of additional requirements)—a course that several member states have engaged in in the transposition of the Services Directive—may substantially change EU regulation, typically by rendering it more complicated.[64] It is not clear whether these changes can be caught by RIA.

---

[60] Kelemen, D., and Menon, A., 'The politics of EC regulation' in Weatherill, S. (ed), *Better Regulation* (Oxford/Portland: Hart Publishing, 2007) 175–89, at 184.

[61] This argument is not spelled out as such but is insinuated in Chittenden, F., Ambler, T, and Xiao, D., 'Impact assessment in the EU' in Weatherill, S. (ed), *Better Regulation* (Oxford/Portland: Hart Publishing, 2007) 271–86, at 275; see also the 2005 Inter-institutional Common Approach to Impact Assessment' (IA), available at <http://ec.europa.eu/governance/impact/;ia_in_other/docs/ii_common_approach_to_ia_en.pdf> (last accessed on 16 November 2011), which clearly states that 'This [RIA] is made without prejudice to the decision-making role and autonomy of each Institution and in line with their respective institutional roles and responsibilities' (para 2).

[62] Meuwese, A., 'Inter-institutionalising EU impact assessment' in Weatherill, S. (ed), *Better Regulation* (Oxford/Portland: Hart Publishing, 2007) 287–309, at 293. In this respect, the 2005 Inter-institutional Common Approach to Impact Assessment (n 61), completing the 2003 Inter-institutional Agreement, 'on Better Regulation', foresees that all proposals and 'substantive' amendments should be subject to RIA—but does not offer any clarification as to when amendments are substantive (para 5).

[63] Ibid, at 295–6.

[64] Olivi, E., 'The EU Better Regulation Agenda' in Weatherill, S. (ed), *Better Regulation* (Oxford/Portland: Hart Publishing, 2007) 191–4, at 194, who refers to a Dutch Study of May 2006, suggesting

ii. Empirical drawbacks of RIA

From an empirical point of view, based on the experience acquired so far, several shortfalls of RIA have been identified. *First*, the factors which impair the effectiveness of RIA are present throughout the process: limitations of material data on the specific topic concerned, the scarcity of information on the positions favoured by the various actors, and the speculative nature of any effort to foresee the reactions of the concerned parties, all transform RIA into a 'heroic guesswork'.[65]

Therefore, *secondly*, RIA is, on many occasions, found to constitute mere 'window dressing' for predetermined decisions.[66] In this regard, it is submitted that unless all OECD conditions for successful RIA are respected (ie political support at the higher level, clear and measurable quality standards, selection of a flexible and administratively feasible methodology, development of an institutional structure with an independent quality control, testing of assumptions through public consultation, integration of analysis into administrative and political decision processes, and building of expertise and skills among regulators),[67] then RIA may not be an efficient tool.

Thirdly, even in countries which deploy a considerable effort to make sure that the above conditions are met, RIAs only play a limited role. Indeed, the UK National Audit Office suggests that there are three types of RIAs: 'those that have no impact on policy development and are produced simply to meet the formal requirement (*pro forma* RIAs); those that have only a limited impact on policy, possibly because they are initiated too late (informative RIAs); and those that inform and genuinely challenge policy development (integrated RIAs)'.[68] From the above three categories the latter is, by far, the most rare.

The combination of these grounds of criticism of RIA does not lead to the conclusion that the effort should be abandoned altogether. On the contrary, it should be streamlined into the regular legislative process—and to a large extent, this is already happening.[69] At the same time, the critique above demonstrates that RIA alone is likely to have a relatively limited impact on the quality and the style of EU regulation. This means that, independently of RIA, other methods that are already in place, especially in the regulation of services, should be considered.

---

that 'more than half the obstacles associated with European legislation result from additional national requirements'; see also Ambler, T., Chittenden, F., and Obodovski, M., *How Much Regulation is Gold Plate? A Study of UK Elaboration of EU Directives* (London: British Chambers of Commerce, 2004).

[65] Baldwin, R., 2007, n 16, at 35.

[66] Andrews, P., 'Are market failure analysis and impact assessment useful?' in Weatherill, S. (ed), *Better Regulation* (Oxford/Portland: Hart Publishing, 2007) 49–81, at 65.

[67] OECD, *Regulatory Impact Analysis: Best Practices in OECD Countries* (Paris: OECD, 1997).

[68] Bihlander, M., 2007, n 53, at 166, who bases his findings on the UK National Audit Office's 2004/05 *Evaluation of Regulatory Impact Assessment Compendium Report*.

[69] Jacobs, S., 'Current trends in the process and methods of regulatory impact assessment: mainstreaming RIA into policy processes' in Kirkpatrick, C., and Parker, D. (eds), *Regulatory Impact Assessment: Towards Better Regulation?* (Cheltenham/Northampton: Edward Elgar Publishing, 2007) 17–35.

2. 'Hybrid' legislation—the use of soft law

Under subheading A of the present chapter, it was noted that the CCM has, especially in recent years, been emasculated through the use of soft law and other means of 'new governance'. Many authors argue, however, that instead of 'emasculated', the appropriate word should be 'enriched'. Indeed, the academic literature that advances the idea of 'hybrid' regulation and its virtues is both very articulate and highly authoritative.[70]

These authors—contrary to the Commission, in its 2001 Governance White Paper—refuse to identify the CCM as the bearer of any intrinsic value which should be preserved at all cost. They further refute the hiatus between the rationalist approach, envisioning law 'as a tool for constraining the behaviour of actors' and the constructivist approach, approaching law 'as a transformative tool capable of changing the behaviour of actors'; rather they believe that *both* propositions are correct.[71] Moreover, they insist on the shortfalls of hard law; they note that a. it tends towards uniformity at a time where diversity is increasingly seen as a value (or, at least, as a necessity); b. it supposes prior knowledge of the basic policy directions to be followed and may not be used in areas requiring constant experimentation and adjustment; c. it solidifies situations which would benefit from fluidity; d. its 'hard' nature does not necessarily translate into stronger compliance.[72] Soft law, according to the same authors, offers several advantages, including lower contracting costs, lower sovereignty costs, enhanced diversity, flexibility, simplicity and speed, broader participation, and incrementalism.[73]

Several EU policy areas have been identified as being subject to 'hybrid' regulation:

- regional policy, where *imperium* (legislation) is combined with *dominium* (financing), through the different funds and programmes;[74]

- fiscal policy coordination, where the Stability and Growth Pact foresees 'soft' coordination, failing which, 'hard' sanctions ensue;[75]

---

[70] See Scott, J., and Trubek, M., 2002, n 28; Trubek, D., Cortell, P., and Nance, M., 2005, n 28; more recently, see Trubek, D., and Trubek, L., 2007, n 28; Maher, I., 2004, n 28; Hatzopoulos, V., 2007, n 28; see also Hervey, T., and Trubek, L., 'Freedom to Provide Health Care Services in the EU: An Opportunity for "Hybrid Governance"' (2007) 13 *Columbia J of Eur L* 623–47.

[71] For a broader discussion of this distinction and the quotations, see Trubek, D., Cortell, P., and Nance, M., 2005, n 28, at 70–4. Indeed, as these authors themselves contend (ibid, at 73) 'from an epistemological standpoint, the constructivist approach is not interested in how things *are*, but in how they *became* what they are' (emphasis in the original).

[72] Ibid, at 67.

[73] On soft law, see Senden, L., and Prechal, S., 'Differentiation in and through Community soft law' in de Witte, B., Hanf, D., and Vos, E. (eds), *The Many Faces of Differentiation in EU Law* (Antwerpen: Intersentia Publishing, 2001) 181–99. For a series of 'para-legal' essays on soft law, see Mörth, U. (ed), *Soft Law in Governance and Regulation, An Interdisciplinary Analysis* (Cheltenham/ Northampton: Edward Elgar Publishing, 2004). For a strictly legal approach, see Senden L., *Soft Law in EC Law* (Oxford/Portland: Hart Publishing, 2004). For a virulent critique of soft law, see Klabbers, J., 'The Undesirability of Soft Law' (1998) 67 *Nordic J of Int L* 381–91.

[74] Trubek, D., Cortell, P., and Nance, M., 2005, n 28, at 81–2.

[75] Hodson, D., and Maher, I., 'Soft Law and Sanctions: Economic Policy Coordination and Reform of the Stability and Growth Pact' (2004) 11 *JEPP* 798–813, also available at <http://eucenter.wisc.edu/OMC/Papers/EconPolCoord/hodsonMaherJEPP2004.pdf> (last accessed on 16

- employment and inclusion policies, where basic EU 'hard' law texts on safety and security at work, working time, equal treatment, and operation of the European Agency for Safety and Health at Work are combined with OMCs and various programmes, especially in the area of inclusion;[76]

- healthcare, where the 'hard' law components of the High Level Reflection Process, the High Level Group on Health and Medical Care, and the dissemination of information insured by the European Monitoring Centre for Drugs and Drug Addiction and the European Medicines Agency, are coupled with CJEU case law and Commission interpretative Communications;[77]

- environmental policy, which is based, to a large extent, on formal and procedural requirements (essential to carrying out an environmental impact assessment), but there are no rules as to whether any specific project should be allowed; at the same time, it bears on Directives, such as the Water Framework Directive,[78] which provide for extensive pooling and reporting of information and for an informal Common Implementation Strategy;[79]

- fundamental rights, where the 2000 non-discrimination Directives[80] work in combination with Action Plans, regular reporting by the European Monitoring Centre on Racism and Xenophobia (EUMC, now reshuffled into the EU Agency for Fundamental Rights, FRA), activity deployed by networks, such as the Racism and Xenophobia Network (RAXEN) and an active role played by non-governmental organizations (NGOs).[81] The EU Charter of Fundamental

November 2011); Maher, I., 'Economic Governance: Hybridity, Accountability, and Control' (2007) 13 *Columbia J of Eur L* 679–703.

[76] Zeitlin, J., and Pochet, P. (eds), *The Open Method of Coordination in Action: The European Employment and Social Inclusion Strategies* (Brussels: Peter Lang, 2005); Kilpatrick, C., 'New EU employment governance and constitutionalism' in de Búrca, G., and Scott, J. (eds), *Law and New Governance in the EU and the US* (Oxford/Portland: Hart Publishing, 2006) 121–51; Jacobsson, K., 'Between deliberation and discipline: soft governance in EU employment policy' in Mörth, U. (ed), *Soft Law and Governance and Regulation: An Interdisciplinary Analysis* (Cheltenham/Northampton: Edward Elgar Publishing, 2004); Ashiagbor, D., 'Soft Harmonisation: The OMC in the EES' (2004) 10 *Eur Public L* 305–32; de la Porte, C., Pochet, P., and Room, G., 'Social Benchmarking, Policy Making and New Governance in the EU' (2001) 11 *J of Eur Social Policy* 291–307; Pagoulatos, G., and Stasinopoulou, M., 'Governance in EU Social Employment Policy: A Survey', Report for the Study on Social Impact of Globalisation in the EU (SIMGLOBE), European Commission and CEPS (VC/2005/0228), 2006, also available at <http://www.eliamep.gr/wp-content/uploads/2009/01/recwowe1.pdf> (last accessed on 16 November 2011).

[77] Hervey, T., 'The EU and the Governance of Health Care' in de Búrca, G., and Scott, J. (eds), *Law and New Governance in the EU and the US* (Oxford/Portland: Hart Publishing, 2006) 179–210; Hervey, T., and Trubek, L., 2007, n 28.

[78] European Parliament and Council Directive 2000/60/EC establishing a framework for Community action in the field of water policy [2000] OJ L327/1.

[79] Scott, J., and Holder, J., 'Law and new environmental governance in the EU' in de Búrca, G., and Scott, J. (eds), *Law and New Governance in the EU and the US* (Oxford/Portland: Hart Publishing, 2006) 211–42.

[80] Council Directive 2000/43/EC implementing the principle of equal treatment between persons irrespective of racial or ethnic origin [2000] OJ L180/22 and Council Directive 2000/78/EC establishing a general framework for equal treatment in employment and occupation [2000] OJ L303/16.

[81] De Búrca, G., 'EU race discrimination law: a hybrid model?' in de Búrca, G. and Scott, J. (eds), *Law and New Governance in the EU and the US* (Oxford/Portland: Hart Publishing, 2006) 97–120;

Rights, to the extent that it also contains non-actionable rights, adds yet another 'soft' layer to the protection of fundamental rights.

It seems undeniable, therefore, that 'hybrid' regulation is at least gradually making inroads into several areas of the EU regulatory space. Is it possible, however, to foresee a generalization—or a horizontal application—of such a trend?

It has been argued above,[82] while examining 'old-fashioned' harmonization, that a. the fact that harmonization constitutes the last solution, after trial and error (or success); b. the increased participation of shareholders; c. the creation of national contact points and their networking at EU level; d. the creation of EU Agencies; e. the general requirement for dissemination (at the national level), and exchange (at the EU level) of important amounts of information; f. the systematic inclusion of cyclical reporting and of 'rendez-vous' clauses into hard law; and g. the increased use of Communications and other means of soft law have all been identified as factors transforming 'old' into 'new governance', or at least into 'new old governance'. Hybridity, therefore, becomes less of a case-specific exception and more of a generalized trend, applicable across services regulation.

This trend is confirmed by the Services Directive (SD), the main legislative text dealing with services in a horizontal manner.[83] It was explained that,[84] after the demise of the country of origin principle (CoOP), the SD is essentially about regulatory reform at the national level. Rather than introducing rules allowing or prohibiting specific measures and practices, it sets the institutional framework for the exchange of information, mutual learning, and for self- and mutual evaluation. The outcome of the SD may not be identified by reading its text and, indeed, it may considerably vary from one member state to another.[85] It is a framework text establishing the necessary mechanisms for the adoption of substantive rules of law, at the national level first (through implementation) and subsequently at the EU level (through evaluation and revision).

This same trend is developed in the Patients' Rights Directive. This text does substantiate, to some extent, the proposal put forward by legal writers of a 'transformative Directive'.[86] It contains two components, a binding one, articulat-

---

Smismans, S., 'New Governance: The Solution for Active European Citizenship, or the End of Citizenship?' (2007) 13 *Columbia J of Eur L* 595–622.

[82] See heading A.

[83] European Parliament and Council Directive 2006/123/EC on services in the internal market [2006] OJ L376/36.

[84] See the discussion in ch 6.

[85] Indeed, the National Reports prepared for the 2008 FIDE Congress on the implementation of the Services Directive clearly show the different approaches and the discrepancies of expected impact between the various member states. See generally, Koeck, H.F., and Karollus, M.M. (eds), *The New Services Directive of the EU, FIDE XXIII Congress 2008, Volume III* (Vienna: Congress Publications, 2008); also the implementation record at the time of writing confirms the existence of startling differences in the way the various member states have transposed the Directive: Bulgaria, Estonia, Greece, and Poland have only adopted one 'omnibus' law, the UK and Lithuania have adopted five legislative acts, France and Malta 15, Denmark 105, Germany 125 and Hungary 307; see <http://ec.europa.eu/internal_market/services/services-dir/implementing_legislation_en.htm> (last accessed 16 November 2011).

[86] Hervey, T. and Trubek, L., n 70.

ing the formal legal rules on cross-border receipt and provision of services, and a non-binding one, creating norms through participatory mechanisms concerning the quality, security, etc of such services.[87] But for the very basic principle that free movement of patients should be enhanced, most of the substantive rules of the Directive will be set at a later stage, through the practice which will develop for the implementation of the Directive (eg centres of reference) and through deliberation in the various bodies the latter sets up (or formally institutionalizes).

'Hybrid' EU regulation seems, therefore, to be already a reality and experiments are expected to increase in the future. T. Hervey and L. Trubek note in this respect:[88]

'the roles of the framework regulation/directive are to set basic principles, objectives, and parameters, and to establish legal duties of transparency and accountability in the sense of "directly deliberative polyarchy". The framework regulation/directive sets legal obligations requiring accountability in the sense of requiring an explanation, not only to a central authority, but also, ideally, to peers. Along with penalty defaults, which are means to induce participation in "soft law" processes and "frameworks for creating rules".'[89]

The virtues of framework directives as means of coping with material and regulatory diversity, especially in the social field, have also been put forward by F. Scharpf.[90] Contrary to F. Scharpf's vision, however, from the analysis above it follows that framework rules need not be confined to defining social standards, but may also steer the internal market itself.

In this respect, previous experience with the Court's case law may serve as a reference model. Through its judgments, the CJEU reshuffles the general 'hard' law framework, but may not adopt generally applicable rules. This function is reserved to the EU legislature. In some occasions, case law-induced rules subsequently take the form of hard law texts. For instance, the Social Security Regulation 1408/71 has been modified several times in response to CJEU judgments.[91] Similarly, the

---

[87] Ibid, at 636.

[88] Ibid, at 628 (fn of the original text omitted).

[89] Ibid, at 628.

[90] Scharpf, F., 'European Governance: Common Concerns vs. the Challenge of Diversity' Jean Monnet Working Paper 07/2001, also available at <http://centers.law.nyu.edu/jeanmonnet/papers/01/010701.html> (last accessed on 16 November 2011).

[91] Indeed, some modifications have been made in order to incorporate CJEU case law into Regulations (see eg see Council Regulation 859/2003/EC incorporating into Regulation 1408/71 the judgment in Joined cases C-95/99–97/99 *Khalil* [2001] ECR I-7413 [2003] OJ L124/1). On the other hand, there have also been amendments made to legislative texts, so as to overturn rules set by the Court (see eg Council Regulation 1390/81/EEC extending to self-employed persons and members of their families Regulation (EEC) No 1408/71 on the application of social security schemes to employed persons and their families moving within the Community [1981] OJ L143/32 and Council Regulation 2793/81/EEC amending Regulation (EEC) No 1408/71 on the application of social security schemes to employed persons and their families moving within the Community and Regulation (EEC) No 574/72 fixing the procedure for implementing Regulation (EEC) No 1408/71 [1981] OJ L275/1). Both amendments expressly overturn the interpretation the Court gave to the Regulation's provisions in Case 117/77 *Bestuur van het Algemeen Ziekenfonds Drenthe-Platteland v G. Pierik* (*Pierik I*) [1978] ECR 825 and, on the same facts, Case 182/78 *Bestuur van het Algemeen Ziekenfonds Drenthe-Platteland v G. Pierik* (*Pierik II*) [1979] ECR 1977.

Citizenship Directive 2004/38,[92] replacing several previous Directives and Regulations, incorporates solutions that follow from jurisprudence. The Services Directive itself, to a large extent, codifies previous case law. The very existence of the Patients' Rights Directive is due to the Court's ingenious case law in this field.

More often than not, however, it is by means of soft law that the EU legislature, in particular the Commission, responds to case law inducements. The *Cassis de Dijon* interpretative Communication was one of the first examples of intervention through soft law.[93] Thereafter, the practice has been generalized and, indeed, diversified to a considerable extent. There are numerous examples, among which one could illustratively state: definition of the scope of the public authority exception under Article 51 TFEU;[94] detailed interpretation of the rules on free provision of services after *Säger* and *Mediawet*;[95] description of the content of the public order, security, and health exceptions in Article 52 TFEU;[96] supplementary rules concerning the mutual recognition of professional qualifications, especially in the field of non-regulated professions (not covered by Directive 89/48, now Directive 2005/36);[97] numerous Action Plans, White or Green Papers, and Reports on legislation already in place, in the area of electronic communications;[98] extensive rules completing (and arguably modifying) the Public Procurement Directives in respect of contracts below the thresholds[99] and in relation to service concessions and institutionalized public-private partnerships (PPPs);[100] principles for the identification of services of general interest (SGIs) and services of general economic interest (SGEIs);[101] rules on the applicability of the state aid rules on

[92] European Parliament and Council Directive 2004/38/EC on the right of citizens of the Union and their family members to move and reside freely within the territory of the Member States amending Regulation (EEC) No 1612/68 and repealing Directives 64/221/EEC, 68/360/EEC, 72/194/EEC, 73/148/EEC, 75/34/EEC, 75/35/EEC, 90/364/EEC, 90/365/EEC and 93/96/EEC [2004] OJ L158/77.

[93] Communication, 'concerning the consequences of the judgment given by the Court of Justice on 20 February 1979 in Case 120/78 (Cassis de Dijon)' [1980] OJ C256/2.

[94] Communication 88/C 72/02, 'on the freedom of movement of workers and access to employment in the public service of the Member States—Commission's action in respect of the application of article 48 paragraph 4 of the EEC Treaty' [1988] OJ C72/2.

[95] Interpretative Communication, 'concerning the free movement of services across frontiers' [1993] OJ C334/3.

[96] Communication COM (1999) 372 final, 'on the special measures concerning the movement and residence of citizens of the Union which are justified on grounds of public policy, public security or public health'.

[97] Communication COM (2002) 694 final, 'Free Movement of Workers: Achieving the Full Benefits and Potential'.

[98] See the list of over 100 texts enumerated on European Telecommunication Standards Institute's (ETSI) website <http://www.etsi.org/WebSite/AboutETSI/RoleinEurope/ECCommunications.aspx> (last accessed on 16 November 2011).

[99] [2005] OJ C297/4; see also the discussion in ch 5.

[100] Communication COM (2005) 569 final, 'on Public-Private Partnerships and Community Law on Public Procurement and Concessions', and Interpretative Communication C (2007) 6661, 'on the application of Community law on Public Procurement and Concessions to Institutionalised Public-Private Partnerships (IPPP)'.

[101] For the most recent, among several communications, see Communication COM (2007) 725 final, 'accompanying the Communication on "A single market for 21st century Europe"—Services of general interest, including social services of general interest: a new European commitment'.

services.[102] Indeed, the examples given represent a tiny proportion of the soft law activity of the Commission: in the field of telecommunications alone, between 2000 and 2007, the Commission has adopted over a hundred COM documents.[103]

Alongside COM documents, recent years have witnessed a proliferation of Staff Documents, published in the form of SEC documents. Indeed, the Commission's recent Communications are rarely longer than a dozen of pages and are limited to general directions and principles; more substantial and technical rules are included in the accompanying SEC documents. A further novelty consists in the publication of FAQs on various topics, such as the application of public procurement rules to social services of general interest (SSGIs),[104] and the application of the *Altmark* Decision 2005/842/EC.[105] Another way of soft steering is through the publication of Handbooks or Guides, the most significant being the Handbook on the Implementation of the Services Directive.[106]

Apart from Communications, COM, SEC, FAQ documents, Handbooks and Guides, the Commission has also issued Recommendations, especially in areas where it has formal decision-making powers: in the field of competition and state aids. Hence, for instance, the Commission's Recommendation on interconnection pricing[107] features as the single most used legal document for practitioners in the field. The same is true for Guidelines, extensively used in the field of competition law.[108]

It would be unwise to speculate further on the future of hard and soft law in the field of services. One final observation needs to be put forward, however. It was mentioned above that the relationship between old and new governance could be

---

[102] Community Framework, 'for State aid in the form of public service compensation', [2005] C297/4.

[103] According to the data published on ETSI's website, see n 98.

[104] Commission Staff Working Document SEC (2007) 1514, 'Frequently asked questions concerning the application of public procurement rules to social services of general interest—Accompanying document to the Communication on "Services of general interest, including social services of general interest: a new European commitment"'.

[105] Commission Staff Working Document SEC (2007) 1516, 'Frequently asked questions in relation with Commission Decision of 28 November 2005 on the application of Article 86(2) of the EC Treaty to State aid in the form of public service compensation granted to certain undertakings entrusted with the operation of services of general economic interest, and of the Community Framework for State aid in the form of public service compensation—Accompanying document to the Communication on "Services of general interest, including social services of general interest: a new European commitment"'.

[106] Available at <http://ec.europa.eu/internal_market/services/docs/services-dir/guides/handbook_en.pdf> (last accessed on 16 November 2011).

[107] Recommendation 1998/195/EC, 'on interconnection in a liberalised telecommunications market (Part 1: Interconnection pricing)' [1998] L73/42. The Recommendation has been modified several times (see 1998/511/EC, 2000/263/EC, 2002/175/EC).

[108] See Guidelines SEC (2010) 411, 'on vertical restraints' [2010] C130/1. Recently, a public consultation has been launched for the assessment of the Guidelines on horizontal cooperation agreements: Guidelines 20011/C 11/01, 'on the applicability of Article 101 of the Treaty on the Functioning of the EU to horizontal co-operation agreements' [2011] OJ C11/01.

described under the gap thesis, the hybridity thesis, and the transformation thesis. While the former does not seem to correspond at all to the reality just described, the other two are by no means contradictory: the hybridity thesis is static and corresponds to a snapshot at a given moment in time, while the transformation thesis is dynamic and accounts for the various evolutions in regulatory techniques.

10

Conclusion: Future Directions—Towards 'Intermodal Homogeneity'?

A. General characteristics of EU regulation of services

The discussion in Chapters 6–9 was aimed at conveying the main characteristics of EU regulation in the field of services. These may be summarized as follows:

i. Unevenness between fields. While some service sectors are extensively regulated and, occasionally, subject to exhaustive harmonization (eg transport, financial services), others are only subject to general free trade clauses, such as the 'internal market clause' (eg e-Directives); at the same time, trade in most services sectors is only covered by general principles developed by the CJEU and inaptly codified by the Services Directive.[1]

ii. Mode-specific regulation. The four modes of cross-border service provision[2] are unevenly dealt with, each one approached through a different regulatory lens. The main bulk of regulation concerns mode 3 of cross-border service provision, ie the establishment of foreign companies in other member states. The relevant legislation is essentially adopted under Article 50 TFEU, which is the legal basis of a different fundamental freedom, the freedom of establishment. Its effects on service provision are often made explicit through texts of soft law and, recently, through the relevant Chapter of the Services Directive. Mode 4, corresponding to the temporary posting of service providers or their personnel, is clearly less regulated: posted workers are dealt with (unsatisfactorily) in one Directive, while the occasional service provision by individual service providers is essentially regulated on a case by case basis by the Court. The same is true for mode 2, namely when the recipient moves towards the service. Finally, mode 1, covering (electronic) provision of services across borders, is, for its part, subject to 'mildly' liberalizing regulation, in the form of the 'internal market clause'.

iii. Dominant role of the CJEU. The vast majority of services rely on the Court's case law for the 'creation' of liberalizing principles and methods; especially so for modes 2 and 4. The occasions in which the legislature has been dragged by case law developments to adopt measures in the field of services are numerous; the Services

---

[1] See the discussion in ch 6.   [2] As described in ch 2.

Directive and the Patients' Rights Directive are just the most recent and striking examples. Nonetheless, several situations still remain in which the Court's case law is the sole aid to free movers.

iv. Variety of regulatory techniques and instruments. The Classic Community Method (CCM) and ensuing harmonization is just one among many techniques employed in the field of services. Mutual recognition, in many versions, is extensively used, despite the fact that, for the time being, it may not seriously be supported by a system of standardization/certification/accreditation. The home country control principle, itself deriving from the principle of mutual recognition, has been modified to take the form of an 'internal market clause' in several Directives, and eventually, the 'country of origin principle' (CoOP) in the draft Services Directive.

Alongside top-down command and control techniques, other more flexible methods are employed. Soft law, in the form of Communications, White and Green Papers, SEC documents, FAQs, Handbooks and Guides is becoming increasingly common. The Open Method of Coordination (OMC) plays its own role in the social field. In other areas, OMC-type procedures (involving periodic exchange of information and mutual evaluation) are also used, while the Lamfalussy process is just one, among several, processes striving to produce new efficient regulation and to increase compliance with existing regulation in the field. Self-regulation, co-regulation, and the use of codes of conduct constitute methods in the same vein.

v. Flexibility/Experimentalism/Dynamism. All these methods and instruments need to be employed in the field of services, because obstacles to services trade are much more numerous and remarkably subtler than in the other fundamental freedoms. This shows that, already at present, services regulation in the EU is far from monolithic and only partly corresponds to the CCM model. Realism (reflected in the Lamfalussy process and the networking of NRAs), experimentalism (demonstrated through the General Systems of mutual recognition), and a sense of trial and error (evidenced by the evolution of financial services regulation), strongly steered by the CJEU case law and the increasing use of soft law, all account for a varied and flexible regulatory patchwork. This trend is expected to be further developed under the ongoing 'better regulation' Agenda, actively promoted within the EU.

In which directions could this dynamism be put to work in the years to come? It is suggested that the regulatory activity of the EU should be directed towards alleviating the modal inequality observed above. The Services Directive (in its Chapter III) sufficiently completes the legal framework for the establishment of companies providing services (mode 3). On the contrary, in the other three modes, regulation is less satisfactory. Regulatory needs in the three remaining modes are briefly presented below, in increasing order of deficiency.

B. Cross-border trade of services (mode 1 GATS)

Mode 1 is currently governed by variants of the 'internal market clause', as expressed in the e-commerce, the electronic signature, and the AVMS Directives.[3] This way of dealing with the electronic provision of services is, at first sight, satisfactory. Under the pressure of technological change and diversification of electronic services, however, the relevant Directives will need to be reviewed—indeed, the transformation of the TVWF Directive into the AVMS Directive testifies to this need.

On such an occasion, two considerations should be taken into account, one material and one normative. At the material level, the 'internal market clause', because of the generality of its terms and the broadness of its enabling effect, may be countered in real life by restrictive administrative practices and/or technical shortcomings. In this respect, it may be desirable, more than 10 years after the first use of this technique in the e-signature Directive, to evaluate it and to identify its shortfalls. At the normative level, the attachment of the 'internal market clause' to strict nationality criteria, in order to determine the requirements with which the provider needs to comply, may need to be reviewed in order to accommodate the commercial combinations of technical means, which are necessary for the provision of electronic services. In addition to the revision of the existing Directives, mode 1 could further benefit from any other instrument of soft or hard law increasing the security of internet users and of transactions over the net. Activity in this field has, up until now, been essentially restricted to support actions and programmes, such as the Safer Internet Programmes (1999–2004, 2005–8, and 2009–13)[4] and the 2006 Communication on fighting spam, spyware, and malicious software.[5] In addition, the creation of the '.eu' top level domain[6] and the adoption of the e-Copyright Directive[7] are both expected to promote the provision of electronic services. Taking this into account, future action in order to facilitate service provision under mode 1 should aim at 'updating' the 'internal market clause' in the main 'e-Directives', as well as creating an environment favourable to electronic commerce, by regulatory means or otherwise.

---

[3] For these Directives, see the discussion in ch 6.

[4] European Parliament and Council Decision 276/1999/EC adopting a multiannual Community action plan on promoting safer use of the Internet by combating illegal and harmful content on global networks [1999] OJ L108/52, European Parliament and Council Decision 854/2005/EC establishing a multiannual Community Programme on promoting safer use of the Internet and new online technologies [2005] OJ L149/1, and European Parliament and Council Decision 1351/2008/EC establishing a multiannual Community programme on protecting children using the Internet and other communication technologies [2008] OJ L348/118, respectively.

[5] COM (2006) 688 final, 'on fighting spam, spyware and malicious software'.

[6] European Parliament and Council Regulation 733/2002/EC on the implementation of the .eu Top Level Domain [2002] OJ L113/1.

[7] European Parliament and Council Directive 2001/29/EC on the harmonization of certain aspects of copyright and related rights in the information society [2001] OJ L167/10; see also European Parliament and Council Directive 2004/48/EC on the enforcement of intellectual property rights [2004] OJ L157/45.

C. Movement of natural persons (mode 4 GATS)

Mode 4 needs urgent attention so far as posted workers are concerned. It was explained above that the Posted Workers Directive 96/71 was adopted partly to codify and partly to contain the CJEU's case law in *Seco v EVI*, *Rush Portuguesa*, and *Vander Elst*.[8] In its recent case law, however, the Court has attempted a reinterpretation of the Directive and has transformed it into a text offering to posted workers a ceiling rather than a floor of rights, although the latter was the legislator's clear will. By the same token, the Court has upset legal certainty to the detriment of both employers and posted workers. It is suggested, therefore, that in view of the importance that mode 4 is due to have in the framework of the enlarged—and ever enlarging—EU, a clarification of the principles applicable on the matter would be desirable. This should take account of the most recent case law of the Court and of the henceforth extremely rich academic literature on regulatory competition. Such a modification of the Posted Workers Directive could be part of a broader package of measures—of both hard and soft law—intended to tame wage disparities and manage regulatory competition, possibly through assistance measures. This features as a highly politicized exercise, as it entails controversial weighing: eg national solidarity (as embodied in national social protection systems) against solidarity at the EU level (which supposedly exists between richer and poorer countries).

D. Consumption abroad (mode 2 GATS)

The Patients' Rights Directive is the first legislative text to promote service recipient's mobility specifically. Hence, it becomes clear that service recipients only recently have become of interest to the EU legislature. This trend, however, is expected to continue. The increased volume of information provided to consumers by virtue of the Services Directive, combined with the facilitation effect of the points of single contact and the important cost differences within the enlarged EU are expected to mobilize larger numbers of service recipients. In this way, the lack of a comprehensive framework for the protection of consumers in service transactions, comparable to the Product Liability Directive for goods,[9] will soon prove to be the single most decisive factor discouraging free movement. This will have to be remedied. By the same token, the existing rules on fair trading and consumer

---

[8] Joined cases 62 & 63/81 *Seco v EVI* [1982] ECR 223; Case C-113/89 *Rush Portuguesa v Office nationale d'immigration* [1990] ECR I-1417; Case C-43/93 *Vander Elst v Office des Migrations Internationales* [1994] ECR I-3803. For these cases, see ch 5.

[9] Council Directive 85/374/EEC on the approximation of the laws, regulations and administrative provisions of the Member States concerning liability for defective products [1985] OJ L210/29.

protection[10] (for distance contracts, etc) should be revised in order to account for new forms—and new platforms—of services. Indeed, such a revision is already under way.[11]

The ongoing financial crisis shows in an unprecedented, acute way the degree of interdependence of EU—and world—economies. The possibility exists that, once the EU gets on its feet again and until its economies stabilize, it may be slow to further open up to international trade in services; therefore the outcome of the WTO Doha round of negotiations seems quite uncertain under the current conjecture. Once the financial situation of EU member states gets stabilized, however, the EU will have no choice than to turn its attention to the 'real' economy. Indeed, it is the fact that—contrary to the Lisbon's ambitious agenda—the EU economy has failed to become the most competitive of the world, that has sparked the waves of aggressive speculation against its member states' economies. Therefore, if the EU is to prosper again, it will need to put its best efforts to better itself on the area it is most competitive in: services. If the findings of this book, based on past experience and integrating current regulatory trends, could contribute, be it by a tiny measure, to the indispensable scholarly and political dialogue, this book will have been a great success.

---

[10] For which see briefly in the introduction to ch 6; for an EU Consumer Law Compendium, see legal documents collected in <http://www.eu-consumer-law.org/index.html> (last accessed on 16 November 2011).

[11] Proposal COM (2008) 614, 'Directive of the European Parliament and of the Council on consumer rights'. The Commission has also launched a public consultation; all relevant documents, including the Commission's proposal, are available in <http://ec.europa.eu/consumers/rights/cons_acquis_en.htm> (last accessed on 16 November 2011); while this book was is production this text was adopted as Directive 2011/83/EU [2011] OJ L304/64.

APPENDIX

Case Law Processed in the Spreadsheet

1.	Case C-155/73 *Sacchi* [1974] ECR 409
2.	Case C-33/74 *Van Binsbergen* [1974] ECR 1299
3.	Case C-36/74 *Walrave and Koch v International Cycliste Asssociation Union* [1974] ECR 1405
4.	Case C-39/75 *Coenen* [1975] ECR 1547
5.	Case C-48/75 *Royer* [1976] ECR 497
6.	Case C-118/75 *Watson and Belmann* [1976] ECR 1185
7.	Case C-13/76 *Dona v Mantero* [1976] ECR 1333
8.	Case C-90/76 *Ufficio Henry van Ameyde* [1977] ECR 1091
9.	Case C-15/78 *Alsacien General Bank Society SA v Koestler* [1978] ECR 1971
10.	Case C-16/78 *Choquet* [1978] ECR 2293
11.	Case C-111/78 *Van Wesemael* [1979] ECR 35
12.	Case C-115/78 *Knoors* [1979] ECR 399
13.	Case C-52/79 *Debauve* [1980] ECR 833
14.	Case C-62/79 *Coditel v Ciné Vog Films* [1980] ECR 881
15.	Case C-246/80 *Broekmeulen* [1981] ECR 2311
16.	Case C-279/80 *Webb* [1981] ECR 3305
17.	Joined cases C-62 & 63/81 *Seco v EVI* [1982] ECR 223
18.	Case C-76/81 SA *Transporoute* [1982] ECR 417
19.	Joined cases C-286/82 & 26/83 *Luisi and Carbone* [1984] ECR 377
20.	Case C-220/83 *Commission v France* [1986] ECR 3663
21.	Case C-251/83 *Haug-Adrion* [1984] ECR 4277
22.	Case C-252/83 *Commission v Danemark* [1986] ECR 3713
23.	Case C-205/84 *Commission v Germany* [1986] ECR 3755
24.	Case C-206/84 *Commission v Ireland* [1986] ECR 3817

25. Case C-96/85 *Commission v France* [1986] ECR 1475

26. Case C-168/85 *Commission v Italy* [1986] ECR 2945

27. Case C-352/85 *Bond van Adverteerders* [1988] ECR 2085

28. Case C-427/85 *Commission v Germany* [1988] ECR 1123

29. Case C-63/86 *Commission v Italy* [1988] ECR 29

30. Case 147/86 *Commission v Greece (private schools)* [1988] ECR 1637

31. Case C-263/86 *Humbel* [1988] ECR 5365

32. Case C-267/86 *Van Eycke v Society Anonymous ASPA* [1988] ECR 4769

33. Case 292/86 *Gullung* [1988] ECR 111

34. Case C-31/87 *Gebroeders Beentjes BV* [1988] ECR 4635

35. Case C-38/87 *Commission v Greece* [1988] ECR 4415

36. Case C-186/87 *Cowan* [1989] ECR 195

37. Case C-196/87 *Steymann* [1988] ECR 6159

38. Case C-305/87 *Commission v Greece* [1989] ECR 1461

39. Case 395/87 *Tournier* [1989] ECR 2521

40. Case C-3/88 *Commission v Italy* [1989] ECR 4035

41. Case C-49/89 *Corsica Ferries France* [1989] ECR 4441

42. Case C-61/89 *Bouchoucha* [1990] ECR I-3551

43. Case C-113/89 *Rush Portuguesa Lda* [1990] ECR I-1417

44. Case C-154/89 *Commission v France* [1991] ECR I-659

45. Case C-180/89 *Commission v Italy* [1991] ECR I-709

46. Case C-198/89 *Commission v Greece* [1991] ECR I-727

47. Case C-260/89 *ERT v DEP* [1991] ECR 2925

48. Case C-279/89 *Commission v UK (fisheries)* [1992] ECR I-5785

49. Case C-288/89 *Stichting Collectieve Antennevoorziening Gouda* [1991] ECR 4007

50. Case C-294/89 *Commission v France* [1991] ECR I-3591

51. Case C-306/89 *Commission v Greece* [1991] ECR 5863

52. Case C-322/89 *Marchandise, Chapuis and Trafitex* [1991] ECR I-1027

53. Case C-340/89 *Vlassopoulou* [1991] ECR I-2357

54. Case C-353/89 *Commission v Netherlands* [1991] ECR I-4069

55. Case C-360/89 *Commission v Italy* [1992] ECR I-3401

56.	Case C-17/90 *Pinaud Wieger Spedition GmbH* [1991] ECR I-5253
57.	Case C-41/90 *Höfner and Elser v Macrotron GmbH* [1991] ECR I-1979
58.	Case C-58/90 *Commission v Italy* [1991] ECR I-4193
59.	Case C-76/90 *Säger v Dennemeyer* [1991] ECR I-4221
60.	Case C-159/90 *Grogan* [1991] ECR 4685
61.	Case C-204/90 *Bachmann* [1992] ECR I-249
62.	Case C-239/90 *SCP Boscher, Studer and Fromentin v SA British Motors Wright* [1991] ECR I-2023
63.	Case C-300/90 *Commission v Belgium* [1992] ECR I-305
64.	Case C-330/90 *Lopez Brea and Hidalgo Palacios* [1992] ECR I-323
65.	Case C-60/91 *Batista Morais* [1992] ECR I-2085
66.	Case C-104/91 *Aguirre Borrell* [1992] ECR I-3003
67.	Case C-106/91 *Ramrath* [1992] ECR I-3351
68.	Case C-147/91 *Ferrer Laderer* [1992] ECR I-4097
69.	Case C-148/91 *Vereniging Veronica Omroep Organisatie* [1993] ECR I-487
70.	Case C-211/91 *Commission v Belgium (cable TV)* [1992] ECR I-235
71.	Case C-272/91 *Commission v Italy, Lottomatica,* [1994] ECR I-1409
72.	Case C-17/92 *Federacion de Distribuidores Cinematograficos* [1993] ECR I-2239
73.	Case C-20/92 *Hubbard* [1993] ECR I-3777
74.	Case C-109/92 *Wirth* [1993] ECR I-6447
75.	Case C-275/92 *Schindler* [1994] ECR I-1039
76.	Case C-319/92 *Haim* [1994] ECR I-425
77.	Case C-375/92 *Commission v Spain (tourist guides)* [1994] ECR I-923
78.	Case C-379/92 *Peralta* [1994] ECR I-3453
79.	Case C-18/93 *Corsica Ferries Italia Srl* [1994] ECR 1783
80.	Case C-23/93 *TV10 SA* [1984] ECR I-4795
81.	Case C-45/93 *Commission v Spain (museums)* [1994] ECR I-911
82.	Case C-55/93 *Van Schaik* [1994] ECR I-4837
83.	Case C-154/93 *Tawil-Albertini* [1994] ECR I-451
84.	Joined cases C-358/93 & C-416/93 *Bordessa, Mari Mellado & Barbero Maestre* [1995] ECR I-361
85.	Case C-381/93 *Commission v France* [1994] ECR I-5145

116. Case C-124/97 *Läärä, Cotswold Microsystems Ltd and Oy Transatlantic Software Ltd* [1999] ECR I-6067

117. Joined Cases C-147/97 & C-148/97 *Deutsche Post AG v Gesellschaft für Zahlungssysteme mbH GZS and Citicorp Kartenservice GmbH* [2000] ECR I-825

118. Case C-224/97 *Ciola* [1999] ECR I-2517

119. Case C-294/97 *Eurowings Luftverkehrs AG* [1999] ECR I-7447

120. Case C-6/98 *Arbeitsgemeinschaft Deutscher Rundfunkanstalten v PRO Sieben Media AG* [1999] ECR I-7599.

121. Joined cases C-49 & 50/98, C-52–54/98 & C-68–71/98 *Finalarte* [2001] ECR I-7831

122. Case C-55/98 *Vestergaard* [1999] ECR I-7641

123. Case C-58/98 *Corsten* [2000] ECR I-7919

124. Case C-97/98 *Jägerskiöld* [1999] ECR I-7319

125. Case C-108/98 *RI SAN Srl* [1999] ECR I-5219

126. Case C-165/98 *Mazzoleni and Inter Surveillance Assistance SARL* [2001] ECR I-2189

127. Case C-225/98 *Commission v France* [2000] ECR I-7445

128. Case C-324/98 *Telaustria Verlags GmbH and Telefonadress GmbH v Telekom Austria AG* [2000] ECR I-10745

129. Case C-355/98 *Commission v Belgium, private security* [2000] ECR I-1221

130. Case C-358/98 *Commission v Italy* [2000] ECR I-1255

131. Case C-368/98 *Vanbraekel and others* [2001] ECR I-5363

132. Case C-405/98 *Konsumentombudsmannnen v Gourmet International Products (GIP)* [2001] ECR I-1795

133. Case C-456/98 *Centrosteel Srl v Adipol GmbH* [2000] ECR I-6007

134. Case C-58/99 *Commission v Italy* [2000] ECR I-3811

135. Case C-68/99 *Commission v Germany* [2001] ECR I-1865

136. Case C-70/99 *Commission v Portugal* [2001] ECR I-4845

137. Case C-94/99 *ARGE Gewässerschutz* [2000] ECR I-11037

138. Case 145/99 *Commission v Italy (lawyers)* [2002] ECR I-2235

139. Case C-157/99 *Smits and Peerbooms* [2001] ECR I-5473

140. Case C-164/99 *Portugaia Construçoes Lda* [2002] ECR I-787

141. Case C-205/99 *Asociacion Profesional de Empresas Navieras de Lineas Regulares (Analir) and others* [2001] ECR I-1271

142.   Case C-232/99 *Commission v Spain (doctor's recognition)* [2002] ECR I-4235

143.   Case 263/99 *Commission v Italy (transport consultants)* [2001] ECR I-4195

144.   Case C-264/99 *Commission v Italy (road haulage)* [2000] ECR I-4417

145.   Case C-283/99 *Commission v Italy (private security)* [2001] ECR I-4363

146.   Case C-298/99 *Commission v Italy (architects)* [2002] ECR I-3129

147.   Case C-309/99 *Wouters et al.* [2002] ECR I-1577

148.   Case C-385/99 *Müller-Fauré and E.E.M. van Riet* [2003] ECR I-4509

149.   Case C-390/99 *Canal Satélite Digital* [2002] ECR I-607

150.   Joined Cases C-430/99–C-431/99 *Sea-Land Service Inc. and Nedlloyd Lijnen BV* [2002] ECR I-5235

151.   Case C-439/99 *Commission v Italy* [2002] ECR I-305

152.   Case C-447/99 *Commission v Italy* [2001] ECR I-5203

153.   Case C-451/99 *Cura Anlagen GmbH v Auto Service Leasing GmbH (ASL)* [2002] ECR I-3193

154.   Case C-493/99 *Commission v Germany* [2001] ECR I-8163

155.   Case C-17/00 *De Coster* [2001] ECR I-9445

156.   Case C-31/00 *Dreessen* [2002] ECR I-663

157.   Case C-60/00 *Carpenter* [2002] ECR I-6279

158.   Case C-92/00 *Hospital Ingenieure Krankenhaustechnik Planungs-Gesellschaft mbH (HI)* [2002] ECR I-5553

159.   Case C-136/00 *Danner* [2002] ECR I-8147

160.   Case C-153/00 *Der Weduwe* [2002] ECR I-11319

161.   Case C-279/00 *Commission v Italy* [2002] ECR I-1425

162.   Case C-294/00 *Deutsche Paracelsus Schulen für Naturheilverfahren GmbH v Gräbner* [2002] ECR I-6515

163.   Case C-295/00 *Commission v Italy* [2002] ECR I-1737

164.   Case C-318/00 *Bacardi-Martini SAS and Cellier des Dauphins v Newcastle United Football Company Ltd* [2003] ECR I-905

165.   Case C-355/00 *Freskot* [2003] ECR I-5263

166.   Case C-435/00 *Geha Naftiliaki EPE et al.* [2002] ECR I-10615

167.   Case C-6/01 *Associaçao Nacional de Operadores de Maquinas Recreativas (Anomar) et al.* [2003] ECR I-8621

168.   Case C-56/01 *Inizan* [2003] ECR I-12403

169. Case C-79/01 *Payroll Data Services Srl et al* [2002] ECR I-8923

170. Case C-92/01 *Stylianakis v Dimosio* [2003] ECR I-1291

171. Case C-131/01 *Commission v Italy* [2003] ECR I-1659

172. Case C-215/01 *Schnitzer* [2003] ECR I-14847

173. Case C-234/01 *Gerritse* [2003] ECR I-5933

174. Case C-243/01 *Gambelli* [2003] ECR I-13031

175. Case C-313/01 *Morgenbesser* [2003] ECR I-13467

176. Joined cases C-317/01 & C-369/01 *Abata y e.a. and Sahin* [2003] ECR I-12301

177. Case C-388/01 *Commission v Italy (museums)* [2003] ECR I-721

178. Case C-422/01 *Försäkringsaktiebolaget Skandia (publ) and Ramstedt* [2003] ECR I-6817

179. Case C-478/01 *Commission v Luxembourg* [2003] ECR I-2351

180. Joined cases C-482/01 & C-493/01 *Orfanopoulos and Oliveri* [2004] ECR I-5257

181. Case C-496/01 *Commission v France (medical laboratories)* [2004] ECR I-2351

182. Case C-8/02 *Leichtle* [2004] ECR I-2641

183. Case C-36/02 *Omega Spielhallen- und Automatenaufstellungs-GmbH* [2004] ECR I-9609

184. Case C-42/02 *Lindman* [2003] ECR I-13519

185. Case C-153/02 *Neri* [2003] ECR I-13555

186. Case C-171/02 *Commission v Portugal (private securities)* [2004] ECR I-5645

187. Case C-200/02 *Zhu and Chen* [2004] ECR I-9925

188. Case C-262/02 *Commission v France* [2004] ECR I-6569

189. Case C-288/02 *Commission v Greece* [2004] ECR I-10071

190. Case C-289/02 *Amok Verlags GmbH v A&R Gastronomie GmbH* [2003] ECR I-15059

191. Case C-313/02 *Meca-Medina and Majcen* [2004] ECR II-3291

192. Case C-334/02 *Commission v France (income tax)* [2004] ECR I-2229

193. Case C-341/02 *Commission v Germany* [2005] ECR I-2733

194. Case C-429/02 *Bacardi France SAS v TF1 et al.* [2004] ECR I-6613

195. Case C-456/02 *Trojani* [2004] ECR I-7573

196. Case C-20/03 *Burmanjer e.a.* [2005] ECR I-4133

197. Case C-60/03 *Wolff & Müller GmbH& Co KG v Pereira* [2004] ECR I-9553

198. Case C-81/03 *Commission v Austria (radiologists)* [2004] nyr

199. Case C-134/03 *Viacom Outdoor Srl v Giotto Immobilier SARL* [2005] ECR I-1167

200. Case C-189/03 *Commission v Netherlands (private security firms)* [2004] ECR I-5645

201. Case C-215/03 *Oulane* [2005] ECR I-1215

202. Case C-219/03 *Commission v Spain* [2004] nyr

203. Case C-231/03 *Consorzio Aziende Metano (Coname)* [2005] ECR I-7287

204. Case C-234/03 *Contse SA et al.* [2005] ECR I-9315

205. Case 264/03 *Commission v France (excluded services)* [2005] ECR I-8831

206. Case C-287/03 *Commission v Belgium* [2005] ECR 3761

207. Case C-323/03 *Commission v Spain* [2006] ECR I-2161

208. Case C-408/03 *Commission v Belgium (financial resources)* [2006] ECR I-2647

209. Case C-445/03 *Commission v Luxembourg* [2004] ECR I-10191

210. Case C-451/03 *Servizi Ausiliari Dottori Commercialisti Srl* [2006] ECR I-2941

211. Case C-458/03 *Parking Brixen GmBH* [2005] ECR I-8585

212. Case C-507/03 *Commission v Ireland* [2007] ECR I-9777

213. Joined cases C-544/03 & 545/03 *Mobistar SA and Belgacom Mobile SA* [2005] ECR I-7723

214. Case C-39/04 *Laboratoires Fournier SA* [2005] ECR I-2057

215. Joined cases C-94/04 & C-202/04 *Cipolla and Meloni* [2006] ECR I-11421

216. Case C-150/04 *Commission v Denmark* [2007] ECR I-1163

217. Case C-151/04 & C-151/04 *Nadin and Durré* [2005] ECR I-1120

218. Case C-168/04 *Commission v Austria (posted workers)* [2006] ECR I-9041

219. Case C-244/04 *Commission v Germany (work visa regime)* [2006] ECR I-885

220. Case C-251/04 *Commission v Greece* [2007] ECR I-67

221. Case C-255/04 *Commission v France* [2006] ECR I-5251

222. Case C-290/04 *FKP Scorpio Konzertproduktionen GmbH* [2006] ECR I-9461

223. Case (ord) C-291/04 *Schmitz* [2006] ECR I-59

224. Joined cases C-338/04, C-359/04 & C-360/04 *Placanica, Palazzese and Sorricchio* [2007] ECR I-1891

225. Case C-345/04 *Centro Equestre da Lezíria Grande Lda* [2007] ECR I-1425

226. Case C-372/04 *Watts* [2006] ECR I-4325

227. Case C-386/04 *Centro di Musicologia Walter Stauffer* [2006] ECR I-8203

228. Case C-410/04 *Associazione Nazionale Autotrasporto Viaggiatori (ANAV)* [2006] ECR I-3303

229. Case C-412/04 *Commission v Italy (below thresholds)* [2008] ECR I-619

230. Case C-433/04 *Commission v Belgium* [2006] ECR I-653

231. Case (ord) C-435/04 *Leroy* [2006] ECR I-4835

232. Case C-452/04 *Fidium Finanz AG* [2006] ECR I-9521

233. Case C-456/04 *Agip Petroli SpA* [2006] ECR I-3395

234. Case C-466/04 *Acereda Herrera* [2006] ECR I-5341

235. Case C-490/04 *Commission v Germany (posted workers)* [2007] ECR I-6095

236. Case C-519/04 P *Meca-Medina* [2006] ECR I-6991

237. Case C-522/04 *Commission v Belgium (occupational pension schemes)* [2007] ECR I-5701

238. Case C-1/05 *Jia* [2007] ECR I-1

239. Case C-65/05 *Commission v Greece (online games)* [2006] ECR I-10341

240. Case 76/05 *Schwarz & Gootjes-Schwarz* [2007] ECR I-6849

241. Case C-208/05 *ITC Innovative Technollogy Center GmbH* [2007] ECR I-181

242. Case (ord) C-242/05 *Van de Coevering* [2006] ECR I-5843

243. Case C-249/05 *Commission v Finland* [2006] ECR I-80

244. Case C-257/05 *Commission v Austria (boiler inspectors)* [2006] ECR I-134

245. Case C-269/05 *Commission v Greece* [2007] ECR I-4

246. Case C-318/05 *Commission v Germany (school fees)* [2007] ECR I-6957

247. Case C-341/05 *Laval un Partneri Ltd* [2007] ECR I-11767

248. Case C-380/05 *Centro Europa 7 Srl* [2008] ECR I-349

249. Case C-389/05 *Commission v France* [2008] nyr

250. Case C-393/05 *Commission v Austria* [2007] ECR I-10195

251. Case (ord) C-395/05 *D'Antonio* [2007] ECR I-24

252. Case C-404/05 *Commission v Germany* [2007] ECR I-10239

253. Case C-432/05 *Unibet (London) Ltd and Unibet (International) Ltd* [2007] ECR I-2271

254. Case C-438/05 *International Transport Workers' Federation and Finnish Seamen's Union v Viking Line ABP and OÜ Viking Line Eesti* [2007] ECR I-10779

255. Case C-444/05 *Stamatelaki* [2007] ECR I-3185

256. Case C-119/06 *Commission v Italy* [2007] ECR I-168

257. Joined cases C-147/06 & C-148/06 *Secap and Santorso* [2008] ECR I-3565

258. Case (ord) C-191/06 *Gallo and Damonte* [2007] ECR I-30

259. Case C-220/06 *Asociación Profesional de Empresas de Reparto y Manipulado de Correspondencia* [2007] ECR I-12175

260. Case C-248/06 *Commission v Spain* [2008] ECR I-47

261. Case C-250/06 *United Pan-Europe* [2007] ECR 11135

262. Case C-281/06 *Jundt* [2007] ECR I-12231

263. Case C-319/06 *Commission v Luxembourg* [2008] ECR I-4323

264. Case C-346/06 *Rüffert* [2008] ECR I-1989

265. Case C-347/06 *ASM Brescia SpA* [2008] nyr

266. Case (ord) C-466/05 *Damonte* [2007] ECR I-27

267. Case (ord) C-466/05 *Di Maggio and Buccola* [2007] ECR I-27

268. Case C-500/06 *Corporación Dermoestética SA* [2008] ECR I-5785

269. Case C-518/06 *Commission v Italy* [2009] ECR I-3491

270. Case C-49/07 *MOTOE v Elliniko Dimosio* [2008] ECR I-4863

271. Case C-169/07 *Hartlauer* [2009] ECR I-1721

272. Case C-205/07 *Lodewijk Gysbrechts and Santurel Inter BVBA* [2008] ECR I-9947

273. Case C-213/07 *Michaniki AE* [2008] ECR I-9999

274. Case C-222/07 *Union de Televisiones Comerciales Asociadas (UTECA)* [2009] ECR I-1407

275. Case C-324/07 *Coditel Brabant SA* [2008] ECR I-8457

276. Case C-330/07 *Jobra* [2008] ECR I-9099

277. Case C-350/07 *Kattner Stahlbau GmbH* [2009] ECR I-1513

278. Case C-564/07 *Commission v Austria* [2009] nyr

279. Case (ord) C-42/08 *Ilhan* [2008] ECR I-83

280. Case (ord) C-104/08 *Kurt* [2008] ECR I-97

281. Joined cases C-155/08 & C-157/08 *X and Passenheim-van Schoot* [2009] ECR I-5093

282. Case C-356/08 *Commission v Austria* [2009] ECR I-108

283. Case (ord) C-364/08 *Vandermeir* [2008] ECR I-8087

Bibliography

BOOKS:

Amato, G., and Ehlermann, C.D., *EC Competition Law: A Critical Assessment* (Oxford/ Portland: Hart Publishing, 2007).

Ambler, T., Chittenden, F., and Obodovski, M., *How Much Regulation is Gold Plate?: A Study of UK Elaboration of EU Directives* (London: British Chambers of Commerce, 2004).

Arrowsmith, S., *The Law of Public and Utilities Procurement* (London: Sweet & Maxwell, 2005).

Ayers, I., and Braithwaite, J., *Responsive Regulation: Transcending the Deregulatory Debate* (Oxford: OUP, 1992).

Baquero Cruz, J., *Between Competition and Free Movement: The Economic Constitutional Law of the European Community* (Oxford/Portland: Hart Publishing, 2002).

—— Closa Montero, C. (eds), *European Integration from Rome to Berlin: 1957–2007: History, Law and Politics* (Bruxelles, etc: PIE Peter Lang, 2009).

Barnard, C., *The Substantive Law of the EU*, 3rd edn (Oxford: OUP, 2010).

—— and Odudu, O. (eds), *The Outer Limits of European Union Law* (Oxford/Portland: Hart Publishing, 2009).

—— and Scott, J. (eds), *The Law of the Single European Market: Unpacking the Premises* (Oxford/Portland: Hart Publishing, 2002).

Barth, R., and Wolff, F. (eds), *Corporate Social Responsibility in Europe: Rhetoric and Realities* (Aldershot: Edward Elgar Publishing, 2009).

Basedow, J., Baum, H., Kanda H., and Kono, T. (eds), *Economic Regulation and Competition: Regulation of Services in the EU, Germany, and Japan* (Hague/London/NY: Kluwer Law International, 2002).

Bauby, P., Coing, H., and de Toledo, A. (eds), *Les services publics en Europe: Pour une régulation démocratique* (Paris: Publisud, 2007).

Baumol, W.J., Panzar, J., and Willig, R., *Contestable Markets and the Theory of Industry Structure* (San Diego: Harcourt Brace Jovanovich, 1982).

Bernaerts, Y., *The 2010 VAT Directive and the Case Law of the Court of Justice of the EU* (Louvain la Neuve: Anthemis, 2010).

Bhagwati, J. and Hisch, M. (eds), *The Uruguay Round and Beyond: Essays in honour of Arthur Dunkel* (Heidelberg: Springer, 1998).

Bigo, D., Carrera, S., and Guild, E., The Challenge Project: Final Policy Recommendations on the Changing Landscape of European Liberty and Security (2009) CEPS Paper available at <http://www.ceps.eu/book/challenge-project-final-policy-recommendations-changing-landscape-european-liberty-and-security>.

Blanpain, R. (ed), *Freedom of Services in the EU, Labour and Social Security Law: The Bolkestein Initiative* (The Hague: Kluwer Law International, 2006).

—— and Swiatkofski, A.M. (eds), *The Laval and Viking Cases: Freedom of Services and Establishment v. Industrial Conflict in the European Economic Area and Russia* (Alphen aan den Rijn: Kluwer Law International, 2009).

Bork, R.H., *The Antitrust Paradox: A Policy at War with Itself* (New York: Free Press, 1993).

Boual, J.C., Brachet, P., and Hiszka, M. (eds), *Les services publiques en Europe* (Paris: Publisud, 2007).

Bourgeois, J., Berrod, F., and Gippini-Fournier, E., *The Uruguay Round Results: A European Lawyer's Perspective* (Brussels: European Interuniversity Press/College of Europe, 1998).

Bovis, C., *EC Public Procurement: Case Law and Regulation* (Oxford: OUP, 2006).

Braconnier, S., *Droit des services publics* (Paris: PUF, 2007).

Breus, F., Fink, G., and Griller, S. (eds), *Services Liberalisation in the Internal Market* (Wien/New York: Springer, 2008).

Breyer, S., *Regulation and Its Reform* (Cambridge MA: Harvard University Press, 1982).

Bryson, J., and Daniels, P. (eds), *The Handbook of Services Industries* (Cheltenham/Northampton: Edward Elgar Publishing, 2007).

Buendia Sierra, J.L., *Exclusive Rights and State Monopolies under EC Law: Article 86 (former Article 90) of the EC Treaty* (Oxford: OUP, 2000).

Capotorti, F., et al (eds), *Du Droit International au Droit de l'intégration: Liber Amicorum Pescatore* (Baden Baden: Nomos, 1987).

Chalmers, D., Davies, G., and Monti, G., *European Union Law: Cases and Materials*, 2nd edn (Cambridge: CUP, 2010).

Collins, H., *Standard Contract Terms in Europe: A Basis for and a Challenge to European Contract Law* (Alphen ann den Rijn: Kluwer Law International, 2008).

Comba, M., and Treumer, S. (eds), *The In House Providing in European Law* (Copenhagen: DJØF Publishing, 2010).

Cossalter, P., *Les délégations d'activités publiques dans l'Union Européenne* (Paris: LGDJ, 2008).

Cox, H., (ed), *Services publics, missions publiques et régulation dans l'UE* (Paris: Pedone/Ciriec International, 1997).

—— Fournier, J., and Girardot, M. (eds), *Les services d'intérêt économique général en Europe: Régulation, Financement, Evaluation, Bonnes Pratiques* (Paris: CEEP/CIRIEC, 2000).

Craig, P., *Administrative Law*, 6th edn (Oxford: OUP, 2008).

—— and de Búrca, G., *EU Law: Texts, Cases and Materials* (Oxford: OUP, 2008).

Curtin, D., *Executive Power of the EU: Law Practices and the Living Constitution* (Oxford: OUP, 2009).

de Búrca, G., and Scott, J. *Law and New Governance in the EU and the US* (Oxford/Portland: Hart Publishing, 2006).

—— and —— (eds), *Constitutional Change in the EU: From Uniformity to Flexibiliy?* (Oxford/Portland: Hart Publishing, 2000).

—— and —— (eds), *The EU and the WTO: Legal and Constitutional Issues* (Oxford/Portland: Hart Publishing, 2001).

de Cannart d'Hamale, E., de Walsche, E., Hachez, N., and Cools, P., *La responsabilité sociale des entreprises: concept, pratiques et droit* (Bruges: Vanden Broele, 2006).

Dehousse, R. (ed), *L'Europe sans Bruxelles?: Une analyse de la Methode Ouverte de Coordination* (Paris: L'Harmattan, 2004).

—— (ed), *The Community Method: Obstinate or Obsolete?* (Basingstoke: Palgrave Macmillan, 2011).

de la Feria, R., *The EU VAT System and the Internal Market* (Amsterdam: IBDF, 2009).

de la Feria, R., and Vogenauer, S. (eds) *Prohibition of Abuse of Law: A New General Principle of EU Law* (Oxford: Hart Publishing, 2011).

Delaunay, J.C., and Gadrey, J., *Les enjeux de la société de service* (Paris: Presses de la Fondation Nationale des Sciences Politiques, 1987).

Delcourt, B., Paye, O., and Vercauteren, P. (eds), *Un nouvel art de gouverner?* (Bruxelles: Bruylant, 2007).

Delimatsis, P., *International Trade in Services and Domestic Regulations, Necessity, Transparency and Regulatory Diversity* (Oxford: OUP, 2008).

Demirag, I. (ed), *Corporate Social Responsibility, Accountability and Governance: Global Perspectives* (Sheffield: Greenleaf, 2005).

de Raulin, A. (ed), *Mélanges en hommage à G. Isaac, Volume I* (Toulouse: Presses de l'Université de Toulouse, 2004).

de Schutter, O., and Deakin, S. (eds), *Social Rights and Market Forces: Is the Open Method of Coordination of Employment and Social Policies the Future of Social Europe?* (Brussels: Bruylant, 2005).

de Witte, B., Hanf, D., and Vos, E. *The Many Faces of Differentiation in EU Law* (Antwerp/Oxford/New York: Intersentia, 2001).

Djelic, M.L., and Sahlin-Andersson, K. (eds), *Transnational Governance: Institutional Dynamics of Regulation* (Cambridge: CUP, 2008).

Dubos, O., and Kauffmann, P., *L'Europe des services: l'approfondissement du marché intérieur* (Paris: Pedone, 2009).

Emiliou, N., *The Principle of Proportionality in European Law* (London: Kluwer Law International, 1996).

Etay, K., *Financial Services in Europe* (Oxford: OUP, 2008).

Fasquelle, D., *Droit américain et droit communautaire des ententes: Etude de la règle de raison* (Paris: Joly, 1993).

Freedland, M., and Sciarra, S. (eds), *Public Services and Citizenship in European Law: Public and Labour Law Perspectives* (Oxford: Clarendon Press, 1998).

Galanis, T., *Droit de la concurrence et régulation sectorielle: l'exemple des communications électroniques* (Bruxelles/Athènes: Sakkoulas/Bruylant, 2010).

Galli, G., and Pelkmans, J. (eds), *Regulatory Reform and Competitiveness in Europe, 1: Horizontal Issues* (Cheltenham/Northampton: Edward Elgar Publishing, 2000).

Gallonj, F., and Djellal, F., *The Handbook of Innovation and Services: A Multi-Disciplinary Perspective* (Cheltenham/Northampton: Edward Elgar Publishing, 2010).

Georgakakis, D., and de Lassalle, M., *La "Nouvelle gouvernance Européenne": Genèses et usages politiques d'un Livre Blanc* (Strasbourg: PUS, 2007).

Gershuny, J.I., and Miles, I.D., *The New Service Economy: The Transformation of Employment in Industrial Societies* (London: Frances Pinter, 1983).

Giovanneti, G., Guerrieri, P., and Quintieri, B. (eds), *Business Services: The New Frontiers of Competitiveness* (Cosenza: Rubbettino Editore, 2010).

Gormley, L., *EU Law of Free Movement of Goods and Customs Union* (Oxford: OUP, 2009).

—— *Prohibiting Restrictions on Trade within the EEC* (The Hague: TMC Asser, 1985).

Gunningham, N., and Grabosky, P., *Smart Regulation* (Oxford: OUP, 1998).

Habisch, A., Wegner, M., Schmidpeter, R., and Jonker, J., *Corporate Social Responsibility across Europe* (Berlin/Heidelberg: Springler, 2005).

Harlow, C., *State Liability: Tort and Beyond* (Oxford: Clarendon Press, 2004).

Hatzopoulos, V., *Le principe communautaire d'équivalence et de reconnaissance mutuelle dans la libre prestation de services* (Athènes/Bruxelles: Sakkoulas/Bruylant, 1999).

Heidenreich, M., and Zeitlin, J. (eds), *Changing European Employment and Welfare Regimes: The Influence of the Open Method of Coordination on National Reforms* (London/New York: Routledge/EUI, 2009).

Hervey, T., and McHale, J., *Health Law and the European Union* (Cambridge: CUP, 2004).

Hoekman, B., English, P., and Mattoo, A. (eds), *Development, Trade and the WTO*, (Washington: The World Bank, 2002).

Howells, G., Micklitz, H.W., and Wilhelmsson, T., *European Fair Trading Law: The Unfair Commercial Practices Directive* (Aldershot/Burlington: Ashgate, 2006).

Janson, J.O., *The Economics of Services: Development and Policy* (Cheltenham/Northampton: Edward Elgar Publishing, 2006).

Joliet, R., *Monopolization and Abuse of a Dominant Position* (The Hague: Martinus Nijhoff, 1970).

Joliet, R., *The Rule of Reason in Antitrust Law: American, German and Common Market Laws in Comparative* (The Hague: Martinus Nijhoff, 1967).

Kaiser, W., Leucht, B., and Gehler, M., *Transnational Networks in Regional Integration: Governing Europe 1945–83* (Basingstoke: Palgrave MacMillan, 2010).

Karagiannis, N., *European Solidarity* (Liverpool: LUP, 2007).

Kieffer, B., *L'OMC et l'évolution du droit international privé* (Bruxelles: Larcier-Droit International, 2008).

Koeck, H.F., and Karollus, M.M. (eds), *The New Services Directive of the EU, FIDE XXIII Congress 2008, Volume III* (Vienna: Nomos, 2008).

Koutrakos, P., *Trade, Foreign Policy and Defence in EU Constitutional Law: The Legal Regulation of Sanctions, Exports of Dual-use Goods and Armaments* (Oxford/Portland: Hart Publishing, 2001).

Krajewski, M., Neergaard, U., and van de Gronden, J. (eds), *The Changing Legal Framework for Services of General Interest in Europe: Between Competition and Solidarity* (The Hague: TMC Asser Press, 2009).

Lang, M., Pistone, P., Schuch, J., and Staringer, C. (eds), *Introduction to European Tax Law: Direct Taxation* (Wien: Spiramus Press, 2008).

Lenoble, J. and de Schutter, O., *Reflexive Governance: Redefining the Public Interest in a Pluralistic World* (Oxford: Hart Publishing, 2010).

Littler, A., and Fijnaut, C., *The Regulation of Gambling: European and National Perspectives* (Leiden: Martinus Nijhoff, 2007).

Louis, J.V. and Rodriguez, S. (eds), *Les services d'intérêt économique général et l'UE* (Bruxelles: Bruylant, 2006).

Madiega, T., *Interaction between EC Competition Law and Sector-specific Regulation in Converging Electronic Communications Markets* EUI PhD Thesis (Florence, 2007).

Majone, G., *Regulating Europe* (Routledge: London, 1996).

—— *Deregulation or Re-regulation* (London: Pinter, 1990).

Marchetti, J., and Roy, M., *Opening Markets for Trade in Services: Countries and Sectors in Bilateral and WTO Negotiations* (Cambridge: CUP, 2008).

Mattera, A., *Le Marché Unique Européen: ses règles, son fonctionnement* (Paris: Jupiter, 1990).

Mattoo, A., Stern, R., and Zanini, G. (eds), *A Handbook of International Trade in Services* (Oxford: OUP, 2008).

McCrudden, C., *Buying Social Justice: Equality, Government Procurement, and Legal Change* (Oxford: OUP, 2007).

Micklitz, H.W., Reich, N., and Rott, P., *Understanding EU Consumer Law* (Antwerpen: Intersentia, 2009).

Morgan, B., and Yeung, K., *An Introduction to Law and Regulation: Text and Materials* (Cambridge: CUP, 2007).

Mörth, U. (ed), *Soft Law in Governance and Regulation: An Interdisciplinary Analysis* (Cheltenham/Northampton: Edward Elgar Publishing, 2004).

Mossialos, E., Permanand, G., Baeten, R., and Hervey, T. (eds), *Health Systems Governance in Europe: The Role of EU Law and Policy* (Cambridge: CUP, 2010).

Mullerat, R. (ed), *Corporate Social Responsibility: The Corporate Governance of the 21st Century* (The Hague: Kluwer Law International, 2005).

Nebbia, P., *Unfair Contract Terms in European Law: A Study in Comparative and EC Law* (Oxford: Hart Publishing, 2007).

Neergaard, U., Nielsen, R., and Roseberry, L. (eds), *The Role of Courts in Developing a European Social Model: Theoretical and Methodological Perspectives* (Copenhagen: DJØF Publishing, 2010).

—— —— and Roseberry, L. (eds), *Integrating Welfare Functions into EU Law: From Rome to Lisbon* (Copenhagen: DJØF Publishing, 2009).

—— —— and —— (eds), *The Services Directive: Consequences for the Welfare State and the European Social Model* (Copenhagen: DJØF Publishing, 2008).

OECD, *Compilation Manual for an Index of Services Production* (Paris: OECD, 2007).

—— *Enhancing the Services Sector* (Paris: OECD, 2005).

—— *Innovation and Productivity in Services: Industry, Services and Trade* (Paris: OECD, 2001).

O'Keeffe, D., and Twomey, P. (eds), *Legal Issues of the Maastricht Treaty* (London: Chancery, 1994).

Oliver, P. et al, *Oliver on Free Movement of Goods in the European Union* (Oxford: Hart Publishing, 2010).

Poiares Maduro, M., and Azoulai, L. (eds), *The Past and the Future of EU Law: The Classics of EU Law Revisited on the 50th Anniversary of the Rome Treaty* (Oxford: Hart Publishing, 2010).

Poltvin-Solis, L., *La libéralisation des services d'intérêt économique général en réseau en Europe* (Bruxelles: Bruylant, 2010).

Prosser, T., *The Regulatory Enterprise, Government, Regulation, and Legitimacy* (Oxford: OUP, 2010).

—— *The Limits of Competition Law: Markets and Public Services* (Oxford: OUP, 2005).

—— *Law and the Regulators* (Oxford: OUP, 1997).

Quaglia, L., *Governing Financial Services in The EU: Banking, Securities and Post-Trading* (London: Routledge, 2010).

Radaelli, C., *The Open Method of Coordination: A New Governance Architecture for the European Union?: Swedish Institute for European Policy Studies (SIEPS) Report No. 1* (Stockholm: SIEPS, 2007).

Rolland, L., *Précis de Droit Administratif* (Paris: Dalloz, 1938).

—— (ed), *Le service public en devenir* (Paris: L'Harmattan/Logiques politiques, 2001).

Rubalcaba, L., *The New Service Economy: Challenges and Policy Implications for Europe* (Cheltenham/Northampton: Edward Elgar Publishing, 2007).

Sakellaropoulos, T., and Berghman, J. (eds), *Connecting Welfare Diversity within the European Social Model* (Antwerpen/Oxford/New York: Intersentia, 2004).

Sauter, W., and Schepel, H., *State and Market in EU Law: The Public and Private Spheres of the Internal Market before the EU Courts* (Cambridge: CUP, 2009).

Sauvé, P., and Stern, R. (eds), *GATS 2000, New Directions in Services Trade Liberalization* (Washington DC: Harvard/Brookings Institution Press) 2000.

Senden, L. *Soft Law in EC Law* (Oxford/Portland: Hart Publishing, 2004).

Shiubhne, N.N. (ed), *Regulating the Internal Market* (Cheltenham/Northampton: Edward Elgar Publishing, 2006).

Snell, J., *Goods and Services in EC Law* (Oxford: OUP, 2002).

Snyder, F. (ed), *The EU and Governance/L'UE et la Gouvernance* (Bruxelles: Bruylant, 2006).

Stephenson, S. (ed), *Services Trade in the Western Hemisphere: Liberalisation, Integration And Reform* (Washington DC: Organisation of American States, Bookings Institution Press, 2000).

Stiglitz, J., *Economics of the Public Sector* (London: WW Norton, 2000).

Stoffaes, C. (ed), *Services publics comparés en Europe: exception française, exigence européenne* (Paris: La documentation française/Ecole Nationale d'Administration, 1997).

Szyszczak, E., *The Regulation of the State in Competitive Markets* (Oxford: OUP, 2007).

Terra, B. and Kajus, J., *A Guide to the European VAT Directives* (Amsterdam: IBFD, 2008).

—— and Wattel, P., *European Tax* Law, 5th edn (Alphen aan den Rijn: Kluwer Law International, 2008).

Thiry, B., and Vandamme, J. (eds), *Les entreprises publiques dans l'UE: entre concurrence et intérêt général* (Paris: Pedone/Ciriec International/TEPSA, 1995).

Tridimas, T., *The General Principles of EU Law*, 2nd edn (Oxford: OUP, 2006).

Tryfonidou, A., *Reverse Discrimination in EC Law* (Alphen aan den Rijn: Kluwer Law International, 2009).

van de Gronden, J. (ed), *EU and WTO Law on Services, Limits to the Realization of General Interest Policies within the Services Markets?* (Alphen aan den Rijn: Kluwer Law International, 2009).

Verhey, L. and Zwart, T. (eds), *Agencies in European and Comparative Perspective* (Antwerp/Oxford/New York: Intersentia, 2003).

Voyez, J. (ed), *VAT in Europe* (Croydon: Tolley Publishing, 2000).

Waterson, M., *Regulation of the Firm and Natural Monopoly* (Cambridge/Massachussets: Blackwell, 1988).

Weatherill, S. (ed), *Better Regulation* (Oxford/Portland: Hart Publishing, 2007).

Weatherill, S., and Bernitz, U., *The Regulation of Unfair Commercial Practices under EC Directive 2005/29* (Oxford: Hart Publishing, 2007).
—— *EU Consumer Law and Policy* (Cheltenham/Northampton: Edward Elgar Publishing, 2005).
Weltz, C., *The European Social Dialogue under Articles 138 and 139 of the EC Treaty: Actors, Processes, Outcomes* (Alphen aan den Rijn: Kluwer Law International, 2008).
Weuwahl, N., and Rosas, A. (eds), *The EU and Human Rights* (The Hague: Martinus Nijhoff, 1995).
Whish, R., *Competition Law*, 6th edn (Oxford: OUP, 2008).
White, R., *Workers, Establishment and Services in the EU* (Oxford: OUP, 2004).
Wittgenstein, L., *Tractatus Logico-Philosophicus* (London: Routledge, 2001 [1921]).
Zeitlin, J., and Pochet, P. (eds), *The Open Method of Coordination in Action: The European Employment and Social Inclusion Strategies* (Brussels: Peter Lang, 2005).

ARTICLES:

Adlung, R., 'L'AGCS: caractéristiques et secteurs principaux' in English, P., Hoekman, B., and Mattoo, A. (eds), *Développement, commerce et Organisation Mondiale du Commerce* (Washington/Paris: The World Bank/Economica, 2004) 191–217.
—— 'Public Services and the GATS' (2006) 9 *J of Int Economic L* 455–85.
—— 'Services trade liberalization from developed and developing countries' in Sauvé, P., and Stern, R. (eds), *GATS 2000, New Directions in Services Trade Liberalization* (Washington DC: Harvard/Brookings Institution Press, 2000) 112–31.
—— and Mattoo, A., 'The GATS' in Mattoo, A., Stern, R., and Zanini, G. (eds), *A Handbook of International Trade in Services* (Oxford: OUP, 2008) 48–83.
—— and Molinuevo, M., 'Bilateralism in Services Trade: Is There Fire Behind the (Bit-) Smoke?' (2008) 11 *J of Int Economic L* 365–409.
Afonso, A., and Gaspar, V., 'Excess Burden and the Cost of Inefficiency in Public Services Provision' (2006) 601 *ECB Working Paper Series* 1–43.
Albors-Llorens, A., 'The Role of Objective Justification and Efficiencies in the Application of Article 82 EC' (2007) 48 *CML Rev* 1727–61.
Allen, B., 'Ladies and Gentlemen, No More Bets Please' (2000) 27 *Legal Issues of Economic Integration* 201–6.
Allot, P., 'European Governance and the Re-branding of Democracy' (2002) 27 *EL Rev* 60–71.
Amato, G., 'Citizenship and public services: some general reflections' in Freedland, M., and Sciarra, S. (eds), *Public Services and Citizenship in European Law: Public and Labour Law Perspectives* (Oxford: Clarendon Press, 1998) 145–56.
Andrews, P., 'Are market failure analysis and impact assessment useful?' in Weatherill, S. (ed), *Better Regulation* (Oxford/Portland: Hart Publishing, 2007) 49–81.
Arkell, J., 'The liberalisation of international trade in services: issues of competence and legitimacy for the GATS—and impact of its rules on institutions' in Basedow, J., Baum, H., Kanda, H., and Kono, T. (eds), *Economic Regulation and Competition: Regulation of Services in the EU, Germany, and Japan* (Hague/London/NY: Kluwer Law International, 2002) 206–30.

Armstrong, K., 'Mutual recognition' in Barnard, C., and Scott, J. (eds), *The Law of the Single European Market: Unpacking the Premises* (Oxford: Hart Publishing, 2002) 225–67.

—— 'Rediscovering Civil Society: The EU and the White Paper on Governance' (2002) 8 *ELJ* 102–32.

—— 'The OMC and Fundamental Rights: A Critical Appraisal' unpublished Paper presented to the seminar 'Fundamental Rights and Reflexive Governance', Columbia Law School, New York (4 November 2005), also available at <http://eucenter.wisc.edu/OMC/Papers/Rights/armstrong.pdf>.

—— and Kilpatrick, C., 'Law, Governance or New Governance?: The Changing Open Method of Coordination' (2007) 13 *Columbia J of Eur L* 649–77.

—— Begg, I., and Zeitlin, J., 'The Open Method of Co-ordination and the Governance of the Lisbon Strategy' (2008) 46 *JCMS* 413–50.

Arnbak, J., 'Multi-utility regulation: yet another convergence?' in Mansell, R., Samarajiva, R., and Mahan, A. (eds), *Networking Knowledge for Information Societies: Institutions and Intervention* (Delft: Delft University Press, 2002) 141–7, also available at <http://lirne.net/resources/netknowledge/arnbak.pdf>.

Ashiagbor, D., 'Collective Labor Rights and the European Social Model' (2009) 3 *J of L and Ethics of Human Rights* 222–66.

—— 'Soft Harmonisation: The OMC in the EES' (2004) 10 *Eur Public L* 305–32.

Audit, M., 'Régulation du marché intérieur et libre circulation des lois' (2006) *Journal des Tribunaux Droit International* 1333–63.

Avbelj, M., 'The European Court of Justice and the Question of Value Choices: Fundamental Human Rights as an Exception to the Freedom of Movement of Goods', Jean Monnet Working Paper No. 6/04, also available at <http://centers.law.nyu.edu/jeanmonnet/papers/04/040601.pdf>.

Ayres, I., and Gertner, R., 'Filling Gaps in Incomplete Contracts: An Economic Theory of Default Rules' (1989) 99 *Yale L J* 87–128.

Azoulay, L., 'The Court of Justice and the Administrative Governance' (2001) 7 *ELJ* 425–41.

Baldwin, R., 'Better regulation: tensions aboard the Enterprise' in Weatherill, S. (ed), *Better Regulation* (Oxford/Portland: Hart Publishing, 2007) 27–47.

—— 'Is Better Regulation Smarter Regulation?' (2005) *Public L* 485–511 (Autumn).

Banks, K., 'The Application of the Fundamental Freedoms to Member State Tax Measures: Guarding Against Protectionism or Second-guessing National Policy Choices?' EUI RSCAS Working Paper No. 2007/31, also available at <http://cadmus.iue.it/dspace/bitstream/1814/7685/1/RSCAS_2007_31.pdf>.

Baquero-Cruz, J., 'Beyond competition: services of general interest and EC law' in de Búrca, G. (ed), *EU Law and the Welfare State: In Search of Solidarity* (Oxford, OUP, 2005) 169–212.

Barbieri, D., and Ongaro, E., 'EU Agencies: What Is Common and What Is Distinctive Compared with National-Level Public Agencies' (2008) 74 *Int Rev of Administrative Sciences* 368–420.

Barents, R., 'New Developments in Measures Having Equivalent Effect' (1981) 18 *CML Rev* 271–308.

Barnard, C., 'Fitting the Remaining Pieces into the Goods and Persons Jigsaw?' (2001) 26 *EL Rev* 35–59.

—— 'Procurement law to enforce labour standards' in Davidov, G., and Langille, B. (eds.), *The Idea of Labour Law* (Oxford: OUP, 2011).

—— 'Restricting Restrictions: Lessons for the EU from the US?' (2009) 68 *Cambridge LJ* 575–606.

—— 'The Social Partners and the Governance Agenda' (2002) 8 *ELJ* 80–101.

—— 'Unravelling the Services Directive' (2008) 45 *CML Rev* 323–94.

—— '*Viking* and *Laval*: An Introduction' (2008) 10 *CYEL* 463–92.

—— and Deakin, S., 'In Search of Coherence: Social Policy, The Single Market And Fundamental Rights' (2000) 31 *Ind Relations J* 331–45.

—— and —— 'Market access and regulatory competition' in Barnard, C., and Scott, J. (eds), *The Law of the Single European Market: Unpacking the Premises* (Oxford: Hart Publishing, 2002) 197–224, Jean Monnet Working Paper No. 9/2001, also available at <http://www.jeanmonnetprogram.org/papers/01/012701.html>.

Bartels, L., 'The Legality of the EC Mutual Recognition Clause under WTO Law' (2005) 8 *J of Int Economic L* 691–720, also available in Shiubhne, N.N. (ed), *Regulating the Internal Market* (Cheltenham/Northampton: Edward Elgar Publishing, 2006) 322–53.

Bartosch, A., 'Is There a Need for a Rule of Reason in European State Aid Law?: Or How to Arrive at a Coherent Concept of Material Selectivity?' (2010) 47 *CML Rev* 729–52.

Basedow, J., 'Economic regulation in market economies' in Basedow, J., Harald, B., Hopt, K., Kanda, H., and Kono, T. (eds), *Economic Regulation and Competition* (The Hague/London/NY: Kluwer Law International, 2002) 1–24.

Bauer, M., 'Limitations to Agency Control in EU Policy Making: The Commission and the Poverty Programmes' (2002) 40 *JCMS* 381–400.

Baumol, W.J., 'Macroeconomics of Unbalanced Growth: The Anatomy of Urban Crisis' (1967) 57 *American Economic Review* 415–26.

—— Bailey, E.E., and Willig, E.D., 'Weak Invisible Hand Theorems on the Sustainability of Multiproduct Natural Monopoly' (1977) 67 *American Economic Rev* 350–65.

—— Panzar, J., and Willig, R., *Contestable Markets and the Theory of Industry Structure* (San Diego: Harcourt Brace Jovanovich, 1982).

Bavasso, A., 'Electronic Communications: A New Paradigm for European Regulation' (2004) 41 *CML Rev* 87–118.

Bergamini, E., 'Freedom of establishment under the Services Directive' in Neergaard, U., Nielsen, R, and Roseberry, L. (eds), *The Services Directive: Consequences for the Welfare State and the European Social Model* (Copenhagen: DJØF Publishing, 2008) 149–69.

Bernard, E. 'La Cour de justice précise les règles du jeu' (2010) 20:11 *Europe* étude No. 12, 7–11.

Bernard, N., 'Discrimination and Free Movement in EC Law' (1996) 45 *Int & Comparative L Q* 82–108.

—— 'La libre circulation des marchandises, des personnes et des services dans le traité CE sous l'angle de la compétence' (1998) 34 *CDE* 11–45.

Bernstein, S., and Hannah, E., 'Non-State Global Standard Setting and the WTO: Legitimacy and the Need for Regulatory Space' (2008) 11 *J of Int Economic L* 575–608.

Besson, S., and Utzinger, A., 'Introduction: Future Challenges of European Citizenship: Facing a Wide-Open Pandora's Box' (2007) 13 *ELJ* 573–90.

Bhaskar, V., 'The Kinked Demand Curve: A Game-Theoretic Approach' (1988) 6 *Int J of Ind Organization* 373–84.

Bihlander, M., 'Better regulation by abdication?: Remarks on parliamentary democracy and governmental law-making' in Weatherill, S. (ed), *Better Regulation* (Oxford/Portland: Hart Publishing, 2007) 149–73.

Biondi, A., 'Recurring cycles in the internal market: some reflections on the free movement of services' in Arnull, A., Eeckhout, P., and Tridimas, T. (eds), *Continuity and Change in EU law* (Oxford: OUP, 2008) 229–42.

—— 'Free Trade, a Mountain Road and the Right to Protest: European Economic Freedoms and Fundamental Individual Rights' (2004) 1 *Eur Human Rights L Rev* 51–61.

Bizioli, G., Balancing the Fundamental Freedoms and Tax Sovereignty: Some Thoughts on Recent ECJ Case Law on Direct Taxation (2008) 3 *European Taxation* 133–40.

Black, J., 'Decentering Regulation: Understanding the Role of Regulation and Self-Regulation in a Post Regulatory World' (2001) 54 *Current Legal Problems* 103–46.

Black, O., 'Per Se Rules and Rules of Reason: What Are They?' (1997) 3 *Eur Competition L Rev* 289–94.

Blankart, C., Baake, P., and Jansen, C., 'Growth and regulation' in Galli, G., and Pelkmans, J. (eds), *Regulatory Reform and Competitiveness in Europe, 1: Horizontal Issues* (Cheltenham/Northampton: Edward Elgar Publishing, 2000) 40–80.

Blanquet, M., 'Le système communautaire à l'épreuve de la 'gouvernance européenne': Pour une "nouvelle gouvernance raisonnée"' in de Raulin, A. (eds), *Mélanges en hommage à G. Isaac: Volume I* (Toulouse: Presses de l'Université de Toulouse, 2004) 239–69.

Boeri, T., Nicoletti, G., and Scarpetta, S., 'Regulation and labour market performance' in Galli, G., and Pelkmans, J. (eds), *Regulatory Reform and Competitiveness in Europe, 1: Horizontal Issues* (Cheltenham/Northampton: Edward Elgar Publishing, 2000) 324–80.

Borràs, S., and Greve, B., 'Concluding Remarks: New Method or Just Cheap Talk?' (2004) 11 *JEPP* 329–36.

—— and Jacobsson, K., 'The Open Method of Co-ordination and New Governance Patterns in the EU' (2004) 11 *JEPP*, 185–208.

Borzel, T., 'What's So Special about Policy Networks?: An Exploration of the Concept and its Usefulness in Studying European Governance' (1997) 1 *Eur Integration Online Papers* No. 16, also available at <http://eiop.or.at/eiop/texte/1997-016a.htm>.

Boulin, P, 'La normalisation dans la construction européenne' (1991) *Révue des Affaires Européennes* 49–54.

Bovis, C., 'The conceptual links between state aid and public procurement in the financing of services of general interest' in Krajewski, M., Neergard, U., and van de Gronden, J. (eds), *The Changing Legal Framework for Services of General Interest* (The Hague: Asser Press, 2009) 149–70.

—— *EC Public Procurement: Case law and Regulation* (Oxford: OUP, 2006).

—— 'Developing Public Procurement Regulation: Jurisprudence and Its Influence on Law Making' (2006) 43 *CML Rev* 461–95.

Bovis, C., 'Financing Services of General Interest in the EU: How Do Public Procurement and State Aids Interact to Demarcate between Market Forces and Protection?' (2005) 11 *ELJ* 79–109.

Boy, L., 'Normes' (1998) 12 *Revue Internationale de Droit Economique* 115–46.

Braun, J.D., and Kühling, J., 'Article 87 EC and the Community Courts: from Revolution to Evolution' (2008) 45 *CML Rev* 465–98.

Breitbarth, T., Harris, P., and Aitken, R., 'Corporate Social Responsibility in the EU: A New Trade Barrier?' (2009) 9 *J of Public Affairs* 239–55.

Breuss, F., 'EU's Services Directive: Macro-economic Impact of a Fuller Integration of the Single Market for Services' Presentation at the Workshop *Liberalisation of Trade in services in the EU*, Vienna, 16/11/2007.

Brousseau, E., and Glachant, J.M., 'The Institutional Economics of Reflexive Governance in the Area of Utility Regulation' EUI/RSCAS Working Paper 2010/90, available at <http://cadmus.eui.eu/bitstream/handle/1814/15168/RSCAS_2010_90.pdf?sequence=1>.

Brown, A., 'EU Primary Law Requirements in Practice: Advertising Procedures and Remedies for Public Contracts outside the Procurement Directives' (2010) 5 *Public Procurement L R* 169–81.

Brown, P., 'The Failure of Market Failures' (1992) 21 *J of Socio-Economics* 1–24.

Bruun, N., 'The Proposed Directive on Services and Labour Law' in Blanpain, R., (ed) *Freedom of Services in the EU, Labour and Social Security Law: The Bolkestein Initiative* (The Hague, Kluwer Law International, 2006) 19–36.

Bryson, J., and Daniels, P., 'Worlds of services: from local service economies to offshoring or global sourcing' in Bryson, J., and Daniels, P. (eds), *The Handbook of Services Industries* (Cheltenham/Northampton: Edward Elgar Publishing, 2007) 1–16.

Büchs, M., 'How Legitimate Is the OMC?' (2008) 46 *JCMS* 765–86.

Cabral, P., 'La libre circulation des soins médicaux dans l'UE' in Hanf, D., and Munoz, R. (eds), *La libre circulation des personnes: Etats des lieux et perspectives* (Bruges: Peter Lang/Cahiers du Collège d'Europe, 2007).

—— 'Cross-border Access to Medical Care: Non-hospital Care and Waiting Lists' (2004) 31 *LIEI* 57–67.

—— 'The Internal Market and the Right to Cross-border Medical Care' (2004) 29 *EL Rev* 673–85.

Cafaggi, F., 'Le rôle des acteurs privés dans le processus de régulation: participation, autorégulation et régulation privée' (2004) 109 *Révue Française d'administration publique* 22–36.

—— 'Private Regulation in European Private Law' EUI RSCAS Working Paper No. 2009/31, also available at <http://cadmus.eui.eu/dspace/bitstream/1814/12054/3/RSCAS_2009_31.pdf>.

—— 'Rethinking Private Regulation in the European Regulatory Space' EUI Law Working Paper No. 2006/13, also available at <http://cadmus.eui.eu/dspace/bitstream/1814/4369/1/LAW2006.13.PDF>.

—— and Muir-Watt, H., 'The Making of European Private Law: Regulation and Governance Design' European Governance Papers (EUROGOV) No. N-07-02, also available at <http://www.connex-network.org/eurogov/pdf/egp-newgov-N-07 02.pdf>.

Cafaro, S., 'La MOC, l'action communautaire et le rôle politique du Conseil Européen' in Vandersanden, G. (ed), *Mélanges en hommage à J.V. Louis, Volume II* (Bruxelles: Editions ULB, 2003) 203–21.

Cass, D.Z., 'The World that Saves Maastricht? The Principle of Subsidiarity and the Division of Powers within the European Community' (1992) 29 *CML Rev* 1107–36.

Catà Backer, L., 'Monitor and Manage: MiFiD and Power in the Regulation of EU Financial Markets' (2008) 27 *YEL* 349–86.

Catchpole, L., and Barav, A., 'The Public Morality Exception and the Free Movement of Goods: Justification of a Dual Standard in National Legislation?' (1980) 7 *LIEI* 1–21.

Chalmers, D., 'Private Power and Public Authority in European Union Law' (2005–6) 8 *CYEL* 59–94.

—— 'Repackaging the Internal Market: The Ramifications of the Keck Judgment' (1994) 19 *EL Rev* 385–403.

—— 'The Single Market: from prima donna to journeyman' in Shaw, J., and More, G. (eds), *New Legal Dynamics of European Union* (Oxford: OUP, 1995) 55–72.

Chanda, R., 'L'AGCS et le mouvement de la main d'œuvre' in English, P., Hoekman, B., and Mattoo, A. (eds), *Développement, commerce et Organisation Mondiale du Commerce* (Washington/Paris: The World Bank/Economica, 2004) 252–62.

Chang, M., Hanf, D., and Pelkmans, J., 'The Services Directive: Trojan Horse or White Knight?' (2010) 32 *European Integration* 97–114.

Charles, W., 'A Theory of Nonmarket Failures' (1979) 55 *The Public Interest* 114–33.

Chavrier, G., 'Etablissement public de santé, logique économique et droit de la concurrence' (2006) 93 *Révue de la Sécurité Sociale* 274–87.

Chiti, E., 'An Important Part of the EU's Institutional Machinery: Features, Problems and Perspectives of European Agencies' (2009) 46 *CML Rev* 1395–442.

Chiti, E., 'The Emergence of a Community Administration: The Case of European Agencies' (2000) 37 *CML Rev* 309–43.

Chittenden, F., Ambler, T., and Xiao, D., 'Impact assessment in the EU' in Weatherill, S. (ed), *Better Regulation* (Oxford/Portland: Hart Publishing, 2007) 271–86.

Citi, M., and Rhodes, M., 'New Modes of Governance in the EU: Common Objectives versus National Preferences' European Governance Papers (EUROGOV) No. N-07-01, also available at <http://www.connex-network.org/eurogov/pdf/egp-newgov-N-07-01. pdf>.

Clergérie, J.L., 'La légalité d'une contrepartie d'obligation de service public' (2003) *Dalloz Juridique* 2814–17.

Coen, D., and Thatcher, M., 'Network Governance and Multi-level Delegation: European Networks of Regulatory Agencies' (2008) 28 *J of Public Policy* 49–71.

Coppel, J., 'Horizontal Effect of Directives, Case C-194/94 *CIA Security International v Signalson*' (1997) 26 *Industrial L J* 69–73.

Cordewener, A., Kofler, G., and Van Thiel, S., 'The Clash between European Freedoms and National Direct Tax Law: Public Interest Defences Available to the Member States' (2009) 46 *CML Rev* 1951–2000.

Craig, P., *Administrative Law*, 6th edn (Oxford: OUP, 2008).

—— 'Democracy and Rulemaking within the EC: An Empirical and Normative Assessment' (2002) 8 *ELJ* 105–30.

Craig, P., 'The Constitutionalisation of Community Administration' (2003) 28 *EL Rev* 840–64.

Craufurd-Smit, R., 'EC media regulation in a converging environment' in Shuibhne, N.N. (ed), *Regulating the Internal Market* (Cheltenham/Northampton: Edward Edgar Publishing, 2006) 105–43.

Cremers, J., Dolvik, J.E., and Bosch, G., 'Posting of Workers in the Single Market: Attempts to Prevent Social Dumping and Regime Competition in the EU?' (2007) 38 *Industrial Relations J* 524–41.

Crespy, A., 'When "Bolkestein" Is Trapped by the French Anti-Liberal Discourse: A Discursive-Institutionalist Account of Preference Formation in the Realm of European Union Multi-level Politics' (2010) 17 *J Europ Public Policy* 1253–70.

Croley, S., 'Theories of Regulation: Incorporating the Administrative Process' (1998) 98 *Columbia L Rev* 56–65.

Curtin, D., and Dekker, I., 'Good governance: the concept and its application by the European Union' in Curtin, D., and Wessel, R.A. (eds), *Good Governance and the European Union: Reflections on Concepts, Institutions and Substance* (Antwerp: Intersentia, 2005) 3–20.

—— Mair, P., and Papadopoulos, Y. (eds), *Special Issue on Accountability and European Governance* (2010) 33 *WEP* 929–1164.

da Cruz Vilaça, J.L., 'On the application of *Keck* in the field of free provision of services' in Andenas, M., and Roth, W.H. (eds), *Services and Free Movement in EU Law* (Oxford: OUP, 2002).

D'Acunto, S, 'Directive services (2006/123/CE): radiographie juridique en dix points' (2007) is. 2 *Revue du Droit de l'Union Europeenne* 261–327.

Damjanovic, D., and de Witte, B., 'Welfare values and welfare integration under the Lisbon Treaty' in Neergaard, U., Roseberry, L., and Nielsen, R. (eds), *Integrating Welfare Functions into EU law: From Rome to Lisbon* (Copenhagen: DJØF Publishing, 2009) 53–94.

Daniele, L., 'Non Discriminatory Restrictions to the Free Movement of Persons' (1997) 22 *EL Rev* 191–200.

Daniels, P., 'A global service economy?' in Bryson, J., and Daniels, P. (eds), *The Handbook of Services Industries* (Cheltenham/Northampton: Edward Elgar Publishing, 2007) 103–25.

Dap, S., 'La prise en compte jurisprudentielle de la position particulière des opérateurs de SIEG sur le marché européen' in Potvin-Solis, L. (ed), *La libéralisation des services d'intérêt économique général en réseau en Europe* (Bruxelles: Bruylant, 2010) 75–99.

Dashwood, A., 'Cassis de Dijon: The Line of Cases Grows' (1981) 6 *EL Rev* 287–90.

—— 'Dual-use goods: (mis)understanding Werner and Leifer' in Arnull, A., Eeckhout, E., and Tridimas, T. (eds), *Continuity and Change in EU Law: Essays in Honour of Sir Francis Jacobs* (Oxford: OUP, 2008) 354–61.

—— '*Viking* and *Laval*: Issues of Horizontal Direct Effect' (2008) 10 *CYEL* 525–40.

Dautricourt, C., and Thomas, S., 'Reverse Discrimination and Free Movement of Persons under Community Law: All for Ulysses, Nothing for Penelope?' (2009) 34 *EL Rev* 433–54.

Davies, G., 'Abstractness and concreteness in the preliminary reference procedure: implications for the division of powers and effective market regulation' in Shuibhne, N.N. (ed), *Regulating the Internal Market* (Cheltenham/Northampton: Edward Edgar Publishing, 2006) 210–44.

—— 'Article 86 EC, the EC's Economic Approach to Competition Law, and the General Interest' (2009) 5 *Eur Competition J* 549–84.

—— 'The Legal Framework of Regulatory Competition', SSRN online paper (2006), available at <http://papers.ssrn.com/sol3/papers.cfm?abstract_id=903138>.

—— 'Process and Production Method-based Trade Restrictions in the EU' (2008) 10 *CYEL* 69–97.

—— 'Welfare as a Service' (2002) 29 *LIEI* 27–40.

—— 'What does Article 86 actually do?' in Krajewski, M., Neergard, U., and van de Gronden, J. (eds), *The Changing Legal Framework for Services of General Interest* (The Hague: Asser Press, 2009) 51–67.

—— 'Posted Workers: Single Market or Protection of National Labour Law Systems?' (1997) 34 *CML Rev* 571–602.

Dawes, A., 'Bonjour Herr Doctor: National Healthcare Systems, the Internal Market and Cross-Border Medical Care within the EU' (2006) 33 *LIEI* 167–82.

Deakin, S., 'Regulatory Competition after *Laval*' (2008) 10 *CYEL* 581–609.

de Búrca, G., 'EU race discrimination law: a hybrid model?' in de Búrca, G., and Scott, J. (eds), *Law and New Governance in the EU and the US* (Oxford/Portland: Hart Publishing, 2006) 97–120.

—— 'The Constitutional Challenge of New Governance in the EU' (2003) 28 *EL Rev* 814–39.

—— 'The institutional development of the EU: a constitutional analysis' in Craig, P., and de Búrca, G. (eds), *The Evolution of EU Law* (Oxford: OUP, 1999) 55–82.

—— 'The Principle of Proportionality and its Applications in EC Law' (1993) 13 *YEL* 105–50.

—— and Scott, J., 'Introduction' in de Búrca, G., and Scott, J. (eds), *Law and New Governance in the EU and the US* (Oxford/Portland: Hart Publishing, 2006).

—— and Zeitlin, J., 'Constitutionalising the OMC: What Should the Convention Propose?' CEPS Policy Brief 31/2003, also available at http://www.ceps.eu/ceps/download/862.

Decker, F., 'Governance beyond the Nation-State: Reflections on the Democratic Deficit of the EU' (2002) 9 *JEPP* 256–72.

Defalque, L. 'Le concept de discrimination en matière de libre circulation des marchandises' (1987) 23 *CDE* 487–510.

—— 'L'harmonisation des législations: une alternative à la jurisprudence' (1994) *Journal de Tribunaux—Droit Européen* 166–70.

Dehousse, F., and van Hecke, K., 'Towards an Audiovisual Media Directive: An Analysis of the Commission Proposal' (2005) 58 *Studia Diplomatica* 139–51, also available at <http://aei.pitt.edu/9087/01/060606-AudioVis.directive.pdf>.

Dehousse, R., 'La méthode communautaire a-t-elle encore un avenir?' in Rey, J.J., and Walebroeck, M. (eds), *Mélanges en l'honneur à J.V. Louis* (Bruxelles: Editions de l'Université Libre de Bruxelles, 2003) 95–107.

Dehousse, R., 'Misfits: EU law and the Transformation of European Governance' Jean Monnet Working Paper 02/2002, also available at <http://centers.law.nyu.edu/jeanmonnet/papers/02/020201.rtf>.

de la Feira, R., 'Prohibition of Abuse of (Community) Law: The Creation of a New General Principle of EC Law Through Tax' (2008) 45 *CML Rev* 395–441.

de la Porte, C., 'Is the Open Method of Coordination Appropriate for Organising Activities at European Level in Sensitive Policy Areas?' (2002) 8 *ELJ* 38–58.

—— Pochet, P., and Room, G., 'Social Benchmarking, Policy Making and New Governance in the EU' (2001) 11 *J of Eur Social Policy* 291–307.

de la Rosa, S., 'The OMC in the New Member States: The Perspectives for its Use as a Tool of Soft Law' (2005) 11 *ELJ* 618–40.

Della Sala, V., 'Stakes and States: Gambling and the Single Market' (2010) 17 *JEPP* 1024–38.

Delimatsis, P., '"Thou shall not . . . (dis)trust": Codes of Conduct and Harmonization of Professional Standards in the EU' (2010) 47 *CML Rev* 1049–87.

—— The non-discrimination principle and the removal of fiscal barriers to intra-community trade' in Cottier, T., and Mavroidis, P. (eds), *Regulatory Barriers and the Principle of Non-discrimination in World Trade Law* (Michigan: University of Michigan Press, 2000) 171–89.

de Pury, D., 'Drawing national democracies towards global governance' in Bhagwati, J., and Hirsch, M. (eds), *The Urugay Round and Beyond: Essays in Honour of Arthur Dunkel* (Heidelberg/New York: Springer, 1998) 171–80.

den Exter, A.P., 'Legal Consequences of EU Accession for Central and Eastern European Health Care Systems' (2002) 8 *ELJ* 556–73.

Derlén, M., and Lindholm, J., 'Article 28 EC and Rules on Use: A Step Towards a Workable Doctrine on Measures Having Equivalent Effect to Quantitative Restrictions' (2010) 16 *Columbia J of Eur L* 191–231.

de Schutter, O. and Francq, S., 'La proposition de directive relative aux services dans le marché intérieur: reconnaissance mutuelle, harmonisation et conflits des lois dans l'Europe élargie' (2005) 41 *CDE* 603–60.

de Streel, A. and Queck, R., 'Services d'intérêt général et communications électroniques' in Louis, J.V., and Rodriguez, S. (eds), *Les services d'intérêt économique général et l'UE* (Bruxelles: Bruylant, 2006) 338–84.

de Vries, S., 'Harmonisation of services of general economic interest: where there is a will there is a way!' in van de Gronden, J. (ed), *EU and WTO Law on Services, Limits to the Realization of General Interest Policies within the Services Markets?* (Alphen aan den Rijn: Kluwer Law International, 2009) 139–58.

de Witte, B., 'Balancing of economic law and human rights by the European Court of Justice' in Dupuy, P.-M., Francioni, F., and Petersmann, E.-U. (eds) *Human Rights in International Investment Law and Arbitration* (Oxford: OUP, 2009) 197–207.

—— 'Setting the Scene: How Did Services Get to Bolkestein and Why?' EUI Law Working Paper No. 2007/20, also available at <http://cadmus.iue.it/dspace/bitstream/1814/6929/1/LAW_2007_20.pdf>.

Do, U., 'La proposition de directive relative aux services dans le marché intérieur...définitivement hors service?' (2006) is. 1 *Revue de Droit de l'Union Européenne* 1–20.

Doig, A., and Wilson, J., 'The Effectiveness of Codes of Conduct' (2002) 7 *Business Ethics: A European Rev* 140–9.

Dony, M., 'Les notions de "service d'intérêt general" et "service d'intérêt économique general"' in Louis, J.V., and Rodriguez, S. (eds), *Les services d'intérêt économique général et l'UE* (Bruxelles: Bruylant, 2006) 4–38.

Dougan, M., 'Expanding the frontiers of EU citizenship by dismantling the territorial boundaries of the national welfare states?' in Barnard, C., and Odudu, O. (eds), *The Outer Limtis of EU Law* (Oxford/Portland: Hart Publishing, 2009) 119–65.

—— 'The spatial restructuring of national welfare states within the EU: The contribution of Union citizenship and the relevance of the Treaty of Lisbon' in Neergaard, U., Roseberry, L., and Nielsen, R. (eds), *Integrating Welfare Functions into EU law: From Rome to Lisbon* (Copenhagen: DJØF Publishing, 2009) 147–87.

—— 'Minimum Harmonization and the Internal Market' (2000) 37 *CML Rev* 853–85.

—— 'The "Disguised" Vertical Effect of Directives?' (2000) 59 *Cambridge LJ* 586–612.

Douglas-Scott, S., 'Annotation: Case *Bosphorus Hava Yollari Turizm Ve Ticaret Anonim Sirketi v. Ireland*' (2006) 43 *CML Rev* 243–54.

—— 'A Tale of Two Courts; Luxembourg, Strasbourg and the Growing European Human Rights Acquis' (2006) 43 *CML Rev* 629–65.

Doukas, D., 'Untying the Market Access Knot: Advertising Restrictions and the Free Movement of Goods and Services' (2007) 9 *CYEL* 177–215.

—— and Anderson, J., 'Commercial Gambling without Frontiers: When the ECJ Throws, the Dice is Loaded' (2008) 27 *YEL* 237–76.

Drai, E., 'Responsabilité sociétale des entreprises: un mouvement créateur de valeur' (2008) 54 *Petites Affiches* 4–8.

Dreyfus, M., 'France' in Krajewski, M., Neergard, U., and van de Gronden, J. (eds), *The Changing Legal Framework for Services of General Interest* (The Hague: Asser Press, 2009) 269–90.

Driguez, L., 'Le détachement des travailleurs après la directive sur les services', (2007) 17: 6 *Europe* 35–9.

Dunne, N., 'Knowing When to See It: State Activities, Economic Activities, and the Concept of Undertaking' (2010) 16 *Columbia J of Eur L* 427–63.

Eberlein, B., and Newman, A., 'Escaping the International Governance Dilemma?: Incorporated Transgovernmental Networks in the European Union' (2008) 21 *Governance* 25–52.

Eckert, G., 'La distinction entre les services d'intérêt général économique et les services d'intérêt général non-économiques' in Potvin-Solis, L. (ed), *La libéralisation des services d'intérêt économique général en réseau en Europe* (Bruxelles: Bruylant, 2010) 3–21.

Economides, N., 'The Economics of Networks' (1996) 16 *Int J of Ind Organization* 673–99, also available at <http://www.stern.nyu.edu/networks/top.html>.

Economides, N., and White, L., 'Networks and Compatibility: Implications for Anti-trust' (1994) 38 *Eur Economic Rev* 651–62.

Economides, N., and White, L., 'One-way networks, two-way networks, compatibility and anti-trust' in Gabel, D., and Weiman, D. (eds), *Opening Networks to Competition: The Regulation and Pricing of Access*, (Amsterdam: Kluwer Academic Press, 1996) 9–29.

Edward, D., and Shuibhne, N.N., 'Continuity and change in the law relating to services' in Arnull, A., Eeckhout P., and Tridimas, T. (eds), *Continuity and Change in EU law* (Oxford: OUP, 2008) 229–42.

Edwards, M., and Croker, M., 'Major trends and issues' in OECD, *Innovation and Productivity in Services: Industry, Services and Trade* (Paris: OECD, 2001) 7–16.

Eeckhout, P., 'After *Keck* and *Mithouard*: free movement of goods in the EC, market access and non-discrimination' in Cottier, T., and Mavroidis, P. (eds), *Regulatory Barriers and the Principle of Non-discrimination in World Trade Law* (Michigan: University of Michigan Press, 2000) 190–206.

—— 'Constitutional concepts for free trade in services' in de Búrca, G., and Scott, J., *The EU and the WTO, Legal and Constitutional Issues* (Oxford/Portland: Hart Publishing, 2001) 211–35.

Eklund, R., 'The *Laval* case, Swedish Court Decision 2005 n. 49' (2006) 35 *Industrial LJ* 202–8.

Epinay, A., 'The Scope of Article 12 EC: Some Remarks on the Influence of European Citizenship' (2007) 13 *ELJ* 611–22.

Evenett, S., and Hoekman, B., 'Government procurement of services and multilateral disciplines' in Sauvé, P., and Stern, R. (eds), *GATS 2000: New Directions in Services Trade Liberalization* (Washington DC: Harvard/Brookings Institution Press, 2000) 143–64.

Faist, T., 'Social Citizenship in the European Union: Nested Membership' (2001) 39 *JCMS* 37–58.

Fallon, M., and Martin, D., 'Dessine-moi une discrimination' (2010) 170 *Journal de droit Européen* 165–73.

Fasquelle, D., *Droit américain et droit communautaire des ententes: Etude de la règle de raison* (Paris: Joly, 1993).

Featherstone, K., 'Soft Co-ordination Meets "Hard" Politics: The EU and Pension Reform in Greece' (2005) 12 *JEPP* 733–50.

Feketekuty, G., 'Improving the architecture of the GATS' in Stephenson, S. (ed), *Services Trade in the Western Hemisphere: Liberalisation, Integration and Reform* (Washington DC: Organisation of American States/Bookings Institution Press, 2000) 19–42.

—— 'Assessing and improving the architecture of GATS' in Sauvé, P. and Stern, R. (eds), *GATS 2000: New Directions in Services Trade Liberalization* (Washington DC: Harvard/Brookings Institution Press, 2000) 85–111.

Fernandez Martin, J.M., and O'Leary, S., 'Judicial exceptions to the Free Provision of Services' in Andenas, M., and Roth, W.H. (eds), *Services and Free Movement in EU Law* (Oxford: OUP, 2002) 163–95.

Fiedziuk, N., 'Towards a More Refined Economic Approach to Services of General Economic Interest' (2010) 16 *Eur P L* 271–88.

Flinders, M., 'Distributed public governance in the EU' (2004) 11 *JEPP* 520–44.

Flower, J., 'Negotiating European Legislation: The Services Directive' (2006–7) 9 *CYEL* 217–38.

Freedland, M., 'Law, public services and citizenship: new domains, new regimes?' in Freedland, M., and Sciarra, S. (eds), *Public Services and Citizenship in European Law* (Oxford: Clarendon Press. 1998) 1–34.

Frenz, W. and Schleissing, P., 'The never ending story of "in-house" procurement' in Krajewski, M., Neergard, U., and van de Gronden, J. (eds), *The Changing Legal Framework for Services of General Interest* (The Hague: TMC Asser Press, 2009) 171–87.

Fuchs, M., 'Free Movement of Services and Social Security—Quo Vadis?' (2002) 8 *ELJ* 536–55.

Funk, L., and Lesch, H., 'Minimum Wage Regulations in Selected European Countries' (2006) 41 *Intereconomics* 78–92.

Gambarale, C., and Mattoo, A., 'Régulations nationales et libéralisation du commerce de services' in English, P., Hoekman, B., and Mattoo, A. (eds), *Développement, commerce et Organisation Mondiale du Commerce* (Washington/Paris: The World Bank/Economica, 2004) 230–51.

Garben, S., 'The Bologna Process: From a European Law Perspective' (2010) 16 *ELJ* 186–210; EUI Working Paper No. 2008/12, also available at <http://cadmus.eui.eu/dspace/handle/1814/8406>.

Garrone, P., 'La Discrimination Indirecte en Droit Communautaire: vers une Théorie Générale' (1994) 30 *RTDE* 42749.

Geach, N., 'Converging Regulation for Convergent Media: An Overview of the AVMS' (2008) 1 *J of Information L and Technology* 1–19, also available at <http://go.warwick.ac.uk/jilt/2008_1/geach>.

Gebski, S., 'Competition First? Application of State Aid Rules in the Banking Sector' (2009) 6 *Competition L Rev* 89–115.

Genschel, P., 'Why No Mutual Recognition of VAT? Regulation, Taxation and the Integration of the EU's Internal Market for Goods' (2007) 14 *JEPP* 743–61.

Georgopoulos, T., 'La MOC européenne: "en attendant Godot"?' McGill Institute for European Studies Working Paper No. 01/2005, also available at <http://www.iee.umontreal.ca/pubicationsfr_fichiers/DIVERS/Georgopoulos-texte.pdf>.

Geradin, D., 'L'ouverture à la concurrence des entreprises de réseau: Analyse des principaux enjeux du processus de libéralisation' (1999) 35 *CDE* 13–48.

—— 'The Liberalization of Network Industries in the European Union: Where Do We Come From and Where Do We Go?' Paper prepared for the Finnish Presidency, 20 September 2006, also available at <http://www.vnk.fi/hankkeet/talousneuvosto/tyo-kokoukset/globalisaatioselvitys-9-2006/artikkelit/Geradin_06-09-20.pdf>.

—— and Petit, N., 'The Development of Agencies at EU and National Levels: Conceptual Analysis and Proposals for Reform' (2004) 23 *YEL* 137–97.

Giesen, R., 'Posting: Social Protection of Workers vs Fundamental Freedoms?' (2003) 40 *CML Rev* 143–58.

Goetschy, J., 'L'apport de la méthode ouverte de coordination à l'intégration Européenne' in Magnette, P. (ed), *La Grande Europe* (Bruxelles: Editions ULB, 2004) 141–66.

Gormley, L., '"Actually or Potentially, Directly or Indirectly?" Obstacles to the Free Movement of Goods' (1989) 9 *YEL* 197–208.

Gormley, L., 'Free Movement of Goods and their Use—What Is the Use of It?' (2010) 33 *Fordham Int'l LJ* 1589–628.

―― 'Reasoning Renounced? The Remarkable Judgment in *Keck & Mithouard*' (1994) 5 *EBL Rev* 63–7.

―― 'The definition of measures having equivalent effect' in Arnull, A., Eeckhout, P., and Tridimas, T. (eds), *Continuity and Change in EU Law* (Oxford: OUP, 2008) 189–205.

Gormley, L., 'The genesis of the rule of reason in the free movement of goods' in Schrauwen, A. (ed), *Rule of Reason: Rethinking another Classic of EC Legal Doctrine* (Groningen: Europa Law Publishing, 2005) 21–33.

―― 'Two Years after *Keck*' (1996) 19 *Fordham Int'l L J* 866–86.

Graham, R. 'Mutual recognition and country of origin in the case law of the ECJ' in Blanpain, R., (ed), *Freedom of Services in the EU, Labour and Social Security Law: The Bolkestein Initiative* (The Hague: Kluwer Law International, 2006) 37–50.

Graz, J.C., 'Diplomatie et marché de la normalisation internationale' (2002) 13 *Economie Politique* 52–66, also available online at <http://www.cairn.info/article.php?ID_REVUE = LECO&ID_NUMPUBLIE=LECO_013&ID_ARTICLE=LECO_013_0052>.

―― 'Quand les normes font loi: Topologie intégrée et processus différenciés de la normalisation internationale' (2004) 35 *Etudes Internationales* 233–60, also available at <http://www.erudit.org/revue/ei/2004/v35/n2/009036ar.html>.

Greer, S., and Williams, A., 'Human Rights in the Council of Europe and the EU: Towards "Individual", "Constitutional" or "Institutional" Justice?' (2009) 34 *EL Rev* 462–81.

Griffin, P., 'The Delaware Effect: Keeping the Tiger in Its Cage—The European Experience of Mutual Recognition in Financial Services' (2001) 7 *Columbia J of Eur L* 337–54.

Griller, S., 'The new services directive of the EU: hopes and expectations from the angle of (further) completion of the internal market' in Koeck, H.F., and Karollus, M.M. (eds), *The New Services Directive of the EU, FIDE XXIII Congress 2008, Volume III* (Vienna: Congress Publications, 2008).

―― and Orator, A., 'Everything under Control? The Way Forward for Agencies in the Footsteps of the Meroni Doctrine' (2010) 35 *EL Rev* 3–35.

Groenleer, M., Versluis, E., and Kaeding, M., 'Regulatory Governance through EU Agencies? The Implementation of Transport Directives' Paper presented at the ECPR Standing Group on Regulatory Governance Conference '(Re)Regulation in the Wake of Neoliberalism: Consequences of Three Decades of Privatization and Market Liberalization', Utrecht, 5–7 June 2008, also available at <http://regulation.upf.edu/ utrecht-08-papers/mgroenleer_eversluis.pdf>.

Gronnegaard Christensen, J., and Lehmann Nielsen, V., 'Administrative Capacity, Structural Choice and the Creation of EU Agencies' (2010) 17 *JEPP* 176–204.

Gunningham, N., and Sinclair, D., 'Designing smart regulation' in Hutter, B. (ed), *The Environmental Regulation Reader* (Oxford: OUP, 1999) 305–34, also available at <http:// www.oecd.org/dataoecd/18/39/33947759.pdf>.

Gyselen, L., 'State Action and the Effectiveness of the Treaty's Competition Provisions' (1989) 26 *CML Rev* 33–60.

Hall, R., and Hitch, C., 'Price Theory and Business Behaviour' (1939) 2 *Oxford Economic Papers* 12–45.

Hancher, L., and Moran, M., 'Organizing regulatory space' in Hancher, L., and Moran, M. (eds), *Capitalism, Culture and Regulation* (Oxford: Clarendon Press, 1989) 271–95.

Hansen, J.L., 'Full Circle: Is There a Difference between the Freedom of Establishment and the Freedom to Provide Services?' in Andenas, M., and Roth, W.H. (eds), *Services and Free Movement in EU Law* (Oxford: OUP, 2002) 197–209.

Harlow, C., 'Deconstructing Government?' (2004) 23 *YEL* 57–89.

—— 'Public service, market ideology and citizenship' in Freedland, M. and Sciarra, S. (eds), *Public Services and Citizenship in European Law: Public and Labour Law Perspectives* (Oxford: Clarendon Press, 1998) 48–56.

Harlow, C., and Rawlings, R., 'Promoting Accountability in Multi-level Governance: A Network Approach' (2007) 13 *ELJ* 542–62.

Hatzopoulos, V., 'Annotation: Case C-250/95, *Futura Participations SA & Singer v. Administration des Contributions (Luxembourg)* [1997] ECR I-2471' (1998) 35 *CML Rev* 493–518.

—— 'Annotation: Case C-326/00 *Ioannidis v IKA* [2003] ECR I-1703' (2003) 40 *CML Rev* 1251–68.

—— 'Annotation: Case C-384/93 *Alpine Investments* [1995] ECR I-1141' (1995) 32 *CML Rev* 1427–45.

—— 'Annotation of Case C-484/93 *Gustavsson & Svensson* [1995] ECR I-3955' (1996) 33 *CML Rev* 659–89.

—— 'Assessing the Services Directive, 2006/123/EC' (2008) 10 *CYEL* 215–61.

—— 'De l'arrêt *Foglia v Novello* à l'arrêt *TWD Textilwerke*: la jurisprudence de la Cour de justice relative à l'admissibilité des renvois préjudiciels' (1994) 3 *Revue du Marché Unique Européen* 195–219.

—— 'Exigences essentielles, impératives ou impérieuses: une théorie, des théories ou pas de théorie du tout?' (1998) 2 *RTDE* 191–236.

—— 'Financing National Health Care in a Transnational Environment: The Impact of the EC Internal Market' (2009) 26 *Wisconsin Int LJ* 761–804.

—— 'Health law and policy: the impact of the EU' in de Búrca, G. (ed), *EU Law and the Welfare State: In Search of Solidarity* (Oxford: OUP, 2005) 123–60.

—— 'Killing National Health and Insurance Systems but Healing Patients?: The European Market for Health Care Services after the Judgments of the ECJ in *Vanbraekel* and *Peerbooms*' (2002) 36 *CML Rev* 683–729.

—— 'Mutual recognition in the field of services' in Lianos, I., and Odudu, O. (eds), *Regulating Trade in Services in the EU and the WTO: Trust, Distrust and Economic Integration* (Cambridge: CUP, forthcoming).

—— 'Le principe de la reconnaissance mutuelle dans la libre prestation de services' (2010) 45 *CDE* 48–93.

—— 'Legal aspects in establishing the internal market for services' in Pelkmans, J., Hanf, D., and Chang, M. (eds), *The EU Internal Market in Comparative Perspective, Economic, Political and Legal Analyses* (Brussels: Peter Lang, 2008) 139–89.

—— 'Liberalising Trade in Services: Creating New Migration Opportunities' *Tidskrift utgiven av Juridiska Föreningen i Finland* (1–2/2010) 39–68.

Hatzopoulos, V., 'L'open network provision' moyen de la dérégulation' (1994) 30 *RTDE* 63–99.

—— 'Public procurement and state aid in national healthcare systems' in Mossialos, E., Permanand, G., Baeten, R., and Hervey, T. (eds), *Health Systems Governance in Europe: The Role of EU Law and Policy* (Cambridge: CUP, 2010) 381–420.

—— 'Que reste-t-il de la directive sur les services?' (2008) 44 *CDE* 299–355.

—— 'Recent Developments of the Case Law of the ECJ in the Field of Services' (2000) 37 *CML Rev* 43–82.

—— 'Services of general interest in healthcare: an exercise in deconstruction?' in Neergaard, U., Roseberry, L., and Nielsen, R. (eds), *Integrating Welfare Functions into EU law: From Rome to Lisbon* (Copenhagen: DJØF Publishing, 2009) 225–52.

—— 'The Evolution of the Essential Facilities Doctrine' in Amato, G., and Elhermann, C.-D. (eds), *EC Competition Law: A Critical View* (Oxford/Portland: Hart Publishing, 2007) 317–58.

—— 'Trente ans après les arrêts fondamentaux de 1974, les quatre libertés: quatre?' in Demaret, P., Govaere, I., and Hanf, D. (eds), *30 Years of European Legal Studies at the College of Europe—30 ans d'études juridiques européennes au Collège d'Europe: Liber Professorum 1973/74–2003/04* (Brussels: Peter Lang, 2005) 185–201.

—— 'Why the Open Method of Coordination Is Bad for You: A Letter to the EU' (2007) 13 *ELJ* 259–92.

—— and Do, U., 'Overview of the Case Law of the ECJ in the Field of Free Movement of Services 2000–2005' (2006) 43 *CML Rev* 923–91.

—— and Stergiou, H., 'Public procurement for healthcare services: from theory to practice' in van de Gronden, J., Krajewski, M., Neergaard, U., and Szyszczak, E. (eds), *Health Care and EU Law* (The Hague: TMC Asser Press, 2011).

—— and —— 'Public procurement law and health care: from theory to practice' in van de Gronden, J., Krajewski, M., Neergaard, U., and Szyszczak, E., *Health Care and EU Law* (The Hague: Asser Press, 2011).

Hay, C., 'What Doesn't Kill You Can Only Make You Stronger: The Doha Development Round, the Services Directive and the EU's Conception of Competitiveness' (2007) 45 *JCMS* 25–43.

Hendrickx, F., 'The Services Directive and the alleged issue of social dumping' in van de Gronden, J. (ed), *EU and WTO Law on Services: Limits to the Realization of General Interest Policies within the Services Markets?* (Alphen aan den Rijn: Kluwer Law International, 2009) 97–117.

Héritier, A., 'Mutual Recognition: Comparing Policy Areas' (2007) 15 *JEPP* 800–13.

—— 'New modes of governance in Europe: policy-making without legislating?' in Héritier, A. (ed), *Common Goods: Reinventing European and International Governance* (Lanham: Rowman and Littlefield Publishers, 2002) 185–206, also available at <http://www.renner-institut.at/download/texte/heritier.pdf>.

Hertig, G., and McCaherty, J., 'Legal options: towards better EC company law regulation' in Weatherill, S. (ed), *Better Regulation* (Oxford/Portland: Hart Publishing, 2007) 219–45.

Hervey, T., 'Co-operation between health care authorities in the Proposed Directive on Patient's Rights in Cross-Border Healthcare' in Van de Gronden, J., Szyszczak, E.,

Neergaard, U., and Krajewski, M. (eds), *Health Care and EU Law* (The Hague: Asser Press, 2011) 159–87.

Hervey, T., 'The EU and the governance of health care' in de Búrca, G., and Scott, J. (eds), *Law and New Governance in the EU and the US* (Oxford/Portland: Hart Publishing, 2006) 179–210.

—— 'The EU's Governance of Health Care and the Welfare Modernization Agenda' (2008) 2 *Regulation and Governance* 103–20.

—— '"Social Solidarity": a buttress against internal market law?' in Shaw, J. (ed), *Social Law and Policy in an Evolving EU* (Oxford: Hart Publishing, 2000) 31–47, also available at <http://aei.pitt.edu/2294/01/002338_1.PDF>.

Hervey, T., and Trubek, L., 'Freedom to Provide Health Care Services in the EU: An Opportunity for "Hybrid Governance"' (2007) 13 *Columbia J of Eur L* 623–47.

Hetsch, P., 'Émergence de valeurs morales dans la jurisprudence de la CJCE' (1982) 18 *RTDEur* 511–25.

Hill, P., 'On Goods and Services' (1977) 23 *Rev of Income and Wealth* 315–38.

Hillgenberg, H., 'A Fresh Look at Soft Law' (1999) 10 *Eur J of Int L* 499–515.

Hilson, C., 'Discrimination in Community Free Movement Law' (1999) 24 *EL Rev* 445–62.

Hinajeros, A., '*Laval* and *Viking:* The Right to Collective Action versus EU Fundamental Freedoms' (2008) 8 *Human Rights L Rev* 714–29.

Hindley, B., and Smith, A., 'Comparative Advantage and Trade in Services' (1984) 7 *The World Economy* 369–89.

Hodge, J., 'Services, libéralisation commerciale et pays en voie de développement' in English, P., Hoekman, B., and Mattoo, A. (eds), *Développement, commerce et Organisation Mondiale du Commerce* (Washington/Paris: The World Bank/Economica, 2004) 173–90.

Hodson, D., and Maher, I., 'Soft Law and Sanctions: Economic Policy Coordination and Reform of the Stability and Growth Pact' (2004) 11 *JEPP* 798–813, also available at <http://eucenter.wisc.edu/OMC/Papers/EconPolCoord/hodsonMaherJEPP2004.pdf>.

Hoekman, B., and Messerlin, P., 'Liberalizing trade in services: reciprocal negotiations and regulatory reform' in Sauvé, P. and Stern, R. (eds), *GATS 2000: New Directions in Services Trade Liberalization* (Washington DC: Harvard/Brookings Institution Press, 2000) 487–508.

Horsley, T., 'Annotation: Case C-110/05, *Commission v Italy (trailers)* [2009] nyr' (2009) 46 *CML Rev* 2001–19.

Hös, N., 'The Principle of Proportionality in the *Viking* and *Laval* Cases: An Appropriate Standard of Judicial Review?' EUI Working Paper No. 2009/06, also available at <http://cadmus.eui.eu/dspace/bitstream/1814/11259/1/LAW_2009_06.pdf>.

House of Lords, 'Amended Proposal for a Directive of the EP and of the Council on Services in the Internal Market', 25 January 2006.

—— 'Completing the Internal Market in Services, Report with Evidence' 6th Report of Session 2005–06, HMSO, 21 July 2005.

Houtepen, R., and Ter Meulen, R., 'New Types of Solidarity in the European Welfare State' (2000) 8 *Health Care Analysis* 329–40.

Howarth, W., 'Aspirations and Realities under the Water Framework Directive: Proceduralisation, Participation and Practicalities' (2009) 21 *J of Environmental L* 391–417.

Howells, J., 'Services and innovation: conceptual and theoretical perspectives' in Bryson, J., and Daniels, P. (eds), *The Handbook of Services Industries* (Cheltenham/Northampton: Edward Elgar Publishing, 2007) 34–44.

—— 'The nature of innovation in services' in OECD, *Innovation and Productivity in Services: Industry, Services and Trade* (Paris: OECD, 2001) 57–82.

Howse, R., and Regan, D., 'The Product/Process Distinction: An Illusory Basis for Disciplining Unilateralism' (2000) 11 *Eur J of Int L* 249–89.

Huysmans, J., 'A Foucaultian View on Spill-over: Freedom and Security in the EU' (2004) 7 *J of Int Relations and Development* 298–314.

Idot, L., 'Concurrence et libre circulation: Regards sur les derniers développements' (2005) is. 3 *Revue des Affaires Européennes* 391–409.

—— 'Droit Social et droit de la concurrence: confrontation ou cohabitation: A propos de quelques développements récents' (1999) 9:11 *Europe* 4–8.

—— 'Les Services d'intérêt général économique et les règles de concurrence' in Louis, J.V., and Rodriguez, S. (eds), *Les services d'intérêt économique général et l'UE* (Brussels: Bruylant, 2006) 39–63.

Iliopoulou, A., 'La méthode ouverte de coordination: un nouveau mode de gouvernance dans l'UE' (2006) 42 *CDE* 315–42.

Ivaldi, G., 'Beyond France's 2005 Referendum on the European Constitutional Treaty: Second-order Model, Anti-Establishment Attitudes and the End of the Alternative European Utopia' (2006) 29 *WEP* 47–69, also available at <http://hal-unice.archives-ouvertes.fr/docs/00/09/02/33/PDF/Ivaldi_WEP2006.pdf>.

Jacobs, F., 'Citizenship of the EU: A Legal Analysis' (2007) 13 *ELJ* 591–610.

Jacobs, S., 'Current trends in the process and methods of regulatory impact assessment: mainstreaming RIA into policy processes' in Kirkpatrick, C., and Parker, D. (eds), *Regulatory Impact Assessment: Towards Better Regulation?* (Cheltenham/Northampton: Edward Elgar Publishing, 2007) 17–35.

Jacobsson, K., 'Between deliberation and discipline: soft governance in EU employment policy' in Mörth, U. (ed), *Soft Law and Governance and Regulation: An Interdisciplinary Analysis* (Cheltenham/Northampton: Edward Elgar Publishing, 2004) 81–102.

Jacqué, J.P., 'The Principle of Institutional Balance' (2004) 41 *CML Rev* 383–91.

Joerges, C., 'A renaissance of the European Economic Constitution?' in Neergard, U., Nielsen, R., and Roseberry, L. (eds), *Integrating Welfare Functions into EU Law* (Copenhagen: DJØF Publishing, 2009) 29–52.

Joerges, C., 'Deliberative Supranationalism: Two Defences' (2002) 8 *ELJ* 133–51.

—— 'Social Market Economy as Europe's Social Model?' EUI Working Paper Law No. 2004/08, also available at <http://cadmus.eui.eu/bitstream/handle/1814/2823/law04-8.pdf?sequence=1>.

—— 'The Commission's White Paper on Governance in the EU: A Symptom of Crisis' (2002) 39 *CML Rev* 441–5.

—— 'What Is Left of the European Economic Constitution?: A Melancholic Eulogy' (2005) 30 *EL Rev* 461–89, also available at <http://www.sv.uio.no/arena/english/research/projects/cidel/old/WorkshopStockholm/Joerges.pdf>.

—— and Neyer, J., 'From Intergovernmental Bargaining to Deliberative Political Processes: The Constitutionalisation of Comitology' (1997) 3 *ELJ* 273–99.

—— and Rödl, F., 'Informal Politics, Formalised Law and the "Social Deficit" of European Integration: Reflections after the Judgments of the ECJ in *Viking* and *Laval*' (2009) 15 *ELJ* 1–19.

—— Mény, Y., and Weiler, J.H.H. (eds), 'Mountain or Molehill?: A Critical Appraisal of the Commission White Paper on Governance' Jean Monnet Working Paper No. 06/2001, also available at <http://centers.law.nyu.edu/jeanmonnet/papers/01/010601.html>.

Joliet, R., 'The Free Circulation of Goods: The *Keck and Mithouard* Decision and the New Directions in the Case Law' (1995) 1 *Columbia J of Eur L* 436–51.

Jönsson, C., and Strömvik, M., 'Negotiations in Networks' in Jönsson, C. (ed), *European Union Negotiations: Processes, Networks and Institutions* (London: Routledge, 2005) 13–26.

Kaarresalo, T., 'Procuring In-house: The Impact of the EC Procurement Regime' (2008) 17 *Public Procurement L Rev* 242–54.

Kaldellis, E., 'Freedom of Establishment versus Freedom to Provide Services: An Evaluation of Case-Law Developments in the Area of Indistinctly Applicable Rules' (2001) 28 *LIEI* 23–55.

Karagiannis, Y. 'Economic Theories and the Science of Inter-Branch Relations' EUI/RSCAS Working Paper No. 2007/4, also available at <http://cadmus.eui.eu/bitstream/handle/1814/6709/RSCAS_2007_04.pdf?sequence=1>.

Karkkainen, B., 'Information-forcing regulation and environmental governance' in de Búrca, G., and Scott, J. (eds), *Law and New Governance in the EU and the US* (Oxford/Portland: Hart Publishing, 2006) 293–321.

Kassim, H., 'Policy Networks, Networks and EU Policy Making: A Sceptical View' (1994) 17 *WEP* 15–27.

Katrougalos, G., 'The (Dim) Perspectives of the European Social Citizenship' Jean Monnet Working Paper No. 2007/05, also available at <http://centers.law.nyu.edu/jeanmonnet/papers/07/070501.html>.

Kaul, I., Grunberg, I., and Stern, M.A., 'Defining global public goods' in Kaul, I., Grunberg, I., and Stern, M.A. (eds), *Global Public Goods: International Cooperation in the 21st Century* (Oxford: OUP, 1999) 2–19.

Keleman, D., 'The Politics of "Eurocratic" Structure and the New European Agencies' (2002) 25 *WEP* 93–118.

—— and Menon, A., 'The politics of EC regulation' in Weatherill, S. (ed), *Better Regulation* (Oxford/Portland: Hart Publishing, 2007) 175–89.

Kenner, J., 'Regulating working time: beyond subordination?' in Weatherill, S. (ed), *Better Regulation* (Oxford/Portland: Hart Publishing, 2007) 195–217.

Keppenne, J.P., and Van Raepenbusch, S., 'Les principaux développements de la jurisprudence de la Cour de Justice et du Tribunal de Première Instance, Année 2003' (2004) 40 *CDE* 439–513.

Kerwer, D., 'Rules that Many Use: Standards and Global Regulation' (2005) 18 *Governance* 611–32.

Kessler, F., 'Droit de la concurrence et régimes de protection sociale: un bilan provisoire' in Kovar, R., and Simon, D. (eds), *Service public et Communauté Européenne: entre l'intérêt général et le marché, Volume I* (Paris: La documentation francaise, 1998) 421–46.

Kilpatrick, C., 'New EU employment governance and constitutionalism' in de Búrca, G., and Scott, J. (eds), *Law and New Governance in the EU and the US* (Oxford/ Portland: Hart Publishing, 2006) 121–51.

―― and Parker, D., 'Regulatory impact assessment: an overview' in Kilpatrick, C., and Parker, D. (eds), *Regulatory Impact Assessment: Towards Better Regulation?* (Cheltenham/ Northampton: Edward Elgar Publishing, 2007) 1–16.

Kitching, J., 'Is less more? Better regulation and the small enterprise' in Weatherill, S. (ed), *Better Regulation* (Oxford/Portland: Hart Publishing, 2007) 155–73.

Klabbers, J., 'The Undesirability of Soft Law' (1998) 67 *Nordic J of Int L* 381–91.

Klamert, M., 'Of Empty Glasses and Double Burdens: Approaches to Regulating the Services Market *à propos* the Implementation of the Services Directive' (2010) 37 *LIEI* 111–32.

Kleiner, C., 'La conception des règles de droit international privé dans la directive services' in (2007) 17:6 *Europe* 48–54.

Knill, C., and Lenschow, A., 'Modes of Regulation in the Governance of the EU: Towards a Comprehensive Evaluation?' (2003) 7 *Eur Integration online Papers* No. 1, also available at <http://eiop.or.at/eiop/texte/2003-001a.htm>.

Kolk, A., van Tulder, R., and Welters, C., 'International Codes of Conduct and Corporate Social Responsibility: Can Transnational Corporations Regulate Themselves?' (1999) 8 *Transnational Corporations* 143–80.

Korah, V., 'The Rise and Fall of Provisional Validity: The Need for a Rule of Reason in EEC Antitrust' (1981) 3 *Northwestern J Int Land Business* 320–57.

Kostakopoulou, D., 'EU Citizenship: Writing the Future' (2007) 13 *ELJ* 623–46.

Kostoris Padoa-Schioppa, F. 'Dominant Losers: A Comment on the Services Directive from an Economic Perspective' (2007) 14 *JEPP* 735–42.

Koutrakos, P., 'On Groceries, Alcohol and Olive Oil: More on the Free Movement of Goods after *Keck*' (2001) 26 *EL Rev* 391–407.

Kovar, R., 'Droit communautaire et service public, esprit d'orthodoxie ou pensée laïcisée' (1996) 32 *RTDE* 215–42 and 493–533.

Kovar, R., 'La Cour de justice et les entreprises chargées de la gestion d'un service d'intérêt économique général: Un pas dans le bon sens vers une dérégulation réglée' (1994) 8–9 *Europe* 1–5 and 1–3.

―― 'La peau du chagrin ou comment le droit communautaire opère la réduction des monopoles publics' (1992) 2:7 *Europe* 1–4.

Krajewski, M., 'Of modes and sectors: external relations, internal debates, and the special case of (trade in) services' in Dashwood, A., and Maresceau, M. (eds), *Law and Practice of EU External Relations: Developments in the EU External Relations Law* (Cambridge: CUP, 2008) 172–215.

―― 'Protecting a shared value of the Union in a globalized world: services of general interest and external trade' in van de Gronden, J. (ed), *EU and WTO Law on Services:*

Limits to the Realization of General Interest Policies within the Services Markets? (Alphen aan den Rijn: Kluwer Law International, 2009) 187–213.

—— and Farley, M., 'Non-economic Activities in Upstream and Downstream Markets and the Scope of Competition Law after *FENIN*' (2007) 32 *EL Rev* 111–24.

Kreher, A., 'Agencies in the EC: A Step towards Administrative Integration in Europe' (1997) 4 *JEPP* 225–45.

Kröger, S., 'The End of Democracy as We Know It?: The Legitimacy Deficits of Bureaucratic Social Policy Governance' (2007) 29 *J of Eur Integration* 565–82.

Krüger, H.K., 'Why the EU Should Accede to the European Convention of Human Rights' Euractiv article (2002, updated in 2010), available at <http://www.euractiv.com/en/future-eu/eu-accede-european-convention-human-rights/article-117174>.

Labory, S., and Malgarini, M., 'Regulation in Europe: justified burden or costly failure?' in Galli, G., and Pelkmans, J. (eds), *Regulatory Reform and Competitiveness in Europe, 1: Horizontal Issues* (Cheltenham/Northampton: Edward Elgar, 2000) 81–126.

Lall, R., 'Why Basel II Failed and Why Basel III Is Doomed' Global Economic Governance Working Paper No. 2009/52, University College, Oxford, available at <http://www.globaleconomicgovernance.org/wp-content/uploads/GEG-Working-paper-Ranjit-Lall.pdf>.

Lamy, P., 'Europe and the Future of Economic Governance' (2004) 42 *JCMS* 5–21.

Laüchli, S., 'The Concept of a Service under the GATS and under the EC Treaty' paper presented for the Master Degree of the College of Europe, Bruges, under the supervision of Eeckhout, P. (2000), available at the Library of the College of Europe, Bruges.

Leitner, K., and Lester, S., 'WTO Dispute Settlement from 1995 To 2005: A Statistical Analysis' (2006) 9 *JIEL* 219–31.

Lejour, A., 'The European market for services: patchwork' in Pelkmans, J., Hanf, D., and Chang, M. (eds), *The EU Internal Market in Comparative Perspective, Economic, Political and Legal Analyses* (Brussels: Peter Lang, 2008) 115–37.

Lemaire, C., 'La directive, la liberté d'établissement et la libre prestation de services: Confirmations, innovations' (2007) 17:2 *Europe* 15–26.

Lemley, M., and McGowan, D., 'Legal Implications of Network Economic Effects' (1998) 86 *California L Rev* 479–611.

Lenaerts, K., 'Regulating the Regulatory Process: Delegation of Powers in the European Community' (1993) 18 *EL Rev* 23–49.

—— 'Respect for Fundamental Rights as a Constitutional Principle of the European Union' (2000) 6 *Columbia J of Eur L* 1–25.

—— and Verhoeven, A., 'Towards a Legal Framework for Executive Rule-making in the EU?: The Contribution of the New Comitology Decision' (2000) 37 *CML Rev* 645–86.

Leroux, E., 'Eleven Years of GATS Case Law: What Have We Learned?' (2007) 10 *J of Int Economic L* 749–93.

Lianos, I., 'Shifting Narratives in the European Internal Market: Efficient Restrictions of Trade and the Nature of "Economic" Integration' (2010) 21 *EBL Rev* 705–60.

Lichère, F., 'Le financement des charges de services d'intérêt économique général' in Potvin-Solis, L. (ed), *La libéralisation des services d'intérêt économique général en réseau en Europe* (Bruxelles: Bruylant, 2010) 60–74.

Lindseth, P., 'Delegation is dead, long live delegation: managing the democratic disconnect in the European market-polity' in Joerges, C., and Dehousse, R. (eds), *Good Governance in Europe's Integrated Market* (Oxford: OUP, 2002) 139–63.

Littler, A., 'The Regulation of Gambling at the European Level: The Balance to Be Found' (2007) 8 *ERA Forum* 357–71.

Lodge, M., 'The Importance of Being Modern: International Benchmarking and National Regulatory Innovation' (2005) 12 *JEPP* 649–67.

Lomincka, E., 'The home country control principle in the Financial Services Directives and the case law' in Andenas, M., and Roth, W.H. (eds), *Services and Free Movement in EU Law* (Oxford: OUP, 2002) 295–319.

Lopatka, J., and Page, W., 'Microsoft, Monopolization and Network Externalities: Some Uses and Abuses of Economic Theory in Antitrust Decision Making' (1995) 40 *Antitrust Bulletin* 317–70.

Lowenthal, P.J., 'The Defence of "Objective Justification" in the Application of Article 82' (2005) 28 *World Competition* 455–77.

Lundblad, C., 'Some legal dimensions of corporate codes of conduct' in Mullerat, R. (ed), *Corporate Social Responsibility: The Corporate Governance of the 21st Century* (The Hague: Kluwer Law International, 2005).

Maher, I., 'Economic Governance: Hybridity, Accountability, and Control' (2007) 13 *Columbia J of Eur L* 679–703.

—— 'Law and the OMC: Towards a New Flexibility in European Policy-Making?' (2004) 2 *J for Comparative Government and Eur Policy* 248–63.

Majone, G., 'Delegation of Regulatory Powers in a Mixed Polity' (2002) 8 *ELJ* 319–39.

—— 'The New European Agencies: Regulation by Information' (1997) 4 *JEPP* 262–75.

—— 'The Regulatory State and Its Legitimacy Problems' (1999) 22 *WEP* 57–78.

Malaret-Garcia, E., 'Public service, public services, public functions and guarantees of the rights of citizens: unchanging needs in a changed context' in Freedland, M., and Sciarra, S. (eds), *Public Services and Citizenship in European Law: Public and Labour Law Perspectives* (Oxford: Clarendon Press, 1998) 57–82.

Malmberg, J., and Sigeman, T., 'Industrial Actions and EU Economic Freedoms: The Autonomous Collective Bargaining Model Curtailed by the ECJ' (2008) 45 *CML Rev* 1115–46.

Manin, P., '"Conclusions" sur la Directive 2006/123/CE' (2007) 17:6 *Europe* 29–30.

Manin, Ph., 'La "méthode communautaire": changement et permanence' in Blanquet, M. (ed), *Mélanges en honneur à Guy Isaac: Cinquante ans de droit communautaire* (Toulouse: Presses Universitaires Sciences Sociales Toulouse, 2004) 213–37.

Marenco, G., 'The Notion of Restriction on the Freedom of Establishment and Provision of Services in the Case-law of the Court' (1991) 11 *YEL* 111–50.

—— 'Pour une interprétation traditionnelle de la notion de mesure d'effet équivalent à une restriction quantitative' (1984) 19 *Cahiers de Droit Européen* 291–364.

Marti, M., Schmidt, M., and Springer, U., 'Libéralisation des services publics: y-a-t-il une convergence en Europe?' (2004) 24 *L'économie politique* 75–89.

Martin, D., '"Discriminations", "entraves" et "raisons impérieuses" dans le traité CE: trois concepts en quête d'identité (partie 1e)' (1998) 34 *CDE* 261–318.

Mattoo, A., 'Négociation des engagements en matière d'accès aux marches des services' in English, P., Hoekman, B., and Mattoo, A. (eds), *Développement, commerce et Organisation Mondiale du Commerce* (Washington/Paris: The World Bank/Economica, 2004) 218–29.

Mattoo, A., Stern, R., 'Overview' in Mattoo, A., Stern, R., and Zanini, G. (eds), *A Handbook of International Trade in Services* (Oxford: OUP, 2008) 3–32.

Mashaw, J., 'Prodelegation: Why Administrators Should Make Political Decisions' (1985) 1 *J of L Economics and Organization* 81–100.

Mathisen, G., 'Consistency and Coherence as Conditions for Justification of Member State Measures Restricting Free Movement' (2010) 47 *CML Rev* 1021–48.

Mattera, A., 'Le principe de la reconnaissance mutuelle: instrument de préservation des traditions et des diversités nationales, régionales et locales' (1998) is. 2 *Révue du Marché Unique Européen* 5–17.

—— 'De l'arrêt *Dassonville* à l'arrêt *Keck*: l'obscure clarté d'une jurisprudence riche en principes novateurs et en contradictions' (1994) is. 1 *Révue du Marché Unique Européen* 117–60.

—— 'L'article 30 du traité CE, la jurisprudence *Cassis de Dijon* et le principe de la reconnaissance mutuelle' (1992) is. 4 *Révue du Marché Unique Européen* 13–71.

—— 'Subsidiarité, reconnaissance mutuelle et hiérarchie des normes européennes' (1991) is. 2 *Révue du Marché Unique Européen* 7–10.

Maurer, A., and Chauvet, P., 'The magnitude of flows of global trade services' in Hoekman, B., English, P., and Mattoo, A. (eds), *Development, Trade and the WTO* (Washington: The World Bank, 2002) 235–45.

—— Marcus, Y., Magdeleine, J., and d'Andrea, B., 'Measuring Trade in services' in Mattoo, A., Stern, R, and Zanini, G. (eds), *A Handbook of International Trade in Services* (Oxford: OUP, 2008) 133–68.

Mavridis, P., 'La libre circulation des patients: la boucle est-elle bouclée ?' Cour de Cassation Française, Cycle de droit Européen 2007, available at <http://www.courdecassation.fr/IMG/File/pdf_2007/02_04_2007/02-04-2007_mavridis.pdf>.

Mayer-Schönberger, V., and Somek, A., 'Introduction: Governing Regulatory Interaction: the Normative Question' (2006) 12 *ELJ* 431–39.

Mazuyer, E., and de la Rosa, S. 'La régulation sociale européenne et l'autorégulation: le défi de la cohérence dans le recours à la *soft law*' (2009) 45 *CDE* 295–333.

McGee, A., and Weatherill, S., 'The Evolution of the Single Market: Harmonisation or Liberalisation' (1990) 53 *Modern L Rev* 578–96.

McMillan, J., 'La "certification", la reconnaissance mutuelle et le marché unique' (1991) is. 2 *Révue du Marché Unique Européen* 181–211.

Merlin-Brogniart, C., 'Compétitivité, innovation et services publics marchands' (2007) 25 *Innovations* 205–22.

Merola, M., and Medina, C., 'De l'arrêt *Ferring* à l'arrêt *Altmark*: continuité ou revirement dans l'approche du financement des services publics' (2003) 39 *CDE* 639–94.

Meuwese, A., 'Inter-institutionalising EU impact assessment' in Weatherill, S. (ed), *Better Regulation* (Oxford/Portland: Hart Publishing, 2007) 287–309.

Meyer, F., 'Libre circulation des travailleurs et libre prestation de services, à propos de la directive "détachement du travailleur"' (1998) is. 1 *Revue Internationale de Droit Economique* 57–73.

Mezanotte, F., 'Interpreting the Boundaries of Collective Dominance in Article 102 TFEU' (2010) 21 *EBL Rev* 519–37.

Michel, Q., 'The European Union Dual-use Export Control Regime' (2008) 40 *ESADRA Bulletin* 41–5, also available at <http://esarda2.jrc.it/db_proceeding/mfile/B_2008_040_10.pdf>.

Micklitz, H.W., 'Regulatory strategies on services contracts in EC law' in Caffagi, F., and Muir-Watt, H. (eds), *The Regulatory Function of European Private Law* (Cheltenham/Northampton: Edward Elgar Publishing, 2009) 16–61.

—— Reich, N., and Rott, P., *Understanding EU Consumer Law* (Antwerpen: Intersentia, 2009).

Miles, I., 'Knowledge-intensive services and innovation' in Bryson, J., and Daniels, P. (eds), *The Handbook of Services Industries* (Cheltenham/Northampton: Edward Elgar Publishing, 2007) 277–94.

Milner, H., 'YES to the Europe I Want; NO to This One; Some Reflections on France's Rejection of the EU Constitution' (2006) 39 *Political Sciences and Politics* 257–60.

Moloney, N., 'EU Financial Market Regulation after the Global Financial Crisis: "More Europe" or More Risks?' (2010) 47 *CML Rev* 1317–83.

—— 'Law-making in EC financial market regulation after the Financial Services Action Plan' in Weatherill, S. (ed), *Better Regulation* (Oxford/Portland: Hart Publishing, 2007) 321–67.

Monteagudo, J., and Diexr, A., 'Economic Performance and Competition in Services in the Euro Area: Policy Lessons in Times of Crisis' European Economy, Occasional Papers No. 2009/53, EU Commission/DG Economic and Financial Affairs, also available at <http://ec.europa.eu/economy_finance/publications/publication15841_en.pdf>.

Morado Foadi, S., 'The Missing Piece of the Lisbon Jigsaw: Is the Open Method of Coordination Effective in Relation to the European Research Area?' (2008) 14 *ELJ* 635–54.

Moravcsik, A., 'The European Constitutional Compromise and the Neofunctionalist Legacy' (2005) 12 *JEPP* 349–86.

Moreau, M.A., 'La recherche de nouvelles méthodes de régulation sociale: quelles fonctions, quelles complémentarités' EUI Working Paper No. 2005/08, also available at <http://www.crimt.org/Publications/IUE_WP_05-08.pdf>.

Morgan, B., and Yeung, K., *An Introduction to Law and Regulation: Text and Materials* (Cambridge: CUP, 2007).

Morijn, J., 'Balancing Fundamental Rights and Common Market Freedoms in Union Law: *Schmidberger* and *Omega* in the Light of the European Constitution' (2006) 12 *ELJ* 15–40.

Mortelmans, K., 'Article 30 of the EEC Treaty and Legislation Relating to Market Circumstances: Time to Consider a New Definition?' (1991) 28 *CML Rev* 115–36.

Mortelmans, K., 'The Common Market, the Internal Market and the Single Market, What's in a Market?' (1998) 35 *CML Rev* 101–36.

Mortelmans, K., 'Toward Convergence in the Application of the Rules on Free Movement and on Competition' (2001) 38 *CML Rev* 613–49.

Mouline, A., 'Libéralisation des services de télécommunications en Europe: Emergence d'une structure oligopolistique dominée par les opérateurs historiques?' in Potvin-Solis, L. (ed), *La libéralisation des services d'intérêt économique général en réseau en Europe* (Bruxelles: Bruylant, 2010) 401–18.

Musgrave, R.A., 'A Multiple Theory of Budget Determination' (1997) 17 *FinanzArchiv* 331–43.

Nebbia, P., *Unfair Contract Terms in European Law: A Study in Comparative and EC Law* (Oxford/Portland: Hart Publishing, 2007).

Neergaard, U., 'In search of the role of "solidarity" in primary law and the case law of the ECJ' in Neergaard, U., Nielsen, R., and Roseberry, L. (eds), *The Role of Courts in Developing a European Social Model: Theoretical and Methodological Perspectives* (Copenhagen: DJØF Publishing, 2010) 97–138.

Neergaard, U., 'Services of general economic interest: the nature of the beast' in Krajewski, M., Neergard, U., and van de Gronden, J. (eds), *The Changing Legal Framework for Services of General Interest* (The Hague: TMC Asser Press, 2009) 17–50.

—— 'Services of general (economic) interest: what aims and values count?' in Neergaard, U., Nielsen, R., and Roseberry, L. (eds), *Integrating Welfare Functions into EU Law* (Copenhagen: DJØF Publishing, 2009) 191–224.

Nenova, M.B., 'The New AVMS Directive: Television *Without* Frontiers, Television *Without* Cultural Diversity' (2007) 44 *CML Rev* 1689–725.

Newdick, C., 'Citizenship, Free Movement and Healthcare: Cementing Individual Rights by Corroding Social Solidarity' (2006) 43 *CML Rev* 1645–68.

Neyer, J., 'Explaining the Unexpected: Efficiency and Effectiveness in European Decision-making' (2004) 11 *JEPP* 19–38.

Nicolaidis, K., 'Trusting the Poles? Constructing Europe through Mutual Recognition' (2007) 15 *JEPP* 682–98.

—— and Schmidt, S., 'Mutual Recognition "on Trial": The Long Road to Services Liberalisation' (2007) 15 *JEPP* 717–34.

—— and Trachtman, J., 'Liberalization, regulation and recognition for services trade' in Stephenson, S. (ed), *Services Trade in the Western Hemisphere, Liberalisation, Integration and Reform* (Washington DC: Organisation of American States/Bookings Institution Press, 2000) 43–71.

Nihoul, P., 'Droit européen, consommateurs et services d'intérêt économique général' in Louis, J.V., and Rodriguez, S., (eds), *Les services d'intérêt économique général et l'Union Européenne* (Bruxelles: Bruylant, 2006) 163–212.

Novitz, T., 'A Human Rights Analysis for the *Viking* and *Laval* Judgments' (2008) 10 *CYEL* 541–62.

Odudu, O., 'Economic activity as a limit to Community law' in Barnard, C., and Odudu, O. (eds), *The Outer Limits of EU Law* (Oxford/Portland: Hart Publishing, 2009) 225–43.

Ogus, A., 'Comparing Regulatory Systems: Institutions, Processes and Legal Forms in Industrialised Countries' Centre on Regulation and Competition Working Paper No.

35/2002, also available at <http://ageconsearch.umn.edu/bitstream/30609/1/cr020035.pdf>.

Ogus, A., 'Competition between National Legal Systems: A Contribution of Economic Analysis to Comparative Law' (1999) 48 *International & Comparative L Q* 405–18.

—— 'The regulation of services and public-private divide' in Caffagi, F., and Muir-Watt, H. (eds), *The Regulatory Function of European Private Law* (Cheltenham/Northampton: Edward Elgar Publishing, 2009) 3–15.

O'Leary, S., 'Developing an Ever Closer Union between the Peoples of Europe? A Reappraisal of the Case Law of the Court of Justice on the Free Movement of Persons and EU Citizenship' (2008) 27 *YEL* 167–93.

—— 'The free movement of persons and services' in Craig, P., and de Bùrca, G. (eds), *The Evolution of EU Law* (Oxford: OUP, 1999) 377–416.

—— and Fernandez-Martin, J., 'Judicially created exceptions to the free provision of services' in Andenas, M., and Roth, W.H., *Services and Free Movement in EU Law* (Oxford, OUP, 2001) 163–96.

Oliver, P. 'Goods and services: two freedoms compared' in Dony, M., and de Walsche, A. (eds), *Mélanges en Hommage à Michel Waelbroeck, Vol. II* (Bruxelles: Bruylant, 1999) 1377–405.

—— 'Of Trailers and Jet-Skis: Is the Case Law on Article 34 TFEU Hurtling in a New Direction' (2010) 33 *Fordham Int'l LJ* 1423–71.

—— 'Some Further Reflections on the Scope of Art. 28–30 (ex 30–36) EC' (1999) 36 *CML Rev* 783–806.

—— and Roth, W.-H., 'The Internal Market and the Four Freedoms' (2004) 41 *CML Rev* 407–41.

Olivi, E., 'The EU Better Regulation Agenda' in Weatherill, S. (ed), *Better Regulation* (Oxford/Portland: Hart Publishing, 2007) 191–4.

Ortino, F., 'Treaty Interpretation and the WTO Appellate Body Report in US-Gambling: A Critique' (2006) 9 *J of Int Economic L* 117–48.

Ortino, M., 'The Role and Functioning of Mutual Recognition in the European Market for Financial Services' (2007) 56 *Int & Comparative L Q* 309–38.

Osborne, D., 'A Duopoly Price Game' (1974) 41 *Economica* 157–75.

Pagoulatos, G., and Stasinopoulou, M., 'Governance in EU Social Employment Policy: A Survey' Report for the Study on Social Impact of Globalisation in the EU (SIMGLOBE), European Commission and CEPS (VC/2005/0228), 2006, also available at <http://www.eliamep.gr/wp-content/uploads/2009/01/recwowe1.pdf>.

Papadopoulos, Y., 'Problems of democratic accountability in network and multi-level governance' in Conzelmann, T., and Smith, R. (eds), *Multi-Level Governance in the European Union: Taking Stock and Looking Ahead* (Baden Baden: Nomos, 2008) 31–52.

Pattberg, P., 'The Institutionalisation of Private Governance: How Business and Non-profit Organizations Agree on Transnational Rules' (2005) 18 *Governance* 589–610.

Pellegrino, P., 'Directive sur les services dans le marché intérieur, Un accouchement dans la douleur' (2007) is. 504 *Revue du Marche Unique Européen* 14–21.

Pelkmans, J., 'Economic approaches of the internal market' in Pelkmans, J., Hanf, D., and Chang, M. (eds), *The EU Internal Market in Comparative Perspective: Economic, Political and Legal Analyses* (Brussels: Peter Lang, 2008) 29–76.

Pelkmans, J., 'Making EU Network Markets Competitive' (2001) 17 *Oxford Rev of Economic Policy* 432–56, also available at <http://people.pwf.cam.ac.uk/mb65/library/pelkmans.2001.pdf>.

—— 'Mutual Recognition in Goods: On Promises and Disillusions' (2007) 15 *JEPP* 699–716.

—— Labory, S., and Majone, G. 'Better EU regulatory quality: assessing current initiatives and new proposals' in Galli, G., and Pelkmans, J. (eds), *Regulatory Reform and Competitiveness in Europe, 1: Horizontal Issues* (Cheltenham/Northampton: Edward Elgar Publishing, 2000) 461–531.

Pernice, I., and Kanitz, R., 'Fundamental Rights and Multilevel Constitutionalism in Europe' Walter Hallstein Institut Working Paper No. 7/04, also available at <www.whi-berlin.de/documents/whi-paper0704.pdf>.

Pescatore, P., 'Les exigences de la démocratie et la légitimité de la CE' (1974) 5 *CDE* 499–514.

Peterson, J., 'Policy Networks and EU Policy Making: A Reply to Kassim' (1995) 18 *WEP* 389–407.

Petit, P. 'The political economy of services in tertiary economies' in Bryson, J., and Daniels, P. (eds), *The Handbook of Services Industries* (Cheltenham/Northampton: Edward Elgar Publishing, 2007) 77–97.

Petreto, A., 'The liberalization and privatization of public utilities and the protection of user's rights: the perspective of economic theory' in Freedland, M., and Sciarra, S. (eds), *Public Services and Citizenship in European Law: Public and Labour Law Perspectives* (Oxford: Clarendon Press, 1998) 99–115.

Picard, E., 'Citizenship, fundamental rights and public services' in Freedland, M. and Sciarra, S. (eds), *Public Services and Citizenship in European Law: Public and Labour Law Perspectives* (Oxford: Clarendon Press, 1998) 83–98.

Picod, F., 'La nouvelle approche de la Cour de justice en matière d'entraves aux échanges' (1998) 34 *RTDEur* 169–89.

Poiares Maduro, M., 'Europe's Social Self: "The Sickness unto Death"' Constitutional Web-paper No. 02/2000, available at <http://eui.academia.edu/MiguelPoiaresMaduro/Papers/523083/Europes_Social_Self_The_Sickness_unto_Death>.

—— 'Harmony and Dissonance in Free Movement' (2001) 4 *CYEL* 315–41.

—— 'Is there any such thing as free or fair trade?' in de Búrca, G., and Scott, J. (eds), *The EU and the WTO: Legal and Constitutional Issues* (Oxford/Portland: Hart Publishing, 2001) 259–82.

Poiares Maduro, M., 'So Close and Yet So Far: The Paradoxes of Mutual Recognition' (2007) 15 *JEPP* 814–25.

Porter, M., and Kramer, M., 'Strategy and Society: The Link between Competitive Advantage and Corporate Social Responsibility' (2006) 84 *Harvard Business Review* 1–15, also available at <http://www.fsg.org/tabid/191/ArticleIId/46/Default.aspx?srpush=true>.

Potvin-Solis, L., 'Accès aux SIEG et libéralisation: des variations au principe' in Potvin-Solis, L. (ed), *La libéralisation des services d'intérêt économique général en réseau en Europe* (Bruxelles: Bruylant, 2010) 23–59.

Prechal, S., 'Fundamental rights and the liberalization of service markets' in van den Gronden, J. (ed), *EU and WTO Law on Services: Limits to the Realization of General*

Interest Policies within the Services Markets? (Alphen aan den Rijn: Kluwer Law International, 2009) 55–73.

—— 'Institutional balance: a fragile principle with uncertain contents' in Heukels, T., Blokker, N., and Brus, M. (eds), *The European Union after Amsterdam* (The Hague: Kluwer Law International, 1998) 273–94.

Princen, S., 'EC Compliance with WTO Law: The Interplay of Law and Politics' (2004) 15 *Eur J of Int L* 555–74, also available at <http://ssrn.com/abstract=803753>.

Prosser, T., 'Self-regulation, Co-regulation and the AVMS Directive' (2008) 31 *J of Consumer Policy* 99–113.

—— 'The Continental tradition of public service' in Prosser, T. (ed), *The Limits of Competition Law: Markets and Public Services* (Oxford: OUP, 2005) 96–120.

Quaglia, L., 'The "Old" and "New" Politics of Financial Services Regulation in the EU' Observatoire Social Européen Research Paper No. 2010/2, also available at <http://www.ose.be/files/publication/OSEPaperSeries/Quaglia_2010_OSEResearchPaper2_0410.pdf>.

—— Eastwood, R., and Holmes, P. 'The Financial Turmoil and EU Policy Cooperation 2007–8', (2009) 47 *JCMS* 1–25.

Racine, J.B., 'Normalisation, certification et droit de la concurrence' (1998) 12 *Revue Internationale de Droit Economique* 147–63.

Radaeli, C., and Meuwese, A., 'Hard Questions, Hard Solutions: Proceduralisation through Impact Assessment in the EU' (2010) 33 *WEP* 136–53.

—— de Francesco, F., and Troeger, V., 'Implementation of Regulatory Impact Assessment in Europe' Speech delivered to the ENBR workshop, University of Exeter, 27–28 March 2008, also available at <http://centres.exeter.ac.uk/ceg/research/riacp/documents/ImplementationofRIAENRworkshop.pdf>.

Reale, A., 'Representation of Interests, Participatory Democracy and Lawmaking in the EU: Which Role and Which Rules for the Social Partners?' Jean Monnet Working Paper No. 15/2003, also available at <http://centers.law.nyu.edu/jeanmonnet/papers/03/031501.html>.

Regan, D., 'An outsider's view of *Dassonville* and *Cassis de Dijon*: on interpretation and policy', in Maduro, M.P., and Azoulai, L. (eds), *The Past and the Future of EU Law: The Classics of EU Law Revisited on the 50th Anniversary of the Rome Treaty* (Oxford: Hart Publishing, 2010) 465–73.

—— 'What Are Trade Agreements For?: Two Conflicting Stories Told by Economists, with a Lesson for Lawyers' (2006) 9 *J Int Economic L* 951–88.

Regent, S., 'The OMC: A New Supranational Form of Governance?' (2003) 9 *ELJ* 190–214.

Reich, N., 'Competition between Legal Orders: A New Paradigm of Law' (1992) 29 *CML Rev* 861–96.

—— 'The "November Revolution" of the European Court of Justice: *Keck, Meng* and *Audi* Revisited' (1994) 31 *CML Rev* 459–92.

Repussard, J., 'Les normes techniques au service de la construction européenne' (1996) 396 *Revue du Marché commun de l'UE* 222–7.

Rhodes, R.A.W., 'Governance and public administration' in Pierre, J. (ed.), *Debating Governance* (Oxford: OUP, 2000) 54–90.

Rhodes, R.A.W., 'The New Governance: Governing without Government' (1996) 44 *Political Studies* 652–67.

Rigaux, A., 'Nouvel épisode de la difficile qualification des mesures d'effet équivalent: le sort des abeilles brunes de Laeso' (1999) 9:3 *Europe* 7–8.

Rodrigues, S., 'Les services d'intérêt économique général et l'UE: Acquis et perspectives' in Louis, J.V. and Rodriguez, S. (eds), *Les services d'intérêt économique général et l'UE* (Bruxelles: Bruylant, 2006) 421–39.

Rodrigues, S. 'Towards a general EC framework instrument related to SGEI?: Political considerations and legal constraints' in Krajewski, M., Neergard, U., and van de Gronden, J. (eds), *The Changing Legal Framework for Services of General Interest* (The Hague: TMC Asser Press, 2009) 255–66.

Roig, E., 'Intricate aspects of the scope [of the services directive] in Spain' Paper delivered at the EIPA/ECR Seminar on *The services directive: The challenge of implementation and management at sub-state level*, Barcelona 19–20 April 2010.

Ronmar, M., 'Free Movement of Services vs National Labour Law and Industrial Relations Systems: Understanding the *Laval* Case from a Swedish and Nordic Perspective' (2008) 10 *CYEL* 493–521.

Ross, M., 'The Value of Solidarity in European Public Services Law' in Krajewski, M., Neergard, U., and van de Gronden, J. (eds), *The Changing Legal Framework for Services of General Interest* (The Hague: Asser Press, 2009) 81–99.

Roth, W.H., 'Annotation: Case C- 205/07 *Gysbrecht*s [2008] ECR I-9947' (2010) 47 *CML Rev* 509–20.

—— 'The ECJ's case law on freedom to provide services: is *Keck* relevant?' in Andenas, M., and Roth, W.H. (eds), *Services and Free Movement in EU Law* (Oxford: OUP, 2002) 1–24.

Rott, P., 'Minimum Harmonisation for the Completion of the Internal Market? The Example of Consumer Sales Law' (2003) 40 *CML Rev* 1107–35.

Rubalcaba-Bermejo, L., and Cuadrado-Roura, J., 'Services in the age of globalisation: explanatory interrelations and dimensions' in Cuadrado-Roura, J., Rubalcaba-Bermejo, L., and Byrson, J.R. (eds), *Trading Services in the Global Economy* (Cheltenham/ Northampton: Edward Elgar Publishing, 2002) 27–57.

Rubio, N., 'Les instruments de *soft law* dans les politiques communautaires: vecteur d'une meilleure articulation entre la politique de concurrence et la politique de cohésion économique et sociale' (2008) is. 4 *RTDE* 597–608.

Rudolph, P., 'The history, variations, impact and future of self-regulation' in Mullerat, R. (ed), *Corporate Social Responsibility: The Corporate Governance of the 21st Century* (The Hague: Kluwer Law International, 2005) 365–84.

Ruiz-Fabri, H., and Crontiras, J.P., 'L'OMC et les services' Rapport IDDRI 2/2003, also available at <http://www.iddri.org/Publications/Collections/Idees-pour-le-debat/id_0310_ruiz&fabri.pdf>.

Sabel, C., and Zeitlin, J., 'Learning from Difference: The New Architecture of Experimentalist Governance in the EU' (2008) 14 *ELJ* 271–327, also available at <http://eucenter.wisc.edu/OMC/Papers/EUC/zeitlinSabelEUGov.pdf>.

Sauer, F. and Fahy, N., 'Malades à la recherche de soins en Europe' (2004) is. 3 *Revue de Droit de l'Union Européenne* 499–508.

Sauter, W., 'Services of General Economic Interest and Universal Service in EU Law' (2008) 33 *EL Rev* 176–93.

—— 'Universal service obligation and the emergence of citizens' rights in European telecommunications liberalization' in Freedland, M., and Sciarra, S. (eds), *Public Services and Citizenship in European Law: Public and Labour Law Perspectives* (Oxford: Clarendon Press, 1998) 117–43.

Sbragia, A., 'The Dilemma of Governance with Government' Jean Monnet Working Paper No. 03/2002, also available at <http://centers.law.nyu.edu/jeanmonnet/papers/02/020301.pdf>.

Schäffer, A., 'A New Effective Form of Governance? Comparing the OMC to Multilateral Surveillance by the IMF and the OECD' Max Plank Institute für Gesellschaftsforchung (MPIfG) Working Paper No. 2004/5, also available at <http://www.mpi-fg-koeln.mpg.de>.

—— 'Resolving Deadlock: Why International Organisations Introduce Soft Law' (2006) 12 *ELJ* 194–208.

Scharpf, F., 'European Governance: Common Concerns vs. the Challenge of Diversity' Jean Monnet Working Paper No. 07/2001, also available at <http://centers.law.nyu.edu/jeanmonnet/papers/01/010701.html>.

—— 'Introduction: The Problem-Solving Capacity of Multi-Level Governance' (1997) 4 *JEPP* 520–38.

—— 'The European Social Model: Coping with the Challenges of Diversity' (2002) 40 *JCMS* 645–70.

—— 'The Only Solution Is to Refuse to Comply with ECJ Rulings' (2009) 4:1 *Social Europe J* 16, also available at <http://www.social-europe.eu/2009/04/interview-the-only-solution-is-to-refuse-to-comply-with-ecj-rulings>.

Schelkle, W., 'EU Fiscal Governance: Hard Law in the Shadow of Soft Law?' (2007) 23 *Columbia J of Eur L* 705–31.

Schepel, H., 'The Public/Private Divide in Secondary Community Law: a Footnote to the European Economic Constitution' (2006) 8 *CYEL* 259–72.

Schmitt, S., 'Mutual Recognition as a New Mode of Governance' (2007) 15 *JEPP* 667–81.

Schout, A., and Jordan, A., 'Coordinated European Governance: Self-Organizing or Centrally Steered?' (2005) 83 *Public Administration* 201–20.

—— and Pereyra, F., 'The Institutionalization of EU Agencies: Agencies as "Mini-Commissions"' (2010) 88 *Public Administration* 1–15.

Schutze, R., 'Subsidiarity after Lisbon: Reinforcing the Safeguards of Federalism' (2009) 68 *Cambridge LJ* 525–36.

Schweitzer, H., 'Competition Law and Public Policy: Reconsidering an Uneasy Relationship: The Example of Article 81' EUI Law Working Paper No. 30/2007, also available at <http://cadmus.eui.eu/dspace/bitstream/1814/7623/3/LAW-2007-30.pdf>.

Sciarra, S., '*Viking* and *Laval*: Collective Labour Rights and Market Freedoms in the Enlarged EU' (2008) 10 *CYEL* 563–80.

Scott, C., 'Regulating private legislation' in Caffagi, F., and Muir-Watt, H. (eds), *The Regulatory Function of European Private Law* (Cheltenham/Northampton: Edward Elgar Publishing, 2009) 254–68.

Scott, C., 'Services of General Interest in EC Law: Matching Values to Regulatory Technique in the Public and Private Sectors' (2000) 6 *ELJ* 310–25.

Scott, J., and Holder, J., 'Law and new environmental governance in the EU' in de Búrca, G., and Scott, J. (eds), *Law and New Governance in the EU and the US* (Oxford/Portland: Hart Publishing, 2006) 211–42.

—— and Trubek, M., 'Mind the Gap: Law and New Approaches to Governance in the EU' (2002) 8 *ELJ* 1–18.

Senden, L., 'Soft Law and Its Implications for Institutional Balance in the EC' (2005) 1 *Utrecht L Rev* 79–99.

—— 'The OMC and Its Patch in the European Regulatory And Constitutional Landscape' EUI RSCAS Working Paper No. 2010/61, also available at <http://cadmus.eui.eu/dspace/bitstream/1814/14436/1/RSCAS_2010_61.pdf>.

—— and Prechal, S., 'Differentiation in and through Community soft law' in de Witte, B., Hanf, D., and Vos, E. (eds), *The Many Faces of Differentiation in EU Law* (Antwerpen: Intersentia Publishing, 2001) 181–99.

Shuibhne, N.N., 'The Resilience of EU Market Citizenship' (2010) 47 *CML Rev* 1597–628.

Silva, F., and Cavaliere, A., 'The economic impact of product liability: lessons from the US and the EU experience' in Galli, G., and Pelkmans, J. (eds), *Regulatory Reform and Competitiveness in Europe, 1: Horizontal Issues* (Cheltenham/Northampton: Edward Elgar Publishing, 2000) 292–323.

Slot, P.J., 'Annotation: Case C-194/94 *CIA Security v Signalson* [1996] ECR I-2201' (1996) 33 *CML Rev* 1035–50.

—— 'Harmonisation' (1996) 21 *EL Rev* 378–97.

—— 'The Application of Articles 3(f), 5 and 85 to 94 EEC' (1987) 12 *EL Rev* 179–89.

—— and Skudder, A., 'Common Features of Community Law in the Network-bound Sectors' (2001) 48 *CML Rev* 87–129.

Smismans, S., 'New Governance: The Solution for Active European Citizenship, or the End of Citizenship?' (2007) 13 *Columbia J of Eur L* 595–622.

—— 'The European Social Dialogue in the Shadow of Hierarchy' (2008) 28 *J Public L* 161–80.

Smith, R., Blouin, C., Drager, N., and Fidler, D., 'Trade in health services and the GATS', in Mattoo, A., Stern, R., and Zanini, G. (eds), *A Handbook of International Trade in Services* (Oxford: OUP, 2008) 437–58.

Snell, J., 'Free movement of services and the Services Directive: the legitimacy of the case law' in van de Gronden, J. (ed), *EU and WTO Law on Services, Limits to the Realization of General Interest Policies within the Services Markets?* (Austin: Kluwer Law International, 2009) 31–54.

Snell, J., 'Freedom to provide services in the case law and in the Services Directive: problems, solutions and institutions' in Neergaard, U., Nielsen, R., and Roseberry, L. (eds), *The Services Directive: Consequences for the Welfare State and the European Social Model* (Copenhagen: DJØF, 2008) 171–97.

—— 'Non-discriminatory Tax Obstacles in Community Law' (2007) 56 *Int & Comparative L Q* 339–70.

—— 'Private parties and the free movement of goods and services' in Andenas, M., and Roth, W.H. (eds), *Services and Free Movement in EU Law* (Oxford: OUP, 2002) 211–44.

—— 'The Notion of Market Access: A Concept or a Slogan?' (2010) 47 *CML Rev* 437–72.

—— 'Who's Got the Power? Free Movement and Allocation of Competences in EC Law' (2003) 22 *YEL* 323–51.

—— and Andenas, M., 'Exploring the outer limits: restrictions on the free movement' in Andenas, M., and Roth, W.H. (eds), *Services and Free Movement in EU Law* (Oxford: OUP, 2002) 69–139.

Snyder, F., 'Soft law and institutional practice in the European Community' in Martin, S. (ed), *The Construction of Europe: Essays in Honour of Emile Noel* (Dordrecht: Kluwer, 1994) 197–225.

Sørensen, E., 'Abuse of Rights in Community Law: A Principle of Substance or Merely Rhetoric?' (2006) 43 *CML Rev* 423–59.

Spaventa, E., 'On Discrimination and the Theory of Mandatory Requirements' (2000) 3 *CYEL* 457–78.

—— 'Public Services and European Law: Looking for Boundaries' (2002) 5 *CYEL* 271–92.

—— 'The outer limits of the Treaty free movement provisions: some reflections on the significance of *Keck*, remoteness, and *Deliège*' in Barnard, C., and Odudu, O. (eds), *The Outer Limits of EU Law* (Oxford/Portland: Hart Publishing, 2009) 245–69.

Spindler, G., 'Market Processes, Standardisation and Tort Law' (1998) 4 *ELJ* 316–36.

Spjut, R.J., 'Fundamental rights, public morality, the margin of appreciation and the Treaty of Rome' in Adams, J. (ed), *Essays for Clive Schmithoff* (Abingdon: Professional Books, 1983) 121–32.

Steindorff, E., 'Article 85 and the Rule of Reason' (1984) 21 *CML Rev* 639–46.

Steiner, J., 'Drawing the Line: Uses and Abuses of Article 30 EEC' (1992) 29 *CML Rev* 749–74.

Steyger, E., 'National Health Care Systems under Fire (But Not Too Heavily)' (2002) 29 *LIEI* 97–107.

Strern, Robert, 'Qualifying barriers to trade in services' in Hoekman, B., English, P., and Mattoo, A. (eds), *Development, Trade and the WTO* (Washington: The World Bank, 2002) 247–58.

Stigler, G., 'The Kinked Oligopoly Demand Curve' (1947) 55 *J Political Economy* 431–9.

Stoffaës, C., 'Towards European Regulation of Network Industries' Discussion Group Report, Initiative for Public Utility Services in Europe, Paris, 2003, also available at <http://www.archives.diplomatie.gouv.fr/europe/pdf/rapportstoffaes.gb.pdf>.

Strauss, P., 'The Place of Agencies in Government: Separation of Powers and the Fourth Branch' (1984) 84 *Columbia L Rev* 573–633.

Stuyck, J., 'Libre circulation et concurrence: les deux piliers du Marché commun' in Dony, M., and de Walsche, A. (eds), *Mélanges en hommage à Michel Waelbroeck, Volume II* (Bruxelles: Bruylant, 1999) 1477–98.

Supiot, A., 'Employment, citizenship and services of general public interest' in Freedland, M., and Sciarra, S. (eds), *Public Services and Citizenship in European Law: Public and Labour Law Perspectives* (Oxford: Clarendon Press, 1998) 157–72.

Swiatkowski, A.-M., 'EU citizenship and the rights of access for welfare state: a comparison with welfare rights guaranteed by the Council of Europe as seen from the perspective of a new Member State' in Neergaard, U., Roseberry, L., and Nielsen, R. (eds), *Integrating Welfare Functions into EU law: From Rome to Lisbon* (Copenhagen: DJØF Publishing, 2009) 123–46.

Szydlo, Marek, 'Sector-Specific Regulation and Competition Law: Between Convergence and Divergence' (2009) 15 *Eur Public L* 257–75.

Szyszczak, E., 'Competition and the liberalised market' in Shuibhne, N.N. (ed), *Regulating the Internal Market* (Cheltenham/Northampton: Edward Elgar Publishing, 2006) 87–104.

Szyszczak, E., 'Experimental Governance: The Open Method of Coordination' (2006) 12 *ELJ* 486–502.

Szyszczak, E., 'Financing Services of General Economic Interest' (2004) 67 *Modern L Rev* 982–92.

Telo, M., 'La gouvernance économique et sociale et la réforme des traités: la MOC' in Vandersanden, G. (ed), *Mélanges en hommage à J.V. Louis, Volume I* (Bruxelles: Editions ULB, 2003) 479–98.

Thatcher, M., 'The Third Force? Independent Regulatory Agencies and Elected Politicians in Europe' (2005) 18 *Governance* 347–73.

Thomson, R. and Hosli, M., 'Who Has Power in the EU? The Commission, Council and Parliament in Legislative Decision-making' (2006) 44 *JCMS* 391–417.

Tholoniat, L., 'The Career of the OMC: Lessons from a "Soft" EU Instrument' (2010) 33 *WEP* 93–117.

Timmermans, C., 'How Can One Improve the Quality of Community Legislation?' (1997) 34 *CML Rev* 1229–57.

Tison, M., 'Unravelling the general good exception: the case of financial services' in Andenas, M., and Roth, W.H. (eds), *Services and Free Movement in EU Law* (Oxford: OUP, 2002) 321–81.

Tomuschat, C., 'Le principe de proportionnalité: *Quis iudicabit?*' (1997) 13 *CDE* 97–102.

Toner, H., 'Non-discriminatory Obstacles to the Exercise of Treaty Rights: Articles 39, 43, 49 and 18 EC' (2004) 23 *YEL* 275–302.

Torriti, J., 'The Standard Cost Model: when "better regulation" fights against red tape' in Weatherill, S. (ed), *Better Regulation* (Oxford/Portland: Hart Publishing, 2007) 83–106.

Tryfonidou, A., 'Further Steps on the Road to Convergence Among the Market Freedoms' (2010) 35 *EL Rev* 3656.

—— 'Reverse Discrimination in Purely Internal Situations: An Incongruity in a Citizen's Europe' (2008) 35 *LIEI* 43–67.

Trubek, D., and Trubek, L., 'New Governance and Legal Regulation: Complementarity, Rivalry and Transformation' (2007) 23 *Columbia J of Eur L* 539–64.

—— and —— 'Hard and Soft Law in the Construction of Social Europe: The Role of the OMC' (2005) 11 *ELJ* 343–64.

—— Cortell, P., and Nance, M., 'Soft Law, Hard law and European Integration: Toward a Theory of Hybridity' Jean Monnet Working Paper No. 02/2005, also available at <http://centers.law.nyu.edu/jeanmonnet/papers/05/050201.pdf>.

Trukeschitz, B., and Schneider, U., 'New Forms of Financing Social Services: The Impact of Service-Contracting on the Provision of Social Services in Austria' Paper delivered at the

Cambridge Journal of Economics Conference, 17–19 September 2003, available at <http://www.econ.cam.ac.uk/cjeconf/delegates/trukeschitz.pdf>.

Valcke, P., and Stevens, D., 'Graduated Regulation of "Regulatable" Content and the European AVMS Directive: One Small Step for the Industry and One Giant Leap for the Legislator?' (2007) 24 *Telematics and Informatics* 285–302, also available at <http://law.kuleuven.be/icri/publications/948ti2007.pdf>.

—— —— Lievens, E., and Werkers, E., 'AVMS in the EU: Next Generation Approach or Old Wine in New Barrels?' (2008) 71 *Communications and Strategies* 103–18.

van de Gronden, J., 'The Services Directive and services of general (economic) interest' in Krajewski, M., Neergard, U., and van de Gronden, J. (eds), *The Changing Legal Framework for Services of General Interest* (The Hague: TMC Asser Press, 2009) 233–54.

van den Abeele, E., 'La proposition de directive sur les services: instrument visionnaire au service de la compétitivité ou cheval de Troie dirigé contre le modèle social européen?' in Degryse, C., and Pochet, P. (eds), *Bilan Social de l'UE 2004* (Brussels: ETUI-REHS/ Observatoire social européen and Saltsa, 2004) 111–50.

van der Mei, A.P., 'Cross-border Access to Health Care within the EU: Some Reflections on *Geraets-Smits and Peerbooms* and *Vanbraekel*' (2002) 9 *Maastricht J of Eur and Comparative Law* 189–213.

—— 'Cross-border Access to Medical Care: Non-Hospital Care and Waiting Lists' (2004) 31 *LIEI* 57–67.

van Gerven, W., 'Constitutional aspects of the European Court's case-law on Articles 30 and 36 EC as compared with the U.S. Dormant Commerce Clause' in Dony, M., and de Walsche, A. (eds), *Mélanges en Hommage à Michel Waelbroeck, Vol. II* (Bruxelles: Bruylant, 1999) 1629–44.

—— 'The Second Banking Directive and the Case Law of the Court of Justice' (1990) 10 *YEL* 57–70.

van Huffel, M., 'The legal framework for financial services and the Internet' in Shuibhne, N.N. (ed), *Regulating the Internal Market* (Cheltenham/Northampton: Edward Elgar Publishing, 2006) 144–80.

van Meerten, H. 'A Comparison of the Services Directive with the Case Law of the Court of Justice: A Case Study' (2006) 2 *Griffin's View* 141–62.

van Raepenbusch, S., 'Les services sociaux en droit communautaire ou la recherche d'un juste équilibre entre l'économique et le social' in Louis, J.L., and Rodriguez, S. (eds), *Les services d'intérêt économique général et l'Union Européenne* (Bruxelles: Bruylant, 2006) 99–161.

van Ooik, R., 'The growing importance of agencies in the EU: shifting governance and the institutional balance' in Curtin, D.M., and Wessel, R.A. (eds), *Good Governance and the European Union: Reflections on Concepts, Institutions and Substance* (Antwerp: Intersentia, 2005) 125–52.

Verheugen, G., 'CSR, Essential for Public Trust in Business' SPEECH 09/53 delivered in the CSR forum, Brussels, 10/02/2009, also available at <http://europa.eu/rapid/pressReleasesAction.do?reference=SPEECH/09/53&format=HTML&aged=1&language=EN&guiLanguage=en>.

Vibert, F., 'Better regulation and the role of EU agencies' in Weatherill, S. (ed), *Better Regulation* (Oxford/Portland: Hart Publishing, 2007) 387–404.

Vickers, J., 'Abuse of Market Power' (2005) 115:504 *Economic J*, F244–F261.

von Bar, C., 'A Common Frame of Reference for European Private Law—Academic Efforts and Political Realities' (2008) 12 *Electronic J of Comparative L*, available at <http://www.ejcl.org/121/art121-27.pdf>.

von Bogdandy, A., 'The European Union as a Human Rights Organisation? Human Rights and the Core of the European Union' (2000) 37 *CML Rev* 1307–38.

—— Arndt, F., and Jürgen, B., 'Legal Instruments in EU Law and their Reform: A Systematic Approach on an Empirical Basis' (2004) 23 *YEL* 91–136.

Vos, E., 'Reforming the European Commission: What Role to Play for EU Agencies?' (2000) 47 *CML Rev* 1113–34.

—— 'The role of comitology in European governance' in Curtin, D.M., and Wessel, R.A. (eds), *Good Governance and the European Union: Reflections on Concepts, Institutions, and Substance* (Antwerp: Intersentia, 2005) 107–24.

—— 'The Rise of Committees' (1997) 3 *ELJ* 210–29.

Vranes, E., 'The WTO and Regulatory Freedom: WTO Disciplines on Market Access, Non Discrimination and Domestic Regulation Relating to Trade in Goods and Services' (2009) 12 *J of Int Economic L* 953–87.

Wachsmann, A. and Berrod, F., 'Les critères de justification des monopoles: un premier bilan après l'affaire *Corbeau*' (1994) 30 *RTDE* 39–61.

Waelbroeck, D., 'L'harmonisation des règles et normes techniques dans la CEE' (1988) 24 *CDE* 243–75.

Waelbroeck, M., 'Les rapports entre les règles sur la libre circulation des marchandises et les règles applicables aux entreprises dans la CEE' in Capotorti, F., Ehlermann, C.D., Frowein, J., Jacobs, F., Joliet, R., Koopmans, T., and Kovar, R. (eds), *Du Droit International au Droit de l'intégration: Liber Amicorum Pescatore* (Baden Baden: Nomos, 1987) 181–203.

Ward, S., and Williams, R., 'From Hierarchy to Networks? Sub-central Government and EU Urban Environment Policy' (1997) 35 *JCMS* 439–64.

Warf, B., 'Embodied information, actor networks, and global value-added services' in Bryson, J., and Daniels, P. (eds), *The Handbook of Services Industries* (Cheltenham/ Northampton: Edward Elgar Publishing, 2007) 379–94.

Warner, M., 'Competition policy and GATS' in Sauvé, P., and Stern, R. (eds), *GATS 2000: New Directions in Services Trade Liberalization* (Washington DC: Harvard/Brookings Institution Press, 2000) 364–98.

Warren, T., and Findlay, C., 'Measuring impediments to trade in services' in Sauvé, P., and Stern, R. (eds), *GATS 2000: New Directions in Services Trade Liberalization* (Washington DC: Harvard/Brookings Institution Press, 2000) 57–84.

Weatherill, S., 'Competence Creep and Competence Control' (2004) 23 *YEL* 1–55.

—— 'The challenge of better regulation' in Weatherill, S. (ed), *Better Regulation* (Oxford/ Portland: Hart Publishing, 2007) 1–17.

—— 'Harmonisation: How much, How Little? (2005) 16 *EBLR* S33–45.

Weiler, J.H.H., 'The constitution of the Common Market Place: text and context in the evolution of the free movement of goods' in Craig, P., and de Búrca, G. (eds), *The Evolution of EU Law* (Oxford: OUP, 1999) 349–76.

Wennerås, P., 'The *De Coster* Case: Reflections on Tax and Proportionality' (2002) 29 *LIEI* 219–30.

Werden, G. 'The Ancillary Restraints Doctrine' Paper presented in the ABA 54th Antitrust Law Spring Meeting (2006), also available at <http://www.abanet.org/antitrust/at-committees/at-s1/pdf/spring-materials/2006/werden06.pdf>.

Wernicke, S., 'Au nom de qui? The ECJ between Member States, Civil Society and Citizens' (2007) 13 *ELJ* 380–407.

—— 'Services of general economic interest in European law: solidarity embedded in the Economic Constitution' in van de Gronden, J. (ed), *EU and WTO Law on Services, Limits to the Realization of General Interest Policies within the Services Markets?* (Alphen aan den Rijn: Kluwer Law International, 2009) 121–37.

—— 'Taking Stock: The EU institutions and services of general economic interest' in Krajewski, M., Neergard, U., and van de Gronden, J. (eds), *The Changing Legal Framework for Services of General Interest* (The Hague: TMC Asser Press, 2009) 69–79.

Wesseling, R., 'The rule of reason and competition law: various rules, various reasons' in Schrauwen, A. (ed), *Rule of Reason: Rethinking Another Classic of EC Legal Doctrine* (Groningen: Europa Law Publishing, 2005) 56–70.

Westen, P., 'The Empty Idea of Equality' (1982) 95 *Harvard L Rev* 537–96.

Whish, R., and Surfin, B., 'Article 85 and the Rule of Reason' (1987) 7 *YEL* 1–38.

White, E.L., 'In Search of the Limits to Article 30 of the EEC Treaty' (1989) 26 *CML Rev* 235–80.

White, J., 'Rethinking Transnational Solidarity in the EU' (2003) 20 *Perspectives* 40–57.

Wilderspin, M., 'Que reste-t-il du principe du pays d'origine? Le regard des internationalistes' (2007) 17:6 *Europe* 26–8.

Williams, C., and Aguilera, R., 'Corporate social responsibility in a comparative perspective' in Crane, A., McWilliams, A., Matten, D., Moon, J., and Siegel, D. (eds), *The Oxford Handbook of Corporate Social Responsibility* (Oxford: OUP, 2008) 522–31.

Wilsher, D., 'Does *Keck* Discrimination Make any Sense? An Assessment of the Non-Discrimination Principle in the European Single Market' (2008) 33 *EL Rev* 3–22.

Wincott, D., 'Beyond Social Regulation? New Instruments and/or a New Agenda for Social Policy at Lisbon?' (2003) 81 *Public Administration* 533–53.

Wölfl, A. 'The service economy in OECD countries' in OECD, *Enhancing the Services Sector* (Paris: OECD, 2005) 27–51.

Wood, D., 'Corporate Social Performance Revisited' (1991) 16 *The Academy of Management Rev* 691–718.

Woolfson, C., and Sommers, J., 'Labour Mobility in Construction: European Implications of the *Laval un Partneri* Dispute with Swedish Labour' (2006) 12 *Eur J of Industrial Relations* 49–68.

Wouters, J., and Coppens, D., 'GATS and domestic regulation: balancing the right to regulate and trade liberalization' in Alexander, K., and Andenas, M. (eds), *The World Trade Organization and Trade in Services* (The Hague: Brill, 2008) 207–236.

Xanthaki, H., 'The Problem of Quality in EU Legislation: What on Earth Is Really Wrong?' (2001) 38 *CML Rev* 651–76.

Yataganas, X., 'Delegation of Regulatory Authority in the EU, The Relevance of the American Model of Independent Agencies' Jean Monnet Working Paper No. 03/2001, also available at http://centers.law.nyu.edu/jeanmonnet/papers/01/010301.html

Zeitlin, J., 'Is the Open Method of Coordination an alternative to the Community Method?' in Dehousse, R. (ed), *The Community Method: Obstinate or Obsolete?* (Basingstoke: Palgrave Macmillan, 2011), also available at <http://eucenter.wisc.edu/OMC/Papers/JZ_Community_Method.pdf>.

Zeitlin, J., 'The OMC in question' in Zeitlin, J. and Pochet, P. (eds.), *The Open Method of Coordination in Action: The European Employment and Social Inclusion Strategies* (Brussels: Peter Lang, 2005) 19–33.

Zumbansen, Peer, 'Spaces and Places: A Systems Theory Approach to Regulatory Competition in European Company Law' (2006) 12 *ELJ* 534–56.

Index